NATIONAL GEOGRAPHIC

DESK
REFERENCE
to
NATURE'S
MEDICINE

NATIONAL GEOGRAPHIC

DESK
REFERENCE
to
NATURE'S
MEDICINE

STEVEN FOSTER AND REBECCA L. JOHNSON

NATIONAL GEOGRAPHIC
WASHINGTON, D.C.

CONTENTS

PRECEDING PAGES: *Echinacea* (Echinacea purpurea), *one of the world's most popular herbs, occurs in the wild in the midwestern United States. However, it is not collected from the wild, as it usually grows in relatively small populations. The entire world's supply of the species is commercially cultivated, as it is here at Trout Lake Farm. This farm in Trout Lake, Washington, is America's largest organic herb farm.* OPPOSITE PAGE: *At a marketplace in Madagascar, a vendor molds finely ground herbs high in iron and other elements for prospective buyers.*

How to Use This Book

Heads provide the plant's standard common name followed by its Latin, or scientific, name. Plants in this book are arranged by common names in alphabetical order, with each plant featured in a two-page spread.

The **Traditional and Current Medicinal Uses** section covers historical (often referred to as traditional) use as well as current use in modern herbal medicine.

Common Names are listed with a plant's standard common name first, as well as other common names used to identify it, both past and present.

Latin Name lists a plant's botanical name and, when appropriate, a synonym commonly used to identify it. Additional botanical names are noted when other species are used as the source of the same herbal ingredient.

Description gives a concise summary of the plant's main physical features.

Habitat describes a plant's indigenous, or native, range as well as where it has naturalized and where it is cultivated commercially.

Range maps show at a glance a plant's native range. The approximate perimeter of the known primary native range is shown. In many cases, the non-native range extends far beyond the native range. Non-native range is not shown. In the case of plants (such as garlic or parsley) used for many centuries, the probable area of origin is shown since the true native range is unknown.

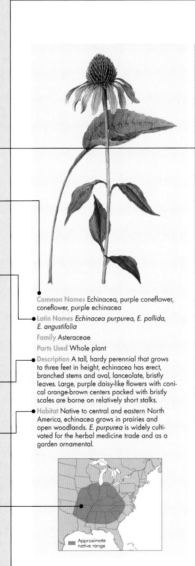

Common Names Echinacea, purple coneflower, coneflower, purple echinacea

Latin Names *Echinacea purpurea, E. pallida, E. angustifolia*

Family Asteraceae

Parts Used Whole plant

Description A tall, hardy perennial that grows to three feet in height, echinacea has erect, branched stems and oval, lanceolate, bristly leaves. Large, purple daisy-like flowers with conical orange-brown centers packed with bristly scales are borne on relatively short stalks.

Habitat Native to central and eastern North America, echinacea grows in prairies and open woodlands. *E. purpurea* is widely cultivated for the herbal medicine trade and as a garden ornamental.

Approximate native range

Echinacea
Echinacea purpurea

ECHINACEA IS A NATIVE NORTH AMERICAN WILDFLOWER often called purple coneflower because of its distinctive color and shape. The genus name, *Echinacea*, comes from the Greek *echinos*, meaning "hedgehog," and refers to the flower's central cone of stiff, upright scales surrounded by striking purple-to-pink petals. It has become one of the most popular and widely used herbs in modern American and European herbal medicine. Three species of the herb are used in herbal medicine products: *Echinacea purpurea, E. angustifolia,* and *E. pallida.*

Traditional and Current Medicinal Uses

ECHINACEA'S USE AS A MEDICINAL PLANT BEGAN HUNDREDS OF years ago with Native Americans, who used it externally for treating wounds and snakebite and internally for more purposes than any other plant. The Choctaw also used preparations of echinacea root to treat coughs and digestive upsets. The Comanche used a root **decoction** to ease the pain of sore throat and held pieces of fresh root against teeth for toothache. The Sioux valued the roots as a cure for rabies. Echinacea was introduced to Western medicine in the 1890s. Then the herb quickly gained a loyal following among American **Eclectic** physicians who incorporated the use of medicinal plants into their practice. It was recommended for respiratory infections and skin problems, as well as meningitis, diphtheria, tonsillitis, sinus infections, indigestion, diarrhea, cholera, and certain types of cancer. By the 1930s, echinacea's popularity began to wane in the United States, especially after the introduction of sulfa drugs and antibiotics. In Germany, in the late 1930s, however, the herb became increasingly popular, largely through the efforts of Dr. Gerhard Madaus, founder of the German pharmaceutical company Madaus AG, who pioneered research into echinacea.

In modern herbal medicine, echinacea is primarily used to reduce the symptoms and duration of colds, flu, and upper respiratory tract infections, and to help boost immune system activity. Echinacea is thought to be an immune system stimulant that promotes healing through its **anti-inflammatory**, antibiotic, antiviral, and detox-ifying effects. It is prescribed for abscesses and other slow-healing wounds, skin diseases,chronic fatigue syndrome, fungal infections, hay fever, asthma, uri-nary tract infections, sinusitis, early stages of cough, flu, and colds, as a gargle for sore throat, and to pre-vent premature aging and skin damage from ultra-violet light.

Cultivation and Preparation

ECHINACEA PURPUREA IS CULTIVATED WIDELY IN THE UNITED States and Europe for the herbal medicine market. It requires rich, somewhat sandy soil and full sun. It can be propagated by seed, root cuttings, or division. Leaves and other above-ground parts are harvested in mid-summer, while the plant is flowering. Roots and **rhizomes** (underground stems) are harvested in autumn and dried. Echinacea—often a mixture of one or more medicinal species—is available in **extracts**, tablets, **tinctures**, capsules, and ointments.

Research

ECHINACEA IS ONE OF THE MOST WELL-STUDIED HERBS IN herbal medicine today. Precisely how preparations of the herb exert their effects, however, is not complete-ly understood. Laboratory and animal studies suggest echinacea contains active substances that stimulate the immune system to counter bacterial, viral, and fungal infections, reduce inflammation, strengthen blood vessels, destroy **free radicals**, increase active white blood cells in circulation, stimulate production of interferon (a natural antiviral substance), and prevent sun damage to the skin. Research has produced con-flicting results. Clinical studies, for example, have shown that echinacea appears to reduce severity and duration of cold and flu symptoms. Other studies have found preparations of the herb did not prevent such infections from developing. More studies are required on the types of preparations and dosages that may deliver predictable, consistent results.

CAUTION High doses of echinacea can cause nausea. Some evidence suggests that echinacea may increase the risk of side effects of drugs used concurrently, including the birth control pill.

See Also: Herbal Medicine Expanded Commission E Monographs by M. Blumenthal, A. Goldberg, J. Brinckmann, American Botanical Council, 2000; A Field Guide to Medicinal Plants & Herbs: Eastern & Central North America, 2nd ed. by S. Foster, J. Duke, Houghton Mifflin, 2000.

THE RISE, FALL, AND RISE OF ECHINACEA

Echinacea was first introduced to conventional med-icine in the U.S. by Dr. John King, an Ohio physi-cian who belonged to the Eclectic School of healing arts, which relied heavily on the use of American medicinal plants in its practices. King mentioned the therapeutic actions of *E. purpurea* in the 1852 edition of *The Eclectic Dispensatory of the United States of America.* Around 1870, Dr. H.C.F. Meyer of Nebraska, having learned of the herb's uses and effects from local Native American tribes, concocted his own special echinacea preparation, which he mar-keted as Meyer's Blood Purifier. He claimed it would cure everything from rattlesnake bite to typhoid. Not until the late 1890s, however, did echinacea's popu-larity really take off in the U.S. In 1895, the pharma-ceutical firm of Lloyd Brothers in Cincinnati, Ohio, began manufacturing the first pharmaceutical prepa-rations of echinacea; shortly thereafter, interest blos-somed. From then until the late 1920s, echinacea became the fastest selling and most widely prescribed remedy derived from a Native American medicinal plant in the U.S. Then, toward the end of the 1920s, echinacea began to fall out of favor in the American medical community along with many other plant-based medicines. Its popularity increased in Ger-many, however. Echinacea continued to be largely ignored as an herbal remedy in the U.S. until the 1970s, when American herbalists "rediscovered" the herb, and herbal product manufacturers began to produce and promote it. Echinacea is now among the top-selling herbal supplements in the U. S. each year.

ECHINACEA PURPUREA | Echinacea

The **Cultivation and Preparation** sec-tion covers growing conditions and methods of preparation for use in herbal medicine, and types of prepa-rations used.

The **Research** section notes recent scientific studies in vitro (in the labo-ratory) or in vivo (with laboratory ani-mals or living organisms), or in human clinical trials or case reports. The sci-ence may confirm or refute thera-peutic claims.

The **Sidebar** offers interesting infor-mation—biology, nomenclature, his-tory, folklore—that adds to a better understanding of human experience with the plant or its relatives.

The **Caution** alerts readers to prob-lems that might arise. Anyone can have a reaction to a plant. Consult a licensed health care provider before using herbs, and inform your health care provider when you use herbs.

The **See Also** feature at the bottom of the spread provides sources of addi-tional information about the herb.

INTRODUCTION

THE WORLD IS EXPERIENCING AN herbal renaissance. Around the globe, nature's medicines are gaining importance not only in traditional herbal medicine but also in providing molecular models for development of new drugs for modern Western medicine. As many as 50 percent of prescription drugs—penicillin, for example, as well as hundreds of others—are based on a molecule that occurs naturally in a plant. Some 25 percent of prescription drugs are derived directly from flowering plants or modeled on plant molecules.

Remarkably, these statistics have not changed even one percent since 1959. Morphine and codeine, derived from the opium poppy, are still important painkillers. Quinine and its derivatives from the bark of the South American red cinchona tree have been primary treatments for malaria for more than four centuries. And as the mosquito-borne protozoa that cause malaria have developed resistance to quinine drugs, a new plant-derived treatment has emerged in world medicine—artemisinin. A derivative of sweet wormwood (*Artemisia annua*), artemisinin is native to Asia but widely naturalized in other parts of the world. It is likely, if you have a home garden in the eastern United States, you pull the plant out as an unwanted weed. Another key herbal medicine, foxglove (*Digitalis purpurea*), along with other *Digitalis* species, is the source of cardiac glycosides such as digitoxin and digoxin. Delivered in minute controlled doses, *Digitalis* strengthens the force of heart contractions while slowing the heart beat and is widely used to treat congestive heart failure and other heart conditions.

Plants also serve as sources of important cancer drugs used in modern chemotherapy. Vincristine and vinblastine are drugs derived from the Madagascar periwinkle (*Catharanthus roseus*). Introduced into chemotherapy in the mid-1960s, vinblastine became a primary treatment for Hodgkin's disease and reversed a near-90 percent mortality rate to a near-90 percent survival rate. Vincristine is primarily used in combination with other drugs for the treatment of acute leukemia in children. Paclitaxel, originally isolated from the Pacific yew (*Taxus brevifolia*) and now made from a semi-synthetic process from related compounds in English yew (*Taxus baccata*)—an ornamental probably planted on your own street—was approved in the 1990s to treat breast and ovarian cancers.

In the pages of this book you will find the history, lore, biochemistry, and medical science of these and many other important medicinal plants used as sources of modern drugs. All were developed out of a scientific field known as pharmacognosy, or knowledge of crude drugs and simples. In the 1970s, Dr. Norman Farnsworth, known to his colleagues as "the grand old man of pharmacognosy," used a rubber stamp on his correspondence that read, "Preserve the endangered species—pharmacognosy." At the time, this academic discipline, once a staple in every college of pharmacy, was disappearing from the curriculum. Now the field is experiencing a rebirth, thanks to scientists like Farnsworth. Head of the Program for Collaborative Research

Foxgloves adorn a field. Digitalis, a complex chemical in foxglove, is widely used for a variety of heart conditions.

in the Pharmaceutical Sciences, at the University of Illinois, Chicago, Farnsworth created the world's largest computer database on medicinal plants, known as NAPRALERT. That database has served countless researchers in many nations, enabling them to target priorities leading to new drugs and to provide the science supporting or refuting traditional claims. According to Farnsworth, "The continuing use of natural products, herbs, and plant materials, such as botanical dietary supplements, will probably go on forever. But the utilization will decrease, unless good science is done to show they work."

For more than five decades, Farnsworth has been helping to make sure good science gets done. In 1976, the World Health Organization (WHO) recognized the potential value of traditional practitioners and folk healers to deliver health care. Noting that up to 80 percent of the world's population relies on traditional medicine, chiefly herbal medicines, WHO designated collaborative research and training centers around the world and developed programs for dissemination of the information. One of the first collaborating centers was Dr. Farnsworth's research team at the University of Illinois.

Farnsworth's lab has collected and screened thousands of plant species worldwide for potential use in cancer, diabetes, AIDS, and virtually every other health condition that afflicts humankind. In the past, most federal funding for medicinal plant research focused on screening plants for anti-cancer or anti-HIV activity, such as the National Cancer Institute's plant screening program that yielded chemotherapy drugs such as camptothecin from happy tree (*Camptotheca acuminata*) and paclitaxel from the Pacific yew (*Taxus brevifolia*). Today, Farnsworth's research focuses on botanicals sold to American consumers as dietary supplements.

He heads two research centers sponsored by the National Institutes of Health—the Center for Botanical Dietary Supplement Research in Women's Health and the Center for Dietary Supplement Research on Botanicals.

Current Research and Development

FOLLOWING PASSAGE OF THE DIETARY SUPPLEMENT Health and Education Act of 1994, herbs and medicinal plant products and consumer information flooded the American market. As part of that legislation, the United States Congress funded two research programs at the National Institutes of Health in Bethesda, Maryland— the Office of Dietary Supplements and the Center for Complementary and Alternative Medicine. These centers, in turn, fund Farnsworth's research programs, which are a microcosm of the broad range of scientific disciplines that must come together to answer questions on the safety and effectiveness of herbal products. Farnsworth's research group focuses on herbal supplements that may benefit women's health, such as black cohosh and red clover for menopausal symptoms. Given the current lack of interest in herbs by pharmaceutical and drug companies, Farnsworth notes that new research on medicinal plants is entirely dependent on available federal money.

Many of the same herbs sold as dietary supplements in the U.S. are sold as drugs in Europe, particularly in Germany, where they are prescribed by physicians and dispensed by pharmacists. Herbal products are routinely sold in pharmacies in modern Russia. Traditional medicine in China, dating back 4,000 years, serves 40 percent of the public health needs of China's urban populace and 60 percent of its rural inhabitants. In India, 300,000 practitioners of Ayurvedic medicine, which has a 6,500-

year tradition, serve the population. In England and Australia, herbalists practice as primary health care providers, tacitly protected under English common law.

An Herbal Sampler

DESK REFERENCE TO NATURE'S MEDICINE INCLUDES a sampling of 150 of the more than 80,000 known medicinal plants worldwide. This book represents a cross-section of herbs used in dietary supplement products in the United States and the European phytomedicine tradition, including popular herbs such as black cohosh, echinacea, ginkgo, and ginseng. It also describes the development of plants currently used in prescription drugs such as foxglove, Pacific yew, and opium poppies, among others. Further, it explores how poisonous plants such as belladonna came to be used as drugs.

Some of the major herbal medicines of traditional medicine in China, such as astragalus and schisandra are sampled here, along with Ayurvedic herbs from India, including ashwagandha and ginger. Kava and noni, plants originating from traditional medicine practices of Oceania, as well as aromatic trees of Australia, such as the eucalyptus and tea tree, are also represented. Readers will learn about herbs from American Indian traditions, such as goldenseal, echinacea, and saw palmetto, now popular in both Europe and North America; readers also will discover the medicinal plants yielded by shamanic traditions of the Amazon Basin, the Andes, and the rain forests of South and Central America—as well as new facts about familiar plants like chocolate. Pomegranates and myrrh originate from the Middle East. The vast deserts and jungles of Africa and Madagascar supply medicinal plants such as devil's claw and Madagascar periwinkle. Africa also gives us a glimpse of "new" medicinal plants from the fledgling field of zoopharmacognosy—revealing how chimpanzees and other primates self-select and self-medicate with aspilia and bitterleaf.

Many of the plants included in this book have been used and cultivated by humans at least since the dawn of recorded history. Garlic, cultivated for at least 7,000 years, is not known from the wild. Its closest wild relatives are believed to have originated on the Asian steppes. Lemongrass, grown throughout tropical and subtropical regions, may have evolved on the Malay Peninsula, but its exact origin is unknown. Flax, which produces the linen cloth, linseed oil, as well as healthful flaxseeds, is widespread in temperate regions around the world. It has been cultivated and utilized for at least 4,000 years—its origins lost in antiquity. Kava, used for at least 3,000 years as the ceremonial drink of South Pacific islanders, is a cultigen—a plant that survives only in cultivation. It does not reproduce on its own. It produces no viable seeds and does not spread through vegetative means; it is entirely dependent on humans for its existence, just as humans throughout history have been dependent on medicinal plants for survival.

Desk Reference to Nature's Medicine provides an essential source of information and imagery on humankind's vast experience with medicinal plants—traditions, descriptions, distribution, history, science, and cautions. Current research is turning up medicinal properties in everything from pomegranates, used as a contraceptive in the ancient world, to the antioxidant benefits of chocolate, to the liver function–enhancing value of dandelions. Who knows? The next cure for cancer or treatment for AIDS may not be hidden in the Amazon rain forest. It may come from your own backyard. ✍

—STEVEN FOSTER

Alfalfa

Medicago sativa

LFALFA, OR LUCERNE AS IT IS OFTEN CALLED IN EURO-
pean countries, is a member of the pea family and
is widely grown throughout the world as a food
crop for animals. The name alfalfa derives from the Arabic name for the plant, *al-fac-facah*, which the Spanish
changed to "alfalfa." Most people associate alfalfa with
animal fodder, but the leaves have been eaten raw or
cooked as a vegetable for centuries in many cultures.
They are rich in protein, calcium and other minerals,
vitamins A, those of the B group, C, D, E, and K. In the
United States, alfalfa sprouts have become a popular
food in salads. As a medicinal plant, alfalfa is less well
known. Preparations of dried alfalfa are incorporated
into herbal supplements that are said to act on the
circulatory and urinary systems to control bleeding,
reduce water retention, and lower cholesterol and
glucose levels in the bloodstream. Alfalfa may also
influence hormones.

Traditional and Current Medicinal Uses

ALFALFA HAS BEEN USED IN HERBAL MEDICINE FOR AT LEAST
1,500 years. In traditional Chinese medicine, physicians
used young alfalfa leaves to treat disorders of the digestive tract and kidneys. **Ayurvedic** physicians of India prescribed leaves and flowering tops of the herb for poor
digestion; a cooling **poultice** was made of the seeds for
boils. Alfalfa was also considered therapeutic to reduce
water retention and for arthritis. Native Americans used
heated alfalfa leaves as a poultice to treat earaches.

In modern herbal medicine, alfalfa is suggested as a
remedy to treat anemia, as an anti-hemorrhagic, for diabetes, to stimulate appetite and promote weight gain,
for indigestion and bladder disorders, as a **diuretic** to
increase urination, as an estrogen replacement to
increase breast milk and alleviate premenstrual syndrome, as a dietary supplement, and to lower blood
cholesterol levels.

Cultivation and Preparation

ALFALFA IS CULTIVATED IN LIGHT, WELL-DRAINED SOIL IN FULL
sun. The leaves and stems are the parts of alfalfa that

Common Names Alfalfa, lucerne, buffalo herb,
purple medic

Latin Name *Medicago sativa*

Family Fabaceae

Parts Used Stems, leaves, seeds, sprouts

Description Alfalfa is a long-lived perennial, typically less than three feet tall with multiple upright
stems and three-part, clover-like leaves, and a
deep root system. It bears clusters of pea-like
flowers that range from reddish-purple to blue.
Fruits are characteristically coiled or sickle-
shaped pods that contain small, shiny seeds.

Habitat Native to southwestern Asia and southeastern Europe, alfalfa is now cultivated and
naturalized in many temperate and tropical parts
of Europe, North America, and North Africa.

Approximate
native range

are used in herbal medicine preparations. These aerial parts are cut before the plant blooms and then dried for use in capsules, **extracts, infusions,** tablets, and teas.

Research

THE BEST RESEARCHED USE OF ALFALFA IN MODERN HERBAL medicine is for helping to control cholesterol. Reductions in blood levels of total cholesterol and **low-density lipoproteins** (LDLs) have been reported in animal studies and in a small number of human cases. **High-density lipoproteins** (HDLs) have remained unchanged in these cases. Several studies in animals report reductions in arterial cholesterol plaques with alfalfa as well. There is some indication that alfalfa's **saponins,** a complex group of chemical compounds present in many plants, decrease intestinal absorption of cholesterol, thus lowering its concentration in blood and helping to prevent **arteriosclerosis.** Although these results are promising, more scientifically based research is needed before a conclusion can be reached about alfalfa's efficacy in reducing cholesterol.

A small number of animal studies report that alfalfa appears to reduce blood sugar levels. Human data are limited, and it remains unclear if the herb would exhibit similar effects in people and would be beneficial in treating diabetes or **hyperglycemia** (high blood sugar). Other chemical compounds found in alfalfa have demonstrated alfalfa's effectiveness in estrogen replacement, but additional studies are required in order to clearly understand alfalfa's action, if any, on hormone levels.

Consuming large amounts of alfalfa seeds has been associated with pancytopenia, a condition in which both red and white blood cell production decreases. Studies have also shown that eating large amounts of alfalfa seeds or alfalfa sprouts can induce systemic lupus erythematosus, an inflammatory connective tissue disease; eating large amounts of alfalfa seeds can also reactivate the disease in cases where it had become dormant. These reactions may be due to the **amino acid** canavanine, a substance which is present in alfalfa seeds and sprouts but is not present in the leaves.

Alfalfa was probably first cultivated in central Asia. From there the herb and its use spread to China, possibly as long as 2,000 years ago. Alfalfa reached Greece in the fifth century B.C. and moved from there into Spain and other parts of Europe and North Africa. Widespread cultivation of alfalfa in Europe began in the 17th century and was an important advance in European agriculture. European settlers brought the plant to America, but it was not widely cultivated until the 1850s. Introduced to California, alfalfa cultivation then spread northward and eastward into other western states. Today, the two most important leguminous forage crops in the United States are alfalfa (*Medicago sativa*) and red clover (*Trifolium pratense*). Both crops provide cattle and other grazing animals with concentrated supplies of nitrogenous compounds. Like other legumes, alfalfa's roots contain symbiotic bacteria that can fix nitrogen, producing a high-protein feed no matter how much nitrogen is in the soil. Having such a nutritious feed available makes it possible for dairies and stockyards to operate on small parcels of land. Alfalfa crops also enable ranches to operate in the dry regions of the western United States, as large amounts of nutritious alfalfa hay can be grown along streams and rivers as well as in irrigated fields and stored for use when the rangeland plants are dormant. In most climates, alfalfa is cut three or four times a year.

MEDICAGO SATIVA | Alfalfa

See Also: *A Field Guide to Medicinal Plants and Herbs: Eastern and Central North America, 2nd ed.* by S. Foster and J. Duke, Houghton Mifflin, 2000; *A Field Guide to Medicinal Plants and Herbs: Western North America* by S. Foster and C. Hobbs, Houghton Mifflin, 2002.

Aloe
Aloe vera

I F THE OLD STORIES ARE TRUE, ONE OF CLEOPATRA'S BEAUTY secrets was aloe. The ancient Egyptians recognized the healing properties of this herb and also used it as one of the ingredients in embalming fluid. The plant was introduced into Europe in the tenth century, where over time it became an important ingredient in many herbal medicines. Aloe arrived in the West Indies in the 16th century and is still widely grown there. The fleshy herb is today a component of modern cosmetics and health care products ranging from hand and face creams to shampoos. In cool climates, aloe is often grown in conservatories or as a houseplant. Potted aloe plants are a common sight in many kitchens, where the leaves are within easy reach to apply to minor burns. Freshly snipped aloe leaves are the ultimate homegrown first aid. They have a soothing effect on minor cuts and burns, dry or chapped skin, sunburn, and insect bites.

Traditional and Current Medicinal Uses

THERE ARE MORE THAN 300 SPECIES OF ALOE, BUT ONLY A FEW have traditionally been used as herbal medicines. These include *Aloe perryi* from northeastern Africa and *A. ferox* from South Africa. But it is *Aloe vera* that tops the list as the aloe with the widest use. Both the Greeks and the Romans used it for treating wounds. During the Middle Ages, the yellow juice found in the leaf skin, was favored as a **purgative**. Throughout history, *Aloe vera*'s value has largely been divided between these two distinct therapeutic roles—as purgative and as leaf gel to heal wounds.

The clear gel found inside the fleshy leaves is used for treating minor burns, wounds, and certain skin conditions such as eczema and ringworm. The healing properties of aloe gel were popularized in Western countries in the 1950s, when much was made of the plant's ability to heal burns—including even radiation burns. The soothing effect of the gel is almost immediate, and it forms a coating over minor wounds that seems to help prevent infection. In Indian **Ayurvedic medicine**, aloe gel is considered an important tonic for excess *pitta* (meaning "fire").

Common Names Aloe, aloe vera, Barbados aloe

Latin Names *Aloe vera*, synonym *A. barbadensis*

Family Asphodelaceae

Parts Used Leaves

Description A succulent, tender perennial, aloe has tough, fleshy, grayish-green leaves that taper to a point like a spear. They have small, spiny teeth along their margins. The leaves arise directly from the root and grow as a circular cluster about two feet tall. Yellow, tubular flowers are produced on a branching flower stalk that rises above the rest of the plant.

Habitat Aloe is native to Mediterranean coastal areas, but grows wild in tropical and subtropical regions where the climate is sunny and dry, including the southern Mediterranean, Latin America, and the Caribbean. It is also extensively cultivated worldwide.

Approximate native range

The source of aloe's other major role in herbal medicine is the bitter, yellow liquid that is derived from the outer layer of its leaves. Known as drug aloe, aloe latex, aloe juice, or aloe sap, it has a powerful purgative effect. (It should not be confused with aloe gel-containing products sold as aloe juice.) Because of its intensely bitter taste, the latex was recommended for a time as a nail-biting deterrent to be painted on the fingertips of children. Aloe is one of the most commonly used herbs in the United States.

Cultivation and Preparation

ALOE NEEDS FULL SUN, WELL-DRAINED SOIL, AND TEMPERatures that do not fall below 40 degrees Fahrenheit. It does well as a potted plant, as long as it is not over-watered and providing the soil is allowed to dry out between waterings. Aloe is propagated by rooting the small plantlets produced by parent plants. Only the leaves are used in herbal medicine. They are cut to collect the gel. The gel is most effective when used immediately from freshly cut leaves. The gel is also commonly available commercially, either as pure gel or as part of creams, lotions, and ointments. It is a common ingredient in over-the-counter skin care products and cosmetics.

Research

ALOE LATEX CONTAINS ANTHRAQUINONES, CHEMICAL COMpounds that stimulate contractions in the walls of the digestive tract, accounting for the herb's laxative properties. Aloe gel is also rich in chemical compounds that speed healing by arresting pain and inflammation, encouraging cellular repair, and stimulating the immune system. The emollient effect of aloe gel is largely attributed to the complex carbohydrate glucomannan. Some preliminary studies on aloe gel indicate it may help lower blood sugar levels in people with Type 2 (adult onset) diabetes, but results are not conclusive and more research is needed. The results of some experiments with whole aloe leaf extracts suggest the plant may have some anticancer properties, and may enhance the effectiveness of some antiviral medications, but more study is needed to confirm, or refute, the findings.

ALOE THROUGH THE AGES

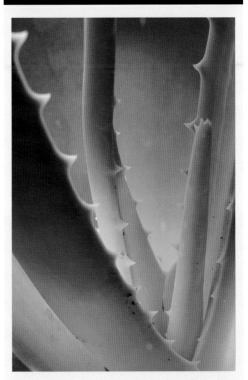

According to some accounts, the first known mention of aloe as a plant with healing powers may be a Sumerian clay tablet written around 2200 B.C. and unearthed in excavations of the ancient city of Nippur. A reference to aloe's use as a medicine is found in the Ebers Papyrus, an ancient Egyptian papyrus scroll dating to about 1550 B.C. that contains some 700 magical formulas and remedies. The Greeks also praised aloe for its medicinal virtues. In fact, it was so prized as a healing herb among the Greeks that, according to one legend, Greek philosopher Aristotle (384–322 B.C.) tried to persuade his pupil Alexander the Great (356–323 B.C.) to conquer the Indian Ocean island of Socotra near the Gulf of Aden for its aloes so that Alexander's armies would have a good supply of aloe for their wounds. Centuries later, Greek physician Dioscorides (A.D. 40–90) gave the first detailed description of aloe in his medical writings, describing aloe's "juices" (aloe latex) as having the power to induce sleep, loosen the belly, and cleanse the stomach. He went on to note that aloe was good for healing bruises, mouth, throat, and eye irritations, and could stop wounds from bleeding.

See Also: World Health Organization (WHO) Monographs on Selected Medicinal Plants, Vol. 1, 1999; Medicinal Herbs History, Use, Recommended Dosages & Cautions by S. Foster, Interweave Press, 1998.

Common Names American ginseng, *xi yang shen*

Latin Name *Panax quinquefolius*

Family Araliaceae

Parts Used Root

Description American ginseng is an herbaceous perennial that likes well-drained, humus-rich soils, north- and east-facing slopes, and forest shade. Above ground, American ginseng has a straight stem about a foot tall with one compound leaf that grows around it in a circle with five serrated leaflets on the subdivisions. In late spring mildly fragrant, yellow or white, umbrella-like flowers grow at the center, which give way to green berries that turn red by late summer.

Habitat American ginseng grows throughout the eastern part of North America in the U.S. and in Canada from Quebec to Alabama and west to Minnesota, Missouri, and Nebraska.

Approximate native range

American Ginseng
Panax quinquefolius

AT LEAST TEN SPECIES OF *PANAX* GROW WORLDWIDE, IN North America and in eastern and southwestern Asia. Asian ginseng (*Panax ginseng*) is considered a close relative to American ginseng (*Panax quinquefolius*). (This is not true of eleuthro or Siberian ginseng, though products may use them interchangeably.) Each year leaves die back in the fall leaving a new scar on the neck of the root indicating the age of the plant. This is important because the root does not have full strength for five years. Mature ginseng root is a scarce resource commanding high prices. In Canada and the U.S. strict laws protect wild ginseng from overharvesting. Most cultivated and wild-harvested ginseng goes to the Orient as part of a multimillion-dollar industry.

Traditional and Current Medicinal Uses

PANAX DERIVES FROM A GREEK WORD MEANING "PANACEA" OR "cure-all." Though ancient texts refer to ginseng's use for cooling and calming, digestive distress, and nutrition, ginseng is widely used today to strengthen the immune system, treat diabetes and cancer, and for energy, strength, stamina, and vigor. The Seneca, Cherokee, Creek, Iroquois, Seminole, and many other Native American tribes used American ginseng for a wide range of ailments. In 1716 a French Jesuit missionary working among the Mohawks north of Montreal reported his discovery of ginseng. Word soon spread via France to China, initiating what would quickly become a huge industry. American ginseng is highly sought after in Asia for its differences from Asian ginseng. American ginseng tastes sweeter and has cooling properties, nourishing the yin, as opposed to the yang of Asian ginseng's heat-raising effects. American ginseng is sought after by consumers in tropical climates for the same cooling effects.

Cultivation and Preparation

GINSENG GROWS FROM SEEDS. THE VALUE OF THE PRODUCT depends on the method and region of growth, and for wild ginseng the size and shape of the root as well. Uncultivated wild ginseng demands by far the most attention and highest price. Ginseng cultivated in the woods, called wild simulated ginseng, is grown from seeds. The least expensive is commercial ginseng, grown in raised beds from seeds, using fertilizers, pesticides, and artificial shade. It takes one to two years of dormancy for seeds to sprout. Flowering begins in the third year and leaves turn bright yellow in the fall before the plant dies back. The highest yields occur at the end of the summer of the fifth year when the root may double in size and weight.

Research

THE PRIMARY ACTIVE COMPONENTS THROUGHOUT THE *PANAX* species are the **saponins**. In the *Panax* genus, they are called ginsenosides. The ginsenosides are thought to be responsible for ginseng's medicinal value. Ginseng is considered an **adaptogen**—a substance that helps the body adapt to stress with few side effects. Most testing has been done on Asian ginseng; American ginseng research is still in its infancy. While there is little evidence of energy-boosting effects, studies suggest that ginseng strengthens the mind and immune system, increases the effect of insulin and regulates glucose in diabetics, counteracts male impotence, helps treat attention deficit (ADHD) in children, and inhibits the growth of cancer in vitro. Another study found that Type 2 (adult onset) diabetics had less of a rise in blood sugar if they took ginseng with sugar. One study comparing two groups suggested American ginseng may reduce cancers of the lungs, liver, pancreas, stomach, and ovaries. Given prior to a flu vaccine, ginseng increased the immune response in trial subjects compared to those given a **placebo**. American ginseng is taken for increased physical performance, but tests on athletes have shown mixed results. Some showed increased strength, others endurance, others reaction time, and others no increased performance at all.

CAUTION *Ginseng has been associated with insomnia, irritability, and nervousness, and is not recommended in combination with caffeine, for people with high blood pressure, or for women who are pregnant or breastfeeding.*

GINSENG ENVY

Most American ginseng (*Panax quinquefolius*) goes to Asia, often packaged in red, white, and blue. So why is American ginseng big in the land that has its own ginseng (*Panax ginseng*)? Several reasons. First, ginseng has been a leading herb in traditional Chinese medicine for millennia. By the early 18th century Asian ginseng was already extremely hard to get—and demand was fierce. Export of American ginseng to China began in the early 1700s. (Though highly regarded by Native Americans, American gingseng was part of the *United States Pharmacopoeia* for only a few decades in the 19th century.) Further, in Chinese medicine, American ginseng plays a complementary role, balancing the powers of Asian ginseng. American ginseng promotes the cold, dark, feminine energy of the yin, while Asian ginseng is the hot, light, masculine, yang energy. American ginseng is taken to reduce a fever, Asian ginseng as a temperature-raising blood circulator. Finally, American ginseng may profit from the good reputation American products enjoy in the Far East (even though much American ginseng comes from the Canadian provinces of Ontario and British Columbia). In the United States, Wisconsin is the biggest producer.

See Also: The ABC Clinical Guide to Herbs by M. Blumenthal, T. Hall, and A Goldberg, American Botanical Council, 2003; A Field Guide to Medicinal Plants and Herbs: Eastern and Central North America, 2nd ed. by S. Foster and J. Duke, Houghton Mifflin Co., 2000.

Common Names Angelica, garden angelica, European angelica

Latin Name *Angelica archangelica*

Family Apiacae

Parts Used Leaves, stems, seeds, roots

Description Angelica is a statuesque biennial that may live for three or more years if not allowed to set seed. In its first year, the plant forms a low-growing rosette of leaves. In the second year, it sends up a hollow, fluted, highly branched green stem. Large, glossy green leaves grow out from the stem on long stalks; each leaf is composed of smaller leaflets that have serrated edges. Large, rounded umbels (umbrella-like clusters) of small, yellow-green flowers are produced in midsummer; the oval seeds ripen in late summer. The entire plant is subtly aromatic.

Habitat *A. archangelica* is widely distributed throughout Asia and Europe, particularly in cool, northern regions. It has also naturalized in parts of the eastern U.S. and is typically found at the edges of woodlands in dappled shade in damp soil, especially near running water.

Approximate native range

Angelica
Angelica archangelica

ANGELICA IS AN ANCIENT HERB WIDELY PRAISED AND USED by the practitioners of both pagan and later Christian religions in northern Europe and England. It was thought to have magical or angelic powers to protect against evil and contagions of all kinds. During the Anglo-Saxon period in England, angelica was used in pagan rituals and worn for protection against evil spirits and spells cast by witches. Throughout northern Europe, it was praised in folklore as an herb that could strengthen and inspire—as well as cure. After the introduction of Christianity, angelica became linked with several of the archangels mentioned in the Bible and associated with various springtime festivals. For some, the connection was to the Archangel Gabriel, who was said to have appeared to the Virgin Mary at the Annunciation, an event traditionally celebrated at the end of March. Alternately, the name of the herb may be in reference to the Archangel Michael who, according to legend, appeared in a vision to relate the herb's protective and curative powers. The traditional feast day of Michael the Archangel is in late May, when the plant is typically in bloom. Whatever the link, angelica was held in such high esteem that it was referred to as "the root of the Holy Ghost" and believed to cure every conceivable malady.

Traditional and Current Medicinal Uses

SINCE ANCIENT TIMES, ANGELICA WAS THOUGHT TO BE A CURE for all ills. The herb was described as a "marvelous medicine" by Paracelsus (1493–1541), the German-Swiss physician and alchemist who established the role of chemistry in medicine. Every part of the plant, including the seeds, was credited with health-giving properties. The roots in particular, but also the leaves, stems, and seeds, were made into preparations used to bring relief from bronchitis, coughs, sore throats, colds, and other respiratory conditions and to act as an **expectorant**. All parts of the plants were considered helpful in stimulating appetite and in relieving indigestion, gas, colic, and bowel complaints. Angelica has been credited with **anti-inflammatory** properties and employed to lower fevers. Often described as a warming, stimulating tonic, the herb has been said to be effective in treating rheumatism and gout, for alleviating nausea, for relieving menstrual cramps, and for diseases of the urinary tract. Herbal medicine practitioners have also prescribed angelica in cases of poor circulation, because the herb is believed to stimulate blood flow to the peripheral parts of the body. Indeed, angelica is considered a specific treatment for Buerger's disease, a condition characterized by inflammation and constriction of the arteries in the hands and feet.

Cultivation and Preparation

ANGELICA REQUIRES DEEP, MOIST, FERTILE SOIL IN DAPPLED shade or part to full sun. It is a hardy plant that can survive severe winter frosts. Left to its own devices, the herb will behave as a true **biennial**, flowering in the second season and then dying. However, if the flowers are removed and the plant is prevented from producing seeds, it will continue to grow for years. Angelica is occasionally cultivated in herb gardens for its culinary uses (see sidebar) and because it attracts pollinating insects. Angelica is best propagated from seed (it self-seeds freely), although the seed does not retain its viability for very long when stored. Medicinally, roots are the plant's most active parts; they are harvested in autumn, cleaned, sliced longitudinally if necessary, and quickly dried. Leaves and seeds are also used in herbal medicine preparations. These are typically harvested and dried in late spring before the plant flowers.

Research

ALL PARTS OF ANGELICA, BUT ESPECIALLY THE ROOTS, contain chemical compounds that can sensitize the skin to light. Subsequent exposure to the ultraviolet radiation in sunlight can lead to inflammation of the skin. Recent research has revealed that *Angelica archangelica* also contains a number of chemicals that act as **calcium-channel blockers** in the heart; one of these is thought to be as potent as verapamil, a commonly used synthetic calcium-channel blocker currently prescribed for treating high blood pressure, angina, and heart arrhythmias.

ON THE SWEET SIDE

Throughout history, angelica has been valued for both culinary and medicinal attributes. Parts of angelica, particularly the roots and stems, possess an unexpectedly sweet, haunting flavor. There is a long tradition of crystallizing the herb's hollow stems in sugar to make a green candied confection eaten as a sweet or used for decorating cakes and puddings. During the 14th century, Carmelite nuns made a sweetish drink known as Carmelite water to treat nervous headache and neuralgia and as a complexion aid. Several centuries later, another form of angelica water, dubbed "the King's Majesty's Excellent Recipe for the Plague" by London's College of Physicians in the mid-1600s, was believed (for a time) to be a cure for that highly contagious disease: Made from nutmeg, treacle (a sweet syrup), and angelica root, the concoction was brewed over a fire and then drunk twice a day as a plague remedy. Angelica roots and seeds were also used for flavoring drinks such as gin, vermouth, and certain liqueurs including Chartreuse and Benedictine. Tender leaves and shoots were used in salads to add a slightly sweet flavor. They were also stewed with tart fruits and berries to reduce their acidity. Angelica roots were commonly made into preserves and the seeds were added to cookies.

See Also: *Herbal Medicine Expanded Commission E Monographs* by M. Blumenthal, A. Goldberg, J. Brinckmann, American Botanical Council, 2000; *A Field Guide to Medicinal Plants & Herbs: Eastern & Central North America, 2nd ed.* by S. Foster, J. Duke, Houghton Mifflin, 2000.

Common Names Arnica, leopard's bane, mountain arnica, mountain tobacco, mountain daisy

Latin Name *Arnica montana*

Family Asteraceae

Parts Used Flowers, root (uncommon)

Description A perennial herb with a creeping rhizome (underground stem), arnica grows to one to two feet. It has an erect, branched, slightly hairy stem that arises from a flat rosette of oval, downy leaves. The stem branches to yellow-orange, daisy-like flower heads that typically bloom in midsummer. Arnica's rhizome is dark brown and covered with rootlets.

Habitat *Arnica montana* is native to the mountains of Europe, central Asia, and Siberia, and is cultivated in North America. Its preferred habitats are sunny mountain meadows, hillside pastures, and open woodlands. It is becoming rare in the wild, possibly due to over-collection as a medicinal herb, and is now protected in many countries.

Approximate native range

Arnica
Arnica montana

THE GENUS NAME *ARNICA* MAY BE DERIVED FROM THE Greek *arnikos*, which means "lamb's skin," possibly an allusion to the soft downy texture of the plant's lower leaves. In parts of the world where arnica is indigenous, it has a history of use as an herbal medicine, especially as an external treatment for bruises and sprains. In North America, Native Americans used indigenous species of the plant (*A. fulgens*, *A. sororia*, and *A. cordifolia*) in much the same way as their European counterparts used *A. montana*. Some tribes also smoked parts of the dried plant in pipes, a practice that led to its nickname "mountain tobacco." Arnica's bright flowers resemble yellow daisies, accounting for another of the herb's common names—"mountain daisy." Today, arnica's medicinal properties are still widely exploited. Several hundred arnica-containing **tinctures**, ointments, and **homeopathic** remedies are currently manufactured for the German herbal medicine market alone.

Traditional and Current Medicinal Uses

ARNICA HAS BEEN USED FOR CENTURIES THROUGHOUT EUROPE and North America to soothe muscle aches, reduce inflammation, and heal bruises, sprains, and wounds. In the late 19th and early 20th centuries, alternative medicine practitioners recommended the herb for bruises and strained muscles, breast pain, and chronic sores or abscesses. Rubbed on the scalp, it was said to promote hair growth. It was also sometimes prescribed for depression, typhoid, pneumonia, anemia, diarrhea, and heart problems.

Currently, arnica is used for a wide range of conditions including bruises, muscle strains, sprains, bunions, dislocations, rheumatic muscle and joint problems, arthritis, wound healing, superficial phlebitis, inflammation from insect bites, and swelling due to bone fractures. It is typically rubbed on the skin in the form of a soothing, healing cream, ointment, or salve. Applied as a salve, it is also considered an effective treatment for chapped lips, acne, and irritated nostrils. In the hands of an experienced homeopathic clinician, arnica preparations may occasionally be used for inflammation of the mouth and throat, angina, and coronary artery disease. These instances are rare, however, and must be carried out only under strict medical supervision. This is because, taken internally, arnica can cause serious side effects including vomiting, increased heart rate, and nervous disorders. Even prolonged external use of arnica can result in toxic skin reactions. Homeopathic preparations are typically very dilute.

Cultivation and Preparation

ARNICA CAN TOLERATE A WIDE RANGE OF SOIL CONDITIONS; it even grows well in very poor or very acidic soils given adequate moisture. Under cultivation, *Arnica montana* thrives in a mixture of loam, peat, and sand. It is propagated by seed or by division of the roots in spring. Full sun is best. *A. chamissonis* is cultivated in addition to *A. montana* in Europe, where demand for arnica-containing herbal medicines is particularly high. All parts of the plant have medicinal value, but it is the fresh or dried flower heads that are commonly used in preparations. Flowers are harvested when fully open and dried.

Research

RECENT RESEARCH HAS DEMONSTRATED THAT WHEN APPLIED externally, arnica possesses **anti-inflammatory**, antiseptic, and **analgesic** properties. It appears to exert some of its effects by stimulating the activity of white blood cells that work within tissues to remove congested blood and by dispersing trapped fluids in bruised tissues, joints, and muscles. **Extracts** of arnica have also been shown to increase circulation. Nevertheless, because it is a severe irritant of the internal organs and can damage the heart, arnica is rarely prescribed for internal use. In fact, for some individuals, external use may also be risky. Eczema, peeling, blisters, and other skin conditions have been reported as a result of long-term use. Arnica should never be used on broken skin.

> **CAUTION:** Arnica should never be taken internally except under strict medical supervision. Repeated external use can cause skin irritation, eczema, and even necroses.

Arnica has long been a popular homeopathic remedy for sprains, bruises, and heart problems in Europe, especially in Germany. The German poet, dramatist, and novelist Johann Wolfgang von Goethe (1749–1832) was known to have drunk arnica tea to relieve his angina; arnica is still widely used in Germany for heart conditions. Despite a large body of anecdotal evidence, however, many claims made for arnica's healing properties have not been supported by scientific research. In 1981, German scientists identified an active ingredient in the herb called helenalin. In lab experiments, helenalin was shown to exhibit anti-inflammatory, analgesic, and mild antibacterial properties. However, subsequent clinical trials have for the most part failed to show any positive effects of arnica preparations in relieving pain from common injuries such as bruises and strained muscles. An exception was a clinical trial conducted in Switzerland in 2002 indicating that fresh arnica gel preparations successfully reduced symptoms in patients who were suffering from osteoarthritis of the knee. Twice a day for six weeks, 53 women and 26 men applied arnica gel to their affected knees. By the end of the testing period, nearly all the participants had experienced significant relief of pain and stiffness as well as increased mobility in osteoarthritic joints. More than three-quarters of them said they would use arnica gel again for relief of symptoms.

See Also: Herbal Medicine Expanded Commission E Monographs by M. Blumenthal, A. Goldberg, and J. Brinckmann, American Botanical Council, 2000; *A Field Guide to Medicinal Plants and Herbs: Western North America* by S. Foster and C. Hobbs, Houghton Mifflin, 2002.

Ashwagandha

Withania somnifera

LIKE GINSENG IN THE CHINESE HERBAL TRADITION, ashwagandha has played a central role in traditional medicine in India for millennia. Though there are by now many wild and cultivated variations, the primary active ingredients appear to be the same in all varieties. It is usually taken as a powder made from the root or the whole plant. Known primarily as a stress reliever and calming tonic, it is considered an **adaptogen**, strengthening the immune system and helping the body to cope with stress of many kinds.

Traditional and Current Medicinal Uses

FOR MORE THAN 3,000 YEARS, ASHWAGANDHA HAS BEEN CONsidered an excellent rejuvenator in India. It is respected as such in the **Ayurvedic, Siddha**, and **Unani** medical traditions. Considered a general tonic for health and recovery from all sorts of ailments, ashwagandha's list of uses is long. Traditionally it has been used as a sedative, **diuretic, anti-inflammatory**, and generally for energy, strength, and endurance. Like ginseng, ashwagandha has a long history as an all-around health enhancer. Unlike ginseng, ashwagandha has a sedative instead of stimulating effect.

In modern herbal medicine, **extracts** can be found in teas, powders, pills, and syrups. Ashwagandha is taken for coughs and colds, ulcers, emaciation, diabetes, epilepsy, insomnia, senile dementia, leprosy, Parkinson's disease, cognitive and nervous disorders, rheumatism, arthritis, intestinal infections, bronchitis, asthma, and sexual enhancement. Leaves, and sometimes the bark of the plant, are applied to bed sores and to swollen, inflamed skin. Leaf juice is used to treat conjunctivitis. Rubbed on the skin, the leaves act as an insect repellent.

Cultivation and Preparation

ASHWAGANDHA LIKES DRY, WARM, SUNNY SPOTS AND WELL-drained, sandy, loamy, or clay soil in the 7.5–8 pH range. It grows up to 5,000 feet above sea level, in hot climates, and needs moist soil but cannot tolerate too much water, shade, or cold, especially as a seedling. Ashwagandha is mostly grown as a production crop, started by seed

Common Names Ashwagandha, winter cherry

Latin Name Withania somnifera

Family Solanaceae

Parts Used Roots, seeds, leaves

Description Ashwagandha is a semi-woody, evergreen shrub that shoots up one to six feet high on a grayish stem and has oval leaves, little greenish or yellow flowers, and red berries.

Habitat It is widely cultivated throughout India, in Africa, the Mediterranean, the Middle East, and around the world.

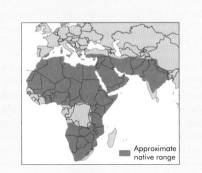

Approximate native range

in the greenhouse and then transplanted to the field a month later. Five to six months after being sown, when the leaves and yellow-red berries dry out, the plant has reached maturity. Then, when the soil is moist, the stems are cut close to the ground, and the roots are harvested with care to preserve spindly, minor roots. Roots are then washed, cut into pieces, and dried. Traditional preparations include a **decoction** of the root in milk, ghee or medicated butter, and medicated oil. A dose of 250 milligrams to 1 gram of the herb per day is generally used.

Research

THOUGH EXTENSIVE RESEARCH HAS BEEN DONE ON ASHWAgandha for decades in India, most has been in test tubes or on animals. The chemical components of the root have been identified, tested, and suggested to have **analgesic**, anti-inflammatory, antimicrobial, aphrodisiac, sedative, and immune-strengthening properties. The leaves also share analgesic, anti-inflammatory, and sedative properties; the seeds are used for diuretic effects. Many studies have been performed. One **double-blind** study performed on underweight 8- to 12-year-old Indian children tested the effects of administering 2 grams of ashwagandha a day. After 60 days, body weight amd red blood cell count improved. When given to a sample of 50-year-old men for a year, red blood cell count, hemoglobin, hair melanin, and sexual performance all improved significantly. In vitro studies have shown that ashwagandha inhibits the growth of cancers of the breast, central nervous system, lung, and colon. Another study suggests that the use of ashwagandha during chemotherapy strengthens the effects of the therapy, leading to less treatment and fewer side effects. Researchers in Switzerland found that albino mice given ashwagandha before and after being exposed to skin cancer-inducing situations had significantly fewer lesions than the control group.

> **CAUTION** Ashwagandha's high iron content may have abortive effects in large doses and should not be taken during pregnancy. A mild depressant, ashwagandha should not be taken with alcohol, sedatives, or other antianxiety drugs.

WITHANIA SOMNIFERA | Ashwagandha

Ayurvedic medicine, dating back more than 6,000 years, has existed longer than any other healing tradition, including Chinese medicine. According to legend, the greatest sages in India met in the mountains of the Himalaya to combine their knowledge into what would be called *ayur* (life) and *veda* (knowledge). The Ayurvedic perspective sees health as harmony between one's mental, physical, and spiritual self and the world. In Ayurvedic thinking, prevention is the best medicine, and in pursuit of a long healthy life, strengthening one's immune system becomes essential. Dietary and herbal prescriptions play a vital role—and ashwagandha is one of the tradition's leading herbs. One Ayurvedic text describes ashwagandha as "that which supports natural immunity by enhancing physical and mental strength, promotes overall health and longevity, is bitter, astringent and warming, and is beneficial for heart-mind-body coordination." In Ayurvedic medicine herbs are rarely recommended alone. Ashwagandha is one of the most commonly used herbs, according to ancient formulas, because it is a synergistic mix of others. For the past 3,000 years, it has been a well-known medicine in India as a rejuvenating tonic, especially for the elderly, said to increase strength and vigor, and to serve as an aphrodisiac. It is a home remedy used throughout India as a geriatric tonic, and for weakness. It is recommended with cooling herbs such as licorice, or cooling foods like sugar, milk, or rice.

See Also: 101 Medicinal Herbs: History, Use, Recommended Dosages & Cautions by S. Foster, Interweave Press, 1998; *Medicinal Plants of the World* by B. van Wyk and M. Wink, Timber Press, 2004.

Asian Ginseng
Panax ginseng

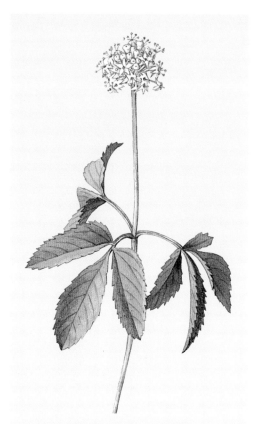

Common Names Asian ginseng, Korean ginseng

Latin Name *Panax ginseng*

Family Araliaceae

Parts Used Root

Description Ginseng is a slow-growing perennial that each year produces a single stem from a short rhizome (underground stem) attached to a fleshy, light tan, gnarled root. The stem gives rise to several oval, toothed leaflets and a single cluster of small white flowers. Each flower develops into a fleshy, bright red fruit.

Habitat Native to mountainous forests of eastern Asia, ginseng is very rare in its historical range but is cultivated extensively in China, Japan, Korea, and Russia.

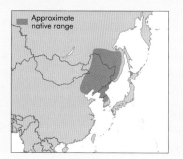

Approximate native range

USED IN CHINA FOR WELL OVER 2,000 YEARS, GINSENG (*Panax ginseng*) is probably the most famous Asian medicinal plant. The earliest written record of ginseng's use and properties is from the *Divine Husbandman's Classic of the Materia Medica (Shen Nong Ben Cao Jing)*, the oldest known comprehensive medical text that dates from the first century A.D. The Chinese—and many other people worldwide—have long regarded ginseng as the ultimate herb, one that can cure all ills. This view is even reflected in the herb's genus name: *Panax*, derived from the Greek words *pan* (all) and *akos* (cure), literally means "cure-all." In herbal medicine, ginseng is considered an **adaptogen**, a substance that strengthens and normalizes body functions, enhancing the body's own natural defenses against disease and stress. In this way the herb is viewed not so much as a medicine but as a substance that revitalizes the body as a whole. Many of the thousands of studies conducted on ginseng over the past 50 years provide some support for the traditional claims made about the benefits of using this herb.

Traditional and Current Medicinal Uses

FOR THOUSANDS OF YEARS IN TRADITIONAL ASIAN MEDICINE, ginseng has been used as a tonic to revitalize and replenish vital energy, or *qi*. Ginseng is believed to build resistance to infection or disease, reduce susceptibility to illness, shorten the time that it takes to recover from illness or surgery, quiet the spirit, promote health and longevity, and give widsom. Ginseng's greatest value is thought to be its normalizing, restorative effects on the whole body, rather than its impact on particular organs or systems or its activity against a certain disease or condition. There is no real equivalent concept or treatment in Western conventional medicine.

Today, ginseng is officially listed in the national **pharmacopeias** of Austria, China, France, Germany, Japan, Switzerland, and Russia. In modern herbal medicine, ginseng is recommended for a remarkably wide variety of conditions (it is difficult to enumerate the uses of an herb said to be a cure-all for nearly every human ailment). Some of the effects ginseng is commonly said to exert include: improving mental performance, enhancing stamina, improving pulmonary function, combating fatigue, lowering blood sugar, stimulating immune cells' activity in the body, preventing cancer, relieving the symptoms of menopause, improving mental health and quality of life (especially in the elderly), fighting chronic illnesses, and combating aging.

Cultivation and Preparation

GINSENG IS DIFFICULT TO GROW. IT REQUIRES MOIST, RICH SOIL in full shade and warm humid conditions in the growing season. Plants take four to seven years to mature. Roots are lifted from mature plants in autumn, washed and steamed, and then dried for use in herbal medicine preparations.

Research

MODERN, WELL-DESIGNED LABORATORY AND CLINICAL STUDies of ginseng seem to support some of the therapeutic applications for which it is recommended. But in most cases, more research is needed to confirm results. Several studies report ginseng can modestly improve mental performance, but there is contrary evidence as well. A number of human studies show ginseng may lower blood sugar levels in patients with Type 2 (adult onset) diabetes, but long-term effects are not clear. Athletes often use ginseng to improve stamina, but results of numerous studies are mixed. Preliminary studies suggest ginseng may lower blood pressure and also relieve menopausal symptoms such as mild depression without changing hormone levels. A few studies indicate ginseng may activate the immune system by stimulating types of white blood cells. And research has suggested ginseng may lower the risk of getting some types of cancers, but more research is needed before conclusions can be drawn.

CAUTION Ginseng is generally not prescribed for pregnant women or those suffering from anxiety, depression, or acute inflammatory disease. Its use is normally restricted to six weeks.

THE YIN AND YANG OF GINSENG

Despite the fact that ginseng has been used medicinally for more than two millennia—and the similar herb, American ginseng (*Panax quinquefolius*), has been used in the West and elsewhere for more than two centuries—modern scientific research on ginseng has yielded mixed results and few answers as to the herb's true effects. However, nearly everyone agrees that the chemical constituents of ginseng that are most active are a complex mixture of saponins called ginsenosides. At least 30 different ginsenosides have been identified in extracts of the plant. The most reliable studies on ginseng have been conducted using extracts containing standardized amounts of these compounds, either 4 or 7 percent. Yet determining precisely what effects different ginsenosides have in the body is a daunting task. One intriguing result of lab research is that the physiological actions of different ginsenosides may work in opposition to one another. For example, in studies with mice, a ginsenoside known as Rg1 has been shown to stimulate central nervous system activity; on the other hand, ginsenoside Rb1 works as a central nervous system depressant. This opposing action may contribute to ginseng's supposed ability to balance bodily functions—much like yin and yang, the two opposing but complementary forces, according to ancient Chinese philosophy, found in all things in the universe.

See Also: *Herbal Medicine Expanded Commission E Monographs* by M. Blumenthal, A. Goldberg, and J. Brinckmann, American Botanical Council, 2000; *World Health Organization (WHO) Monographs on Selected Medicinal Plants, Vol. 1,* 1999.

Aspilia
Aspilia mossambicensis

ASPILIA IS NOT A PLANT REFERENCED IN THE ANCIENT herbal texts of Europe and Asia. It is sometimes classified in the genus *Wedelia*. Aspilia is native to Africa and its use as a medicinal plant was largely unknown outside of that continent until the 1980s. When aspilia did capture the attention of the scientific world, it was the result of a chance observation of the feeding habits of chimpanzees in Gombe National Park and in Mahale Mountains National Park in western Tanzania. In1983, Richard Wrangham of Harvard University and Toshisada Nishida of Kyoto University in Japan reported in a jointly authored scientific paper that chimpanzees—specifically individuals that looked ill—methodically picked, folded, and swallowed leaves of *Aspilia mossambicensis*. The scientists were intrigued by the fact that the leaves passed through the chimpanzees' digestive tracts undigested and intact. A few years later, a scientist at Cornell University reported that he had isolated a chemical substance, thiarubrine, from *Aspilia mossambicensis* leaves, that appeared to have strong antibiotic, antiparasitic, and antifungal properties. This finding led Wrangham and Jane Goodall, Gombe's pioneer chimpanzee researcher, to suggest that chimps might be eating aspilia leaves to rid themselves of intestinal parasites. They hypothesized that the chimps were self-medicating. The hypothesis turned out to be true—but not entirely as was first supposed.

Traditional and Current Medicinal Uses

IN THE 1990s, WRANGHAM AND OTHER RESEARCHERS WORKing in Gombe and Mahale conducted extensive field work on chimpanzees and their diets. They identified the species of plants that chimps were eating and also analyzed the animals' droppings. The researchers discovered that many chimpanzees suffering from heavy infestations of parasitic intestinal worms were also ingesting aspilia leaves. The chimps did not appear to enjoy eating the leaves, as they did other plants in their diet. Instead, they held aspilia leaves in their mouths for a few seconds before gulping them down whole,

Common Names Aspilia, wild sunflower

Latin Names *Aspilia mossambicensis, A. africana,* synonym *Wedelia mossambicensis*

Family Asteraceae

Parts Used Leaves

Description Aspilia is a perennial, semi-woody herb or small shrub. It has large, pointed, lance-shaped leaves with serrated edges and very rough-textured surfaces. The roughness is due to the presence of tiny hairs called trichomes.

Habitat Aspilia is native to East Africa and is found throughout tropical and subtropical Africa, including Madagascar.

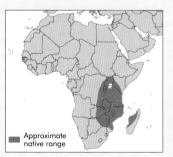

■ Approximate native range

without chewing—often consuming several dozen leaves at a sitting. Intrigued, the researchers examined the intact leaves that they found in chimp feces. Analyses revealed that the aspilia leaves not only remained whole and undigested, but they were teeming with parasitic worms. Many of the worms were caught in the flexible hairs that cover the surface of the leaves. The scientists concluded that aspilia leaf swallowing was acting to remove parasites from the chimps' digestive tracts. The roughness of the leaf surfaces, which some researchers dubbed the "velcro effect," had a purging effect, physically dislodging parasites as the leaves passed through the chimps' bodies. Researchers also noted that chimps at Gombe swallowed more aspilia leaves during the rainy season, when parasitic infections tend to increase. The observations seemed to support the idea that the chimps were selecting and eating the leaves as part of a self-medicating strategy to rid themselves of intestinal parasites.

In the same region of East Africa, some people also use aspilia leaves medicinally—not to scour their intestines, but in treating infections, malaria, and scurvy, as well as conditions such as sciatica and lumbago.

Cultivation and Preparation

Although Aspilia is not cultivated as a garden plant it is important in projects to restore degraded woodlands in East Africa (see sidebar). The leaves, when used as a traditional medicine, are made into a tea.

Research

THE INITIAL REPORT OF THE PRESENCE OF THIARUBRINE IN aspilia leaves has not been confirmed by other researchers. Many additional samples, taken from different locations in Mahale and Gombe National Parks at different times of the year, showed no trace of thiarubrine, though small amounts were found in the plants' roots. This inconsistency has yet to be explained. However, two potent stimulators of uterine contraction have been isolated from the leaves. Their presence may lend support to the idea that wild chimps eat the leaves for their pharmacological and physical properties, but much more research remains to be done.

Aspilia is native to east Africa and is now found throughout much of tropical Africa. *Aspilia* is a genus in the aster family with more than a hundred species that occur in warm and tropical regions. A perennial, semi-herbaceous plant or small woody shrub, the plant is quick to become a dominant species in dense, shrubby undergrowth. It is particularly useful in natural or wild areas that have been degraded either by overgrazing by animals or by the activities of humans who have cut down trees for producing charcoal for burning or for firewood. Once the overgrazing by livestock such as cattle or goats or the forest destruction by humans has stopped, aspilia is one of the first succession plants to appear. The plants help to form a thick undergrowth that creates a favorable layer so that trees begin to re-establish themselves. If these areas are left alone for a period of three to four years, they recover and woody species begin to grow to a height tall enough that they cannot be browsed and overgrazed by goats and other livestock.

See Also: "Biologically Active Diterpenes Fom *Aspilia mossabicensis,* a Chimpanzee Medicinal Plant," by J. Page and F. Balza, *Phytochemistry* 31 (10): 3437-9, 1992.

Astragalus

Astragalus membranaceus

ASTRAGALUS MEMBRANACEUS IS INDIGENOUS TO CHINA. It is a legendary plant whose root, called *huang qi* (meaning "yellow leader"), has been used in herbal medicine for more than 2,000 years. One of the earliest references to huang qi and its healing powers comes from what was perhaps the first **pharmacopoeia** of Chinese herbal medicine, the *Divine Husbandman's Classic of the Materia Medica*, which dates to the first century A.D. Most herbs cited in this ancient herbal can still be found in standard Chinese herbal textbooks and herbal pharmacies. Huang qi is today one of the most popular tonic herbs in traditional Chinese medicine, used to increase vitality and strengthen resistance. It has recently been recognized in North America for its immune system-stimulating properties, particularly in cancer patients.

Traditional and Current Medicinal Uses

THE DIVINE HUSBANDMAN'S CLASSIC OF THE MATERIA MEDica established basic Chinese herbal theory, including the principles of the four *qi*—cold, hot, warm, and cool. Considered on par with, or even superior to, ginseng as a tonic, preparations made from astragalus root are believed to warm and replenish a person's *wei qi*, an energy force that underlies the skin and is thought to protect the body from environmental influences, especially cold. Practitioners of traditional Chinese medicine consider astragalus to be a true tonic that can strengthen debilitated patients, increase energy levels, and increase resistance to disease.

Bundles of thinly sliced huang qi roots are regularly sold in pharmacies in China. The roots are boiled along with other herbs or broth to create a tonic or medicinal soup. Preparations of huang qi have been used to control excessive sweating, as in night sweats, as a **diuretic** to alleviate **edema** (swelling) by increasing urination, to reduce thirst, and to lower blood pressure. Other conditions for which the herb is considered a remedy include the common cold and similar viral infections, chronic diarrhea, uterine bleeding, abscesses and chronic ulcers, diabetes, and nephritis.

Common Names Astragalus, *huang qi*

Latin Name *Astragalus membranaceus*

Family Fabaceae

Parts Used Rhizomes (underground stems)

Description Astragalus is a small, half-hardy, multi-stemmed perennial that grows one to two feet tall. The herb's compound leaves have hairy stems; each leaf is made up of 12 to 18 pairs of smaller, pointed, bright-green leaflets. Mature plants have yellow, pea-like flowers that bloom in long clusters during early summer. Tough, fibrous, branching roots (rhizomes) are dark brown to black with a yellowish core. They have a peculiar odor and a slightly sweet taste.

Habitat Native to Mongolia and northern China, astragalus is now cultivated in several Asian countries, as well as in Canada and the U.S. It grows in sandy, well-drained soil and needs full sun.

Approximate native range

In contemporary Chinese medicine, astragalus is a major component in *zheng fu* therapy, a treatment involving combinations of herbs and designed to restore immune function in cancer patients undergoing radiation or chemotherapy. In Western medicine, astragalus has been shown to increase production of white blood cells and so may be of help in restoring immune function in immunocompromised patients.

Cultivation and Preparation

ASTRAGALUS NEEDS VERY GOOD DRAINAGE AND FULL SUN. IT is drought tolerant, but requires adequate moisture to grow well. Plants can be propagated easily from seed, but once established they do not like to have their roots disturbed. The roots are not harvested until the autumn of a plant's third to fifth year. Roots are typically harvested by hand or by machine. The crown and any lateral roots are trimmed from the main root, which is cleaned and partially dried, cut into thin slices, and dried further. For medicinal purposes, the herb is marketed as dried roots, ground roots in capsule and tablet, as a liquid **extract,** or as an ingredient in herbal teas.

Research

MUCH OF THE RESEARCH ON THE MEDICINAL PROPERTIES OF astragalus has been conducted in China. Chinese studies have confirmed that the herb acts as a diuretic and lowers blood pressure. A study of 1,000 patients in China showed that astragalus exhibits a prophylactic effect against colds and upper respiratory infections. Other research has focused on the herb's ability to boost the immune system by increasing production and activity of white blood cells. Research also indicates that astragalus may stimulate production of antibodies and interferon, a signaling agent that causes white blood cells to either multiply or fight infection. Studies in the U. S. suggest that cancer patients undergoing chemotherapy and radiation recover faster and live longer if astragalus is administered with other anticancer drugs. Clinical studies have shown astragalus provides benefits in the treatment of **ischemic** heart disease as well as in heart conditions such as myocardial infarction, heart failure, and relief of anginal pain.

A DIVERSE GROUP

Astragalus membranaceus is one of 2,000 species of annuals, perennials, and small shrubs belonging to the genus *Astragalus.* Within this diverse collection—in addition to *A. membranaceus*—are some with medicinal properties. One of these is *A. complanatus,* known as *sha yuan* in traditional Chinese medicine. Employed since the 12th century, the seeds of sha yuan are used to make preparations that serve as liver and kidney tonics and improve visual acuity; the herb is also known to lower blood pressure. Another group of *Astragalus* species, including *A. gummifer,* produces a rubbery, mucilaginous sap that is the source of a natural, water-soluble gum called gum tragacanth. Gum tragacanth has been used for thousands of years to treat persistent cough, diarrhea, and as an aphrodisiac. It is used in modern pharmaceuticals as an adhesive agent for pills and tablets, and for suspending oil in lotions, creams, and pastes. Other *Astragalus* species include plants that accumulate high concentrations of the mineral selenium or produce toxic compounds and so are poisonous to cattle and grazing animals. Termed "locoweeds," these species induce bizarre or "loco" behavior in animals, including weakness, loss of nervous control, staggering, and convulsions; large doses can be fatal.

See Also: World Health Organization (WHO) Monographs on Selected Medicinal Plants, Vol. 1, 1999; Herbal Emissaries: Bringing Chinese Herbs to the West by S. Foster and Y. Chongxi, Healing Arts Press, 1992.

Common Names Autumn crocus, naked ladies, meadow saffron

Latin Name *Colchicum autumnale*

Family Liliaceae

Parts Used Corms, seeds

Description A small perennial about a foot in height, autumn crocus has tulip-like leaves that grow up from a brown, scaly bulb, or corm. The leaves emerge in spring, together with the fertilized fruit—an elliptical capsule filled with small brown seeds—that was produced the previous growing season. By midsummer, these above-ground parts have died back, but in autumn, several light purple, crocus-like flowers emerge from the now leafless plant.

Habitat Autumn crocus is native to North Africa and Europe, but is widely cultivated as an ornamental in England, the United States, and Canada. In the wild, it grows well in wet meadows, as well as in woodland clearings and shady rocky habitats up to an altitude of about 6,500 feet above sea level.

Approximate native range

Autumn Crocus
Colchicum autumnale

ONE OF THE MORE INTRIGUING NICKNAMES FOR AUTUMN crocus is "naked ladies." The name refers to the plant's odd flowering habit: Flowers appear in the autumn long after the leaves have died and disappeared, making them seem strangely naked as they emerge from the ground. Referred to as autumn crocus and also meadow saffron, this lovely—and potentially deadly—herb is neither related to real crocus (*Crocus* spp.) nor saffron and should never be used as a saffron substitute in cooking. That's because the plant contains colchicine, an extremely poisonous **alkaloid**. Eating the plant's seeds, corms, or flowers can be fatal. Nevertheless, autumn crocus has long been valued in herbal medicine as a painkiller and as a specific treatment for gout, a form of arthritis caused by an accumulation of uric acid crystals in the joints.

Traditional and Current Medicinal Uses

THE ANCIENT GREEKS KNEW OF AUTUMN CROCUS'S DEADLY nature. But in the fifth century A.D. Byzantine herbalists discovered the plant could be effective in treating rheumatism—characterized by inflammation or pain in the muscles, joints, or fibrous tissue; about the same time, their counterparts in Arabia began using the herb as a remedy for gout. Autumn crocus was also discovered to be, in very small doses, a stimulant that possessed **cathartic**, **diuretic**, and **emetic** properties. Over the years it has been used to treat heart palpitations, gonorrhea, enlarged prostate, fever, various inflammatory conditions, chronic bronchial complaints, nausea, and some nervous ailments. A paste made from the bulb was said to be a folk remedy for tumors, a **poultice** made of the leaves supposedly helped eliminate corns, and a **decoction** of seeds was said to be effective in treating leukemia. But throughout the history of its use, its primary success has been as a treatment for rheumatism and gout.

Today extracts of the herbs are still used in carefully measured and administered doses to treat acute gout attacks. The herb's most active ingredient, colchicine, is a very effective painkiller with **anti-inflammatory** properties that specifically prevents certain types of white blood cells from migrating into the inflamed joints typically associated with acute gout attacks.

Cultivation and Preparation

WHILE NATIVE TO SOUTH, WEST, AND CENTRAL EUROPE, AND parts of North Africa, autumn crocus is cultivated throughout much of the world as an outdoor ornamental and for its medicinal value. Seeds are harvested in early summer; corms are harvested in mid- to late summer when the above-ground plant parts have died back completely. The powdered seeds are used in herbal preparations, as are **tinctures** of the seeds and corms. Fresh corm preparations are also used.

Research

THE PRIMARY ACTIVE INGREDIENT IN AUTUMN CROCUS IS the poisonous alkaloid colchicine, which is found in all parts of the plant, although corms and seeds contain the highest concentrations. In the treatment or prevention of attacks of gout (also called gouty arthritis), colchicine appears to exert its therapeutic effects by reducing inflammation in affected joints. Research has shown that colchicine affects cells by inhibiting cell division. Specifically, the alkaloid interferes with the development of spindle fibers as cell nuclei are dividing. As a result of its cell division-inhibiting properties, colchicine was initially considered as a potential anticancer drug. A derivative of the poisonous alkaloid was used for a time in the treatment of chronic leukemia. But due to severe side effects, currently colchicine is not used in cancer therapy in humans, although it is occasionally used in veterinary medicine to treat cancers in some animals. Colchicine is used, however, in cancer research, in studies where the division of cancerous cells needs to be stopped at a particular point in the cell cycle.

CAUTION Autumn crocus is very poisonous. No part of the plant should ever be collected or used for self-medication, and herbal preparations containing colchicine should never be used without expert medical supervision.

Colchicine is a deadly poison that can become a therapeutic medicine if carefully administered in small doses. But colchicine is also used in plant breeding research to induce polyploidy, a situation in which cells contain multiple, complete sets of chromosomes—for instance, twice or four times the normal number. Although polyploidy is rare and usually lethal in animals, it occurs naturally in plants. Plant breeders induce polyploidy in plants by treating them with colchicine under controlled conditions. This usually involves immersing the roots or terminal buds of a plant in a colchicine solution. Chromosomes duplicate inside these colchicine-treated cells, but the cells cannot complete division. As a result, cells with two or more sets of chromosomes are produced. When a plant is removed from the colchicine solution, normal cell division resumes. But the resulting daughter cells of colchicine-altered cells contain extra sets of chromosomes. These cells are then cultured to produce fully polyploid plants—which have abnormally large cells and are larger than others of the species.

Discovery of colchicine's effects on cells has led to the deliberate creation of polyploid varieties of many plants including daylilies, watermelons, marigolds, and snapdragons. In ornamentals, polyploid plants have exceptionally large blossoms. In food plants, polyploid varieties often produce higher yields.

See Also: Medical Botany: Plants Affecting Human Health by W. Lewis and M. Elvin-Lewis, John Wiley & Sons, 2003; *Medicinal Plants of the World* by B. van Wyk and M. Wink, Timber Press, 2004.

COLCHICUM AUTUMNALE | Autumn Crocus

Bearberry

Arctostaphylos uva-ursi

FOUND WIDELY ACROSS THE NORTHERN TEMPERATE ZONE, bearberry is indigenous to rocky shrublands and open woodlands in northern Europe, Scandinavia, Russia, northern Asia, Japan, and North America—as far north as the Arctic Circle and as far south as New Jersey, Wisconsin, and northern California in the U.S. The long genus name, *Arctostaphylos*, comes from the Greek words *arctos staphyle* and means "bear's grapes." The species name, *uva-ursi*, means the same thing in Latin. Presumably the names refer to the fact that bears ate the small red fruits, although they are extremely sour. Bearberry was first mentioned as a medicinal herb in a 13th-century Welsh herbal. Its therapeutic use, primarily for kidney and bladder problems, continued in Europe throughout the Middle Ages. In North America, Native Americans used bearberry as well; it was employed medicinally and the dried leaves were mixed with those of tobacco and smoked. Bearberry was considered one of the best natural remedies available for urinary infections until the 1940s, when it was largely replaced by sulfa drugs and antibiotics. In modern herbal medicine, however, bearberry remains useful in treating infections and inflammation of the urinary tract.

Traditional and Current Medicinal Uses

BEARBERRY HAS BEEN USED FOR CENTURIES FOR ITS **ASTRINGENT**, antiseptic, and mildly **diuretic** properties. In Europe, the leaves were typically brewed to make a tea taken for inflammatory diseases of the bladder and kidney. It was also used to treat kidney stones; its mild diuretic action has a flushing action on the kidneys and bladder. Bearberry was widely used by many Native American tribes. It was mixed with fat and used as a salve for rashes, boils, burns, and skin sores, made into a mouthwash for canker sores, and placed as a poultice on wounds and cuts for rapid healing. **Infusions** of bearberry leaves were taken for back pain, to stimulate menstruation, as a wash for rheumatism, as a diuretic, and as a tonic for the bladder and kidneys. The berries were eaten to prevent scurvy and the dried leaves, mixed with tobacco, were smoked; the mixture was called *kinnikinnick*.

Common Names Bearberry, uva ursi, bear's grape, kinnikinnick, mountain box

Latin Name *Arctostaphylos uva-ursi*

Family Ericaceae

Parts Used Leaves

Description A creeping evergreen shrub, bearberry has long, rooting branches that gradually spread to form a dense mat. Its small, oval, leathery leaves are dark green above and pale below. Clusters of tiny, white or pink, bell-shaped flowers give rise to small, shiny red fruits.

Habitat Bearberry thrives in acid soils of open, rocky hillsides and mountain slopes throughout the Northern Hemisphere.

Approximate native range

Bearberry berries were an important winter food for many tribes.

Modern use of bearberry developed in the 1700s, and it was widely recommended for urinary tract infections including chronic cystitis and urethritis, as well as for nephritis, kidney and gallstones, gout, and gonorrhea. More recently bearberry has also been suggested by herbal practitioners for vaginitis and for treating cases of chronic cystitis in disabled individuals that are often resistant to conventional antibiotics.

Cultivation and Preparation

BEARBERRY GROWS BEST IN COOL SURROUNDINGS AND IN ACID, rocky, well-drained soil in full sun or light shade. It is propagated by cuttings or layerings; propagation by seed is difficult. For commercial use, bearberry leaves are collected by hand in spring or summer entirely from wild plants, primarily in Scandinavia, Spain, Italy, and Russia. Overcollecting has led to protection of wild populations in Germany. Leaves are dried for use in liquid **extracts**, medicinal teas, infusions, and tablets.

Research

BEARBERRY LEAVES CONTAIN FLAVONOIDS, TANNINS, organic acids, and an active compound called arbutin. In the body, arbutin is converted to other forms—hydroquinones and their derivatives—that have been shown in lab experiments with animals to have strong antibacterial and antifungal properties. They are effective against several bacterial pathogens known to cause urinary tract infections, including *Escherichia coli* and *Staphylococcus aureus*. They also have an antiseptic and astringent effect on linings of the urinary tract. Arbutin and its breakdown products only work well as antibacterial agents when urine is alkaline, so herbal practitioners often suggest excluding fruits, juices, and acidic foods from the diet while taking bearberry preparations. Limited clinical studies have been conducted on bearberry's urinary disinfectant effects.

CAUTION In large doses, hydroquinones can be toxic. Bearberry preparations should only be used for short periods (not more than a week). This herb should not be used by pregnant women, children, and individuals with kidney disease.

Native Americans often smoked tobacco, or tobacco mixed with other herbs, as part of ceremonies with religious significance. Smoking could be carried out by burning materials in a smudge pot, like incense, or using a sacred pipe. Either way, the smoke rising into the sky was thought to carry the smoker's prayers or thoughts to the Great Spirit. A smoking ceremony might be conducted to seal a pact, quiet a thunderstorm, or seek relief from disease or drought. Smoking was also a part of rituals associated with dances, games, and festivals that fulfilled ceremonial practices. The word "kinnikinnick" was originally associated with a mix of bearberry and tobacco. The word originates from Chippewa and Cree dialects of the Algonquian word that means "that which is mixed." The term later came to include mixtures of tobacco and leaves of many herbs, including leaves of sumac, laurel, or squaw bush, and the inner barks of the red willow, dogwood, cherry, poplar, or birch. A typical kinnikinnick mixture might have included sumac or red willow bark, native tobacco, spicebush, and bearberry. Bark used in a kinnikinnick was prepared by peeling away the outer bark and shaving the inner bark into thin strips. These were toasted over an open fire. Bearberry and other herb leaves were generally toasted as well and then added to the final mixture to be smoked.

See Also: Herbal Medicine Expanded Commission E Monographs by M. Blumenthal, A. Goldberg, and J. Brinckmann, American Botanical Council, 2000; World Health Organization (WHO) Monographs on Selected Medicinal Plants, Vol. 2, 2002.

Bee Balm
Monarda didyma

Common Names Bee balm, Oswego tea, scarlet bergamot, mountain mint

Latin Name *Monarda didyma*

Family Lamiaceae

Parts Used Leaves

Description Bee balm is a hardy perennial growing to four feet in height with square stems, lance-shaped, toothed leaves and bright crimson, tubular flowers produced on crowded terminal heads. The entire plant exudes a citrus-like fragrance.

Habitat Native to eastern North America, *Monarda didyma* is found in damp woodlands and along rivers and streams. It is introduced and widely grown elsewhere.

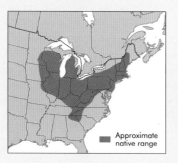

Approximate native range

ABOUT 15 SPECIES MAKE UP THE NATIVE NORTH AMERIcan genus *Monarda*, which belongs to the mint family, Lamiaceae. Most have brightly colored flowerheads that attract bees and butterflies, hence the common name "bee balm." The genus *Monarda* was named for Spanish physician and botanist Nicholas Monardes (1512–1588), who authored one of the first European books on American plants. The work was later translated into English in 1577, with the title *Joyfull Newes out of the Newe Founde Worlde*. The joyful news about *Monarda didyma* was not really news to Native Americans. Tribes in what is now the eastern United States had been using the leaves of the herb and several related species for centuries medicinally. European colonists learned of bee balm from Native Americans. When settlers found *M. didyma* growing on the banks of the Oswego River near Lake Ontario, the refreshing drink they brewed from its leaves became known as Oswego tea. After the Boston Tea Party, the leaves were used as a black tea substitute. Bee balm is still used in herbal medicine today, primarily for digestive complaints.

Traditional and Current Medicinal Uses

BEE BALM AND ITS RELATIVES, ESPECIALLY *M. FISTULOSA*, WERE widely used medicinally by Native Americans. The Cherokee used the herb for weak stomachs and intestinal troubles, flatulence, and colic. A **poultice** of the leaves was applied to relieve colds and headaches. Tea brewed from the leaves and flower heads was administered to bring out measles pustules, to induce sweating to break fevers, for heart trouble, and as a mild sedative to induce restful sleep. The Chippewa and Meskwaki used the leaves and flower heads of *M. fistulosa* as a cold remedy. They were ingredients in tea brewed by the Teton Dakota for easing stomach pain, in preparations the Winnebago used for skin eruptions, and in **infusions** the Ojibwa made for treating fevers and convulsions. Other conditions that were treated with bee balm preparations included colic, nosebleeds, insomnia, bronchial problems, fainting, and sore eyes. In early

American folk medicine, bee balm had a reputation for being effective in treating colds and sore throats. Inhaling the fumes given off by steamed leaves was credited with clearing sinuses and relieving congestion. American **Eclectic** physicians used bee balm and its relatives for flatulence, nausea, vomiting, to reduce muscle spasms, and as a **diuretic** in treating some types of urinary disorders. Tea made from bee balm leaves was also drunk as a refreshing, stimulating beverage.

In modern herbal medicine, bee balm is used as an aromatic, stimulant, **expectorant** herb to relieve nausea, flatulence, and other minor digestive complaints, and for coughs, sore throats, and menstrual cramps.

Cultivation and Preparation

BEE BALM PREFERS FAIRLY RICH, MOIST, SLIGHTLY ACID, and highly organic soil in partial shade or full sun. It spreads freely by root runners (stolons) and can form large clumps. In three to four years, a clump of bee balm may expand to more than three feet across. Bee balm can be started from seed, by division of existing plants, or by cuttings. For use in herbal medicine, the leaves and other plant parts are cut before flowering begins. (After blooming the leaves are more pungent and bitter.) These are used fresh or dried for infusions.

Research

LITTLE SCIENTIFIC RESEARCH HAS BEEN DONE ON BEE BALM. The leaves and other above-ground plant parts of the related horsemint (*M. punctata*) are a rich source of an **essential oil** that contains large amounts of thymol and similar compounds. Several of these compounds have known antiseptic properties and are effective in killing bacteria. Thymol, a powerful antibiotic, is probably best known as an ingredient in mouthwashes (such as Listerine) and other oral bacteria-killing gargles and cough drops, as well as in antibacterial ointments. Thymol is also strongly fungicidal and **anthelmintic** (used for expelling parasitic worms). Thymol was first discovered in 1719 in thyme oil. *Monarda punctata* was once cultivated for its thymol content (it contains more thymol than thyme). Today, however, the chemical compound is largely synthesized in the lab.

Bee balm is also known as scarlet bergamot because its scent is similar to that of the bergamot orange (*Citrus bergamia*), a member of the citrus family. Scarlet bergamot (bee balm) and bergamot orange are often confused. Bergamot orange, a small tree that produces a yellow citrus fruit with a pear-like shape, has its own interesting story. Bergamot oil is extracted from the fruit's rind. True bergamot oil—not to be confused with the oil extracted from the leaves of *Monarda didyma* or its relatives—is one of the most widely used oils in the perfume and toiletry industries. It is the main flavoring in Earl Grey tea. The tea is named after Charles Grey (1764–1845), the second Earl Grey, who was also Britain's Prime Minister from 1830 to 1834. According to legend, the earl sent a trade delegation to China and while there a member of the delegation earned the gratitude of a Chinese mandarin. In appreciation the mandarin gave the diplomat a gift of tea to present to the earl. The tea became a favorite of the earl and he went so far as to give a sample to his tea merchants, Twinings in the Strand, hoping they could create a tea that would be a close match. The result was a blend of unsteamed Chinese black teas flavored with oil of bergamot that was sold as "Earl Grey's tea." Today Earl Grey tea is typically a blend of Sri Lankan and Indian teas, but it is still flavored with bergamot.

See Also: A Field Guide to Medicinal Plants and Herbs; Eastern and Central North America, 2nd ed. by S. Foster and J. Duke, Houghton Mifflin, 2000; Herbal Renaissance: Growing, Using, and Understanding Herbs in the Modern World by S. Foster, Gibbs-Smith, 1993.

Belladonna
Atropa belladonna

IN GREEK MYTHOLOGY, ATROPOS IS ONE OF THE THREE Fates endowed with the power of life and death over mere mortals. It was she who wielded the shears that could cut the thread of human life. And so can *Atropa belladonna*, if it is not handled with great care. All parts of this deceptively lovely plant are extremely poisonous as one of its common names, "deadly nightshade," implies. It is one of the most toxic plants to be found in the Western Hemisphere. Children have been poisoned by eating less than a half dozen of the berries. One small leaf can be a fatal dose for an adult. Yet, when used correctly, *Atropa belladonna* is a valuable herbal medicine, one that has anesthetic, sedative, **analgesic**, and antispasmodic properties. Strangely enough, it is even used as an antidote to some other poisons.

Traditional and Current Medicinal Uses

DESPITE ITS DEADLY POTENTIAL, *ATROPA* HAS A HISTORY OF medicinal use covering a wide range of applications. Traditionally the herb was used to dilate the pupils for eye examinations and eye operations and its **alkaloids** are used for the same purposes today. As a powerful smooth muscle relaxant, it is employed to relieve pain and muscular spasms in the stomach, intestines, and bile ducts, to treat peptic ulcers, and as a local anesthetic in both herbal and conventional medicine. It can serve as an antidote to poisoning by some types of mushrooms, certain insecticides, and nerve gas. The alkaloid atropine is a valuable remedy for treating asthma, bradycardia (slow heart beat), whooping cough, hay fever, and most importantly, to alleviate the symptoms of Parkinson's disease. It can noticeably reduce tremors and paralysis as well as improve mobility and speech in patients with this debilitating disease.

Cultivation and Preparation

ATROPA IS HARVESTED WILD IN SOME PLACES, BUT IT IS MORE commonly cultivated as a commercial crop for the pharmaceutical industry, especially in Eastern Europe, for the

Common Names Belladonna, deadly nightshade

Latin Name *Atropa belladonna*

Family Solanaceae

Parts Used Leaves, roots

Description A bushy perennial, *A. belladonna* grows three to five feet tall with a large, turnip-like root and spreading, branching stems. Its dull-green leaves are large, soft, and oval. Reddish-purple, bell-shaped flowers grow out singly from the leaf axils. They are succeeded by glossy black berries about the size of cherries, each of which is cupped in the former flower's spreading sepals.

Habitat Native to Europe, western Asia, and northern Africa, *A. belladonna* is naturalized and cultivated worldwide. It grows in wooded areas or waste places such as along roadsides, preferring alkaline soil and part shade.

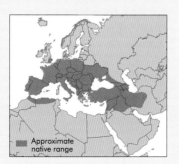

Approximate native range

medically active compounds it contains. The plant requires rich, moist soil, plenty of fertilizer, and a weed-free environment; warm, dry conditions increase the plant's alkaloid content. Harvesting of the plant is done when it is in full bloom. The leaves are harvested in early summer, while the roots are collected in autumn. Both are then dried for medicinal use.

Research

THE KEY CONSTITUENTS OF *ATROPA* INCLUDE VARIOUS alkaloids, including atropine—discovered in 1833 by the German chemist Friedrich Ferdinand Runge (1795–1867)—along with belladonnine, scopolamine, and others. These substances act quite specifically on the parasympathetic nervous system, which controls involuntary body activities, by first stimulating the nervous system and then depressing it. Carefully controlled doses of these compounds can inhibit the production of certain bodily fluids, such as nasal mucus, and secretions in the digestive tract, lungs, and urinary system. They can stop perspiration and slow the movement of food through the digestive tract. They can also relax the muscles of the pupil to cause dilation and can increase heart rate.

Atropine is available as a prescription drug. Atropine is used to help restore or control heart function and is an important drug in cardiopulmonary resuscitation (CPR). In combination with other drugs, atropine is prescribed to treat other health problems including diarrhea and excessive saliva production, nausea, and vomiting. Atropine drops are used to dilate pupils for eye exams. The line between a therapeutic dose of atropine and its related compounds and a fatal dose is very fine. Another of the comounds contained in the plant, scopolamine, is a widely prescribed drug to control motion sickness. Excessive amounts of these substances, or of *Atropa* plant parts or extracts, can result in respiratory and cardiac failure, coma, and death—in half an hour.

CAUTION *A. belladonna* is an extremely poisonous plant. It should never be collected, and used only under the strict supervision of a qualified practitioner. Even small doses can be fatal.

ATROPA BELLADONNA | Belladonna

*A*tropa is an herb that features prominently in ancient stories of intrigue, lustful behavior, and even witchcraft. The Romans supposedly used the plant to contaminate the food stocks of their enemies. Some historians postulate that the famous Bacchanalian orgies of ancient Rome could not have been induced by alcohol alone—the hallucinogenic effects of *Atropa* were well known at the time. There is also a legend that the Scottish army defeated the Danes by putting an extract of the herb in the enemy's liquor supply, and then murdered them in their drug-induced slumber. *A. belladonna* was often linked with witches and sorcerers, who were thought to brew it along with other ingredients into concoctions that would allow them to fly. In the 16th century in Italy, *Atropa* was widely known as *herba bella donna*, which translates as "the plant of the fair lady." The name refers to a practice common at the time among fashionable Italian women. By placing a tiny drop of the plant's sap in their eyes, they could dilate their pupils to give their eyes a dark-eyed brilliance thought to be irresistible. (Little did they know that this practice can cause glaucoma!) Belladonna's deadly powers, however, were certainly known at the time: The name that apothecaries gave the plant—still commonly used today—was *solatrum mortale*, which translates as "deadly nightshade."

See Also: *Medical Botany: Plants Affecting Human Health* by W. Lewis and M. Elvin-Lewis, John Wiley & Sons, 2003; *A Field Guide to Venomous Animals and Poisonous Plants of North America Exclusive of Mexico* by S. Foster and R. Caras, Houghton Mifflin, 1994.

Bethroot
Trillium erectum

ALTHOUGH BETHROOT IS A WOODLAND WILDFLOWER, IT is often grown as an ornamental plant in shade gardens, where its slender, erect stalks emerge from the damp ground in early spring bearing three triangular leaves. These are followed—usually before leaves appear on trees—by stunning dark red or white flowers produced above the foliage; each flower has three colored petals framed by three green or reddish-green sepals. This emphasis on three is reflected in the genus name, *Trillium*, which comes from the Latin word *trilix*, for "triple." *Trillium erectum* blooms for several weeks before its flowers gradually fade. The scent of the flowers is the source of another common name: "stinking benjamin." The flowers have an unpleasant smell when they first open, emitting a scent that reminds some people of rotting meat and others of the smell of a wet dog. By summer's end, bethroot's above-ground parts have died down and it has all but disappeared from the garden. The name "bethroot" is a corruption of "birth root." Bethroot was traditionally used by Native Americans of the eastern United States as an aid in childbirth and to treat menstrual disorders. Today it plays a minor, but similar, role in modern herbal medicine.

Traditional and Current Medicinal Uses

THE RHIZOMES OF BETHROOT WERE USED BY NATIVE American tribes, including the Abnaki, Cherokee, and Iroquois, to make a root tea that was used to induce childbirth, aid in labor, treat menstrual disorders, ease the symptoms of menopause, and soothe sore nipples. The herb was also used to combat cough, control bleeding, and for bowel complaints. **Poultices** of the entire plant were a remedy for ulcers, inflammation, and cancerous tumors. Small pieces of the rhizome were eaten as an aphrodisiac. Early settlers adopted bethroot as a medicinal herb, using it much like Native Americans. Chewing the root was thought to slow down heart palpitations. Sniffing the fetid-smelling flowers was supposed to stop a nosebleed. The plant was introduced into the American medical community in the early 1800s,

Common Names Bethroot, red trillium, birthroot, wake robin, stinking benjamin

Latin Name *Trillium erectum*

Family Liliaceae

Parts Used Rhizomes (underground stems)

Description A rhizomous perennial that rarely exceeds 15 inches in height, bethroot has simple stems topped by a whorl of three triangular leaves. In spring, a single tri-petalled flower that ranges from dull red to white appears above the leaves.

Habitat Bethroot is indigenous to damp, shady woodlands of eastern North America.

Approximate native range

and was recommended for childbirth and labor as well as hemorrhage, asthma, labored breathing, chronic lung disorders, snakebite, insect bites, and various skin irritations and conditions including the control of gangrene. The rhizomes, boiled in milk, were taken for diarrhea and dysentery. Bethroot was listed in the United States National Formulary until 1947.

Today bethroot is still considered a valuable herbal remedy for facilitating childbirth and controlling unusually heavy menstrual flow, including bleeding associated with fibroids in the uterus.

Cultivation and Preparation

BETHROOT GROWS IN THE RICH SOIL OF DAMP AND SHADY woodlands. It can be cultivated as a garden plant; it is usually started by division of existing plants, as seeds can take three years to germinate. It needs moist, well-drained, slightly acid soil and part shade. Bethroot blooms in April and May, but most plants do not begin to flower until they are at least five years old (though fertilizing can speed development). Rhizomes are harvested in early autumn, when leaves have died back. They are dried for use in different kinds of herbal preparations. *Trillium erectum* is endangered and protected in some states, as are several other *Trillium* species.

Research

THE RHIZOMES OF *TRILLIUM ERECTUM* ARE RICH IN **steroidal saponins** (particularly diosgenin and trillarin) that exhibit hormonal effects. This may explain the herb's action in inducing labor and regulating various aspects of menstruation. Steroidal saponins can also be **precursors** in the production of cortisone. Almost no scientific research has been carried out on bethroot. Some herbalists suggest that bethroot may be a safer alternative to blue cohosh (*Caulophyllum thalictroides*), which is an herb commonly used to induce labor. Much more research is needed to analyze bethroot and to explore its actions and its potential side effects.

CAUTION Bethroot should not be taken during pregnancy except under professional supervision.

TRICKY TRILLIUMS

The fetid smell for which the flowers of bethroot and other trilliums are famous may be repulsive to most people. But that smell is precisely what attracts trillium's primary pollinators. Flies fancy blossoms that emit the essence of carrion or dung. Among their favorites are trilliums, which early naturalists christened "stinking benjamins" because of their stench. Once trillium flowers have been pollinated by flies and seeds begin to form, the plants have another trick. They have an intriguing method of seed dispersal in which ants play a crucial role. When the seed-containing fruits of trillium mature in late summer, they fall to the ground and split open, exposing the seeds. Each seed is equipped with a structure that botanists call an elaiosome. It is a little appendage that is rich in fat as well as chemicals that mimic the smell of ant prey. Chemically deceived by this hoax, ants carry trillium seeds back to their nests, eat the high-fat "ant snacks" attached to them, and then discard the seeds in the tunnels of their mounds. When all is said and done, the ants have dispersed the seeds of the trillium plant in a secure underground spot (out of the reach of most seed-eaters) where germination can safely take place. Other spring-flowering "ant plants" found in similar woodland habitats include bleeding heart and wild ginger.

See Also: *A Field Guide to Medicinal Plants and Herbs: Eastern and Central North America, 2nd ed.* by S. Foster and J. Duke, Houghton Mifflin, 2000; *Native American Ethnobotany* by D. Moerman, Timber Press, 1998.

Bilberry
Vaccinium myrtillus

A CLOSE RELATIVE OF CRANBERRY (*VACCINIUM MACRO-carpon*), bilberry is a small perennial shrub that produces a profusion of dark, sweet berries with a taste similar to American blueberries. The name "bilberry" is derived from a Danish word, *bollebar*, which means "dark berry." Eaten fresh or dried, bilberries have traditionally been stewed into jams and jellies, baked into tarts and pies, and made into wine or used to add color to wines made from other fruits. Medicinally, bilberry was prized for centuries in Europe as an **astringent** herbal treatment good for relieving both constipation and diarrhea, particularly in children. In modern herbal medicine, however, bilberry is better known as a potent source of **antioxidants** that enhance circulation through the body's smallest blood vessels—an effect thought to help combat eye problems such as macular degeneration and diabetic retinopathy, a major cause of blindness in people with diabetes.

Common Names Bilberry, whortleberry, huckleberry, European blueberry

Latin Name *Vaccinium myrtillus*

Family Ericaceae

Parts Used Fruits, leaves

Description Bilberry is a small, branching, deciduous shrub that rarely grows more than 18 inches high. It has oval, glossy green leaves and white or pinkish bell-shaped flowers that are followed by blue-black berries.

Habitat Native to the temperate regions of the Northern Hemisphere, bilberry grows in damp woods and forest meadows throughout northern and mountainous regions of Europe as well as western Asia.

Traditional and Current Medicinal Uses

BILBERRY HAS HAD A PLACE IN THE HERBAL MEDICINE CHEST of European traditional healers for many centuries. Hundreds of years ago, tea made from bilberry leaves was a folk remedy for treating diabetes. Bilberry leaf tea was also given to alleviate diarrhea, vomiting, stomach cramps, and cough. In the Middle Ages, herbalists recommended bilberry fruits as a mild laxative and gentle anti-diarrheal aid. Preparations of the berries were also given to treat stomach complaints, bladder infections, kidney stones, scurvy, coughs, and inflammations of the mouth and throat. In the 1700s, bilberry was prescribed for typhoid fever, gout, and rheumatism; it remained a widely respected cure for diarrhea and dysentery. During the Second World War, British fighter pilots reported notable improvement in their eyesight, especially night vision, after eating bilberry jam. Research into the fruit's effects led to bilberry preparations being prescribed to treat a variety of eye-related disorders and to improve circulatory system health.

In modern herbal medicine, bilberry fruits are recommended for improving visual acuity, preventing and

Approximate native range

treating macular degeneration, glaucoma, and diabetic retinopathy, and for preventing cataracts. Bilberry **extracts** are also used as a remedy for varicose veins, atherosclerosis, hemorrhoids, bruising, and Raynaud's disease (a vascular disorder). Preparations of the herb are also still employed to treat diarrhea and stomach upsets, and for inflammations of mucous membranes of the mouth, throat, stomach lining, and urinary tract.

Cultivation and Preparation

BILBERRY DOES BEST IN MOIST, PEATY OR SANDY SOIL IN FULL sun or partial shade. It is typically propagated by seeds or cuttings. Although bilberry is cultivated in many parts of the world, the berries (and to a lesser extent the leaves) are primarily wild harvested for the herbal medicine trade. Berries are gathered in late summer when ripe; they are used fresh or dried, or their juice is extracted and further processed into powdered concentrate that is used in capsules and pills.

Research

THE KEY ACTIVE COMPOUNDS IN BILBERRY FRUITS ARE **flavonoids** known as anthocyanosides. Derivatives of the pigments that give bilberries their bluish purple color, anthocyanosides are powerful antioxidants that scavenge **free radicals**—destructive particles formed in the body. Bilberry anthocyanosides appear to strengthen capillaries, the smallest blood vessels, by protecting them from free radical damage and by stimulating growth of healthy connective tissue. Bilberry anthocyanosides also appear to regenerate rhodopsin, a pigment found in the retina critical to night vision. Many human studies suggest that bilberry anthocyanosides prevent diabetic retinopathy and improve visual acuity and retinal function. Research carried out in Italy and France in the 1960s and 1970s appeared to support anecdotal evidence that bilberry can improve night vision. However, recent clinical trials with bilberry extracts found no short- or long-term improvements in night vision attributable to the herb. More research is needed. In other studies, bilberry extracts have been shown to reduce **platelet aggregation** (thus reducing the risk of atherosclerosis) and to inhibit the growth of certain types of cancers.

Many of the dyes that color modern clothes have been created in the laboratory. However, prior to 1856—when the first synthetic dye, known as mauveine or aniline purple, was discovered accidentally by a chemist trying to synthesize the antimalarial drug quinine—dyes for clothing and paper came entirely from natural sources, including many plants. Dyers were often also herbal healers, since many of the plants they used for dyeing cloth were also used medicinally in folk remedies. Bilberry juice was the source of a dye used for centuries in the British Isles to color wool and other fabrics. In Ireland bilberry fruits were known as *fraughan*, from the Gaelic word *fraochán*. Depending on the mordant used (the substance used to help bond, or fix, a dye to the fibers of a fabric), bilberry juice dyed cloth a deep blue, purple, or purplish-gray. Another ancient source of blue color was woad (*Isatis tinctoria*), a hardy biennial native to northern Europe. The source of woad's blue dye is the chemical indigotin, also found in much greater quantities in true indigo (*Indigofera tinctoria*), a subtropical plant native to India and southeastern Asia. After the invention of synthetic dyes, most plant-derived dyes were abandoned. But in recent years, many traditional coloring agents—including bilberry juice—have been making a comeback, especially with manufacturers specializing in clothing made from natural and organically grown fibers.

VACCINIUM MYRTILLUS | Bilberry

See Also: Herbal Medicine Expanded Commission E Monographs by M. Blumenthal, A. Goldberg, and J. Brinckmann, American Botanical Council, 2000; *The ABC Clinical Guide to Herbs* by M. Blumenthal, T. Hall, and A. Goldberg, American Botanical Council, 2003.

HEALING PLANTS OF
Africa

I N A RURAL HAUSA VILLAGE IN NORTHERN NIGERIA, SHEHU TREATS HIS stomachache with a plant **decoction** prescribed by Laraba, who is a specialist in diseases caused by the heat of the dry season. After seven days without improvement, Laraba suspects that healing is being obstructed by sorcery or witchcraft, and directs her ailing neighbor to Musa, who specializes in removing disease agents that have been inserted into the body. The healer applies a hollow goat's horn to the foot (the lowest part of the body), puts his mouth against the horn tip, and creates suction by drawing air into his lungs. This causes the flesh to rise in a welt; then Musa cuts the welt to promote bleeding—evidence that disease agents have exited the body. Next, an **infusion** of African mahogany bark (*Khaya senegalensis*) and other bitter plants is applied to the cut so that disease agents cannot re-enter the patient's body. Now the original healing process resumes: Laraba mixes baobab fruit and leaves (*Adansonia digitata*) with the root of Cape lily (*Crinum ornatum*)—the combination is both tonic and antimicrobial. Then an infusion is prepared for Shehu to be taken by the patient three times a day. Within four days Shehu feels better and has resumed his ordinary activities.

MEDICAL PRACTICES IN AFRICA

AFRICA, THE WORLD'S SECOND LARGEST CONTINENT IN BOTH AREA AND POPULATION, IS home, and adopted home, to enormous botanical and cultural diversity. Traditional medical practices are the primary source of health care for many of Africa's people. In this context of diverse physical environments and human communities, healing practices nevertheless have some common themes. Throughout the continent, medicine commonly overlaps with religion. Even where Islam and Christianity now predominate, aspects of folk religions persist, as they continue to serve some of the most challenging of life's circumstances. Many African cultures attribute disease to the actions of

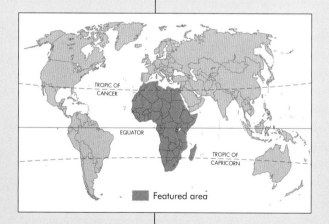

agents such as gods, spirits, ghosts, ancestors, sorcerers, and witches. The sick person is thought to be the target of aggression or punishment directed personally against him or her; hence the ailing person experiences both familiar symptoms of physical distress and other afflictions such as hysteria, tremors, and misfortunes in social and business affairs. Some of the social tensions of polygamous Hausa households in Nigeria and Niger, for

A Hausa healer applies a hollow goat's horn to suction disease from his patient's body. This therapeutic measure is indicated when ordinary treatments fail, suggesting to the healer that witchcraft or sorcery is impeding the healing process. Later, an infusion of bitter plants, including mahogany bark, is applied to the same spot to ensure that disease agents do not re-enter the patient's body. Finally, a tonic and antimicrobial medicine is administered, made from the root of Cape lily and the fruit and leaves of the baobab tree.

PRECEDING PAGES: Fleshy, tapering leaves surround the blooming stalks of an aloe plant in Madagascar's Spiny Desert. Since ancient times healers the world over have used aloe—primarily its gel and leaves—to treat an array of ailments.

example, are reflected in accusations of sorcery and witchcraft commonly exchanged among co-wives. The Abron of Ivory Coast attribute specific diseases to one of a host of agents—bush devils, ghosts, sorcerers, and a supreme deity who acts alone or through the medium of lesser gods. In Zimbabwe, the Shona attribute severe mental illness to witches and somewhat less troubling psychological problems to ancestral spirits.

These illnesses commonly require interventions different from, or in addition to, those for organic disorders. This is the province of shamans, diviners, and those adroit in mediating spirits, witches, and sorcerers. In South Africa the priest-diviner is the personification of an ancestral spirit, and serves his community by providing treatment of physical and psychological problems. He also interprets dreams and provides counsel for misfortune, bereavement, and other matters. Among the Dogon of southern Mali the diviner foretells good and bad fortune for his village by interpreting the patterns in fox tracks. In traditional !Kung religion a great god inhabits the eastern sky where the sun rises, and a lesser god the western sky. Neither is all good or all bad, both sending favors and misfortunes. The great god gives healing powers to medicine men and to medicine songs that accompany community dances during which the sick are cured and imminent misfortunes avoided by driving away the spirits of the dead. In these circumstances, medicinal plants play a prominent role in various healing measures. Plant remedies range from incense and fumigants to drive away bad spirits or appease the ancestors, to **purgatives** and **emetics** that expel disease agents from the body, to plants whose pharmacologic actions cure symptoms.

It is common as well in African medical practices to link disease to tangible features of the environment. Principles of equilibrium explain illness as imbalances of hot-cold, sweet-sour, and dry-wet. For example, the Hausa in Nigeria use the mahogany tree—ascribed the principle of cold—to treat fever, a hot disease. They attribute difficult childbirth to accumulations of sugar or salt, and malaria in children to excess moisture in the rainy season. Similarly, in Ghana, fever medicines that ward off cold include bushmint (*Hyptis pectinata*), African basil (*Ocimum gratissimum*), and croton (*Croton penduliflorus*).

Traditional healers also are mindful of the physical properties (acidic, bitter), physiologic actions (anti-emetic, stimulant), and the growth forms and locations of plant medicines. In Liberia, Mano healers point to natural causes for what they regard as simple illnesses such as bone fracture or digestive disorders. Healers administer chile pepper (*Capsicum annuum*) enemas to relieve babies of constipation, which is understood to result from exposure to cold winds or rainfall. Traditional Amhara medicine men in Ethiopia point to dirt and contagion as causes of skin disorders and use a variety of cleansing plants such as castor oil seeds (*Ricinus communis*) and bitter apple fruit (*Citrullus colocynthis*) to relieve symptoms and rid the body of dirt.

Africa's Medicinal Plants

Diverse African healing practices find an analogue in the widespread use of various medicinal plants. For example, aloe (*Aloe vera, Aloe* spp.), a familiar ingredient in moisturizers and cosmetic products in the West, is used in traditional African medicine as wound dressing or to treat rash and other skin disorders. The leaf jelly is swallowed to relieve constipation.

Traditional uses of the baobab tree include bark infusions for cough and intestinal distress, and as a treatment to aid in childbirth. In some cultures, spirits are thought to dwell in openings in the huge trunks of the trees. The fruit and leaves are edible and are made into decoctions to treat fever, and in Western laboratories have been shown to have antibacterial and antifungal properties.

In South Africa the characteristic claw-like fruit and tuber of devil's claw (*Harpagophytum procumbens*) are infused and administered as a drink for the relief of fever and for joint and blood disorders. A tonic made from the tuber is applied to sprains and sores. Pharmacologic studies report constituents in devil's claw that reduce blood cholesterol and diminish arthritic pain. Today, devil's claw supplements and complementary medicines are widely marketed in the United States and in Western Europe as well.

In West Africa kola nuts (*Cola acuminata*), which contain caffeine, are chewed as tonics and stimulants, and for stomachache, sore throat, and nausea. A seed extract from the kola nut was used in the early 1900s (along with coca plant extract) in the original formulation of the popular beverage Coca Cola.

Alkaloids from the Madagascar periwinkle (*Catharanthus roseus*) make important contributions to contemporary cancer treatments: Vincristine is used to treat childhood leukemia, and vinblastine to treat Hodgkin's disease. Traditional healers also use Madagascar periwinkle as a laxative and for stomach upsets. Less commonly, periwinkle is used to treat diabetes; pharmacologists have determined that water extracts of Madagascar periwinkle are weakly effective.

AFRICA'S CHANGING MEDICAL TRADITIONS

OVER TIME AFRICA'S DIVERSE MEDICAL TRADITIONS HAVE CHANGED AS LOCAL GROUPS communicate across regions and even across continents today. Since colonial times, African traditional healers have been influenced by the introduction of Western medical ideas. It is not unusual for today's traditional healers to use stethoscopes and other medical technology, to mix **extracts** made from plants and pharmaceuticals, and to use injection needles to deliver medicines. Many traditional healers are eager to incorporate into their practice what scientists in the West, and in their own countries, have discovered about African medicinal plants. African healers also have to contend with challenges for which the knowledge of earlier generations did not prepare them. In earlier times, these included health problems attendant on slavery and colonial interventions; today this involves diseases of war and displacement, new diseases such as HIV/AIDS, and the revival of old ones such as malaria.

Traditional Hausa (northern Nigeria) plant medicines are often used in conjunction with Western medical drugs and technology. This mixing of traditions is depicted here in the juxtapostion of the items in the woven basket and on the mat: a Hausa metal knife for simple surgery (right), medicinal plants, edible medicinal clay (white ball, center), exotic barks purchased in the market (in plastic bag), pharmaceutical capsules, a syringe, and a bottle of injectable penicillin. The Hausa learned about injecting penicillin from government agricultural extension workers who helped villagers cure diseases affecting their cattle and other livestock.

In addition to collaborating with Western doctors, traditional healers in Africa want to retain their autonomy and have created a professional Traditional Healers Organization for Africa. Regional and national counterparts also exist: Zimbabwe National Traditional Healers Association, Congo National Union of Tradi-Therapists, Ghana Federation of Traditional Medicine Practitioners Association, and South Africa Natural Therapeutic Practitioners Association. Many traditional healers are drawn into more formal primary health care as they work alongside biomedical doctors and serve as community liaisons.

Over the last several decades scientists have established that many African medicinal plants are effective against diseases ranging from infection, to physical trauma, to psychological distress. Especially in rural areas where other medicines are not affordable, traditional healers and their Western counterparts have begun to collaborate to ensure that healers treat their community with the most effective plant medicines.

In the fight against malaria as a health threat throughout Africa (and the world), several native and introduced African plants have proven promising. Neem (*Azadirachta indica*), a proven antimalarial since the early 1900s, was introduced from India to forestation programs in Africa and rapidly adopted into local medical traditions for fevers. In Mali, a traditional three-plant antimalarial treatment is now produced by the National Institute of Public Health Research as a standardized medicine. Known as Malarial-5, this remedy includes leaves of coffee senna (*Cassia occidentalis*) and tea bush (*Lippia chevalieri*), and paracress flowers (*Spilanthes oleracea*). Similarly, in Ghana, the traditional antimalarial yellow root (*Cryptolepis sanguinolenta*) was introduced to the Center for Scientific Research into Plant Medicine (CSRPM) some 20 years ago and has since been incorporated into several products sold in Ghanaian markets for malaria and other fevers. At present, the World Health Organization is collaborating with Ghana's CSRPM to develop a standardized extract to treat malaria for use throughout Africa. Elsewhere, sweet wormwood (*Artemisia annua*), a traditional Chinese antimalarial plant, has been cultivated in Africa and incorporated into local medical practices.

As an extension of these practices, research collaborations are exploring traditional insect repellents. Several have been confirmed as repellents of mosquitoes, which transmit malaria and other infections: aromatic grasses (*Bothriochloa* spp.), rose geranium (*Pelargonium graveolens*), mango (*Mangifera indica*), wild ginger (*Siphonochilus aethiopicus)*, and lantana (*Lantana camara*). Collaborations among Western and African scientists and traditional healers to discover new therapies offer great public health potential for Africa. ✔

OPPOSITE PAGE: *This itinerant seller travels among villages in northern Nigeria selling medicines. She makes nonlocal products available to people in villages across the region. Most of the small bags contain plant medicines; a few contain animal parts and products as well as minerals. Customers ask for medicinal plants or medicines by name, or they report symptoms and ask for the appropriate treatments or preventives.*

Bitterleaf
Vernonia amygdalina

Common Names Bitterleaf, *ewuro* (Nigeria); *mujonso* (Tanzania)

Latin Name *Vernonia amygdalina*

Family Asteraceae

Parts Used Leaf, twigs, roots

Description *Vernonia amygdalina* is a drought-tolerant shrub or small tree growing to about 20 feet in height. Its dark green leaves have a distinctive odor and bitter taste.

Habitat Native to sub-Saharan Africa, bitterleaf grows in a variety of habitats in several countries, from Ghana and Cameroon in the west to southern Ethiopia and Tanzania in the east.

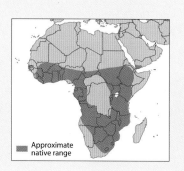

Approximate native range

I N THE LATE 1980s, BIOLOGISTS STUDYING CHIMPANZEES IN Tanzania's Mahale Mountains National Park noticed an interesting behavior in one of their primate subjects. A chimp that appeared to be sick carefully plucked leaves from *Vernonia amygdalina*, a small, shrubby tree known as bitterleaf. Bitterleaf was not part of the chimp's normal diet. After meticulously removing the leaves and outer bark from several young shoots, the sick chimp chewed on the exposed pith and sucked out the extremely bitter juice. The next day, the researchers noticed that the chimp appeared to be fully recovered. Intrigued, they analyzed droppings from the chimp before and after the pith-eating incident. They found a common intestinal parasite in both samples. But the sample collected the day after the chimp had eaten bitterleaf contained far fewer parasites. The researchers concluded that they had witnessed an example of **zoopharmacognosy**—an animal eating something to cure itself of an illness. Other researchers have confirmed both the behavior and the hypothesis. Chimps suck the pith of bitterleaf in order to reduce the number of parasites in their digestive tracts. In short, they consume the plant for its medicinal rather than nutritional benefits.

Interestingly, people in many parts of sub-Saharan Africa also use bitterleaf medicinally. About half of traditional bitterleaf cures are for ridding the body of intestinal parasites. In the past few years, chemical compounds extracted from bitterleaf have been shown to possess powerful antiparasitic, antibacterial, and anticancer properties. Research is under way to explore the potential of this "new" herbal medicine to fight breast cancer, malaria, and other human diseases.

Traditional and Current Medicinal Uses

BITTERLEAF LEAVES ARE EATEN AS A VEGETABLE (AFTER BEING soaked and washed to reduce bitter compounds and toxicity) in many areas where the plant is common. They are also dried and used as a seasoning. In traditional herbal medicine, *Vernonia amygdalina* has more than 25 known uses among the peoples of sub-Saharan

Africa, for both humans and livestock. These traditional cures utilize the pith of twigs and small branches, the leaves, and in some cases the tree's roots. In Tanzania, the leaves are soaked in water to create a **tincture** drunk to cleanse the body of intestinal worms. In addition to bitterleaf's antiparasitic action, the herb is also used to treat fever and diarrhea, stimulate digestion, soothe stomachaches, lower high blood pressure, and as a malaria cure. In Cameroon, the leaves are made into a bitter-tasting dish called *ndole* said to be a strength-restoring tonic. Bitterleaf is also used as topical medicine against leeches, said to transmit the disease bilharzia, along with snails, in some areas. Preparations of bitterleaf are also used as insecticide.

Cultivation and Preparation

BITTERLEAF IS HARVESTED IN THE WILD AND CULTIVATED for herbal remedies. Trees are usually propagated by cuttings. The leaves of bitterleaf contain high levels of toxic compounds. Other important physiologically active compounds are extracted in the laboratory.

Research

IN ANALYZING BITTERLEAF, RESEARCHERS ISOLATED A HIGHLY toxic compound, vernodalin, from the leaves. Traditional methods of preparing bitterleaf leaves for eating apparently remove much of this toxin. Chemical analysis of bitterleaf also led to the discovery of a new class of chemical compounds, called vernoniosides, from the pith of twigs and branches. One of these, called vernonioside B1, exhibits antiparasitic, antitumor, and antibacterial properties. A number of studies using bitterleaf extracts have yielded promising results in terms of bitterleaf's therapeutic effects. For instance, in animal experiments, extracts from bitterleaf leaves and root bark showed significant antimalarial activity against drug-sensitive *Plasmodium berghei* (one species of malaria parasite). Extracts of bitterleaf have also been shown to inhibit DNA synthesis in certain types of human breast cancer cells.

A NEW BREW?

On a hot day in a hot climate, the thirst-quenching taste of a cold beer can be especially welcome. But in many parts of Africa, the cost of importing conventional brewing ingredients not locally grown, such as barley and hops, is often prohibitively expensive. This has led some enterprising individuals to explore the use of locally available products as substitutes in the brewing process. Sorghum is now a common substitute for barley in making beer in countries such as Nigeria, where it is used in both malted and unmalted forms. Finding a substitute for hops was more challenging, but one possible candidate seems to be bitterleaf. The plant is widely cultivated in Nigeria as a food source. Much to the delight of Nigerian brewers, bitterleaf resembles hops in the brewing process not only in its bitter flavor but also in its antimicrobial properties. In experiments with bitterleaf in brewing sorghum beer, it was discovered that bitterleaf extract is actually more effective at inhibiting the growth of bacteria that can ruin beer than the formaldehyde-containing solution that is now commonly used. At the same time, bitterleaf does not harm the brewer's yeast cells that are so essential to the fermentation process. In taste comparisons, beer brewed using bitterleaf extract as a hops substitute was found to be nearly as good as hopped beer brewed from the same sorghum malt.

VERNONIA AMYGDALINA | Bitterleaf

See Also: Nature's Medicine: Plants that Heal by Joel Swerdlow, National Geographic, 2000; *Medical Botany: Plants Affecting Human Health* by W. Lewis and M. Elvin-Lewis, John Wiley & Sons, 2003.

Black Cherry
Prunus serotina

Common Names Black cherry, rum cherry, bird cherry

Latin Name *Prunus serotina*

Family Rosaceae

Parts Used Bark

Description Wild black cherry is a fast-growing, medium-sized deciduous tree (60 to 80 feet) with oval, finely toothed, shiny leaves. Slender, drooping clusters of fragrant white flowers bloom in spring, followed by small purple-black fruits (drupes) with a large pit.

Habitat Native to North America, black cherry grows in dry woods from Nova Scotia to Florida and west to the Dakotas, Kansas, and Arizona.

Approximate native range

THERE ARE MORE THAN 200 SPECIES IN THE GENUS *Prunus*. Many are the source of familiar fruits, including plums, peaches, almonds, apricots, and cherries. Wild black cherry (*Prunus serotina*) produces small, dark, bittersweet, and vaguely wine-flavored cherries that are loved by birds and some people, too. They have been simmered and stewed, baked into puddings and pies, and made into jellies and jams. Wild black cherry fruits have also been used to flavor spirits and liqueurs, including rum, which is the source of one of the tree's common names (rum cherry) and a southern liqueur known as cherry bounce. Wild black cherry is also known for its wood, which is a rich, reddish-brown color, and strong, hard, and close-grained. It is one of the most valued woods indigenous to North America—second only to black walnut—and is used for cabinets and fine quality furniture, as well as veneers, paneling, and scientific instruments. Wild black cherry was used extensively by Native Americans as a medicinal herb. In American folk and herbal medicine, it was used primarily in treating coughs. Authentic wild cherry cough syrup is still made from extracts of the inner bark of wild black cherry.

Traditional and Current Medicinal Uses

NATIVE AMERICANS WERE THE FIRST TO USE WILD BLACK cherry medicinally. The aromatic inner bark of the tree was used by many tribes to brew a tea or syrup good for relieving coughs and colds. **Infusions** of the bark were also taken as a blood tonic, as a wash for sores and ulcers, for reducing fever, to ease childbirth, control diarrhea, cure headaches, and ease laryngitis. Concoctions of the root were used to expel worms, treat burns, and heal ulcers. Wild black cherry was also respected as a remedy for fever, sore throat, lung ailments bronchitis, pneumonia, inflammatory diseases, upset stomach, poor circulation, general debility, and lack of appetite. It was also a mild sedative. Early colonists learned about wild black cherry from Native Americans and adopted it as an herbal medicine for many of the same ailments. In Appalachia, the tree's inner bark was widely used for brewing wild cherry bark tea, a folk remedy for coughs, colds, and cholera. A century ago, wild black cherry bark was still being used as an excellent **expectorant** in treating coughs. It was also added to cough lozenges to create the classic wild cherry cough drops. Wild black cherry syrup, made from a mixture of wild cherry bark extract, glycerin, sucrose, alcohol, and water, was widely used as a flavoring vehicle for other, less palatable drugs.

Contemporary herbalists still recommend wild black cherry bark for chronic and dry coughs, whooping cough, bronchitis, nervous indigestion, diarrhea, to relieve pain, and as a tonic for those recovering from convalescence.

Cultivation and Preparation

WILD BLACK CHERRY IS USUALLY A SMALL TO MEDIUM TREE, although it can sometimes grow up to 80 feet tall. It can also live up to 150 years. Wild black cherry can tolerate a wide variety of soils, but it is not very tolerant of shade. In herbal medicine, the root bark is the most highly prized, but inner bark from the trunk and branches is also used. Bark must be collected each season because its therapeutic constituents deteriorate if stored longer than a year. The inner bark smells faintly of almonds and has a bitter, acidic taste. The bark is stripped in autumn and winter and dried for herbal preparations.

Research

WILD BLACK CHERRY BARK, LEAVES, AND SEEDS CONTAIN A cyanide-like **glycoside** called prunasin. Prunasin relieves coughs by quelling spasms in the smooth muscles lining the **bronchioles** (branching air tubes) of the lungs, thus quieting the cough reflex. Due to its powerful sedative action, wild black cherry is especially useful for treating irritating and persistent coughs when expectorant action is needed, as is the case with bronchitis and whooping cough. Although wild black cherry is a commonly used ingredient in cough syrups and has been used in traditional and homeopathic medicine for centuries, there are no published clinical trials in humans to support its use as a cough reliever.

Like the inner bark of the black cherry tree, the leaves of wild black cherry contain prunasin. When the leaves are damaged by such things as frost, drought, wilting, blow-down during storms, or trampling by animals or people, the prunasin is broken down and the poison cyanide released. Most animals can eat small amounts of healthy wild black cherry leaves without a problem. The same is true of a few nibbles of bark and fruits, including seeds. But when hungry animals eat even small amounts of damaged leaves, the effects can be deadly. There are many reported cases of animals being poisoned after eating damaged wild black cherry leaves. This can easily happen if animals have no other plants to eat, or in the case of pets, when they are confined or bored and the fallen leaves of wild black cherry are within easy reach. Many other plants in the rose family (Rosaceae) contain prunasin and so have the potential to produce toxic levels of cyanide under certain conditions as well. Cyanide interferes with cells' ability to use oxygen. Although animals (and people) who ingest cyanide can still breathe for a while, internally their cells and tissue quickly begin to "suffocate." The symptoms of cyanide poisoning appear within minutes of ingesting too much of the toxin. If the dose is large enough, the outcome is a violent death from respiratory or cardiac arrest.

See Also: *A Field Guide to Medicinal Plants and Herbs: Eastern and Central North America, 2nd ed.* by S. Foster and J. Duke, Houghton Mifflin, 2000; *Native American Ethnobotany* by D. Moerman, Timber Press, 1998.

PRUNUS SEROTINA | Black Cherry

Black Cohosh
Cimicifuga racemosa

Common Names Black cohosh, black snakeroot, bugbane, bugwort, macrotys

Latin Names *Cimicifuga racemosa,* synonyn *Actaea racemosa*

Family Ranunculaceae

Parts Used Roots, rhizome

Description Black cohosh is a member of the buttercup family, a robust perennial that forms imposing clumps four to seven feet in height. The leaves are divided into threes, with three-lobed terminal leaflets. Around midsummer, black cohosh sends up tall spires of feathery white flowers. It has a knobby, black root (rhizome) that emits a slightly resinous scent.

Habitat A native of eastern North America, black cohosh has a range that extends from Maine to Ontario and from Wisconsin south to Missouri and Georgia. It grows in moist woodlands, typically in deep shade.

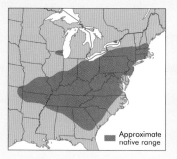

Approximate native range

NATIVE TO EASTERN NORTH AMERICA, BLACK COHOSH was first described by botanists in 1705. Less than 30 years later, it was being widely planted in England as a garden perennial. Black cohosh is a stately herb with brilliant-white flower stalks that tower above other plants in the midsummer garden. Insects avoid it, however, which may account for its common names "bugbane" and "bugwort" as well as its genus name; *Cimicifuga* comes from the Latin *cimex*, meaning "bug," and *fugare*, meaning "to drive away." The striking stems and flower stalks grow up from a twisted, blackish rhizome, which, with only a slight stretch of the imagination, could be considered snakelike in appearance. For centuries, Native Americans used the gnarled roots of black cohosh in remedies designed to treat rheumatism and various gynecological complaints. In the past few decades, black cohosh has gained tremendous popularity in modern herbal medicine as an effective treatment for symptoms associated with menopause. It also shows promise in alleviating high blood pressure, asthma, and tinnitus (ringing in the ears).

Traditional and Current Medicinal Uses

CENTURIES BEFORE EUROPEANS CAME TO NORTH AMERICA, Native Americans were incorporating the roots of black cohosh into medicines. The Delaware added black cohosh to an herb concoction drunk as a woman's tonic. The Algonquin used it for kidney troubles. The Iroquois bathed aching joints with it. The Cherokee found it useful in all these ways and also as a **diuretic** and a treatment for tuberculosis and fatigue. European colonists learned the use of the plant from Native Americans and were soon employing it to treat conditions including general malaise, malaria, sore throat, rheumatism, kidney function, menstrual irregularities, and childbirth. Throughout the 19th century, black cohosh was a common ingredient in many patent medicines and prescribed for menstrual difficulties, pain following childbirth, and for nervous disorders and arthritis. By the 1930s, use of black cohosh was fading in the

United States, but its popularity grew in Europe, particularly in Germany, where it was prescribed primarily for menopausal symptoms.

In recent years, black cohosh has become increasingly popular as a dietary supplement in the U.S. for reducing symptoms associated with menopause, including hot flashes, irritability, anxiety, mood swings, and sleep disturbances.

Cultivation and Preparation

THE RHIZOMES AND ATTACHED ROOTS OF BLACK COHOSH ARE used in herbal medicine preparations. Most of the supply comes from wild-harvested plants, but some black cohosh is grown commercially in Europe. The roots are harvested in the autumn, dried, and then used in various preparations. Black cohosh is typically available in capsules, tablets, as a liquid **tincture** that can be mixed with water, and as dried root.

Research

CONSIDERABLE RESEARCH HAS BEEN CONDUCTED ON THE effects and chemical actions of the herb. Many studies have looked at the therapeutic effects of black cohosh extracts on menopausal symptoms. Many, although not all, clinical studies have shown that taking black cohosh significantly reduces the severity of certain premenopausal and menopausal symptoms, including hot flashes, excessive sweating, depression, and anxiety. As a result, some experts recommend black cohosh as a safe and effective alternative to hormone replacement therapy. Nevertheless, the American College of Obstetricians and Gynecologists (ACOG) has criticized some of these studies as not investigating the safety and effectiveness of black cohosh beyond six months of use. Both ACOG and Germany's Commission E, a panel of scientific experts who make recommendations on herbal medicines, approve black cohosh for relieving hot flashes and some other menopausal symptoms—but only for periods of six months or less.

CAUTION Black cohosh should not be confused with blue cohosh (*Caulophyllum thalictroides*), an herb that exhibits some similar activities but has not been thoroughly tested for safety.

In 1820, black cohosh was listed in the *Pharmacopoeia of the United States*, the nation's official drug reference book, under the name "black snakeroot." During this time, the herb was also called macrotys, especially among medical practitioners who focused on an eclectic approach to medicine. These Eclectic medical professionals, as they were known, actively promoted the use of black cohosh as an herbal remedy. One of the plant's most vocal advocates was Dr. John King (1813–1893). King was a professor of obstetrics at The Eclectic Medical College in Cincinnati, Ohio. Black cohosh was one of King's favorite herbal remedies. He prescribed it in his own practice for decades for nervous disorders and rheumatism as well as for menstrual irregularities and menopause. Although black cohosh gradually fell out of favor as an herbal remedy during the early 1900s (it was dropped from the *Pharmacopoeia of the United States* in 1926), King's promotion of the herb caught the attention of the medical community in Germany. German researchers conducted many of the early studies of black cohosh and its medicinal effects; intensive clinical studies continue there today. And it is commonly taken there for relief of various menopausal symptoms. In Germany black cohosh has been sold under the trade name Remifemin since 1955.

See Also: *Herbal Medicine Expanded Commission E Monographs* by M. Blumenthal, A. Goldberg, and J. Brinckmann, American Botanical Council, 2000; *World Health Organization (WHO) Monographs on Selected Medicinal Plants, Vol. 2,* 2002.

Black Haw
Viburnum prunifolium

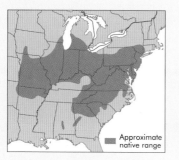

Common Names Black haw, smooth black haw, sloe-leaved viburnum, cramp bark

Latin Name *Viburnum prunifolium*

Family Caprifoliaceae

Parts Used Bark

Description Black haw is a large woody shrub or small tree that can reach 15 feet in height. It has glossy, dark green, elliptical, finely toothed leaves and flat clusters of small white flowers that are followed by blue-black fruits.

Habitat Native to the central and eastern parts of the United States, black haw inhabits moist woods, thickets and stream banks. It is also widely cultivated as an ornamental shrub.

Approximate native range

ROUGHLY 150 SPECIES MAKE UP THE GENUS *VIBURNUM*, which includes many familiar shrubs that are widely grown as ornamentals, some for their showy flower clusters and others for their colorful fall berries. *Viburnum prunifolium* is native to the central and eastern United States. It is prized for its brilliant reddish-purple fall color. Black haw is also known to bear the largest fruits of any species in the genus; the fruits often persist into the winter and are devoured by birds. People eat the fruits, often called haws, as well and they are locally used in making jams and preserves, sauces, and drinks. Native Americans used black haw medicinally, primarily as a pregnancy and childbirth aid and to treat menstrual difficulties. The herb was adopted into conventional medicine in the United States, and during the 19th century was particularly popular among American **Eclectic** physicians, who used herbs extensively in their practices and prescriptions. Although not widely used today, black haw is still included in the herbal medicine **pharmacopoeia**, primarily for relieving menstrual cramps and also for preventing miscarriage.

Traditional and Current Medicinal Uses

THE CHEROKEE AND SEVERAL OTHER NATIVE AMERICAN TRIBES used the bark of the stems and roots of black haw to brew a medicinal tea that was taken to relieve painful menstruation, prevent miscarriage, and ease uterine spasms after childbirth. Some tribes also used black haw to strengthen female reproductive organs, prevent or calm muscle spasms, promote sweating, treat fever and smallpox, and as a wash for sore mouths. European settlers adopted black haw for many of the same conditions. During the 19th century, American Eclectic physicians valued black haw for its sedative effects on the nervous system. They found it to slightly depress respiration and lower blood pressure. It was often prescribed to prevent spontaneous abortion in women who had a history of miscarriage by regulating uterine functions and soothing muscular irritation. Black haw was also considered helpful in treating asthma, painful menstruation, bleeding, nervous irritation, and muscle spasms in any part of the body.

Today, black haw is still used in herbal medicine for its antispasmodic and **astringent** properties. Perhaps its most recognized use is for menstrual pain and cramping. It is also recommended for easing the symptoms of menopause, to treat false labor pains, and to calm uterine muscles in cases of threatened miscarriage. Other therapeutic uses of black haw include treating uterine prolapse, morning sickness, colic, heavy menstruation, lowering blood pressure, and as an antispasmodic in treating asthma as well as cramping pains in the gallbladder and digestive and urinary tracts.

Cultivation and Preparation

BLACK HAW IS EASILY GROWN IN AVERAGE, DRY TO MOIST, well-drained soil in full sun to part shade. It is very drought tolerant. Propagation is typically done by seed or cuttings. Bark is harvested for use in herbal medicine by stripping it from stems of the plant either in spring (before the leaf buds open) or in autumn (before the leaves turn color). The bark is dried and used in a variety of preparations ranging from **decoctions** and liquid **extracts** to **infusions** and powders.

Research

A WIDE VARIETY OF CHEMICAL COMPOUNDS CAN BE FOUND IN black haw bark, including the chemical compounds scopoletin and aesculetin, which have both been shown to have a sedative effect on the uterus—one that counteracts muscle contractions. Scopoletin is also a known antibacterial agent as well as an **anti-inflammatory** that is useful in treating bronchial conditions, including asthma. Scopoletin also plays a role in the secretion of the hormone **serotonin**, which helps to reduce anxiety and depression. Further, black haw contains salicin, an **analgesic** substance that is chemically similar to aspirin and has similar pain-relieving effects.

CAUTION Individuals who are allergic to aspirin should not take black haw. Eating black haw fruits has been known to produce nausea and other forms of intestinal discomfort.

ANOTHER CRAMP BARK

One of black haw's other common names is cramp bark, obviously derived from the fact that preparations of the bark were a folk remedy for muscle, and especially uterine muscle, cramps. However, there is another cramp bark in herbal medicine—the closely related *Viburnum opulus*, which also goes by the names "guelder rose" and "highbush cranberry." *Guelder* comes from Gueldersland, a Dutch province, where the wild *V. opulus* was first cultivated. Highbush cranberry is something of a misnomer, because cramp bark bears no relation to true cranberry, *Vaccinium macrocarpon*. However, the ripe fruits of cramp bark are bright crimson. They are edible and were sometimes used as a substitute for cranberries, hence the common name. Cramp bark is native to Europe and naturalized in North America. Like black haw, cramp bark is used as an antispasmodic for treating cramping muscles. It is sometimes used interchangeably with black haw, although black haw is thought to have a more specific action on the uterus; its effects are also somewhat stronger. Cramp bark is often recommended in cases of arthritis in which painful joints have led to muscles that are nearly rigid from constant contraction. Lotions made from cramp bark are applied to the joints, causing the muscles to relax and renewing normal blood flow to the joint and surrounding tissues.

See Also: *A Field Guide to Medicinal Plants and Herbs: Eastern and Central North America, 2nd ed.* by S. Foster and J. Duke, Houghton Mifflin Co., 2000; *Nature's Medicine: Plants that Heal* by Joel Swerdlow, National Geographic, 2000.

VIBURNUM PRUNIFOLIUM | Black Haw

Bloodroot

Sanguinaria canadensis

THERE IS LITTLE MYSTERY ABOUT THE ORIGIN OF BLOOD-root's most common name. Pluck a leaf from this herb or cut the root and a red sap will ooze from the wound, like blood. Its genus name, *Sanguinaria*, is a reference to the red sap as well; it comes from the Latin word *sanguis*, which means "blood." Native to eastern North American woodlands, bloodroot was used by Native Americans as a source of blood-red coloring that made ideal war paint and a dye that turned cloth a similarly rich red color. But bloodroot was also used medicinally to induce vomiting and treat a number of ailments. Yet it was never used in excess, because bloodroot is quite toxic. Today bloodroot is an important source of an **alkaloid**—sanguinarine—with proven antibacterial effects. It is widely used in commercial preparations to counteract dental plaque and gum disease. It is also used in small doses to treat congestive coughs and respiratory ailments.

Traditional and Current Medicinal Uses

NATIVE AMERICANS USED BLOODROOT TO TREAT A VARIETY OF complaints. A tea was made from the roots and drunk to ease sore throat, fevers, and rheumatism. Somewhat larger doses were used to induce vomiting. Some tribes chewed the roots and spat the resulting juice-and-saliva mixture on burns, sores, and fungal infections such as ringworm. Other tribes used the sap to help heal skin tumors and cancerous sores. The Cherokee used very small doses of the root for lung inflammations and coughs. The Ojibwa put a drop or two of the red root juice onto a lump of maple sugar to suck as a lozenge in easing sore throats. Native Americans introduced Europeans settlers to the therapeutic powers of bloodroot. It quickly became a folk remedy for many ailments. Bloodroot was found to be an excellent **expectorant** for bronchitis and other lung conditions characterized by coughs. The dried roots went into preparations for soothing skin ulcers and various kinds of sores and for killing ringworm and other fungal growths. Bloodroot was also sometimes suggested for stomach upsets, heart conditions, and nervous irritation,

Common Names Bloodroot, Indian paint, red paint root, red puccoon

Latin Name *Sanguinaria canadensis*

Family Papaveraceae

Parts Used Rhizome (underground stem)

Description Bloodroot is a small perennial herb that exudes a red sap or latex. Rounded, lobed, solitary leaves arise from buds on the fleshy, creeping, red rhizome. Naked flower stalks that are shorter than the leaves bear a white flower with up to 16 petals arranged in whorls. The fruit is a two-valved capsule full of small seeds.

Habitat Native to eastern North America, bloodroot grows in rich open woodlands.

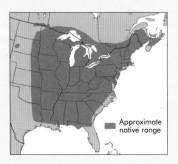

Approximate native range

and to induce vomiting—even a small dose of the fresh root would bring on severe nausea.

In modern herbal medicine, bloodroot is used in minute doses, administered by professionals, primarily as an expectorant and spasmolytic (for relief of spasms) to treat bronchitis, asthma, croup, laryngitis, and other ailments of the respiratory tract. Bloodroot preparations can be used externally for sores, eczema, and other skin problems; preparations of the herb remain a folk treatment for warts, nasal polyps, and benign skin tumors but should not be used without medical supervision.

Cultivation and Preparation

BLOODROOT DOES BEST IN MOIST SOIL THAT IS RICH IN DECAYED organic matter and in part shade. Propagation from seed can be difficult; division of the **rhizome** is easier. The brittle rhizomes are harvested after flowering when leaves are mature and dried for use in **extracts, tinctures,** and ointments.

Research

BLOODROOT IS RICH IN ALKALOIDS; BY FAR THE MOST ABUNDANT is sanguinarine. Studies have shown this compound to exhibit broad-spectrum antibacterial activity, as well as antispasmodic, antifungal, and expectorant effects. Sanguinarine is also known to stimulate respiration, raise blood pressure, and increase **peristalsis** in the intestines. The alkaloid is an ingredient in toothpastes and mouthwashes for killing oral bacteria and plaque leading to tooth decay and gum disease. Clinical and toxicological studies have been conducted to test the effectiveness and safety of these products. Results have been mixed. Sanguinarine is also found in cough medicines and expectorants. Herbal practitioners caution that products containing bloodroot should not be used without professional supervision. Further, sanguinarine has been shown to readily induce mutations in DNA; its prolonged use in oral hygiene products may be potentially harmful.

CAUTION Bloodroot is a toxic herb and no part of it should be ingested. Fresh root and root juice can burn skin and damage underlying tissue. Use only under the guidance of a medical professional.

STATE-OF-THE-ART SUNSCREEN?

Sanguinarine has been shown to have anti-bacterial, anti-fungal, and anti-inflammatory properties. Now, recent laboratory research at the University of Wisconsin, Madison, has revealed another potential medicinal use for the sanguinarine extracted from bloodroot: protection against skin cancer. According to new studies, sanguinarine was shown to enhance production of proteins that induce cell death in cells damaged by ultraviolet-B (UVB) radiation. The alkaloid also restricts certain proteins that stimulate skin cell production. Based on these findings, researchers believe that sanguinarine may protect skin from cells that have been genetically damaged by radiation and are beginning to make the normal-to-cancerous cell transition. That would make sanguinarine a "chemopreventive" agent against skin cancer, and potentially a very valuable ingredient in state-of-the-art sunscreens. Interestingly, sanguinarine simply applied to the skin had no effect on skin cells. But when the skin was exposed to UVB rays, then the alkaloid began to exhibit its cell-killing effects. More research is needed to confirm this new discovery and its true therapeutic value.

See Also: *A Field Guide to Medicinal Plants & Herbs: Eastern & Central North America 2nd ed.* by S. Foster & J. Duke, Houghton Mifflin, 2000; *A Field Guide to Venomous Animals & Poisonous Plants of N. America Exclusive of Mexico* by S. Foster & R. Caras, Houghton Mifflin, 1994.

Blue Cohosh
Caulophyllum thalictroides

Common Names Blue cohosh, papoose root, squawroot, blueberry root

Latin Name *Caulophyllum thalictroides*

Family Berberidaceae

Parts Used Root (rhizome)

Description A perennial that arises from thick, twisted rhizomous roots, blue cohosh may reach three feet in height. The plant has smooth stems and leaves that are typically divided into three, lobed leaflets. Terminal clusters of greenish-yellow or greenish-purple flowers appear in spring, followed by small round seeds that resemble dark-blue berries.

Habitat Blue cohosh grows in the deep rich loam of shady woodlands primarily in eastern North America from New Brunswick to South Carolina and westward to Nebraska. It is particularly abundant in the Allegheny Mountain region.

Approximate native range

NAMED FOR ITS STRIKINGLY BLUE, BERRY-LIKE SEEDS, blue cohosh, if encountered in the woods, is a plant to be treated with respect. The bright blue seeds are poisonous and the roots, including powdered root, are known to be skin and mucous membrane irritants. Just touching the leaves and stem of the plant can cause skin irritations in some people. In addition to its blue seeds, the herb's stems and leaves are covered with a bluish-green film or "bloom" early in the summer, a coloration that gradually fades during the season. The name "cohosh" may be derived from an Algonquian word meaning "rough," referring to the texture of the plant's **rhizome**, a gnarled yellow-brown mass covered with matted roots that is the source of blue cohosh's medicinal power.

Traditional and Current Medicinal Uses

A NUMBER OF NATIVE AMERICAN TRIBES TRADITIONALLY USED the root of *Caulophyllum thalictroides* to treat various ailments but especially to promote childbirth by hastening labor. The dried root was typically ground into a powder, which was added to make a therapeutic tea. Root preparations were also applied as a **poultice** or wash. The Cherokee used blue cohosh root preparations to induce labor and alleviate uterine inflammation, as well as for anxiety, rheumatism, toothache, and externally as an antidote to poison oak or poison ivy. The Chippewa considered the herb a remedy for indigestion, stomach cramps, and lung conditions. A number of tribes also took blue cohosh for fever, to increase perspiration, to ease cramps accompanying painful or profuse menstruation, to reduce spasms, to treat genitourinary dysfunction and venereal disease, for colic and sore throat, and as a general tonic. The herb became a folk remedy among European settlers for many of the same conditions for which Native Americans used it. Western medicine also adopted blue cohosh for a time, where its primary use was in facilitating childbirth, encouraging menstruation, and treating chronic uterine diseases. Early physicians in the United States also used blue cohosh to treat kidney infections and arthritis. Blue cohosh was listed as an approved medicinal herb, and included in *Pharmacopoeia of the United States*, the nation's official drug reference book, until the early 20th century.

In modern herbal medicine, blue cohosh is used to ease false labor pains, induce labor or ensure an easy delivery once labor begins, and bring on delayed or suppressed menstruation while relieving the pain that may accompany it. The herb is also used in situations calling for an antispasmodic, such as nervous coughs and colic, and for easing rheumatic pain.

Cultivation and Preparation

BLUE COHOSH NEEDS MOIST, RICH, HUMUSY SOIL AND PARTIAL or full shade. The easiest way to propagate the herb is to divide plants in spring, as germination of seeds is slow and erratic. For the herbal medicine market, only the roots are used. Roots are collected at the end of the growing season in autumn, when they contain the greatest concentration of active ingredients. They are dried for inclusion in powders, liquid **extracts**, and other medicinal preparations.

Research

BLUE COHOSH CONTAINS A NUMBER OF ACTIVE COMPOUNDS including caulosaponin, a powerful stimulator of uterine contractions. This compound is the source of the herb's use in inducing labor and encouraging menstruation. Blue cohosh is also thought to be a potential **abortifacient** because of the strong uterine muscle contractions it can induce. Studies indicate that the root exhibits **estrogenic** activity and may also induce muscle spasms. Research in India has suggested that the herb may act as a contraceptive by interfering with embryo implantation. In animal studies, the herb has been shown to have some **anti-inflammatory** effects. It also contains an **alkaloid**—methylcytisine—that, like nicotine, increases blood pressure, raises blood sugar levels, and stimulates the small intestine, thereby increasing movement in the digestive tract.

> CAUTION Blue cohosh should not be used without the advice of a qualified medical practitioner. It should not be used during pregnancy.

Blue cohosh is not an herbal remedy to be taken casually. It should never be taken during pregnancy because of its potential to interfere with the mother's natural schedule for labor. Nevertheless, when used carefully under the knowledgeable guidance of an experienced herbal medicine practitioner, blue cohosh is often suggested in situations where labor needs to be speeded up, especially in cases where the mother is exhausted and uterine contractions are weakening. In such situations, blue cohosh is considered by some to be no more dangerous than oxytocin, a labor-promoting hormone that has been widely used for many years in delivery rooms around the world. At normal levels oxytocin (which is produced naturally by the body) has little effect on uterine contractions. When synthetic oxytocin is injected in larger amounts, however, it causes the smooth muscles in the wall of the uterus to contract—precisely the effect blue cohosh has as well.

CAULOPHYLLUM THALICTROIDES | Blue Cohosh

See Also: A Field Guide to Medicinal Plants and Herbs: Eastern and Central North America, 2nd ed. by S. Foster and J. Duke, Houghton Mifflin, 2000; Medicinal Herbs History, Use, Recommended Dosages & Cautions by S. Foster, Interweave Press, 1998.

Borage
Borago officinalis

TAKE BORAGE FOR COURAGE. THAT WAS THE ADVICE OF many ancient herbalists. A gray-green herb with small but strikingly blue flowers, borage was valued for centuries for its ability to impart bravery and courage. Knights going off to fight in the Crusades were given cups of wine sprinkled with borage flowers. If the borage did not allay their fears of the hardships and battles that lay ahead, perhaps the wine did. The herbalists might have also prescribed borage for any family members and friends that felt despondent as they watched their brave crusaders ride off, for borage was also thought to banish sorrow, drive away depression, and bring joy to the heart. Borage was recognized as a cooling, soothing, **anti-inflammatory** herb with **diuretic** and **diaphoretic** (sweat-promoting) effects. Modern herbalists still use borage as a medicinal herb based on these characteristics. And although it is no longer prescribed for courage, some practitioners do consider it a mild antidepressant.

Traditional and Current Medicinal Uses

LONG BEFORE THE CRUSADES, ROMAN AND CELTIC WARRIORS consumed borage for courage and strength. Both the Greek physician Dioscorides and the Roman scholar Pliny recommended borage to relieve depression and instill feelings of joy and exhilaration. Medieval herbalists continued to promote borage for its mood-lifting benefits, but they also used the herb for treating more concrete ailments. They prescribed borage to promote sweating in cases of fever, for lung infections, as a diuretic, and for inflammation of mucous membranes. **Poultices** made of borage leaves and flowers were applied to soothe dry skin and external inflammations, bruises, and swellings. **Infusions** of borage were used to bathe sore eyes.

Modern herbalists recommend borage for relieving fevers and bronchial infections, liver complaints, urinary tract infections, as a mild sedative, and also a mild antidepressant. Borage oil is considered an alternative to evening primrose oil and is used for treating rheumatism, skin conditions, and hormonal complaints.

Common Names Borage, burrage, star flower

Latin Name *Borago officinalis*

Family Boraginaceae

Parts Used Flowers, flowering tops, seed oil

Description A robust annual, borage has succulent hollow stems and thick gray-green leaves; both stems and leaves are densely covered with stiff, rough hairs. Small, star-shaped, bright blue flowers are produced in nodding clusters.

Habitat Borage is native to southern Europe and the Mediterranean region, where it thrives in rich soil in full sun. Long cultivated in herb gardens, it has become naturalized in much of Europe and England. It continues to be cultivated worldwide.

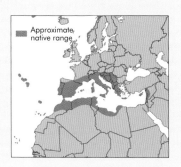

Approximate native range

Washes of borage extract are used to soothe various irritations of the eye, mouth, and skin.

Cultivation and Preparation

BORAGE IS VERY EASY TO GROW IN GOOD GARDEN SOIL IN FULL sun or light shade; it self-sows profusely. For use in herbal medicine, the flowering tops are cut just as the flowers are starting to open. Borage seeds are harvested when they are ripe for the extraction of the oil they contain. Borage is widely cultivated for its seed oil, which is also used in conventional medicine as an ingredient in some pharmaceuticals and in the cosmetics industry.

Research

BORAGE'S PRIMARY CONSTITUENTS ARE TANNINS, SAPONINS, **mucilage**, organic acids, and minerals, including calcium and potassium nitrate. The tannins in borage account for its slight **astringent** properties. The mucilage is a mild **expectorant** and has soothing properties. Potassium nitrate and some of the organic acids probably account for the herb's mild diuretic effects. On the whole, however, the therapeutic properties of borage plant extracts are slight. The seed oil, on the other hand, is a rich source of gammalinolenic acid (GLA), a fatty acid that the body uses to fight inflammation and boost immunity. Borage oil has been considered a good substitute for evening primrose oil in treating eczema and a variety of other conditions that have been thought to respond to GLA supplementation. However, at least one recent clinical study involving 124 subjects showed that borage oil, which contains more GLA than evening primrose oil, had no effect on eczema. Additional research in this area is needed. Some studies carried out in cardiac stress tests suggest that borage oil may slow heart rate and lower blood pressure. A note of caution: Borage leaves have been shown to contain small amounts of **alkaloids** that are known to cause liver damage as well as liver cancer. (Borage oil contains none of these alkaloids, and the flowers contain only trace amounts.) Nevertheless, herbalists do not recommend consumption of borage leaves or preparations made from the leaves, such as herbal teas.

WHAT'S IN A NAME?

The modern names of many herbs can clearly be traced back to their linguistic roots. But borage is definitely not such an herb. The origin of its very similar common and genus names is quite obscure. Some researchers suggest that both borage and *Borago* are corruptions of the Latin *corago*, which is based on *cor*, meaning "heart," and *ago*, meaning "I bring." This might be a reference to borage's use as a restorative drink, one that supposedly banished melancholy and conferred both happiness and courage. Other authorities point to the fact that borage is spelled "burrage," in some places. This is a clue, they maintain, that the word stems from the Italian *borra*, the French *bourrache*, and the Latin *burra*, which all refer to a condition of rough hairiness—a reasonable link to the herb's distinctive covering of tiny, prickly hairs. Because borage has so long been connected with imparting courage, it also has been suggested that the name comes from the Celtic word *barrach*, which translates as "a man of courage." A fourth possibility involves a link to the Arabic phrase *'abu 'arak*, which means "father of sweat" and may be a reference to borage's reputation as a sweat-promoting herb that was used to break fevers.

See Also: *A Field Guide to Medicinal Plants and Herbs: Eastern and Central North America, 2nd ed.* by S. Foster and J. Duke, Houghton Mifflin, 2000; *Medicinal Herbs History, Use, Recommended Dosages & Cautions* by S. Foster, Interweave Press, 1998.

Brazil Nut
Bertholletia excelsa

Common Names Brazil nut, *castanheiro do para* (Brazil), creamnut, castaña

Latin Name *Bertholletia excelsa*

Family Lecythidaceae

Parts Used Nut, seed pod, bark

Description An enormous rain forest tree with its branches high in the canopy, *Bertholletia* can grow to 150 feet and live 500 to 800 years. It produces cream-colored flowers that are about the size of grapes. Fruits that develop from the flowers are large, round woody capsules or pods, each about the size of a coconut; a single pod can weigh nearly five pounds. Wedged inside each pod are 12 to 25 three-sided Brazil nuts, each within its own shell.

Habitat Brazil nut trees are found throughout the warm, humid forests of the Amazon Basin, including Brazil, Peru, Colombia, Venezuela, and Ecuador.

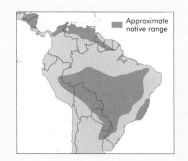

Approximate native range

MOST PEOPLE IN THE UNITED STATES ARE FAMILiar with Brazil nuts only as the delicious, oily nuts that are typically the largest in a can of mixed nuts. Their creamy white flesh is a remarkable 70 percent fat. That's so much fat that fresh Brazil nuts will actually burn like small candles when lit with a flame. While such a high fat content may be the bane of people who are counting calories, it is part of what made Brazil nuts an invaluable staple in the diet of many indigenous rain forest tribes in South America. The protein content of nuts is also very high. In addition to being a wonderful food source, the nuts were also crushed to extract their oil, which was used for cooking, lamps, and to make soap. Brazil nuts were so important to indigenous people that they were once traded like money. As an herbal medicine, Brazil nuts are rich source of vitamin E, lecithin, and the **antioxidant** mineral selenium, which may enhance circulation, fight arthritis, and protect against cataracts.

Traditional and Current Medicinal Uses

IN BRAZILIAN FOLK MEDICINE, THE HUSKS OF THE BRAZIL NUT pods were used to make a tea considered to be a good remedy for stomachaches. A **decoction** of the tree's bark was drunk as a treatment for liver diseases. In the Amazon rain forest, indigenous people applied the oil from the nut to treat some skin conditions.

Modern research has revealed that Brazil nuts are very high in the trace mineral selenium, a nutrient that is essential to good health. Selenium is incorporated into proteins to make selenoproteins, which are important antioxidants. The antioxidant properties of selenoproteins help prevent cellular damage from **free radicals**. Brazil nuts may be the richest natural source of selenium currently known. The average Brazil nut contains 70 micrograms of selenium, which exceeds the Daily Value recommended by the U.S. Food and Drug Administration. Some herbal and plant health experts recommend eating one or two Brazil nuts a day as an easy way to get a rich supply of selenium. The nuts are also high in vitamin E (another antioxidant). Brazil nut oil remains an important ingredient in many soaps, skin creams, and hair conditioners as it has both detergent and moisturizing properties.

Cultivation and Preparation

ALMOST ALL BRAZIL NUTS ARE HARVESTED FROM TREES GROWING in the wild. The Brazil nut may be the only tropical product consumed worldwide that comes exclusively from wild populations. Cultivation is rare. One reason for this is that the trees are very slow-growing; it may be 30 years before a tree will begin to produce fruit. In Brazil, several Brazil nut plantations have been established, but the nut production of the trees remains low. This may be due to the fact that *Bertholletia* flowers are pollinated only by euglossine ("orchid") bees, which do not tend to frequent areas of disturbed forest and so may avoid plantation-style environments. In the wild, the pods remain on branches high in the rain forest canopy for more than 15 months. When finally ripe, they fall from the canopy like cannonballs. Brazil nut collection is typically delayed until most of the fruits have fallen, as the risk of being killed or seriously injured by these free-falling projectiles is considerable.

Research

THE SELENIUM CONTENT OF BRAZIL NUTS MAKES THEM AN important, easy-to-ingest source of this nutrient. Selenium is one of several antioxidants that may help limit the oxidation of **low-density lipoprotein** (LDL) cholesterol and thereby help to prevent coronary artery disease. As an antioxidant, selenium may help to relieve symptoms of arthritis by curbing free radicals. Current findings are considered preliminary, however, and further studies are needed before selenium supplements can be recommended for arthritis sufferers. Researchers continue to investigate the relationship between selenium and HIV/AIDS, including how selenium levels in the body affect progression of the AIDS virus. Brazil nuts are also a rich source of lecithin, which contains the chemical compound choline. Both choline and lecithin have been studied—with encouraging but still inconclusive results—in helping to improve memory in Alzheimer's patients.

Brazil nut trees cover more than 10 million acres of Amazonian Peru and even larger areas in Bolivia and Brazil. These parts of the Amazon Basin are among the world's most biologically diverse ecosystems. In this region, vast expanses of Brazil nut-rich forest link protected areas such as Manu, Madidi, and Bahuaja-Sonene National Parks in Peru and Bolivia and similar reserves in Brazil. Even though these concentrations of Brazil nut trees lie outside of parks and reserves, they are vital to the future of the protected zones in that they provide incentives for forest conservation. The reason for these incentives is vast stands of Brazil nut trees at the sites of *castañales*, or Brazil nut harvesting concessions. These areas, which range from several hundred to a few thousand acres, are allotted to local families or to larger landholders for harvesting Brazil nuts. The nuts are gathered by local harvesters (*castañeros*). Typically a family lives in the *castañal* or moves in during the harvesting season. The harvesters sell the nuts to local shelling factories, which pack them for export overseas. Brazil nuts are the most profitable non-timber forest products in the southwestern Amazon, and the Brazil nut harvest represents more than half the yearly income for thousands of families in these areas. When a forest is managed for Brazil nut collection, it also can be legally defended from alternative land-use practices such as cattle ranching and logging. It will remain protected as long as it is being harvested for nuts.

See Also: *Food Plants of the World* by Ben-Erik van Wyk, Timber Press, 2005; *Food Plants of China* by S. Hu, Hong Kong University Press, 2005.

BERTHOLLETIA EXCELSA | Brazil Nut

Buchu

Agathosma betulina

Common Name Buchu

Latin Names *Agathosma betulina,* synomyn *Barosma betulina*

Family Rutaceae

Parts Used Leaves

Description A twiggy, somewhat angular shrub, buchu grows to six feet in height. Its oval, leathery leaves are a pale yellow-green and have fine-toothed edges; their undersides are dotted with tiny oil glands. The leaves are strongly aromatic. In spring, the delicate branches bear tiny white or pink flowers with purple anthers that are succeeded by small, shiny black seeds.

Habitat Buchu is native to the mountain slopes of South Africa. It is widely cultivated there and in parts of South America.

Approximate native range

B UCHU IS THE COMMON NAME GIVEN TO SEVERAL SPECIES of heavily scented evergreen shrubs that are native to the Cape region of South Africa. A number of the native tribes of the western Cape, including the Khoi San (referred to as Bushmen by colonial Europeans) and the Khoi Khoi (called Hottentots by the Dutch after their curious-sounding language), were probably the first to use buchu medicinally. The herb has a long history as a remedy for urinary tract ailments and as a **diuretic.** The leaves contain a **volatile oil** and have a distinctive aroma and taste, minty to some but more reminiscent of black currant to others. The Khoi Khoi used powdered preparations of the leaves to perfume their skin as well as using it medicinally. The herb was first exported to Britain in 1790. By 1821 its name had been added to the official list of medicinal herbs in the *British Pharmacopoeia,* the official drug reference of Britain. Several decades later, the herb had reached America. One of its most vocal promoters was Henry T. Hembold, a New York entrepreneur who successfully marketed his Buchu Fluid Extracts across the country. Hembold's buchu was a watered-down version of the traditional formula. Hembold and his agents claimed the patent medicine would cure a host of ailments. He even warned that by not using his extract, people risked such afflictions as epilepsy, consumption, and insanity!

Traditional and Current Medicinal Uses

BUCHU'S TRADITIONAL USE AMONG INDIGENOUS PEOPLE OF South Africa's Cape region was as a stimulating tonic and a diuretic. The leaves were brewed to make a tea that was known to alleviate burning urination and some types of digestive complaints. The volatile oils produced in the leaves, when mixed with vinegar to make a lotion, were used as a soothing application for bruises and sprains. The oil was also used as an insect repellent. Dutch colonists were introduced to the herb by the Khoi Khoi, and they quickly adopted it, expanding its applications to the treatment of a variety of urinary tract infections, kidney stones, arthritis, muscle aches, and even cholera. In Europe it was used to treat gout. In England, after its introduction there as a medicinal herb in the late 18th century, buchu was primarily prescribed for cystitis, nephritis, and urethritis (inflammation of the bladder, kidneys, and the urethra, respectively).

Three hundred years later, the African herb's role in herbal medicine remains much the same. It is typically prescribed for urinary tract infections and as a diuretic. When used in combination with other herbs, it is said to be especially effective in curing acute cystitis—and, if taken on a regular basis—to help prevent recurring infections. It is also used for inflammation of the prostate, rheumatism, colds and flu, stomach cramps and colic, to reduce high blood pressure, and to treat diabetes, chills, and anxiety.

Cultivation and Preparation

ADAPTED TO DRY CONDITIONS, BUCHU DOES WELL ON SUNNY hillsides in well-drained soil. It is grown from cuttings planted in late summer. Leaves harvested for medicinal purposes are picked when the plant is flowering or has just begun to set fruit. After picking, the leaves are dried; they retain their pleasant scent remarkably well. The herb's volatile oil is obtained from steam distillation of the leaves.

Research

THE DARK YELLOW VOLATILE OIL EXTRACTED FROM THE leaves of buchu includes a number of important compounds, including diosphenol, the key active ingredient. It is probably responsible for buchu's antiseptic and diuretic actions. Although the oil has also been credited with exhibiting antibacterial activity, one in vitro study using buchu oil found no significant antibacterial effect. Germany's Commission E, a panel of scientific experts who make recommendations on herbal medicines, classifies buchu as an unapproved herb because there is insufficient evidence to support its use in the treatment of urinary tract infections and inflammation. However, traditional herbal practitioners continue to prescribe it for these conditions, and the herbal medicine continues to grow in popularity.

BUCHU FOR BUCKS

Agathosma betulina is widely cultivated in South Africa and is the foundation of a multimillion dollar industry there. But the growing demand for buchu has a downside for South Africa as well. Increasingly, wild buchu plants are being poached from nature reserves in the western Cape of South Africa region. Illegal collecting has already brought about the extinction of the plants in some areas. To counteract this trend and to create employment opportunities in poor rural communities, a pilot project was launched in 2004 to enable small-scale farmers to grow buchu to supply the herbal market. With funding from the United States Agency for International Development and with the participation of several conservation agencies and companies, the project will help farmers near the communities of Elandskloof and Goedverwacht in South Africa propagate and cultivate buchu. If the project turns out to be a success, it will go quite a long way toward protecting wild stocks of Agathosma betulina while at the same time raising the standard of living for people in these communities.

See Also: A Field Guide to Venomous Animals and Poisonous Plants of North America Exclusive of Mexico by S. Foster and R. Caras, Houghton Mifflin, 1994; Nature's Medicine: Plants that Heal by Joel Swerdlow, National Geographic, 2000.

Butterbur
Petasites hybridus

GROWING THROUGHOUT EUROPE AS WELL AS PARTS OF Asia and North America, butterbur is a moisture-loving perennial that prefers marshy ground in damp forests or adjacent to rivers and streams. Its leaves are reminiscent of those of rhubarb and are unexpectedly large: They may reach 2 to 3 feet across. The size and shape of the leaves is reflected in the herb's genus name, *Petasites*, which comes from the Greek *petasos*, meaning "a large, broad-brimmed hat." The common name, "butterbur," may be derived from the practice, in the time before refrigeration, of using the huge leaves to wrap up butter on warm summer days. Other common names for butterbur are "pestilence wort" and "coughwort." During the Middle Ages, the herb was thought to banish plague, the worst form of pestilence known at that time. It is unlikely that butterbur had any effect against that dreaded disease. But the name coughwort is well-deserved, as parts of butterbur have been used for centuries to treat coughs and respiratory disorders. Today, butterbur is still used in herbal medicine to treat asthma, chronic coughs, and bronchial spasms as well as spasms of the gastrointestinal and urinary tracts. Recent research has also shown butterbur to be very effective in reducing the frequency and severity of migraine headaches.

Traditional and Current Medicinal Uses

HISTORICALLY, BOTH THE **RHIZOMES** AND LEAVES OF BUTTERbur were used medicinally. **Infusions** were given to treat coughs, hoarseness, urinary disorders, and to expel intestinal parasites. During the Middle Ages, butterbur was used primarily to treat plague and fever as well as spasms of the digestive tract associated with colic and bile flow obstructions. In the 17th century, fresh butterbur leaves were commonly made into **poultices** and applied directly to skin wounds as well as swellings, rashes, swollen veins and glands, and rheumatic joints. Dried butterbur plant parts were also smoked to relieve coughs.

In modern herbal medicine, butterbur's primary therapeutic uses are for the treatment of migraine headaches and as an antispasmodic to relieve asthma, bronchial

Common Names Butterbur, common butterbur, coughwort, pestilence wort

Latin Name *Petasites hybridus*

Family Asteraceae

Parts Used Rhizomes, leaves

Description Butterbur is a robust perennial with a creeping rhizome (underground stem) and very large leaves that are green above and woolly grey on the undersides. Erect flowering shoots emerge in spring before the leaves and bear club-shaped clusters of reddish-violet tubular flowers.

Habitat Native to Europe and northwestern Asia, butterbur grows on damp ground in wet meadows, along roadsides, and beside streams. The herb was introduced into North America.

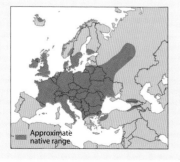

Approximate native range

spasms, and chronic cough; it is often combined with horehound or marshmallow in cough remedies. Butterbur has also been successfully used to prevent gastric ulcers, to treat patients with irritable bladder and urinary tract spasms, and to relieve nerve pain. There is some evidence that butterbur may also be helpful in alleviating seasonal allergic rhinitis.

Cultivation and Preparation

BUTTERBUR THRIVES IN DAMP HABITATS. IT GROWS BEST IN deep, moist, humusy soil, typically in shade or part shade. Butterbur rhizomes spread quickly, making it a very invasive plant. Butterbur flowers are **dioecious**, that is, individual flowers are either male or female, but only one sex is found on any one plant. Thus, for seeds to be produced, both male and female plants must be grown in close proximity. Butterbur is easily propagated by division of the rhizomes. Extracts of butterbur are prepared from the rhizomes and leaves. The herb is best taken as a standardized **extract** certified to be free of pyrrolizidine **alkaloids** (see sidebar).

Research

THE MAIN THERAPEUTIC INGREDIENTS OF BUTTERBUR ARE sesquiterpenes called petasin and isopetasin. Isopetasin appears to impact **prostaglandins** in the body, which are important mediators in the **inflammatory response**. Petasin is thought to reduce smooth muscle spasms, particularly in the walls of blood vessels. It also exerts **anti-inflammatory** effects. Studies have also shown that petasin has an affinity for acting in blood vessels of the brain, which may explain butterbur's effectiveness in relieving migraines. Two clinical studies using a standardized butterbur extract over three months demonstrated its efficacy as a preventive for migraines. Both studies were **double blind** and **placebo** controlled. Results showed as much as 60 percent reduction in frequency of migraine attacks compared to placebo; pain and duration of migraines were also reduced. A number of studies have shown butterbur extracts to reduce bronchial spasms in asthma and bronchitis patients. Several studies have found extracts of butterbur as effective as commonly prescribed antihistamines in relieving hay fever and allergic rhinitis.

Although butterbur contains at least two remarkably therapeutic compounds, petasin and isopetasin, the herb does have a darker side in that it also contains pyrrolizidine alkaloids, or PAs for short. PAs are very toxic compounds that can be dangerous even in small doses. They are known to cause serious liver damage and their effects are cumulative. They are also potential carcinogens and have been associated with fatal blood clots and chronic scarring of lung tissue. Butterbur extracts are now available, however, from which these toxic alkaloids have been removed. In the United States, where herbs and supplements are not well-regulated, it is important to make sure that butterbur extract preparations are certified to be PA-free. Butterbur is not the only plant in the herbal medicine chest that contains PAs. Several other members of the botanical family Asteraceae, the family to which butterbur belongs, contain these compounds as well, including the medicinal herbs boneset (*Eupatorium perforatum*), golden ragwort (*Senecio aureus*), and coltsfoot (*Tussilago farfara*). Virtually all the plants in the family Boraginaceae (including borage, *Borago officinalis*) contain detectable levels of PAs, as doseveral members of the family Fabaceae. As isthe case with butterbur, manufacturers of herbal preparations are working to create PA-free extracts of these herbs that might otherwise pose a health risk.

See Also: Herbalgram, American Botanical Council, *www.Herbalgram.org/default.asp?c–8043; Herbalgram*, American Botanical Council, *www. Herbalgram.org/default.asp?c-petadolex.kids.*

PETASITES HYBRIDUS | Butterbur

Calabar Bean

Physostigma venenosum

Common Names Calabar bean, ordeal bean, esere bean, doomsday plant

Latin Name *Physostigma venenosum*

Family Fabaceae

Parts Used Seed

Description Calabar bean is a perennial woody climber that can reach 20 feet and has three-part pointed leaves. Pinkish purple pea-like flowers are succeeded by six-inch pods that contain two to three dark reddish-brown seeds, each just over an inch long.

Habitat Native to West Africa, calabar bean grows under warm, tropical conditions. It is cultivated in India and parts of South America.

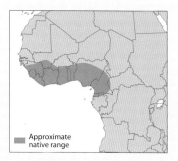

Approximate native range

CALABAR BEAN IS A VIGOROUS WOODY VINE THAT PROduces long pods. Sheltered inside the pods are large seeds that look a bit like oversized kidney beans. But unlike kidney beans, calabar beans are extremely toxic. Centuries ago, this toxicity was put to an interesting use in the Calabar Province of present-day Nigeria in West Africa. There, the calabar bean was the key ingredient in ritualistic ordeals by poison designed to determine the guilt or innocence of individuals accused of witchcraft or other crimes. Those who survived ingesting a dose of the crushed beans, called esere, were pronounced innocent. By the 1860s, specimens of calabar bean had found their way back to botanic gardens in Edinburgh, Scotland. In the spirit of self-experimentation that characterized 19th-century scientific and medical research, a professor of medicine at the University of Edinburgh tried the poison on himself to document its effects. Fortunately for Robert Christison, he ingested a small dose and survived. His assistant went on to discover that **extract** of calabar bean, applied to the eye, causes the pupil to contract. This discovery foreshadowed the plant's modern use in treating eye diseases. Although a poison itself, calabar bean is an antidote to other poisons and is used to treat some neuromuscular diseases.

Traditional and Current Medicinal Uses

WHEN CHRISTISON'S ASSOCIATE, THOMAS FRASER, NOTICED that an extract of calabar bean caused contraction of the eye's pupil, he was excited. Calabar bean's effect was precisely the opposite of that caused by atropine eye-drops (see Belladonna, page 36). Atropine causes the pupil to dilate. In the years that followed Fraser's discovery, this pupil-contracting substance was isolated and named eserine, which was later changed to physostigmine. Now largely synthesized in the laboratory, physostigmine is widely used to treat glaucoma (disease marked by pressure in eyeball that can lead to blindness). By causing a sudden contraction of muscles in the pupil, the pressure in the eye is quickly reduced. In the past, calabar bean was also used as an intestinal stimulant for chronic constipation and to control muscle spasms and seizures associated with epilepsy, cholera, and tetanus. More recently, physostigmine has been used to treat neuromuscular diseases (particularly the muscle-weakening disease myasthenia gravis) and as an antidote to certain poisons, notably atropine. It can be effective in reversing the effects of anesthesia, decreasing the incidence of hallucinations, and controlling agitated body movements. Physostigmine has also been prescribed to arrest the progression of Alzheimer's disease.

Cultivation and Preparation

CALABAR BEAN REQUIRES RICH, WELL-DRAINED SOIL AND FULL sun. Ripe seeds are collected and dried for use in preparations and for extraction of key chemical constituents.

Research

THROUGHOUT THE HUMAN BODY, MUSCLES, GLANDS, AND nerve cells are stimulated by nerve impulses that travel across switching centers called **synapses**. Nerve impulses are transmitted across synapses by a chemical called acetylcholine. Transmission is halted by an **enzyme** called acetylcholinesterase. These important chemical reactions go on constantly in the body, with acetylcholine making nerve impulse transmission possible and acetylcholinesterase counteracting it. Physostigmine is an **alkaloid** that acts as an inhibitor of acetylcholinesterase (the enzyme that halts transmission of impulses). By inhibiting the enzyme, the action of acetylcholine is prolonged and nerve impulses continue to be transmitted. Physostigmine is therapeutic in situations in which the activity of acetylcholine needs to be prolonged to restore normal function (or alleviate negative symptoms). Dementia associated with Alzheimer's is thought to be caused by acetylcholinesterase's inhibition of nerve impulse transmission in the brain. Physostigmine was one of the earliest known acetylcholinesterase inhibitors used to treat Alzheimer's. Patients showed modest improvement in cognitive function, but therapeutic effects were short-lived and the drug had significant side effects. Research continues with newer formulations of this calabar bean **phytochemical.**

The power of the calabar bean in African folk medicine lay in its supposed ability to reveal and destroy witches in a poisoning ordeal. One of the first accounts by a Westerner of the use of calabar bean in such a "trial" came from William Freeman Daniel, a medical officer in the British Army. Daniel witnessed one of these events among the Efik tribe in the Calabar Province in what is now Nigeria, and wrote about the experience in 1846. In the ritual, an accused person was forced to drink a milky-looking preparation of eight crushed calabar beans and water. After swallowing a portion, the accused was ordered to walk around until the effects of the poison became evident—typically a matter of minutes. It could not have been a pretty sight, because one of the first signs of physostigmine poisoning is twitching of the mouth and extreme salivation. The judges and onlookers carefully watched what happened next. If the accused could raise his or her right hand and quickly vomit up the poison, then the person was pronounced innocent and allowed to go free. However, if the person succumbed to the poison (which is typically what happened), a horrible death from paralytic asphyxia ensued and guilt was assumed. By the late 1800s, the practice of trial by ordeal for witchcraft was outlawed in Africa, though the practice doubtlessly continued. Today calabar beans are sometimes used as protective charms. They are often kept with money to guard against theft by witches.

See Also: *Nature's Medicine: Plants that Heal* by Joel Swerdlow, National Geographic, 2000; *Medical Botany: Plants Affecting Human Health* by W. Lewis and M. Elvin-Lewis, John Wiley & Sons, 2003..

PHYSOSTIGMA VENENOSUM | Calabar Bean

Common Names Calamus, sweet flag, sweet sedge, sweet rush, myrtle grass

Latin Name *Acorus calamus*

Family Acoraceae

Parts Used Root (rhizome)

Description Calamus is an aquatic, reed-like plant with erect, sword-shaped leaves that resemble those of irises. Growing to three feet in height, the plant spreads via thick, branching rhizomes (underground stems). Calamus produces a solid, cylindrical flower spike (spadix), two to four inches long, that is covered with small, tightly packed, greenish-yellow flowers. Plants growing in Europe and other cool northern climates typically do not produce fruit.

Habitat Various forms of the plant originate from Asia, Europe, and North America. It prefers wet soil and grows in marshes, ditches, and along shallow, somewhat stagnant waterways.

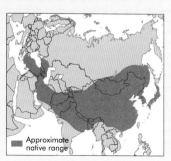

Approximate native range

Calamus
Acorus calamus

C ALAMUS AND ITS VARIETIES ORIGINATE IN INDIA, Europe, and North America. Calamus has been widely used in all regions where it grows. Its sword-like leaves are similar to the leaves of yellow flag (*Iris pseudoacorus*) and other irises, but the two types of plants are not botanically related. All parts of calamus emit an aromatic fragrance that has been described as somewhat cinnamon-spicy and also reminiscent of the aroma of crushed tangerines. *Acorus calamus* var. *americanus* is native to the United States. Because of its sweet smell, it was for a time a popular strewing herb. The ground root was also added to potpourris, sachets, and hair powders. The **volatile oil** extracted from the roots is still used in perfumery today. Medicinally, calamus roots have been used to produce aromatic, bitter tonics used primarily to settle stomach and intestinal upsets.

Traditional and Current Medicinal Uses

CALAMUS HAS LONG BEEN USED IN HERBAL MEDICINE, AND IS taken both internally and externally. In ancient India and Egypt, it was regarded as an aphrodisiac. In Europe, the herb was widely used as a digestive aid. In North America, Native Americans used calamus preparations to quiet stomach cramps, relieve colic, and reduce fevers. The root was chewed for toothache and to clear phlegm from the throat. Sweet flag was so valued as a source of medicine by tribes of the Great Plains region that it appears to have been intentionally planted around village sites and along trails, thus ensuring that the herb would always be close at hand. Calamus was used medicinally at least 2,000 years ago in India and still is an important traditional herbal remedy used in **Ayurvedic medicine** for stroke victims, in preparations used to treat epilepsy, as a nervous system tonic, and a remedy for digestive problems.

Among modern Western herbalists, *Acorus calamus* has been used for treating a wide range of digestive complaints; it is credited with stimulating the appetite, relieving bloating and flatulence, regulating stomach acid production, calming indigestion, and dispelling intestinal worms. The herb is also a mild sedative and some herbalists recommend chewing on small pieces of calamus root to quell motion sickness. The North American variety, *Acorus calamus* var. *americanus*, has antispasmodic effects and relieves intestinal cramps. *A. gramineus* is a much smaller species that is native to the Far East and used in Chinese medicine (as *shi ch'ang pu*) for many of the same ailments as *A. calamus*. Externally, *A. calamus* can be used as a rub to soothe aching muscles and is often added to bath preparations to help alleviate fatigue and nervous exhaustion.

Cultivation and Preparation

CALAMUS TYPICALLY GROWS IN A SUNNY POSITION IN SHALlow water or very wet soil. The flowering spadix appears in midsummer on a curved triangular stalk (spathe) about midway up the leaves. Vigorous in habit, the herb is easy to propagate in spring or autumn by dividing healthy **rhizomes** into small pieces, each with two or three intact buds, and planting them in muddy ground. Fresh rhizomes are harvested as needed. They are stripped of their roots, cleaned, and then dried, a process that renders them strongly aromatic and brittle. Dried rhizome is taken internally in powdered form in Ayurvedic medicine; it is also taken in **tinctures** and **decoctions**.

Research

THE CONSTITUENTS OF CALAMUS INCLUDE AN **ESSENTIAL OIL** to which the herb owes its aromatic scent and medicinal properties. The oil contains forms of the chemical compound asarone as its primary components. Most research has been focused on asarone in the essential oil, which is considered carcinogenic (laboratory rats fed large doses of *A. calamus* root preparations developed tumors). Although it has been used in India for thousands of years without any link to cancer, some herbal medicine practitioners now caution against its use. The United States Food and Drug Administration has prohibited the use of powdered *Acorus* root as a food additive.

> CAUTION Since some strains of calamus contain the carcinogen beta-asarone, it should not be taken internally.

Both the grasslike leaves and spongy roots of calamus exude a sweet spicy fragrance with overtones of musk—no other herb smells quite like it. No doubt because of its haunting aroma, calamus was an ingredient in the incense of the Egyptians and many ancient cultures. Remains of calamus were found in the tomb of Tutankhamen. In the Middle Ages, fresh calamus leaves were scattered on the floors of medieval churches and houses to both freshen the air and to drive off insects, as the herb also exhibits insecticidal properties. In addition to scenting and freshening the air, calamus was believed to purify and sweeten water where it grew. As invading tribes from Mongolia swept across parts of Asia and the Middle East centuries ago, it was their habit to plant calamus in and near bodies of water they intended to drink from. Ironically, the herb came to be called Mongolian poison among the people whose lands had been invaded. Throughout its history, calamus has also had a reputation as a stimulant to boost stamina. Some North American Indians chewed pieces of calamus root much as South American Indians chewed coca leaves for their stimulating sensation. Native American tribes ascribed mystical powers to calamus and it was used in various ceremonies. It was said to instill energy and clarity of mind. Many familiar with calamus consider it to be psychoactive, and possibly hallucinogenic, due to the presence of asarone, which can have hallucinogenic effects if taken in sufficient quantities.

See Also: A Field Guide to Medicinal Plants and Herbs: Eastern and Central North America, 2nd ed. by S. Foster and J. Duke, Houghton Mifflin, 2000; A Field Guide to Medicinal Plants and Herbs: Western North America by S. Foster and C. Hobbs, Houghton Mifflin, 2002.

ACORUS CALAMUS | Calamus

Common Names Calendula, pot marigold, poet's marigold, gold

Latin Name *Calendula officinalis*

Family Asteraceae

Parts Used Flowers

Description A low-growing, branching annual, typically 12 to 20 inches tall, with lance-shaped, slightly pale green leaves. Both leaves and stems are covered with fine hair and are rough and slightly sticky to the touch. Large, orange-yellow or yellow flowers are produced from early summer to late autumn; they resemble daisies, with the petals radiating from a pronounced center.

Habitat Calendula is native to countries bordering the Mediterranean, both north and south. It is cultivated in most temperate parts of the world as both an herb and a long-blooming cottage garden flower. Calendula flourishes in full sun in almost any type of soil.

Approximate native range

Calendula
Calendula officinalis

CHEERFUL, FAMILIAR CALENDULA IS A PARTICULARLY versatile herb, valued through many centuries for its medicinal, culinary, and cosmetic attributes. This is a plant that never seems to stop blooming. That characteristic, in fact, is reflected in its botanical name: *Calendula* is a diminutive of the Latin word *calendae* and so means "little calendar or little clock." This is a reference to the belief that these bright flowers were always in bloom on the first day—the *Calends*—of each month. Hindus used the intensely bright flowers to decorate altars in temples and adorn their favorite gods. Both the ancient Greeks and Persians used the flower's petals to garnish and flavor foods. In Europe during the Middle Ages, calendula was a popular flavoring agent in stews, soups, and drinks. In markets, grocers and spice sellers had barrels filled with the dried petals for these culinary uses. Dubbed "poor man's saffron," dried flower parts were also added to rice and chowders calling for the far more expensive saffron, and baked into breads and cookies. Calendula also lent its warm, yellow-gold color to butter and "marigold" cheese, and the fresh petals were sprinkled on salads to add both color and zesty flavor.

Traditional and Current Medicinal Uses

THE ANCIENT EGYPTIANS VALUED CALENDULA AS A HEALING plant and over the centuries it has never lost its popularity as an essential inclusion in the herbal medicine chest. One herbalist in the 12th century recommended simply gazing at the flowers to improve eyesight and lighten the spirit. Folk medicine practitioners in Europe employed calendula to induce menstruation, encourage sweating to break a fever, and to cure jaundice. During the Civil War, doctors on the battlefield used the leaves of the herb to treat open sores, burns, and superficial wounds. Physicians of the day also found calendula helpful in treating conjunctivitis (pink eye), stomach ulcers, and liver complaints.

The **anti-inflammatory** and antiseptic properties of the herb have made it a time-honored ingredient in a variety of ointments and lotions for soothing irritated, chapped or cracked skin, healing eczema, and cooling sunburn. The plant's **essential oil** is said by some herbal medicine practitioners to be an effective antifungal agent in treating vaginal yeast infections. **Extracts** and **tinctures** are sometimes employed to heal stubborn wounds such as bed sores and to treat varicose veins, gum inflammations, and bruises. Today calendula is a common additive in complexion creams and lotions that soothe, soften, and clean the skin. In the pharmaceutical industry, the bright orange pigments of calendula petals are added to some medicinal preparations to give a pleasing color.

Cultivation and Preparation

GROWING CALENDULAS IS AN EASY TASK. SEEDS SOWN IN early spring, in any good soil with plenty of sun, will quickly germinate. Flowering begins typically in June and will continue until frost. Regular deadheading ensures a steady supply of fresh blossoms. Plants with single or double flowers are grown for medicinal use— selected for the highest concentrations of active compounds. Flowers are harvested in summer. Depending on the preparation, the entire flower head or just the florets may be used, either fresh or dried.

Research

Calendula's mechanism for wound healing remains poorly understood. Studies have demonstrated that calendula preparations appear to foster tissue regeneration. These observations may explain the herb's success in treating lesions and other slow-healing sores and wounds. Some clinical studies have demonstrated that calendula is helpful in the early treatment of stomach ulcers, although more research is called for. There is evidence that the herb stimulates the immune system; it also exhibits antiviral action, including potentially therapeutic activity against the human immunodeficiency virus (HIV). Applications of calendula preparations, along with other plant extracts, have been reported to help reduce pain in postmastectomy lymphedema. In clinical studies, calendula has also been shown to be highly effective in preventing acute dermatitis in patients undergoing postoperative irradiation for breast cancer.

In medieval England, people referred to calendula flowers simply as "golds." At some point, however, the name "marigold" became more common. Initially this may have been a corruption of the Anglo-Saxon name *merso-meargealla*, the name for marsh marigolds (*Caltha palustris*). Later, however, the "mari" in marigolds came to be associated first with the Virgin Mary and later still with the English monarch Queen Mary. Calendula, or pot marigold, should never be confused with the completely unrelated French or garden marigolds of the genus *Tagetes*. About 30 species make up the genus *Tagetes*, and there are many cultivars, some of which commonly crowd the flats of annuals on display at garden shops and greenhouses every spring. French marigolds are native to South and Central America. Many of them are toxic and should not be consumed in any form. One obvious difference between *Calendula* and *Tagetes* marigold plants is the aroma. *Tagetes* marigolds have a strong, rather unpleasant odor, while calendula's scent is far less pronounced and quite mild.

See Also: Herbal Medicine Expanded Commission E Monographs by M. Blumenthal, A. Goldberg, and J. Brinckmann, American Botanical Council, 2000; World Health Organization (WHO) Monographs on Selected Medicinal Plants, Vol. 2, 2002.

Cascara Sagrada

Frangula purshiana

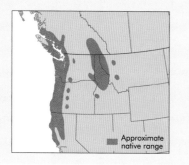

Common Names Cascara sagrada, cascara buckthorn, sacred bark, California buckthorn

Latin Names *Frangula purshiana*, synonym *Rhamnus purshiana*

Family Rhamnaceae

Parts Used Bark

Description Growing to 40 feet, cascara sagrada is a large deciduous shrub or small tree with reddish-gray bark. It has deeply veined leaves and umbels of small, greenish flowers that are followed by red fruits that turn black as they ripen.

Habitat Found in moist soils in evergreen forests, cascara sagrada is native to the Pacific Northwest in North America. It is commercially cultivated on plantations in the United States, Canada, and Kenya.

Approximate native range

THE GENUS *FRANGULA* IS MADE UP OF MORE THAN A hundred **deciduous** and evergreen shrubs and small trees that inhabit primarily the northern temperate regions of the world. The fruits and bark of a number of *Frangula* species contain substances that have a powerful purgative effect on the digestive tract and so have been used as herbal laxatives. The fruits of buckthorn were eaten as long ago as the ninth century for their cleansing effects. The bark of *Frangula purshiana*, which is native to North America's Pacific Northwest, was used by many Native American tribes as a remedy for constipation. Native Americans introduced their remedy to Spanish explorers, who gave the plant the name *cascara sagrada*, which means "sacred bark." Since the late 1800s, cascara sagrada has been a widely used stimulant laxative in the United States and Europe. Today it is marketed in the form of pills and powders as well as in herbal preparations and herbal supplements.

Traditional and Current Medicinal Uses

MANY NATIVE AMERICAN TRIBES IN THE PACIFIC NORTHWEST traditionally used cascara bark as a laxative. The Flathead of northwest Montana and the Kutenai of Montana, Idaho, and British Columbia made **infusions** of the bark to drink as a laxative tea. The Sanpoil, Shuswap, Skagit, and Yurok tribes made **decoctions** of the bark to administer for constipation. The bark was also chewed directly for its laxative effects. The use of cascara bark was adopted by herbal medicine practitioners throughout the United States in the 19th century as an effective, as well as a relatively mild, stimulant laxative.

It is still widely used today in herbal medicine for the treatment of chronic constipation. Cascara sagrada is also taken as a remedy for colitis (inflammation of the colon), stomach upsets, hemorrhoids, liver problems, and jaundice. The herb is a component in several hundred different medicinal products, ranging from flavored fluid extracts to various pills and powders. Although effective as a laxative, cascara tea is not widely consumed because of its bitter taste. Cascara sagrada is also used in veterinary medicine.

Cultivation and Preparation

CASCARA SAGRADA REQUIRES MOIST, FERTILE SOIL AND FULL sun to partial shade and can be started from seed or cuttings. The bark is harvested in spring and early summer from the trunk and stems of plants that are at least a year old. Fresh bark has a stronger action (it causes nausea and cramping) than bark that has been allowed to cure, so freshly harvested bark is typically stored for at least one year, or artificially aged by drying at 100 degrees Celsius for an hour to achieve the same effect as 12 months of storage. In the herbal medicine market, cascara sagrada is available as capsules, **extracts**, and as dried bark that is often sold as rolls or "quills" like cinnamon sticks.

Research

DRIED, AGED CASCARA SAGRADA BARK WAS WIDELY ACCEPTED as a mild and effective treatment for chronic constipation for centuries. However, on November 5, 2002, the U.S. Food and Drug Administration banned stimulant laxatives containing cascara sagrada or aloe, deeming them not generally recognized as safe or effective. The active ingredients that give the bark its laxative properties are various anthraquinones (chemical compounds that stimulate contractions in the walls of the digestive tract). In the digestive tract, these compounds are transformed by intestinal bacteria into substances that increase peristalsis (rhythmic intestinal contractions), speeding up the movement of material through the colon and reducing the absorption of liquid.

The mildest of the known anthraquinone stimulant laxatives, cascara sagrada is considered the least likely to cause undesirable side effects such as intestinal cramping. The few clinical studies that have been done on cascara sagrada have investigated its effectiveness as a colon cleanser for colonoscopies and to treat elderly patients who are suffering from chronic constipation. In vitro studies have also shown that extracts of the bark contain an active ingredient, emodin, which may have anticancer effects.

The name "cascara sagrada" (sacred bark) was given to this plant in the 1600s by Spanish explorers traveling in the Pacific Northwest. They encountered many Indian tribes that used the bark for a number of medicinal purposes, but primarily as a remedy for constipation. The fact that the Spanish dubbed the source of the remedy as *sacred* bark may give some indication as to its effectiveness! Settlers of the American West also later adopted it as a remedy. They typically soaked pieces of the bark overnight in cold water to make a laxative tea. The infusion was also drunk as a tonic. By 1877 the American medical community was using cascara sagrada in preparations made by the pharmaceutical company Parke-Davis. Cascara sagrada powders and extracts soon found their way into European medicine, creating a new market for this sacred bark. Indiscriminant stripping of the bark greatly damaged wild populations of the plant in North America in the early 1900s. The laxative properties of the bark vary greatly in plants grown outside their native region, and active ingredients can be lower in the bark from cultivated plants versus that harvested from wild trees. Today, bark is still harvested from wild trees in the forests of Oregon, Washington, and British Colombia, but trees are also cultivated elsewhere in the United States, Canada, and Kenya.

FRANGULA PURSHIANA | Cascara Sagrada

See Also: *Herbal Medicine Expanded Commission E Monographs* by M. Blumenthal, A. Goldberg, and J. Brinckmann, American Botanical Council, 2000; *World Health Organization (WHO) Monographs on Selected Medicinal Plants, Vol. 2,* 2002.

Common Names Castor bean, castor oil plant, Mexico seed, *bofareira, palma Christi*

Latin Name *Ricinus communis*

Family Euphorbiaceae

Parts Used Seed oil

Description In its natural habitat, castor bean is an evergreen, perennial that has very large, red-tinged, palm-shaped leaves. Flowering stalks bear both male and female flowers. The fruit is a capsule covered with soft spines that contains large, shiny, bean-like seeds with variable brownish mottling on a cream-colored background.

Habitat Native to western Asia and northeastern Africa, castor bean has its origins in tropical climates and is widely naturalized and cultivated in warm regions of the world.

Approximate native range

Castor Bean
Ricinus communis

CASTOR BEAN IS QUITE A VARIABLE PLANT WITH A DIS-tinctly tropical look. Grown in the tropics, it is a perennial shrub that can attain a height of nearly 30 feet. Plant its seeds in a Mediterranean climate and the result will be a smaller shrub that might live two to three years. In more northern climates, where cold temperatures and shorter days control the length of the growing season, castor bean flourishes briefly as an annual, one that can fill the role of a dramatic accent plant, form an impressive backdrop for other plants, or provide a fast-growing screen to disguise an eyesore in the garden. For non-gardeners, castor bean may be familiar as the source of castor oil, the foul-tasting, evil-smelling oil once regularly given to children and the elderly as a gentle laxative when the practice of regular purging was considered essential for good health. The oil is safe in small quantities and still plays a minor role in herbal medicine. But castor bean is not to be trifled with—the seeds from which the oil is extracted are deadly poisons and other parts of the plant can cause serious allergic reactions.

Traditional and Current Medicinal Uses

IN ANCIENT EGYPT, CASTOR BEAN OIL WAS USED AS A COS-metic for hair and skin and for treating wounds. It was also administered to induce labor. At least as long ago as 2000 B.C., the oil was used in traditional medicine in India as a laxative. Both castor bean seeds and their oil were used in traditional Chinese medicine as well. The ancient Greeks reserved the oil for external use only. Throughout the Middle Ages, castor bean oil was valued as both liniment and lubricant, but still not taken internally. It was only in the 1780s that castor bean oil became widely used as a laxative in the West. During the 18th and 19th centuries, castor oil was given freely and regularly to "clear" the digestive tract. **Poultices** of the roots and leaves were also folk remedies for treating wounds, boils, and sores and encouraging milk flow in nursing mothers. Other folk uses for castor bean oil included expelling worms and treating colds, colic, convulsions, fever, gout, nerve pain, rheumatism, swellings, tumors, and warts. It also was employed at times to induce labor.

In modern **Ayurvedic medicine** in India, castor oil is used to treat nervous disorders. In the West, castor bean oil is still sometimes prescribed in modern herbal and conventional medicine as a laxative, especially in cases of food poisoning or before x-ray diagnostic tests of the lower intestine. The oil is also used in contraceptive creams as well as in medicinal preparations designed to treat skin conditions such as ringworm, sores, and abscesses and to soothe eye irritations.

Cultivation and Preparation

CASTOR BEAN IS EASILY GROWN IN GOOD SOIL IN SUN OR PART SHADE. The plant is cultivated for its seed oil primarily in China, India, and Brazil. The ripe seeds are collected, peeled, and then pressed for the oil they contain. Although the use of castor bean oil in herbal medicine is limited, this oil is widely employed in industry as a lubricant, in varnishes, and as the starting point for certain types of polymers.

Research

THE OIL EXTRACTED FROM CASTOR BEAN SEEDS IS MADE UP primarily of ricinoleic acid, which is not toxic. In the body, it acts to reduce fluid uptake in the intestinal tract and to increase peristalsis (rhythmic intestinal contractions), which accounts for its laxative effects. Castor bean seeds themselves contain two poisonous substances: ricinine and ricin. Ricin is one of the most poisonous naturally occurring substances known today. Eating a single castor bean seed can be fatal to a child. Modern cancer research is trying to harness ricin's toxicity, however. In the lab, ricin molecules can be bioengineered to attach to antibodies that bind to certain types of cells, such as cancer cells. When the antibodies bind to these cells, the ricin destroys the cell. The same technique is being tested on cells infected with the human immuno-deficiency virus (HIV/AIDS). Treatments are still in the experimental stage.

> CAUTION All parts of the castor bean plant, but especially the seeds, are poisonous if taken internally. Prolonged or repeated contact with the leaves or seeds can lead to skin irritations and allergic reactions.

THE DEADLY BEAN

The common and scientific names associated with castor bean have an interesting history. "Castor" was the name given to the plant by English traders who confused the oil of the castor bean seed with the oil of another shrub, *Vitex agnus-castus* (the chasteberry or chaste tree), which the Spanish and Portuguese in Jamaica called *agno-casto.* Over time, the *casto* became *castor.* The genus name, *Ricinus,* was given to the plant by the 18th-century Swedish naturalist Carolus Linnaeus. *Ricinus* is Latin for "tick." Linnaeus thought that castor bean seeds looked a lot like ticks, with their small heads and mottled bodies. *Communis* means "common" in Latin. By Linnaeus' day, castor bean plants were aggressively naturalizing in many parts of the world where they had been introduced. They will grow in almost any warm area where the soil contains enough nutrients to support them. Castor bean grows so well, in fact, that it is classified as a noxious weed in the southwestern United States. Castor bean seeds are only toxic if the outer shell is broken or chewed, releasing the ricin toxin inside. It has been estimated that gram for gram, ricin is 6,000 times deadlier than cyanide. An amount of pure ricin that is roughly equivalent to the weight of a single grain of table salt is enough to kill a person weighing 160 pounds.

See Also: A Field Guide to Medicinal Plants and Herbs: Eastern and Central North America, 2nd ed. by S. Foster and J. Duke, Houghton Mifflin, 2000; *A Field Guide to Medicinal Plants and Herbs: Western North America* by S. Foster and C. Hobbs, Houghton Mifflin, 2002.

HEALING PLANTS OF

Australia and
New Zealand

SAILING ON THE H.M.S. *ENDEAVOUR* IN HIS FIRST VOYAGE AROUND THE world, Captain James Cook and his crew landed at 11 locations on the eastern coast of Australia between April 19 and August 26, 1770. Among the crew were British naturalists Joseph Banks and Daniel Solander. Impressed by the aromatic eucalyptus forests shrouded in morning mist near what is now Sydney, they named the site Botany Bay. Even among plants new to them—as well as to science—Banks' and Solander's botanical knowledge gave them a sense of which plants could be eaten or used as medicine. This onboard botanical information source for the crew of the *Endeavour* resulted in a remarkable achievement in maritime history: Not one of the 95 people aboard, including 11 civilians as well as the crew, died of scurvy. After an absence of nearly three years, the *Endeavour* returned to England on July 13, 1771. Scurvy, which is caused by a diet lacking in vitamin C, had plagued sailing voyages for centuries before its cause was discovered. The presence of the botanists on board allowed Captain Cook and his men to use edible plants more effectively than any previous voyage had been able to do.

Herbal Medicine in Australia and New Zealand

DID COOK'S MEN, LIKE THE AUSTRALIAN ABORIGINES, EAT THE TENDER SPROUTING tips of beach morning glory (*Ipomoea pres-caprae*) as a tender green? According to Australian naturalist Tim Low, the beach morning glory was widely used medicinally by Australian Aborigines. The leaves and stems, heated over a fire, are commonly applied to the forehead to treat headache. The plant has other uses as well. An ethno-botanical project in Australia's Northern Territory, documenting uses from 12 Aboriginal communities, notes that morning glory leaves are used to treat stings, boils, sores, pains, and swelling. Captain Cook and his crew probably encountered it at every stop—the rangy plant, with conspicuous purple trumpet flowers and floating seeds, occurs on sandy beaches throughout the Pacific.

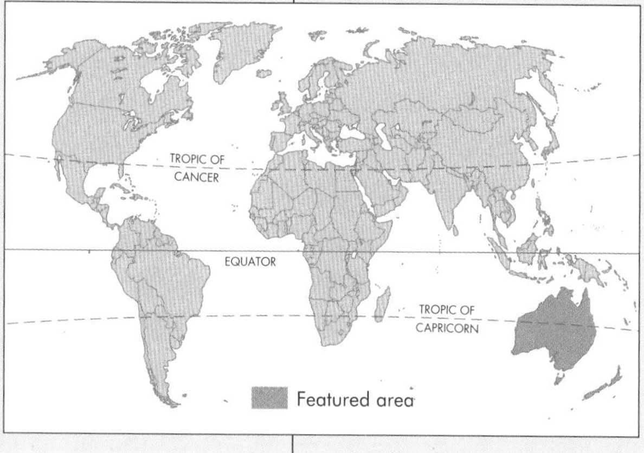

Cook and his men also may have encountered the plant at a previous stop before reaching Australia—the islands of New Zealand. On October 6, 1769, the *Endeavour*'s crew sighted New Zealand. Quiet botanical pursuits were not the order of the day, as the original contact with the islands' native inhabitants, the Maori, turned violent. But before sailing eastward toward

TROPIC OF CANCER

EQUATOR

TROPIC OF CAPRICORN

Featured area

Australia two months later, Banks and Solander had made collections of at least 100 native plant specimens of New Zealand. In his journal, Banks remarked that the health of the Maori was so good that they had little need for formal medical intervention. On his second voyage of discovery in 1774, Cook observed the Maori heating a stone and placing fresh ground herbs on it to treat a woman with the steam. This herbal delivery method also was observed by other early explorers.

Since New Zealand stood isolated for millions of years, at least 80 percent of its native flora occurs nowhere else on Earth. The most spectacular specimens are the massive kauri trees (*Agathis australis*), a pine family member; some grow up to 24 feet in diameter with the lowest branches starting 80 feet up. The tree is full of resin, but collecting the resin kills the tree. However, the first settlers found that the forest soil was full of fossilized resin of the kauri trees. Simply sticking an iron rod in the ground yielded chunks of the dark brown amber-like resin. It became the first important plant product exported from New Zealand in the late 19th century. In 1899, 11,000 tons of the fossilized gum were exported, most sold as New Zealand copal, and primarily used as an ingredient in making molds for dentures. The Maori burned the gum to make *map-blak*, from which they made a tattooing

Beach morning glory (Ipomoea pes-caprae) occurs on beaches in warmer regions of the world, including the Gulf Coast of the United States. Beach morning glory's wide distribution in warmer waters is attributed to the ability of the seeds to float across oceans, and sprout on a suitable beach.

PRECEDING PAGES: *Of the more than 600 species of eucalyptus (Eucalyptus spp.), the vast majority orginate in Australia. The Eucalyptus genus produces some of the world's largest trees, such as the evergreen giant pictured on the previous pages. The tree is one of many large eucalyptus trees at Neilson Park in the eastern suburbs of Sydney.*

pigment. Remarkable for their tattoos, sometimes covering the entire body, the Maori used them as ritualistic ornament and to frighten enemies.

The practice of Maori herbal medicine, as with Australian Aborigines, was primarily external—in the form of poultices, pastes, and steam baths. Serious disease was thought to be caused by unseen spirits, and the Maori shaman, the *tohunga*, was called in to deal with serious illness. The Tohunga Suppression Act of 1907 sought to put an end to their influence. The law was repealed in 1963, and the tohunga's role restored in Maori culture.

The aromatic essential oil glands glisten on the leaves of tea tree (Melaleuca alternifolia), *a tree found in a narrow range in eastern Australia. Recent clinical studies on* M. alternifolia, *particularly in Australia, show potential value for treating acne and various skin infections. Studies have shown conflicting results on the oil's effectiveness as an antibacterial. Tea tree oil is found in a broad range of products.*

MEDICINAL PLANTS IN AUSTRALIA AND NEW ZEALAND

FROM THE LATE 1790S ONWARD, NEW ZEALAND WAS SETTLED BY whalers and missionaries, but the real influx began when the British annexed New Zealand in 1840. Within 50 short years, most of the native kauri forests and other native plant habitats were cleared for timber, burned, or turned into pasture. In *Plants of New Zealand* (1906), R. M. Laing and E. W. Blackwell lament that in 1893 the area still covered in native bush was only 20 million acres, which by 1906 was being reduced at a rate of 200,000 acres per year. "Of course, only a very small proportion of timber is removed and utilized. Most of it is burned on the spot. . . . However necessary this clearing may be, it cannot fail to leave the lover of nature with a feeling of sadness," they write.

European settlement of Australia began in January 1788; 11 ships carrying 1,350 people landed with instructions to establish the first British colony. Contact with Aborigines was at first friendly, with exchanges of food, water, cloth, and tools. By 1790, however, clans of the Eora group, living near what is now Sydney, led raids against the colonists. As more settlers arrived, Aborigines were driven into the dry interior, and their traditional ways, including their knowledge of medicinal plants, was lost to history.

Undoubtedly, the Australian flora captured the imagination of early European explorers and colonists. The color and variety of the vegetation, the strange plant forms, and the diversity of habitats from alpine to tropical rain forests make Australian flora unique in composition and structure. Two plant types dominate Australian vegetation: the acacia and eucalyptus. It is the eucaluptus that typifies Australia. And among Australia's medicinal plants, it is the most well known.

The genus *Eucalyptus* contains more than 600 species, mostly indigenous to Australia. *Eucalyptus globulus*, perhaps the most familiar species, is commonly known as the blue gum. It was also introduced to other countries and is common in east Africa, parts of India, the Mediterranean region, California, and even the Peruvian Andes. First described by French botanist Jacques Julien Houtton de Labillardiere in 1798, it is said that the trees he first encountered in Tasmania were so tall he could only see the flowers through a telescope. What is thought to be the tallest tree ever known was a eucalyptus felled in Gippsland, Victoria, in 1872, measuring 435 feet tall.

Blue gum and other eucalyptus trees such as the blue mallee (*Eucalyptus polybractea*) and the peppermint tree (*Eucalyptus piperita*) are best known for their **essential oils**. The first oil still, or distillery, was built in 1852 at Dandenong Creek by Melbourne pharmacist Joseph Bosisto. By 1865 he began exports of the oil to London, and soon partnered with the Australian pharmacy Felton Grimwade & Company to produce and distribute these oils. Today in Melbourne, more than 150 years later, Felton Grimwade & Bickford Ltd. still produces Bosisto's Parrot Brand Eucalyptus Oil, said to "help ease cold and flu symptoms, relieve arthritic and muscular pain, and eliminate stubborn stains and grease marks."

Eucalyptus oil was touted as a cure for everything from diarrhea to malaria. *Eucalyptus globulus* was even described as an "antimiasmic"—used to rid an area of "miasma" caused by marsh and malarial fevers. Extensive eucalyptus plantings in Australia are credited with keeping its early settlements nearly malaria-free. Because the tree absorbs large quantities of water from the soil, it was thought that eucalyptus disinfected the soil by dessicating malarial "germs." In fact, the plantings eliminated standing water—breeding grounds for malaria-carrying mosquitos.

Introduced into Santa Barbara, California, in 1852, eucalpytus leaves soon became a folk remedy for the treatment of colds and digestive problems. Preparations made from the leaves and essential oils, such as candies, cold remedies, hair restorers, and lozenges for sore throat and hoarseness, also appeared on the market. A product called Mission Lozenges was popular among singers and public speakers. Eucalyptus oil was used as a nonprescription drug in topical pain-relievers, expectorant products for colds, and insect repellants. However, the United States Food and Drug Administration no longer allows eucalyptus oil products to carry labels claiming therapeutic benefits, though the oil is still widely used as a flavor and fragrance ingredient in a wide range of products.

As ubiquitous and important to Australia as the eucalyptus are 60 or more species of the *Melaleuca* genus known as tea trees. The story of the tea tree begins during the patent medicine era of the late 19th century. The Ti Ta Volatile Oil Company of Brisbane made a product called ti-ta, hailed as a panacea to "cure all diseases." The product was hyped for a few years, then it disappeared for a while, but the stage was set for the future development of Australia's "ti-tree."

Scientific interest in tea tree oil emerged in the 1920s when researchers at the Museum of Technology and Applied Sciences in Sydney found that the oil had up to 13 times greater antiseptic activity than carbolic acid, a well-known germicide agent at that time. *The Medicinal Journal of Australia* published an article in 1930 claiming that when the oil was applied to carbuncles and infections, the oil's antibacterial action dried up the sores without damaging surrounding tissues. This led to further studies and catapulted the oil to prominence as a disinfectant ingredient for soaps, and a topical treatment for parasitic skin diseases, wounds, and more. Commercial preparations were quick to follow. The essential oil was marketed as ti-trol, or in aqueous suspension, as melasol, and it also gained a reputation among dentists for the treatment of pyorrhea, gingivitis, and oral bleeding.

Eventually the market was limited by the source of supply. The leaves were harvested from wild trees, which grow in a relatively limited range of about 100 square miles of swamp in the northeastern corner of New South Wales. Commercial interest in the oil flourished through World War II. Used by the Australian Army, it was added to first-aid kits for soldiers operating in tropical regions to help reduce fungal disease and as an antiseptic. After the war, interest in Australian tea tree oil declined.

In the mid-1970s tea tree oil was revived. Entrepreneur Christopher Dean started a tea tree plantation near Bunagawalbyn Creek in New South Wales where the tree grows wild. By the early 1980s, the Deans were bottling their own tea tree oil product, touting it as "a medicine chest in a bottle," and selling it in pharmacies and health food stores across Australia.

The oil is considered a good antibacterial and is promoted for treating boils, abscesses, sores, cuts, abrasions, and wounds. Other conditions for which use has been promoted include arthritis, bruises, burns, sunburn, dermatitis, fungal infections, herpes, insect bites, muscle aches, respiratory tract infections, vaginal infections, and acne. Clinical studies have cautiously confirmed claims of effectiveness in the treatment of acne, athlete's foot, psoriasis, and vaginal infections. Today tea tree oil products abound in the U.S. and elsewhere, including the pure essential oil, topical first-aid gels, ointments, medicated shampoos, mouthwash, feminine douches, throat sprays, hand soaps, hand creams, sunscreens, even tea tree-impregnated toothpicks.

With less then two centuries of European settlement in Australia and New Zealand, there is still much to learn. Medicinal plants down under remain a treasure trove awaiting rediscovery. ✒

*OPPOSITE PAGE: The tea tree has long been a traditional Aboriginal remedy for colds and stuffy noses. Here, in Charles Point, Northern Territory, Australia, Tobias Ferguson and son Colin sniff the crushed leaves of the weeping tea tree (*Melaleuca leucadendron*).*

Catnip
Nepeta cataria

CATNIP—ALSO COMMONLY CALLED CATMINT—IS A widely grown herb that has a well-earned reputation for driving cats crazy. One whiff of the bruised leaves of this mounding, rather coarse-looking perennial and many (but not all) cats will do everything they can to anoint themselves with the fragrance. The species name, *cataria*, is from the Latin word *catari*, meaning "of a cat" and reflecting the special attraction catnip has for felines. On humans, however, catnip has a calming rather than stimulating effect. For centuries, people have cultivated catnip, cooked with it, and used it medicinally. The leaves and shoots have gone into sauces, soups, and stews. Catnip tea dates to medieval England, where it was a popular drink prior to the importation of teas from Asia. After catnip's introduction into North America, Native Americans adopted it for treating colds, fevers, and a variety of other conditions. Today, catnip continues to play a role, although a minor one, in herbal medicine as a treatment for fevers, colds, stomachaches, and headaches.

Traditional and Current Medicinal Uses

IN BOTH EUROPE AND ENGLAND DURING THE MIDDLE AGES, catnip was commonly used as a relaxing, multipurpose tonic before real tea reached these regions. It was one of the main healing herbs grown by monks in monastery gardens. Medieval herbalists recommended a **decoction** of catnip, sweetened with honey, for relief of coughs. Preparations of the leaves were also used for treating bruises, scalp irritations, and skin lesions. Often given to children, catnip was respected for its ability to help ease colicky pain, gas, spasms, and restlessness. In America, the Cherokee used catnip for spasms, colds and coughs, hives, boils, and swellings, for relief of stomach upsets, and to rid the body of worms. The Chippewa administered catnip as a fever reducer, while the Delaware, Ontario, and Iroquois used it in preparations—often for children and infants—to treat diarrhea, headache, vomiting, chills, stomachaches, and sore throats and to encourage restful sleep. Catnip has traditionally been chewed, often with other herbs, as a

Common Names Catnip, catmint, catnep, catswort

Latin Name *Nepeta cataria*

Family Lamiaceae

Parts Used Leaves, flowers

Description A perennial in the mint family, catnip grows one to three feet tall with erect branching stems. The coarse, hairy leaves are ovate and gray-green, with serrated edges. From midsummer to autumn, small, mauve to purple flowers are borne in whorls in upper leaf axils. The plant gives off a pungent, mint-like odor.

Habitat Native to parts of Europe and Asia, catnip has been introduced and become naturalized in temperate regions, including much of North America. It grows at the edges of meadows and fields and is widely cultivated in herb gardens.

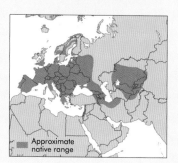

Approximate native range

remedy for toothaches. In the 18th century, inhabitants of southern Appalachia used catnip primarily for colds. **Poultices** made from catnip leaves have been applied to joints to ease pain, to the sore breasts of nursing mothers, and to the neck for tonsillitis.

In modern herbal medicine, catnip is recommended to settle upset stomachs and ease colic. As a hot tea it relieves colds, flu, and fever; it controls the symptoms of diarrhea and powerfully stimulates sweating. Herbal practitioners also recommended catnip for headaches, especially those related to digestive upsets. Catnip is considered helpful as well for arthritis, rheumatism, hemorrhoids, eye inflammation, and allergies. Recently, because of its mild sedative effects, catnip has also been suggested for treating attention deficit hyperactivity disorder in children.

Cultivation and Preparation

CATNIP IS A HARDY PERENNIAL. IT GROWS WELL IN FULL SUN in somewhat sandy soil. The herb can be propagated by seed or by root division of established plants. The flowering tops are harvested when the plant is in full bloom. Cuttings are then dried for extraction of oil, or they are processed further into finely cut or powdered forms. Catnip herbal preparations include tablets, capsules, fluid **extracts, tinctures**, ointments, and powders. Dried catnip is also incorporated with other herbs into herbal teas—and used to stuff or scent cat toys.

Research

CATNIP'S MAIN ACTIVE CONSTITUENT, FOUND IN ITS ESSENTIAL **oil**, is a **phytochemical** called nepetalactone. The calming effect that catnip has on people is thought to be due to nepetalactone. In studies with mice, nepetalactone was shown to significantly increase sleeping time. Catnip oil has also been shown to depress the central nervous system in humans. Laboratory experiments conducted at Iowa State University indicated that the volatile compounds that give catnip its pungent aroma are highly effective mosquito repellents—as good as high concentrations of DEET (diethyl-meta-toluamide), the compound used in many insect repellents on the market today.

The aroma of catnip has a strange, stimulating effect on most cats, from domestic tabbies to lions, tigers, leopards, and jaguars. This catnip response, as it is sometimes called, involves sniffing and licking behavior that typically escalates to head shaking, chin rubbing, full body rubbing, and, ultimately, enthusiastic rolling and carousing on the source of the scent. For the herb gardener, the catnip response leads to crushed and tattered catnip plants. It is the source of the folk wisdom that encourages gardeners to sow catnip seed rather than set out the plant. Plants raised from seed are spared, but transplants attract cats. The reason is that even the slightest bruising of catnip leaves releases the essential oils that are so attractive to felines. Some people have hypothesized that the scent of the plant may be similar to the scent of tomcat urine and cats may associate this smell with courtship and behave accordingly. All that is really known is that something in the essential oil triggers crazy behavior in cats—at least most of them. Research has revealed that about a third of all domestic cats do not respond to catnip at all. It appears that the catnip response is an inherited trait carried on a dominant gene. Cats that lack the proper genes also lack the response.

NEPETA CATARIA | Catnip

See Also: *A Field Guide to Medicinal Plants and Herbs: Eastern and Central North America, 2nd ed.* by S. Foster and J. Duke, Houghton Mifflin., 2000; *A Field Guide to Medicinal Plants and Herbs: Western North America* by S. Foster and C. Hobbs, Houghton Mifflin, 2002.

Cat's Claw
Uncaria tomentosa, U. guianensis

Common Names Cat's claw, Peruvian cat's claw, hawk's claw, *una de gato*

Latin Names *Uncaria tomentosa, U. guianensis*

Family Rubiaceae

Parts Used Bark, root

Description Cat's claw usually refers to two closely related species of large, woody vines (*Uncaria tomentosa* and *U. guianensis*) that get their names for their claw-like thorns that hook into a tree, allowing the vine to climb up to 100 feet into the rain forest canopy. *U. tomentosa* has small, yellow-white flowers and *U. guianensis* has small, reddish-orange flowers and thorns that are more curved than those of *U. tomentosa*.

Habitat Cat's claw is indigenous to the Amazon rain forest of South and Central America and other tropical regions of Peru, Colombia, Ecuador, Venezuela, Costa Rica, Guatemala, Panama, Trinidad, Guyana, and Suriname.

Approximate native range

THIRTY-TWO SPECIES OF THE *UNCARIA* GENUS ARE found throughout tropical Asia and Africa; only two live in South America, *Uncaria tomentosa* and *U. guianensis*, known there as *una de gato*, or cat's claw. This woody vine climbs high into the Amazon rain forest canopy with its cat-like claws. Both species grow mainly in Peru, where they have been used for centuries by native tribes that cultivate and harvest them as an important part of their medicine and livelihood. Bundles of the reddish-brown dried bark are a common sight in the marketplaces of Peru. *U. guianensis* is also exported to Europe, where it has been popular for decades. In the United States, *U. tomentosa* is one of the most popular Amazonian herbal remedies. European and American science is still catching up with cat's claw's popularity and reputation in South America. Decades of research have come a long way in isolating and identifying the medicinal compunds found in cat's claw. But as demand rises, native stewards of the land and crops are steadily displaced. The market will have to find sustainable solutions to prevent the overharvesting of cat's claw and the clearing of the rain forest it relies upon.

Traditional and Current Medicinal Uses

FOR MORE THAN 2,000 YEARS, PERUVIAN TRIBES OF THE Amazon such as the Asháninka, Cashibo, Conibo, and Shipibo Indians have used these two *Uncaria* species for healing. The Asháninkas are the largest producers of cat's claw in Peru and the leading exporter. They have used the bark for asthma, urinary tract infections, arthritis, rheumatism, bone pain, recovery from childbirth, kidney cleansing, deep wounds, inflammation, gastric ulcers, and cancer. It has been used by other tribes for diabetes, hemorrhages, menstruation, cirrhosis of the liver, fever, abscesses, and intestinal problems. Some tribes use cat's claw to treat gonorrhea, others use it as a contraceptive. Indigenous Colombian and Guianan natives use it to treat dysentery.

In modern herbal medicine, cat's claw is usually taken to boost the immune system. It is also taken for arthritis, rheumatism, all kinds of inflammation, gastritis, ulcers, neuralgias, intestinal problems, viral diseases like shingles, and as a complement to cancer treatments. Since the early 1990s, cat's claw has also been used in Peru and Europe for treatment of HIV and other diseases or disorders of the immune system.

Cultivation and Preparation

ALMOST ALL HARVESTING OF CAT'S CLAW OCCURS IN THE RAIN forest from both wild and cultivated crops. Most propagation occurs by means of cuttings, which grow easily in moist rain forest soil. Eight-inch sections are inserted into the soil and the canopy above is often thinned out to allow enough light for new growth. Rising demand and increasingly precious rain forest area are making sustainable management of cat's claw an important issue. Currently the root is rarely harvested. When the vine has reached a sufficient diameter for harvesting the bark, usually after at least eight years, the vine is cut one to three feet off the ground and stripped. Then the bark is cut into sections and dried in the open air. From the dried bark, teas and other **infusions** are made. Cat's claw is also available as an **extract** in liquid or pill form.

Research

FROM THE EARLY 1970S THROUGH THE 1980S, AUSTRIAN journalist and ethnologist Klaus Keplinger did the first comprehensive research on cat's claw, which led to its use in Austria and Germany. Worldwide interest and the first U.S. patents for the immune-enhancing **alkaloids** followed, along with research in Spain, France, Japan, Germany, Peru, and Canada that confirmed Keplinger's conclusions. In 1974, researchers in London identified major alkaloids in the stem and leaves. In 1985, an independent German study isolated oxidole alkaloids unique to *U. tomentosa* that stimulate the immune system by enhancing phagocytosis, the process by which white blood cells destroy invaders. A recent Austrian study found that these alkaloids also slow the growth of leukemia cells.

> CAUTION Cat's claw is an immune system stimulant. Before taking cat's claw, consult a physician. Adverse reactions may include hypotension (abnormally low pressure) and diarrhea.

The Asháninka are the second largest ethnic group inhabiting the Peruvian rain forest—and were the first to use, cultivate, and produce cat's claw. Preservation of their heritage and the rain forest go hand in hand. They have a long history as stewards of the land and still live by cultivating cat's claw, Murmuru nuts, stingless bees, and the seeds of dozens of native species like mahogany and cedar. The Asháninka have been defending their dense Amazonian jungle at the heart of Peru for centuries. Tragically, this also means they have been killed or kidnapped, tortured, and forced into servitude or prostitution. Since the 1500s, the Asháninka have been assaulted by one group or another trying to take their land. First, they fought off Spanish soldiers and Franciscan missionaries. A century later, the Peruvian ruling class displaced the Asháninka and tried to turn their lands into British coffee plantations. From 1980 to 2000, the Asháninka were terrorized by the Maoist guerrilla group, the Shining Path, among others. In 2003, the Peruvian Truth and Reconciliation Commission issued a report documenting human rights abuses that the Asháninka had suffered—from the assassination of tribal leaders to hundreds of tribe members in hiding. The report concludes that terrorists have killed at least 6,000 members of the tribe. Along with the Asháninka, the rain forest itself is a victim. Hopefully, the rising popularity of cat's claw will help support efforts toward sustainable cultivation of the rain forest that the Asháninka have practiced for centuries.

See Also: Herbal Medicine Expanded Commission E Monographs by M. Blumenthal, A. Goldberg, and J. Brinckmann, American Botanical Council, 2000; *The ABC Clinical Guide to Herbs* by M. Blumenthal, T. Hall, and A. Goldberg, American Botanical Council, 2003.

Cayenne

Capsicum annuum

R ED OR GREEN, SWEET OR HOT, PEPPERS ARE A COMMON sight in many home gardens, with their glossy fruits hanging from the branches of bushy plants. There are several species and hundreds of varieties, ranging from mild Hungarians and sweet bells to flaming jalapeños and bonnets so hot they bring tears to the eyes. Stripped of their seeds many are eaten raw in salads and salsas or cooked as a vegetable. The dried, powdered fruits of sweet varieties give us the spice paprika, while potent chili powder and cayenne pepper come from hotter forms. Peppers belong to the genus *Capsicum*, a name that is possibly derived from the Latin *capsa*, meaning "case," or from the Greek *kapto*, meaning "I bite." From a medicinal standpoint, a pepper's bite is a barometer for the amount of capsaicin it contains. Capsaicin is the key to cayenne's healing powers and cayenne (*Capsicum annuum*) is probably the best-known source of this remarkable **phytochemical** (plant chemical).

Traditional and Current Medicinal Uses

CAYENNE MADE ITS WAY TO EUROPE FROM THE NEW WORLD in the 15th century. Spanish and Portuguese explorers had noticed that Native Americans not only ate cayenne and other peppers but also used them as pain relievers. The Maya of Central America used cayenne to halt infections. The Aztecs used the herb to treat toothache and scabies. A warming stimulant, the herb was traditionally used to dull pain and increase circulation, which made it an appropriate remedy for headaches, arthritis, rheumatism, neuralgia, menstrual cramps, and muscle pain. Cayenne has also been employed to encourage sweating, stimulate the appetite, relieve gas and colic, and otherwise aid digestion. It has even been used as a remedy for sore throats: A small amount of cayenne mixed with water makes a healing, **analgesic** gargle, and it may help to open bronchial passages and ease colds and fevers. Purified compounds from the herb have also been shown to be helpful in treating psoriasis (a skin disease characterized by red patches and scales) and herpes infections, including shingles.

Common Names Cayenne, cayenne pepper, red pepper, capsicum, chili pepper

Latin Name *Capsicum annuum*

Family Solanaceae

Parts Used Fruit

Description Cayenne is an annual in temperate climates, but a perennial in the tropics. Reaching two to four feet in height, it has an erect, branching stem, elliptical dark-green leaves, and short-stalked, white flowers with yellow centers. Flowers are succeeded by elongated, conical fruits (berries) that are initially green but ripen to red and contain seeds on thin, fleshy inner partitions.

Habitat Native to tropical and subtropical regions of the Americas, cayenne and other *Capsicums* are now widely cultivated throughout the world.

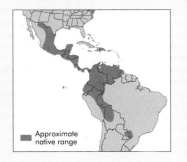

Approximate native range

Cultivation and Preparation

MORE THAN A THOUSAND CULTIVARS OF *CAPSICUM* ARE grown around the world, producing fruits that vary in shape, size, and degree of heat or pungency. Cayenne and its kin are cultivated from seed sown in early spring. Plants grow best in rich, moist soil under humid, warm conditions. Fruits are harvested when ripe in late summer. For the herbal medicine market, they are dried and powdered. (Grinding of dried fruits is always done with great care, because the straight powder can be a strong irritant of the skin and mucous membranes.) Preparations of cayenne are made into creams and ointments, or mixed with oil to make therapeutic massage oils.

Research

THE PRIMARY ACTIVE INGREDIENT OF CAYENNE IS CAPSAICIN, a pungent principle that gives peppers their heat. Modern research has established that capsaicin is an effective painkiller. It desensitizes nerve endings by depleting them of the chemical neurotransmitter that enables pain messages to be sent to the brain. The nerves are overwhelmed by the capsaicin and are unable to transmit pain sensations for an extended period of time. Capsaicin also stimulates blood flow and has well-established antibacterial activity. While many people believe that eating hot, spicy foods will induce stomach ulcers, research has shown that capsaicin provides protection against them; lab animals fed high, ulcer-inducing doses of aspirin did not develop ulcers when they also received capsaicin. Experiments indicate that cayenne also benefits the cardiovascular system by reducing **triglyceride** levels and **platelet aggregations** in the blood. Applied to the skin in various preparations, the phytochemical is a mild **analgesic.** In addition to capsaicin, cayenne and other peppers contain **carotenoids** and **flavonoids** and are also rich in vitamins A, B1, B2, C, and E, several minerals, and **antioxidants,** which can help fight cardiovascular disease.

> CAUTION Cayenne and other hot peppers can inflame and irritate skin and mucous membranes. Wear gloves when handling them and avoid touching the face, especially the eyes. In large doses, cayenne may cause digestive disorders.

WHEN YOU'RE HOT, YOU'RE H-O-T

Comparing the heat of peppers may seem a purely subjective undertaking. But in 1912, pharmacist Wilbur Scoville developed a system for measuring the hotness of cayenne and other peppers somewhat scientifically. The result was the Scoville Scale. To construct the scale, Scoville carried out a series of tests with whole ground chili peppers mixed in a solution of water and sugar. He assembled a panel of five testers and asked each tester to sip increasingly dilute solutions until he or she reached a solution that no longer burned the mouth. A number was then given to each tested pepper based on how much it had to be diluted before effects of capsaicin could not be felt. From this, Scoville developed a measure of pepper heat (capsaicin content). He rated one part of pepper heat per one million drops of water as 1.5 Scoville heat units (SHU). Since tasters' perceptions of hot were never in complete agreement, Scoville averaged his panelists' estimates. Although there are now accurate lab techniques for measuring capsaicin content in peppers, the Scoville scale is still used by spice companies and sauce manufacturers worldwide. On the Scoville scale, sweet bell peppers have less than 100 SHU while a Mexican habañero earns a fiery 350,000. Pure capsaicin tops the scale at a daunting 16 million!

See Also: *Herbal Medicine Expanded Commission E Monographs* by M. Blumenthal, A. Goldberg, and J. Brinckmann, American Botanical Council, 2000; *The ABC Clinical Guide to Herbs* by M. Blumenthal, T. Hall, and A. Goldberg, American Botanical Council, 2003.

Chamomile
Matricaria recutita

Common Names Chamomile, German chamomile, Hungarian chamomile, wild chamomile

Latin Names *Matricaria recutita,* synonyms *M. chamomilla, Chamomilla recutita*

Family Asteraceae

Parts Used Dried flower heads, oil

Description A branching, annual herb, chamomile grows to two feet. It has finely divided feathery foliage and small, daisy-like flowers. The entire plant is sweetly scented, with an aroma reminiscent of fresh apples.

Habitat Native to eastern Europe, northern Africa, and western Asia, chamomile is widely cultivated in both hemispheres and naturalized in North America.

Approximate native range

HAMOMILE IS ONE OF THE WORLD'S MOST WELL-known medicinal herbs. Not only does it rank among the most widely used components of herbal teas, but it is also a popular ingredient in health and beauty aids. There are two species of chamomile used in herbal medicine: German or Hungarian chamomile (*Matricaria recutita*) and Roman or English chamomile (*Chamaemelum nobile* syn. *Anthemis nobilis*). Both herbs have been used medicinally for centuries in similar ways. Roman chamomile is preferred in Great Britain, but worldwide German chamomile is far more widely used and more extensively researched. (Although Roman and German chamomile have historically been used for similar purposes, their **essential oils** and chemical components are quite different.) Chamomile is today a classic remedy—especially in the form of chamomile tea—for calming digestive upsets and jangled nerves, relaxing tensed muscles, and soothing irritations of all kinds.

Traditional and Current Medicinal Uses

THE ANCIENT EGYPTIANS VALUED CHAMOMILE AS A REMEDY FOR the fever and chills that accompany malaria. In ancient Rome, the herb was often recommended to relieve headaches and disorders of the bladder, liver, and kidneys. Chamomile was used medicinally in Europe as early as the first century A.D. Medieval herbalists recommended it for easing pain and combating weariness, as a **diuretic**, for colic and nervous stomach, and to dissolve gallstones and kidney stones. During the 19th century, chamomile was an important drug prescribed by American **Eclectic** physicians, particularly for treating digestive and skin problems in young children.

In modern herbal medicine, chamomile is used much as it has been for centuries: as a treatment for colic, bloating, flatulence, indigestion, irritable bowel syndrome, gastrointestinal spasms, and heartburn; as a soothing remedy to calm nervous tension and dispel restlessness or sleeplessness (especially in infants and young children); to ease tense muscles and menstrual cramps; and to heal irritations of the mouth and gums as well as skin inflammations, including eczema. The herb is sometimes suggested for relieving pain after dermabrasion (including tattoo removal) and alleviating swelling and irritation in mucous membranes caused by chemotherapy and radiation treatments. Chamomile flowers are an official drug in the **pharmacopoeia**, or drug references, of 26 countries.

Cultivation and Preparation

GERMAN CHAMOMILE IS EASILY RAISED FROM SEED, SOWN where it will grow, in dry, light soil in full sun. For herbal medicine, the flower heads are picked in summer, when in full bloom. They may be used fresh or dried; the extracted essential oil has a deep-blue color.

Research

CHAMOMILE EXHIBITS **ANTI-INFLAMMATORY**, ANTIBACTERIAL, antifungal, antiseptic, and antispasmodic effects. The herb contains an essential oil, **flavonoids**, and many other compounds. More than 120 components have been identified from the essential oil alone; two of these, alpha-bisabolol and chamazulene, appear to be particularly active therapeutically. Many commercial German chamomile preparations are standardized as to their chamazulene and alpha-bisabolol content. In lab studies, the flavonoid apigenin recently was found to inhibit growth of *Helicobacter pylori*, a bacterium that causes peptic ulcers in humans. This finding may suggest a wider use of chamomile in long-term management of peptic ulcers. Chamomile extracts have also been shown to accelerate wound healing by reducing inflammation and promoting tissue regeneration. Scientific studies support the effectiveness of chamomile extracts in many applications, though chamomile tea does not measure up as well as its reputation would suggest. Most of the beneficial effects of the herb are derived from its essential oil; even chamomile tea that has been steeped for a long time contains only a small amount of the essential oil. Chamomile preparations made from the flowers, which contain pollen, have been shown to cause allergic reactions, especially in those sensitive to ragweed and other members of the Asteraceae (daisy) family. But such reactions are rare.

For centuries, chamomile has been prized not only for its medicinal value but also for many other virtues. The Egyptians apparently thought so highly of the herb that they made offerings of it to their gods. To the Anglo-Saxons, chamomile, or *maythen* as they called it, was one of the sacred herbs of the god of war, Woden. It was a charm believed to counter the effects of "flying venom" and "loathful things" that roamed the countryside. In medieval England, the fresh fragrance of chamomile made it a popular strewing herb to freshen the air—probably a necessity in a time when bathing was fairly uncommon. The Spanish called the herb *manzanilla*, meaning "little apple," and used it to flavor their best sherries. Before the days of refrigeration, meat on the edge of spoiling was soaked in chamomile tea to mask its rancid taste. The herb also had a reputation for being a good insect repellent. For hundreds of years, women have used chamomile tea to accentuate natural blond highlights in their hair. Even today, the herb is often included in shampoos and conditioners that are advertised as being specifically for blonds. And despite the scientific research, many people still believe that there is not much that chamomile cannot cure. The Germans use the phrase *alles zutraut*—"capable of anything"—to describe what they revere as a remarkable herb.

See Also: *Herbal Medicine Expanded Commission E Monographs* by M. Blumenthal, A. Goldberg, and J. Brinckmann, American Botanical Council, 2000; *World Health Organization (WHO) Monographs on Selected Medicinal Plants, Vol. 1,* 1999.

MATRICARIA RECUTITA | Chamomile

Chaparral

Larrea tridentata

CHAPARRAL IS ONE OF THE MOST COMMON PLANT species in the Mojave, Sonoran, and Chihuahua Deserts of North America. Highly adapted to arid conditions, chaparral can withstand long periods of drought thanks to a root system that is extremely efficient at absorbing water. The leaves of chaparral exude a sticky, strong-smelling resin. After a rain, the resin oozes from the leaves, and the desert air becomes strongly tinged with a pungent, acrid, creosote-like aroma—hence the common names "creosote bush," "stinkweed," and *hedionilla*, which in Spanish means "bad little stinker." Chaparral is useless to ranchers since cattle will not eat it and it is poisonous to sheep. For farmers, the presence of chaparral means generally poor soil. Yet chaparral was highly prized by many Native American tribes of the Southwest as a valuable medicinal herb.

Traditional and Current Medicinal Uses

CHAPARRAL HAS A LONG HISTORY OF USE AS A TRADITIONAL medicine by Native Americans. It was considered an excellent remedy for rheumatic pain. Ground leaves were rubbed into affected joints or were bathed with a **decoction** made from the leaves. A salve made from the leaves was used as an antiseptic for wounds, cuts, sores, and bruises. A tea brewed from the leaves and stems of the plant was used to treat stomach and intestinal disorders, bronchitis, colds and flu, cramps and diarrhea, kidney and urinary tract problems, and tuberculosis. Twigs were chewed to relieve toothache; heated resin was also dripped into tooth cavities to alleviate pain. European settlers found chaparral plants to be a useful remedy for venereal disease as well as for skin conditions.

In the 1960s and 1970s, chaparral gained a reputation in herbal medicine for many of the same conditions for which it had been used traditionally, as well as for a treatment for acne and as a folk cancer cure (particularly leukemia). In 1992, several cases of acute non-viral hepatitis were linked with the consumption of chaparral as a dietary supplement. The United States

Common Names Chaparral, creosote bush, stinkweed, *hedionilla*, *gobernadora*

Latin Name *Larrea tridentata*

Family Zygophyllaceae

Parts Used Leaves, twigs

Description Chaparral is a woody, vase-shaped shrub with slim stems that grow to three to ten feet in height. It has tiny, bifurcated, olive green leaves that exude an aromatic resin. Small yellow flowers are followed by fruits that are fuzzy, pea-sized capsules.

Habitat A common inhabitant of deserts of the southwestern United States and northern and central Mexico, chaparral thrives under hot, arid conditions and can tolerate extreme drought.

Approximate native range

Food and Drug Administration ultimately issued a health warning against chaparral and the herb industry voluntarily suspended the sale of the herb for internal use until a medical review could be conducted. In 1995 the suspension was lifted when the review concluded that there was no direct causal relationship between chaparral ingestion and liver damage. Chaparral preparations are now widely available in health food stores. Nevertheless, many herbal medicine authorities continue to recommend against the internal use of chaparral, especially in those cases of individuals who have a history of liver disease.

Cultivation and Preparation

CHAPARRAL DOES NOT FLOURISH OUTSIDE ITS NATIVE habitat in the southwestern U.S. and northern Mexico. It can be propagated from seed but chaparral is difficult to transplant. For use in herbal medicine, the young leafy twigs are cut and used fresh for teas and **tinctures**, or they may be dried for use in other preparations.

Research

CHAPARRAL'S MOST ACTIVE INGREDIENT IS THOUGHT TO BE one of the **lignans**: nordihydroguaiaretic acid (NDGA). NDGA is a potent **antioxidant**. Researchers once thought NDGA might be a potential anti-cancer drug because of its powerful antioxidant properties. In initial studies with rats, NDGA and a leaf **extract** of a South American subspecies of chaparral were found to exhibit antitumor effects. Another study, however, suggested that NDGA may stimulate tumor growth. Clinical trials, therefore, are still needed to establish whether chaparral is a safe and effective treatment for people with cancer. Reports continue to link liver damage with use of chaparral. Although a retrospective study indicated that low doses of chaparral tincture appeared to have no adverse effects, correlation between the length of exposure and possible risks has not yet been determined. Other reported effects for chaparral include **anti-inflammatory** properties as well as antimicrobial actions in test tubes. However, these effects have not been established in human clinical trials.

THE OLDEST LIVING THING?

Chaparral is extremely well-adapted to the hot, arid deserts in which it is found. In many parts of its range, it covers large areas in practically pure stands. This characteristic of taking over the landscape may be the source of one of the plant's common names, *gobernadora*, which means "governess" in Spanish. Chaparral has an interesting growth habit. Individual plants produce new stems from an underground crown taproot. New stems arise from the outer edges of the root, while older, more central stems gradually die off. Over time, an individual plant grows outward as a ring of what look like separate plants, though all are attached to the same root and share the same genetic material. As expansion continues, the ring breaks up into groups of plants that, although separate, are essentially clones of the original plant. Researchers found that chaparral clone rings grow and expand very slowly. Using carbon-14 and other dating techniques, researchers determined that a ring of chaparral 20 feet across is roughly 3,000 years old. One of the oldest chaparral clone rings discovered is the 11,700-year-old "King Clone" in the Mojave Desert; an even larger clone ring in the Sonoran Desert in Arizona is thought to be an astounding 18,000 years old. If the clones are considered part of the original plant, these plants have the distinction of being the oldest living things on Earth. The seeds from which the original plants sprouted would have germinated at the end of the last Ice Age.

See Also: *A Field Guide to Medicinal Plants and Herbs: Western North America* by S. Foster and C. Hobbs, Houghton Mifflin, 2002; *Medicinal Herbs History, Use, Recommended Dosages & Cautions* by S. Foster, Interweave Press, 1998.

LARREA TRIDENTATA | Chaparral

Chaste Tree
Vitex agnus-castus

CHASTE TREE IS A STRIKING, OPEN SHRUB WITH ELEGANT compound leaves that are dull green on their upper surfaces and a downy gray below. At the height of summer the plant is covered with spikes of slender, fragrant, mauve-colored flowers. The dark reddish-brown to black fruits that follow resemble peppercorns. The resemblance is more than skin deep, as the fruits also have both a pepper-like aroma and flavor. Used medicinally since at least the sixth century B.C., chaste tree is a relaxant herb with pain-relieving properties. But its greatest value lies in its power to regulate the balance of hormones in the body linked to gynecological health. Preparations of ripe chaste tree fruits are used by European gynecologists and Western herbal medicine practitioners for treating various menstrual disorders and irregularities, premenstrual syndrome (PMS), and infertility as well as for promoting lactation in nursing mothers.

Common Names Chaste tree, chaste berry, monk's pepper, agnus castus

Latin Name *Vitex agnus-castus*

Family Verbenaceae

Parts Used Fruits

Description Chaste tree is a large shrub or small tree with characteristically palmate leaves; each has up to nine oblong leaflets radiating out from the leaf stalk. Upright clusters of small, tubular, purplish flowers are succeeded by tiny, hard, red-black fruits.

Habitat Native to the Mediterranean region of southern Europe and western Asia, chaste tree grows in dry, coastal habitats as well as along riverbanks and creek beds. It is now naturalized and cultivated in many tropical and subtropical parts of the world.

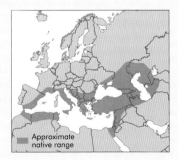
Approximate native range

Traditional and Current Medicinal Uses

CHASTE TREE HAS BEEN USED AS A REMEDY PRIMARILY FOR gynecological problems for at least 2,500 years. In the fourth century B.C., Hippocrates recommended the herb for staunching bleeding following childbirth and aiding in the passing of the afterbirth. Three hundred years later, the Roman physician Pliny wrote about the benefits of using chaste tree for promoting both normal menstruation and lactation. The Greek physician Dioscorides recommended chaste tree to lower libido. During the Middle Ages, chaste tree was used to relieve menstrual cramps and to bring on menstruation. It was also used at various times throughout history to treat flatulence, constipation, fevers, and hangovers. In the 19th century, American **Eclectic** physicians recommended chaste tree for a variety of menstrual difficulties and to stimulate lactation.

Today, chaste tree remains one of the most important herbs in Western herbal medicine for balancing female hormones. Preparations of chaste tree are used primarily for managing a variety of menstrual disorders, including irregular or absent periods, PMS, breast pain (mastalgia), and the treatment of infertility resulting from low progesterone levels. Chaste tree preparations are also given for menopausal problems including hot flashes, problems such as acne and migraine that are linked to the menstrual cycle, and to treat impotence, depression, and inadequate milk secretion.

Cultivation and Preparation

CHASTE TREE DOES WELL IN MOST TYPES OF SOIL AND IS drought tolerant. It is propagated by seeds or cuttings. Ripe fruits are gathered in autumn and are used fresh or dried in various preparations, including dry extracts and liquids used to create **tinctures** or **infusions**.

Research

FOR MORE THAN 30 YEARS, RESEARCHERS HAVE BEEN INVES-tigating chaste tree fruits and their effects on the body. The fruits are known to contain a variety of **alkaloids** and **flavonoids** as well as compounds that are **precursors** to **steroidal hormones**. However, no single component is apparently responsible for the herb's activity; various compounds are most likely acting together to bring about its effects. Studies have shown that chaste tree fruit preparations act primarily on the pituitary gland. Compounds in the fruit stimulate the pituitary gland to reduce the amount of follicle-stimulating hormone (FSH) being released from the anterior pituitary while increasing the release of luteinizing hormone (LH) and prolactin. This, in turn, leads to an increase in the production of the hormone progesterone during the second half of a woman's menstrual cycle, normalizing the balance of hormones that regulate menstruation, fertility, and other processes. Numerous clinical trials on women suffering from menstrual disturbances and PMS have shown that chaste tree preparations help significantly to restore normal menstruation and alleviate many symptoms of PMS, including headaches, breast tenderness, bloating, anxiety, and mood swings. As an added benefit, chaste tree treatment for these problems, unlike treatment with steroidal hormones, produces few if any side effects.

CAUTION Chaste tree is not recommended for use during pregnancy, and should not be taken together with any form of hormone therapy.

A SYMBOL OF CHASTITY

Since ancient times, chaste tree has been associated with chastity. In Greek mythology, the goddess Hera, a champion and protector of marriage and married couples, was said to have been born in the shade of a chaste tree. The wives of Greek soldiers scattered chaste tree fruits on their beds when their husbands went to war as a sign of their faithfulness. When the Greeks held festivals honoring Demeter, the goddess of fertility, women who remained "pure" during the festival adorned themselves with chaste tree blossoms. Demeter's temples were decorated with blossoms and branches of the shrub as well. In Rome, vestal virgins often carried chaste tree twigs as a sign of their self-imposed chastity. Later, this symbolic link between herb and chaste behavior was adopted by the Christian church in much of Europe. Novice monks followed a path strewn with chaste tree blossoms to the monastery during initiation ceremonies—a tradition that still survives in parts of Italy. Because chaste tree fruits were said to suppress sexual desire, the dried fruits were ground and used as a pepper substitute in monasteries, fostering one of the herb's common names: "monk's pepper." Despite this folk use, however, there is no scientific evidence that chaste tree fruits have any effect on libido.

See Also: Herbal Medicine Expanded Commission E Monographs by M. Blumenthal, A. Goldberg, and J. Brinckmann, American Botanical Council, 2000; The ABC Clinical Guide to Herbs by M. Blumenthal, T. Hall, and A. Goldberg, American Botanical Council, 2003.

Chaulmoogra
Hydnocarpus kurzii

Common Names Chaulmoogra, kalaw tree, *da feng zi*

Latin Name *Hydnocarpus kurzii*

Family Flacourtiaceae

Parts Used Seeds

Description Chaulmoogra trees are large, growing to 100 feet, with pale yellowish bark and long, leathery lanceolate leaves. Male and female flowers are borne separately and succeeded by brownish, velvety fruits that contain a dozen or more inch-long seeds embedded in an oily pulp.

Habitat Native to Southeast Asia, chaulmoogra grows in moderately humid forest environments.

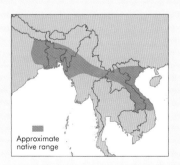

Approximate native range

THROUGHOUT HISTORY, LEPROSY—SOMETIMES CALLED Hansen's disease—has been one of the most feared and misunderstood of human diseases. Records of its existence date from at least 1350 B.C. in Egypt. Leprosy is caused by a bacterium (*Mycobacterium leprae*) that affects the skin, nerves, and mucous membranes, causing terribly disfiguring lesions and swellings. For centuries it was considered incurable, although leprosy patients were subjected to a wide variety of treatments, ranging from strychnine and arsenic to x-rays and electric shock. Only chaulmoogra oil, a remedy first used by Indian and Chinese herbal practitioners, was of any real value in treating leprosy until the introduction of sulfa drugs and other antibiotics in the 1940s. Chaulmoogra has not been widely used in Western herbal medicine since that time.

Traditional and Current Medicinal Uses

THE COMMON NAME "CHAULMOOGRA" IS THE BENGALI NAME for *Hydnocarpus kurzii*, as well as two other closely related species, *H. anthelmintica* and *H. wightiana*. All three trees are a source of chaulmoogra oil. The first mention of chaulmoogra as a treatment for leprosy appeared in Chinese medical literature dating from 1347. The Chinese called the seeds from which chaulmoogra oil is derived *da feng zi*. They used the oil for treating a number of serious skin diseases including leprosy. The oil of chaulmoogra seeds was also used in traditional **Ayurvedic medicine** for the same purposes. British physician Frederic John Mouat introduced chaulmoogra oil to Western medicine in 1854. Mouat ran across the use of the oil in his medical practice in India. He administered the oil to several patients with leprosy and described its healing effects as remarkable. Chaulmoogra's reputation spread, and by the turn of the century the oil was being prescribed for leprosy around the world. Taking the oil internally, rather than applying it externally, gave better results but caused debilitating nausea. After much experimentation, it was found that mixing the oil with camphor and injecting it gave very good results. Some patients treated in this way appeared to be cured; many others showed marked improvement. Chaulmoogra became the treatment of choice for leprosy. It was also used for open sores, wounds, sprains, and bruises. As chaulmoogra's use became more widespread, demand for the oil increased. Concerned about a possible shortage, the United States Department of Agriculture sent Joseph Rock, a botany professor from the College of Hawaii, to Southeast Asia to find and collect chaulmoogra seeds. The seeds he collected were used to establish a chaulmoogra plantation on Oahu in 1921. Chaulmoogra was widely used to treat leprosy until the 1950s, when it was replaced by antibiotics.

In modern herbal medicine, chaulmoogra is considered a treatment for lowering fevers, for expelling intestinal worms, and for skin conditions such as scabies, eczema, psoriasis, and ringworm. However, its use is uncommon.

Cultivation and Preparation

CHAULMOOGRA GROWS BEST IN RICH, MOIST, WELL-DRAINING soil in warm, humid climates. The seeds are separated from the ripe fruits, then washed and dried in the sun. They can be used whole for **decoctions**, powdered for pills, or crushed so the oil they contain can be extracted. Chaulmoogra oil has the consistency of butter, a nauseating smell, and an acrid taste. It is mixed with paraffin, walnut oil, or sesame oil when it is used as an ointment.

Research

THE FIRST COMPREHENSIVE CHEMICAL ANALYSIS OF CHAULmoogra oil was carried out in the early 1900s. The oil was found to contain unique fatty acids, including chaulmoogric and hydnocarpic acid. Although little research has been done on chaulmoogra's mechanism of action against leprosy, some studies have shown it is a potent antibiotic. Chaulmoogra oil and preparations may cause vomiting, dizziness, respiratory difficulty, and may act as a cardiac depressant.

> WARNING High doses of chaulmoogra can cause nausea. Some evidence suggests that chaulmoogra may increase the risk of side effects of drugs used concurrently, including birth-control pills.

HYDNOCARPUS KURZII | Chaulmoogra

IDYLLS OF THE KING (AND PRINCE)

A number of traditional stories have been passed down through the centuries concerning how chaulmoogra came to be used in the treatment of leprosy. According to one tale in Burmese folklore, a Burmese prince who had contracted leprosy was advised by the gods to withdraw from civilization and retreat to the forest to meditate. The prince did as he was told. One day while walking through the woods, the gods directed the prince to a tree with large round fruits. The prince was told to eat the seeds of the fruits. He did, and was subsequently cured of his leprosy. An Indian version of the story attributes the discovery of chaulmoogra's powers to Rama, king of Benares (now Varanasi) in Uttar Pradesh, one of India's northern states. When Rama contracted leprosy, he stepped down from his throne and put his son in his place. Then Rama fled into the forest, where he lived off herbs and roots. One of the fruits he ate came from the kalaw tree; it was filled with many seeds. Rama improved and he attributed his cure to the kalaw tree's fruit. As Rama continued to wander through the forest, he came upon a young princess named Piya, who had been banished to the forest because she, too, had leprosy. Rama encouraged Piya to eat kalaw fruits, and she was cured of the disease as well. According to the legend, the miraculous kalaw tree was one of several types of trees that scientists later recognized as belonging to the genus *Hydnocarpus*.

See Also: Medical Botany: Plants Affecting Human Health by W. Lewis and M. Elvin-Lewis, John Wiley & Sons, 2003; *Nature's Medicine, Plants That Heal* by Joel Swerdlow, National Geographic, 2000.

Chicory
Cichorium intybus

HICORY IS A PLANT THAT HAS YET TO FIND ITS NICHE in modern herbal medicine though it has been used as both food and folk medicine for at least 2,000 years. The first-century Roman physician Pliny the Elder notes that "chicory" was an Egyptian word, later adopted by the Greeks. Its meaning is lost in history. The species name "intybus" derives from *intubus*, Latin for "endive," referring to the closely related *Cichorium endivia*, source of endive leaves used in salads. The leaves, long recognized for their cooling properties, according to Pliny were taken in food or applied as liniments to cool inflammation. The juice of the boiled down leaves was used to benefit the liver, kidneys, and stomach. Taken in honey wine, the root was used by the Romans to alleviate painful urination and treat jaundice. Pliny also writes that Zoroastrian priests, one of the world's oldest priesthoods, mixed the juice of the entire plant with oil and anointed themselves with it. A lofty realm for a plant "generally regarded in the light of a noxious weed," as Phillip Miller put it in the final edition of *The Gardener's and Botanist's Dictionary*, published in 1807.

Traditional and Current Medicinal Uses

CHICORY ROOT, USED IN DECOCTIONS, WAS SAID TO INCREASE the appetite and aid digestion. It was valued in England as a digestive tonic. The root was also used for cleansing the blood, cooling heat in the body, and toning the intestines. Leaves were considered a **diuretic** and useful against scurvy. The Cherokee adopted the root as a tonic for the nerves and the Iroquois used it as a **poultice** to treat lesions in the early stages of syphilis. Chicory was grown as a fodder crop in France and England—the fast-growing leaves in the cool weather of spring provided greens for sheep and horses, when other plants were dormant. Chicory root's greatest fame is as an additive to coffee. "The French maintain that the quality of Coffee is improved by the addition of the succory root if not in too large a quantity," writes British botanist John Lindley in his 1838 *Flora Medica*. He adds, "It certainly affords a most harmless means of adulterating it."

Common Names Chicory, succory, wild succory

Latin Names *Cichorium intybus*

Family Asteraceae

Parts Used Whole herb, leaves, roots

Description A two-to-six-foot perennial, chicory has long, narrow leaves that resemble those of dandelion. The fleshy taproot is milky within. Sky-blue flowers hug the stems in clusters of two to three and unfurl fully on cloudy or rainy days or in early morning sun. Chicory blooms in mid- to late summer until the first frost.

Habitat Native to Europe and Asia, chicory is widely naturalized in North America and elsewhere. It is a common sight along roadsides, fencerows, fields, and gardens.

Approximate native range

In modern German phytomedicine, chicory herb and root are approved for therapeutic use in the treatment of indigestion and loss of appetite.

Cultivation and Preparation

CHICORY NEEDS WELL-DRAINED SOIL BUT IS OTHERWISE undemanding. It grows best in full sun to partial shade and is drought tolerant, but prefers a cooler climate. It is propagated by sowing seeds in late spring, or for autumn greens, planted in mid-summer. For use as an herbal medicine, the plants are not allowed to go to seed; roots are harvested in the fall of the second or third years. After harvest, the roots are cured on the ground for two weeks before final drying.

Research

CHICORY, WHILE APPROVED AS A THERAPEUTIC AGENT IN Germany, is a neglected medicinal plant, most often thought of as a weed. Most new research on it is coming from the Middle East, where it is a widely used folk remedy. Recently, researchers in Turkey have ascribed liver-protecting properties to the seeds. In Iran researchers found that ethanol **extracts** of the plant had significant immune system-stimulating activity in lab studies. The root is high in inulin, a large sugar-like molecule comprising up to 8 percent of the dried root weight. Inulin itself, when the root is roasted, is responsible for the coffee-like aroma of chicory. It also contains maltol, known to intensify the flavor of sugar. There is some evidence that, when mixed with coffee, chicory may reduce available caffeine in coffee. Water-soluble fractions have been shown to have a mild sedative effect, perhaps counteracting the stimulant effects of coffee. Studies on rats have shown that the inulin from chicory enhances calcium content in the large intestine. A water extract of chicory root was shown to have an **antioxidant** effect on **low-density lipoprotein** (LDL). LDL is among the so-called "bad cholesterol" fatty substances. Future research will perhaps reveal new uses from this weed turned **phytomedicine**.

CAUTION Rare allergies and allergic skin reactions are reported for chicory. In cases of gallstones, use only under the direction of a physician.

NO SUBSTITUTES, PLEASE

To some, roasted chicory root is a great additive to coffee, creating a slightly bitter brew. To others, the addition of chicory root is simple adulteration—stretching a more expensive commodity with a far cheaper ingredient. That tradition arose in France. According to an 1885 account by Francis Thurber in *Coffee: From Plantation to Cup*, "Consumption of chicory in France is traceable to the practice of economy in small things, so characteristic of the middle and lower classes in that country, and not to the gratification of a peculiar taste." To make his point, Thurber recounts a story of M. Grévy, President of France from 1879–1887, in which Grévy and a companion got lost on a hunting trip, and emerged from the forest near a small winery. The President asked for a cup of coffee. But first he asked the proprietor if he had any chicory. When the proprietor replied yes, Grévy asked the proprietor to bring him some. Then Grévy asked if he had more chicory and asked him to bring it him. Again, he asked if there was still more chicory in the establishment, and this time, Grévy requested that the proprietor bring him all of the chicory he had. Finally Grévy asked, "You have no more?" and the proprietor acknowledged that indeed he had no chicory left. "Very well," the President said, "Now make me a cup of coffee."

See Also: A Field Guide to Medicinal Plants and Herbs: Eastern and Central North America, 2nd ed. by S. Foster, J. Duke, Houghton Mifflin Co., 2000; A Field Guide to Medicinal Plants and Herbs: Western North America by S. Foster and C. Hobbs, Houghton Mifflin, 2002.

Common Names Chinese rhubarb, Turkey rhubarb, Indian rhubarb, *da-huang*

Latin Names *Rheum palmatum*

Family Polygonaceae

Parts Used Stalk, root

Description *Rheum palmatum* is distinguished from the garden rhubarb we eat mainly by its size. Garden varieties grow to a few feet. Chinese rhubarb has thick, deep roots, a six- to ten-foot jointed stalk, and loose panicles of flowers along the top that bloom yellow or white and turn red. Around it fall tapering branches that hold out large, jagged, hand-shaped leaves two to three feet wide.

Habitat Chinese rhubarb is native to the borderlands of western China, northern Tibet, and the Mongolian Plateau.

Approximate native range

Chinese Rhubarb
Rheum palmatum

CHINESE RHUBARB IS NOT THE SOURCE OF THE FAMILiar red stems in American gardens used to make rhuarb pie. Rather, the root historically has been the source of an important laxative in herbal medicine. Today *Rheum palmatum* along with *R. tanguticum* and *R. officinale* are the sources of the Chinese drug known as *da-huang*, consisting of the dried roots and **rhizome** of these three species. Until the 18th century, live plants of these species were not known in European gardens; in fact, the identity of the source plant of Chinese rhubarb root was not known in Europe until the 18th century, despite the fact that the herb had been used in Europe for hundreds of years. Only the species of *Rheum* with lobed leaves is used for medicinal rhubarb. Species or varieties with wavy or undulating leaves are not considered medicinal. Common garden rhubarb (*R. rhubarbarum*) is not used medicinally.

Traditional and Current Medicinal Uses

ANCIENT CHINESE WRITINGS DATE CHINES RHUBARB TO 2700 B.C. when it was first used for purging. It was taken for fever with noted respect for its potency by an emperor of the Liang dynasty (557–579), presented as a gift to an emperor of the Tang dynasty (618–907), taken for the plague during the Song dynasty (960–1127), and even taken to commit suicide by a general of the Ming dynasty (1368–1644). In 1731, the imperial Russian state began a monopoly in rhubarb trade from China via the Asian steppes to Moscow and St. Petersburg, where the root was shipped to the rest of Europe. The "Rhubarb Office" controlled European imports of rhubarb for more than 125 years until Chinese ports opened to the West allowing direct export of the roots. The common names of "Russia rhubarb," "Turkey rhubarb," and "Indian rhubarb" were once used in European commerce to refer to the trade routes for rhubarb produced in China. Traditionally rhubarb was taken in China as a remedy for stomach complaints and as a **cathartic** and used as a **poultice** for fevers and **edema** (swelling). Through Chinese merchants, seeds of the plant were received in European botanical gardens around 1750. *Rheum palmatum* was given its Latin name by Swedish botanist Carolus Linnaeus in 1759. A live flowering specimen was described in a 1767 publication. Seeds of the plant were introduced to British botanical gardens around 1762. The root was a famous **astringent** cathartic (as well as a strong laxative); the **tannins** in the root caused an astringent action making it useful in the early stages of diarrhea, dysentery, and other intestinal problems.

Chinese rhubarb has been used as an antibacterial and as a remedy for constipation, diarrhea, dysentery, toothaches, shingles, fevers, hypertension, burns, acute appendicitis, acute infectious hepatitis, conjunctivitis, swelling and pain of gums, and sores of the mouth or tongue. While still an important pharmaceutical laxative in China, in the West it has largely been replaced by other plant-derived and synthetic laxatives.

Cultivation and Preparation

IN CHINA PLANTS THREE OR MORE YEARS OLD ARE DUG IN September and October. The root is cleaned, and lateral rootlets and the crown removed. The rough outer bark is scraped off and roots are cut into cubes for drying. Traditionally in China, the root is wild harvested, but wild supplies have been depleted. In the past 30 years it has been extensively cultivated in China.

Research

LITTLE HUMAN RESEARCH HAS BEEN DONE ON *RHEUM palmatum*. In China, research has been done using combinations of rhubarb and other herbs. Experiments in animals have shown rhubarb **extracts** to be effective in preventing and treating gastric bleeding and ulcer formation. Another rhubarb extract, emodin, has been found to be a strong inhibitor of leukemia cells and other cancer cells in mice. In humans, rhubarb has been shown to prevent and delay renal failure and reduce symptoms of nausea and **anorexia nervosa**.

> CAUTION The leaves contain oxalic acid crystals in high enough concentration to be poisonous, causing, in higher quantities, the tongue and throat to swell, eventually preventing breathing. It is not recommended for patients with arthritis, kidney problems, inflammatory bowel disease, or intestinal obstruction. Rhubarb may cause uterine stimulation and therefore should not be consumed by pregnant women.

Chinese rhubarb is a famous traveler. It was commonly traded along the Silk Road—which could have been called the Rhubarb Road. Marco Polo wrote about it as he traveled to China at the end of the 13th century. Writing about the city of Su-chau (now Jiuquan), he reported, "In the mountains belonging to this city, rhubarb and ginger grow in great abundance." Polo returned to Venice with rhubarb and is often credited with having brought it to Europe. In fact, it was already being used as a medicine in European pharmacies. Rhubarb export was so common by the mid-19th century that when the emperor of China could not stop the import of British opium, he threatened to stop exporting rhubarb to Britain. Today rhubarb inspires travelers to participate in rhubarb gatherings all over the world. In 1990, the first International Symposium on Rhubarb was held in China. The theme was scientific confirmation of what had been long prescribed by Chinese pharmacopoeias. Rhubarb festivals take place all over the U.S., Canada, England, and Australia. The Rosy Rhubarb Festival, in Shedden, Ontario, just celebrated its 13th year, attracting rhubarb buffs from as far south as Florida. Marco Polo would understand.

See Also: Herbal Emissaries: Bringing Chinese Herbs to the West by S. Foster and Y. Chongxi, Healing Arts Press, 1992; *Tyler's Honest Herbal, 4th ed.* by S. Foster and V. Tyler, The Haworth Herbal Press, 1999.

Chocolate
Theobroma cacao

MANY PEOPLE WHO LOVE CHOCOLATE WOULD ENTHU-siastically agree that the Swedish naturalist Carolus Linnaeus was right on target in 1753 when he gave cacao the scientific name *Theobroma,* which translates as "the food of the gods." Cacao is the source of cocoa, chocolate, and creamy cocoa butter. The plant is native to the Americas and played an integral role in Olmec, Inca, Maya, and Aztec cultures. It was both food and medicine, and so valuable that cacao seeds were used as currency. In 1502, Christopher Columbus was the first European to encounter cacao. When Cortez landed on the coast of Mexico a few years later, Montezuma's attendants served the explorer a cup of cocoa—in a solid gold cup. By 1544, cocoa drinks had been introduced into Europe and within a century the French and Spanish had established cacao planta-tions in the Caribbean and Philippines, respectively. In the form of cocoa and chocolate, cacao remained a deli-cious delicacy. But in Western cultures it has also been used medicinally since the 16th century. Today, cacao is a known source of protective **antioxidants** as well as chemicals that give a sense of well-being and alertness.

Traditional and Current Medicinal Uses

CENTURIES AGO IN MESOAMERICA, COCOA DRINKS WERE CON-sumed to treat intestinal complaints, calm the nerves, and as stimulants. Combined with the bark of a type of rubber tree (*Castilla elastica*), cacao was given to cure infections and lung congestion. Cacao beans mixed with maize and other herbs were used to alle-viate fever, shortness of breath, and heart palpitations. Cacao flowers were consumed to treat fatigue. Cocoa butter was used in many Mesoamerican cultures to soothe burns, cracked lips, wounds, and skin irrita-tions. European herbals and medical manuals dating from the 16th to the 20th century list dozens of uses for cacao. It was given to convalescing patients to pro-mote weight gain, administered as a nervous system stimulant, used to improve digestion and stimulate the kidneys. Preparations were also recommended for ane-mia, mental fatigue, tuberculosis, bronchitis, fever,

Common Names Chocolate, cocoa, chocolate tree

Latin Name *Theobroma cacao*

Family Sterculiaceae

Parts Used Seeds

Description Cacao is a small tree, with pale brown bark and large glossy leaves, that grows to 25 feet. Clusters of yellow flowers emerge directly from the trunk and main branches. These produce large yellow, brown, or reddish ribbed pods with many seeds surrounded by a sweet, buttery pulp.

Habitat Native to lowland tropical forests in the Americas, cacao is cultivated in tropical regions worldwide.

Approximate native range

gout, kidney stones, inflammation, and as a general tonic for good health. Cacao butter was used as a base for ointments, salves, and suppositories. Chocolate-coated medicines became popular in the 1800s and are still used today.

In modern herbal medicine, cocoa powder is used to treat angina (chest pain) and high blood pressure. Cocoa butter is widely used for chapped skin, burns, and irritations. Cocoa and chocolate are rich sources of antioxidants.

Cultivation and Preparation

CACAO IS A SMALL TROPICAL TREE THAT NEEDS WARMTH, HIGH humidity, fertile soil, and protection from direct sunlight and wind. Trees can be started from seed, by air layering, or from cuttings. The seed pods are harvested twice a year. Seeds separated from the pulp are processed to produce chocolate, cocoa, and cocoa butter.

Research

STUDIES HAVE SHOWN THAT CACAO SEEDS CONTAIN MORE than 300 different chemical compounds. They are particularly rich in the well-known stimulant caffeine along with theobromine, an **alkaloid** that has a calming effect on the brain and an energizing effect on the nervous system. Both caffeine and theobromine are proven **diuretics**. Theobromine also tends to relax smooth muscles in the bronchial passages (making breathing easier), in the digestive tract, and in the walls of blood vessels (slightly lowering blood pressure). Other components of cacao include at least two stimulant compounds that raise blood sugar levels and slightly raise blood pressure; they tend to reduce depression and induce a slight sense of euphoria in some people. Cacao is also high in powerful antioxidant compounds and may help prevent or delay the onset of some degenerative diseases such as cancer and heart disease. In a study comparing the antioxidant action of tea, red wine, and cocoa, cocoa exhibited the highest activity. A study conducted at the University of California-Davis found that cocoa consumption has the same effect as aspirin in reducing **platelet aggregation**, with potential cardiovascular system benefits.

The word "cacao" is thought to have originated with the Olmec culture, the earliest civilization that occupied the lowland regions of the eastern Mexican Gulf coast beginning around 1200 B.C. Cacao is the Europeanized spelling of the original word, which is thought to have been pronounced "kakawa." (Over the centuries cacao eventually became cocoa.) Very similar names were given to the cacao tree and its seeds by the Maya and Aztec cultures that flourished in the region several centuries after the Olmecs. The Aztec word for the plant was *cacahuatl*. In all three cultures, cacao was considered a sacred plant. The Maya believed that the Feathered Serpent god gave cacao to people after he created them from maize. Their cacao god, Ek Chuah, was honored every spring by the sacrifice of a dog with cacao-colored markings. According to Aztec folklore, the god Quetzalcoatl discovered cacao inside a mountain with other plant foods. Cacao seeds were offered to the gods as hallowed sacrifices; the seeds were sometimes covered in the blood of priests who ceremonially cut themselves. Before Europeans arrived in Mesoamerica in the 1500s, drinks made from cacao seeds were sacred ceremonial beverages that only adult males such as priests, government officials, and warriors were allowed to drink. They were also given to sacrificial victims to comfort and calm them prior to their execution. Cacao was considered too intoxicating—and too valuable—to give to women and children.

See Also: *Medical Botany: Plants Affecting Human Health* by W. Lewis and M. Elvin-Lewis, John Wiley & Sons, 2003; *The Chocolate Tree: A History of Cacao* by A. Young, The Smithsonian Press, 1994.

Common Names Cinnamon, Ceylon cinnamon

Latin Name *Cinnamonum verum*

Family Lauraceae

Parts Used Bark

Description Cinnamon is a bushy tropical ever-green tree, growing 15 to 25 feet high, with soft, reddish-brown aromatic bark and leathery, oval, green leaves. Small greenish-white, rather unpleasantly scented flowers produce small, oblong, dark purple fruits. An older scientific name for the plant is *Cinnamonum zeylanicum*.

Habitat Cinnamon is native to humid tropical forests in southwestern India and Sri Lanka, but is cultivated in Indonesia, the West Indies, the Seychelles, and parts of Africa, and South America.

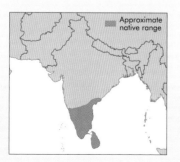

Approximate native range

Cinnamon
Cinnamonum verum

ALMOST EVERYONE IS FAMILIAR WITH THE DELICATELY fragrant aroma and warm, sweet flavor of cinnamon. Whether in the form of cinnamon sticks, a fine powder, or an intensely scented oil, the source of this wonderful and widely used spice, flavoring, and perfume ingredient is *Cinnamonum verum*, a modest-size tree belonging to the laurel family. Once more precious than gold, cinnamon was regarded as a present fit for kings. The ancient Egyptians valued cinnamon as an essential ingredient in the embalming process and in witchcraft. In medieval Europe, the powdered herb was used as flavoring and in religious ceremonies. Cinnamon was what brought traders with the Dutch East India company to Sri Lanka (then called Ceylon), where they established an outpost in 1638. Captains of Dutch East India ships claimed the scent of cinnamon wafting out to sea from the island was so strong that they could smell it from miles away. This claim is questionable, as the tree as a whole does not give off a strong fragrance of cinnamon and most people find the scent of its flowers quite disagreeable. Cinnamon is less known as an herbal medicine, but it is a time-honored remedy, particularly for gastrointestinal upsets of various kinds.

Traditional and Current Medicinal Uses

THE USE OF CINNAMON AS A MEDICINAL HERB MAY EXTEND back several millennia, at least to 500 B.C. Traditionally, cinnamon has been taken as a remedy for colds, flu, and other respiratory afflictions, but especially for digestive problems. It was widely used for treating flatulence, loss of appetite, gastric upsets, nausea, vomiting, intestinal cramping, and diarrhea. The herb was considered a warming tonic, one that can help bring heat to cold hands and feet by increasing circulation to the extremities. The 17th-century English herbalist Nicolas Culpeper advised ingesting a daily dose of cinnamon as a protection against scurvy. In India, cinnamon was sometimes prescribed as a contraceptive for women who had recently given birth. In China and Japan, *Cinnamonum aromaticum*, a closely related species, is used in much the same way as true cinnamon is used.

In modern herbal medicine, cinnamon is still recognized for its ability to soothe digestive complaints and to treat inflammation, rheumatism, colds, nausea and vomiting, and menstrual problems. Cinnamon is also used to make the taste and scent of other medicinal products more appealing.

Cultivation and Preparation

THE WORLD'S FINEST CINNAMON IS SAID TO COME FROM SRI Lanka and India, although *Cinnamonum verum* is cultivated in a number of other countries in different parts of the world. Cinnamon trees grow best under conditions of constant warmth and moisture—they thrive in tropical forests at an altitude of about 1,500 feet. Propagation is usually accomplished by planting cuttings. Trees are coppiced (cut back to just above ground level) to produce a crop of young shoots that grow up from the stump. These are cut and rubbed to loosen the bark, which is peeled off. The outer bark is scraped away, leaving thin sheets of aromatic inner bark that are rolled together to form quills. These are then allowed to dry. The dried bark can be sold as quills (cinnamon sticks) or can be pulverized into powder; **essential oil** is also extracted from the bark.

Research

CINNAMON BARK CONTAINS FROM 0.5 TO 1 PERCENT ESSENtial oil. This is the source of cinnamon's pungent taste and scent. Its main active ingredient is the compound cinnamaldehyde. Research has documented that the oil has antispasmodic, antifungal, antibacterial, and **carminative** properties. Cinnamaldehyde appears to be responsible for cinnamon's antispasmodic characteristics, while some of the other active compounds in the essential oil are the source of its antimicrobial effects. Several studies have revealed that cinnamon oil inhibits the growth of many types of oral bacteria, and may be useful in treating certain types of oral infections, particularly those caused by *Candida* species. Other research points to significant **antioxidant** capacity in cinnamon oil, especially oil extracted from the fruit stalks of the trees.

A TRUE BLUE TEST

True or Ceylon cinnamon (*Cinnamonum verum*) is a much more expensive spice than its close relative Chinese cinnamon or cassia (*Cinnamonum aromaticum*). Cassia is widely cultivated in China, Indonesia, and Vietnam. The dried quills of cinnamon and cassia are fairly easy to tell apart. But when ground into a powder, the difference is harder to spot. Spice merchants have long taken advantage of the similarity between these two ground spices by mixing costly cinnamon with less expensive, and rather harsh-tasting, cassia. A simple chemical test can reveal the deception. All that is needed is an eye dropper and a vial of tincture of iodine. True cinnamon contains very little starch unlike cassia. Iodine turns starch blue. A few drops of iodine added to pure ground cinnamon should have little or no effect. But add the drops to ground cassia and a characteristic blue color will appear. When testing a "cinnamon" sample, the intensity of the blue color produced will depend on the proportion of cassia to cinnamon in the mix. Despite differences in taste and starch content, cinnamon and cassia have very similar pharmacological effects and are used in much the same way in herbal medicine, with one exception. Herbal medicine practitioners caution against using cinnamon medicinally during pregnancy; high doses can induce abortion. Cassia is regarded as safe, even during pregnancy.

See Also: Herbal Medicine Expanded Commission E Monographs by M. Blumenthal, A. Goldberg, J. Brinckmann, American Botanical Council, 2000; *World Health Organization (WHO) Monographs on Selected Medicinal Plants, Vol. 1*, 2000.

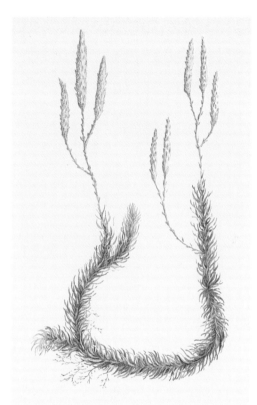

Common Names Clubmoss, common clubmoss, ground pine, stag's horn moss, running pine, wolf's claw moss

Latin Name *Lycopodium clavatum*

Family Lycopodiaceae

Parts Used Whole plant, spores

Description Clubmoss is a primitive evergreen perennial with narrow, creeping runners and upright branches that are thickly covered in small, scale-like leaves. Clubmoss reproduces by minute, dust-like spores produced in tiny spore-containing cones (strobili).

Habitat Clubmoss is native to forests and Arctic habitats in both the Northern and Southern Hemispheres. It grows in dry shaded woodlands, open thickets, rocky slopes, pine forests, and occasionally around the edges of swamps and bogs.

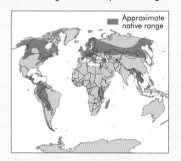

Approximate native range

Clubmoss
Lycopodium clavatum

DESPITE THEIR NAME, CLUBMOSSES ARE NOT RELATED TO true mosses at all. They are primitive plants with small scale-like leaves that flourished during the Carboniferous period some 360 million years ago. About 400 species of clubmoss make up the genus *Lycopodium*. Many of these can be found creeping along forest floors or tundra terrain. Their creeping stems send up small vertical branches that at first glance might be mistaken for pine tree seedlings. This resemblance has earned the plant the common name "ground pine." The shape of the small branching stems has also been likened to deer antlers, hence the name "stag's horn moss." The common name "wolf's claw moss" grew out of the genus name; *Lycopodium* means "wolf's foot" in Latin. Clubmoss reproduces by spores instead of seeds. The very fine, yellow spores are produced in special structures called strobili that develop from the tips of branches. Although entire clubmoss plants were used medicinally in ancient times, only the spores have been employed in herbal medicine since about the 17th century. They have sedative, antibacterial, and **diuretic** properties and are used primarily in treating skin diseases, rheumatism, and bladder and kidney disorders.

Traditional and Current Medicinal Uses

SEVERAL THOUSAND YEARS AGO, CLUBMOSS PLANTS WERE DRIED and used whole by ancient physicians as a remedy for stomach disorders and as a diuretic in treating kidney ailments. The Druids, an ancient Celtic priesthood, used clubmoss as a laxative and **purgative**. Native Americans used clubmoss for postpartum pains, weakness and fever, to stop bleeding from wounds, and to stimulate nosebleeds to relieve headaches. Beginning around the 17th century, only the spores were used in medicinal preparations. Their primary therapeutic value was as a diuretic in cases of **edema** (swelling), as a laxative but also to control diarrhea and dysentery, for relief of gout and scurvy, for bladder irritability, to treat wounds, and to ease the pain of rheumatism. They were also used as a sedative, an aphrodisiac, and to stop bleeding. Externally the spores made an ideal dusting powder to prevent skin chafing in infants and to relieve eczema and other skin diseases and irritations.

In modern herbal medicine, clubmoss is taken for urinary and kidney disorders, cystitis, stomach upsets, diarrhea, and skin conditions. Two closely related clubmoss species are used in traditional Chinese medicine. *Lycopodium cernuum* is employed in treating rheumatoid arthritis and traumatic injuries as well as spasms in the legs and arms. The related *Huperzia serrata* may help delay the symptoms of Alzheimer's disease.

Cultivation and Preparation

LYCOPODIUM IS RATHER DIFFICULT TO GROW. NEW PLANTS MAY be propagated by sowing spores on damp sphagnum moss or by dividing mature plants and cultivating them in damp, acidic soil. Clubmoss is harvested year-round. Spores are shaken out of strobili-covered plants cut in summer. Clubmoss was once widely used for Christmas decorations and in some areas has been over-collected, endangering wild populations. Gathering of some species is subject to restrictions in some places.

Research

MORE THAN 100 DIFFERENT **ALKALOIDS** HAVE BEEN ISOLATED from *Lycopodium* and related *Huperzia* species, along with acids and other compounds. Recent studies have found that *Lycopodium clavatum* contains an **enzyme** that may help improve memory and reverse dementia in Alzheimer's patients. Two species of clubmoss once used by the Chippewa also contain a substance known as huperzine, which is also recognized as a potential treatment for Alzheimer's disease. Huperzine inhibits the breakdown of acetylcholine in the brain. Acetylcholine is a **neurotransmitter** thought to play an important role in recognition, reasoning, and memory. *Lycopodium clavatum* is generally considered safe. However, it has been shown to contain some toxic alkaloids that with prolonged use may irritate the lining of the mouth, throat, stomach, and intestines and cause vomiting and diarrhea. It is also easily confused with *Huperzia selago*, which can lead to poisoning characterized by sweating, vomiting, diarrhea, dizziness, cramps, and slurred speech.

PILLS, POWDERS, AND FLASH POWER

Clubmoss spores, also called vegetable sulfur and lycopodium powder, have several remarkable properties. They form an amazing barrier against water because a waxy substance in the spores renders them, and whatever they coat, water repellent. If a person dusts his or her hands with the powdery spores, and then plunges them into water, the skin will stay dry. This property made clubmoss spores especially useful in treating intertrigo, a type of dermatitis caused by the build-up of moisture between skin folds. Pharmacists also exploited the water-repellent traits of clubmoss spores in the past by coating pills with vegetable sulfur to seal in unpleasant tastes and to keep the pills from getting damp and sticking together. The spores are still used today as a drying powder inside some types of rubber and latex products, and as a body powder for babies and bedridden patients. Clubmoss spores also burn with explosive violence. If a small amount of the powder is brought into contact with a flame, it catches fire with a vivid flash and a hissing explosion. Because of this, the spores played an important role in the development of flash photography. They were used as "flash powder," the forerunner of flashbulbs and strobe lights to light up subjects in front of the camera.

See Also: A Field Guide to Medicinal Plants and Herbs: Eastern and Central North America, 2nd ed. by S. Foster and J. Duke, Houghton Mifflin, 2000; A Field Guide to Medicinal Plants and Herbs: Western North America by S. Foster and C. Hobbs, Houghton Mifflin, 2002.

Coca
Erythroxylum coca

THE LEAVES OF COCA HAVE PLAYED A VITAL ROLE—RELIgiously, socially, and physiologically—in the lives of the indigenous people of Peru, Bolivia, and northern Argentina for thousands of years. Coca was a symbol of royalty and also had great religious significance. Coca leaves were offered to the gods as gifts and burned to produce smoke at special religious events. Near Nazca, Peru, 2,000-year-old mummies have been found with bags of coca leaves hung around their necks. In rural areas in these regions, people still chew, or more precisely, gently crush and suck on, coca leaves as a stimulant to relieve hunger and fatigue and to help their bodies adapt to a high-altitude existence. The leaves are the source of the **alkaloid** cocaine, a powerful stimulant that became the world's first commercial anesthetic but is now far better known as an illegal narcotic.

Traditional and Current Medicinal Uses

IN RURAL ANDEAN VILLAGES IT IS STILL NOT UNCOMMON TO SEE people carrying a small pouch containing a day's supply of coca leaves together with a little powdered lime. A small amount of lime is added to a few leaves that are rolled up and tucked into the cheek like a quid of chewing tobacco. The lime helps release cocaine from the leaf, and it is swallowed throughout the day. Coca leaves are also used to brew *mate de coca*, or coca tea. Chewing coca leaves or drinking coca tea has an energizing effect on the body, relieving fatigue and masking hunger. It also produces a numbing effect in the mouth and on the lips. The practice of chewing coca leaves may have arisen out of necessity in high Andean regions, making life bearable in places where food was often as scarce as oxygen in the thin mountain air. Cocaine, the active ingredient in coca leaves, was isolated in 1855. Not long after, it was being used as an ingredient in cough drops and other patent medicines, as well as in "medicinal" coca wines (called Vin Mariani and Cocas de Inca). These stimulating tonics became very popular in Europe. In the United States, a drink developed in 1886 by John S. Pemberton, and called Coca Cola, combined the

Common Names Coca, cuca, cocaine

Latin Name *Erythroxylum coca*

Family Erythroxylaceae

Parts Used Leaves

Description Coca is a perennial evergreen shrub with reddish-brown bark and light green, elliptical leaves with a pronounced midrib. Clusters of small white flowers are followed by bright red berries. The herb grows to six feet in cultivation, but to fifteen feet in the wild.

Habitat Native to Peru and Bolivia, coca was traditionally cultivated at lower altitudes on the eastern slopes of the Andes.

Approximate native range

stimulating effects of both cocaine and caffeine. (In 1902, cocaine was dropped as an ingredient.) Around the same time, cocaine's value as an anesthetic was discovered. It was used as a local anesthetic in delicate eye, ear, nose, and throat surgeries, but has been almost entirely replaced in Western medicine by synthetic local anesthetics such as benzocaine.

Today cocaine ointments are used for eczema, itching, nettle rash, painful hemorrhoids, and facial neuralgia. Cocaine may be combined with morphine as a pain reliever in terminally ill patients. Coca tea is sometimes recommended for altitude sickness.

Cultivation and Preparation

TRADITIONALLY, COCA IS CULTIVATED IN SMALL PLOTS THAT are somewhat sheltered from the sun, such as in forest clearings. The plants thrive in warm, humid conditions. Leaves are harvested several times a year and are picked when they break if bent. The leaves are dried, often in the sun. Coca leaves (not cocaine) are used in the food and cosmetics industries. Cocaine is extracted from the leaves and used in some medicinal preparations and as a local anesthetic in some countries. The cultivation, harvesting, and processing of coca plants and leaves is subject to legal restrictions worldwide.

Research

COCA LEAVES CONTAIN MORE THAN 18 ALKALOIDS, ALTHOUGH cocaine is the primary one. As a naturally occurring anesthetic, cocaine works by blocking sodium channels in neurons and thereby interfering with nerve impulses. As a stimulant, cocaine travels to the brain, where it binds to dopamine receptors. Dopamine is a **neurotransmitter** and neurohormone produced naturally in the body and commonly associated with the brain's "pleasure system." Cocaine interferes with normal dopamine uptake, which leads to intense feelings of exhilaration along with increased heart rate and elevated blood pressure. The effect is temporary, and is often followed by feelings of depression and anxiety. Persistent, excessive use of cocaine (but not coca leaves) causes tremors, convulsions, delusion, hyperactivity, loss of memory, and emaciation.

HABITS OF THE RICH AND FAMOUS

In the late 19th century, cocaine was a fashionable drug. There was no stigma associated with it, and many wealthy and prominent people used cocaine openly. Some of the more well-known cocaine users of that period included Ulysses S. Grant, Popes Leo XIII and Saint Pius X, Britain's Queen Victoria, and Sigmund Freud, the father of psychoanalysis. Freud discovered that cocaine relieved his own chronic depression. In 1884, he published an article titled *Über Coca* ("About Coca") in which he referred to it as a magical drug—with no side effects. Like many other medical professionals of his day, Freud believed that cocaine could be used to treat a variety of illnesses, including alcohol and morphine addictions. Cocaine was widely available at the time. In the U.S., the drug manufacturer Parke-Davis sold cocaine in various forms, including a mixture—with needle included—that could be injected. Freud recommended cocaine to a number of his patients, some of whom became addicted to the drug. So did Freud. But by 1904, Freud had kicked his habit and stopped using cocaine. By then, the destructive downside to cocaine was obvious. Cocaine abuse began to capture public attention in many countries. In the U.S., the Harrison Narcotics Tax Act heavily regulated cocaine in 1914, and in 1922 it was outlawed as a narcotic.

See Also: Medical Botany: Plants Affecting Human Health by W. Lewis and M. Elvin-Lewis, John Wiley & Sons, 2003; *Nature's Medicine, Plants That Heal* by Joel Swerdlow, National Geographic, 2000.

Comfrey
Symphytum officinale

A MEMBER OF THE BORAGE FAMILY, COMFREY HAS A LONG history of medicinal use, primarily for healing wounds and mending broken bones. Its genus name, *Symphytum*, comes from the Greek *symphyo*, meaning "to unite" while the common name, "comfrey," is derived from the Latin *confervia*, meaning "to heal" or "to boil together." Some of the herb's other common names, such as "knitbone" and "boneset," also reflect comfrey's reputation for promoting healing in broken, bruised, torn, or damaged tissues. Used since at least 400 B.C., comfrey enjoyed popularity as an herbal remedy until the late 1970s, when researchers raised concerns about its potential to cause liver damage, due to the presence of certain toxic **alkaloids** in leaves and roots. Comfrey-containing herbal products for internal consumption were banned in the U.S. in 2001. The United Kingdom, Australia, Canada, and Germany have also banned oral comfrey products. Topical preparations are still available.

Traditional and Current Medicinal Uses

THE GREEKS WERE AMONG THE FIRST USERS OF COMFREY; they employed it to staunch heavy bleeding and to treat bronchial problems. In the first century B.C., the Greek physician Dioscorides recommended comfrey for healing wounds and mending broken bones. Both the Greeks and Romans made **poultices** out of comfrey leaves and roots to treat external wounds, and drank comfrey tea for stomach disorders, internal bleeding, diarrhea, and other ailments. Comfrey was popular during the Middle Ages as a healing poultice applied to fractures, bruises, and wounds. Comfrey tea was also drunk as a remedy for internal injuries. Centuries later, comfrey remained a popular treatment for a wide variety of ailments. It was considered a gentle remedy for diarrhea and dysentery, an effective treatment for bronchitis, whooping cough, and tuberculosis, and good for internal bleeding, ulcers, and hemorrhoids. Ointments and other preparations of the roots and leaves were applied to bruises, sprains, strains, broken bones, torn ligaments, severe cuts, boils and burns, arthritis, gangrene, and

Common Names Comfrey, common comfrey, knitbone, boneset, slippery root, blackwort

Latin Name *Symphytum officinale*

Family Boraginaceae

Parts Used Leaves, roots

Description Comfrey is a hardy, upright, leafy perennial growing up to three feet high from thick taproots. Its rough, slightly hairy leaves are dark green and lance-shaped. Nodding clusters of bell-shaped white, cream, pink, or purple flowers are followed by small, hard, glossy-black fruits.

Habitat Native to Europe and western Asia, comfrey has been introduced and naturalized elsewhere, including the eastern United States and Canada. In the wild, it grows along stream banks and in moist meadows.

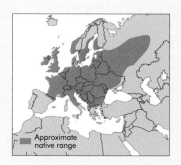

Approximate native range

almost any kind of inflamed swelling. Since 2001, only preparations designed for topical use (where skin is unbroken) in treating bruises, swellings, and some skin conditions have been approved for sale in the U.S.

Cultivation and Preparation

ALTHOUGH COMFREY PREFERS DAMP SOIL IN THE WILD, IT does well in any good garden soil in full sun or light shade. It can be propagated easily by division of the roots. Comfrey roots have a black exterior and fleshy whitish interior that exudes a slimy, mucilaginous juice (hence the common names "blackwort" and "slippery root"). Just a small piece of root will give rise to a new plant. For this reason, comfrey is invasive and almost impossible to eradicate once established. Leaves are harvested in summer while the roots are lifted in autumn. Fresh or dried leaves and roots are used to make poultices, ointments, **infused oils**, and **tinctures**.

Research

COMFREY CONTAINS TWO PRIMARY THERAPEUTIC CON-stituents: allantoin, which scientists call a cell prolif-erant, and rosmarinic acid. Allantoin causes cells to multiply and thereby enhances growth and regenera-tion of damaged tissues. Applications of allantoin cause wounds, burns, sores, and similar injuries to heal faster; allantoin is a fairly common ingredient in ointments and creams used to treat skin problems. Rosmarinic acid is an **anti-inflammatory** agent. Despite the presence of these positive ingredients, comfrey also contains a number of toxic pyrrolizidine alkaloids, or PAs. Although PAs help stop bleeding, they have been shown in experiments using lab animals to damage the liver and cause cancerous liver tumors. Despite its long history of use in herbal medicine, no clinical studies have documented any positive effects of comfrey. Many studies, however, have demonstrated its liver toxicity.

CAUTION Comfrey contains toxic substances that can cause severe liver damage, cancerous tumors, and possibly even death. Neither com-frey nor comfrey-containing products should ever be ingested in any form. Topical comfrey preparations should be used only on unbroken skin and under the supervision of a knowledgeable healthcare provider. Pregnant and breastfeeding women and children should not use com-frey products under any circumstances.

COMFREY CONCERNS

Initial concerns about the safety of comfrey were raised in 1978, when Japanese researchers pub-lished the report of a study in which laboratory rats were fed dried comfrey leaves and roots. Within 180 days, the rats began to show signs of liver damage. After six months, all of the rats had developed liver tumors. Subsequent studies of the toxic compounds responsible for the liver damage—pyrrolizidine alka-loids, or PAs, for short—revealed that PAs initially lead to an insidious and difficult-to-diagnose condition known as hepatic veno-occlusive disease (HVOD). With this condition, the blood vessels around the liver gradually become blocked. Symptoms are subtle. As the liver enlarges due to HVOD, a victim might expe-rience some degree of abdominal pain just below the right side of the rib cage. By this time, however, the disease could be quite advanced. Left untreated, HVOD can lead to liver failure and even death. In the years that followed the groundbreaking research on HVOD, several fatal cases of the disease in people who had consumed comfrey over various periods of time came to light in Europe and the United States. These cases prompted the U.S. Food and Drug Admin-istration to recommend in 2001 the removal of all com-frey-containing products from the marketplace. In defense of the ban, the FDA cited evidence that PAs are toxic to the liver, may damage other body tissues and organs, and may potentially cause cancer.

See Also: *A Field Guide to Medicinal Plants and Herbs: Eastern and Central North America, 2nd ed.* by S. Foster and J. Duke, Houghton Mif-flin, 2000; *A Field Guide to Medicinal Plants and Herbs: Western North America* by S. Foster and C. Hobbs, Houghton Mifflin, 2002.

Common Privet

Ligustrum vulgare, Ligustrum lucidum

P RIVET BRINGS TO MIND DENSE, LEAFY GREEN ENCLOSURES for lawns and gardens. This member of the olive family—there are about 50 species in the genus *Ligustrum*—is a wonderful hedge plant. The name "privet" probably is derived from "private," referring to its centuries' old use as a plant that could be easily trimmed to create living screens and barriers. The genus name *Ligustrum* is the Latin word used by first century Roman botanist and physician Pliny the Elder for privet and may have come from *ligare*, meaning "to tie." The flexible twigs of the herb were long ago used as cords for lashing. Privet has been grown as a hedge plant in Europe since the 16th century. It was introduced to North America from England—and soon escaped the bounds of gardens to become naturalized in the wild. In some states, it is classified as an invasive weed that can displace native species. Yet it is still widely planted as a common landscaping shrub. Less familiar is privet's medicinal value. Both *L. vulgare* and *L. lucidum* have been used in traditional herbal medicine, but in recent years Chinese privet (*L. lucidum)* has gained attention for its value in treating cancer chemotherapy patients.

Traditional and Current Medicinal Uses

COMMON PRIVET HAS ASTRINGENT PROPERTIES. DECOCTIONS of the leaves were used in treating chronic intestinal complaints such as diarrhea, stomach ulcers, and bladder problems. It was especially known for its use as a gargle or mouthwash for sore mouths and throats, and for mumps. Preparations of the leaves were also used to treat chapped lips and as a wash for skin problems. Privet was also a folk remedy for tumors of the uvula. Privet tea was administered to improve appetite and digestion. The closely related Chinese privet has been used in traditional Chinese medicine for well over 1,000 years. The leaves and bark are used in preparations to expel phlegm, stop coughs, and treat bronchitis. The leaves alone have traditionally been used to treat headaches, dizziness, sore eyes, swellings, ulcers, burns, and mouth irritations. The small seeds, called *nu zhen zi* in Chinese, are also used in herbal preparations.

Common Names Common privet, European Privet, prim, primwort, privy (*L. vulgare*); Chinese privet, glossy privet (*L. lucidum*)

Latin Names *Ligustrum vulgare, L. lucidum*

Family Oleaceae

Parts Used Leaves, berries, bark (*L. lucidum*)

Description Privet is a large shrub or small tree with dark green, oval, pointed leaves and small creamy white flowers that bloom in dense, pyramidal panicles. The fruit is a black, shiny berry.

Habitat *Ligustrum vulgare* is native to western Asia, North Africa, and Europe, while *L. lucidum* is indigenous to eastern Asia. Both species are commonly cultivated as hedge plants.

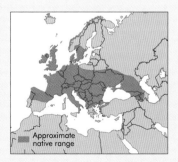

Approximate
native range

Traditionally these were taken as a tonic for conditions thought to be associated with weak kidney and liver energy, such as premature aging (especially graying of the hair), premature menopause, vision problems, cataracts, rheumatic pains, backache, tinnitus, heart palpitations, and insomnia.

More recently, Chinese privet has been used to prevent bone marrow loss in cancer chemotherapy patients. It has also been used with notable success in treating Parkinson's disease, early cataracts, hypertension (high blood pressure), certain types of respiratory tract infections, and hepatitis, and appears to potentially be effective against AIDS.

Cultivation and Preparation

PRIVET GROWS BEST IN WELL-DRAINED, MOIST SOIL IN SUNNY locations. Some species can be started reliably from seed (not cultivars, which may not breed true). The plants can also be started from cuttings. Leaves can be harvested at any time. Berries are collected when ripe in late summer. They are typically dried before being used in herbal medicine preparations; privet is often mixed with other herbs. Although privet fruits can be toxic when consumed in large quantities, toxicity in herbal preparations is considered to be low.

Research

PRIVET, PARTICULARLY CHINESE PRIVET, IS THOUGHT TO exhibit antibacterial, antiseptic, **diuretic**, and antitumor properties. The major chemical constituent is ligustrin (oleanolic acid). According to a number of studies in China, *Ligustrum lucidum* appears to reduce inflammation. It also enhances the number of white blood cells in the bloodstream in cancer patients who are undergoing chemotherapy or radiotherapy treatments that have induced leucopenia (reduced white cell count). *Nu zhen zi* preparations raise the white counts in chemotherapy patients back to normal levels. Extracts of the fruit also seem to stimulate normal immune system functioning. Other research indicates that Chinese privet preparations can increase blood flow through coronary arteries. Extracts have also been shown to inhibit cervical cancers in mice.

HEPATITIS AND LIGUSTRUM

Hepatitis B is a serious disease caused by a virus that attacks the liver. The virus can lead to life-long infection, cirrhosis (scarring) of liver tissue, liver cancer, liver failure, and death. Hepatitis B is endemic in Southeast Asia with 20 percent of the population infected in some areas; a major concern in other parts of the world, it has been spreading in almost epidemic proportions over the past several decades. A vaccine is available to prevent infection. In the U.S., hepatitis B vaccine has been recommended for everyone under 18 years of age since 1997. For millions worldwide, however, a vaccine is simply not available. Historical records indicate that a disease similar to hepatitis B was known to doctors in China 1,800 years ago and treated with a combination of herbs. In the mid-20th century, Chinese and Japanese researchers began doing studies of herbal medicines used to treat viral hepatitis. In clinical trials, the effectiveness of these herbs has been documented. Herbs most often used in hepatitis B preparations are *Glycyrrhiza, Schisandra, Salvia, Polygonum cuspidatum, Curcuma, Silybum marianum, and Ligustrum lucidum. Ligustrum* is rich in oleanolic acid, a substance that enhances immune response and seems to act as a liver-protecting agent, thereby combating liver infections. *Ligustrum* appears to be remarkably effective in treating hepatitis, with a cure rate of up to 70 percent for the acute form of the disease.

See Also: *Herbal Emissaries: Bringing Chinese Herbs to the West* by S. Foster and Y. Chongxi, Healing Arts Press,1992; *Tyler's Honest Herbal 4th ed.* by S. Foster and V. Tyler, The Haworth Herbal Press, 1999.

HEALING PLANTS OF
Central and
South America

ROSITA ARVIGO BECKONED TO HER APPRENTICE TO HELP HER CARRY IN wood to build a fire. Rosita was making a healing bath for a patient waiting on her front porch in the heart of Belize's Maya Mountains. The morning fog hung in the mountain valleys, outlining the Macal River below, winding like a snake in the rain forest. Rosita wielded a two-foot long stick as she went to the wood pile. She carefully picked up each stick of wood by her fingertips, then flung it onto the concrete porch. Six-inch-long, black scorpions darted from the wood as she whacked at them with her stick.

A doctor of naprapathic medicine, a discipline akin to chiropractic medicine, Rosita is a natural healer. She came to Belize from Chicago in 1981 and bought a tract of 35 acres in the rain forest near the border with Guatemala. In the ensuing years there were many times when Rosita found tropical homesteading and her dream of using herbs of the rain forest to heal people a bit too challenging. But one day that changed. On that day, a short, slightly hunched, elderly Maya man with bright youthful eyes came to visit. He had heard of her interest in herbs. The visitor was Don Elijio Panti, a name she recognized from the locals as the most revered—and feared— Maya medicine man in Central America. They soon became friends, and Rosita Arvigo became the healer's apprentice until he died at age 103 in 1996.

Her journey as a medicine man's apprentice led her to remedies and treatments for cancer, diabetes, and dozens of common ailments. She joined Dr. Michael J. Balick, director of the New York Botanical Garden's Institute of Economic Botany, in documenting and collecting more than 2,000 plant species, 500 of which were used by Don Elijio Panti for anti-AIDS and anticancer screening by the National Cancer Institute. Rosita Arvigo and Michael Balick researched the economics of medicinal plants to demonstrate that the sustainable harvest of medicinal plants from tropical rain forests in Belize had a greater economic value than would timber sales were the same piece of land clear cut. In 1993, at Rosita Arvigo's behest, the government of Belize created a 6,000-acre medicinal plant reserve, Terra Nova Medicinal Plant Reserve. Currently, many of the herbs that Arvigo uses in her clinical practice in San Ignacio Town, a few miles away, can be found here along the Ix Chel Medicine Trail at Chaa Creek, the first medicine trail in Central America open to the public.

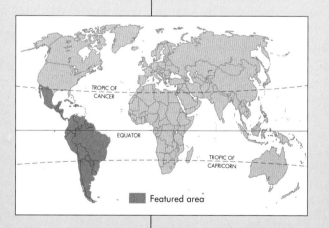

TROPIC OF CANCER

EQUATOR

TROPIC OF CAPRICORN

Featured area

HOME OF
RAINFOREST REMEDIES
Stand Up For Your Roots!

TRADITIONAL MEDICINE IN LATIN AMERICA

MANY OF THE SECRETS OF TRADITIONAL MEDICINE PRACTICED BY INDIAN TRIBES IN LATIN America are still to be discovered. Medieval and Renaissance herb traditions of Europe can be found in illuminated herbals such as the 1597 *Herball* of John Gerarde. In 1552, 60 years after Columbus arrived in the New World and 45 years before Gerarde's *Herball* was published, the first herbal from the Americas—indeed the first medical book—was produced at the Santa Cruz College of Tlaltelolco, Mexico. Recorded in his native language by Martín de la Cruz, an Aztec physician who learned the value of medicinal plants from his elders, the document (later translated into Latin) is known as the *Badianus Manuscript*. Practically unknown for 350 years, it was re-discovered in the Vatican Library in 1929. The *Badianus Manuscript* shows that the Aztecs' knowledge of medicinal plants was comparable to that of their European conquerors. De la Cruz recorded uses of native medical remedies, with colored illustrations, and detailed procedures for the preparation of medicines. Most were relatively simple, intended for common ailments, though some were exceptionally elaborate such as a prescription with 27

Natural healer and shaman's apprentice Rosita Arvigo stands at the entry of the small factory where medicinal plant products are manufactured in San Ignacio Town in western Belize. Arvigo brought to the attention of the world—and the National Cancer Institute—the herbal remedies of her shaman mentor, Don Elijio Panti.

PRECEDING PAGES: Morning fog outlines the Macal River's serpentine path through the Maya Mountains in Belize near the Guatemalan border. The diverse tropical rain forest here is home to dozens of medicinal plants.

plant, animal, and mineral ingredients intended to bestow strength, reduce fatigue, and fortify the hearts of those administering the government. In 1990, after visiting Mexico, Pope John Paul II returned the manuscript to the Mexican people. According to Dr. Carlos Viesca of the National Autonomous University of Mexico, the leading authority on the *Badianus Manuscript*, 90 percent of the plants depicted are still used as herbal medicines in Mexico today. The *Badianus Manuscript* is the first detailed record of uses of plants by the indigenous peoples of Latin America.

*In an impromptu demonstration in the Peruvian Amazon rain forest, ethnobotanist James A. Duke applied a natural insect repellant containing citronella (*Cymbopogon nardus*) and other essential oils to a small area of this fly-covered cap. The result: Fewer flies on the crown of the cap where the oils were applied.*

PLANT MIGRATIONS

COLUMBUS'S ARRIVAL ON NEW WORLD SHORES OPENED THE WAY for migration of Europeans to the Americas. It also marked the beginning of widespread, unabated, and continuous transoceanic movement of plants by humans. We think of potatoes as Irish, but they were unknown to Europeans prior to their arrival in the Andes. Columbus was the first European to encounter the Caribbean's Arawak Indians. In his journal he refers to *panizo*—a broadleaf, waist-high grass cultivated as a grain by the Arawak. We know it as corn, a dietary staple for much of the world's population.

When Columbus and his men departed the Canary Islands on September 6, 1492, he wanted to find a westward route to the Spice Islands. He sought black pepper (*Piper nigrum*); dining with the Arawak, Columbus experienced another pepper. He became the first European known to taste red pepper—a member of the genus *Capsicum*, which gives us bell pepper, pimiento, paprika, chili, cayenne, and more. In pre-Columbian Latin America five *Capsicum* species had already been domesticated. The compound capsaicin, which gives cayenne (*C. annuum*) its bite, is now used in over-the-counter topical drug products for the treatment of pain associated with post-herpetic neuralgia (persistent pain at the site of an infection that has apparently healed), diabetic neuropathy (nerve damage), and *Herpes zoster* (shingles). Columbus's taste of a red pepper was a mere glimpse of the botanical wealth in the rain forests just to the west.

LATIN AMERICA'S MEDICINAL PLANTS

DR. JAMES A. DUKE AND HIS SHAMAN COLLEAGUE DON ANTONIO STAND IN A SMALL clearing in the Peruvian rain forest with medicinal plants spread out for pharmacists and physicians attending the American Botanical Council's annual "Pharmacy From the Rain Forest" program. Flies swarm so thick that Duke's students cannot sit still. Duke stands barefoot, oblivious to insects, describing in his Alabama drawl the the herbs Don Antonio is preparing. Noticing his student's discomfort—and ever the experimenter—he takes out a natural insect repellant containing citronella and other **essential oils**. A sweat-soaked hat hangs by a tree, covered with the brown flies plaguing his students. Spreading some of the oil on part of the hat, Duke enjoys watching as the flies settle on the hat away from the area where he spread the oil.

Duke considers the Amazon his home away from home, having traveled there more than 50 times in the last several decades. Early in his career Duke lived among the Cuna and Choco Indian tribes of Panama, studying their ethnobotany. As Chief of the U.S. Department of Agriculture's (USDA) Germplasm Resource Lab, he spearheaded government efforts to find a replacement crop in the Andes for coca (source of cocaine), study genetic diversity of opium poppies in Iran, and collect plants for the National Cancer Institute (NCI) plant screening program. In July 1960 NCI contracted with USDA to begin collecting plant materials to screen for new anticancer compounds. Over the next 20 years, about 35,000 species of flowering plants were analyzed. Some 3,000 demonstrated reproducible activity. A fraction (including mayapple and yew derivatives) were chosen for clinical trials.

Ethnobotanist James A. Duke, accompanied by Amazonian shaman and colleague Don Antonio, explains a traditional preparation used as a divination aid by shamans in Amazonia. Duke is lecturing to pharmacists attending the American Botanical Council's "Pharmacy From the Rain Forest" education series.

Duke takes groups to the Amazon several times a year to study medicinal plants. As he speaks to the American Botanical Council attendees on this trip, his love of the Amazon is evident. He plows barefoot through the rain forest, oblivious to the ants, insects, or occasional reptile that might lurk beneath the understory. Emphasizing the diversity of the rain forest, Duke explains that here in the Peruvian rain forest alone there are more than 300 woody species per hectare, in comparison to about 30 species of woody plants per hectare in the woods near his Maryland home. In the 2,700,000 square miles that are home to the world's most extensive rain forest, botanists estimate there are as many as half a million species of plants. Some estimate as many as 80,000 plant species may occur in the Amazon Basin alone.

Duke points to a liana, close to where Don Antonio is preparing his brew. "That's cat's claw," he says, then lets the Latin name, *Uncaria guianensis,* and the Spanish *una de gato* roll off his tongue. Details of medicinal uses of cat's claw are revealed in *Amazonian Ethnobotanical Dictionary,* published in 1995, one of Duke's more than 30 books. A bark **decoction** of *U. guianensis* is used in Peru as an **anti-inflammatory**, antirheumatic, and a contraceptive, as well as for treating gastric ulcers and tumors. In Colombia and Guiana, Indian groups use it for the treatment of dysentery.

Reports of successful use of cat's claw's in South America as a folk cancer remedy prompted scientists in Germany, Austria, and Italy to take a closer look at the plant. In the 1970s chemical compounds called proanthocyanidins were found to inhibit tumor growth in animals. Studies at the University of Munich in 1985 found several alkaloids in the root of the related *U. tomentosa* with significant immuno-stimulant activity. In Germany and Austria, standardized cat's claw extracts have been given to cancer patients as immune system stimulants. The extracts also have been used to treat rheumatoid arthritis, allergies, herpes infections, gastric ulcers, gastritis, and AIDS. The products are registered prescription drugs in Germany, Austria, and Italy.

The Amazon Basin and other areas of Latin America continue to fascinate those interested in new drug discovery. Latin America has given us many important drugs, including quinine (from *Cinchona* species) whose derivatives have been used as antimalarials for 300 years; curare (from *Strychnos* species) whose derivatives are used as muscle relaxants in surgical procedures; cocaine (from *Erythroxylum coca*) famous for its abuse but also for providing the chemical structure for many anesthetics; and pilocarpine (from *Pilocarpus jaborandi*) used to treat glaucoma. Columbus never found the Spice Islands. Instead, he was the first European to taste the wealth of the Americas and the gifts they would bestow. ✎

OPPOSITE PAGE: A family stops on a trail along the Napo River, a tributary of the Amazon in eastern Peru. The family is collecting wild herbs for local markets and gathering the bounty that the rain forest provides.

Common Names Cranberry, bog cranberry, crane berry, bounce berry

Latin Name *Vaccinium macrocarpon*

Family Ericaceae

Parts Used Fruits

Description Cranberry is a low, mat-forming evergreen shrub with small, dark green, oval leaves. Pink, bell-shaped flowers are followed by slightly egg-shaped, dark red fruits.

Habitat Native to eastern North America, cranberry thrives in acidic bogs and similar wet habitats. It is widely cultivated in the northeastern and north-central United States.

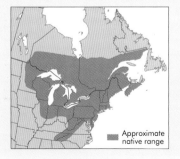

Approximate native range

Cranberry
Vaccinium macrocarpon

C RANBERRY GROWS IN PEATY BOGS AND WETLANDS IN eastern North America, from Newfoundland to Manitoba, south to Virginia and west to Ohio. Many Americans associate cranberries with fall festivals and Thanksgiving feasts. But long before Europeans set foot on the continent, Native Americans feasted on these dark red fruits every year as fall drew to a close. Some tribes boiled the berries and sweetened them with maple sugar. Many added ground cranberries to a mixture of meat and fat to make a nutritious staple called pemmican that would carry them through the long, cold days of winter. Native Americans also used cranberry medicinally. Early settlers adopted cranberry both as a food and a source of medicine, particularly for bladder and kidney complaints. Scientific study of the use of cranberry to treat disorders of the urinary tract began in the 1800s. By the early 1900s, cranberry's healing powers were well-documented. Cranberry is now widely accepted for the treatment and prevention of urinary tract infections.

Traditional and Current Medicinal Uses

NATIVE AMERICANS USED RAW CRANBERRIES PRIMARILY AS A dressing for wounds and to treat lung infections. Early settlers from England learned to use the berries both raw and cooked for a number of ailments, including digestive problems, blood disorders, liver problems, appetite loss, and scurvy. A mixture of boiled cranberries and seal oil was a common folk remedy in New England for treating gallbladder attacks. Cranberries were also valued for their **astringent** properties and as a **diuretic** for helping to prevent kidney stones. Cranberry's reputation for clearing up urinary tract infections blossomed during the late 1800s. Early investigations into this beneficial effect led researchers to hypothesize that cranberry cured urinary tract infections by making urine more acidic; the bacterium that causes most of these infections, *Escherichia coli*, was known to be inhibited by an acidic environment. In the decades that followed, however, this hypothesis was disputed. Nevertheless, cranberry, usually in the form of cranberry juice, was widely recommended by herbalists and conventional doctors to treat urinary tract infections, particularly for women who suffered bouts of the infection.

In 1984 new research revealed that cranberry combats urinary tract infections by preventing bacteria from clinging to the lining of the urinary tract. Since *E. coli* bacteria cannot proliferate in the urinary tract unless they attach to its lining, cranberry appears to prevent them from multiplying and causing infection. In modern herbal medicine, cranberry is used for treating and preventing urinary tract infections. It is also suggested for kidney and bladder stones, incontinence, and for problems associated with enlarged prostate.

Cultivation and Preparation

CRANBERRIES ARE WIDELY CULTIVATED IN SANDY MARSHES AND damp coastal meadows in Massachusetts, New Jersey, Oregon, Washington, and Wisconsin. The fruits are harvested in late summer. Some are pressed for juice. Others are dried for **decoctions**, liquid **extracts**, and capsules of powdered juice concentrate. Pure cranberry juice is acidic and quite sour. Most commercial cranberry juices contain limited amounts of cranberry juice and lots of sweetener. Many herbalists suggest capsules of powdered juice extract as an effective way to take this herb.

Research

CRANBERRY IS RICH IN **TANNINS** (INCLUDING PROANTHO-cyanidins), **flavonoids**, and vitamin C. Researchers have identified proanthocyanidins as the anti-adherence factors in cranberry—substances that prevent infectious *E. coli* from sticking to the lining of the urinary tract. These anti-adhesion effects could potentially help prevent peptic ulcers as well. Many ulcers are caused by infection with *Helicobacter pylori*, and a recent study has shown that the adhesion of several strains of *H. pylori* was inhibited by cranberry. By the same token, cranberry could prevent gum diseases by preventing plaque-causing bacteria from sticking to teeth and gums. However, research is just beginning in these areas and many more studies and clinical trials are needed. Proanthocyanidins, like vitamin C, are also powerful **antioxidants**.

A BERRY GOOD THING

Cranberry belongs to the genus *Vaccinium*, which includes around 450 species of shrubs and trees that occur on several continents in a wide range of habitats. A number of these shrubs produce some of the world's favorite berries. The name *Vaccinium* comes from an ancient Greek word that means a berry-producing plant. In addition to cranberries, *Vaccinium* includes blueberries, whortleberries, huckleberries, cowberries, and bilberries. How cranberries got their common name is not entirely clear. The word "cranberry" first appeared in a letter written by Cape Cod missionary John Eliot in 1647. One folkloric story suggests that colonists dubbed the fruits "crane berries" because cranes congregated in cranberry bogs and gorged themselves on huge quantities of the berries when they were ripe. Another nickname for cranberry is "bounce berry," thought to have been given to the fruit because of the way it tends to bounce or jump when dropped onto a hard surface. Wild cranberries were harvested by Native Americans for centuries. Settlers joined in the harvest enthusiastically when they arrived in eastern North America—perhaps too enthusiastically in some places. In New Jersey, for example, legislation was enacted in the 1700s to make it illegal to pick cranberries before they were ripe. In the U.S., cranberries were not cultivated as a commercial agricultural crop until 1816. Today, Wisconsin, Massachusetts, and New Jersey lead the country in cranberry production.

See Also: *The ABC Clinical Guide to Herbs* by M. Blumenthal, T. Hall, and A. Goldberg, American Botanical Council, 2003; *A Field Guide to Medicinal Plants and Herbs: Eastern and Central North America, 2nd ed.* by S. Foster and J. Duke, Houghton Mifflin, 2000.

VACCINIUM MACROCARPON | Cranberry

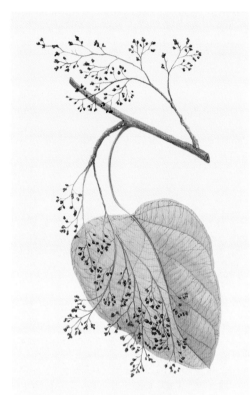

Common Names Curare, velvet leaf, *woorari, grieswurzel, pareira*

Latin Name *Chondrodendron tomentosum*

Family Menispermaceae

Parts Used Leaf, root

Description Curare is a tropical, woody vine that winds its way up into the rain forest canopy, sometimes to a height of 100 feet. It has large, heart-shaped leaves with undersurfaces that are covered with velvety soft white hairs. Small, greenish white flowers grow in clusters and are succeeded by small, bitter-sweet, fleshy fruits that are black or red.

Habitat A South American native, curare grows wild in the Amazon Basin, including Brazil, Peru, Bolivia, Colombia, Ecuador, and Guiana, as well as on some Caribbean islands.

Approximate native range

Curare
Chondrodendron tomentosum

THE LARGE, VELVETY SOFT LEAVES OF THE CURARE VINE give no hint as to the potentially deadly nature of the substances that circulate through their veins. But **extracts** of curare leaves and roots have long been used by indigenous tribes in the Amazon River Basin in South America as an extremely potent arrow poison. "Curare" and "woorari" are Indian names that refer to any number of poisonous mixtures made from curare and other toxic ingredients and into which the tips of darts and arrows were dipped for hunting wild game. The active substance extracted from the curare vine is not actually a toxin, but rather a remarkably strong muscle relaxant. Used carefully, curare has been a valuable surgical tool. It also has a variety of other uses in traditional herbal and conventional medicine.

Traditional and Current Medicinal Uses

AS PART OF THE HERBAL MEDICINE TRADITIONS OF INDIGENOUS tribes in Brazil and Peru, curare root was used to reduce fever, promote menstruation, and increase urine flow. It was also considered a remedy for **edema** (swelling), kidney stones, and inflammation of the testicles. Crushed leaves of the curare vine were applied to bruises and for snakebites. As the plant became known to Europeans, curare found a place in herbal medicine traditions there. Over the centuries it was recommended for urinary infections, kidney stones, rheumatism, as a **diuretic**, and for gonorrhea.

In modern herbal medicine, curare is considered relatively safe as long as preparations containing it are ingested; the powerful muscle-relaxing substance in curare extract typically exerts its deadly effects when introduced directly into the bloodstream. In herbal medicine, **decoctions** of the plant's roots are used for persistent infections of the urinary tract, prostate, and testicles. Curare derivatives have also been widely used in modern conventional medicine as muscle relaxants administered in conjunction with general anesthesia during certain kinds of surgical procedures. They are also used to treat some chronic conditions, including muscle spasms, acute arthritis, and polio.

Cultivation and Preparation

CURARE VINES THRIVE IN THE WARM, HUMID RAIN FOREST environments such as those found in the Amazon River Basin. The herb's leaves and roots are the plant parts used in herbal medicine. In modern conventional medicine, it is curare derivatives that are most often employed.

Research

TUBOCURARINE IS AN **ALKALOID** THAT IS THE ACTIVE COMPONENT of curare. It works to relax muscles by interfering with the transmission of nerve impulses between the nerve axon and the contraction mechanism of a muscle cell. Specifically, it interferes with the normal activity of a certain type of **neurotransmitter** called acetylcholine. In 1844, French physiologist Claude Bernard made the initial discovery that curare extract blocks nerve impulses from being transmitted to muscles, leaving the muscles unable to contract. Tubocurarine was not successfully isolated from curare until 1897, and it was not until 1935 that the compound was obtained in crystalline form. In 1942 a tubocurarine derivative was first used as a muscle-relaxing adjunct to clinical anesthesia. This was a tremendous breakthrough in surgery because it provided doctors with a way to induce safe, short-term, localized relaxation of certain muscles.

Today, tubocurarine has been largely replaced by a number of curare-like compounds that have similar effects but with fewer side effects. In various types of surgeries during which a patient's breathing can be controlled artificially, these compounds are being used along with a general anesthetic to limit muscle contractions. Tubocurarine derivatives are also used to treat paralysis caused by tetanus, a bacteria-caused disease that results in uncontrollable muscle contractions throughout the body.

The chemical actions of the drug tubocurarine are also being investigated for their role in blocking serotonin, a neurotransmitter that is believed to play an important part both in depression and bipolar disorder, as well as in reducing vomiting, in alleviating symptoms of drug withdrawal, and as an anti-anxiety drug.

A POTENT—BUT FLEETING—POISON

In the 1500s, Sir Walter Raleigh and a number of other early explorers were among the first Europeans to report on curare poisons and their effects. But it was Alexander von Humboldt, an adventurous German naturalist who spent five years exploring South America from 1799–1804, who may have been the first non-Indian to witness how curare poisons were prepared. The ingredients varied, but typically included crushed stems and roots of curare vine, along with poison-containing barks of other plants and a bit of venom from snakes, ants, or frogs added for good measure. The mixture was boiled gently for several days until it was reduced to a dark, syrupy paste. Darts and arrows were then tipped with the mixture and used for hunting. Animals pierced by these poisoned weapons would begin to feel the powerful muscle-paralyzing effects of curare as soon as it hit their bloodstream, but death, ultimately from asphyxiation, took from two to twenty minutes depending on the size of the animal. Curare poisoning typically affects the muscles of the toes, ears, and eyes first, then the neck and limbs, and finally, the muscles that control respiration. Curare poisoning is terrifying to contemplate—as it would be possible to feel paralysis spreading through the body until the muscles controlling breathing cease to contract. Interestingly, the effects of curare are not permanent; the poison is cleansed from muscle tissue in about 90 minutes. If breathing is sustained through artificial resuscitation, a victim will recover.

See Also: *Medical Botany: Plants Affecting Human Health* by W. Lewis and M. Elvin-Lewis, John Wiley & Sons, 2003; *Pharmacognosy*, 9th ed. by V. Tyler, L. Brady, J. Robbers, Lea & Febiger, 1998

Dandelion
Taraxacum officinale

FOR MOST PEOPLE, DANDELION IS LITTLE MORE THAN A common and annoying lawn weed. But in the history of herbal medicine, dandelion has played no small role. Although its medicinal values were recognized by the ancient Chinese, dandelion did not become a part of Western herbal medicine until the 10th or 11th century, when it was introduced into Europe by Arab physicians. The French called dandelion *dents de lion*, or "lion's tooth," in reference to the deeply jagged shape of the plant's leaves. They also called it *pissenlit*, which translates as "piss in bed," a linguistic nod to dandelion's strong **diuretic** action. For many centuries, dandelion was used as a detoxifying herb and as a healthful tonic. The leaves were eaten as a vegetable (thought to resemble endive), the roots brewed into a coffee substitute and fermented into beer, and the flowers used to make wine. In herbal medicine today, dandelion is still recommended to stimulate liver and kidney function and for its diuretic, laxative, and anti-rheumatic effects.

Traditional and Current Medicinal Uses

THE FIRST RECORDED REFERENCE TO DANDELION IN CHINESE medical texts was in A.D. 659. The herb was used to treat digestive disorders, appendicitis, breast inflammation, to stimulate milk flow, and to reduce abscesses in the breast and intestines. By the tenth century, Arabian physicians were writing about dandelion in their medical journals. Once introduced to Europe, dandelion became a prized medicinal plant. European herbalists incorporated it into remedies for fever, boils, eye problems, diabetes, and diarrhea. They also used it for liver complaints. Native Americans used dandelion **decoctions** to treat kidney disease, swellings, skin problems, heartburn, and dyspepsia.

In traditional Chinese medicine today, dandelion is prescribed for lung and breast tumors, jaundice and hepatitis, mastitis, abscesses, and urinary tract infections. In Western herbal medicine, the herb is considered a remedy for a wide range of conditions that can benefit from mild diuretic action, including poor digestion, liver disorders, urinary tract infections, and high

Common Names Dandelion, lion's tooth, blowball, *pu gong ying*, swine snout, wild endive

Latin Name *Taraxacum officinale*

Family Asteraceae

Parts Used Leaves, flowers, root

Description A small perennial with a stout taproot, dandelion has long, toothed leaves that form a basal rosette. Yellow, solitary flowers are followed by spherical, fluffy "seed" heads. All parts of the plant exude a somewhat bitter, milky latex.

Habitat Native to Europe and Asia, dandelions grow almost everywhere throughout the world's temperate regions. They thrive in nitrogen-rich soil in pastures, gardens, and lawns and are cultivated in Germany and France.

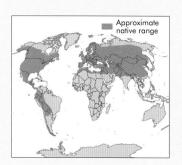

Approximate native range

blood pressure. Fresh or dried dandelion preparations are used to stimulate appetite and ease stomach distress. Dandelion root is used as a mild laxative and to improve digestion, as well as to treat gallstones, jaundice, and other liver problems. Dandelion is also used for chronic joint complaints, rheumatoid arthritis, gout, and skin conditions such as eczema, psoriasis, and acne. It is still respected as one of the best tonic herbs for building the blood and combating anemia. The juice of dandelion root is used to treat diabetes.

Cultivation and Preparation

PROPAGATION OF DANDELIONS IS NOT DIFFICULT; SIMPLY SOW the seeds on any good, somewhat nitrogen-rich soil. In Chinese herbal medicine, plants are cut in spring and used in decoctions. In Western herbal medicine, leaves are harvested any time for fresh use. Roots are lifted in autumn, as the plant is dying back. Roots are pressed for juice and also dried for use in various preparations.

Research

DANDELION CONTAINS A VARIETY OF ACIDS, SUGARS, and other nutrients (iron, zinc, boron, calcium, silicon, and especially potassium), and vitamins A, B complex, C, and D. Despite the fact that dandelion has long been recommended as a diuretic, studies of its potent diuretic properties have yet to identify the substance or substances that are responsible for this action. Some researchers have proposed that dandelion's diuretic activity may simply be the result of the high potassium content of its leaves and roots. While most conventional diuretics cause a loss of potassium from the body, dandelion contains so much potassium that despite its diuretic effects, potassium levels do not generally decline. Some preliminary animal studies on diabetic mice suggest that dandelion may help normalize blood sugar levels. Extracts of dandelion have been shown to have antimicrobial and antibacterial effects, and some animal studies have shown it to have moderate **anti-inflammatory** and **antioxidant** properties. In test tube studies, dandelion **extracts** have also shown antitumor activity against liver, colon, and melanoma cancer cell lines.

BLOWIN' IN THE WIND

Dandelion is a seemingly ubiquitous plant, so it is not surprising that quite a number of superstitions, sayings, and practices are associated with it. The common name "swine snout" comes from the fact that poised-to-open dandelion flowers reminded some people of pig snouts. The nickname "blowball" refers to the fluffy spheres of dandelion fruits (achenes), each of which is fitted with a parachute-like tuft. Making a wish on a dandelion seed head is a common custom, with many variations. It is said that if you can blow all the tufted fruits off in one breath, your wish will come true. Another version of this tradition holds that if you can blow all the fruit off with one blow, you are loved with a passionate love. If some remain, however, your lover has reservations about the relationship. Blowing the fruits off a dandelion head is also thought to be a way to carry your thoughts and dreams to your loved one. On a different note, the number of breaths it takes to denude the seed head was supposed to give the time of day. The flowers were time tellers, too. They were said to close at dusk before the evening dew could dampen them and open again at dawn to greet the sun. The blowball was also thought to predict the weather. In fine weather, it was open and extended. If rain was on its way, though, the fluffy structure would supposedly shut up like an umbrella.

See Also: *Herbal Medicine Expanded Commission E Monographs* by Blumenthal, Goldberg, Brinckmann, American Botanical Council, 2000; *A Field Guide to Medicinal Plants and Herbs: Eastern and Central North America, 2nd ed.* by S. Foster and J. Duke, Houghton Mifflin, 2000.

Devil's Claw
Harpagophytum procumbens

WHEN YOU SEE THE FRUITS OF *HARPAGOPHYTUM procumbens* (botanically they are called capsules), you realize that devil's claw is a perfect name for this African herb. Roughly three inches across, each capsule is studded with long, slightly curved projections that really do resemble the claws of some dreadful creature. Each claw is further armed with sharp thorns that look like small grappling hooks. It is hard to imagine how a plant that produces something so wicked looking could be anything but dangerous. Yet the bulbous underground tubers of devil's claw are the source of herbal remedies that many claim can relieve the pain and inflammation of arthritis and rheumatism. The Khoikhoi of the Kalahari Desert and other indigenous peoples of the region used devil's claw as a healing herb for thousands of years. It was introduced into Western medicine in the early 1900s. Today devil's claw is widely used in Europe and Canada as a treatment for arthritis pain. And although studies that attempt to substantiate its effects are still far from conclusive, the popularity of devil's claw as a pain reliever is also growing in the United States.

Common Names Devil's claw, grapple plant, grapple apple, wood spider

Latin Name *Harpagophytum procumbens*

Family Pedaliaceae

Parts Used Secondary roots

Description A trailing perennial with creeping stems up to five feet long, devil's claw has a thick, carrot-like primary root surrounded by tuberous secondary roots. Its stems bear grayish green leaves, tubular violet flowers, and barbed, woody fruits.

Habitat Devil's claw is native to arid savannahs of the Kalahari and Transvaal regions of southern Africa and to Madagascar. It often grows where natural vegetation has been removed.

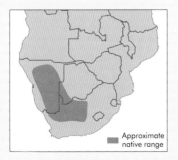

Approximate native range

Traditional and Current Medicinal Uses

INDIGENOUS CULTURES OF SOUTHERN AFRICA USED DEVIL'S CLAW root in remedies to treat pain, digestive complaints, migraine, fever, allergic reactions, and pain during childbirth. Ointments made from devil's claw root were applied to heal sores, boils, ulcers, and other skin problems. In recent years, devil's claw has become a popular remedy in Europe, Canada, and the U.S. for easing the pain of rheumatism and arthritis. It is also taken as a general tonic and for many other conditions. Germany's Commission E, a panel of experts that makes recommendations on herbal medicine, has approved use of devil's claw root as an appetite stimulant, to ease stomach upsets, and to treat degenerative disorders of the musculoskeletal system. Herbal practitioners also recommend devil's claw root for tendinitis, blood diseases, headache, allergies, lower back pain, neuralgia, fever, and topically for ulcers, boils, and skin lesions.

Cultivation and Preparation

DEVIL'S CLAW GROWS IN SANDY SOIL IN FULL SUN. THE BARBED capsules are designed to catch in the fur and feet of animals and in the process, disperse the seeds of the parent plant. Devil's claw can be propagated from seed, but so far attempts at cultivating it outside its native habitat have been largely unsuccessful. Nearly all devil's claw available commercially is wild harvested. The secondary storage roots, or tubers, of the plant are used in herbal medicine. These are harvested when the plant is dormant and sliced and dried for use in various preparations, from **tinctures** to tablets.

Research

DEVIL'S CLAW TUBERS CONTAIN A NUMBER OF ACTIVE CHEMIcal constituents that have been studied extensively in the laboratory. One of the most important of these initially appeared to be harpagoside, which belongs to a general group of compounds known as **iridoid glycosides**. The secondary tuberous roots of the devil's claw plant contain roughly twice as much harpagoside as the primary roots and are the chief source of devil's claw used medicinally and in research. In several animal studies and a few clinical studies, **extracts** of the tubers that contained primarily harpagoside have demonstrated **anti-inflammatory** and **analgesic** effects. For example, in one trial devil's claw extract was found to reduce pain associated with osteoarthritis as effectively as a well-known analgesic drug. Another study involving about 200 men and women with chronic low back pain reported that subjects who received daily doses of devil's claw extract experienced less pain than those who received a **placebo**. However, other studies on arthritis patients have found devil's claw extracts to be ineffective in reducing either pain or inflammation. As researchers try to sort out these conflicting results, one thing has become clear: Harpagoside alone is less helpful for alleviating pain than whole extracts of the tuber, indicating that other compounds are involved in the herb's effects. In other studies, devil's claw has been shown to exhibit significant **antioxidant** activity. There is also good evidence that the herb stimulates digestion and may help lower both blood pressure and heart rate.

MYSTERY MEDICINE

Use of devil's claw as a medicinal herb was a well-kept secret among the indigenous tribes that inhabit the arid regions of southern Africa where this plant can be found hugging the sandy, rocky ground. Europeans became aware of devil's claw's medicinal value during the very early 1900s. According to one story, G. H. Mehnert, a farmer in South Africa, observed a case in which a Khoikhoi man was treated and cured of a serious illness by a tribal doctor in 1904. Curious to know the cure, Mehnert pressed the tribal healer for information and learned that the tuberous root he used to cure the ill man came from the devil's claw plant. Mehnert began advocating the use of the tubers as a medicinal tea. News of this African herb reached Europe by way of Germany. In the 1950s, scientists began investigating the chemical make-up of devil's claw tubers and over the next few decades, considerable research was carried out on the effects of extracts of the roots as well as their various active components. This research continues, but a clear understanding of devil's claw and how—or if—it works remains elusive.

See Also: *Herbal Medicine Expanded Commission E Monographs* by M. Blumenthal, A. Goldberg, and J. Brinckmann, American Botanical Council, 2000; *Medicinal Herbs History, Use, Recommended Dosages & Cautions* by S. Foster, Interweave Press, 1998.

Dog Rose

Rosa canina

THE DOG ROSE IS THE CLASSIC WILD ROSE OF ENGLISH hedgerows and rambling cottage gardens. Its simple, single flowers are sweetly scented. As the flowers fade, the fleshy receptacles at their bases swell to contain numerous hairy seeds and to form the familiar red rose hips (a name derived from the Anglo-Saxon *hiope*). Sometimes called "dagger rose" because of the sharpness of its jagged thorns, the origin of this rose's other common name—"dog rose"—is less clear. One popular explanation is that it is a corruption of the medieval Latin name *rosa canina*, which came from the ancient Greek word *cynorrhodon*, the belief that the plant's roots could cure the bite of a rabid dog. It may be that "dagger" was shortened to "dag" and then "dog." Other sources suggest that the term "dog" was derogatory, implying that this rose was of little value in a garden. What is known is that the dog rose has great value in herbal medicine. Both its vitamin C-rich hips and oil-laden petals have been used for centuries to treat colds and stomach upsets, minor infections, scurvy, and stress.

Traditional and Current Medicinal Uses

THE REMAINS OF ROSE HIPS HAVE BEEN FOUND AT PREHISTORIC dwellings sites, suggesting that people have valued roses since before recorded history. Roses have been cultivated for thousands of years, both as food and medicine. Asian species were used in traditional Chinese medicine and other types of roses were used medicinally by the ancient Greeks, Romans, and Persians. The Greek poet Anacreon referred to their therapeutic value in his poems, and in A.D. 77 the Roman botanist and physician Pliny the Elder listed more than 30 disorders for which there were known rose remedies. Roses were widely grown in the Middle Ages for their medicinal value. Rose petals were used to treat diarrhea, sores, coughs and colds, aching joints, nervous tension, lethargy, and a host of other complaints. Roses were believed to staunch blood in any part of the body. Rose water, invented in the first century A.D. by the Persian physician Ibn Sina, was prescribed for eye inflammation and

Common Names Dog rose, dagger rose

Latin Name *Rosa canina*

Family Rosaceae

Parts Used Fruits (hips), seeds, petals, oil

Description A shrub with arched, downward-curving branches, Rosa canina has thorny stems, smooth green leaves, and clusters of five-petaled flowers that are white or tinged with pink. The flowers are followed by large, oval, scarlet hips.

Habitat Native to Europe and Asia, *R. canina* is also naturalized in North America. It grows wild in hedges, along roadsides, and at the edges of meadows and woodlands.

Approximate native range

to refresh the spirit and strengthen the heart. Rose oil, also known as attar (or otto) of roses, was applied to chapped and irritated skin. The seeds of roses were traditionally used as a **diuretic** and a remedy for various disorders of the urinary tract. During the 1800s in Britain, rose petals were used as an **astringent** and in other pharmaceutical preparations, including as a flavoring for medicines. When citrus fruits have been scarce, as in World War II, rose hips have been used as a source of vitamin C to prevent scurvy.

In modern herbal medicine, rose hips and petals are used in various preparations to treat colds, bronchial infections, gastrointestinal complaints, diarrhea, and skin irritations. The hips are mildly diuretic and have a slight laxative effect. They are also a source of vitamin C (richer than oranges) and an ingredient in rose hip tea and many "natural" vitamin preparations. Rose petals are often used in tonics and gargles for sore throats and mouth sores. Rose oil is widely used in aromatherapy for depression and nervous tension.

Cultivation and Preparation

ROSES CAN BE PROPAGATED FROM SEEDS, CUTTINGS, OR BUDDINGS. They do best in fairly heavy clay loam that is slightly acidic and enriched with organic matter. At least six hours of sun per day are required for roses to flourish. For herbal preparations, rose hips are gathered when ripe; the seeds and irritant hairs they contain are removed. Petals are collected from newly opened flowers; they are used fresh, crushed, dried, or distilled for rose oil and rose water preparations. Oil can also be extracted from the seeds.

Research

ROSE HIPS CONTAIN A SIGNIFICANT AMOUNT OF VITAMIN C, AS WELL AS vitamins A, B, E, and K. They also contain **flavonoids**, sugars, **tannins**, organic acids, and pectin. The acids and pectin are largely responsible for rose's mild laxative and diuretic properties. The petals contain tannins, which make them mildly astringent. Rose oil contains citronellol, a compound with antirheumatic action. One recent clinical study showed that powdered *Rosa canina* reduced pain and improved well-being in patients with osteoarthritis.

Roses have been cultivated for their fragrance and beauty, as well as their medicinal value for centuries. The ancient Greeks may have introduced roses from Greece to southern Italy, beginning a long tradition of rose cultivation in Europe. That first rose is thought to possibly have been the red *Rosa gallica*. The Romans cultivated *R. gallica*, using it lavishly in ceremonies and celebrations. It became both a symbol of love and of secrecy. As early as 477 B.C., the Romans practiced the custom of suspending a red rose above a council table to indicate a meeting was confidential and that all topics discussed *sub rosa*— "under the rose"—were to be kept secret and confidential. Even today, the ornate plaster decoration in the center of a ceiling, often located in the dining room, is known as a rose and is a throwback to this custom. The Romans introduced roses to England, and centuries later the rose is still the emblem of that country. In addition to being associated with love, the rose also became a symbol of sweetness in both life and death. In England, it was a custom to plant a rose bush on the grave of a lover who died before marriage. The rose and its thorns were thought to possess many powers useful in love divination, charms, and potions. The symbolism continues today. Florists still emphasize that roses' colors have special meanings: Red roses represent true, undying love; yellow roses symbolize friendship; white roses stand for purity.

ROSA CANINA | Dog Rose

See Also: *Medicinal Plants of the World* by B. van Wyk and M. Wink, Timber Press, 2004; *Herbal Medicine, 2nd ed.* by R. Weiss and V. Fintelmann, Thieme, 2000.

Dong Quai
Angelica sinensis

Common Names Dong quai, *dang gui, tang kwei/kuei*

Latin Name *Angelica sinensis*

Family Apiaceae

Parts Used Roots

Description A sturdy, erect perennial that grows three to seven feet tall, dong quai has large bright green leaves with slightly serrated edges and hollow, fluted, purplish stems. It produces umbrella-shaped clusters (umbels) of greenish-white flowers followed by winged fruits. The large, yellow-brown roots (rhizomes) have creamy white interiors and are highly branched, with multiple, tentacle-like extensions.

Habitat Native to cool, damp, mountainous regions of China, Korea, and Japan, the herb grows at high altitude along riverbanks and in moist ravines. It is widely cultivated in China and Japan.

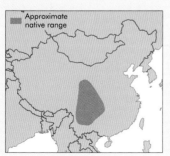

Approximate native range

For more than two thousand years, *Angelica sinensis* has been used as a medicine, tonic, and spice throughout China, Korea, and Japan. The Chinese name for this herb, *dong quai*, translates as "proper order." Fittingly, preparations made from its dried roots have been used in traditional Chinese medicine as a means to help restore proper order and health to the human body. The herb is sometimes called "female ginseng" because it is the most commonly prescribed Chinese herbal medicine used to treat the health complaints of women. Among several species in the genus *Angelica*, dong quai is considered the most valuable medicinally. Japanese angelica (*Angelica acutiloba*) has similar properties to *A. sinensis* and is used in many of the same ways.

Traditional and Current Medicinal Uses

In traditional Chinese medicine, dong quai is said to have sweet, acrid, bitter, and warm properties. It is used in treating a variety of reproductive, circulatory, and respiratory conditions. *A. sinensis* has been used for centuries for menstrual pain and cramping, regulating and balancing the menstrual cycle, and alleviating menopausal symptoms. The herb is considered helpful in preventing anemia in women who experience significant blood loss as a result of heavy menstrual flow. As a "warming" herb, it is thought to increase circulation, especially to the extremities, to help decrease chest pain associated with heart disease, to lower blood pressure, and to regulate irregular heartbeat. Traditionally, dong quai has also been prescribed for abdominal pain and injuries, arthritis, migraine headaches, liver ailments, constipation, and to fight infection and promote sleep.

More recently, the herb is prescribed for alleviating premenstrual syndrome (PMS) and, because it contains **phytoestrogens** (plant estrogens), as an estrogen replacement in postmenopausal women to relieve symptoms of menopause, especially hot flashes. In general, dong quai is prescribed for chronic conditions and as a preventative, and is used in combination with other herbs; it is rarely, if ever, prescribed in cases of severe illness.

Cultivation and Preparation

DONG QUAI CAN BE GROWN IN FERTILE, MOIST SOIL FROM seed sown in spring; it does well in shade or sun. The plant flowers in late summer and the seeds ripen in autumn. It takes three years for the plant to reach maturity, at which time the **rhizomes** (underground stems) are lifted, sliced and dried, and then made into tablets, powders, and other medicinal forms. Chopped, dried rhizomes are often added to soups in China. Drinking a daily glass or two of a tonic made from dong quai and other bitter herbs is also common.

Research

A SIGNIFICANT NUMBER OF LABORATORY AND ANIMAL studies have been carried out on *A. sinensis*, many of them in Asia where the herb is widely used. However, concrete scientific evidence regarding its effects in people is still weak; more human studies are needed. The herb's pharmacological actions are partly due to its **volatile oil** and partly to various compounds, including phytoestrogens and **coumarins**, extracted from the root with hot water. Physiologically, the phytoestrogens exert some estrogen-like effects in the body when normal levels of natural estrogens are low, as is the case in menopausal and postmenopausal women. Coumarin compounds are known vasodilators and antispasmodics; they may also stimulate certain types of immune system cells and probably are the source of the herb's **anti-inflammatory** effects. Certain components of dong quai appear to act as **calcium-channel blockers,** causing smooth muscles to relax. This may account for the relief of uterine and other muscle tissue cramping as well as migraines. By dilating blood vessels, it may also increase blood flow and lower blood pressure. According to some animal research, dong quai may relieve pain better than aspirin. This **analgesic** activity, combined with the herb's muscle-relaxing properties, could support its use for muscle cramps, headaches, migraines, and arthritis.

CAUTION Dong quai contains substances that may induce photosensitivity in some people. Among its active ingredients are psoralens and safrole, both of which are thought to be carcinogenic in high doses. In an in vitro study carried out in 2002, dong quai induced the growth of the MCF-7 Breast Cancer cell line independent of estrogenic activity.

THE "PROPER ORDER" HERB

Many herbs are named for their association with legends or folktales, and dong quai is no exception. In the case of this important Chinese herb—so the story goes—a young, newly married Chinese man decided to leave his beloved wife and go into the mountains. He was not keen to be a hermit but instead wanted to prove to men in the village, who had questioned his manliness, that he was strong. Before setting out, the young husband and his wife agreed that if he had not returned after three years, she would accept this as a sign he had not survived and would take another husband. The young man left and the years rolled by. After three years passed and there was no sign of her husband, the wife accepted her fate and remarried. She was horrified and heartbroken when her husband returned a short time later, and was so saddened by this turn of events that she fell seriously ill. The husband made an herbal medicine from a plant root brought with him from the mountains. His wife took it and was cured. The herb was given the name "dong quai" in honor of the tale, which can be translated as "should come back" and "missing the husband" as well as "proper order."

See Also: World Health Organization (WHO) Monographs on Selected Medicinal Plants, Vol. 2, 2002; Herbal Emissaries: Bringing Chinese Herbs to the West by S. Foster and Y. Chongxi, Healing Arts Press, 1992.

ANGELICA SINENSIS | Dong Quai

Echinacea
Echinacea purpurea

E CHINACEA IS A NATIVE NORTH AMERICAN WILDFLOWER often called purple coneflower because of its distinctive color and shape. The genus name, *Echinacea*, comes from the Greek *echinos*, meaning "hedgehog," and refers to the flower's central cone of stiff, upright scales surrounded by striking purple-to-pink petals. It has become one of the most popular and widely used herbs in modern American and European herbal medicine. Three species of the herb are used in herbal medicine products: *Echinacea purpurea, E. angustifolia,* and *E. pallida.*

Traditional and Current Medicinal Uses

ECHINACEA'S USE AS A MEDICINAL PLANT BEGAN HUNDREDS OF years ago with Native Americans, who used it externally for treating wounds and snakebite and internally for more purposes than any other plant. The Choctaw also used preparations of echinacea root to treat coughs and digestive upsets. The Comanche used a root **decoction** to ease the pain of sore throat and held pieces of fresh root against teeth for toothache. The Sioux valued the roots as a cure for rabies. Echinacea was introduced to Western medicine in the 1890s. Then the herb quickly gained a loyal following among American **Eclectic** physicians who incorporated the use of medicinal plants into their practice. It was recommended for respiratory infections and skin problems, as well as meningitis, diphtheria, tonsillitis, sinus infections, indigestion, diarrhea, cholera, and certain types of cancer. By the 1930s, echinacea's popularity began to wane in the United States, especially after the introduction of sulfa drugs and antibiotics. In Germany, in the late 1930s, however, the herb became increasingly popular, largely through the efforts of Dr. Gerhard Madaus, founder of the German pharmaceutical company Madaus AG, who pioneered research into echinacea.

In modern herbal medicine, echinacea is primarily used to reduce the symptoms and duration of colds, flu, and upper respiratory tract infections, and to help boost immune system activity. Echinacea is thought to be an immune system stimulant that promotes healing through

Common Names Echinacea, purple coneflower, coneflower, purple echinacea

Latin Names *Echinacea purpurea, E. pallida, E. angustifolia*

Family Asteraceae

Parts Used Whole plant

Description A tall, hardy perennial that grows to three feet in height, echinacea has erect, branched stems and oval, lanceolate, bristly leaves. Large, purple daisy-like flowers with conical orange-brown centers packed with bristly scales are borne on relatively short stalks.

Habitat Native to central and eastern North America, echinacea grows in prairies and open woodlands. *E. purpurea* is widely cultivated for the herbal medicine trade and as a garden ornamental.

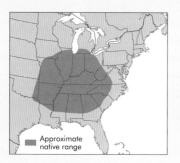

Approximate native range

its **anti-inflammatory**, antibiotic, antiviral, and detoxifying effects. It is prescribed for abscesses and other slow-healing wounds, skin diseases,chronic fatigue syndrome, fungal infections, hay fever, asthma, urinary tract infections, sinusitis, early stages of cough, flu, and colds, as a gargle for sore throat, and to prevent premature aging and skin damage from ultraviolet light.

Cultivation and Preparation

ECHINACEA PURPUREA IS CULTIVATED WIDELY IN THE UNITED States and Europe for the herbal medicine market. It requires rich, somewhat sandy soil and full sun. It can be propagated by seed, root cuttings, or division. Leaves and other above-ground parts are harvested in mid-summer, while the plant is flowering. Roots and **rhizomes** (underground stems) are harvested in autumn and dried. Echinacea—often a mixture of one or more medicinal species—is available in **extracts**, tablets, **tinctures**, capsules, and ointments.

Research

ECHINACEA IS ONE OF THE MOST WELL-STUDIED HERBS IN herbal medicine today. Precisely how preparations of the herb exert their effects, however, is not completely understood. Laboratory and animal studies suggest echinacea contains active substances that stimulate the immune system to counter bacterial, viral, and fungal infections, reduce inflammation, strengthen blood vessels, destroy **free radicals**, increase active white blood cells in circulation, stimulate production of interferon (a natural antiviral substance), and prevent sun damage to the skin. Research has produced conflicting results. Clinical studies, for example, have shown that echinacea appears to reduce severity and duration of cold and flu symptoms. Other studies have found preparations of the herb did not prevent such infections from developing. More studies are required on the types of preparations and dosages that may deliver predictable, consistent results.

> CAUTION High doses of echinacea can cause nausea. Some evidence suggests that echinacea may increase the risk of side effects of drugs used concurrently, including the birth control pill.

THE RISE, FALL, AND RISE OF ECHINACEA

Echinacea was first introduced to conventional medicine in the U.S. by Dr. John King, an Ohio physician who belonged to the Eclectic School of healing arts, which relied heavily on the use of American medicinal plants in its practices. King mentioned the therapeutic actions of *E. purpurea* in the 1852 edition of *The Eclectic Dispensatory of the United States of America*. Around 1870, Dr. H.C.F. Meyer of Nebraska, having learned of the herb's uses and effects from local Native American tribes, concocted his own special echinacea preparation, which he marketed as Meyer's Blood Purifier. He claimed it would cure everything from rattlesnake bite to typhoid. Not until the late 1890s, however, did echinacea's popularity really take off in the U.S. In 1895, the pharmaceutical firm of Lloyd Brothers in Cincinnati, Ohio, began manufacturing the first pharmaceutical preparations of echinacea; shortly thereafter, interest blossomed. From then until the late 1920s, echinacea became the fastest selling and most widely prescribed remedy derived from a Native American medicinal plant in the U.S. Then, toward the end of the 1920s, echinacea began to fall out of favor in the American medical community along with many other plant-based medicines. Its popularity increased in Germany, however. Echinacea continued to be largely ignored as an herbal remedy in the U.S. until the 1970s, when American herbalists "rediscovered" the herb, and herbal product manufacturers began to produce and promote it. Echinacea is now among the top-selling herbal supplements in the U. S. each year.

See Also: Herbal Medicine Expanded Commission E Monographs by M. Blumenthal, A. Goldberg, J. Brinckmann, American Botanical Council, 2000; A Field Guide to Medicinal Plants & Herbs: Eastern & Central North America, 2nd ed. by S. Foster, J. Duke, Houghton Mifflin, 2000.

Common Names Elecampane, elfdock, elfwort, scabwort, horseheal

Latin Name *Inula helenium*

Family Asteraceae

Parts Used Rhizomes (underground stem), roots

Description A four-to-eight-feet tall, robust perennial, *Inula* has thick rhizomes, erect, softly hairy stems, and large, pointed, irregularly toothed leaves with woolly undersides. Yellow flowers, three to four inches in diameter and shaped like shaggy daisies, bloom in summer.

Habitat Native to southeastern Europe, *Inula* has been naturalized throughout Europe, in North America, and in eastern Asia. It is cultivated in eastern Europe and China. It grows around the edges of fields, woods, and roadsides and is planted as a garden ornamental.

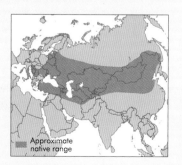

Approximate native range

Elecampane
Inula helenium

LONG PRIZED AS A GENTLE TONIC ESPECIALLY USEFUL FOR respiratory ailments, elecampane can trace its history as a medicinal plant back to ancient Greece and Rome. There it was commonly used as a bitter vegetable, eaten after a heavy meal to relieve indigestion. A strikingly statuesque plant, elecampane most likely moved beyond the borders of its original habitat through widespread planting as a garden plant as well as a medicinal herb. Whatever the case, the herb is now naturalized in temperate parts of Europe, the British Isles, the eastern United States, and eastern Asia. In addition to its medicinal value, the roots of elecampane were often candied and old herbals contain many recipes for conserves made from the plant.

Traditional and Current Medicinal Uses

ELECAMPANE'S RELATIVES HAVE LONG BEEN A PART OF **Ayurvedic medicine**. In India, it is known as *pushkaramula* and used as a lung tonic and **analgesic**. The closely related species, *I. cappa* and *I. racemosa*, are used in traditional medicine in southern China and the Himalaya region, respectively, primarily for bronchial complaints and skin infections. Herbalists throughout Europe used elecampane as a folk remedy for lung ailments such as pneumonia, whooping cough, asthma, and bronchitis. It was widely employed as a cure for skin infections and to calm upset stomachs, relieve diarrhea, and cleanse the intestines of certain types of parasitic worms. Elecampane tea was used to quiet coughing and stimulate digestion. The herb also was said to relieve dropsy (edema).

Elecampane is seldom used in modern herbal medicine for its **expectorant** and **diuretic** properties. It is prescribed for bronchitis, hay fever, coughs, asthma, tuberculosis, tonsillitis, pleurisy, and weak digestion. Rarely used alone, the herb is typically added to compound medicines for treating these conditions, often in the form of syrups, lozenges, or pills. In Chinese medicine, it is used to treat certain cancers. Topically, the herb has been used to heal skin inflammations and for facial neuralgia and sciatica.

Cultivation and Preparation

ELECAMPANE THRIVES IN FAIRLY RICH, MOIST CLAY SOIL IN A sunny or partly shaded position. Although slow to start from seed, it is easily propagated by division of roots in spring or autumn. Only the root is used in herbal medicine. Roots are typically harvested from two-year-old plants in autumn. They can be used fresh to make **extracts** and syrups, sliced and dried for use in various preparations, or distilled for oil.

Research

THE ROOTS OF ELECAMPANE CONTAIN UP TO 44 PERCENT OF the **polysaccharide** inulin, which has been shown to have expectorant properties. Nevertheless, the efficacy of elecampane for bronchial-related conditions has not yet been experimentally substantiated. Elecampane has been shown to aid in maintaining a good balance of intestinal bacteria and in soothing inflamed tissue. The herb is slightly sweet, and has been sometimes recommended for diabetics. (It should not be confused with the hormone insulin.) Elecampane also contains an **essential oil** that contains alantolactone. In Germany, experiments carried out in the late 1990s showed that alantolactone was active against tuberculosis. Both alantolactone and the essential oil exhibit **anti-inflammatory** and antiseptic properties and have been shown to stimulate the immune system. Alantolactone has also proved useful in treating roundworm, hookworm, whipworm, and threadworm infections in children and adults. When administered to laboratory mice, extracts of elecampane acted as a sedative. In other animal experiments, the herb influenced both blood sugar levels and blood pressure. In one clinical trial of chemotherapy patients with malignant tumors, a **decoction** containing *Inula* extract helped prevent chemotherapy-induced nausea and vomiting without any side effects.

CAUTION In large doses, the lactones contained in elecampane can be toxic. Even medicinal doses can irritate mucous membranes and cause skin sensitization and allergic dermatitis. Germany's Commission E lists elecampane as an unapproved herb in light of the risks of allergic reactions and since the activity of the herb and its preparations have not been adequately substantiated for bronchial-related conditions.

Considerable, and sometimes confusing, folklore surrounds the origin of elecampane's scientific and common names. The genus name, *Inula*, is believed to be a Latinized version of the Greek word *helenion*. Some sources suggest that this name, in turn, is a reference to Helenus, son of Priam. Other sources believe it refers to the lovely Helen of Troy. One story has it that Helen was gathering the herb when she was abducted by Paris. Another version describes how elecampane sprang from her tears on the same occasion—or from the tears of the goddess Helena. Yet another legend suggests that the "Helen" in question was actually the island of Helena, where the herbs grew especially well. The origin of the common name "elecampane" is somewhat more straightforward. It comes from medieval apothecaries' Latin name for the herb, *enula* and *campana*, meaning "fields." In short, elecampane means "*Inula* of the fields." Other nicknames have come into use through the centuries. Some were based on the herb's medicinal powers, not just in people but also in animals. "Scabwort" developed from the herb's alleged effectiveness in healing scabs on sheep. "Horseheal" grew out of the belief that elecampane cured skin ailments of horses. In the British Isles, the herb (known as "elf-dock" or "elfwort") was thought to be a favorite plant of the little people.

INULA HELENIUM | Elecampane

See Also: *A Field Guide to Medicinal Plants and Herbs: Eastern and Central North America 2nd ed.* by S. Foster and J. Duke, Houghton Mifflin, 2000; *Medicinal Plants of the World* by B. van Wyk and M. Wink, Timber Press, 2004.

Common Names Eleuthero, Siberian ginseng, *ci wu jia*, Russian ginseng, touch-me-not

Latin Name *Eleutherococcus senticosus*, synonym *Acantopanax senticosus*

Family Araliaceae

Parts Used Roots, stems, bark

Description Eleuthero is a woody shrub with a thick, twisted root, very prickly stems, and large, palmately divided compound leaves. Umbels (umbrella-like clusters) of tiny inconspicuous flowers are followed by small blue-black berries.

Habitat Native to northern Asia, eleuthero grows in the taiga forests of southeastern Russia, northern China, Korea, and Japan.

Approximate native range

Eleuthero
Eleutherococcus senticosus

ELEUTHERO IS OFTEN CALLED SIBERIAN GINSENG BECAUSE it belongs to the same family, Araliaceae, as true ginsengs (*Panax* spp.) and like them is considered an **adaptogen**—a substance that helps the body adapt to stress and is more important for maintaining good health than treating disease. Eleuthero attracted attention in herbal medicine in the 1940s, when Russian researchers began promoting the herb as a cheaper alternative to ginseng with similar benefits. However, eleuthero does not contain the same chemical compounds known to be the active ingredients in ginseng. Nevertheless, eleuthero has gained a reputation as an invigorating tonic—enthusiastically endorsed by Russian cosmonauts and athletes—that is recommended for reducing physical and mental stress, alleviating fatigue, improving concentration, and as a performance enhancer under stressful conditions. A growing body of scientific evidence suggests that some of the claims made about eleuthero as a therapy for stress and stress-related illnesses are grounded in fact.

Traditional and Current Medicinal Uses

THE CHINESE HAVE USED ELEUTHERO FOR AT LEAST 2,000 YEARS. Called *ci wu jia* in traditional Chinese medicine, the root and root bark were used in preparations designed to prevent respiratory infections, colds and flu, and heart ailments. Eleuthero was prized as a tonic that could restore vigor and vitality, improve general health, restore memory, promote healthy appetite, and increase stamina. Farther north, people living in parts of southeastern Russia used eleuthero in folk remedies that were said to fight infection and increase performance, stamina, and general good health. In the 1940s, Russian scientists studied eleuthero extensively. Use of the herb became very popular in Russia and other European countries. Eventually, enthusiasm for the herb spread to the U.S. Today eleuthero is recommended as a tonic to counter fatigue and improve strength and stamina, to improve physical performance and memory, to prevent colds and flu, to stimulate the immune system and counter chronic fatigue syndrome, to restore health following convalescence, chemotherapy, or radiation exposure, and to combat viruses, including herpes simplex.

Cultivation and Preparation

IDEAL CONDITIONS FOR GROWING ELEUTHERO INCLUDE RICH, moist, well-drained soil and full sun or light shade. Starting new plants from seed is difficult, as germination is slow and erratic. Most propagation is done by stem and root cuttings. The roots are used in herbal preparations. They are harvested in autumn and dried. Dried root powder is used to make **tinctures** and **decoctions;** pills and capsules are also available. Most eleuthero imported to the U.S. comes from Russia.

Research

THE ACTIVE INGREDIENTS IN ELEUTHERO ROOT ARE SEVERAL eleutherosides—which include different kinds of compounds. Until recently, most research carried out on eleuthero took place in Russia. Although large, randomized trials on the herb have yet to be conducted, smaller studies have supported eleuthero's claimed therapeutic effects in a number of areas. As an immune-stimulating agent, eleuthero appears to energize the body's defenses, particularly by stimulating specific types of immune cells called helper T-lymphocytes and natural killer cells. This immune cell-stimulating effect suggests that eleuthero may prove valuable in long-term treatment of immune system diseases, such as chronic fatigue syndrome, lupus, and HIV. Eleuthero has also been shown to decrease the severity, duration, and frequency of attacks of herpes simplex infections and slow replication of viruses causing influenza and the common cold. In animal studies, eleuthero has been shown to exert a protective effect against toxins and damaging chemicals, including chemotherapy drugs and radiation. Some studies have shown eleuthero to improve memory. Results of investigations into whether the herb enhances physical stamina and performance, however, have been mixed.

CAUTION Most herbalists recommend using eleuthero for no more than three months. It should be avoided by individuals with high blood pressure.

THE RUSSIAN TONIC

Thirty years ago, eleuthero was largely unknown in the West. Russian botanists first described and named the herb *Hedra sentocosa* in 1856, but later realized it belonged elsewhere in the taxonomic scheme and changed its name to *Eleutherococcus senticosus.* In the 1940s, Russian scientist I. I. Brekhman mounted an intensive investigation into the plants of Russia in the hopes of finding new adaptogens similar to Asian ginseng in their effects. The quest turned up eleuthero as a likely candidate. For decades, Brekhman and several colleagues studied eleuthero's effects in animals and people. Clinical research supporting the herb's supposed effects on stamina and endurance was so highly regarded that eleuthero became an integral part of Russian life. While American astronauts used amphetamines to help their bodies tolerate the stress of being in space, Russian cosmonauts took eleuthero. Soviet athletes used the herb as they trained for the 1984 Moscow Olympics, and excelled in many endurance events. Soon, many Russians, from divers and sailors to miners and explorers, were using eleuthero—anyone whose job and life depended on being able to perform under physically stressful conditions. In 1986, when the Chernobyl nuclear reactor exploded, thousands around and downwind from ground zero were given eleuthero to counter the effects of radiation. Eleuthero was first marketed in the United States in the 1970s, and is now one of the top-selling herbal dietary supplements in the country.

See Also: Herbal Medicine Expanded Commission E Monographs by M. Blumenthal, A. Goldberg, and J. Brinckmann, American Botanical Council, 2000; *Herbal Emissaries: Bringing Chinese Herbs to the West* by S. Foster and Y. Chongxi, Healing Arts Press, 1992.

Common Names English lavender, common lavender

Latin Name *Lavandula angustifolia*

Family Lamiaceae

Parts Used Flowers, essential oil

Description Growing as a small, brittle shrub, lavender has a much-branched woody stem and narrow gray-green leaves. Small bluish-purple flowers are borne on slender spikes that rise up above the foliage. All parts of the plant are aromatic.

Habitat Lavender is native to the mountains of the Mediterranean region. It flourishes in sunny, stony habitats and now grows throughout much of Europe and is widely cultivated in the United States and Australia. There are many cultivated varieties.

Approximate native range

English Lavender
Lavandula angustifolia

THE CLEAN, POWERFUL, BUT PLEASING AROMA OF LAVENder is familiar to most people as a scent in many soaps, shampoos, sachets, and potpourris. It is a classic fragrance that has been associated with bathing—and purity of the spirit as well as the body—since ancient Rome. The Romans and the Libyans were said to have scented their bathwater with lavender, a fact that is reflected in the Latin root of the herb's name: *lavare* means "to wash." The ancient Egyptians used the herb as a perfume. In herbal medicine, lavender has long been respected for its calming, relaxing effects. Today it is used much as it has been for centuries, to soothe digestive upsets, ease headaches, and relieve anxiety, tension, and stress.

Traditional and Current Medicinal Uses

IN THE MEDICINAL TRADITIONS OF ANCIENT PERSIA, GREECE, and Rome, lavender was recognized for its antiseptic properties. It was used to disinfect sick rooms and hospitals. Use of lavender spread from the Mediterranean to India, and later to Tibet. In both regions, lavender gained a reputation for helping quell anxiety and clear the mind. In Tibet, lavender was, and still is, used in traditional treatments for mental illness. In **Ayurvedic medicine** the herb was valued in treating depression associated with digestive dysfunction. By the late Middle Ages, lavender was commonly grown in monastery gardens, where it was always at hand for use in medicinal preparations. It was used, distilled in oil, for dressing wounds and cuts, bites, stings, coughs and colds, chest infections, rheumatic aches, and flatulence. As a soothing tonic, such as lavender water or lavender tea, the herb was prescribed to relieve insomnia, tension, and depression. A sprig of fresh lavender tucked behind the ear was believed to cure headaches.

In modern herbal medicine, lavender is most commonly prescribed as a mild, calming sedative for insomnia and sleep disorders, to settle indigestion and nervous intestinal complaints, and to treat minor nervous ailments. Lavender oil is widely used in aromatherapy, for relieving headaches, migraines, and emotional upsets, as a rub for circulatory disorders and rheumatic ailments, and as a mild antiseptic to treat wounds, burns, skin ailments, fungal infections, sunburn, and muscle pain. It is also used in other medicines to mask unpleasant odors.

Cultivation and Preparation

LAVENDER REQUIRES VERY WELL-DRAINED SOIL AND PLENTY of sun. Because different species and varieties of lavenders hybridize easily, they rarely come true from seed. For this reason, the herbs are typically propagated from cuttings taken from the side shoots of mature lavender plants in mid- to late summer. The flowers contain the highest levels of the plant's **essential oil**. They are harvested in summer, when the petals have just begun to open. The flowers are used fresh, distilled to produce essential oil, or dried for **infusions, tinctures,** and other preparations.

Research

LAVENDER CONTAINS MANY CHEMICAL COMPOUNDS; THE most important medicinally may be linalool and linalyl acetate. These compounds are rapidly absorbed through the skin or mucous membranes. They are believed to depress the central nervous system, slowing nerve impulses and thereby slightly deadening pain and reducing irritability. This has been supported in animal studies. In other animal studies, lavender oil has been shown to exhibit antispasmodic effects on smooth muscle tissue. This may correlate in part to its relaxing effects on people. In vitro studies indicate that lavender is an effective antibiotic, but no clinical studies have been conducted to support this in humans. Animal studies have also shown that lavender lowers cholesterol levels. A lavender isolate called perillyl alcohol has been shown to prevent tumor development and caused tumors to regress in lab animals. Perillyl alcohol is undergoing human trials to assess its anticancer potential, possibly as a substitute for tamoxifen in treating breast cancer.

THE CHARMS OF LAVENDER

In ancient times, lavender was said to avert the "eye of evil." It was a flower and essence dedicated to Hecate, the goddess of witches and sorcerers. Lavender was also purported to invoke ecstasy and constancy in love. In the Middle Ages, lavender was also associated with love in various ways: It was thought to be an aphrodisiac, and at the same time it was believed that sprinkling lavender water on someone's head would keep him or her chaste. Sipping lavender dew on Saint Luke's Day while chanting to the saint was thought to ensure that a maiden would see her true love in a dream. It was also believed that spouses who placed sprigs of lavender between their bedsheets would never quarrel and that pillows filled with lavender would help the restless fall asleep. (Considerable observational evidence seems to support that the aroma of lavender may enhance sleep.) In medieval England, peddlers hawked lavender as a charm against evil. A cross made of lavender was often hung on the door to ward off evil spirits. Lavender was also thought to be a remedy for the plague. In fact, lavender was one of the essential ingredients in a concoction called Four Thieves' Vinegar, which was supposed to provide those who applied it to their bodies sufficient immunity to safely rob the bodies of plague victims. People also tied lavender bunches to their wrists to guard against infection.

See Also: *Herbal Medicine Expanded Commission E Monographs* by M. Blumenthal, A. Goldberg, and J. Brinckmann, American Botanical Council, 2000; *Herbal Emissaries: Bringing Chinese Herbs to the West* by S. Foster and Y. Chongxi, Healing Arts Press, 1992.

LAVANDULA ANGUSTIFOLIA | English Lavender

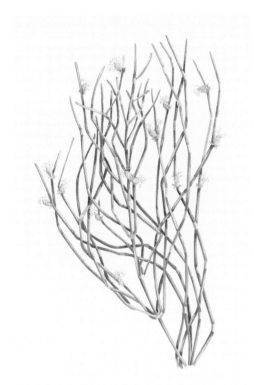

Ephedra
Ephedra sinica

Common Names Ephedra, desert tea, *ma huang*, Chinese ephedra

Latin Names *Ephedra sinica, E. equisetina, E. intermedia*

Family Ephedraceae

Parts Used Stems

Description Ephedra is a wiry, grayish-green, perennial shrub growing to three feet with long, thin stems and much-reduced, almost scale-like leaves. Minute male flowers are borne in small clusters; female flowers form small, fleshy, bright-red cones.

Habitat Native to China, *Ephedra sinica* grows in dry, desert habitats.

Approximate native range

EPHEDRA IS A PERENNIAL ASIATIC SHRUB ADAPTED TO ARID regions of western China. Known as *ma huang* in Chinese, the herb is a natural source of the **alkaloids** ephedrine and pseudoephedrine, which are powerful stimulants of the central nervous system that mimic the effects of the hormone epinephrine (adrenaline) in the body. Zen monks were said to use preparations of ephedra to help stay awake and alert during long sessions of meditation and prayer. According to legend, Genghis Khan's soldiers used the plant in a similar way during night watches—as the penalty for sleeping while on duty was death. Throughout the long history of its use, ephedra has been considered an important herbal remedy for coughs, colds, asthma, and a variety of other respiratory conditions. Today, synthetic ephedrine and pseudoephedrine are common ingredients in over-the-counter medicines for colds, coughs, and allergies. During the 1990s, ephedra became controversial as a major ingredient in certain types of dietary supplements, including those marketed as weight loss aids and athletic performance enhancers. It was ultimately banned in these kinds of products in the United States, due to the health risks associated with it.

Traditional and Current Medicinal Uses

EPHEDRA HAS BEEN USED FOR THOUSANDS OF YEARS IN TRADItional Chinese medicine for the treatment of asthma, bronchitis, colds, flu, coughs and wheezing, fever, chills, aching joints and bones, and nasal congestion. It is listed in one of China's oldest herbals, the *Shen Nong Ben Cao Jing* that was compiled around 206 B.C. for use in inducing perspiration and to counter the symptoms of allergies. It is possible that ancient Greeks knew of ephedra and its medicinal properties. Pliny the Elder, a Roman scientist and historian from the first century A.D., described a plant called *ephedron* that was used by the Greeks for coughs, asthma, and colic.

Current herbal uses of ephedra in China are very similar to what they have been historically. Ephedra is often taken to relieve chills, fevers, and coughs. In Western herbal medicine, ephedra is typically used as a decongestant, for asthma, hay fever, colds, flu, to raise blood pressure, and for the pains of rheumatism.

Cultivation and Preparation

EPHEDRA IS THE NAME GIVEN TO THREE SPECIES OF THE HERB used medicinally: *Ephedra sinica, E. equisetina,* and *E. intermedia.* All ephedra species prefer well-drained, almost dry soil in full sun. The herb can be propagated from seed or by division in fall or spring. The stems are most often used in herbal medicine. Collected in autumn, when active compounds are most concentrated, the stems are dried for use in **decoctions, tinctures,** powders, or liquid **extracts.**

Research

THE MINUTE LEAVES AND STEMS OF EPHEDRA CONTAIN MANY potentially active compounds, but it is the alkaloids ephedrine, pseudoephedrine, norephedrine, and norpseudoephedrine that are valued for therapeutic properties. Ephedrine, the most potent, is by far the most abundant in stems of the herb. It was first isolated in 1885 by Japanese scientists. Research has shown that ephedrine and pseudoephedrine stimulate heart rate. They cause narrowing in peripheral blood vessels, leading to an increase in blood pressure. The two alkaloids also relax bronchial muscles, making them effective as decongestants and for the temporary relief of shortness of breath caused by asthma. Ephedrine and pseudoephedrine stimulate the central nervous system, much like an **amphetamine.** They increase sweating and ephedrine may also dull the appetite—actions that made these substances attractive as weight loss aids. However, evidence from clinical trials supports the conclusion that ephedrine, particularly when taken with caffeine, significantly increases the risk of nausea, vomiting, anxiety, mood swings, hyperactivity, and heart palpitations. Research indicates that ephedrine and its related compounds are potentially addictive and can disrupt regular heart rhythm, raise blood pressure, and potentially induce cardiac arrest.

CAUTION Ephedra or its alkaloids may cause insomnia, high blood pressure, or hypertension, and in high doses may be fatal. Ephedra has been banned by the U.S. Food and Drug Administration.

THE EPHEDRA CONTROVERSY

In the early 1990s, the United States Food and Drug Administration raised concerns about the safety of ephedra and ephedra-based products. Because ephedra is a herb, products that included it as an ingredient were sold as dietary supplements. Because of its stimulant properties, ephedra was included in many popular herbal "fen-phen" products used for weight loss, as energy boosters, and to enhance athletic performance. Reports about serious side effects from these products, ranging from high blood pressure and heart rate irregularities to seizures, strokes, and cardiac arrest, fueled fears. As problems and even deaths accumulated, the U.S. Food and Drug Administration issued warnings about ephedra-containing products and imposed stricter limits on recommended dosages. In 2001 the National Football League prohibited players from using supplements that contained ephedra. In June 2003, the health food chain GNC stopped selling ephedra-containing supplements in its stores. In December 2003, the FDA announced a ban on the uncontrolled sale of ephedra supplements. Synthetic ephedrine is still available as an ingredient in some over-the-counter medications that are clearly labeled in accordance with Food and Drug Administration regulations. In April 2005, however, the ban on ephedra-containing supplements and similar products was struck down by a federal judge in Utah.

See Also: Herbal Medicine Expanded Commission E Monographs by M. Blumenthal, A. Goldberg, and J. Brinckmann, American Botanical Council, 2000; *Nature's Medicine, Plants That Heal* by Joel Swerdlow, National Geographic, 2000.

Common Names Eucalyptus, blue gum, Tasmanian blue gum, Australian fever tree

Latin Name *Eucalyptus globulus*

Family Myrtaceae

Parts Used Leaves, oil

Description *Eucalyptus globulus* is a tall (150-200 feet), spreading evergreen tree with creamy white, shedding bark and rounded, bluish-green juvenile leaves but narrow, lance-shaped adult leaves. Large, cream-colored flowers are followed by globe-shaped, woody fruits.

Habitat Native to the Australian states of New South Wales, Victoria, and Tasmania, *E. globulus* thrives in moist valleys of upland areas. It is widely cultivated in many other parts of the world.

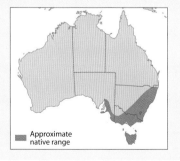

Approximate native range

Eucalyptus
Eucalyptus globulus

MORE THAN 600 SPECIES OF DISTINCTLY AROMATIC, evergreen trees and shrubs make up the genus *Eucalyptus*. Most are indigenous to Australia, where they are commonly called gum trees, or simply gums. Many of Australia's *Eucalyptus* species are among the fastest growing and tallest trees in the world, with some exceeding 300 feet in height. They are also rich in **volatile oils**. Australian Aborigines have included eucalyptus in their herbal medicine tradition for millennia, using the trees' bark, leaves, oils, and resins as remedies for a variety of ailments. Many eucalyptus oils exhibit antiseptic properties. The oil of *Eucalyptus globulus*, the blue gum, is also highly aromatic with a pungent, haunting fragrance. It is used worldwide for its decongestant, **expectorant**, and fever-reducing properties.

Traditional and Current Medicinal Uses

AUSTRALIAN ABORIGINES WERE VERY LIKELY THE FIRST PEOPLE to discover that eucalyptus has powerful medicinal properties. Eucalyptus oil, derived from the tree's mature leaves as well as the roots and bark, is antiseptic and **astringent**. Traditionally, Aborigines used topical ointments containing eucalyptus oil to heal wounds and fungal infections. Teas brewed from eucalyptus leaves were used to reduce fevers. The therapeutic value of eucalyptus spread across many continents, and the herb became incorporated into the traditional medicine systems of China and India. In China, eucalyptus was used externally to treat nerve pain. In the Indian **Ayurvedic** tradition, it was employed as a mild expectorant, and topically for headache due to colds. Commercial production of eucalyptus oil began in Australia in 1852 and quickly found its way into Western herbal and conventional medicine. Eucalyptus was also widely used to treat coughs and colds, as it still is today.

Teas made from fresh or dried leaves are helpful in soothing sore throats and treating bronchitis and sinusitis. Ointments containing eucalyptus oil applied to the nose or chest help relieve congestion and loosen phlegm. Ointments or **poultices** are helpful in treating minor wounds and skin abscesses. Some herbalists also recommend eucalyptus **tinctures** for bad breath. Diluted eucalyptus oil can be used as a soothing rub for rheumatism, neuralgia, bruises, sprains, and sore muscles. It also is recommended for some types of skin conditions.

Cultivation and Preparation

EUCALYPTUS GLOBULUS IS EXTENSIVELY CULTIVATED FOR ITS leaves and oil, especially in Mediterranean and subtropical climates. Australia, Spain, and Morocco are among the largest suppliers of eucalyptus products for the herbal medicine market. It is also grown in California. Eucalyptus requires fertile, well-drained soil and full sun. Propagation is by seed. Mature leaves contain the highest concentrations of the **essential oil.** They are harvested and dried or distilled for oil. Eucalyptus oil is used in ointments and liquids. Dried leaves are incorporated into teas. Eucalyptus oil or its primary active ingredient, cineole, is added to over-the-counter cough drops and cough syrups, chest rubs, vaporizer preparations, toothpaste, and mouthwash.

Research

EUCALYPTUS OIL'S PRIMARY ACTIVE INGREDIENT, CINEOLE (sometimes called eucalyptol), has documented antiseptic properties. Eucalyptus oil actively dilates bronchioles in the lungs, making it easier to breathe. It is also effective against many bacteria, especially *Staphylococcus.* The cooling sensation of eucalyptus is thought to result from stimulation of cold receptors in the skin. An herbal tincture containing eucalyptus has shown promise in experiments in treating chronic ear infections. Eucalyptus has traditionally been used as a diabetes remedy. In several studies involving mice, eucalyptus leaf extracts have been shown to exhibit anti-diabetic effects. In mice with experimentally induced diabetes, the extracts reduced blood sugar levels and stimulated insulin production. Further study is needed to confirm preliminary research. In other research, leaf extracts appear to exhibit **diuretic** and antitumor activity.

> CAUTION Pure, or applied undiluted to the skin, eucalyptus oil is toxic and should never be taken internally.

The genus name *Eucalyptus* comes from the Greek word *eucalyptos,* which means "well covered." The reference is to the flowers of the many trees and shrubs that make up the genus. *Eucalyptus* species are so abundant in Australia that they constitute three-quarters of the vegetation on the continent. It is not surprising that eucalyptus has played an important role in the lives of Aborigines and later European settlers in Australia. Roots of some smaller species were ground and used as food by indigenous tribes and early colonists. The leaves of several species, including *E. mannifera* and *E. viminalis,* exude a sugary secretion when damaged by insects. Called "lerp" or "manna," it was found to make a good base for certain foods and beverages. Aborigines also learned that eucalyptus trees store water in their roots. All that was needed to slake a serious thirst was to dig up a length of root and blow the water out of its vessels. Ironically, many explorers and colonists perished from thirst in Australia, never realizing that water was at hand in the tree roots all around them. In a number of countries, *Eucalyptus globulus* was imported to help eradicate malaria. The trees absorb huge quantities of water and were planted in mosquito-infested marshes to help dry up the land. This earned the eucalyptus the nickname "fever tree."

See Also: *Herbal Medicine Expanded Commission E Monographs* by M. Blumenthal, A. Goldberg, and J. Brinckmann, American Botanical Council, 2000; *World Health Organization (WHO) Monographs on Selected Medicinal Plants, Vol. 2,* 2002.

Common Names European elder, elderberry, black elder, common elder, pipe tree, bore tree

Latin Names *Sambucus nigra, S. nigra* var. *canadensis*

Family Caprifoliaceae

Parts Used Flowers, fruits

Description Elder is a deciduous shrub or small tree, growing to 30 feet, with pithy branches and gray-brown, furrowed, corky bark. It has dull-green, unpleasant-smelling leaves and flat clusters of cream-colored flowers that are followed by shiny black fruits on red stalks.

Habitat Native to Europe, Asia, North Africa and eastern North America, elder is found in subtropical and temperate regions worldwide. Its preferred habitat is moist woodlands, hedges, ditches, and in waste places.

Approximate native range

European Elder
Sambucus nigra

SINCE ANCIENT TIMES, ELDER HAS BEEN VALUED FOR ITS cosmetic, culinary, household, and medicinal uses. The Romans used the dark juice from its purplish-black berries as a hair dye. Elder water was said to ensure a fair complexion. Elder flowers were made into cordials and tea. Elderberries have been baked into pies and tarts, cooked into jellies, jams, chutneys, and preserves, and fermented into famous elderberry wine. The wood from the trees is finely grained and easily cut and has been used in centuries past for making fences, pegs, needles, mathematical instruments, and children's toys. The easily bored-out twigs made ideal pipe stems—hence the common names "bore tree" and "pipe tree." The name "elder" comes from the Anglo-Saxon word *aeld*, meaning "fire," because the hollowed stems were once used for getting fires going. In times past, elder was credited as being a cure for nearly everything. In modern herbal medicine the herb is gaining popularity as a cold and flu medicine that has scientifically substantiated antiviral and immune system-stimulating properties.

Traditional and Current Medicinal Uses

ELDER HAS BEEN USED MEDICINALLY SINCE THE DAYS OF ANCIENT Rome, when Hippocrates recommended it to promote vomiting and purging. Many medieval herbals celebrated elder's ability to cure essentially all known illnesses. All parts of the plant were used at one time or another. Elder roots were used as a **diuretic** in treating **edema**; their juice was a respected **purgative**. The leaves went into making ointments for treating bruises, sprains, and wounds; they were also made into nauseatingly effective purgatives. Tea made from the leaves has long been a traditional cure for coughs, colds, and inflammation of mucous membranes as well as reducing swelling and promoting sweating. Elder flower water was applied to the eyes and skin for its mildly **astringent** effects, and tea made from the flowers was considered a spring tonic that could purify the blood. Elder berries were used to treat rheumatism and serious skin rashes and were praised as a diuretic and laxative. Dried elderberry tea was recommended for colic and diarrhea. A sweetened syrup made from the juice of elderberries was another traditional remedy for colds, coughs, and bronchial ailments. Native Americans used elderberry in treating colds, rheumatism, and fever as well as sores, skin problems, swollen limbs, and boils. Various tribes also used the herb as a diuretic and strong laxative and to stop bleeding.

In modern herbal medicine, elder is used primarily in treating influenza, colds, and feverish conditions, and as an immune system stimulant. It is also prescribed for allergies, congestion, ear and throat infections, burns, inflamed skin and mucous membranes, and for arthritis and rheumatism.

Cultivation and Preparation

ELDER NEEDS MOIST, FERTILE SOIL AND FULL SUN TO PART shade. It is propagated from cuttings in spring; the plants also sucker freely. Clusters of flowers are harvested in early spring; berries are picked in early autumn, when ripe, and used fresh, for juice, or dried.

Research

ELDER CONTAINS VARIOUS FLAVONOIDS, TRITERPENES, organic acids, **essential oils**, and more. The flavonoids and triterpenes appear to be the main biologically active constituents, although their mechanism of action is not fully understood. In laboratory studies, preparations made from the elder tree have demonstrated **anti-inflammatory**, antiviral, and diuretic actions. Clinical trials have been conducted to test elder's efficacy in treating influenza. In these studies, patients receiving elderberry **extract** recovered from the flu several days earlier than control groups; their symptoms were also less severe. The extract also stimulated antibody production. Because of the elder's strong immune system-stimulating properties, some researchers have suggested that elder may also be beneficial in treating patients with weak immune systems, such as those with cancer. In preliminary studies, elder extracts have also been shown to neutralize the West Nile virus, suggesting that it may be useful as a prophylactic agent during seasons when mosquitoes are a threat.

Elder is an herb steeped in superstition and folklore. According to legend, the cross on which Christ was crucified was made of elder wood. Judas, the disciple who betrayed Christ, supposedly hung himself from an elder tree. These associations made elder a symbol of sorrow and death and it was often planted in graveyards. Predating these Christian superstitions were beliefs that elder provided protection from witches and evil. Elder branches were buried in graves to protect the dead from evil spirits. In some regions, hearse drivers carried horse whips made of elder wood. Elder trees were planted near cottages and their branches nailed to windows and doors to keep evil out of the house. Yet it was an omen of death to bring elder indoors. Elder branches were affixed to stables, too, to keep the animals safe. Another very common belief was that elder shrubs and trees were inhabited by supernatural beings, particularly a tree spirit known as Elder Tree Mother, who dwelled in the tree and watched over it. Before an elder tree could be cut down or any branch or twig removed, it was necessary to kneel down and ask forgiveness and permission, or misfortune would follow. Even then, there were those who would not risk offending this tree-dwelling spirit and would neither cut down or prune an elder tree or burn its wood. The Tree Mother's wrath could be formidable. She was believed to haunt the owners of furniture made from elder wood and harm babies sleeping in elder wood cradles.

SAMBUCUS NIGRA | European Elder

See Also: *Herbal Medicine Expanded Commission E Monographs* by M. Blumenthal, Goldberg, and J. Brinckmann, American Botanical Council, 2000; *World Health Organization (WHO) Monographs on Selected Medicinal Plants, Vol. 2,* 2002.

European Mistletoe
Viscum album

Common Names European mistletoe, birdlime

Latin Name *Viscum album*

Family Viscaceae

Parts Used Leaves, twigs

Description Mistletoe is a semi-parasitic, evergreen shrub that grows on trees. It has thick, leathery leaves, male and female flowers borne on separate plants, and small white berries with sticky flesh and a single seed.

Habitat *Viscum album* is native to Europe and Asia. Three recognized subspecies are associated with different types of trees; one parasitizes apple, ash, and other broadleaf trees; another grows on pines and larches; and the third, on firs.

Approximate native range

MISTLETOE HAS LONG BEEN ASSOCIATED WITH mystery and magic—and more recently with medicine. This strange herb with its symmetrically branched stems and fleshy leaves grows high in the branches of trees. It seems to appear in these aerial perches spontaneously and mysteriously survives without roots that draw water and nutrients from the ground. What seemed magical to ancient cultures was eventually explained by observant botanists. Mistletoe's sticky seeds are spread from tree to tree by birds. The seeds sprout and produce thread-like roots that dig into branches and tap into a tree's resources. Mistletoe's leaves, and especially its berries, are poisonous. Nevertheless, beginning in the 1600s, mistletoe was used as a medicinal herb, initially to treat epilepsy and nervous disorders. Today mistletoe is recognized as an immune system stimulant and cancer cell inhibitor. In Europe, drugs made from mistletoe **extracts** are used to treat certain cancers, but these have not been approved in the U.S.

Traditional and Current Medicinal Uses

HERBAL WRITINGS FROM AROUND 1680 INDICATE THAT FRENCH herbalists prescribed mistletoe preparations for epilepsy, St. Vitus' dance, and other nervous disorders. Powdered mistletoe, added to water, wine, or milk, was taken after seizures. Mistletoe was used to treat delirium, dizziness, hysteria, and nerve pain. Because mistletoe slightly slowed the heartbeat and lowered blood pressure, it was also used for certain heart conditions. Applying the sticky juice of the berries was a remedy for skin ulcers and sores.

Mistletoe is still valued in modern herbal medicine, but because of the plant's toxicity, it is best taken only under the direction of a qualified practitioner. The herb's primary uses today are in the supportive treatment of cancer, for arteriolosclerosis, in cases of arthritis and other forms of degenerative inflammation, for hepatitis (especially hepatitis C) and HIV/AIDS, as a sedative for nervous tension and panic attacks, and as an immune system stimulant.

Cultivation and Preparation

MUCH OF THE MISTLETOE USED IN HERBAL MEDICINE IS HARvested from the wild. New mistletoe plants can be "cultivated" by crushing ripe fruits into crevices in the bark of trees so the seeds will germinate and "infect" the trees as new hosts. The fleshy leaves and tender stems are harvested in autumn and dried for use in herbal preparations or for extraction of their chemical constituents.

Research

IN LABORATORY STUDIES, EXTRACTS OF MISTLETOE HAVE BEEN shown to stimulate the immune system and to kill cancer cells. The most active ingredients in mistletoe are lectins and viscotoxins. Both of these seem to play a major role in the herb's immune-stimulating effects, especially at low concentrations. At higher concentrations, lectins and viscotoxins exhibit cytotoxic (cell-killing) effects and, consequently, anticancer activity. Viscotoxins also lower blood pressure and decrease intensity of the heartbeat. In Europe, mistletoe preparations have been used for decades to complement conventional therapies in treating cancer patients. In Germany, nearly 40 percent of cancer patients use mistletoe preparations, usually in the form of an injectable serum. The Food and Drug Administration has not approved the use of such products in the United States. Mistletoe's effectiveness as a cancer treatment has been investigated in clinical studies, although some of these have been criticized for their small size and results that have not been confirmed in controlled trials. Nevertheless, some studies have shown mistletoe to be an effective complementary therapy in the treatment of certain types of tumors. An injectable form of mistletoe lectins has also demonstrated the ability to reduce the frequency and intensity of clinical signs and symptoms in patients with hepatitis.

CAUTION All parts of mistletoe, but especially the berries, are toxic if eaten. Large doses can lead to coma, seizures, and death.

UNDER THE MISTLETOE

The custom of kissing under the mistletoe at Christmastime is ages old. Some experts believe that it comes from the ancient Celtic belief that mistletoe could ward off evil. It was hung in homes for protection and used to welcome the new year. The Druids (Celtic priests) collected mistletoe in an elaborate ceremony that involved white-robed figures scouring forests in winter, peering upward through the bare branches as they searched for dangling green clumps of the plant. Mistletoe living in oak trees was highly prized. Once a suitable specimen was located, it was cut down by a priest wielding a golden sickle while the other members of the search party chanted in unison. As the mistletoe fell from the treetops, it was carefully caught in a cloth spread out beneath the tree. Allowing the plant to touch the ground meant that all manner of misfortune would ensue. Historians suggest that the modern mistletoe custom is derived from Scandinavian mythology, specifically the story of Balder, the god of peace. According to legend, Balder was killed by an arrow made of mistletoe. But he was brought back to life and to commemorate this resurrection, mistletoe was given to the goddess of love. She decreed that anyone who passed beneath it should receive a kiss to show that mistletoe was no longer associated with death, but was now a symbol of love.

See Also: Herbal Medicine Expanded Commission E Monographs by M. Blumenthal, A. Goldberg, and J. Brinckmann, American Botanical Council, 2000; *A Field Guide to Medicinal Plants and Herbs: Western North America* by S. Foster and C. Hobbs, Houghton Mifflin, 2002.

Common Names Evening primrose, tree primrose, sundrop, German rampion, king's cure-all

Latin Name *Oenothera biennis*

Family Onagraceae

Parts Used Seed, oil, leaves

Description Evening primrose is an erect biennial or short-lived perennial with a thick, yellowish taproot and a rosette of basal leaves from which the flowering stems arise. These have lance-shaped leaves topped by yellow, lemon-scented flowers that open in the evening. Downy seed capsules contain many minute seeds.

Habitat Original to North America, evening primrose has been introduced and naturalized through much of Europe and other temperate regions. It is found in open areas of poor sandy soil, such as embankments, dry meadows, roadsides, and disturbed areas.

Approximate native range

Evening Primrose

Oenothera biennis

EVENING PRIMROSE IS NATIVE TO NORTH AMERICA, where it grows like a weed along roadsides and in abandoned places. On a summer day, this herb looks fairly uninteresting. But as evening falls, its delicate, sunny yellow flowers begin to unfurl, opening to welcome the moths that pollinate them. Each flower lasts for only one night. Traditionally known largely as an edible wild plant, evening primrose was food for Native Americans and later Europeans when it was introduced into Continental gardens. The herb was something of a minor medicinal plant in American history for several centuries until the 1980s, when scientific research revealed that the oil from its seeds showed promise in treating a number of serious complaints.

Traditional and Current Medicinal Uses

EVENING PRIMROSE WAS USED AS AN HERBAL MEDICINE BY A number of Native American tribes. The Ojibwa made **poultices** of the entire plant and applied them to bruises. The Potawatomi used the seeds as medicine. Various preparations of evening primrose were used by the Cherokee for weight reduction, boils, and as a stimulant and muscle strengthener. In American folk medicine, evening primrose was highly regarded as a treatment for wounds. Like the Native Americans, settlers applied poultices of the herb on wounds, bruises, painful swellings, and tumors. Evening primrose was especially prized for treating skin eruptions of infants. The roots of the plant were sold commercially by the Shakers for use in medicinal preparations. In the 1800s, evening primrose was suggested as a treatment for skin problems in infants, skin ulcerations, gastrointestinal disorders, dyspepsia, kidney problems, diarrhea, dysentery, and chronic asthma.

Modern herbal practitioners prescribe the seed oil for eczema and certain other skin diseases including allergic dermatitis, for rheumatoid arthritis, fatigue, and diabetic neuropathy (nerve degeneration). Evening primrose has also been suggested for lowering blood pressure, digestive problems, asthma, alcohol-related liver disease, weight loss in cases where there is a family history of obesity, and multiple sclerosis.

Cultivation and Preparation

THE HERB IS EASILY PROPAGATED BY SOWING SEEDS ON TOP of the soil (it requires light for germination). Evening primrose thrives in full sun or part shade and poor, sandy, relatively dry soil; in fact, plants grown in rich soil produce seeds with lower gammalinolenic acid content (see sidebar at right). Leaves can be collected in summer and used fresh, but seeds are not harvested until ripe in late summer and pressed to extract their oil.

Research

EVENING PRIMROSE OIL IS BECOMING ONE OF THE MOST widely used botanical supplements in the world, sold in more than 30 countries. The oil contains gamma-linolenic acid, or GLA, an unsaturated fatty acid that functions as a **precursor** in the production of hormone-like substances called **prostaglandins**. Hundreds of lab and clinical studies have been carried out, particularly on the GLA-rich oil from its seeds. Much of this research supports the plant's use for treating conditions related to deficiencies or imbalances in essential fatty acids and their relationship to hormone production. Several clinical studies have supported the success of the oil in treating eczema. Clinical research has also shown the oil to be significantly therapeutic in cases of rheumatoid arthritis and a promising long-term therapy in delaying the onset and slowing progression of diabetic neuropathy (nerve damage). Results of studies on benefits of evening primrose oil in relieving premenstrual syndrome have been mixed; studies on relieving menopausal symptoms have failed to confirm significant effects. The effect of evening primrose oil on a number of conditions, including breast cancer, heart disease, high cholesterol, attention deficit hyperactivity disorder, and stomach ulcers is currently under scientific investigation.

Oenothera biennis and several closely related species were a source of food for many Native American tribes at one time. The entire plant is edible. The Apache, Chiricahua, and Mescalero used the seeds in soups and gravies. The seeds were also chewed as a special treat. The Cherokee cooked the leaves and ate them as greens, and boiled the roots like potatoes. When evening primrose was introduced to Europe in 1619, it was more as a culinary herb than a medicinal one. (They were dubbed "primroses" because their flowers resembled the yellow spring primrose of Britain; the two types of plants are not related, however.) Young leaves were eaten in salads; the yellow flowers made a pretty edible garnish with a slight lemon-pepper taste. The seeds were used atop breads and rolls, similar to the way in which poppy and sesame seeds were used. Young seedpods could also be steamed and added to vegetables for a tasty side dish. Evening primrose was cultivated in England and Germany especially for its large taproots, which were boiled as a vegetable and said to have a nutty flavor somewhat similar to parsnips with a hint of pepper. The roots of the herb became so popular as a vegetable in Germany that they were given the nickname "German rampion," a reference to another European plant with a white, edible root.

OENOTHERA BIENNIS | Evening Primrose

See Also: The ABC Clinical Guide to Herbs by M. Blumenthal, T. Hall, and A. Goldberg, American Botanical Council, 2003; World Health Organization (WHO) Monographs on Selected Medicinal Plants, Vol. 2, 2002.

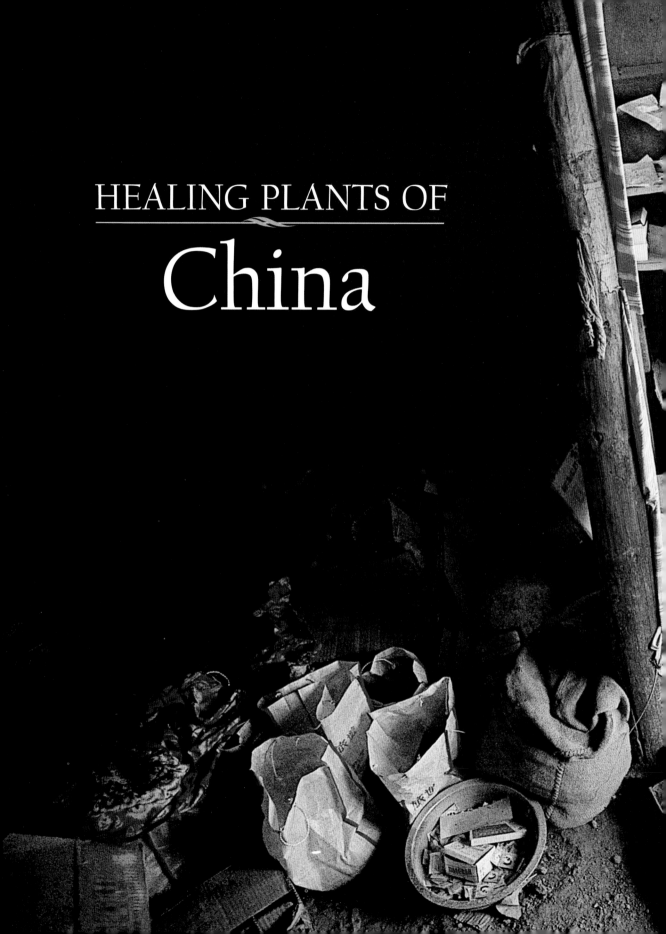

HEALING PLANTS OF
China

CHINA IS A COUNTRY OF CONTRASTS WHERE PROGRESS STRUGgles upstream against its own history. It is a mysterious creature with a life of its own. Although the government rules with an iron hand, the soul of China seems to have its own destiny. The congested traffic—cars and trucks interlaced with weaving bicycles and hurrying pedestrians—blends and separates all at once. It is chaos gliding like a swan and darting like a squirrel.

In the study of medicinal plants few human beings embody the blend of ancient Chinese culture with an understanding of modern China's role better than Dr. Shiu Ying Hu. A Chinese-born botanist who has spent her career at Harvard University's Arnold Arboretum, Dr. Hu is regarded, both in the U.S. and China, as a liaison between American and Chinese botanists. Raised on a small communal homestead on the south bank of the Yellow River near Xuzhou, where famines followed floods and war, she learned to use wild plants for food and medicine. Before leaving her village to study in Nanjing, she had never eaten a bowl of rice. As a youth, she vowed to pursue a life of learning to help rural people overcome the hardships she experienced.

In 1946 Dr. Hu became the first Chinese woman to receive a scholarship to Harvard University to pursue a Ph.D. in botany. Over the last six decades she has inspired hundreds of students and colleagues with new ways of looking at familiar plants—many of them Chinese medicinal plants, such as peonies, daylilies, ginkgo trees, forsythia, mallows, and the sacred lotus. From completion of her master's thesis, "The Chinese Esculent Plants Used for the Conservation of Health," in 1937, to publication in 2005 of her magnum opus, *Food Plants of China*, no other person has contributed more to bridging understanding of Chinese herbs to the West. Her personal use of plants has yielded positive results: In 2005, Dr. Hu, still an active lecturer and writer in Hong Kong, turned 100 years old.

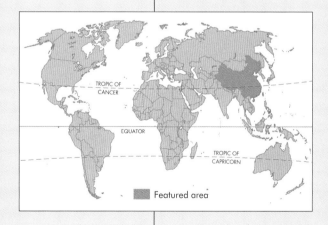

TRADITIONAL MEDICINE IN CHINA

SINCE DIPLOMATIC RELATIONS WITH CHINA BEGAN IN THE MID-1970S, AMERICANS have been fascinated with things Chinese. Foremost among those fascinations is the 2,000-year-old medical system known as Traditional Chinese Medicine (TCM), which combines the use of herbal prescriptions,

acupuncture, and other practices. In just the past 30 years, acupuncture has gone from fantastic reports of sticking needles into the body to a recognized medical discipline with most states licensing non-physician acupuncturists.

In tandem with the use of acupuncture in the U.S. has been the introduction of many herbs commonly used in TCM to health food stores. Not only do these herbs have a 2,000-year written history of continuous use, but they also are backed by more than 50 years of Western-style research efforts by Chinese scientists, including clinical reports, pharmacological and chemical research, and quality assurance systems, to develop sources of high-quality supplies for Chinese consumption as well as export.

With 5,000 years of cultural evolution, the Chinese possess one of the oldest herbal traditions in the world. From the beginning of the Christian era to the end of the rule of the last emperor at the end of the Qing dynasty in 1911, more than 400 herbals had been written. One of the main works providing a basis for the most widely used medicinal plants in modern TCM is the nearly 2,000-year-old classic, *Shen Nong Ben Cao Jing.* (A *ben cao* is an herbal.) This work is attributed to the mythical plowman-emperor, Shen Nong, thought to have lived some 5,000 years ago. In Chinese drawings Shen

Lotus plants fill a pond on the grounds of the historic imperial Summer Palace on the outskirts of Beijing. The roots, leaves, stems, seeds, and other parts of the sacred lotus (Nelumbo nucifera) all supply separate herbal ingredients in the practice of Traditional Chinese Medicine.

PRECEDING PAGES: A healer palpates the stomach of a woman with recurring abdominal pain. She has come to his office on the western Tibean Plateau. Traditional herbal medicines and Western drugs sent to the outpost by the Chinese government litter the floor, but they are often outdated and patients frequently must resort to home remedies.

Nong is depicted as a horned, Pan-like figure. The book survives as a list of 365 herbs divided into three classes based on their importance as medicinal plants. Shen Nong's herbal, along with the16th-century classic *Ben Cao Gang Mu*, serves as the basis for plant drugs used in modern TCM.

As a system of medicine, TCM is employed by nearly a quarter of the world's population. Since the mid-1950s, the communist governments ruling China have spearheaded the revitalization of this ancient system by making TCM a part of China's public health care policy. Recognizing that Western medicine was too expensive to meet the needs of China's people, research efforts were established to document TCM from a scientific perspective. The effort included setting up colleges of traditional medicine in each of China's provinces, using Western scientific methods to document source plants of Chinese drugs in all parts of China, and performing botanical, pharmacological, and clinical studies. The effort has resulted in a large body of modern scientific literature on Chinese drug plants.

One of China's leading research institutes is the Academy of Traditional Chinese Medicine in Beijing. It is China's main scientific arm for research in traditional medicine, including herbs and acupuncture. It employs more than 3,300 workers in 16 departments, including 2 hospitals. One of the Academy's many achievements includes isolating a substance from sweet wormwood (*Artemisia annua*). Grown in the U.S. for making herbal wreaths, it is used clinically in China for treating malaria resistant to quinine drugs, with a reported success rate of more than 90 percent in treating 10,000 cases.

At a processing plant near the eastern city of Ningbo, workers sort recently harvested ginseng. They will wash and scrape the root, then allow it to dry naturally. Studies show that ginseng can stimulate the immune system, increase alertness, and help to relieve stress.

MEDICINAL PLANTS IN CHINA

PROFESSOR YUE CHONGXI IS A LEADING LIGHT at the Academy of Traditional Chinese Medicine. Now retired, he spent his career as a researcher at the Institute of Materia Medica at the Academy, beginning work there when the institution opened in 1956. Like Dr. Hu, Professor Yue is a bridge between modern Chinese medicinal plant research and ancient traditions. Yue Chongxi's ancestors were pharmacists in Beijing for 400 years. Before the communist government took power in 1949, the Yue family owned China's oldest drug store, Tong-Ren-Tang, which still operates today at its original 1667 location. The Yue family, which once owned half of the drug stores in Beijing, served as pharmacists for China's emperors from the end of the Ming dynasty in 1644 through the Qing dynasty in 1912, the last era of imperial rule.

According to Professor Yue, the Chinese make a clear distinction between plants used as drugs and those considered herbs (also called folk medicines or nationality medicines) that are used by people in the countryside but not recognized as drugs in TCM. The distinction is as clear as that between herbal medicine and Western medicine in the U.S. In addition to about 500 medicinal plants serving as official drugs in TCM, 4,500 herbs or folk medicines are documented as being used by the Chinese people. In China there are more than 100 nationalities. The Han people comprise about 98 percent of the population. The remaining 2 percent includes groups such as the Dai people of Southwest China, the nomadic tribes of Inner Mongolia to the north, and the Tibetan people to the west. Each of the minority populations has its own distinct traditional medicine and medicinal plants.

An herbalist in a remote village may take pride in being able to cure a disease that doctors of TCM may not have success in treating. Part of Professor Yue's work has been to travel to remote regions to follow up on reports of folk cures. When he and several colleagues went to Hainan Island in the South China Sea to follow up on a report of an herb considered successful as a contraceptive, the researchers found that it was used primarily by women in their mid-40s (a group presumably less fertile at that age) and had less than a 40 percent success rate. Corroborating traditional knowledge with modern scientific research has been a major part of Professor Yue's work.

In TCM, root drugs are most important, seeds and fruits second, and leaf drugs the least important. Unlike Western herbalism, where most herbs are used singly, Dr. Yue explains that a major characteristic of TCM is that plants are used in combinations of three, ten, or even a hundred herbs. A notable exception is ginseng, which is often used alone.

If you could dig a tunnel to the central Chinese mountains from the Appalachians you might end up in a forest that looks a lot like where you started. For more than 200 years, plant geographers have recognized a phenomena known as the disjunct eastern Asiatic-eastern North American range. Similar plant populations separated by thousands of miles in the east of both continents are believed to be remnants of an ancient forest covering the Northern Hemisphere some 70 million years ago. There are more than a hundred genera of plants that only occur in eastern Asia and eastern North America, including well-known medicinal plants such as sassafras, witch hazel, hickory, blue cohosh, and the famous ginseng (*Panax* spp.).

American ginseng (*Panax quinquefolius*) and Asian ginseng (*Panax ginseng*) are considered distinct medicinal plants. In Chinese tradition,

American ginseng is considered more yin, helping to reduce the heat of the respiratory and digestive systems. Asian ginseng is stronger and more yang—a heat-raising tonic for the blood and circulatory system, as understood in TCM. Since American ginseng is a cold or mild tonic, reducing "heat" in the system and acting as a general rejuvenator, it is often preferred by the elderly and people in subtropical and tropical areas of Asia.

According to Dr. Shiu Ying Hu, the word "ginseng" is the French romanization of the Chinese name *ren-shen*. In Chinese ethnobotany, fleshy root-stocks with tonic effects are *shen*. *Ren* signifies "man." Hence the name translates as "the essence of Earth, dwelling in a root with a man-like form." Following the age-old belief in the **Doctrine of Signatures**—in which medicinal use of a plant is suggested by the resemblance of a plant part to an organ—ginseng is regarded as a tonic for the whole body.

American ginseng is first mentioned in the Chinese work *Ben Cao Gang Mu Shi Yi* (*Omissions from Ben Cao Gang Mu*) by Zhao Xue-min, published in 1765, about 50 years after its discovery by a Jesuit missionary in Quebec. It is a "new drug" by Chinese standards. The earliest reference to Asian ginseng is in *Shen Nong Ben Cao Jing*, compiled about A.D. 200. Dr. Shiu Ying Hu translates Shen Nong's account as: "It is used for repairing the five viscera, quieting the spirit, curbing the emotion, stopping agitation, removing noxious influence, brightening the eyes, enlightening the mind, and increasing the wisdom. Continuous use leads one to longevity with light weight."

Recent studies deem the herb **adaptogenic**—implying that it helps the body adapt to stress and increase endurance. It is also thought to enhance mental capacity. Wild ginseng from northeast China is exceedingly rare—and expensive. In the department store-size Tong-Ren-Tang drug store, one can find wild ginseng roots, handsomely displayed in neat, gold-gilded boxes on red silk with a price tag of about $8,000!

With the richest flora in the temperate world—some 30,000 species of flowering plants—China has 50 percent more species than North America. So for a Chinese botanist like Dr. Hu coming to America for the first time, the transition was not so difficult. She found much that was familiar. Over the past 200 years, temperate East Asia—with a similar climate and half again as many plant species as temperate North America—has been the primary source of garden ornamentals for the American garden. Many ornamental plants of Chinese origin, such as balloon flower, daylily, forsythia, and gardenia, are also sources of Chinese drugs. Dr. Hu and her colleagues have documented more than a thousand Chinese medicinal plants in American horticulture. Take away the difficult-to-pronounce Chinese names, and many Chinese herbs are already familiar to you. They grow all around you. ✍

OPPOSITE PAGE: *Traditional Chinese Medicine is not limited to China. Traditional Chinese drugs—ranging from the reishi mushroom (*Ganoderma lucidum*) to dried seahorses and starfish—are offered in a market in the Chinatown section of Ho Chi Minh City (Saigon), Vietnam. Today in the United States, there are more than 20,000 licensed acupuncturists and 400 companies specializing in Chinese herbal medicine products. Chinese herbal medicine is practiced in more than 120 countries.*

Eyebright
Euphrasia officinalis

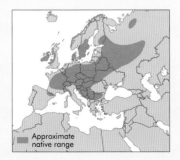

Common Names Eyebright, euphrasia

Latin Name *Euphrasia officinalis*

Family Scrophulariaceae

Parts Used Leaves, stems

Description Eyebright is a creeping, semiparasitic, annual herb that only grows about a foot high. It has small, deeply toothed leaves and strikingly marked flowers—white or pink with a central yellow spot and purple lines that converge in the throat of the blossom.

Habitat Native to Europe as well as parts of western Asia, eyebright grows in meadows and pastures in poor soil.

Approximate native range

I F YOU USE YOUR IMAGINATION—OR IF YOUR EYESIGHT IS NOT very good—you might think that the petite and pastel flowers of eyebright resemble tiny eyes. Bloodshot eyes, perhaps, because of the purplish "veins" that lead toward the dark center. Eyebright was first introduced as a medicinal "eye herb" in the 1100s by the European theologian, visionary, and herbalist Hildegard von Bingen (1098–1179). Later herbalists promoted eyebright for eye ailments as well, no doubt encouraged by a belief in the **Doctrine of Signatures**, the idea that the way a plant looks indicates the ailments for which is should be used in herbal medicine. The Doctrine of Signatures was very popular during the 1500s and 1600s, when many medieval herbalists were espousing eyebright's ocular benefits. The plant's genus name, *Euphrasia*, comes from the Greek *euphraino*, meaning "to gladden," a possible reference to the joy patients might experience at having their eyesight improved or restored. Although no research has established eyebright's value in treating eye diseases, the herb remains popular in herbal medicine and is prescribed for various eye ailments.

Traditional and Current Medicinal Uses

SINCE THE 12TH CENTURY, EYEBRIGHT HAS BEEN COMMONLY employed to treat various inflammations and infections of the eyes. Leaves and flowers were typically used to make a soothing wash for bathing sore eyes or compresses were steeped in the mixture and applied to the eyes. By the 14th century, eyebright's effectiveness was considered so extensive that herbalists praised it as being able to cure "all evils of the eye." Preparations of the herb were both applied to the eyes directly or taken internally as a syrup or mixed with wine. Eyebright tea was popular during the 1700s for clearing the sight and strengthening the memory; it was also taken for headache, hysteria, and insomnia. During the reign of England's Queen Elizabeth I, there was even an eyebright ale. Dried eyebright leaves were once incorporated into British "herbal tobacco," which was smoked to cure bronchial infections.

Modern herbalists still recommend eyebright preparations for a variety of eye irritations and disorders including conjunctivitis (an inflammation of the mucous membranes covering the eyeball and lining the eyelids) and blepharitis (a painful condition characterized by inflamed eyes and scaly eyelids). Eyebright is also suggested for treating sties, poor vision, eye strain, sensitivity to light, and eye ulcers. Some herbal practitioners recommend **infusions** of eyebright for sinus infections, hay fever, allergic rhinitis, coughs, and stomach upsets. It is also applied to the skin to soothe certain types of irritations as well as eczema.

Cultivation and Preparation

IN THE WILD, EYEBRIGHT THRIVES IN MEADOWS, PASTURES, and grasslands where the soil is poor and dry. It is abundant in the wild in eastern European countries. But since it is a semiparasitic and dependent on various grasses, it is not cultivated. Eyebright is harvested while in bloom, in late summer and early autumn. The plant is cut off just above the roots and the stems, leaves, and flowers are dried and used in various preparations.

Research

DESPITE EYEBRIGHT'S LONG HISTORY FOR TREATING EYE AILments, its effectiveness has never been verified scientifically. None of the traditional uses of eyebright have been tested in clinical studies. Some herbal texts suggest that the **astringent** actions of eyebright may reduce eye irritation or reduce mucous drainage. Other sources suggest that eyebright may have antibacterial actions. To date, however, there have been no studies to support or refute such claims. Eyebright contains a number of potentially active chemical compounds, including various **glycosides, tannins,** and **flavonoids**. Some of these components are known to have limited antibacterial and **anti-inflammatory** effects. But none have been proven to have specific effects on eye inflammation or irritation. Because there is limited information on eyebright's chemical make-up and because anything applied to the eyes should be sterile, many herbalists discourage using homemade eyebright preparations. Even over-the-counter eyebright drops may not be sterile.

A PLEASANT PARASITE

You would never know it just by looking, but eyebright lives off other plants. Botanists classify it as a semiparasitic plant because it only gets part of the nutrients it needs to survive from the host plants to which it attaches. The chloroplasts in eyebright's tiny bright green leaves make the rest of the food it needs. One of eyebright's preferred hosts is grass, so it is no wonder that eyebright plants are commonly found in meadows, pastures, and other grassy habitats. Beneath the soil's surface, tiny root suckers spread out from eyebright's roots. When the tips of the suckers encounter grass roots, they adhere to them and form tiny nodules that grow into the root tissue. Cells in the nodules are specialized for absorption, and they draw off sugars and other nutrients flowing through the host plant's roots. What is taken is not enough to harm the host, however, and the invading sucker tips do not penetrate the host's roots very deeply so they do no real damage. Furthermore, being an annual, eyebright does not develop into a persistent pest, and its drain on its host's resources ends with the coming of winter. In general, grasses survive eyebright's parasitism quite well. By the following spring they are usually ready to withstand another season of "nutrient sharing" when the seeds of the previous year's eyebright plants sprout and begin the cycle anew.

See Also: A Field Guide to Medicinal Plants and Herbs: Eastern and Central North America 2nd ed. by S. Foster and J. Duke, Houghton Mifflin, 2000; Medicinal Herbs History, Use, Recommended Dosages & Cautions by S. Foster, Interweave Press, 1998.

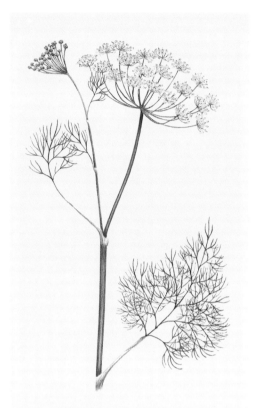

Fennel
Foeniculum vulgare

FENNEL IS A BEAUTIFUL PLANT. IN AN HERB GARDEN, ITS graceful stems and filigreed leaves soften the edges of fences and walls and provide a cloudlike backdrop for other plants. Fennel emits a wonderful fragrance that is clearly reminiscent of anise. The Romans called the plant *foeniculum*, which is derived from the Latin, *foenum*, meaning "hay"—possibly a reference to this fresh scent. *Foeniculum* became *fanculum* during the Middle Ages, which in turn gave rise to one of the herb's common names: "fenkel." Fennel has been a popular culinary herb throughout European history. The Romans ate the plant's seeds and young shoots, and the Anglo-Saxons included various parts of the herb in many recipes. Today fennel is still widely used in cooking and in the food industry. As an herbal medicine, fennel is most famous as an aid to digestion.

Traditional and Current Medicinal Uses

THE ROMANS ENJOYED FENNEL NOT ONLY AS A CULINARY PLANT but also as a medicinal. In the first century A.D., Pliny the Elder listed fennel as a remedy for more than 20 specific complaints. The Greek physicians Dioscorides (A.D. 40–90) and Hippocrates (460–377 B.C.) both recommended fennel to stimulate the flow of breast milk. In ancient times, the herb was widely used to treat menstrual disorders, gastrointestinal upsets, flatulence, and coughs. It seems also to have been effective as an aid to weight loss, by deadening hunger pangs. In fact, an ancient Greek name for fennel is *marathron*, from *maraino*, which means "to grow thin." Another reference to fennel's appetite-suppressing effects is found in the 17th-century botanical writings of William Coles, in which he mentions that fennel used in broths and drinks could help slenderize people who were overweight. Fennel seeds were brewed to make the famous "gripe water" of olden days, which was given to babies to cure colic and relieve gas. Fennel tea was also gargled as a breath freshener, to ease sore throats, and to heal infected gums. It was drunk to expel intestinal worms and applied as an eyewash to cure eye infections.

Common Names Fennel, wild fennel, fenkel, sweet fennel, finocchio

Latin Names *Foeniculum vulgare, F. vulagre var. dulce*

Family Apiaceae

Parts Used Seeds

Description Fennel is a four-to-five-foot, semi-hardy perennial often cultivated as an annual. Finely divided, feathery leaves have fleshy sheaths at their bases. Umbels (umbrella-like clusters) of small yellow flowers are succeeded by oval, ribbed, gray-brown fruits. The tapering root resembles a carrot.

Habitat Native to the Mediterranean, fennel is widely cultivated in Europe, temperate parts of Asia, India, Australia, and North America.

Approximate native range

In modern herbal medicine, fennel is widely recommended for menstrual disorders, to relieve bloating and settle upset stomachs, for flatulence, to relieve coughs, and to reduce the cramping effects of laxatives. Fennel preparations are used as remedies for skin diseases and conjunctivitis (an inflammation of the mucous membranes covering the eyeball and lining the eyelids). The herb also is incorporated into preparations used to increase the flow of breast milk in nursing mothers.

Cultivation and Preparation

COMMON FENNEL IS EASILY GROWN FROM SEED IN WELL-drained to sandy soil in full sun. Sweet fennel requires richer soil and plenty of water to produce the swollen stems that are used in cooking. *F. vulgare* is the species primarily used in herbal medicine. While active constituents are found in the plant's leaves, stems, and roots, the most concentrated source is the seed. Ripe seeds are harvested in autumn. They are used whole, ground, or distilled for oil.

Research

FENNEL OIL IS EXTRACTED PRIMARILY FROM THE SEEDS OF *F. vulgare*. Its active ingredients include sweet-tasting anethole (also the chief constituent of anise oil) and bitter-tasting fenchone and estragole. The proportions of these three compounds vary in fennel plants, depending both on the species and where they are cultivated. Studies have shown that anethole has antispasmodic and **anti-inflammatory** properties. It also increases motility in the digestive tract. Both anethole and fenchone are proven stimulants that promote secretions in the respiratory tract, helping to break up chest congestion and facilitate breathing. In laboratory experiments, fennel oil has shown antimicrobial effects. In studies with lab animals, fennel extracts also exhibit **estrogenic** (estrogen-promoting) action. Fennel preparations are generally safe, but the pure **essential oil** should be avoided. It has been known to cause not only skin irritations but also vomiting, seizures, and respiratory problems. Fennel is not suitable for pregnant woman and acts as a uterine stimulant in large doses.

FENNEL FOR LONG LIFE

The ancient Greeks and Romans believed fennel bestowed strength, courage, and long life on those who consumed and used it. Fennel was one of nine herbs held sacred by the Anglo-Saxons and believed to possess the power to cure diseases, which were thought to be the result of poisons carried on the wind. In medieval monasteries and churches, fennel was a strewing herb for sweetening the air. Inserted in keyholes or hung over doors, the herb was said to ward off witches and evil spirits during the Middle Ages. Fennel was eaten with fish dishes during Lent, perhaps to aid digestion as much as to flavor the food; fennel seeds were also eaten during Lent to allay hunger. The emperor Charlemagne (742–814 A.D.) is credited with introducing fennel from its Mediterranean homeland to central and northern Europe, where it was cultivated on his imperial farms. Fennel remains widely cultivated today. Two of the common culinary forms are *Foeniculum vulgare* (common or wild fennel) and *F. vulgare* var. *dulce* (sweet fennel, Florence fennel, or finocchio). Both have a taste similar to anise, but sweet fennel is sweeter. Fennel leaves are common in salads. The stems, especially the celery-like stems of sweet fennel, are eaten raw or cooked as a vegetable. Whole, cracked, or ground seeds are used to flavor breads, sausages, cucumber dishes, stuffing, and liqueurs. Both seeds and leaves are used to make anise-flavored tea.

See Also: *Herbal Medicine Expanded Commission E Monographs* by M. Blumenthal, A. Goldberg, J.Brinckmann, American Botanical Council, 2000; *A Field Guide to Medicinal Plants and Herbs: Eastern and Central N. America, 2nd ed.* by S. Foster, J. Duke, Houghton Mifflin, 2000.

FOENICULUM VULGARE | Fennel

Feverfew
Tanacetum parthenium

IT IS NOT HARD TO GUESS ONE OF THE ORIGINAL USES FOR feverfew—the common name comes from the Latin *febris*, for "fever," and *fugure*, meaning "to chase away." Feverfew has been used as a medicinal herb since ancient Greece not only for keeping fevers at bay but also for treating a range of complaints, including headache. Although it was included in many old herbals, feverfew was not widely used during the last century. Then in 1974 a Welsh doctor's wife gained relief from her chronic migraine headaches by eating fresh feverfew leaves. The discovery sparked a flurry of research that revealed that this rather unassuming herb may be a potential long-term treatment for easing and preventing migraine headaches and a possible pain reliever for arthritis as well.

Traditional and Current Medicinal Uses

FEVERFEW WAS MENTIONED BY THE ANCIENT GREEK PHYSICIAN Dioscorides as an herb valued for its effects on the uterus; it was used to help expel the placenta after childbirth and ease menstrual irregularities. Feverfew was also a remedy for stomach upsets, headaches, and inflammation. In the centuries that followed, feverfew was considered a cure for a variety of ills, including stomach disorders, toothache, headache, and menstrual complaints. It was often mixed with honey or sweet wine to disguise its bitter taste. In the 1600s and 1700s, feverfew's value as a headache cure continued. European colonists introduced feverfew to the Americas. In South America, the herb was used for morning sickness, stomachache, and for easing kidney pains and colic. In parts of Central America, it was employed as a digestive aid and to promote menstruation. In the last century, some herbalists used feverfew for relieving pain and treating fevers, but it gradually fell into obscurity.

In the 1970s, discovery of feverfew's ability to relieve headaches, particularly migraines, brought it back as an alternative to conventional medicine's treatment of these conditions. Since then, feverfew has undergone considerable scientific study and in many cases has been found to be helpful in treating migraine headaches, as well as

Common Names Feverfew, featherfew, bachelor's buttons, featherfoil

Latin Name *Tanacetum parthenium*

Family Asteraceae

Parts Used Leaves, flowering tops

Description A member of the daisy family, feverfew is a strong-smelling, branching perennial with oval, lobed, yellow-green leaves and numerous diminutive, daisy-like flowers.

Habitat Feverfew is native to central and southern Europe, but has been naturalized in most parts of the temperate zone, including North America. It thrives in dry, stony soils along roadsides and woodland borders and in abandoned places.

Approximate native range

the nausea and vomiting that often accompanies them. Feverfew is also taken for rheumatism and for menstrual problems.

Cultivation and Preparation

DROUGHT-TOLERANT FEVERFEW GROWS WELL IN ORDINARY soil and full sun. The herb is best propagated by seed or by division. Leaves are harvested for fresh use. The entire plant is cut during flowering and dried for use in pills, capsules, **tinctures**, and other preparations.

Research

FEVERFEW CONTAINS A **VOLATILE OIL** THAT INCLUDES CAMphor, and many chemical compounds, including parthenolide, thought to be key in terms of the herb's ability to relieve migraines. Migraines seem to be triggered by abnormal aggregation of **platelets** in the bloodstream and their subsequent release of **serotonin** and inflammatory substances. In lab studies, feverfew has been shown to deter **platelet aggregation** and inhibit production of inflammatory substances. These actions may explain feverfew's ability to reduce the severity, duration, and frequency of migraines in many cases. They could also account for the herb's historical use as an **anti-inflammatory**. Feverfew's active ingredients also inhibit smooth muscle contractions, particularly those in the walls of blood vessels in the brain; constriction of these vessels is thought to be a major contributor to migraine headaches. Clinical trials have found feverfew helpful in relieving the severity and frequency of migraines, but other studies have shown no benefit. No clinical studies have yet been shown to support the use of feverfew in the treatment of rheumatoid arthritis. More research is needed in both these areas. For now, herbal practitioners suggest feverfew may be most appropriate for migraine sufferers who have not improved using conventional therapies or who cannot tolerate standard medications because of side effects. Most authorities who advocate feverfew for migraines suggest using high quality dried leaf extracts. Chewing the fresh leaves of the plant, or drinking tea made from them, has led to mouth ulceration and swelling of the tongue and mouth tissues in some individuals.

A BUG-OFF HERB

About 70 species make up the genus *Tanacetum*. Many of them, including feverfew, are pungently aromatic. They contain volatile oils and other compounds that cause allergic reactions in some people. They also contain pyrethrins, which are natural insecticides that repel and kill insects. The highest concentrations of pyrethrins are found in tiny oil-containing glands of the seed case in the tightly packed flower heads of many *Tanacetum* species. The first pyrethrin-based insecticide was made in the early 19th century from one of feverfew's close cousins, red pyrethrum (*T. coccineum*) and was known as Persian or Caucasian Insect Powder. More experimentation led to the discovery that another species, *T. cinerariifolium*, was the best source for these insecticidal compounds. Natural pyrethrins are contact poisons. They penetrate the body of an insect and affect its nervous system. Pyrethrins are very fast acting. Minutes after coming into contact with these chemicals, an insect cannot move or fly away. A large dose will kill it. But a small dose is swiftly detoxified by the insect's own enzymes, enough so that it can recover. In modern pyrethrin-based insecticides, compounds such as organophosphates that delay the action of enzymes are added to pyrethrin mixtures to make them more effective. Pyrethrins decompose rapidly in the environment and in general are not toxic to people and other vertebrates. Pyrethrin dusts are commonly used to kill insects that feed on crops and ornamentals. They are also used to control lice, mosquitoes, cockroaches, beetles, and flies.

See Also: The ABC Clinical Guide to Herbs by M. Blumenthal, T. Hall, and A. Goldberg, American Botanical Council, 2003; *World Health Organization (WHO) Monographs on Selected Medicinal Plants, Vol. 2*, 2002.

Flax

Linum usitatissimum

FLAX IS ONE OF THE WORLD'S OLDEST CROP PLANTS, HAVing been cultivated since at least 5,000 B.C., first by the ancient Mesopotamians and then by the Egyptians. The Romans were probably responsible for spreading flax as a crop plant throughout Europe. *Linum* is the original Latin name for the plant, which in turn was derived from its Greek name, *linon*. Flax is a multipurpose herb. Its slender stalks are a source of strong, supple fibers used for countless centuries to make rope, nets, sacks, bowstrings, sails, and, of course, linen fabrics. Linseed oil from the crushed seeds has long been used in paints and was once the essential ingredient in linoleum. The seeds have been baked into breads since ancient Greece and Rome. Both seeds and oil have been used medicinally in many cultures. Still respected today in both herbal and conventional medicine, flax is used for promoting digestive and respiratory health, for its soothing and emollient properties, and as a source of cancer-fighting **lignans** and heart-healthy essential fatty acids.

Traditional and Current Medicinal Uses

HIPPOCRATES RECOMMENDED FLAX FOR COLDS, AND THE HERB is a centuries-old remedy employed to relieve coughs and colds and soothe sore throats. Flax seed has long been recognized as a useful laxative. Since the Middle Ages, the oil from flax seed has also been prescribed for constipation, as well as urinary tract infections and respiratory ailments. In the eighth century, the emperor Charlemagne was so convinced of the therapeutic properties of flax that he demanded his subjects eat flax seeds regularly to maintain good health. **Poultices** made from boiled, crushed seeds were commonly applied to swellings, burns, boils and other skin eruptions, and to ease aches and pains in muscles and joints. A thick, mucilaginous liquid extracted from the seeds was also used as a poultice applied to burns and other types of inflammation. Native Americans used flax for stomach disorders, kidney disease, coughs, diseases of the lungs, and for urinary infections, as well as for skin and eye problems.

Common Names Flax, common flax, flaxseed, linseed, lint bells

Latin Name *Linum usitatissimum*

Family Linaceae

Parts Used Seed, oil

Description A slender annual herb, flax has a solitary, erect stem that branches at the top and narrow, spear-shaped, gray-green leaves. Simple, five-petaled pale blue flowers are followed by seed capsules that contain small, shiny, flattened brown seeds.

Habitat Thought to be a native of Asia, flax is cultivated worldwide.

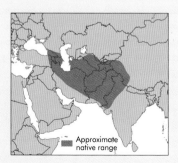

Approximate
native range

In modern herbal medicine, flax is recommended as a safe, gentle laxative for chronic constipation, irritable bowel syndrome, and diverticulitis. The herb is used to treat coughs, sore throats, bronchitis and emphysema, gastric disorders, and urinary tract infections, including chronic cystitis (inflammation of the bladder). Flax is also used to treat rheumatoid arthritis, menstrual problems, atherosclerosis, skin conditions, and in fighting endometrial, colon, breast, and prostate cancer.

Cultivation and Preparation

FLAX IS EASILY GROWN FROM SEED SOWN IN SPRING INTO WELL-drained, sandy, slightly dry soils in full sun. It is cultivated in the northwestern United States, Canada, and Europe. The plants are cut when mature for extracting the fibers they contain. The seed is used medicinally. Seeds are collected when they are ripe, and sold whole or pressed to extract their oil. The oil is often marketed in health food stores as soft-gel capsules.

Research

FLAX SEED OIL CONTAINS LARGE AMOUNTS OF AN OMEGA-3 fatty acid known as alpha-linolenic acid, a compound closely related to the beneficial essential fatty acids found in fish oils. An estimated 80 percent of all Americans are deficient in omega-3 fatty acids. Research has shown that omega-3 oils combat inflammation, stimulate immune system function, and protect against kidney disease, heart problems, and cancer. Flax is also one of the most concentrated sources known of plant lignans; the seeds contain 100 to 800 times the amount found in most other plant foods. Lignans have been shown to reduce the concentration in the bloodstream of certain forms of estrogen that promote tumor growth in endometrial and breast cancers. Clinical studies support the use of flax in preventing breast cancer and its metastasis (spread). Other studies have demonstrated positive effects of flax in treating endometrial, colon, and prostate cancers. Research has also shown that flax supports brain function, reduces cholesterol levels, **platelet aggregation** that can lead to blood clots, and inflammation, and protects against degenerative diseases.

FLAX FACTS AND FOLKLORE

It is impossible to know exactly how long flax fibers have been used by people, but they have been unearthed in prehistoric archeological sites. The Egyptians wrapped their mummies in linen and adorned tombs with paintings and carvings of the plant. There are many references to linen clothing in the Bible. Most medieval English monasteries and nunneries cultivated small fields of flax that were a source of fiber for making napkins, cloths, and wimples for nuns. The inferior fibers were used to make lamp wicks and stuffed into building cracks to keep out drafts. Many old herbals describe the process of turning flax stems into fiber for making clothing, sheets, sails, fishing nets, thread, rope, sack, bags, and even bowstrings. For at least 200 years, flax was a main source of fabric in the American colonies, in the form of homemade "linsey-woolsey" made from linen and wool.

Flax is rich in folklore as well as fiber. In German myths, the flax plant was protected by the goddess Hulda, credited with having taught mortals the art of growing flax and spinning and weaving cloth from it. In the Middle Ages, flax flowers were said to protect against witchcraft. Before planting flax, superstitious farmers sat on the bags of seed three times and faced east to ensure a good crop. Ringing church bells on Ascension Day and jumping over midsummer fires were also thought to encourage a healthy flax crop.

See Also: *The ABC Clinical Guide to Herbs* by M. Blumenthal, T. Hall, and A. Goldberg, American Botanical Council, 2003; *A Field Guide to Medicinal Plants and Herbs: Eastern and Central North America, 2nd ed.* by S. Foster and J. Duke, Houghton Mifflin, 2000.

Forskohlii
Plectranthus barbatus

THE GENUS *PLECTRANTHUS* COMPRISES SOME HUNDRED species of mostly tropical and subtropical plants. Many are widely grown ornamentals due to their bright variegated foliage that comes in hues of red, yellow, lime green, and purple—and their remarkable tolerance for shade. Forskohlii, with its undistinguished green leaves, is not a particularly striking member of the genus. But it has been a part of the Indian herbal medicine tradition for centuries. In the 1970s, forskohlii captured the attention of practitioners in conventional medicine as well when a chemical compound called forskolin was isolated from the herb's roots and found to have a variety of therapeutic effects.

Traditional and Current Medicinal Uses

ANCIENT SANSKRIT TEXTS MENTION FORSKOHLII AS A TRADITIONAL remedy for digestive complaints. It also has a long history in Indian and Asian folk medicine as a treatment for heart and lung conditions (including asthma), intestinal spasms, convulsions, skin problems, and insomnia.

Modern interest in forskohlii's medicinal properties began in 1974, when researchers from Hoechst Pharmaceuticals, in collaboration with the Indian Central Drug Research Institute, were screening herbs used in traditional medicine for potential new drugs. In studies of root **extracts** from forskohlii, the researchers discovered that the extract calmed muscle spasms and lowered blood pressure. Intensive analysis of the extract resulted in the isolation of a chemically active ingredient, forskolin, thought to be the substance responsible for the root extract's beneficial effects. Now available in supplement form and as a prescription drug, forskolin is often recommended for treating hypothyroidism, a condition in which the thyroid gland produces too little thyroid hormone. It is also suggested as a treatment for asthma, for skin conditions such as eczema and psoriasis, and for conditions characterized by muscle cramping, such as spastic colon, angina, and bladder pain due to urinary tract infections. Forskolin has also been shown to lower high

Common Names Forskohlii, makandi, Kaffir potato

Latin Names *Plectranthus barbatus,* synonym *Coleus forskohlii*

Family Lamiaceae

Parts Used Leaves, roots

Description A perennial member of the mint family, forskohlii has tuberous roots and bright green leaves with irregularly serrated margins borne on erect stems. The herb grows to approximately two feet in height and gives off an aroma of camphor.

Habitat Forskohlii is indigenous to relatively dry hillsides and lower-elevation mountain slopes in India, Nepal, Thailand, and Sri Lanka.

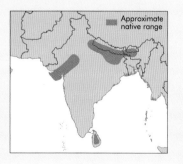

Approximate native range

blood pressure and reduce pressure inside the eyes brought on by glaucoma.

Cultivation and Preparation

FORSKOHLII GROWS BEST IN WELL-DRAINED SOIL IN A SUNNY or partly shaded location. Propagation is by root division or stem cuttings in summer. Both the leaves and roots of forskohlii are harvested in autumn for their medicinal properties, when active ingredients are most concentrated. Medicinal preparations include **decoctions** of the dried root and **infusions** of the leaves. Because forskohlii root contains only small amounts of forskolin, many who use this herb medicinally take supplements standardized for forskolin content. Pure forskolin is a prescription medication.

Research

STUDIES HAVE SHOWN THAT FORSKOLIN EXERTS A VARIETY of effects because it activates an important **enzyme** that raises levels of a substance called cyclic adenosine monophosphate, or cAMP; this substance (cAMP) then activates other chemicals that help carry out the complex effects of hormones in the body. In this way, forskolin is thought to stimulate the release of thyroid hormone, relieving many symptoms associated with hypothyroidism, such as depression, fatigue, weight gain, and dry skin. By raising levels of cAMP, forskolin also relaxes smooth muscles, thus helping to lower blood pressure by dilating blood vessels and to decrease lung spasms associated with asthma and other bronchial conditions (by relaxing smooth muscles in air passages). Forskolin has also been shown to inhibit production of substances that trigger the body's **inflammatory response**, making it potentially useful in the treatment of asthma, eczema, and other allergic conditions. The compound has also been proposed for psoriasis, which seems to be partly related to low levels of cAMP in skin cells. Applications of an ophthalmic preparation of forskolin reduce the intraocular pressure of glaucoma by stimulating better blood flow inside the eyes. Most current research being done on forskohlii relates to forskolin; scientific support for using preparations of the herb itself in the treatment of disease is much weaker.

THE PLANT WORLD'S CINDERELLA

Forskohlii has recently been placed in the genus *Plectranthus* and is more widely known under the name *Coleus forskohlii*. It is a plant somewhat weedy in habit that had attracted little attention. The species name, *forskohlii*, which has come to be used as a modern common name, honors the Finnish botanist Petrus Forsskal (1732–1763), who traveled extensively in the Middle East on plant surveys until he died of plague at the age of 31. Unlike most herbs currently used in Ayurvedic medicine, forskohlii is not a major medicinal plant of Indian traditions; rather its importance emerged as the result of scientific screenings in the 1970s. In the search for new compounds that might have future value as a prescription drug, Hoechst India Limited led a screening program of medicinal plants of India based on a combination of medical, chemical, and botanical criteria. The plant, then known to botanists as *Coleus forskohlii*, was screened because of its botanical relationship to *Coleus amboinicus*, the source of a traditional Ayurvedic drug known as *pashanbhed*. Ethnobotanical information on forskohlii was scant at the time. When the compound forskohlin was discovered in the screening program, *C. forskohlii* was thrust into prominence due to its unique pharmacological mechanism of action discovered in the early 1980s. Despite extensive efforts to find the compound in other plants, forskohlin has only been found in *Plectranthus barbatus* (*Coleus forskohlii*).

See Also: Medical Botany: Plants Affecting Human Health by W. Lewis and M. Elvin-Lewis, John Wiley & Sons, 2003; *Medicinal Plants of the World* by B. van Wyk and M. Wink, Timber Press, 2004.

PLECTRANTHUS BARBATUS | Forskohlii

Foxglove
Digitalis purpurea

Common Names Foxglove, purple foxglove, finger-hut, folksglove, dead men's bells

Latin Name *Digitalis purpurea*

Family Scrophulariaceae

Parts Used Leaves

Description A biennial or short-lived perennial, foxglove produces a dense rosette of large, downy leaves in its first year. In its second year, one or more spectacular, one-sided flower stalks emerge that can reach six feet in height. Flowers are bell-shaped and range from pink to mauve with dark purple spots on the inside.

Habitat Foxglove is native to the Mediterranean region and Europe, where it grows wild in woodland clearings, heaths, and on mountain slopes. Foxglove has been naturalized in the British Isles and many parts of North and Central America and is widely cultivated as a garden plant.

Approximate native range

F OXGLOVE IS A MEMBER OF THE FIGWORT FAMILY. ITS ELE-gant flower spires decorate woodland clearings, roadsides, and meadows all over Europe and England. The common name for the plant in German is *fingerhut* (literally "finger hat"), which means "thimble." In 1542, the German botanist Leonard Fuchs gave foxglove its Latin name, *Digitalis*, based on this resemblance (digit = finger). The origin of the name foxglove is less straightforward, however. Some sources say it has to do with a Northern European legend that claims foxes wore the flowers on their feet to muffle their footsteps while out hunting at night. Another suggests that the name comes from an Anglo-Saxon word, *foxesglew*, meaning "fox music" in reference to the flower's resemblance to an ancient musical instrument. Many other sources propose that the name "foxglove" was originally "folksglove," a reference to the fairy folk that supposedly inhabited the forests. Although it is extremely poisonous, foxglove is a potent source of the powerful chemicals that have long been used to treat congestive heart failure in both herbal and conventional medicine.

Traditional and Current Medicinal Uses

FOXGLOVE WAS CULTIVATED FOR USE AS AN HERBAL MEDICINE as long ago as A.D. 1000. In Great Britain and on the European continent, foxglove was used for centuries as an **expectorant** in treating coughs, for epilepsy and paralysis, to reduce swelling in lymph glands, especially those in the neck, and to cleanse, dry, and heal sores, skin ulcers, and wounds. Many European herbalists, including Gerard, Culpeper, and Fuchs, wrote about foxglove and its medicinal roles. The herb was introduced into the *London Pharmacopoeia* in 1650. However, it was not until the late 1700s that foxglove's value in treating the symptoms of a weak heart (a condition then known as dropsy) came to light. After that, the herb quickly found a place in conventional as well as herbal medicine. It was widely prescribed by physicians for controlling the **edema** (swelling) associated with congestive heart failure, as well as for cardiac insufficiency and abnormalities in the heartbeat. Its beneficial effects are derived from several **steroid glycosides** that act as cardiac stimulants and are very effective in treating congestive heart failure as well as certain congenital heart defects.

Cultivation and Preparation

FOXGLOVE THRIVES IN RICH, MOIST, WELL-DRAINED SOIL IN full sun or light shade. It can be started from seed, and it self-sows readily. The leaves are used in herbal medicine and they are typically harvested just as the flower stalk is beginning to bloom. The leaves are dried for the commercial extraction of the medicinally important chemical compounds they contain.

Research

IN PHARMACEUTICAL TERMS, *DIGITALIS* ONCE REFERRED TO the powdered leaf of *Digitalis purpurea*, made into pills. However, the raw leaf is no longer widely used. Instead, the most medicinally active glycosides, including digitoxin, digoxin, and gitoxin, are extracted and formulated into prescription drugs that allow for precisely controlled doses. Research has shown that digitoxin and digoxin are effective in treating congestive heart failure because they strengthen the force of heart contractions while at the same time slowing the heart beat so the period of relaxation between beats is lengthened. The heart muscle is thus able to rest even though it is working harder. This also helps to reduce high venous blood pressure but to increase low arterial blood pressure caused by impaired heart function. The improved circulation helps alleviate the fluid retention and edema that characterize congestive heart failure. Both pure digitoxin and digoxin are considerably more powerful than the powdered leaves of the herb itself. Digoxin is more rapidly excreted and less cumulative in the body, and thus very widely prescribed for heart conditions. Preparations of this glycoside are also employed in treating muscular dystrophy and in helping reduce eye pressure in people suffering from glaucoma.

CAUTION All parts of the foxglove plant are extremely poisonous. *Digitalis* preparations should never be used for self-medication.

Although foxglove had a place in folk traditions, it did not become an important medicine until the late 1700s. English physician and botanist William Withering (1741–1799) is credited with the introduction of foxglove to medicine. Withering practiced in Stafford, England, and in 1775 became chief physician at the Birmingham General Hospital. In that year, Withering examined a woman suffering from a case of dropsy, a heart-related condition in which fluid accumulates and causes swelling in tissues and body cavities. The woman's condition was so severe that Withering expected her to die shortly; he was surprised to hear some weeks later that she was much improved. She credited her recovery to an herbal drink given her by a woman who claimed it was a family recipe for dropsy. Withering got the recipe and discovered it included foxglove as an ingredient. For the next ten years, he experimented with extracts of the plant and its effects. He deduced that foxglove contained compounds that relieved fluid buildup in the body and strengthened the heart. In 1785, Withering published *An Account of the Foxglove and Some of its Medical Uses*, summarizing his extensive clinical trials. The account thrust foxglove into the forefront of conventional medical treatments for some types of heart disease. Withering died in 1799 after a battle with tuberculosis. A monument to him in Birmingham bears the fitting symbol of a foxglove.

DIGITALIS PURPUREA | Foxglove

See Also: *Nature's Medicine, Plants That Heal* by Joel Swerdlow, National Geographic, 2000; *A Field Guide to Medicinal Plants and Herbs: Eastern and Central North America, 2nd ed.* by S. Foster and J. Duke, Houghton Mifflin, 2000.

Garlic

Allium sativum

A VALUABLE FOOD, SEASONING, AND MEDICINAL HERB, garlic has been part of human culture for at least 5,000 years. It was a dietary staple in ancient Egypt and Mesopotamia. Roman soldiers were given garlic to sustain them on long marches. In terms of its medicinal properties, garlic was recognized long ago for its healing powers, especially in battling infections. Garlic is in the same genus, *Allium*, as onions, chives, and leeks. *Allium* is Latin for "onion." It may, in turn, have its origins in the Celtic word *all*, which means "burning or smarting" and could refer to the pungent and distinctive taste characteristic of garlic and its relatives.

Traditional and Current Medicinal Uses

HERBALISTS OF THE ANCIENT WORLD HAD MUCH PRAISE FOR garlic. In the first century A.D., Pliny the Elder wrote that garlic was an antidote for snakebites and certain poisons and good for treating asthma, as a cough suppressant, and to rid the body of intestinal parasites. Known as *da-suan* in China, garlic was being used as a medicinal herb at least by A.D. 500 for treating colds, tuberculosis, dysentery, and digestive ailments as well as fungal infections of the skin. It was used in both India and China for its beneficial effects on circulation and the heart. Long before the discovery of antibiotics, garlic was renowned for its success in treating infections. In 1858 French microbiologist Louis Pasteur investigated garlic's antibacterial properties in his laboratory. Garlic was widely used during World War I to dress wounds, and Albert Schweitzer used the herb to treat amoebic dysentery in Africa. Over the centuries, the list of ailments and conditions that are helped by garlic has grown considerably.

Modern herbalists use garlic in treating external and internal bacterial, viral, and fungal infections. It is prescribed for reducing nasal congestion and easing the symptoms of colds and a variety of other respiratory conditions. As garlic tends to inhibit blood clotting, it is used to promote circulatory system health by helping to prevent coronary heart disease, thrombosis, and

Common Name Garlic

Latin Name *Allium sativum*

Family Liliaceae

Parts Used Bulb, separated into cloves

Description Garlic is a hardy, bulbous perennial. Each parent bulb is surrounded by several bulblets or cloves, enclosed by a papery casing. Mature bulbs are two to three inches in diameter. Long, flat green leaves hug a central, rounded stem that can reach two to three feet. In spring, a terminal cluster of small whitish flowers develops at the top of the stem, initially enclosed in a papery bract. Small black seeds are produced (seeds do not mature in cultivated varieties).

Habitat Garlic is thought to have originated in Central Asia, but today it is found worldwide and widely cultivated, although it does not flourish in cold climates.

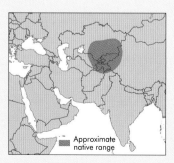

Approximate native range

strokes. It also lowers blood sugar levels and may be helpful in treating diabetes.

Cultivation and Preparation

GARLIC GROWS BEST IN RICH, MOIST, SANDY SOIL WITH plenty of sun in a warm climate. It is grown as an annual and can be planted in spring or autumn. Bulbs are separated into individual cloves; these are planted, flat end down, about three inches deep. Much of the garlic cultivated commercially in the U.S. comes from central California, where the harvest exceeds several hundred million pounds annually. Garlic bulbs are harvested in summer. For medicinal purposes, garlic cloves are used whole, chopped, or crushed. Cutting and macerating the cloves releases active compounds from the plant tissues.

Research

WITHIN THE NEAT PACKAGE OF A GARLIC BULB LIES A STORE-house of chemically active substances. Intact garlic cloves are rich in an odorless, sulfur-containing compound called alliin. When cloves are cut or crushed, alliin comes into contact with the enzyme alliinase, which quickly transforms alliin into allicin. Allicin and its breakdown products are largely responsible for garlic's beneficial actions in the body. They exhibit notable antibiotic, antiviral, and antifungal properties. Since the 1960s, considerable laboratory and clinical research has been carried out on garlic and its effects in the U.S., Germany, Japan, and many other countries. Hundreds of research papers support the long-held belief that garlic can improve circulatory health. It works by lowering blood cholesterol, acting as an antioxidant to protect blood vessels from free radicals, lowering levels of **low-density lipoproteins** (LDLs) in the blood (thereby increasing the proportion of HDLs in circulation), increasing the flow of blood to capillaries (slightly lowering blood pressure), reducing the tendency of blood to clot, and enhancing a physiological process called fibrinolysis, which works to remove plaque and clots from blood vessels. Other studies have investigated garlic's antiviral effects, including anti-HIV activity, as well as the herb's role in reducing the risk of certain cancers.

A POTENT PACKAGE

It is the allicin and other sulphur-containing compounds in garlic that are largely responsible for garlic's strong odor. And, as anyone who has ever eaten garlic knows, that odor tends to linger on the breath. This is because garlic's aromatic compounds are excreted from the body via the lungs, and to a lesser extent, through the skin. The problem of having "garlic breath" is not a new phenomenon. The Roman poet Horace (65–8 B.C.) was revolted by the smell of garlic, on the breath or otherwise, and considered it a sign of vulgarity. Herbalists in the Middle Ages recommended chewing parsley to help eliminate garlic's odor on the breath. Chewing a leaf of basil (*Ocimum*), mint (*Mentha*), or thyme (*Thymus*) may also counteract it. If time and circumstances allow, taking a long bath in fairly hot water may help as well, as this is thought to hasten the evaporation of aromatic garlic compounds that are being excreted through the skin. For people who want to enjoy the beneficial health effects of garlic but worry about having garlic breath (and its social ramifications), garlic capsules and tablets are widely available. However, garlic's active compounds in these forms may not be as effective as they are in the fresh herb itself.

See Also: The ABC Clinical Guide to Herbs by M. Blumenthal, T. Hall, and A. Goldberg, American Botanical Council, 2003; *Herbal Emissaries: Bringing Chinese Herbs to the West* by S. Foster and Y. Chongxi, Healing Arts Press, 1992.

Gentian

Gentiana lutea

GENTIAN WAS NAMED FOR THE SUPPOSED DISCOVERER of its medicinal powers in the second century B.C., King Gentius of Illyria, a country on the Balkan Peninsula that was situated approximately where modern Albania and Bosnia are now. But the use of gentian in herbal medicine predates Gentius, the Illyrian king. An Egyptian papyrus from 1200 B.C. mentions gentian as an ingredient in medicines. Both the Arabs and the Greeks were familiar with the herb as well. The species name, *lutea*, is from a Latin word meaning "yellow" and refers to the brilliant yellow flowers of this stately herb that is native to the slopes of the Alps, Carpathians, Pyrenees, and other mountain ranges in central Europe and western Asia. But for many centuries, gentian has been prized far more for its intensely bitter-tasting root than for its flowers. Bitter substances have long been used in herbal medicine as bitter tonics or "stomachics" to improve both the appetite and digestion by stimulating the flow of gastric juices. Gentian remains popular in modern herbal medicine as a bitter tonic used to treat indigestion, poor appetite, and **anorexia**.

Traditional and Current Medicinal Uses

ANCIENT ARAB AND GREEK HERBALISTS AND PHYSICIANS REComended preparations of gentian for stomach and liver ailments, to kill intestinal worms, and to guard against infectious diseases. The Roman physician Pliny wrote that gentian was effective against stomach complaints, digestive disorders, ulcers, and certain infections and irritations of the skin. By the Middle Ages, gentian had been introduced into the British Isles. It was cultivated in monastic gardens there and in Europe and preparations of the roots were prescribed as a remedy for reducing fever and stimulating the flow of digestive juices and bile. The herb was also used to cleanse and disinfect wounds and was considered an antidote to some poisons. In the 1700s, gentian wine was drunk in Germany as an aperitif before dinner; a variety of other gentian-based bitter tonics and aperitifs were popular in many countries. In the 1800s,

Common Names Gentian, yellow gentian, bitterwort

Latin Name *Gentiana lutea*

Family Gentianaceae

Parts Used Roots

Description A hardy perennial growing to six feet, gentian has a thick taproot, sturdy erect stems, and fleshy, ribbed leaves that grow in pairs joined at the base. Bright yellow, star-shaped flowers emerge in whorls from the leaf axils of the uppermost leaf pairs on each stem.

Habitat Native to Europe and western Asia, gentian grows in the wild in high mountain meadows up to 8,000 feet. It has been overcollected and is protected in parts of its former range.

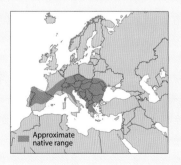

Approximate native range

gentian was commonly used to improve appetite, strengthen digestion, cure indigestion, treat diarrhea and debility, improve circulation, and as a remedy for gout, jaundice, menstrual problems, exhaustion from chronic disease, hysteria, and worms.

Today, gentian is still used in herbal medicine to stimulate appetite, relieve stomach and intestinal upsets, and for liver complaints. It is sometimes recommended to reduce fever and treat anemia.

Cultivation and Preparation

GENTIAN PREFERS MOIST, WELL-DRAINED, HUMUSY SOIL AND strong, direct sunshine. It can be propagated from seed, but frost (or cold treatment) is needed for germination. Gentian plants also can be propagated by division. The roots are harvested in late summer or autumn and thoroughly cured by drying. Good quality gentian roots are a dark red-brown and have an unpleasant odor and a taste that is initially sweet and then intensely bitter. Gentian is endangered in much of its native range due to overcollecting. Wild collecting is subject to strict controls. The herb is also cultivated on a small scale at lower altitudes in parts of France, Germany, Italy, and Austria, but most of the gentian used in herbal medicine is still wild collected. Some gentian is also cultivated in the northwestern United States and Canada.

Research

THE ACTIVE INGREDIENTS IN GENTIAN ARE BITTER COMPOUNDS, particularly gentiopicroside and amarogentin, which is more than 3,000 times more bitter than gentiopicroside. These substances stimulate the taste buds and promote, as a nerve-directed reflex response, the flow of saliva, gastric juices, and bile from the liver and from the gallbladder. This activity is what stimulates both appetite and encourages normal functioning of the digestive tract. Laboratory studies have shown gentian extracts to exhibit antimicrobial and immune-stimulating properties. The herb also appears to stimulate the production of red blood cells. In experiments using laboratory animals, there are some indications that gentian may also increase bronchial secretions.

THE BITTEREST SUBSTANCE KNOWN

Gentian is what is known as a "pure" bitter in herbal medicine. The bitter taste of the plant's roots is so strong that it survives drying, grinding to a powder, and repeated dilution. In fact, the bitter taste of gentian can still be detected at dilutions of at least 1:20,000—one part herb for every 20,000 parts water. Another way of saying that is that gentian root has a bitterness value of 20,000. Much of gentian's bitter nature is due to the presence of small amounts of a glycoside known as amarogentin. It has a bitterness value of an astounding 58,000,000, making it possibly the most intensely bitter substance known. Gentian is a prized ingredient for making bitter aperitifs that many take to aid digestion, especially before a heavy, fatty meal. Some of the most famous include Enzian schnapps, a traditional Austrian brandy, and Angostura bitters, a flavoring in cocktails and foods. Angostura bitters was developed in 1824 by Johann Gottlieb Benjamin Siegert, a German physician and scientist living in Venezuela. Confronting his patients' stomach and intestinal disorders, Siegert eventually concocted a unique blend of herbs to bring relief. The fruit of his labors was Angostura bitters, named after the town of Angostura on the Orinoco River. The bitters became famous as a tonic and flavoring and some two centuries later is marketed worldwide. Although gentian is a known ingredient, the trademark blend remains a closely guarded secret.

See Also: *Herbal Medicine Expanded Commission E Monographs* by M. Blumenthal, A. Goldberg, and J. Brinckmann, American Botanical Council, 2000; *Medicinal Herbs History, Use, Recommended Dosages & Cautions* by S. Foster, Interweave Press, 1998.

Ginger
Zingiber officinale

Common Names Ginger, African ginger, *sheng jiang/gan jiang*

Latin Name *Zingiber officinale*

Family Zingiberaceae

Parts Used Rhizomes (underground stems)

Description Ginger is a tender, creeping perennial that grows three to four feet high. Its thick, aromatic, knotty, tuberous rhizomes produce erect stems with long, narrow, lance-shaped leaves. Sterile but fragrant white flowers are streaked with purple and grow in spikes.

Habitat Native to tropical Asia, ginger is widely cultivated in tropical regions worldwide, but especially in China, India, Nigeria, Australia, Haiti, and Jamaica.

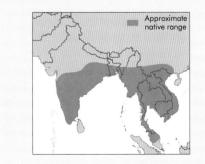

Approximate native range

S PICY TO THE TONGUE, YET SOOTHING TO THE DIGESTIVE tract, ginger has been prized for centuries as a culinary and medicinal herb. At least 4,500 years ago, ginger was an ingredient in specialty breads baked in ancient Greece. The Romans loved ginger as well, and like the Greeks, imported it from China and India. Ginger's name in Greek was *zingiberis*; in Latin it was *zingiber*. Both names were derived from the Sanskrit word, *singabera*, meaning "horn-shaped" and referring to the shape of the herb's **rhizomes**. Even today, ginger remains one of the world's most popular culinary flavorings, used in everything from ginger ale to spicy Asian cuisine. The tuberous rhizome of the plant is used fresh or dried in foods from China, Indonesia, Japan, India, the Caribbean, and North Africa. As a medicinal herb, ginger was important in both ancient Chinese and **Ayurvedic medicine**. In the Ayurvedic tradition, ginger is known as "the great or universal medicine." During the Middle Ages, ginger's powers were so highly prized it was thought to have come from the Garden of Eden. In modern herbal medicine, ginger is used as a digestive aid and to help prevent or treat nausea and vomiting.

Traditional and Current Medicinal Uses

IN CHINA, GINGER HAS BEEN USED TO AID DIGESTION AND TREAT stomach upset, diarrhea, and nausea for roughly 2,000 years. Ginger was also used to help treat arthritis, colic, and heart conditions. Ginger was widely used by the Greeks and Romans; eating ginger was a way to eliminate or guard against intestinal parasites, and it was widely used by the Romans for that purpose. During the Middle Ages, ginger was prescribed to promote perspiration, warm the stomach, treat colds, flu, and bronchitis, and improve circulation to the extremities. Ginger was also used to stimulate digestion, improve liver function, banish flatulence, cure colic, ease nausea, and relax muscle spasms. Added to massage oil, ginger was renowned for relieving muscular strains and rheumatic pain, and for stimulating circulation in painful joints.

In modern herbal medicine, ginger is considered an excellent remedy for digestive complaints such as nausea and indigestion. It relieves motion sickness, morning sickness, and postoperative and chemotherapy-induced nausea. Because it exhibits antiseptic action, ginger is often suggested for infections of the gastrointestinal tract, and for treating food poisoning. Fresh ginger root can be chewed for sore throat. Ginger preparations are also taken for the common cold, as well as for chills and feverish infections, flu, and headaches.

Cultivation and Preparation

GINGER IS A SHADE-LOVING TROPICAL PLANT THAT GROWS best in moist, fertile soil under warm and humid conditions. It is cultivated commercially throughout the tropics and propagated by division of the rhizomes. Rhizomes are harvested when plants are 10 to 12 months old. Ginger products are made from fresh or dried ginger rhizomes or from steam distillation of the oil.

Research

GINGER'S RHIZOMES CONTAIN CHEMICALS KNOWN AS GINgerols and shogaols. They stimulate the flow of saliva, bile, and gastric secretions, quell stomach upsets, and encourage gentle muscle contractions that move food through the digestive tract. They are also responsible for ginger's antinausea effects; they inhibit violent muscle spasms in the digestive tract and curb diarrhea. Clinical studies have shown that ginger is effective in reducing symptoms associated with motion sickness. Ginger has also been shown in clinical studies to relieve nausea linked to pregnancy. Research concerning ginger's efficacy in reducing nausea following surgery and chemotherapy also has been positive. Ginger extract has long been used in herbal medicine to decrease inflammation; the active compound responsible for this effect is zingibain, an **enzyme** that counteracts inflammation. One study suggests ginger may have protective effects against Alzheimer's disease by protecting nerve cells in the brain. Preliminary studies also suggest that ginger may lower cholesterol, act as an **antioxidant** to prevent arterial plaque, and prevent **platelet aggregation** that can lead to blood clots.

Ginger is an extremely important medicinal herb in Asian medicine, and has been for thousands of years. Ginger was first noted in the *Shen Nong Ben Cao Jing*, an ancient Chinese herbal thought to be written by the divine plowman emperor, Shen Nong, who lived about 200 B.C. Fresh ginger was first listed in *Ming Yi Bie Lu* (*Miscellaneous Records of Famous Physicians*) and *Ben Cao Jing Ji Zhu* (*Collection of Commentaries on the Classics of Materia Medica*) around A.D. 500. In traditional Chinese medicine, fresh and dried ginger are considered different medicines used for treating different complaints. (Indian Ayurvedic medicine also recognizes "two" gingers.) As fresh ginger rhizomes dry, some of the gingerols they contain break down to form shogaols. Shogaols are twice as pungent as their parent compounds, making dried ginger much "hotter" than fresh ginger. Fresh ginger is known as *sheng jiang* in Chinese medicine, while dried ginger is *gan jiang*. Fresh ginger is used to promote sweating, to warm the spleen and stomach and alleviate vomiting, and to warm the lungs and alleviate coughs. Dried ginger is used as a treatment for pains in the stomach and abdominal regions, for vomiting and diarrhea, poor appetite, listlessness, chills, asthma, cough, and weak pulse. Studies conducted using fresh ginger show it to initially reduce stomach secretions and to exhibit analgesic and anti-inflammatory effects.

See Also: *World Health Organization (WHO) Monographs on Selected Medicinal Plants, Vol. 1, 1999; Herbal Emissaries: Bringing Chinese Herbs to the West* by S. Foster and Y. Chongxi, Healing Arts Press, 1992.

ZINGIBER OFFICINALE | Ginger

Ginkgo
Ginkgo biloba

Common Names Ginkgo, maidenhair tree, *yin-hsing, bao gou* (female seeds)

Latin Name *Ginkgo biloba*

Family Ginkgoaceae

Parts Used Leaves, seeds

Description Ginkgo is a large (100+ feet), long-lived (1,000 years), deciduous tree with furrowed gray bark. The leaves are fan-shaped and deeply notched to form two lobes—hence the species name, *biloba*. Male and female flowers and fruits are borne on separate trees.

Habitat Native to China, ginkgo is cultivated in China, France, Japan, and the southeastern United States. It is also a popular ornamental tree.

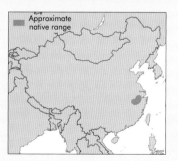

Approximate native range

THE ONLY SURVIVING MEMBER OF THE GENUS *GINKGO*, the ginkgo tree is considered a living fossil. Ginkgo trees date to the Paleozoic period more than 225 million years ago, when dinosaurs were flourishing, but mammals had not yet appeared on the scene. The ginkgo has remained relatively unchanged over that enormous span of time, making it the oldest living tree species on the planet today. Long a sacred plant in China and Japan, the genus name *Ginkgo* is derived from the Japanese word *gingkyo*, which is thought to be a corruption of the Chinese *yin-hsing*, meaning "silver apricot." The name refers to the fleshy fruits produced by the female trees. Another colloquial Chinese name for ginkgo is *kung-sun-shu*, which means "grandfather and grandson tree," referring to the fact that ginkgo trees planted by one generation will not produce fruit for at least one or two generations. Ginkgo leaves and seeds have been used in traditional Chinese medicine for many centuries. Modern research has discovered impressive healing compounds in ginkgo leaves that were previously unknown.

Traditional and Current Medicinal Uses

TRADITIONALLY, THE CHINESE USED THE SEEDS OF GINKGO FOR lung-related ailments, particularly asthma, tuberculosis, coughs, and certain other bronchial conditions. Seeds were traditionally used to treat skin sores and urinary problems. Ginkgo leaves were included in remedies to strengthen the heart and lungs and to treat chilblains. In Western herbal medicine, ginkgo leaves have played a role for only about 40 years and attention has been focused on ginkgo's ability to improve circulation, particularly to the brain and the extremities.

Ginkgo leaf extract is now widely prescribed to improve cognitive function in people with symptoms of age-related mental decline, including memory loss and the early stages of Alzheimer's disease. It is also thought to improve concentration and mental sharpness in healthy people over the age of 50. Extracts of the leaf are given to treat irregular heartbeat, varicose veins, Raynaud's disease, hemorrhoids, and leg ulcers. The herb is a recognized, effective remedy for claudication, a circulatory condition most common in the elderly characterized by severe cramping and pain in the lower legs while walking or exercising. Because of its pronounced **antioxidant** effects in the central nervous system, ginkgo is considered effective in prevention and early treatment of age-related eye disorders such as cataracts, macular degeneration, and diabetic retinopathy, and in circulatory conditions leading to heart disease and stroke. Ginkgo is also recommended for tinnitus (ringing in the ears), vertigo, and some types of sexual dysfunction.

Cultivation and Preparation

FEW, IF ANY, GINKGOS REMAIN IN THE WILD, BUT GINKGO TREES are extensively cultivated on several continents. Ginkgos need fertile, well-drained soil and full sun. Leaves are harvested as they turn from green to yellow in the autumn and then dried and made into **extracts**.

Research

IN THE PAST FEW DECADES, HUNDREDS OF LABORATORY, animal, and clinical studies have been conducted on standardized ginkgo extracts, concretely establishing the herb's therapeutic value. Ginkgo contains many active compounds, but gingkolides and bilobalide are unique to the herb. These substances are known to improve blood flow to the brain and other parts of the body. Gingkolides not only enhance circulation but inhibit platelet "stickiness" and improve elasticity of blood vessels. The well-documented action of ginkgo in improving circulation to the brain and central nervous system accounts for the herb's widespread use in preventing and managing memory loss and circulatory disorders in the elderly. Studies have shown that ginkgo's active ingredients also stabilize the structure of brain and nerve cells and protect them from oxidative damage by **free radicals**. Extracts of the herb contain a number of **anti-inflammatory** compounds as well as seven natural **antihistamines**, making it an effective treatment for allergies and asthma.

CAUTION Ginkgo leaves and seeds are considered toxic. Only complex standardized leaf extracts (with toxic components removed) should be used.

GROWING GINKGOS

The first record of ginkgo being cultivated in Asia dates to the Song dynasty in China in the 11th century. Ginkgo was regarded as the source of a rare and precious fruit at that time, and ginkgo seed was sent as a tribute from what is now China's Anhui province to the emperor residing in the country's ancient capital of Kaifeng. Cultivation of ginkgo began there in earnest and slowly spread to other parts of China. Ginkgo was first mentioned in Chinese herbals in the 1200s, although it was probably widely used in folk medicine long before that. Native to China, ginkgo was known and used in Asia for centuries before making its way to the Western world. The tree was introduced to Europe in the early 1700s with seeds brought from China or Japan; its botanical characteristics were recorded in 1712 by a German surgeon who was working for the Dutch East India Company. In 1771 Swedish botanist Carolus Linnaeus gave ginkgo its scientific name, *Ginkgo biloba*. The first ginkgo was planted in North America in 1784 as an ornamental at an estate near Philadelphia. Ginkgo's gingkolides were discovered by Japanese researchers in 1932. One of the active compounds, gingkolide B, was synthesized in the 1980s by a team of chemists at Harvard. Still widely used in Asian medicine, ginkgo is a commonly prescribed herbal medicine in Europe and one of the 10 best-selling herbal supplements in the U.S.

See Also: Herbal Medicine Expanded Commission E Monographs by M. Blumenthal, A. Goldberg, and J. Brinckmann, American Botanical Council, 2000; *Herbal Emissaries: Bringing Chinese Herbs to the West* by S. Foster and Y. Chongxi, Healing Arts Press, 1992.

Goat's Rue
Galega officinalis

A MEMBER OF THE LEGUME FAMILY, GOAT'S RUE HAS BEEN a popular garden plant in Europe and the U.S. for many years. It was supposedly introduced to the British Isles from France as a garden ornamental and so earned the nickname, "French lilac," although it is not related to true lilacs. The common name "goat's rue" provides a clue as to the plant's scent. When bruised, the foliage gives off a rank odor. The genus name *Galega* is derived from the Greek *gala*, meaning "milk." The reference is to the fact that goat's rue, when fed to domestic animals, was found to increase the amount of milk the animals produced. In European folk medicine, an infusion of the herb was given to improve lactation in nursing mothers. Historically, goat's rue has also been used as an antidiabetic herb and to treat a variety of other conditions.

Traditional and Current Medicinal Uses

GOAT'S RUE WAS USED IN THE MIDDLE AGES AS A REMEDY for plague, fevers, and other infectious diseases. The Germans called it *pestilenzkraut*, literally "pestilence herb." A tea made from the leaves was said to induce sweating, helping fevers to break. Goat's rue was used in treating intestinal worms and was thought to cure the bites of snakes and other poisonous animals. In addition to its use in promoting milk flow in nursing mothers, goat's rue was also a traditional folk remedy for diabetes and was used in a variety of antidiabetic preparations. It was also a weak **diuretic**.

In modern herbal medicine, goat's rue is no longer widely prescribed, especially in treating diabetes, primarily because it is difficult to determine accurate, therapeutic doses from plant material that may be variable in its chemical composition. Diabetes is a serious condition, and safer, modern treatments are available. Goat's rue is, however, still used to treat skin ulcers, to help increase milk flow, and in ointments to hasten healing after plastic surgery. In combination with other herbs, goat's rue preparations are also used to stimulate the adrenal glands and pancreas and for intestinal complaints, caused by a lack of digestive **enzymes**.

Common Names Goat's rue, French lilac, professor weed, Italian fitch

Latin Name *Galega officinalis*

Family Fabaceae

Parts Used Flowering stems

Description Goat's rue is a hardy, bushy perennial that can reach three feet in height. It has compound leaves with bright green, lanceolate leaflets and spikes of white, pink, or purple pea-like flowers. Each flower produces a red-brown pod that contains several dull yellow seeds.

Habitat Native to southern and eastern Europe and western Asia, goat's rue grows in moist meadows and pasturelands.

Approximate native range

Cultivation and Preparation

GOAT'S RUE WILL GROW IN MOST SOILS, BUT IT NEEDS MOIST conditions. Planted in rich, fertile soil and given plenty of water, it will not only thrive but spread rapidly and even invasively. Goat's rue is easily started from seed in spring, in full sun or light shade. The flowering stems are most often used in herbal medicine. They are cut as flowering begins and dried for use in liquid **extracts, tinctures, infusions,** and powders.

Research

AS A FOLK MEDICINE, GOAT'S RUE WAS USED FOR CENTURIES to relieve the symptoms of diabetes. Scientific studies have shown that one of the herb's main active components is the **alkaloid** galegine, which in laboratory tests lowers blood sugar levels. Galegine and a synthetic derivative called guanidine lowered blood sugar in both alcoholic and water extracts in animal studies conducted in Russia in 1974. A 1995 study by researchers in Belgium evaluated a relatively high dose of goat's rue herb water and alcoholic extracts in laboratory mice and found that it significantly lowered blood glucose levels. Unfortunately, the goat's rue extract produced **anorexia** (eating disorder) in the mice. Since the plant is known to cause fetal toxicity, lung congestion, and **abortifacient** effects in laboratory animals and livestock, it is not recommended for human use. For this reason, goat's rue is classified as an unapproved herb by Germany's Commission E, a scientific panel that investigates and classifies herbal medicines, and most herbal practitioners no longer consider goat's rue an appropriate treatment for diabetes. A number of studies have shown that goat's rue exhibits significant antibacterial activity against certain types of bacteria. It also inhibits blood clotting. Although the herb is sometimes sold as a dietary supplement in the U.S., it is not sold in other countries such as the United Kingdom (due to toxicity issues) or Germany, because of health risks and availability of more effective drugs.

> CAUTION Goat's rue had been found to be toxic to some animals. It should only be used under qualified medical direction, especially in the treatment of diabetes.

FROM FEED TO WEED

Historically in its native habitats, goat's rue was considered a good forage plant for livestock because of the resulting increase in milk production it was said to bring about. Claims about higher milk yields in goat's rue-eating cows were validated by French researchers in 1873. They discovered that cattle fed the herb experienced a 35 to 50 percent increase in milk production. Perhaps because of this finding, goat's rue was introduced into the western United States in the late 1800s as a potential new forage crop for livestock. It turned out, however, that cattle and sheep left to graze on lands where goat's rue was growing avoided the herb entirely. In feeding trials, however, sheep were poisoned by eating the plant. Because cattle and sheep rarely nibble on goat's rue as they graze on pasturelands, the possibility of their being poisoned is not a major concern.

A much greater problem is that by cropping grasses and other plants around clumps of goat's rue, the animals are indirectly encouraging an invasive species to spread. And spread it has. In 1980, goat's rue was designated as a noxious weed by federal authorities. Now listed as a noxious weed in at least a dozen states, considerable money and time have been spent trying to eradicate it.

See Also: Nature's Medicine, Plants That Heal by Joel Swerdlow, National Geographic, 2000; *Herbal Medicine, 2nd ed.* by R. Wiess and V. Fintelman, Thieme, 2000.

Common Names Goldenseal, yellow root, eye root, wild turmeric, ground raspberry, Indian dye, Indian paint

Latin Name *Hydrastis canadensis*

Family Ranunculaceae

Parts Used Rhizome (underground stem), roots

Description Goldenseal is a small perennial with a knotty rhizome that sends up two or more erect, hairy stems, each typically ending in a fork with two leaves. The large, soft leaves are deeply divided into five to seven lobes. A small, solitary greenish-white flower is produced at the end of each stem that develops into an inedible rasp-berry-like fruit.

Habitat Native to eastern North America, goldenseal grows wild in the rich soil of damp meadows and shady, moist woodlands from Connecticut to Minnesota and southward. It is also cultivated to some extent for the herbal medicine market.

Approximate native range

Goldenseal
Hydrastis canadensis

GOLDENSEAL IS A HIGHLY PRIZED MEDICINAL HERB THAT has been collected from the forests of eastern North America for hundreds of years. The slim stems of the herb arise from a fleshy rhizome about two inches long; it is yellowish-brown on the outside, but bright yellow inside. The outside of the **rhizome** is also marked with seal-shaped scars—hence the herb's most common name, goldenseal—from the flowering stems of previous years. Native Americans introduced European settlers to the medicinal properties of goldenseal. The Cherokee and other tribes used the herb primarily for treating skin problems and as an eyewash for sore eyes. They also used it to produce a golden-yellow dye—the source of the names "Indian dye" and "Indian paint." By the early 1900s, goldenseal became such a popular medicinal herb that it was severely overharvested in the wild. It remains one of the top-selling herbal supplements sold in natural food stores in the U.S., despite the fact that there have been surprisingly few clinical studies conducted to document the validity of claims made about it.

Traditional and Current Medicinal Uses

THE CHEROKEE USED THE BITTER-TASTING ROOT OF GOLDENSEAL as an antiseptic for inflammation, as a general health tonic, to settle stomach upsets and improve appetite, and as a cancer treatment. Goldenseal was used by the Iroquois in similar ways, and also to cure diarrhea, as drops for earaches and sore eyes, as a fever reducer, to treat whooping cough and pulmonary problems, and for heart and liver troubles. Adopting the herb into their medicinal folk tradition, early European settlers used goldenseal preparations primarily as an eyewash and to treat sore throats and digestive complaints; they also chewed the root to relieve mouth sores. In the late 1800s, physicians of the American **Eclectic** school, who used medicinal herbs in their practice, promoted goldenseal as a treatment for inflammation, stomach upsets, and as a general cure-all.

In modern herbal medicine, goldenseal is marketed as a tonic to help digestion and soothe upset stomach, as an antiseptic and **astringent**, as a mouthwash for canker sores, infected gums, sore throat, and more. It is also considered a natural antibiotic and is often mixed with *Echinacea purpurea* in immune system-boosting preparations.

Cultivation and Preparation

GOLDENSEAL IS A SENSITIVE PLANT NEEDING VERY SPECIFIC environmental conditions to grow well. It needs rich, moist, loamy soil with good drainage and full shade. New plants are most successfully started from pieces of rooted rhizome. Plants take up to four years to reach harvestable size. Rhizomes from mature plants are lifted in autumn, washed, and dried for preparations.

Research

TWO ALKALOIDS, BERBERINE AND HYDRASTINE, ARE AMONG the primary constituents responsible for goldenseal's medicinal activity. Most research has been conducted on berberine. Lab studies have shown that berberine exhibits significant activity against a wide range of bacteria, including *Staphylococcus*, and several intestinal parasites, including *Giardia* and tapeworms. This documented antimicrobial action may explain goldenseal's effectiveness in treating diarrhea, eye inflammation, and similar infections. (Berberine-containing herbs are used in traditional Chinese medicine to treat dysentery as well as infectious forms of diarrhea.) In the laboratory, berberine has been shown to be toxic to fungal cells and to some types of cancer cells; it also appears to activate white blood cells to fight infection. Berberine has also been shown to have antispasmodic effects, and both hydrastine and berberine exhibit activity shown to be beneficial to the circulatory system and heart. It is important to note that oral doses of goldenseal contain only trace amounts of berberine and hydrastine. More research is needed on the effects of whole goldenseal **extracts** and preparations. In large doses, hydrastine is dangerously toxic.

CAUTION Goldenseal is poisonous in large doses. It should not be used by pregnant women or people with high blood pressure. Goldenseal destroys beneficial intestinal microorganisms and so should be taken only for limited periods of times.

BY POPULAR DEMAND

After introduction to the folk medicine tradition of colonial America, goldenseal became so popular that by the mid-1800s a commercial demand for the root had developed. People headed into eastern forests to collect goldenseal roots; they sold for about 8 cents a pound. As early as 1884, dramatic declines in the wild population due to overharvesting were becoming obvious. Yet collecting continued. As wild stocks declined, the price soared. In 1909, the root brought $1.50 per pound. Attempts were made to protect wild populations of goldenseal by encouraging cultivation. But the assault went on. In 1997, the herb was listed on Appendix II of the Convention for International Trade on Endangered Species (CITES). In some states, harvesting goldenseal on public lands is illegal. Some goldenseal is being cultivated, and to protect wild stocks, only products made with cultivated goldenseal should be used. Because of the price that the root still commands today, products containing it are susceptible to adulteration. Some supplements sold as "goldenseal herb" may contain goldenseal leaves rather than roots. The leaves have approximately one-tenth the amount of active alkaloids found in the roots.

See Also: The ABC Clinical Guide to Herbs by M. Blumenthal, T. Hall, and A. Goldberg, American Botanical Council, 2003; *A Field Guide to Medicinal Plants and Herbs: Eastern and Central North America, 2nd ed.* by S. Foster and J. Duke, Houghton Mifflin Co., 2000.

Gotu Kola
Centella asiatica

Common Names Gotu kola, centella, Indian pennywort, *brahmi, luei gong gen*

Latin Name *Centella asiatica*

Family Apiaceae

Parts Used Leaves, stems

Description Gotu kola is a trailing evergreen perennial with slender stems and rounded leaves. Clusters of tiny white or light purple-to-pink flowers are borne beneath the leaves and succeeded by small oval fruits.

Habitat Gotu kola is native to tropical climates in Asia, Africa, Madagascar, North and South America, and Australia. The plant thrives in and around water.

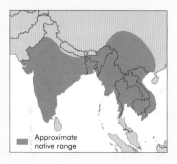

■ Approximate native range

GOTU KOLA HAS BEEN USED AS A MEDICINAL HERB FOR thousands of years in India, China, and Indonesia. It is a common plant in tropical parts of these countries, hugging the ground in wet places around paddy fields and along the margins of ponds and lakes. In India, gotu kola is one of the most important herbs in **Ayurvedic medicine**. It is also revered as an aid to meditation. It may be for this reason that the herb is called *brahmi* in Hindi, which means "bringing the knowledge of Brahman." In Ayurvedic medicine, gotu kola is highly regarded as a blood purifier and multifunctional tonic, one that can be used to treat many diseases and afflictions. Long ago in Sri Lanka, people noticed that elephants ate large quantities of gotu kola. Since elephants are long-lived—and also are said to have good memories—gotu kola was credited with enhancing longevity and mental clarity. As it turns out, there may be some truth to this notion, as scientific studies have supported many of the traditional claims made for gotu kola's therapeutic effects, including its ability to increase mental function. Gotu kola is no "elixir of life," but it has been shown to be remarkably effective in treating a wide range of human illnesses.

Traditional and Current Medicinal Uses

IN AYURVEDIC MEDICINE, GOTU KOLA WAS TRADITIONALLY USED to heal wounds and revitalize the nerves and brain cells, thus improving concentration and memory. In Chinese medicine, the herb (known as *luei gong gen*) was used for fever and respiratory diseases. Throughout Asia, gotu kola was valued for its effectiveness in treating skin diseases such as leprosy and lupus, and skin conditions such as eczema and psoriasis. Eastern healers also looked to gotu kola as a remedy for depression and other emotional disorders that were believed to be caused by physical problems, and for treating stomach ulcers, syphilis, hepatitis, mental fatigue, epilepsy, diarrhea, and asthma. Based on these many traditional indications, gotu kola was accepted as a drug in France in the 1880s. British physicians working in Africa used a special extract of gotu kola to treat leprosy there.

Today, American and European herbalists use gotu kola primarily for healing wounds, burns, and ulcers, and for preventing the formation of scar tissue following surgery. The herb is also suggested for disorders that cause connective tissue swelling, such as scleroderma. In recent years, gotu kola has also been recommended for lowering high blood pressure, treating varicose veins and chronic venous insufficiency (pooling of blood in the veins), and for improving memory, easing anxiety, and treating insomnia.

Cultivation and Preparation

BEING A TROPICAL PLANT, GOTU KOLA THRIVES UNDER WARM conditions in moist to wet, rich, somewhat sandy soil. Full sun or light shade is best. Although the herb is typically collected from the wild, gotu kola can be propagated by seeds or by division of its long runners; these send down roots at each node. For the herbal medicine market, either the leaves or the entire plant is harvested and used fresh or dried in a variety of preparations.

Research

GOTU KOLA CONTAINS A MIX OF VARIOUS CHEMICAL components, but its most active ingredients appear to be a number of **triterpenoids** that have been shown to exert complex effects on cells and tissues. In animal studies on wound healing, these compounds have been shown to stimulate the production of collagen (a protein associated with tissue building and wound healing), increase the blood supply to damaged tissues, and somehow concentrate **antioxidants** in the wound. Several small but well-designed clinical studies have shown triterpenoids to reduce venous pressure in cases of venous insufficiency and improve the "tone" of distended blood vessels, such as varicose veins, that have lost their elasticity. A number of clinical trials have confirmed that gotu kola can lower blood pressure; it also displays sedative, **anti-inflammatory**, and antimicrobial effects. Gotu kola has also been shown in several animal studies and one **double-blind, placebo-**controlled clinical study to significantly increase mental function. In both laboratory and animal studies, gotu kola **extracts** have exhibited anticancer effects.

Many clinical studies over several decades have established that gotu kola is an excellent skin and tissue rejuvenator. It may also offer symptomatic relief to people suffering from scleroderma, a rare, chronic disease characterized by excessive, progressive deposits of collagen in their tissues. Scleroderma comes from the Greek *sclero*, meaning "hard," and *derma*, meaning "skin." The first documented case of scleroderma was in Italy in 1754. The patient was a young woman whose skin was becoming so taut and hard that she could barely move her limbs, close her eyelids, or open her mouth. Such extreme cases are rare, but hardening and scarring of the skin is one of the most visible symptoms of this condition. In mild cases, only small areas of skin are affected. In severe cases, large parts of the body are involved, affecting not just the skin but what underlies it. Muscles, blood vessels, and organs get bound up with scar tissue to the point that limbs waste away and organs fail. Scleroderma is thought to be an autoimmune disease, for which there is currently no cure. A number of drugs are known to relieve pain, joint stiffness, and other symptoms of scleroderma. Gotu kola appears to be a promising alternative to more conventional treatments. In a recent, small clinical study of 13 scleroderma patients, 11 experienced better movement in fingers, less joint pain, and a reduction in hardness of their skin after taking gotu kola. Research into the herb and its effects on scleroderma continues.

See Also: *World Health Organization (WHO) Monographs on Selected Medicinal Plants, Vol. 1, 1999; Medicinal Herbs History, Use, Recommended Dosages & Cautions* by S. Foster, Interweave Press, 1998.

Guaiacum
Guaiacum officinale

GUAIACUM IS THE NATIONAL FLOWER OF JAMAICA. When in bloom, which is most of the time, a guaiacum tree's rounded canopy of dark green leaves is dotted with clusters of intensely blue, star-shaped flowers. The old flowers fade to a silvery-blue and then give way to small, heart-shaped yellow fruits. Fruits and flowers often cover the tree at the same time, creating a striking contrast. The name of the genus, *Guaiacum*, comes from the Spanish *guayaco*, an adaptation of a Taino Indian word for the tree. Long before Europeans arrived in the West Indies, native inhabitants were using guaiacum as a source of medicine. When the Spanish and other explorers arrived, the Indians introduced them to the tree. One of its most common names, *lignum vitae*, means "wood of life" in Latin and reflects the high regard people had for guaiacum's medicinal value in the past. Although not widely employed in herbal medicine these days, it is used—along with a closely related species, *G. sanctum*—primarily as an **anti-inflammatory** and to promote circulation and clear toxins from tissues.

Traditional and Current Medicinal Uses

GUAIACUM WAS USED BY NATIVE CARIBBEAN ISLANDERS AND indigenous tribes of Central and South America to treat various tropical diseases and later syphilis when it was introduced by Europeans in the late 1400s. The Spanish began exporting guaiacum to Europe in the early 1500s where it quickly gained a reputation as a syphilis cure (as a **decoction** mixed with mercury). It was used as such for nearly two centuries, until more effective treatments for venereal diseases were developed. In Europe and England, guaiacum also gained a reputation as a remedy for sore throat, gout, palsy, leprosy, dropsy, and epilepsy.

More recently, guaiacum has been primarily employed as a treatment for chronic rheumatism; it is said to increase circulation and to ease pain when rubbed into painful joints. The resin from guaiacum is also highly recommended for gout, certain skin diseases, tonsillitis and upper respiratory infections,

Common Names Guaiacum, lignum vitae, guayacan, pockwood

Latin Name *Guaiacum officinale*

Family Zygophyllaceae

Parts Used Resin, wood

Description Guaiacum is a slow-growing tropical evergreen tree that can attain a height of about 30 feet. It typically has a crooked trunk with knobby, twisted branches that are covered with dark green, glossy, oval leaves. Deep-blue flowers, produced almost year-round, are followed by yellow-orange capsule-like fruits.

Habitat Now rare in the wild, guaiacum is native to the West Indies, Central America, and the northern coast of South America where it grows in dry, coastal areas. The tree is widely planted as an ornamental for its large clusters of beautiful blue flowers.

Approximate native range

as a mild laxative, to induce sweating, and as a mild **diuretic**.

Cultivation and Preparation

A COASTAL SPECIES, GUAIACUM NEEDS FULL SUN TO PART SHADE and can be grown in a wide variety of soils. It can survive periods of flooding and drought as well as exposure to salt spray. Propagation is by seed. The dark, greenish-brown heartwood is harvested when trees are cut. It is processed into chips and shavings that are heated to extract the resin they contain—about 20 percent by weight. (Centuries ago, indigenous people extracted the resin by cutting yard-long sections of the trunk, boring a hole through the center, setting fire to one end, and catching the liquefied resin that ran out the hole at the other end.) Guaiacum resin, sometimes called gum guaiacum, is dark-brown or greenish-brown in color. It smells slightly balsamic, and when heated it is quite fragrant. Harvested resin is formed into various sized blocks. Medicinal preparations are made from powdered resin or, somewhat less commonly, by boiling very small shavings of resin-containing heartwood in water to make a decoction.

Research

THE MEDICINAL PROPERTIES OF GUAIACUM WERE FIRST OUT-lined by Sir Hans Sloane (1660–1753), whose extensive collections—including books, prints, botanical specimens, and other items—became the basis of the British Museum. Modern chemical analyses reveal that guaiacum resin contains numerous **lignans**, plant compounds containing an **essential oil** whose primary constituent is guajol. Guajol can be converted into guaiazulene, which is a valuable compound now used in aromatherapy. Guaiacum resin is said to have **anti-inflammatory**, antirheumatic, and diuretic properties; guaiazulene, in particular, has demonstrated strong anti-inflammatory effects. However, studies indicate that one of the lignans appears to induce the formation of kidney stones. Because of the herb's high resin content, herbal practitioners do not recommend guaiacum for people with stomach problems because the resin can turn out to be an irritant.

HEAVY-DUTY BEAUTY

Underneath the furrowed, grayish bark of a guaiacm tree lies some of the world's densest and heaviest wood. Instead of floating like most other types of timber, guaiacum wood sinks under its own weight, largely the result of its extremely high resin content. The wood is remarkably hard; tough plant fibers cross each other diagonally, making guaiacum lumber almost impossible to split. On account of its hardness, density, and durability, guaiacum trees have long been valued as a source of wood for objects that must withstand great stress and impact, such as ships' pulleys and propeller shafts, mallets, and wooden pestles. It is also used for carving. The Spanish began exporting guaiacum wood to Europe shortly after they arrived in the West Indies. The trees were cut and shipped so intensively that in 1701 the government of Martinique passed laws to protect them. Today CITES, the Convention on International Trade in Endangered Species, lists *Guaiacum officinale* as a species that is not currently threatened with extinction worldwide, but may become extinct if trade is not regulated. Export permits are required in countries where guaiacum trees are harvested to certify that trade is not detrimental to survival of the species. However, dry coastal tropical forest habitats, where guaiacum trees grow naturally, are threatened around the globe and protecting the remaining wild populations will depend on preserving these habitats.

See Also: *Medical Botany: Plants Affecting Human Health* by W. Lewis, and M. Elvin-Lewis, John Wiley & Sons, 2003; *Nature's Medicine, Plants That Heal* by Joel Swerdlow, National Geographic, 2000.

Guarana
Paullinia cupana

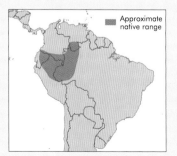

Common Names Guarana, guarana gum, Brazilian cocoa, guarana seed, zoom cocoa

Latin Name *Paullinia cupana*

Family Sapindaceae

Parts Used Seeds

Description Growing to 30 feet long, guarana is a woody vine that climbs by means of coiled tendrils. It has glossy compound leaves with five large pointed leaflets with toothed edges and pronounced veins. Spikes of small, yellowish flowers are succeeded by bright-red fruits that contain shiny brown seeds.

Habitat Native to Brazil, Venezuela, and Uruguay, guarana grows in damp forested regions near the Amazon, Madeira, and Tapajos Rivers. It is cultivated in the Amazon Basin and other parts of Brazil, but rarely elsewhere.

Approximate native range

GUARANA IS A TROPICAL VINE THAT CLIMBS THROUGH the trees of the Amazon rain forest. The name "guarana" comes from the Guarani Indians of northern Brazil, who, like other indigenous tribes in the central Amazon River Basin, have long used the fruits of the vine for making a stimulating drink known as guaraná. The fruits are bright red capsules that split open when ripe, revealing a shiny black seed (sometimes two or three) that is partially embedded in a thin white pulp. From a distance, the split fruits look disturbingly like large, open eyes staring down from the leafy canopy. Guarana seeds are rich in caffeine and authentic guarana made from them has three or four times the caffeine content of a strong cup of coffee. Traditionally, guarana was used by Amazonian natives as an invigorating stimulant. Over the past few decades, guarana has become popular worldwide as an ingredient in soft drinks and energy drinks, as well as in dietary supplements that are promoted for increasing mental alertness and energy levels and suppressing appetite.

Traditional and Current Medicinal Uses

AMAZONIAN TRIBES WERE USING GUARANA LONG BEFORE THE arrival of Europeans to South America. The traditional method of preparing and using guarana was to harvest and dry the seeds, grind them to a powder, add a little water to make a paste, and then form the paste into sticks that were dried and smoked. The drink was made by grating part of a guarana stick into hot water and drinking the **infusion** like tea. Guarana was taken mainly as a powerful stimulant and for chronic diarrhea. Ethnobotanical studies of the herb's modern use by indigenous Amazon tribes reveal that the herb was also traditionally used as a pain reliever and blood tonic, and for hypertension, fever, and headaches. By the 1700s, guarana use had moved beyond the forests and was widespread throughout Brazil. It was recommended for protecting against malaria and amoebic dysentery, and as an aphrodisiac. Guarana extracts were added to carbonated drinks in the early 1900s, and by the 1940s, guarana soda had become Brazil's national drink.

Guarana also went into candy, syrups, and many herbal products.

Today, millions of Brazilians take guarana as a daily tonic to combat fatigue and premature aging, and as a blood purifier. It is also used for flatulence, dyspepsia, diarrhea, fever, headaches and migraine, neuralgia, arteriosclerosis, and as an appetite suppressant. Use of guarana has spread to Europe and North America. In the U.S., guarana is marketed for its ability to increase mental alertness, fight fatigue, increase stamina and endurance, suppress appetite, relieve headaches, tone and strengthen the heart, prevent blood clots, and to enhance sexual performance.

Cultivation and Preparation

MUCH OF THE WORLD'S COMMERCIAL PRODUCTION OF guarana paste still comes from the Amazon Basin. Guarana is still cultivated in an ecologically sustainable way by indigenous tribes. Young wild seedlings are transplanted from the rain forest and trained onto trellises. Guarana is also grown on commercial plantations; cultivated plants tend to form shrubby bushes rather than vines. The seeds are harvested when ripe, then roasted, ground, and stored as dried powder or paste.

Research

WHEN GUARANA WAS FIRST ANALYZED CHEMICALLY IN THE 1700s, chemists isolated a substance with stimulating properties they called guaranine. Further study showed that guaranine is nothing other than caffeine. Guarana seeds contain a lot of caffeine (from 4 to 8 percent), along with **tannins** and other chemical compounds. Caffeine's effects on the body are well documented. It stimulates the central nervous system, increases heart rate, raises blood glucose levels, and acts as a **diuretic** and appetite suppressant, which may contribute to weight loss. Many therapeutic effects ascribed to guarana, therefore, are explained by its caffeine content. In research studies in Brazil, guarana has been shown to inhibit **platelet aggregation**, lending some support to the herb's traditional use as a blood tonic. Guarana's tannins are thought to be responsible for its antidiarrheal effects.

Guarana is one of the best-loved fruits in Brazil and considerable folklore has grown up around it. Perhaps the most famous story explains the appearance of the edible fruit that, when ripe, has an uncanny resemblance to a human eye peering out of the split in the bright-red capsule. There are different versions of the legend but most relate the story of Onhiamuacabe, a beautiful young woman with a great knowledge of rain forest plants who belonged to the Satare-Maue Indian tribe. Onhiamuacabe had given birth to a boy fathered by a mysterious being. Before giving birth, she had planted a tree so that when her son was born, he could eat its delicious fruits. By the time the child was old enough to speak, he was clamoring to eat the fruits that his mother had told him about. But the brothers of Onhiamuacabe, unhappy that the child had been born, had posted guards around the tree with orders to kill whoever came near it. Eventually the guards caught the boy in the act of eating the tree's fruits and beheaded him. When Onhiamuacabe discovered her son had been killed, she took his right eye from his severed head and planted it while calling upon the spirit of the trees for help. A few days later, the guarana plant sprouted from where the eye had been planted and its fruits looked like the eyes of Onhiamuacabe's son. The name of the plant reflects this connection, as *guara* means "human" and *na* means "like."

See Also: Medical Botany: Plants Affecting Human Health by W. Lewis and M. Elvin-Lewis, John Wiley & Sons, 2003; *Tyler's Honest Herbal*, 4th ed. by S. Foster and V. Tyler, The Haworth Herbal Press, 1999.

HEALING PLANTS OF
Europe

THE PHONE RANG. DR. ANKE STRENGE-HESSE, A GERMAN PHYSI-
cian specializing in liver disease, answered it and calmed
the frantic voice on the other end. It was another physician
in an emergency room in Prague. He had just diagnosed a
patient with death cap (*Amanita*) mushroom poisoning,
responsible for more than 90 percent of all mushroom
fatalities. At least half the time people who ingest deathcap mushroom die—
or they did, until a new treatment was introduced in the 1970s. Dr. Strenge-
Hesse listened, hung up the phone and quickly made a call to arrange for a
shipment of silybinin, extracted from the seeds of milk thistle (*Silybum marianum*). The plant medicine was to be shipped in the cockpit of the next plane
from the nearby Cologne airport to Prague.

The purified silybinin extract from milk thistle, delivered as an intra-
venous drip, saved the life of the patient. Its use is just one example of the
way in which traditional herbal knowledge is embraced in today's Europe to
help deliver modern health care. The use of milk thistle over the last 40 years
has reduced death cap mushroom fatalities by more than 80 percent.

HERBAL MEDICINE IN EUROPE

IN GERMANY, ON THE EAST SIDE OF THE RHINE RIVER FROM FRANKFURT TO
Cologne, stretches an endless array of thousand-year-old castles towering
over bullet trains speeding by in the valley below. Their newness blends with
the ancient sentinels of Germanic culture, reminders of continuity amid endless change. And so it is with herbal medicine.
The past is part of the here-and-now. In a
conversation about herbal medicine, one is
likely to hear the name of Hildegarde of Bingen evoked as if she were someone's grandmother—rather than an 11th-century nun.

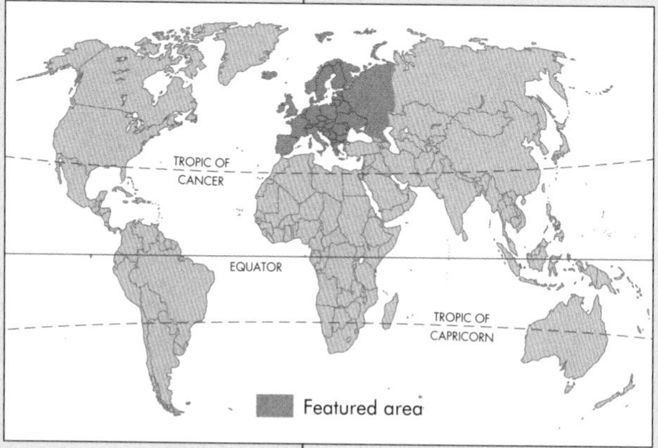

Hildegarde, author of *Physica* (*Natural
Science*), is considered the mother of German
botany and was the first woman to write an
herbal. Her *Physica* existed in manuscript
form for four centuries until published in
1533. Hildegarde also knew, and wrote, of
milk thistle, which she called *vehedistel* (Venus thistle). She recommended it
for tumors and for erysipelas (a bacterial disease causing fever and localized
inflammation). She warned, however, that the tea should never be kept long
on the stove—according to medieval superstition, this would lead to household quarrels.

TROPIC OF
CANCER

EQUATOR

TROPIC OF
CAPRICORN

Featured area

For more than 2,000 years, milk thistle (Silybum marianum) has been used for the prevention and treatment of mild to severe toxic liver damage. Its use as a liver-protecting herb dates to the earliest references to the plant by the Greeks. Pliny the Elder (A.D. 23–79), the first-century Roman physician and naturalist, recognized the use of milk thistle for liver problems and wrote that the juice of the plant, mixed with honey, is excellent for "carrying off bile."

PRECEDING PAGES: *In traditional dress, a resident of Plav in Montenegro, near the Albanian and Kosovo borders, harvests fruits of bilberry (Vaccinium myrtillus). The three-week-long wild harvest season in the Balkan Mountains of Montenegro yields 300 metric tons of the fresh berries. The berrries are used in herbal products to improve microcirculation to the extremities as well as in the eyes.*

The status of modern herbal medicine in Germany began a century ago. A 1901 law in Germany, reaffirmed in 1961, allowed for the sale of herbal medicines as drugs, giving them special status as medicinal agents. Throughout the 20th century and beyond, herbs sold to cure, alleviate, or prevent disease have been known as phytomedicines. The prefix "phyto" originates from the Greek *phyton* meaning "plant." Phytomedicines are therapeutic agents derived from plants or parts of plants, or preparations made from them. They are not single compounds. Phytomedicines represent the totality of chemical constituents contained in the whole plant or plant part, rather than a single chemical compound. This is a key difference between plant preparations used in herbal medicine and isolated plant compounds used as drugs in conventional medicine. Phytomedicines have been valued in a traditional sense for their benefits; their medicinal value was known before research was conducted on them. Subsequently, traditional or folk use has been verified by pharmacological experiments and clinical studies.

According to Heinz Schilcher of the Institute of Pharmaceutical Biology at Berlin Independent University, herbal medicine's survival in Germany rests on the use of herbs as a component of orthodox medicine and is not seen as an alternative or complementary approach. Further, a major reason German physicians accept phytotherapy is the existence of the scientifically supported Commission E monographs.

From 1978 to1994, the German government's Commission E produced 380 monographs or articles on specific herbs with details on the name of the herb, constituents, indications for use, contraindications (if any), side effects (if known), interactions with other drugs (if known), dosage, method of dosing, and the herb's therapeutic value. The monographs serve as the basis for information in product inserts or on product labels. According to the late Dr. Varro Tyler of Purdue University, author of *Tyler's Honest Herbal*, "These monographs constitute some of the most up-to-date and useful information extant on the safety and efficacy of plant drugs." In 1998 the complete text of all German Commission E monographs was translated and published in English by the American Botanical Council. The project, initiated and edited by Mark Blumenthal, Executive Director of the American Botanical Council, took more than six years to complete.

As integration of currencies, law, and trade proceeds across Europe, the German Commission E monographs serve as the foundation of scientifically accepted uses of herbal medicine throughout the European Union. However, though the Germans provided the lead for European herbal medicine, each country has its own traditions, its own herbals, and its own way of

*The flowers of German chamomile (*Matricaria recutita*) are harvested with a specialized tool, designed for harvesting berries and flowers. The German name for chamomile translates as "capable of anything."*

melding past and present. In 2005, several universities in England, including the University of Middlesex and Westminister University, matriculated their first four-year graduates in herbal medicine. Upon graduation, these students become members of the National Institute of Medical Herbalists. Founded in 1864, it is the oldest professional body of practicing herbalists in the Western world. The graduates are licensed and may open a clinic and hang out their shingle offering their services as medical herbalists to the English public.

In England a fractious relationship between the medical establishment and herbal practitioners began centuries ago. King Henry VIII ruled on the issue nearly 500 years ago in a 1543 decree known as the Herbalists' Charter. In it he ordained it lawful for those "having Knowledge and Experience of the Nature of Herbs, Roots, and Waters . . . to practice, use, and minister . . . according to their Cunning, Experience, and Knowledge . . . without suit, vexation, trouble, penalty, or loss of their goods." And so it was, until the English Parliament defied Henry VIII with the Pharmacy Act and made herbal medicine illegal. Not until the passage of the Medicine Act in 1968 was the right of herbalists to practice and prescribe herbs reinstated.

MEDICINAL PLANTS IN EUROPE

THE ROOTS OF EUROPEAN HERBAL MEDICINE RUN DEEP. THE EVOLUTION OF EUROpean herbal practice began along the Mediterranean, blending the wisdom of ancient Greece and the wide influence of the Romans. In the first century, a Greek physician in the army of the Roman emperor Nero explored medicinal plants and practices of the Roman Empire. His name was Dioscorides, and his work *De Materia Medica* was the result. Completed in A.D. 77, it contained detailed botanical descriptions and the medical properties of 600 plants. His careful description of plants, their habitats, how they should be gathered, their edible, poisonous, and medicinal attributes, along with recipes and formulas, became the foundation of herbal medicine, indeed medical practice itself, for more than 1,500 years.

The mold of Dioscorides was finally broken in 1542 when the German Leonard Fuchs wrote *De Historia Stirpium*, describing 400 plants native to northern Europe not found in the work of Dioscorides. But the influence of Mediterranean herbal use had already become well established. Herbs of the mountains of Greece and Italy along the Mediterranean and Adriatic coasts had become the mainstay of herb gardens. Rosemary, sage, thyme, lavender, oregano, marjoram, and many others, known today for their flavor and fragrance, became mainstays of medieval monastery herb gardens. But their medicinal use is not relegated to history. Thyme, common in the wild throughout Europe, is approved for therapeutic use in Germany for treatment of bronchitis, whooping cough, and congestion. Sage leaf is approved for inflammation of mucous membranes of the nose and throat. Rosemary is approved for dyspepsia and for supportive treatment of circulatory problems and rheumatic conditions.

The former communists states of Bulgaria, Romania, Hungary, Albania, and the former Yugoslavian states of Croatia, Bosnia-Herzegovina, and Montenegro abound with wild herbs. Some 2,000 species of medicinal plants are still used in European herbal medicine. About 1,300 of those are native to Europe, and Eastern Europe is the main source for many wild-harvested medicinal herbs. Over the last 17 years, following the transition of the former Eastern Bloc countries from state-controlled economies to market economies, some medicinal plants collected in the region have declined significantly, leading to conservation concerns for future sustainable harvests. One such herb is gentian root (*Gentiana lutea*), used for digestive disorders, loss of appetite, and flatulence. Overharvesting has led to a ban of its collection in Montenegro along the Adriatic coast.

Veselin Vucinic, an herb dealer in the small Balkan village of Mojkovak near Tara River Canyon National Park, is trying to remedy that problem. Once a dealer in gentian root before its harvest was banned, he used to purchase 60,000 kilograms (132,300 pounds) of the root per year from wild harvesters. For the past five years Mr. Vucinic has been distributing seed of gentian to seasonal shepherds and villagers of Mount Sinjajevina—the same people who used to collect it for him.

Mount Sinjajevina is a high mountain plain in the central highlands of Montenegro. Far from the nearest road, villagers scratch a living tending sheep, taxed only by the mountain wolves who take about 10 percent of the flock each season. Water is obtained by hiking to higher elevations, chipping the frozen flow from ice packs, and backpacking it down to the village. Here, as in much of the Balkans, hay is still cut with a scythe and raked by hand into haystacks.

Wild herb harvest brings significant supplementary cash for the shepherds. And after five years of seed distribution by Veselin Vucinic and others, the central plateau now boasts hundreds of new stands of gentian. Veselin Vucinic has even trained the villagers to avoid cutting the gentian plants when they are harvesting their hay. Consequently, newly cut hay fields are dotted with flowering gentian in early August. His regeneration efforts for the threatened yellow gentian are an excellent example of how conservation efforts can be implemented for the practical benefit of both plants and people. ✍

OPPOSITE PAGE: Foxglove (Digitalis purpurea), a poisonous plant, widely planted garden biennial, and source of drugs used in the treatment of congestive heart failure, is indigenous to Europe. It is naturalized in the United States and grows wild in the Northeast and in the Pacific Northwest.

Happy Tree
Camptotheca acuminata

THE TALL AND GRACEFUL HAPPY TREE IS NATIVE TO forests of southern China and Tibet. There it goes by many names, including *xi shu*, which can be translated as "happy tree," *tian zi shu* (heaven wood tree), *jia shu* (fine tree), and *long shu* (dragon tree). For many people who are battling cancer, the name "tree of life" may be most appropriate. In the late 1960s, a chemical substance called camptothecin was isolated from extracts of *Camptotheca*. As it turned out, camptothecin has powerful anticancer properties. It was subsequently modified in the laboratory to create a number of cancer-fighting drugs that modern medicine has added to its anticancer arsenal.

Traditional and Current Medicinal Uses

FOR HUNDREDS OF YEARS *CAMPTOTHECA* PLAYED A MINOR role in traditional Chinese medicine. It was employed as a remedy for psoriasis (a chronic skin disease characterized by red, scaly patches) as well as diseases of the stomach, spleen, gallbladder, and liver.

Western science and medicine knew little about the plant's therapeutic potential, however, until 1958 when Monroe Wall, then with the U.S. Department of Agriculture (later, at the Research Triangle Institute), and Jonathan Hartwell, of the National Cancer Institute, discovered *Camptotheca*'s tumor-fighting properties in the course of a screening project to identify new sources of **steroids** to make cortisone. In 1966 Wall and Mansukh Wani isolated this active anti-cancer compound in **extracts** from *Camptotheca* bark. They called it camptothecin. (Wall and Wani are also famous for their discovery of Taxol in 1971.) By the early 1970s, a camptothecin-based drug was being tested on patients with stomach and intestinal cancers. The drug was so toxic that its side effects in patients were too severe for clinical trials to be completed. In the years that followed, researchers focused their efforts on trying to understand how camptothecin killed tumor cells. As the work progressed, the National Cancer Institute provided funding for experiments designed to find less toxic derivatives of the **alkaloid**. By the late 1980s the

Common Names Happy tree, *xi shu*, tree of joy, cancer tree

Latin Name *Camptotheca acuminata*

Family Nyssaceae

Parts Used Bark, leaves, fruit

Description *Camptotheca* is a large deciduous tree that may reach 80 feet in height. It has red-brown bark and large, oval, pointed, green leaves with pronounced venation. Umbels (umbrella-like clusters) of tiny white flowers are borne on short twigs.

Habitat *Camptotheca* is native to south China and Tibet.

Approximate native range

research had borne fruit, and in the 1990s several cancer-destroying camptothecin derivatives had been developed. Because of their toxicity, however, only a couple of these derivatives—topotecan and irinotecan—have been approved by the United States Food and Drug Administration. Topotecan and irinotecan are now used in the United States for treating advanced ovarian cancer and metastatic colorectal cancer, respectively, especially in cases where treatment with other chemotherapy drugs has not been successful. Topotecan has been approved for the treatment of recurrent ovarian and small-cell lung cancers in several dozen other countries. In China, camptothecin derivatives have been used to treat leukemia and cancers of the liver and stomach.

Cultivation and Preparation

INITIALLY, CAMPTOTHECIN WAS OBTAINED FROM EXTRACTS made from most parts of the *Camptotheca* tree. Additional research revealed that very young leaves contain the highest concentrations of the compound. However, current camptothecin derivatives and drugs are synthesized in the laboratory. The tree is sometimes grown as a specimen or shade tree, particularly in southeast Texas and Louisiana. It is not hardy in more northern climates.

Research

CHEMICALLY, CAMPTOTHECIN AND ITS CANCER-FIGHTING derivatives are unique in their ability to kill tumor cells by interfering with a particular **enzyme** known as topoisomerase I. During DNA replication (copying) inside cells, topoisomerase I is responsible for the unwinding of super-coiled DNA that makes up chromosomes. Camptothecin-based drugs prevent topoisomerase from carrying out this unwinding task in tumor cells; these drugs keep DNA molecules wound up tight. Since the chromosome cannot unwind, DNA cannot be transcribed and the cells cannot make the critically necessary proteins that sustain life. The result is death of the cells. Because cancer cells reproduce much faster than normal cells, they are more susceptible to topoisomerase interference by camptothecin derivatives than are normal, healthy cells.

*C*amptotheca was never an important herb in traditional Chinese medicine. Rather, the dried root and fruit were considered a folk medicine from Zhejiang Province in south-central China, a region where many trees unique to China occur. The ginkgo may have come from the mountains just to the west. The dried winged fruit (*xi-shu-guo*) of the tree was used to disperse stagnant blood and inhibit cancers. The first mention of medicinal use of the plant came very late by Chinese standards in *Illustrated Investigations of the Names and Natures of Plants* (*Zhi Wu Ming Shi Du Gao*) by Wu Chi-Jun, published in 1848 in Beijing. *Camptotheca* was one of 1,700 species illustrated in this important work. By the 1920s, the tree is mentioned only in passing in Chinese works on trees, though in full bloom its beauty caught people's attention. The clean gray bark and globose heads of small white flowers of wild *Campotheca* trees growing along steams in west-central China were extolled by the famous Chinese plant hunter Ernest "Chinese" Wilson in his 1913 book, *A Naturalist in Western China*. At the time, the soft, white wood was used only for fuel. Today it is an example of a new herbal drug in China, which, like ginkgo leaves, came to the attention of Chinese herbalists following discovery of the active constituents by Western scientists.

See Also: *Medical Botany: Plants Affecting Human Health* by W. Lewis and M. Elvin-Lewis, John Wiley & Sons, 2003; *Medicinal Plants of the World* by B. Wyk and M. Wink, Timber Press, 2004.

Hawthorn

Crataegus laevigata

ALTHOUGH HAWTHORN BELONGS TO THE ROSE FAMILY, ITS flowers are far from sweetly scented. Their aroma, in fact, has been likened to the odor of decaying fish. The genus *Crataegus* is a large one, comprised of some 280 species that have a widespread distribution throughout most temperate regions of the Northern Hemisphere. Several species of hawthorn have made their way into herbal medicine; the English hawthorn (*C. laevigata*) and the one-seed hawthorn (*C. monogyna*) are the most widely used in the West. In China, *C. pinnatifida* (*shen-za*) is used.

Traditional and Current Medicinal Uses

HAWTHORN HAS LONG BEEN AN IMPORTANT HERB IN BOTH Eastern and Western herbal medicine traditions. The herb and its effects were mentioned in the *Tang-Ben-Cao*, a Chinese herbal dating to A.D. 659. For centuries, hawthorn preparations have been used in China to treat high blood pressure, **arteriosclerosis** (condition characterized by fatty deposits in the arteries), and heart pain. The small, dry fruits were eaten as a cure for scurvy (disease caused by vitamin C deficiency) and for various stomach ailments. In North America, hawthorn was widely respected by Native Americans as a healing herb to treat stomachache, to relieve various female complaints, as a **diuretic** that could relieve kidney and bladder problems, as an **astringent**, and as a strengthener of the heart. In Europe, the beneficial actions of hawthorn on the heart were mentioned in the writings of the Greek physician Dioscorides and later, during the 1500s, by the Swiss physician Paracelsus. Hawthorn did not gain popularity in Europe as a treatment for cardiovascular disorders until the 19th century—and not until 1898 in the United States.

Hawthorn has remained a well-regarded treatment for the early stages of congestive heart failure, to aid long-term recovery from heart attack, for high blood pressure, arteriosclerosis , and mild heart arrhythmias. It is also still used as a diuretic as well as to treat digestive problems, nervous tension, insomnia, and for sore throat.

Common Names Hawthorn, May tree, quickset, whitethorn, bread and cheese tree

Latin Names *Crataegus laevigata*, synonym *C. oxyacantha*

Family Rosaceae

Parts Used Leaves, flowers, fruits

Description Hawthorn is a large shrub or small tree with branches that are studded with spines. Foliage consists of dark green, wedge-shaped, deeply lobed leaves. Dense clusters of white, strong-smelling flowers are produced in spring and succeeded by bright to dark red, mealy but edible fruits (berries) that resemble crabapples.

Habitat *Crataegus laevigata* is native to Europe and Asia, while the closely related *C. monogyna* is indigenous only to Europe. Both species grow in open woodlands and pastures in sun to partial shade.

Approximate native range

Cultivation and Preparation

HAWTHORN IS NOT FUSSY ABOUT SOIL; IT CAN GROW EVEN in heavy clay. Trees are usually started from cuttings, as seeds can take a long time to germinate. Flowering tops—thought to be the most valuable medicinally—are harvested in late spring, as blooming typically begins in May. Berries are gathered in late summer. Hawthorn leaf and flower extracts are approved for use in Germany. Hawthorn preparations are available as capsules, **tinctures**, and as both fluid and solid **extracts**.

Research

HAWTHORN'S ACTIVE INGREDIENTS INCLUDE **FLAVONOIDS** and oligomeric procyanidins, also known as OPCs. Flavonoids act to dilate blood vessels, and both flavonoids and OPCs are known to have potent **antioxidant** effects. Hawthorn has been extensively studied in Germany. There and elsewhere, clinical studies have demonstrated that hawthorn's active compounds enhance the strength of heart muscle contractions, help increase the amount of blood pumped with each contraction, and foster a stable, rhythmic heart beat. In studies of people with congestive heart failure, hawthorn has been shown to improve heart function and relieve symptoms such as shortness of breath and fatigue. Hawthorn preparations appear to dilate coronary arteries, permitting a freer flow of blood and oxygen to heart muscle, thus combating chest pain (angina). Active ingredients in the herb also seem to prevent the release of angiotensin, a substance which activates an **enzyme** known to cause high blood pressure. However, the herb should not be considered a substitute for other blood pressure medications. Hawthorn extracts have been shown to improve circulation to the extremities by helping to reduce resistance in the peripheral blood vessels. In both laboratory and animal studies, hawthorn's antioxidant properties have been shown to be effective in protecting against the formation of plaque in blood vessels, thus helping to combat atherosclerosis. Research has also indicated that the preparations from the hawthorn tree may help remove "bad" **low-density lipoproteins** (LDLs) from the bloodstream.

FROM HAWS TO HEDGES

The small, apple-like fruits of hawthorn are called haws. Combine that with the plant's thorny branches, and one might assume that was the source of the name "hawthorn." However, some scholars believe the common name is a corruption of the Anglo-Saxon name for the tree, *hagathorn*, or possibly the German *hagedorn*. Both words translate as "hedge thorn." Hawthorn does indeed make a formidable, fast-growing barrier or hedge. The common name "quickset" is a reference to the fact that the thorny trees were grown to create thorny, living barriers. Another common name, "whitethorn," refers to the grayish-white coloring of the bark. In hard times, the tree's buds were eaten by European peasants, a practice that perhaps spawned the name "bread and cheese" tree. The genus name, *Crataegus*, comes from the Greek *kratos*, meaning "strength," an allusion to the remarkable hardness of the hawthorn tree's wood.

In addition to having a host of common names, hawthorn has been associated with both superstition and sacredness over the centuries. The Romans tied sprigs of hawthorn to cradles to protect babies against evil and disease. In medieval times, the branches were hung over doorways to keep away evil spirits. Hawthorn trees have been associated with both the Virgin Mary and Jesus Christ. Hawthorn was thought to be the source for Christ's crown of thorns.

See Also: *Herbal Medicine Expanded Commission E Monographs* by M. Blumenthal, A. Goldberg, and J. Brinckmann, American Botanical Council, 2000; *World Health Organization (WHO) Monographs on Selected Medicinal Plants, Vol. 2*, 2002.

Heal All
Prunella vulgaris

HEAL ALL IS AN EXTREMELY COMMON HERB—SOME might call it a weed—that spreads by creeping **rhizomes** and can be found growing in sunny, open ground all over Europe, England, and much of North America. Heal all has a long history in herbal medicine, both in China and in Europe and later the United States. Yet it was used quite differently in the East and the West. Although heal all does appear in the important Chinese herbal *Shen Nong Ben Cao Jing*, the author, Shen Nong, placed it in the third class, considering it a low-grade herb. In traditional Chinese medicine, heal all was associated with "liver energy" disorders. In Western herbal medicine, the herb was primarily used to heal wounds and throat infections. The generic name, *Prunella*, is thought to be a corruption of the word *brunella*, which in turn came from the German *Braüne*, which means "a throat affliction." The flower was also thought to resemble a throat, so it followed that it should be used for treating throat problems. Heal all's longstanding tradition as a wound herb is reflected in many of its other common names: "self heal," "hock heal," "carpenter's weed," and of course, "woundwort."

Traditional and Current Medicinal Uses

HEAL ALL IS A PLANT WITH AN ANCIENT HISTORY IN CHINESE herbalism. It was first mentioned in Chinese medical literature almost 2,000 years ago, described in the Shen Nong herbal that was written (actually compiled) during the Han dynasty (206 B.C.–A.D. 23). The Chinese regarded heal all as an herb for complaints associated with liver disturbances; it was used to treat heat in the liver and aid in circulation. In China, heal all was also used as a **diuretic** for kidney problems, for boils and skin ulcers, and for conjunctivitis (pink eye). A tea made from the plant was considered cooling. Although the ancient Greeks and Romans appear either to have been unaware of heal all or to have not used it at all, it was a widely used medicinal herb in medieval Europe and thought to be a good activator of the body's natural defenses. A tea made from the leaves was used as a

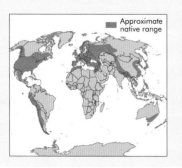

Common Names Heal all, self heal, woundwort, prunella, hock heal, blue curls, carpenter's weed, *xia ku cao*

Latin Name *Prunella vulgaris*

Family Lamiaceae

Parts Used Flowering stems

Description Heal alll is a low-growing perennial with a creeping rhizome (underground stem) that sends up square, red-tinged stems. It has small oval leaves and compact spikes of blue-violet, two-lipped flowers that are much loved by bees.

Habitat Native to Europe, Asia, and North Africa, heal all has also been naturalized in North America. It grows on sunny banks, dry grasslands, open woodlands, and waste places.

Approximate native range

gargle or mouthwash for sore throats, throat infections, and mouth ulcers, and was drunk to help heal internal wounds. It was also taken for fever and diarrhea. As a wash, heal all preparations were applied to wounds, bruises, sores, skin ulcers, and irritations. Heal all was believed to aid in curing convulsions and fits and to expel intestinal worms. Centuries later, European colonists took heal all with them to America, where it was grown and quickly became naturalized. There it was called "heart of the earth" and "blue curls." Heal all still has a place in modern herbal medicine. In China, it is often taken with chrysanthemum for fevers, headaches, high blood pressure, mumps, dizziness and vertigo, mastitis, and hyperactivity in children. In modern Western herbal medicine, it is used to soothe sore throats and inflamed gums, to help heal burns, minor injuries, skin inflammation, bites, bruises, and hemorrhoids, and for hemorrhage and excessive menstruation. Because heal all has **antioxidant** properties, some herbalists recommend it to help maintain immune system function in people who are HIV-positive.

Cultivation and Preparation

A RATHER INVASIVE PERENNIAL, HEAL ALL IS GROWN FROM seed sown in spring or by division of the creeping rhizomes or of entire plants. Flowering stems are typically cut in autumn and dried for use in a number of preparations.

Research

THE MAIN CONSTITUENTS OF HEAL ALL INCLUDE TANNINS, bitter compounds, **essential oil, saponins**, and a **glycoside** called aucubin. These substances give the herb **astringent, anti-inflammatory**, antiseptic, and blood-staunching properties. Research in China supports heal all's value as a moderately effective antibiotic against a range of bacteria and suggests that it may also lower high blood pressure. Other studies indicate that heal all contains ursolic acid, a known diuretic that also has anti-tumor actions. Heal all has been shown to be rich in natural antioxidant components such as rosmarinic acid; in fact, heal all contains more rosmarinic acid than rosemary itself.

Many herbals from the Middle Ages and later expound on the virtues of heal all. The English herbalist John Gerard (1545–1612) declared that "there is not a better wounde herbe in the world." A few decades later, another English herbalist, Nicholas Culpeper (1616–1654), who wrote *The Complete Herbal* and *English Physician Enlarged* in the mid-1600s, described heal all as a wound herb that "whereby when you are hurt you may heal yourself." He went on to explain that use of heal all had confirmed a proverb known at the time that claimed whoever used heal all needed neither a physician nor a surgeon. In Ireland, the herb, known as "heart's-ease" was historically considered an important remedy. Three principle uses persist in folk medicine in different parts of Europe: to stop bleeding, to ease respiratory conditions, and to treat heart troubles. But since the 18th century the herb has been largely ignored. Perhaps the Chinese name for the herb is most appropriate—*xia ku cao*—meaning "herb withered after summer," a moniker a lot less hyperbolic than heal all. The dried flower spike, harvested after the plant had withered in the fall, is the part used in China. Recently, a Korean research group discovered anti-allergenic constituents in the plant as well as anti-inflammatory activity. Perhaps those early herbalists knew what they were talking about after all.

See Also: A Field Guide to Medicinal Plants and Herbs: Eastern and Central North America 2nd ed. by S. Foster and J. Duke, Houghton Mifflin, 2000; *A Field Guide to Medicinal Plants and Herbs: Western North America* by S. Foster and C. Hobbs, Houghton Mifflin, 2002.

Hemp
Cannabis sativa

Common Names Hemp, Indian hemp, marijuana, pot, dagga, ganja, hashish, neckweed

Latin Names *Cannabis sativa, Cannabis indica*

Family Cannabaceae

Parts Used Flowering tops, leaves, seeds

Description An annual that grows to six to twelve feet or more in height, *Cannabis* has an erect stem and narrow leaves composed of three to eleven leaflets that have sharply serrated edges. Male and female flowers are greenish and inconspicuous and are borne on separate plants. The fruits are small, shiny, and grayish-green.

Habitat *Cannabis* is native to western and central Asia, northern India, and southern Siberia but is now widely grown in temperate and tropical regions worldwide.

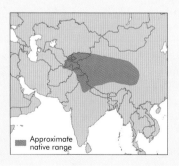

■ Approximate native range

C ANNABIS HAS A VERY LONG HISTORY AS A MULTIUSE plant, valued for its tough hemp fibers and as a medicine and mind-altering drug. Ancient texts from China, Persia, India, and Greece confirm that the herb's medicinal and psychoactive properties were recognized thousands of years ago. *Cannabis* continued to be used as both medicine and drug in many countries, including the United States, up until the end of the 1800s and early 1900s. It was readily available as a **tincture** from medical practitioners, primarily as a painkiller. After the turn of the century, however, *Cannabis*' popularity as a medicine faded as other drugs such as aspirin came onto the scene. Still, it was used without stigma until the 1930s, when negative media attention and lobbying by various groups led to *Cannabis* products becoming illegal in most parts of the world; they remain so today. Yet modern medicine still recognizes the herb's medicinal value. In addition, genetic selections with no mind-altering chemical constituents are grown for fiber.

Traditional and Current Medicinal Uses

FOR PERHAPS AS MUCH AS 5,000 YEARS, *CANNABIS* HAS BEEN cultivated for various purposes. As a medicinal herb it was typically smoked or eaten to relieve pain and as a sedative. Other ancient remedies employed *Cannabis* for treating gastrointestinal disorders, insomnia, and headaches. During the Middle Ages, it was widely grown in monastic herb gardens. For a time, applications of the seed, as a paste or ointment, were a folk remedy for cancerous ulcers. A **decoction** of the root was thought to heal hard tumors and relax knots in the joints. Few herbs, in fact, have had a greater array of folk medicine applications; at some time or another the herb has been used for treating everything from anthrax and blood poisoning to lockjaw and snakebite. In the 1800s, many medical practitioners recommended *Cannabis* for insomnia, depression, neuralgia, migraine, and asthma. Queen Victoria's doctors prescribed it for her menstrual pains. It was also widely used as a local anesthetic in dentistry.

More recently, *Cannabis* has been found to be a very effective anti-**emetic** for relieving nausea and pain associated with cancer chemotherapy and HIV/AIDS. *Cannabis* exhibits therapeutic value in the treatment of migraines, epilepsy, and malaria, for improving appetite in AIDS, cancer, and anorexia nervosa patients, and for suppressing muscular spasms in multiple sclerosis.

Cultivation and Preparation

CANNABIS IS PROPAGATED BY SEED, SOWN IN EARLY SPRING IN fertile, moist, neutral to slightly alkaline soil. Plants are ready for harvesting four to five months later. Those with male flowers are typically harvested for hemp fibers (the world's strongest, most durable natural fibers). Plants with female flowers have the highest concentrations of medicinally active compounds. The female flowers and small leaves are picked and dried. A dark resin can also be extracted from the leaves.

Research

THE MAIN ACTIVE CONSTITUENTS OF *CANNABIS*—TETRA-hydrocannabinol (THC), cannabinol, cannabidiol—give the herb sedative, **analgesic**, and antispasmodic properties. THC is the primary psychoactive ingredient in *Cannabis*. Its actions are the result of its binding to certain receptors in the brain and body. Effects include relaxation, euphoria, alteration of visual, auditory, and olfactory senses, disorientation, and appetite stimulation. Recent research has shown the herb also may block the spread of cancer-causing herpes simplex viruses. Synthetic THC is available as an experimental prescription drug in the U.S. and elsewhere. It is considered to be non-narcotic and to have low risk of physical or mental dependence. The question of dependence with use of *Cannabis* itself, however, is more controversial. Some studies suggest prolonged use is associated with memory loss and depression, although these findings are disputed. Recently, a mouth spray for alleviating the pain of multiple sclerosis was approved by Canadian authorities. The drug contains THC and cannabidiol, making it the first *Cannabis*-based prescription drug in the world.

> CAUTION Restrictions on growing and using *Cannabis* for medical purposes vary from country to country. It is illegal in the United States to grow, possess, or sell *Cannabis*.

SO MANY NAMES

Call it zambi, grass, skyf, kaartjie, pill, bhang, sense of knowledge, ganja, ma fen, Kentucky laughing grass, dagga, marijuana, or hundreds of other names—it is still *Cannabis sativa*. Perhaps because *Cannabis* has so long been part of the human culture, and has narcotic properties, it has picked up more names along the way than other medicinal herbs. Its primary common name, "hemp," derives from the Anglo-Saxon name for the plant, *henep*. The genus name, *Cannabis*, it thought to have its origins in the Greek *kannabis*, which in turn may come from the Arabic *kinnab* or Persian *kannab*. These words may have an older origin in the language of the Scythians, an ancient people of central Asia. *Cannabis* was apparently used in Scythian funeral rites, as seeds have been found in funerary urns dating back to the fifth century B.C. Another name, "hashish" is widely used for the compressed, concentrated resin collected from the leaves and flowers of a mature, flowering *Cannabis* plant. According to one hashish legend, Marco Polo in his travels came upon a band of robbers in 1271, near the Caspian Sea, who were consuming *Cannabis* to become fearless. They were called *ashishin* (from "assasin"), which may be derived as well from the word "hashish." But not all of *Cannabis*' names reflect medicinal uses. "Neckweed" along with "gallowsgrass" were names the plant acquired in medieval England, where hemp provided the ropes used by hangmen for the gallows.

See Also: *A Field Guide to Medicinal Plants and Herbs: Eastern and Central North America 2nd ed.* by S. Foster and J. Duke, Houghton Mifflin, 2000; *A Field Guide to Medicinal Plants and Herbs: Western North America* by S. Foster & C. Hobbs, Houghton Mifflin, 2002.

Herb-Robert
Geranium robertianum

INTRODUCED INTO NORTH AMERICA FROM EUROPE, herb-Robert grows wild in rocky woodlands from Nova Scotia south to Pennsylvania and west to Manitoba and Missouri. It is a small, short-lived plant that has unpleasant-smelling, red-tinged leaves, and distinctive fruit capsules that look like the heads of tiny cranes or storks with long, pointed beaks. The genus name, *Geranium*, comes from the Greek word *geranos*, meaning "a crane." The bird beak-shaped fruits explain two of *Geranium robertianum*'s common names: "cranesbill" and "storkbill." (It is important not to confuse cranesbills with plants in the genus *Pelargonium*; these species are commonly referred to as "scented geraniums.") But who is the "Robert" in herb-Robert? It is thought that the name may be a corruption of the Latin word *ruber*, meaning "red," which could be a reference to the color of the flowers or the red tint of the leaves and stems. Some sources suggest, however, that the name may be a reference to Robert, Duke of Normandy, or St. Robert, an 11th-century French religious figure. Herb-Robert was once associated with magical practices. It has also traditionally been used as an herbal medicine to treat diarrhea and stop bleeding.

Traditional and Current Medicinal Uses

HERB-ROBERT IS A BITTER, ASTRINGENT, AND MILDLY **diuretic** herb—and not pleasant to handle. The entire plant is quite hairy and smells fetid when the foliage is bruised. For centuries, though, herb-Robert has been used to stop nosebleeds and bleeding from cuts and wounds, to treat severe diarrhea, and as a remedy for kidney and bladder disorders, including urinary tract infections. Other conditions for which the herb has been traditionally used include gastrointestinal ailments, peptic ulcers, boils and other skin eruptions, eczema, slow-healing wounds, inflamed gums, tonsillitis and sore throats, malaria, and tuberculosis. A hot **poultice** of boiled herb-Robert leaves was said to be good for bladder pains, bruises, and persistent skin problems and infections. Crushed fresh leaves were

Common Names Herb-Robert, wild cranesbill, storkbill, dragon's blood, stinking cranesbill

Latin Name *Geranium robertianum*

Family Geraniaceae

Parts Used Leaves, stem, roots

Description Herb-Robert is a strong-smelling annual or biennial with thin branched stems, reddish-green, deeply cleft leaves, and purplish-red or rose-colored flowers. Flowers are followed by pointed seed capsules that are reminiscent of a bird's long beak.

Habitat Native to Europe and Asia, herb-Robert has been introduced and naturalized in North and South America. It grows best in poor, dry soils in woods, thickets, and on rocky ground.

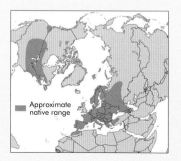

Approximate native range

also applied directly to parts of the body to relieve pain and inflammation. An herbal tea made from the leaves was sometimes recommended as a gargle for inflammation in the mouth and as an eyewash. Herb-Robert is said to be helpful in treating heavy menstrual bleeding and irritable bowel syndrome, and is also a folk cancer remedy; preparations of herb-Robert are externally applied to tumors and ulcers. When freshly picked leaves are crushed and rubbed on the skin, the peculiar odor released is said to repel mosquitoes.

Cultivation and Preparation

HERB-ROBERT DOES BEST IN WELL-DRAINED, DRY SOIL IN SUN or light shade. It can be propagated by seed, and it self-sows freely. The plant has a long blooming period, from as early as May all throughout the summer into October. For use in herbal medicine, the leaves and above-ground parts of the plant are cut as soon as flowering begins. These can be dried for use in **infusions**, liquid extracts, **tinctures, decoctions**, powders, and tablets. Fresh leaves and stems are also used in some remedies.

Research

THE CHEMICAL CONSTITUENTS OF HERB-ROBERT INCLUDE AN **essential oil** that has an unpleasant smell, various **tannins**, and the bitter compound geraniin. Tannins have been shown to be astringent agents that have both antiseptic and **anti-inflammatory** properties. They also exert antidiarrheal action because they tend to form a protective layer on skin and mucous membranes while at the same time causing small blood vessels to constrict, thereby reducing the loss of fluid. Herb-Robert is no longer commonly used in contemporary herbal medicine. However, fresh extracts of the herb have been found to be active against vesicular stomatitis virus (VSV), which is in the same family as the rabies virus. Although harmless to people, VSV infects insects and some mammals. It is also a common laboratory virus used in experiments to study the activities of viruses as well as to trace their evolution. Herb-Robert extracts also have exhibited a number of antibacterial effects.

THE CRANESBILL CROWD

In the genus *Geranium*, there are several species and many varieties of cranesbills. In addition to *Geranium robertianum*, a number of these other cranesbills are used in herbal medicine. Two of the most common are *Geranium maculatum* and *G. dissectum*. Like herb-Robert, these cranesbills are high in tannins, making them important astringent remedies that are good for emergency treatment of minor injuries and diarrhea. *Geranium maculatum* (wild geranium or spotted cranesbill) was widely used by Native Americans in much the same way as herb-Robert was used in Europe. The Cherokee, for example, used wild geranium to cleanse open wounds, heal canker sores, and to check bleeding in wounds. The Chippewa used the roots to cure diarrhea, as did the Iroquois, and others. Many tribes used the herb to treat venereal diseases. European colonists adopted the use of wild geranium from indigenous peoples; in 1820 it was added to the *United States Pharmacopoeia*, where it remained until 1990. *Geranium dissectum* (cut-leaf cranesbill) is a European species with similar healing properties. A native cranesbill of China, *G. wilfordii*, is used to treat rheumatism, diarrhea, and gastrointestinal complaints. In addition to their use in folk medicine, cranesbills are popular garden plants with attractive leaves and delicate flowers that bloom for an extended period.

See Also: *A Field Guide to Medicinal Plants and Herbs: Eastern and Central North America 2nd ed.* by S. Foster and J. Duke, Houghton Mifflin, 2000; *Herbal Medicine, 2nd ed.* by R. Weiss and V. Fintelmann, Thieme, 2000.

GERANIUM ROBERTIANUM | Herb-Robert

Common Names Hops, common hop, hop plant

Latin Name *Humulus lupulus*

Family Cannabaceae

Parts Used Female flowers (strobiles)

Description Hop plants are perennial, twining vines with clinging, hairy stems and deeply lobed leaves resembling those of grapes. Male and female flowers are borne on different plants. Hops are the pale green, cone-like, female flower cluster.

Habitat Hops are found in Europe, western Asia, and North America, and are widely distributed in northern temperate zones.

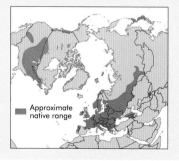

Approximate
native range

Hops
Humulus lupulus

THE HOP PLANT IS A VIGOROUS VINE THAT BEARS SCALY, cone-like fruits that are technically referred to as strobiles, but are better known as hops. In the first century A.D., Pliny the Elder named the hop plant *Lupus salictarius*, meaning "willow wolf," for its habit of climbing up willow trees and strangling them. Hops are famous as a bitter flavoring and preservative for beer. They have been used in brewing for more than a thousand years, but their medicinal values did not go unnoticed. Back when hops were harvested by hand, people observed that hops pickers were often drowsy. When the link was made between hop residues and this relaxed state, hops gained a reputation as a sleep-inducing drug. Throughout the history of herbal medicine, hops has been put to many uses. But it is still valued mainly for its calming, sedative effects.

Traditional and Current Medicinal Use

ONLY THE DRIED FEMALE FRUITING BODIES CALLED STROBILES are used in herbal medicine. They have a spicy aroma and a bitter taste. Over the centuries, hops have been used to treat a wide variety of conditions wherever the plants were found. Native Americans used hops for insomnia and pain. In European herbal medicine they were recommended as a general tonic, to relieve rheumatism and painful joints, cure fevers, as an **expectorant**, to get rid of intestinal worms, to remove obstructions of the spleen, as a **diuretic**, and as a sedative. Hops were also prescribed to treat jaundice, hysteria, nervous heart conditions, flatulence, intestinal cramps, diarrhea, and many kinds of skin infections and conditions, including boils. Hops are no longer viewed as a remedy for most of these ailments. But they are still used in herbal medicine as a treatment for sleeplessness and anxiety.

A sachet of dried hops placed under a pillow at night is said to be very effective in combating insomnia and promoting a good night's sleep. Blended with other herbs, hops have a reputation for effectively relieving stress, irritability, tension, and headaches. When applied as a **poultice**, hops are known to reduce inflammation. They also act as an antispasmodic to relieve certain types of asthma and menstrual cramps. Hops are also known to be good for digestion by increasing stomach secretions and stimulating appetite. They ease muscle spasms in the digestive tract and may be helpful in treating irritable bowel syndrome.

Cultivation and Preparation

HOPS ARE A TEMPERATE ZONE PLANT. THEY PREFER MOIST, well-drained soil in full sun or partial shade but are vigorous enough to grow well under most conditions. Hops are propagated by seed, by softwood cuttings in spring, or by leaf-bud cuttings in summer. They flower from July to August. The female flowers, or strobiles, are about an inch long and covered with translucent, papery bracts (a leaf grown on a floral axis). They are picked in early autumn and used fresh or carefully dried for use in making **infusions**, liquid **extracts**, tablets, **tinctures**, and oils. Extracts of hops have become especially popular as an ingredient in sleep-promoting herbal teas as well as in other sedative remedies.

Research

RIPE HOPS CONTAIN A YELLOW GRANULAR SUBSTANCE CALLED lupulin that clings to the hairs of the female flowers. Lupulin contains the active chemical compounds that give hops its medicinal properties. Two of the most important compounds are lupulone and humulone. These chemical substances, or their breakdown products, are largely responsible for hops' bitter taste as well as its antibacterial action; they are also what act as preservatives in beer. A **volatile oil** that escaped detection for some time in laboratory tests is believed to account for the plant's sedative effects. This oil is present in fresh hops in fairly small quantities, but the concentration is significantly increased when hops are dried. A number of studies have also shown that hops contain bitter principles that strongly stimulate gastric secretions and thereby stimulate appetite and proper digestion.

CAUTION Handling hops can cause dermatitis. Dislodged hairs from the plant can cause eye irritations, and the resin from the strobiles may cause allergic reactions in some individuals.

THE "BREWHAHA" OVER HOPS

B eer has been part of human culture for as long as 7,000 years. In Europe, beer was originally flavored with mixtures of bitter herbs, including *Glechoma hederacea* (now most familiar as a lawn weed often called ground ivy). In the ninth century, hops began to be cultivated in France and brewers started adding hops to beer in the brewing process to clear, flavor, and preserve it. Thanks to hops' preservative action, beer could be kept longer before it was sold. (We now know that hops have an antibiotic effect in fermenting beer that favors the activity of brewer's yeast over less desirable microorganisms.) The use of hops caught on in France and Germany in the ninth and tenth centuries. The oldest surviving written record of the use of hops in brewing dates from 1067. Brewers in other European countries resisted the use of this new ingredient; in Britain, people believed hops would spoil the taste of traditional ales. Several British kings went so far as to ban the use of hops in beer. Not until the 16th century were the bans lifted and hops added to English ales. In 1516, a Bavarian duke enacted the *Reinheitsgebot* (purity law), which may be the oldest food regulation still in use today. The law stated that beer could only have three ingredients: water, barley, and hops (yeast was added to the list in 1857). Althought the regulation has been updated to reflect more modern trends in beer brewing, it is still considered a mark of purity in beers.

See Also: *Herbal Medicine Expanded Commission E Monographs* by M. Blumenthal, A. Goldberg, J. Brinckmann, American Botanical Council, 2000; *A Field Guide to Medicinal Plants & Herbs: Eastern & Central North America 2nd ed.* by S. Foster, J. Duke, Houghton Mifflin, 2000.

Horse Chestnut
Aesculus hippocastanum

L EGEND HAS IT THAT CARRYING CONKERS (HORSE chestnut seed capsules) in your pocket is good luck. The rich deep-brown, shiny-smooth seed capsules are appealing. In Britain children play a game with them: They tie the conkers to strings and compete to see who can burst open their opponents' conker first. Known for their beauty, color, and shape, horse chestnut trees are impressive trees adorning parks and streets. In spring, panicles of white bloom appear. The flowers have a faint perfume that smells of honey. The green, spiky fruits that grow from the panicles contain the seed capsules (or conkers). The horse chestnut tree arrived in Europe from Asia in 1576 and traveled to the New World in the 1700s. Horse chestnut **extracts** have been used medicinally for centuries, but recently horse chestnut seed extract has also been shown to be as effective as any standard treatment for varicose veins and chronic venous insufficiency in the legs (a condition that may include swelling, aching, tiredness, and nocturnal cramping of calf muscles).

Traditional and Current Medicinal Uses

W ITHIN A FEW CENTURIES OF THE HORSE CHESTNUT TREE'S arrival in Europe—by the early 1800s—extracts from horse chestnut seeds were being used in France. The Iroquois used Native American species as an **analgesic** and for chest pain. The Mohegan and Shinnecock carried conkers in their pockets for rheumatism (which may have led to the belief that this would bring good luck). While the extract from horse chestnut seeds has only recently gained attention in the U.S. for vascular problems, the Europeans have long valued horse chestnut products as a treatment for many vascular conditions as well as an effective treatment for sports injuries. In India, a paste made from the bark is applied externally for joint pain. Parts of the horse chestnut tree have also been used for nocturnal leg cramps, to improve circulation, as well as to treat phlebitis, varicose veins, chronic venous insufficiency, rheumatism, neuralgia, diarrhea, cellulite, backache, arthritis, and swelling from injuries such as sprains or following surgery.

Common Names Horse chestnut, Spanish chestnut, chestnut, escine, aescin

Latin Name *Aesculus hippocastanum*

Family Hippocastanaceae

Parts Used Seeds, leaves, flowers, bark

Description The deciduous horse chestnut tree, with its columnar trunk and tall, domed crown of branches grows rapidly to about 50 feet, blooming quickly in three to four weeks from spring to early summer.

Habitat The horse chestnut tree grows throughout the temperate Northern Hemisphere. It is native to Persia and northern India.

Approximate native range

Cultivation and Preparation

HORSE CHESTNUT TREES ARE GENERALLY GROWN FROM SEEDS collected in the fall and planted in fall or early spring when the ground is not too wet. To prevent mold rot, conkers can be kept in sand for the winter and, to germinate, soaked in water 24 hours prior to planting. Thriving in most soils, the trees do best in deep, sandy, loamy soil in full sun or light shade.

Horse-chestnut seed extracts are a complex **phytomedicine**, well-defined chemically. Some 16–20 percent of the extract is made up of a group of compounds called **triterpene glycosides**. According to Germany's Commission E, a panel of experts that labels and regulates herbal plant medicines, the average daily dose corresponds to 100 mg of aescin. Aescin is not a single compound but a mixture of triterpene glycosides found in the horse chestnut. It is usually taken in two doses per day of extract. The extract is usually formulated in tablets to deliver it in a delayed time-release form. In the European and American markets, liquid extracts and other forms of the product are formulated to deliver the equivalent amount of aescin.

Research

OF THE 13 SPECIES OF *AESCULUS* ONLY THE EUROPEAN HORSE chestnut (*Aesculus hippocastanum*) has been studied for its high aescin content. Aescin protects the walls of veins; it also works with other active chemicals to improve circulation and reduce inflammation. Horse chestnut seed extract has grown in popularity as a result of many recent studies documenting its efficacy for vascular disorders such as varicose veins and chronic venous insufficiency. At least 13 **placebo-controlled double-blind** studies on the use of horse chestnut extract for chronic venous insufficiency have been published since 1973. A recent review of these studies concluded that horse chestnut seed extract is safe and effective for decreasing **edema** (swelling) and reducing pain, fatigue, and tension (in the legs). The reviewers concluded that horse-chestnut extract was superior to placebo and equally effective as the standard treatment. Another trial suggested the horse chestnut extract is as effective as compression stockings as well.

FOR BRUISERS AND BRUISES

Horse chestnut preparations are among the best kept secrets in European herbal medicine. If you looked into the first-aid kits of most professional and amateur soccer players in Europe, you would find a big tube of horse chestnut gel, used for reducing the pain, bruising, and swelling that results from sprains and other sports injuries. Similar to the mechanisms of action in oral dosage products, topical products containing aescin act by diminishing the number or diameter of tiny openings in capillary walls, helping to "seal" the outflow of fluid surrounding tissue, hence thwarting swelling and bruising. This action makes topical horse chestnut extracts useful not only for soccer players but also for the everyday treatment of sprained ankles, smashed fingers, and a host of other injuries suffered by children and adults. In addition, injectable forms are used in German trauma centers for the treatment of acute head injuries or brain trauma. Topical horse chestnut extract products (usually in the form of a gel or a cream) are widely available in Europe and other parts of the world as well. The extracts are not available in the U.S. because they are not on the Food and Drug Administration (FDA) approved list of GRAS (generally regarded as safe) drug products.

See Also: Herbal Medicine Expanded Commission E Monographs by M. Blumenthal, A. Goldberg, and J. Brinckmann, American Botanical Council, 2000; World Health Organization (WHO) Monographs on Selected Medicinal Plants, Vol. 2, 2002.

Ignatius Bean
Strychnos ignatii

NATIVE TO THE PHILIPPINES, IGNATIUS BEAN IS A SOURCE of the violently poisonous plant **alkaloid**, strychnine. Strychnine is also extracted from another, closely related medicinal plant, *Strychnos nux-vomica*, which is native to tropical India and parts of Indonesia. Despite its toxicity, strychnine has therapeutic value when carefully administered by professionals in minute doses. Ignatius bean was used traditionally in the Philippines as an effective folk remedy for cholera. The seeds were sold in bazaars in Manila. Extracts of the seeds were also used by indigenous tribes as an arrow poison. Ignatius bean was introduced to the West by Jesuit missionaries working in the Philippines in the latter half of the 1600s. It is believed to have been named for St. Ignatius of Loyola, the founder of the Jesuit Order.

Traditional and Current Medicinal Uses

IGNATIUS BEAN WAS ONCE A COMMON MEDICINE IN MANY Filipino households. In addition to its reputation as a cure for cholera, the seeds of the plant were mixed with wine and prescribed to improve appetite and digestion. Ignatius bean seeds, along with the bark of the plant, were also used to treat fevers and to relieve some types of paralysis. Ignatius bean entered into a number of drug references, or **pharmacopoeias**, in Europe around 1800, and in America in 1830. Its actions and uses were quite similar to those of *Strychnos nux-vomica*, but Ignatius bean preparations were considered to be generally more stimulating. Ignatius bean was considered valuable in treating nervous debility, hysteria, and melancholy. It was also promoted as a remedy for digestive disorders and to stimulate appetite, for headaches characterized by stabbing pain, for ovarian, uterine, and rectal pain in women, to treat impotence and sterility, and to relieve muscle twitching in the face and eyelids.

Ignatius bean is used in some cultures—in very small doses—for acute emotional and mental afflictions, such as grief, shock, hysteria, and acute depression, as well as for tension headaches, indigestion,

Common Names Ignatius bean, St. Ignatius bean, *katbalonga, faba ignatii*, poison nut

Latin Names *Strychnos ignatii*, synonyms *Ignatia amara, Strychnos ignatia*

Family Loganiaceae

Parts Used Seed

Description Ignatius bean is a woody climbing shrub with large, shiny, oval green leaves and tubular white flowers. Smooth, yellow-brown, apple-sized fruits contain 20 or so hard, oval seeds about the size of olives embedded in a yellow pulp.

Habitat Indigenous to the Philippines, Ignatius bean grows in tropical forest environments and is found throughout Southeast Asia; it is especially common in the Philippines and Vietnam.

Approximate native range

insomnia, painful hemorrhoids, dry coughs, and sore throat.

Cultivation and Preparation

IGNATIUS BEAN GROWS WELL IN WELL-DRAINED, RICH SOIL IN sun or part shade. It is a tropical plant, and cannot survive temperatures lower than about 60 degrees Fahrenheit. Ripe seeds are collected and dried for use in pills and **tinctures** and for the commercial extraction of the alkaloids they contain.

Research

THE ALKALOID STRYCHNINE WAS DISCOVERED BY THE FRENCH chemists Joseph-Bienaimé Caventou and Pierre-Joseph Pelletier in 1818 in extracts of Ignatius bean. It is a colorless, crystalline powder with a bitter, metallic taste. In therapeutic doses, this extreme bitterness simulates the flow of gastric juices, thereby stimulating appetite and improving digestion. Carefully administered, minute amounts of strychnine can also deepen respiration and decrease the strength of the heart's contractions, as well as raise the levels of the hormone epinephrine (adrenaline) in the blood and increase blood pressure. These actions can help to prevent cardiac failure—and are the reason that strychnine is sometimes administered in cases of chloroform poisoning, surgical shock, and cardiac arrest.

Research has shown that strychnine increases the reflex irritability of the spinal cord. Taken in large enough quantities (a fraction of an ounce), the chemical interferes with the normal inhibition of the body's motor neurons and causes muscles to contract violently. Strychnine poisoning begins with muscle cramping that quickly escalates into powerful and agonizing convulsions. The convulsions come in waves that briefly subside but recur at the slightest stimulus, such as a touch or a noise. Death is usually due to asphyxiation resulting from continuous spasms of the respiratory muscles. Strychnine is also commonly used as a rat poison.

CAUTION Seeds of the Ignatius bean plant are extremely poisonous. Ignatius bean preparations should only be taken under the supervision of qualified medical practitioners.

The man often credited with the "discovery" of Ignatius bean is Georg Joseph Kamel, a German Jesuit missionary with a flair for the natural sciences. Born in Brünn, in Moravia, in 1661, Kamel was enrolled in a Jesuit mission school in Vienna, Austria, at the age of 21. After his ordination, he was sent to the Spanish-colonized Philippines as a Jesuit missionary in 1688. Kamel served as a physician to indigenous people of the region, but also gathered a tremendous amount of information about the Philippine flora. His investigations of the plants and natural history of the islands were published in the "Philosophical Transactions of the British Royal Society." Kamel also wrote extensively about the medicinal plants of the Philippines. One of the plants he described was St. Ignatius bean, the seeds of which were commonly used by Filipinos as a folk remedy for cholera. Kamel died of unknown causes in 1706 in Manila. He is most remembered, however, for his association with the lovely flowering evergreen shrubs called camellias (genus *Camellia*). Kamel was not their discoverer—he never traveled to Japan or China, where they are indigenous—but he was well-known in Europe for this work on Eastern plants. It was Carolus Linnaeus, father of the modern biological classification system, who named camellias after Kamel, with a slight Latinization of the missionary's last name.

See Also: *Medical Botany: Plants Affecting Human Health* by W. Lewis and M. Elvin-Lewis, John Wiley & Sons, 2003; *Pharmacognosy, 9th ed.* by V. Tyler, L. Brady, J. Robbers, Lea & Febiger, 1988.

Jaborandi
Pilocarpus pennatifolius

I N THE LATE 1500S AND EARLY 1600S, EUROPEAN naturalists who were eager to learn of the botanical treasures of the New World encountered many indigenous tribes in the rain forests of Brazil who had great knowledge of the medicinal value of local plants. A number of tribes used the leaves of small shrubby trees with long, pendulous clusters of flowers to treat everything from colds to kidney stones. The leaves were also used to promote profuse sweating, urination, and salivation to rid the body of toxins in cases of poisoning. The Tupi tribe called the plant *jaborandi*, which translates as "what causes slobbering." At least four closely related species are known as jaborandi in herbal medicine: *Pilocarpus jaborandi*, *P. pennatifolius*, *P. microphyllus*, and *P. racemosus*. The leaves of all four species are used in herbal medicine for a wide range of ailments. In conventional medicine, an **alkaloid** isolated from the leaves of jaborandi, pilocarpine, is also an important drug for treating glaucoma and dryness of the mouth and throat.

Traditional and Current Medicinal Uses

INDIGENOUS TRIBES USED JABORANDI AS A NATURAL REMEDY for fever, often to promote sweating. An **infusion** of the leaves could induce profuse sweating in just a few minutes. The herb was also used in treating influenza, pneumonia, bronchitis, diphtheria, laryngitis, epilepsy, convulsions, gonorrhea, intestinal and stomach disorders, kidney problems, edema, hepatitis, and skin conditions. It was applied to the hair to prevent hair loss and open pores in the scalp, and to the skin to ease psoriasis (a skin ailment characterized by red, scaly patches). Jaborandi was introduced into Western medicine in the 1870s and became popular in Europe as a remedy for fever, stomach and intestinal problems, laryngitis, bronchitis, flu, pneumonia, and psoriasis. Jaborandi found a home in American medicine as well, where it was used to treat lung congestion, asthma, bronchitis, dry cough, diphtheria, edema, fever, rheumatism, nephritis, psoriasis and other skin conditions, hard labor, kidney diseases, and to counter the effects of belladonna and

Common Names Jaborandi, Paraguay jaborandi

Latin Names *Pilocarpus pennatifolius* and other *Pilocarpus* species

Family Rutaceae

Parts Used Leaves

Description Jaborandi is a small shrubby tree with large, leathery leaves, smooth gray bark, and small pink or reddish flowers produced in long, slender clusters.

Habitat Native to tropical South and Central America and the West Indies, jaborandi grows in tropical forests under warm, humid conditions.

Approximate native range

other types of poisoning. By 1875, the alkaloid pilocarpine had been isolated from jaborandi and was shown to be responsible for the herb's ability to induce salivation and perspiration. It soon was discovered that pilocarpine was helpful in treating the eye disease glaucoma by reducing internal pressure in the eyeball.

Today, pilocarpine remains a widely used prescription drug for treating glaucoma. For many years, pilocarpine was also used as a **diuretic** to treat **edema**. Jaborandi is also used in modern herbal medicine to treat syphilis, as well as psoriasis and similar skin conditions, to increase hair growth, and to alleviate dryness of the mouth and throat caused by radiation therapy in cancer patients.

Cultivation and Preparation

JABORANDI IS STILL LARGELY HARVESTED BY HAND FROM THE wild. Heavy demand has raised concerns about the sustainability of jaborandi populations in the wild. There are now several jaborandi plantations in Brazil. The leaves are harvested during the dry season and dried for the extraction of alkaloids and for use in other preparations.

Research

THE ACTIVE PRINCIPLE IN JABORANDI IS THE ALKALOID pilocarpine, discovered almost simultaneously by two researchers working independently in France and England in 1875. The chemical constricts the pupil of the eye, thus reducing intraocular pressure in the eyeball. Pilocarpine remains a mainstay in ophthalmology for treating glaucoma. Pilocarpine also causes the sudden release of fluid from glandular tissue, making it a stimulant for profuse sweating and salivation. In 1994, the United States Food and Drug Administration approved pilocarpine for treating xerostomia (dry mouth). Pilocarpine's use in products marketed as preventing baldness is based on its ability to relax and open skin pores, increase circulation around hair follicles, and promote the uptake of other compounds thought to stimulate hair growth. Research has also shown that pilocarpine may be helpful in combating the side effects of morphine in cancer patients who are terminally ill.

Jaborandi is one of Brazil's most important commercial plant species. Small stands of these shrubby trees can be found throughout the tropical part of the country, although most are concentrated in the state of Maranhão, which is the source of about 95 percent of the country's total jaborandi crop each year. Traditionally, jaborandi leaves have been harvested by hand by indigenous peasants, providing them with a small but relatively reliable source of income. For a period of about six months each year, leaves are picked, dried, and packaged for sale to prescription drug companies. (Pilocarpine has yet to be fully synthesized in the laboratory; the majority of all pharmaceutical pilocarpine is still extracted from jaborandi leaves.) As demand for the leaves has risen, overharvesting of the limited jaborandi resource has had a negative effect on wild plants. The situation became serious enough for Brazil to list jaborandi as a threatened species within its borders. In order to safeguard wild population from further damage, drug companies have been investing in the "domestication" of jaborandi. Jaborandi cultivars are now being grown on plantations in Brazil. The domestication of jaborandi may ensure the survival of the plant in the wild. But it may seriously impact the livelihood of the local people who have long depended on the wild harvest of jaborandi leaves for their own survival.

See Also: *Medical Botany: Plants Affecting Human Health* by W. Lewis, and M. Elvin-Lewis, John Wiley & Sons, 2003; *Medicinal Plants of the Worlds* by B. Wyk and M. Wink, Timber Press, 2004.

PILOCARPUS PENNATIFOLIUS | Jaborandi

Juniper
Juniperus communis

Common Names Juniper, common juniper

Latin Name *Juniperus communis*

Family Cupressaceae

Parts Used Cones ("berries")

Description Juniper is a hardy, shrubby, evergreen conifer, usually growing up to 15 feet, with reddish-brown bark and flexible reddish-brown twigs that are covered with dense whorls of gray-green, needle-like leaves. Male and female flowers form on separate plants. Female flowers produce spherical green "berries," actually fleshy cones, that ripen to blue-black.

Habitat Juniper is native to northern temperate regions of Europe, Asia, and North America, where it grows on mountain slopes, moors, dry woods, and hills. It is also widely cultivated.

■ Approximate native range

ONE OF OVER 50 SPECIES IN ITS GENUS, *JUNIPERUS communis*, or common juniper, is indeed common. It can be found growing wild in most temperate regions of the Northern Hemisphere. Junipers are also cultivated, in many different varieties, as durable landscape shrubs and small trees that require little care. Tucked among the prickly leaves of female junipers are small, spherical, fleshy cones that are almost universally known as "juniper berries." When crushed, the berries give off a pungent, cedar-like aroma. Many people are familiar with juniper berries as the flavoring source for gin. The name is derived from an abbreviation of "Holland's Geneva," as the Dutch-invented drink was first known. Juniper's uses have not been confined to the gin industry, however. Juniper berries have traditionally been used in cooking and employed as a folk medicine for treating rheumatism, kidney and bladder disorders, and to relieve indigestion.

Traditional and Current Medicinal Uses

IN ANCIENT ROME, PLINY THE ELDER (23–79 A.D.) HAD CONsiderable respect for juniper's warming properties and its ability to relieve the aches and pains of rheumatism. Roman physicians prescribed preparations of the berries for stomach and chest pains, flatulence, coughs and colds, tumors, and uterine disorders. Coating the body with a juniper berry **extract** was thought to protect against snakebite. Medieval herbalists recommended juniper as an antidote against poisons and to ward off the plague, and also as a cure for a wide range of conditions, from flatulence to feeble-mindedness. The berries were sometimes eaten as an **abortifacient**. In North America, various Native American tribes used juniper for stomach pain, heartburn, coughs, colds and flu, high fevers, tuberculosis, venereal disease, ulcers, wounds, arthritis, muscle aches, as a blood tonic, and for kidney problems. In Western folk medicine, juniper berries were used to relieve indigestion and flatulence and to stimulate the appetite. They were also recommended to relieve the aches of rheumatism, dropsy (edema), bronchitis, cystitis, and some types of cancer. In the early 1900s, juniper was often prescribed as a **diuretic** for treating edema, for cystitis, kidney problems, and gonorrhea. Externally in ointments it was a remedy for eczema, ringing in the ears, hay fever, and chapped skin.

In modern herbal medicine, juniper is recognized for its diuretic and antiseptic properties. Preparations of the herb are used for cystitis, edema (except in cases of kidney disease), for stomach upsets, arthritis, gout, and rheumatic conditions.

Cultivation and Preparation

JUNIPER IS A HARDY PERENNIAL THAT TOLERATES MOST SOILS but needs full sun to grow well. It is propagated by seed or cuttings. Juniper berries take two to three years to ripen. Only the dark bluish-black berries are harvested. They are used fresh for oil distillation or dried and crushed or powdered for **infusions**, **decoctions**, **tinctures**, and tablets.

Research

JUNIPER BERRIES CONTAIN FLAVONOIDS, TANNINS, A BITTER compound known as juniperin, and a **volatile oil** composed of more than a hundred constituents. Scientific studies on juniper's therapeutic activity have been performed primarily on laboratory animals. Research has revealed that it is the volatile oil in juniper that is responsible for its diuretic action. Constituents of the oil irritate the kidneys, increasing urine production and, ultimately, fluid loss. Because this irritant action can potentially damage the kidneys, use of juniper is not recommended for people with acute or chronic kidney disease or for pregnant women. No one taking juniper should do so for more than four to six weeks. Studies have shown that juniper exhibits some **anti-inflammatory** and antispasmodic activity, making it helpful in treating urinary tract infections. Juniper also contains several substances that have been shown to combat viruses, and other compounds that are potentially active as **antioxidants**.

> CAUTION Prolonged use or overdosing may cause kidney damage. Juniper oil may cause blistering of the skin.

A BERRY GOOD LUCK CHARM

Since ancient times, juniper has been more than a folk medicine and flavoring agent. It has also been valued for its power in protecting people from evil spirits, spells, and bad luck. In biblical times, junipers symbolized protection, and there are many references in the Bible to people using juniper trees for shelter. Juniper branches were also burned in temples as a purifying herb. In medieval Europe, juniper wood was burned to banish evil spirits and to ward off the plague. A widely held superstition was that cutting down a juniper would bring death to a family member within a year. In England, branches of juniper were often strewn on floors to sweeten the smell of rooms and to cleanse the air of infection and disease. Juniper was also thought to protect against witches. According to one legend, a juniper planted beside the front door of a dwelling would keep witches out. The only way a witch could get past the shrub and into the house was by correctly counting its thousands of tiny, needle-like leaves. Native Americans also believed that juniper possessed cleansing and protecting powers. The Cheyenne burned juniper in ceremonies, particularly to ease the fear of thunder. The Navajo burned juniper to produce "good luck smoke" for hunters, and the Kitasoo rubbed sprigs of juniper on their backs to ensure good fortune.

See Also: Herbal Medicine Expanded Commission E Monographs by M. Blumenthal, A. Goldberg, J. Brinckmann, American Botanical Council, 2000; A Field Guide to Medicinal Plants & Herbs: Eastern & Central North America, 2nd ed. by S. Foster and J. Duke, Houghton Mifflin, 2000.

Common Names Kava, kava kava, 'awa, ava pepper

Latin Name *Piper methysticum*

Family Piperaceae

Parts Used Rhizome (underground stem), roots

Description A sparingly branched evergreen shrub that grows 6 to 20 feet high, kava has thick, succulent stems with swollen nodes and very large, smooth, heart-shaped leaves. The stout, fleshy rhizome can weigh up to 15 pounds. Small male and female flowers are borne on separate plants.

Habitat Kava is native to Polynesia, from which it spread to many western Pacific islands. It is cultivated in the United States and Australia.

Approximate native range

Kava
Piper methysticum

FOR PERHAPS AS LONG AS 3,000 YEARS, THE DRIED **RHI-zomes** of kava, a member of the pepper family, have been used to make a social and ceremonial beverage important in the cultures of many Pacific islanders. Traditionally, the rhizomes were chewed or ground into a pulp mixed with cold water to create a thick brew that would slightly numb the mouth and produce feelings of well-being, tranquility, and contentment. Kava ceremonies were special events held to welcome visiting royalty or honored guests. When Captain James Cook made his first voyage into the Pacific in the 1760s, he and his crew encountered kava for the first time and went on to introduce the herb to Europe. As an herbal medicine, kava became immensely popular in the West during the 1990s for treating anxiety, insomnia, and related nervous disorders and as an effective alternative to prescription tranquilizers and antidepressants. However, reports linking kava with rare cases of liver damage prompted the U.S. Food and Drug Administration and various regulatory agencies in Europe and Canada to warn consumers of potential risks associated with the herb. Kava's safety is still being studied and debated.

Traditional and Current Medicinal Uses

FOR CENTURIES, PACIFIC ISLANDERS FROM PAPUA NEW GUINEA west to Hawaii have drunk kava to calm nerves, promote relaxation, and fight fatigue. Taken in large quantities, it produced a state of euphoria. Considered a strengthening tonic, it was given to combat feelings of weakness and nervous exhaustion as well as chills and head colds. Kava was administered as a remedy for urinary tract disorders and infections, asthma, rheumatism and arthritis, stomach upsets, headaches, cramps, muscle pain, boils, and for syphilis and gonorrhea. Preparations of the rhizome were also said to deaden pain, prevent infection, and act as an aphrodisiac. The roots were chewed to relieve sharp, blinding headaches. The buds of the plant were chewed by children as a general restorative. A **decoction** of the whole plant was taken for lung ailments and related conditions. In

Western herbal medicine, kava was recognized for its value as a strong **diuretic** useful for gout, rheumatism, bronchial and other ailments and for its calming effect for treating anxiety and nervous tensions.

Kava's role in modern herbal medicine is mainly as an antianxiety aid. It is also recommended to combat sleep disorders, for stress and restlessness, and as a muscle relaxant.

Cultivation and Preparation

KAVA REQUIRES WELL-DRAINED, ROCKY SOIL AND PROTECTIVE shade. The plant is typically propagated by runners that emerge from the rhizomes. Kava does not produce viable seed and does not reproduce on its own. It is entirely dependent on humans for its existence.

Research

KAVA CONTAINS A NUMBER OF CHEMICALLY ACTIVE COMpounds known collectively as kavalactones. Research has shown that kavalactones bind to various neuroreceptors in the brain, including dopamine receptors. This action largely explains the herb's sedative, muscle relaxant, tranquilizing, and mild **analgesic** effects. Several well-conducted, controlled clinical trials have demonstrated kava's efficacy in the treatment of anxiety, tension, and agitation. The herb appears to be as effective in treating anxiety as popular prescription tranquilizers such as diazepam. Unlike prescription drugs for anxiety, kava does not appear to interfere with mental alertness, upset the stomach, or foster a dependency on the herb. However, over the past few years, concerns about possible liver toxicity resulting from the use of kava have grown, based on several reports of liver damage, including hepatitis, cirrhosis, and liver failure in Europe. The quality of these case reports has been variable. The United States Food and Drug Administration and similar regulatory bodies in other countries have issued warnings to consumers and physicians. However, a recent ban on kava in Germany has been rescinded (see Oceania essay, page 346). Research continues.

CAUTION Use of kava is not recommended for pregnant or breastfeeding women.

KAVA CULTURE

The name "kava" may be derived from the Hawaiian name for the plant, 'awa, which means "bitter." Kava was originally a bitter brew reserved primarily for priests, chiefs, and other members of royal families on South Pacific islands. It was also drunk to welcome honored guests, acknowledge preparation for or completion of an event, validate status in the community, for public atonement of misdeeds, to restore goodwill, in naming ceremonies and initiations, and to observe births, marriages, and deaths. One of the traditional ways of preparing kava was for the rhizome to be chewed by children or by a young woman, preferably a virgin, and then spat into a vessel and mixed with water to prepare the drink. Missionaries to the South Pacific were appalled by the practice of preparing kava in this way and pressured islanders to replace chewing with grating the herb or pounding it. Kava was also of great religious significance. The drink was viewed as a way to connect with ancestors or the gods. It was not merely an offering or sacrifice to the spirits but a way of gaining access to the spirit world or obtaining hidden or esoteric knowledge. Kava was also widely used in healing as well as in ceremonies to divine the future or the meaning of certain events. In Hawaii, native priests called kahunas would read the bubbles on the surface of a cup of kava—much like tea leaves are read in other cultures—to predict the sex of an unborn child or the cause of illnesses.

See Also: The ABC Clinical Guide to Herbs by M. Blumenthal, T. Hall, and A. Goldberg, American Botanical Council, 2003; World Health Organization (WHO) Monographs on Selected Medicinal Plants, Vol. 2, 2002.

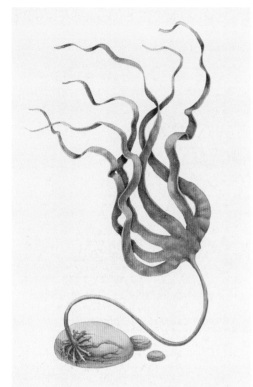

Common Names Kelp, oarweed, tangleweed, *kombu*

Latin Names *Laminaria digitata* and other *Laminaria* species

Family Laminariaceae

Parts Used Blade

Description Kelp is a common brown marine alga. It grows attached to rocky substrates with a dome-shaped cluster of root-like structures known as holdfasts. The smooth and flexible stem (stipe) gives rise to a broad, leathery frond (blade) that is divided into ribbon-like segments.

Habitat *Laminaria digitata* occurs in cold coastal waters along rocky shorelines in the northern Atlantic Ocean in the lower intertidal to subtidal zone. Closely related species, such as *Laminaria japonica*, grow in similar habitats along northern Pacific coasts.

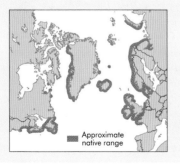

■ Approximate native range

Kelp
Laminaria digitata

KELP IS NOT A TRUE PLANT, BUT A TYPE OF MARINE ALGA (seaweed) that grows in large beds in offshore waters along many coastlines. It anchors itself to rocks on the sea floor by means of an extremely tough structure known as a holdfast. The strap-like blades of *Laminaria digitata* can grow three to four feet long and float upward, toward the water's surface and the sunlight. The scientific name, *Laminaria digitata,* is derived from Latin words meaning "finger-like leaves." The common names "oarweed" and "tangleweed" probably originated as a result of kelp's habit of floating in dense, tangled masses near the shore where people and boats encountered it. The blades (fronds) and stipes (stems) are covered with numerous mucus-producing glands that give it a slippery, slimy feel. The mucus acts to prevent water loss when kelp is exposed to air, as often happens at low tide. Kelp is one of several types of edible marine algae. It is rich in organic iodine and has been used in herbal medicine primarily to treat thyroid disorders.

Traditional and Current Medicinal Uses

KELP HAS BEEN EATEN AS A "SEA VEGETABLE" IN JAPAN, CHINA, and Korea for thousands of years. Japanese and Chinese folk cultures attributed a number of healing virtues to the alga, especially in treating thyroid disease and lowering blood pressure. In Japan, bathing with strips of kelp was said to help ease nervous disorders.

In modern herbal medicine, kelp is often incorporated into nutritional supplements as a source of vitamins and minerals, and a rich source of organic iodine. (Iodine is the chief component of thyroid hormones and is essential for their production.) Kelp-containing herbal supplements are often suggested for the treatment of high blood pressure, thyroid hormone deficiencies, arthritis, and to promote weight loss.

Cultivation and Preparation

MOST KELP IS HARVESTED WILD FROM THE OCEAN. IN THE PAST, harvesting was done primarily by hand, and the kelp blade was cut off just above the stipe or stem (the blade quickly regenerates). Currently, most kelp is mechanically harvested using boat-mounted devices to pull the algae up from the seabed. Blades are spread on screens to dry. Dried kelp is used in many herbal preparations.

Research

ANALYSIS OF KELP REVEALS THAT IT IS A GOOD SOURCE OF FOLIC acid (a B vitamin) as well as several other vitamins, minerals such as potassium, magnesium, calcium and iron, carotene, and, of course, iodine. Kelp contains all the essential **amino acids** necessary in the human diet, making it a valuable source of protein (about 9 percent by weight). It is also a source of a fine, very sweet sugar known as mannitol, which is sometimes used as a sweetener in diabetic foods. Despite the claims made by some supplement manufacturers, very little research has been carried out on kelp to support its supposed therapeutic effects. In cases of iodine deficiency, kelp may be beneficial because of its high iodine content. But thanks to iodized salt, few people in Western countries suffer from iodine deficiencies. Ingesting too much iodine, on the other hand, can interfere with normal thyroid function. The results of preliminary test tube and animal studies on kelp indicate that some of its constituents may help to prevent infection by several types of viruses, including influenza, herpes simplex, and HIV. There is also weak evidence that kelp exhibits anticancer effects and may slightly lower blood pressure. However, far more research, including **double-blind, placebo**-controlled studies, are needed to determine kelp's true medicinal value.

Recently, kelp has been marketed as a weight loss product, but there have been no meaningful scientific studies conducted to indicate that it is effective for this purpose. Kelp supplements should not be taken by individuals who are using thyroid hormone medications. Use of kelp has been linked with low blood pressure and depressed **platelet** counts in some people. It may also aggravate acne, and elevated urinary arsenic concentrations have been traced to the ingestion of kelp tablets. Prolonged use of kelp in large quantities may reduce gastrointestinal iron absorption and affect absorption of sodium and potassium, resulting in diarrhea.

Kelp is a rich source of alginate, a carbohydrate that is widely used commerically as a thickening agent. In the textile industry, alginate is used to thicken dyes used in screen and roller printing of fabric. Alginate makes dyes easier to handle and enhances how strongly dyes bond to fabric fibers. Once the dying process is complete, alginate easily washes out of the finished textile. In the food industry, alginate is widely used to thicken products like ice cream, ice cream toppings, jellies, sauces, syrups, pie fillings, and toothpaste. Adding alginate to icing makes it less sticky, allowing iced baked goods to be covered with plastic wrap without a mess. Water-in-oil emulsions such as mayonnaise and salad dressings are less likely to separate into their original oil and water phases if thickened with alginate. Alginate improves the texture, body, and sheen of yogurt. Small amounts of alginate can thicken and stabilize whipped cream. Added to ice cream, alginate does more than just thicken; it also reduces the formation of ice crystals during freezing and inhibits the formation of large, crunchy ice crystals each time ice cream softens slightly and is then refrozen, which is what happens when ice cream is purchased at the supermarket and then later popped into the home freezer. Alginate gels also are used in various types of food products where small pieces of meat are bound together and formed into shapes, such as little loaves of pet food and the chicken nuggets sold in fast-food restaurants.

LAMINARIA DIGITATA | Kelp

See Also: Seaweeds: Their Environment, Biogeogrpahy, and Ecophysiolgy by Klaus Lüning, John Wiley & Sons, 1990; Limu: An Ethnobotanical Study of Some Hawaiian Seaweeds by I. A. Abbott, National Tropical Botanical Garden, 1996.

Lemon Balm
Melissa officinalis

THOUGH YOU MAY KNOW IT ONLY AS ONE OF THE SCENTS emanating from your aunt's potpourri, lemon balm has been cultivated around the Mediterranean coast for more than 2,000 years for its many pleasing and healing properties. It was mentioned often in Greek and Latin classics, popular as a drink in medieval times, naturalized in England, and important to Native and colonial Americans. Many in the Arab world attribute increased intelligence to all who eat it, both man and animal. For most of its long history, lemon balm has been used as a sedative, antispasmodic, and antibacterial. The genus name, *Melissa*, comes from the Greek word for "bee" because plants belonging to this genus are so attractive to honeybees.

Traditional and Current Uses

IN ADDITION TO BEING CONSIDERED A CURE-ALL, LEMON BALM has been used to heal wounds, soothe bites and stings, to prevent and treat cold sores, to relax nerves, for sleeping disorders, digestion, depression, and generally for strengthening the memory and mind. The ancients commonly steeped lemon balm in wine for fevers and to lift the spirits. Greek physician Dioscorides prescribed it in the first century in his *De Materia Medica*. In the Middle Ages, it was used for stress and anxiety, sleeplessness, lack of appetite, and digestive discomfort. Ibn Sina (Avicenna), a Muslim physician and philosopher (980-1037), prescribed it for wounds and ulcers. The 16th-century physician Paracelsus thought it so powerful as to revivify patients close to death and prescribed lemon balm's healing powers for "all complaints supposed to proceed from a disordered state of the nervous system." In America, the Cherokee used lemon balm as a remedy for colds, fever, and chills, as well as for treating typhus. The Costanoan Indians of northern California used it as a gastrointestinal aid. It was also a part of the colonial garden: When lemons were scarce, lemon balm was used instead for jams and jellies. Thomas Jefferson grew it in his Virginia garden at Monticello.

Today it is still used as a garnish or spice and as a substitute for lemongrass, lemon peel, or sassafras. What

Common Names Lemon balm, sweet balm, blue balm, garden balm, cure-all, dropsy plant, honey plant, sweet melissa, sweet mary, balm mint

Latin Name *Melissa officinalis*

Family Lamiaceae

Parts Used Leaf

Description This hardy perennial grows into a bush two to three feet high with crinkly, serrated, heart-shaped leaves, which taste and—when rubbed—smell of lemon. It blooms all summer and into the autumn. Lemon balm is a shallow-rooted member of the mint family.

Habitat Native to southern Europe and western Asia, lemon balm likes the mountains, but has also been naturalized in southern England. It is now grown worldwide.

Approximate native range

the Europeans have known about lemon balm's medicinal effects is gaining acceptance in the United States, where it continues to grow in popularity and is now being used for Alzheimer's or dementia. The German government allows lemon balm preparations to be prescribed for difficulty in falling asleep due to nervous conditions and for spasms of the digestive tract.

Cultivation and Preparation

LEMON BALM GROWS IN ANY WELL-DRAINED SOIL, AND TOL-erates poor, sandy soils and full sun. In hotter climates, it prefers some midday shade. It can be propagated by seeds, cuttings, or root division in spring or fall. Seed propagation can be slow. The seeds need light and moisture for several weeks for germination. When plants reach a height of several inches, they can be planted in sun with partial shade. Lemon balm prefers moist soil and is susceptible to mildew, especially in winter when it must be kept dry. Unlike many herbs, lemon balm is best harvested in the afternoon when oils are strongest.

Research

CURRENT RESEARCH CONFIRMS THAT COMPONENTS IN LEMON balm's **volatile oils**—such as citral and citronellal—exhibit anti-spasmodic properties and have a calming effect on the central nervous system. Lemon balm has been shown to be effective for insomnia and anxiety in combination with valerian. It is unknown whether these effects come from the lemon balm alone or from the combination of the two, but patients with minor sleep disorders reported sleeping better than those who took a **placebo**. Some of the strongest evidence of lemon balm's medicinal efficacy comes from a **double-blind** study of 115 patients with genital or oral herpes. Lemon balm reduced duration of sores and increased length of time between outbreaks. Its antiviral action is not known, but it is thought that lemon balm inhibits protein synthesis and blocks virus receptors on host cells .

> CAUTION No side effects or symptoms are known but lemon balm should not be taken by pregnant or breastfeeding women. Consult a doctor when taking with other medication.

A "SPIRITUAL" LIFT

Starting around the 16th century, lemon balm reached widespread use as part of an alcoholic infusion, known as Carmelite water, first produced by Carmelite nuns. This medicine was regarded as an effective cure for headaches and neuralgia. It also became known as King Charles's water after Emperor Charles V of Spain, who drank it daily. It was used externally as an after-bath rub as well, and was among the first alcohol-based perfumes. Carmelite water basically consists of two pounds of fresh lemon balm leaves steeped in a half gallon of orange blossom water and a gallon of alcoholic spirits for two weeks. After that, various other herbs, such as nutmeg, coriander, cinnamon, and cloves are added to various recipes. The 17th-century herbalist Culpeper suggested the herb "be kept in every gentlewomans house. . . . It causeth the Mind and Heart to become merry . . . and driveth away troublesome cares." Modern gentlewomen who keep it in their houses often make a lemon balm tea by adding 1–2 teaspoonfuls of cut and sifted dried leaves to 1 cup of hot water, then steeping for ten minutes. It is sold and taken in Germany but with citronella instead of lemon balm, making it cheaper, but less fragrant.

See Also: *Herbal Medicine Expanded Commission E Monographs* by M. Blumenthal, A. Goldberg, and J. Brinckmann, American Botanical Council, 2000; *World Health Organization (WHO) Monographs on Selected Medicinal Plants, Vol. 2,* 2002.

MELISSA OFFICINALIS | Lemon Balm

Lemongrass
Cymbopogon citratus

RUSH THE NARROW, SOFTLY ARCHING LEAVES OF lemongrass and the air will be filled with the intense aroma of fresh lemons. This tall, clump-forming tropical grass is native to India and Sri Lanka and is widely used in their cuisines as well as those of several of their nearest neighbors, including Thailand, Vietnam, and Indonesia. The clean, lemony fragrance is really no surprise, since lemongrass contains in its **essential oil** some of the same aromatic compounds found in lemon peel. The oil of *Cymbopogon citratus* is widely used in perfumery and aromatherapy. Along with the oils of several related species, it is also an effective insect repellent. Lemongrass's genus name, *Cymbopogon*, comes from the Greek *kymbe*, meaning "boat," and *pogon*, meaning "beard." The reference is thought to be to the shape of the grass's tiny flowers that emerge on branched stalks. Medicinally, this stately grass has been used in its native homeland for many centuries for its soothing, calming properties. It is, however, a relatively new addition to Western herbal medicine where it is it used primarily for digestive and nervous complaints.

Traditional and Current Medicinal Uses

LEMONGRASS HAS BEEN USED MEDICINALLY FOR CENTURIES IN Indonesia and Malaysia. It has long been a part of the Indian **Ayurvedic** tradition, in which it was administered, primarily in teas, for fighting fevers, combating depression, and treating nervous and digestive disorders. **Poultices** of the leaves were applied to kill fungal infections of the skin. As part of Surinam's folk medicine tradition, lemongrass was given for coughs, cuts, asthma, bladder disorders, and as a **diaphoretic** to promote sweating. It was also a headache cure.

In Western herbal medicine, lemongrass is said to be good for colds, indigestion and other digestive problems (especially in children), to promote sweating and reduce fever in feverish illnesses, for relief of menstrual troubles and nervous conditions, as a **diuretic**, and as a stimulating tonic. Lemongrass oil is applied topically to ease rheumatic pain and for the treatment

Common Names Lemongrass, fever grass, *sera* (Hindi), *takrai* (Thai)

Latin Name *Cymbopogon citratus*

Family Poaceae

Parts Used Leaves, young stems, oil

Description Lemongrass is an aromatic tropical grass with clumped, bulbous stems that give rise to long, linear leaf blades that form clumps up to six feet tall.

Habitat Indigenous to southern India and Sri Lanka, lemongrass grows wild and is cultivated in tropical and subtropical regions around the world.

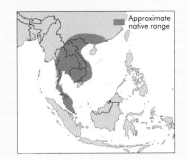

Approximate native range

of athlete's foot, ringworm, scabies, and lice. The herb also is used as a mild sedative.

Cultivation and Preparation

LEMONGRASS GROWS AS A PERENNIAL IN WARM, TROPICAL climates, but as an annual outside of these regions. It prefers well-drained, fertile soil, lots of moisture, and full sun. Under ideal growing conditions, lemongrass will bloom, producing clusters of small, greenish flowers tinged with red at the end of a curving stalk. Unfortunately, lemongrass flowers are usually only seen in plants growing in their native lands. Lemongrass is easily propagated by dividing the large, dense root clumps, but it can also be grown from seed. The herb is extensively cultivated throughout Southeast Asia, southern India, Sri Lanka, central Africa, Brazil, Guatemala, the West Indies, and the United States (primarily in Florida and California). To harvest lemongrass for use in herbal medicine, well-established plants are cut at ground level. Oil is extracted from these fresh leaves and stems, or they can be dried and powdered for various preparations. Several closely related members of the *Cymbopogon* genus are also cultivated for their oils (used largely in the perfume industry rather than in herbal medicines); these include East Indian lemongrass (*C. flexuosus*), citronella (*C. nardus*), and geranium grass (*C. martini*). Citronella oil is also used to ward off insects.

Research

LEMONGRASS OIL CONTAINS LARGE AMOUNTS OF CITRAL (also the active ingredient in lemons). Citral exhibits sedative action. Laboratory studies have shown that lemongrass oil has significant antiseptic and antibacterial properties. Other research studies have demonstrated that lemongrass is also a powerful antifungal agent, one that exhibits antifungal activity against a wide range of common fungal species that cause infections in human skin, such as athlete's foot and ringworm.

CAUTION Pure lemongrass oil can be toxic or even lethal if ingested in large doses.

A MOVEABLE FEAST

In addition to its medicinal uses, lemongrass is an essential ingredient in many foods, in aromatherapy, and in perfumes and cosmetics. The herb is a classic, essential flavoring for many Indian, Indonesian, Malaysian, Vietnamese, Thai, and Caribbean dishes. The taste it imparts is refreshing and light, with a hint of ginger. Used in small amounts, lemongrass adds an intriguing, lemony essence to various foods without the acidic "bite" that lemon juice or lemon peel would bring with it. This quality allows lemongrass to blend well with garlic, chilies, cilantro, and other ingredients common to Southeast Asian, and in Caribbean curries, marinades, stews, and seafood soups. Lemongrass is also used as the basis of a popular tropical drink and a refreshing tea. Typically, the fresh lower stems (first gently bruised) are added to flavor dishes. Powdered lemongrass, called *sejeh*, is added to curry pastes and used in beverages. Pure lemongrass oil is added to massage oil for use in aromatherapy. The scent is considered to be very calming. Cosmetically, lemongrass oil preparations are used to cleanse oily skin. The herb's oil is also added to perfumes and forms one of the most common lemon scents used commercially in soaps and other bathproducts, scented candles, and sachets.

See Also: Medicinal Herbs History, Use, Recommended Dosages & Cautions by S. Foster, Interweave Press, 1998; *Medicinal Plants of the World* by B. van Wyk and M. Wink, Timber Press, 2004.

Licorice
Glycyrrhiza glabra

FOR THOUSANDS OF YEARS, LICORICE HAS BEEN PRIZED IN both Eastern and Western traditional medicine for the sweetness of its roots as well as its therapeutic value. In ancient China, licorice was credited with rejuvenating powers and thought to impart strength and life. The ancient Egyptians put licorice into funeral jars—some was even found in the burial chamber of Tutankhamen. Roman legionnaires chewed the herb's roots on the battlefield, and many centuries later, Napoleon adopted the same habit in his military exploits, claiming it had a calming effect on his nerves. Today licorice has the distinction of being the most commonly used herb in traditional Chinese medicine. Licorice's sweet-tasting roots are the parts of the plant used in herbal medicine, primarily as a remedy for lung, stomach, and intestinal ailments.

Traditional and Current Medicinal Uses

IN TRADITIONAL CHINESE MEDICINE, LICORICE WAS USED FOR sore throat and food poisoning. The herb's role in **Ayurvedic medicine** was as a cure for stomach disorders, sore throat, respiratory infections, and as first aid for snake or scorpion bites. In Greece during the fourth century B.C., the philosopher Theophrastus wrote about licorice root's effectiveness in easing coughs and relieving thirst. Roman scholar and naturalist Pliny the Elder (A.D. 23–79) also noted the herb's ability to calm coughs, while Greek physician Dioscorides (A.D. 40–90) recommended it to clear the voice and mellow the mood. In the Middle Ages and beyond, licorice was widely used in Europe and England to soothe coughs and hoarseness, to relieve bronchial infections, and as a treatment for stomach upsets. Across the Atlantic, Native Americans used licorice for sore throat, coughs, chest pains, diarrhea, stomachache, fevers in children, and—in at least one tribe—to create a strong voice for singing.

In modern herbal medicine, licorice is still valued for its ability to relieve coughs and sore throat, inflammation of mucous membranes, asthma, bronchial problems and lung congestion, for stomach upsets, peptic and duodenal ulcers, arthritis, bladder and kidney

Common Names Licorice, liquorice, licorice root, sweet licorice

Latin Name *Glycyrrhiza glabra*

Family Fabaceae

Parts Used Rhizome (undergrond stem)

Description Licorice is a perennial herb that grows to three feet tall and has a woody, branching, brown rhizome (underground stem) that is yellow inside. Compound leaves are composed of three to seven pairs of small oblong leaflets, while purplish flowers bloom in terminal spikes. Fruits are smooth, reddish-brown pods.

Habitat Native to southern Europe and western and central Asia, *Glycyrrhiza glabra* is now cultivated in many temperate regions worldwide, including parts of North and South America and Australia.

Approximate native range

ailments, and for the rare endocrine disorder called Addison's disease. Licorice is also prescribed for skin sores, herpes, shingles, sunburn, insect bites, and as a mild laxative.

Cultivation and Preparation

LICORICE REQUIRES DEEP, RICH, MOISTURE-RETENTIVE, somewhat sandy soil, and full sun. Plants can be started from seed or by division. **Rhizomes** and roots are harvested from plants that are three to four years old. They are dried for liquid **extracts** and **decoctions**, powdered, or crushed and boiled to produce a sweet, sticky juice that, when concentrated, is shaped into cakes or sticks.

Research

CONSIDERABLE LABORATORY AND CLINICAL RESEARCH HAS been carried out on licorice and its effects. The **saponin** glycyrrhizin (the source of licorice's sweet taste) has been shown to exhibit **anti-inflammatory** and anti-arthritic properties similar to those of hydrocortisone and other corticosteroid hormones. It stimulates the production of cortisol by the adrenal glands, but also seems to inhibit some of the more damaging effects that this natural hormone can exert in the body. Licorice has proven antiviral properties against a wide variety of viruses, including herpes, hepatitis, and HIV. It also exhibits antibacterial properties and toxic effects on tumor cells. Studies have documented that licorice protects the liver, helps heal liver damage, and is effective in treating chronic hepatitis and cirrhosis. It stimulates the immune system and, in women, may slightly raise estrogen levels. Licorice has been shown to be highly effective in healing canker sores. It acts to prevent the buildup of the sugar sorbital in the body, which is a complication in diabetes that can lead to cataracts and vision deterioration, kidney problems, and nerve damage. Some studies have found that licorice or extracts may work as well in treating ulcers as prescription antacids and as well in calming coughs as codeine.

> **CAUTION** Excessive, prolonged use of licorice can lead to water retention, high blood pressure, and other complications. It should be administered by qualified medical practitioners only.

LICORICE, SWEET LICORICE

In Sanskrit, licorice is called "sweet stalk." The Greeks named it "sweet root." And the Chinese, who may have known about it the longest, named it *gan cao*, or "sweet herb." Much loved in many cultures, licorice is often said to be 50 times sweeter than table sugar, but some researchers believe it may be several times sweeter than that. Licorice's sweetness is reflected in it genus name, *Glycyrrhiza*, which comes from the Greek *glukos*, meaning "sweet," and *rhiza*, meaning "root." Over the centuries, this was corrupted to "gliquiricia," "liquiritia," and then "licorice." From the Mediterranean region, licorice and love for it spread north. By the 1100s, the herb was cultivated in Europe. In England, it was grown in monastery gardens for its medicinal value. In the 16th century, the monks of Pontefract Abbey in Yorkshire made lozenges out of licorice extract for coughs and stomachaches. In 1760, George Dunhill, a Pontefract apothecary, hit on the idea of adding sugar and flour to an extract of licorice. The result was a soft, chewy, intensely flavored candy known as a "Pontefract cake" or "Yorkshire penny." Pontefract cakes are still manufactured today, and licorice remains a popular ingredient in confections in England and worldwide.

GLYCYRRHIZA GLABRA | Licorice

See Also: World Health Organization (WHO) Monographs on Selected Medicinal Plants, Vol. 1, 1999; Herbal Emissaries: Bringing Chinese Herbs to the West by S. Foster and Y. Chongxi, Healing Arts Press, 1992.

HEALING PLANTS OF
India

ONCE UPON A TIME AN APPRENTICE TO AN INDIAN HERBAL DOCtor was given a final exam. "Go to the surrounding hills and forest," the teacher instructed, "and collect any plants without medicinal uses."

The apprentice wandered the surrounding fields and forests for several days before returning to his master. With his head hanging down, he murmured, "Master, I have failed, I could not find any plants without medicinal use."

His teacher smiled broadly and exclaimed, "You've passed the test!"

India is a country like no other. The extremes of topography and of weather are unmatched anywhere on the globe, resulting in one of the most diverse collections of medicinal plants on Earth. In the world's tallest mountain range, the Himalaya, temperatures may dip to −50° Fahrenheit, and in some areas Arctic conditions prevail year round. Desert areas such as the Rajputana may receive less than 5 inches of rain a year with temperatures climbing to 126° Fahrenheit. In the moisture-saturated air of the Assam, rainfall may total 430 inches per year. This great diversity of habitats sustains more than 45,000 species of flowering plants. About 3,000 plant species are used medicinally in India. Medicinal herb markets can be found in every village, town, and city, offering herbal medicines originating out of local traditions to herbs used in the traditional medicine system of India—*Ayurveda*.

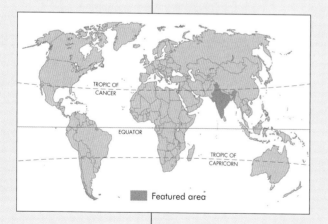

TRADITIONAL MEDICINE IN INDIA
DATING BACK SOME 6,500 YEARS, AYURVEDA translates as "the science of life," from the Sanskrit *ayu* meaning "life" and *veda* meaning "knowledge." **Ayurvedic medicine** is the oldest medical system in the world, predating traditional Chinese medicine, according to some estimates, by 2,000 years.

Ayurvedic medicine cannot be understood through a simple delineation of medical principles. It is too complex and too much a part of spiritual traditions, in addition to its medical concepts, to be understood in a neatly defined context. Ayurveda does not use the critical analytical approach of modern Western medicine. Rather, it follows a broad-based integration of life, health, and disease. One of the classic texts of Ayurvedic medicine, the *Caraka Samhita*, declares that it is not possible or necessary to name every disease. Each patient is considered unique, and the imbalance of a patient's illness requires a precise clinical

assessment and individual treatment. Ayurveda, therefore, looks at illness in terms of the nature of the disease rather than a named disease.

Ayurveda is much more than the use of herbs. It strives to promote the quality of life and increase life span. Emphasis is placed on preventing disease and promoting health by strengthening mind, spirit, body, and tissues to withstand stresses. Changing or adjusting lifestyle and diet and the use of herbs and other therapeutic techniques that restore equilibrium are among the means to a healthy life. The nuances of Ayurvedic classification of body types, body systems, and energetics require a lifetime of study.

During the British occupation of India, from the 18th century until independence in 1947, use of the Sanskrit language and knowledge conveyed in the ancient Vedic texts was suppressed. This slowed the translation of the ancient Sanskrit Ayurvedic texts into English. However, in the last century, most works on Ayurvedic medicinal plants and a vast body of scientific literature on Ayurvedic herbs have been published in English.

More than 3,000 herbs have been described in ancient Ayurvedic texts. Today, between 250 and 300 are commonly used. Ayurveda is only one traditional medical system recognized in India. Others include the **Unani-**

Water hyssop yields its juices as two herbal practitioners prepare a medicinal infusion at the Poonkutil Mana Hospital, an Ayurvedic treatment center in Karala, India. The medicine will be used to relieve anxiety in mentally ill patients.

PRECEDING PAGES: Munni Bibi of Lucknow, India, has spent much of her life collecting medicinal plants. The plant she holds possesses strongly bioactive chemicals.

Tibb (traditional Islamic medicine), Siddha (limited mostly to Tamil Nadu and adjacent regions of south India), and Yoga. Homeopathy, introduced by the British in the 19th century, is also widely practiced in India (with more than 125,000 practitioners). Ayurveda, with more than 300,000 practitioners is the most widespread traditional medicine system in India. Institutionally recognized by the government with more than a hundred graduate training colleges, it is practiced in 1,500 Indian hospitals. Ayurvedic physicians are licensed by state licensing boards.

Ayurvedic practitioners, however, are not confined to India. In the United States, Ayurveda is becoming increasingly integrated into complementary and alternative health care. In the last 20 years, Ayurvedic medicine has been popularized in the U.S. through the writings and lectures of physicians such as Deepak Chopra, Andrew Weil, and Maharishi Mahesh Yogi, founder of the Transcendental Meditation movement. Dr. Vassant Lad, director of the Ayurvedic Institute in Albuquerque, New Mexico, also has been instrumental in educating a new generation of Ayurvedic practitioners in the West. Ayurvedic healing and treatment centers are located across the U.S., especially in cities and regions where alternative medicine practitioners are commonplace, such as New York City, Washington, D.C., California, Hawaii, and New Mexico. Loren Israelsen, a leading consultant in the American herbal products industry, asked recently about the future of the herb business, replied in one word: "Ayurveda."

MEDICINAL PLANTS IN INDIA

SINCE 2000, THE NATIONAL CENTER FOR COMPLEMENTARY AND ALTERNATIVE Medicine and the Office of Dietary Supplements at the National Institutes of Health (NIH) in Bethesda, Maryland, has funded seven university research centers to study various aspects of botanical medicine. The seven centers comprise the NIH Botanical Research Center Program. One such research group is the Center for Phytomedicine Research at the University of Arizona College of Pharmacy in Tucson. Researchers in the Arizona group, led by Dr. Barbara N. Timmermann, focused on botanical uses in Ayurvedic medicine for the treatment of inflammatory diseases and arthritis, including ginger, turmeric, and boswellia. The $7.9 million five-year grant, issued in 2001, has helped to reveal some of the chemical constituents and mechanisms of action related to Ayurvedic herbs' anti-inflammatory activity.

Boswellia (*Boswellia serrata*), a small tree found in dry hilly areas in India (also known as the Indian olibanum tree) is valued for its gum resin, which resembles frankincense. In Ayurveda, boswellia is valued as a traditional anti-inflammatory used to relieve arthritic and low back pain. The active chemical compounds in the resin are said to have effects comparable to anti-inflammatory agents such as aspirin. These compounds have been found to inhibit the breakdown of connective tissue, increase blood supply to the joints, and help restore the structure of blood vessels.

Small clinical studies have suggested boswellia also could be effective in the treatment of bronchial asthma, ulcerative colitis, arthritis, and related inflammatory conditions. But results are conflicting. One clinical study showed significant reduction in swelling, pain, and morning stiffness in rheumatoid arthritis patients. Boswellia has been shown to reduce stiffness and associated inflammation two to four weeks after taking the herb. The herb has an advantage over conventional nonsteroidal anti-inflammatory agents in that it has a much reduced rate of side effects, especially in terms of gastric irritation and ulcer-inducing activity. However, a recent study showed that long-term use could lead to liver damage. Despite the long history of traditional use in India and an improved scientific understanding of how the herb works, more research is needed, especially clinical studies, to show whether or not the herb is suitable for use.

Gotu kola (Centella asiatica) is found in ditches and along waterways throughout warmer parts of Asia and beyond. Eating a few leaves daily is thought to revitalize worn-out bodies and brains.

Another popular Indian herb on the American market is gotu kola (*Centella asiatica*). Although widely used by the herb-consuming public for benefiting memory, scientific evidence supporting this use is scant to nonexistent. In India, gotu kola has also been used as a topical anti-inflammatory and to promote wound healing. Much of the scientific literature deals with its topical use for skin conditions. Studies have shown that it relieves inflammation, strengthens tissue at wound sites, and helps to rebuild damaged skin tissue.

In Ayurvedic traditions, gotu kola is used as a rejuvenating herb. It is prescribed to increase intelligence, longevity, and memory while retarding senility and aging. Pharmacological studies in India seem to confirm its benefits in improving memory and overcoming stress and fatigue. Two studies involving a small number of patients from India reported that gotu kola helped improve general mental abilities and behavior in mentally retarded children. Small experimental studies like this one show a trend toward confirming the traditional use of the herb to benefit brain function; however, these isolated studies are hardly the basis for making a scientifically proven claim for its use.

Ashwagandha or withania (*Withania somnifera*) is another herb from Ayurvedic tradition that is sold at health food stores across the U.S. In Sanskrit *ashwagandha* means "smelling like a horse or mare." In Ayurvedic texts, use of the herb dates back 3,000 years. Numerous uses for the herb were noted as early as 1000 B.C. In 100 B.C. a famous Ayurvedic physician, Charaka, prescribed it for female disorders and hiccups. For the past 2,000 years, it has been a well-known medicine in India as a tonic, especially for the elderly, to increase strength and vigor. It also has been used as a general tonic for debility and sexual dysfunction, nervous exhaustion, convalescence, loss of memory, lack of muscular energy, overwork, insomnia, fatigue, anemia, and infertility. It is also used as a sedative, hence the species name *somnifera*, which means "to make one sleep."

Modern interest in the herb arose in India during the mid-1950s, when its traditional use as a sedative was first investigated. A comparative pharmacological study with ashwagandha and Asian ginseng showed that ashwagandha stimulated the appetite. Ashwagandha also was found to have comparable anti-stress activity. Most studies on this ancient herb have been limited to pharmacological studies in animals or in the laboratory, with few clinical studies published outside of India. Studies tend to confirm positive benefits. But the real evidence for ashwagandha's status in herbal medicine comes from thousands of years of use, even reverence, in India. (Ashwagandha is the flagship of Ayurvedic herbs adopted in the West.)

India produces more medicinal and aromatic plants than any other country in the world and also educates more professionals in sciences such as ethnobotany, economic botany, and alternative medicine systems, such as Ayurveda, than any other nation. The National Medicinal Plants Board in India estimates 2005 exports of medicinal plants at $685 million, up from exports of about $102 million in 2000. This increase is prompting conservation concerns, particularly in four states of the Himalayan region where 500 medicinal plant species are collected from the wild. Approximately 90 percent of the medicinal plants from these and other regions are wild collected. With an annual export growth rate of 20 percent in the last few years, the Indian government, research institutions, and state governments are promoting medicinal plant cultivation by small farmers in the Himalayan foothills. Some 50 million people are engaged in medicinal plant collection in the Himalaya region alone. As India bridges past with present, world supplies of Ayurvedic herbs will depend on cultivation of plants now collected from the wild. As the Ayurvedic master taught his student, all plants may have medicinal value—and must be protected. Who knows what herbal remedy may hold the next cure for cancer or next treatment for AIDS?

OPPOSITE PAGE: *Swami Brahmananda, a Siddha healer living in Bangalore, India, tests a combination of minerals and herbs that have been mixed together and heated. Siddha is an ancient medical system of the Tamil culture in southern India. Preparing a Siddha remedy can take up to 30 days, following rules written centuries ago. In Siddha belief, as in northern India's Ayurvedic medicine, healers are holy men.*

Lobelia
Lobelia inflata

A QUICK GLANCE AT SOME OF LOBELIA'S COMMON NAMES— "pukeweed," "gagwort," and "vomitwort"— reveals that this is an herb with powerful **emetic** properties. Large doses induce vomiting. Lobelia was a traditional Native American remedy for many conditions, including asthma. It was smoked to quiet the spasms of asthma and bronchitis and as a tobacco substitute to break the tobacco habit, hence the nicknames "asthma weed" and "Indian tobacco." At least four other lobelia species were also used medicinally by Native American tribes. Indians introduced lobelia to European settlers. During the 19th century, lobelia was widely prescribed by some American herbal practitioners, primarily to induce vomiting. In the 1970s, the herb's popularity was renewed when it gained a reputation for producing feelings of well-being and mental clarity, and as an aid to quit smoking. Because of its toxic effects on the central nervous system, however, lobelia's use in modern herbal medicine is limited.

Traditional and Current Medicinal Uses

NATIVE AMERICANS SMOKED THE LEAVES OF LOBELIA FOR asthma and bronchitis, and chewed the leaves for sore throat and coughs. Leaves and **poultices** made from the roots were used to relieve body aches and stiff necks. Various preparations of the plant soothed skin irritations, stings, and sores. Lobelia was used to induce vomiting, but in very small doses, and also to treat colic in infants. The herb was taken to cure both habitual tobacco and alcohol use, and to treat dysentery. Lobelia was added to the drug reference volume, or **pharmacopoeia,** of American herbalist physicians in the late 1700s and widely promoted during the early 1800s as a muscle relaxant in childbirth, for healing ulcers, and for treating epilepsy, diphtheria, dysentery, whooping cough, and tetanus. Many practitioners believed strongly in the "cleansing" action of vomiting that lobelia induced.

In more recent times, lobelia has been smoked, brewed as a tea, or used in powdered form to relieve asthma, bronchitis, and whooping cough, as an **expectorant** and sedative, and to treat fevers, sprains,

Common Names Lobelia, Indian tobacco, pukeweed, asthma weed, gagwort, vomitwort, bladderpod

Latin Name *Lobelia inflata*

Family Campanulaceae

Parts Used Leaves, stems, flowering tops

Description Lobelia is a highly branched annual that grows one to three feet high and contains a milky sap. It has soft, pointed leaves and loose, terminal spikes of small pale-blue flowers. The fruit is a puffy capsule (hence the species name *inflata*) filled with tiny black seeds.

Habitat Native to North America, lobelia grows wild in pastures, meadows, and around the edges of cultivated fields. It is cultivated in North America, Russia, and India.

Approximate native range

bruises, and insect bites. One of lobelia's active ingredients, the **alkaloid** lobeline, was formerly used in some oral anti-smoking aids.

Cultivation and Preparation

LOBELIA INFLATA PREFERS ACID SOIL IN SUN OR PARTIAL SHADE. It is propagated by seed. The above-ground plant parts are usually cut in early autumn after flowering when the lower seed capsules are developed and ripe. Lobelia is typically dried for use in herbal preparations and is also incorporated into pills containing other herbs. The potency of the herb deteriorates rapidly after drying.

Research

LOBELIA CONTAINS MORE THAN A DOZEN ALKALOIDS, WITH lobeline (a cousin of nicotine) the most active. Like nicotine, lobeline has been shown to initially stimulate and then depress the central nervous system. Research has shown that the alkaloid activates nicotine-like receptors in the brain, exerting physiological activity similar to nicotine without its addictive effects. Experiments have indicated that lobelia's toxicity may be enhanced when combined with nicotine, and clinical studies evaluating the herb for smoking cessation do not support its use. Research into other aspects of lobeline has shown that the alkaloid accelerates respiration and acts as a bronchodilator, making breathing easier. Lobelia extracts were formerly injected as resuscitation treatments for apnea (cessation of breathing) and asphyxia in infants. But there were side effects and results were considered unreliable. Preparations from the whole leaf have shown lobelia to be an effective antispasmodic. In precise, appropriate doses, lobelia is considered safe when administered by qualified practitioners. Even small overdoses, however, slow respiration and can quite drastically lower blood pressure. Large overdoses—as little as 50 milligrams of the dried herb—can lead to severe nausea and vomiting, stupor, convulsions, and, ultimately, fatal respiratory failure.

> CAUTION Lobelia can be poisonous and has been implicated in deaths from improper use as a home remedy. It is for use by qualified practitioners only.

LOBELIA'S DAY IN THE SUN

The American botanic physician Samuel Thomson (1769–1843) is a controversial figure in American medical history. When his wife almost died due to a conventional medical treatment, Thomson turned to herbal remedies as cures for disease. He practiced his own approach to medicine (called the Thomsonian System) and had many followers in the early 1800s. One of Thomson's fundamental beliefs was that cold was responsible for many illnesses and that by restoring the body's "natural heat," health could be restored. In treating patients, Thomson recommended steam baths, cayenne pepper, and lobelia to induce vomiting. Thomson called lobelia his "Number 1" herb. He incorporated it into his patented medicines and carefully guarded the formulas. Thomson was critical of conventional medical practitioners and their treatments and most, in turn, resented Thomson's popularity. In 1809, Thomson was accused of murdering a patient, Ezra Lovett, by administering a fatal dose of lobelia. Ultimately, Thomson was acquitted on grounds of insufficient evidence that he intended to harm Lovett or that lobelia was a poison. The defense also showed that one of the prosecution's exhibits, labeled "Lobelia," was actually marsh rosemary. The trial prompted some states to pass laws prohibiting the sale of lobelia and of similar patent medicines. However, most were repealed by the 1820s.

See Also: A Field Guide to Medicinal Plants and Herbs: Eastern and Central North America, 2nd ed. by S. Foster and J. Duke, Houghton Mifflin, 2000; Tyler's Honest Herbal 4th ed. by S. Foster and V. Tyler, The Haworth Herbal Press, 1999.

Common Names Madagascar periwinkle, rosy periwinkle, church flower, Cape periwinkle, old maid

Latin Name *Catharanthus roseus*

Family Apocynaceae

Parts Used Flowers, leaves, roots

Description A bushy, fleshy annual (or in tropical climates, a semi-woody evergreen perennial), Madagascar periwinkle has glossy, dark green, oval leaves and five-petaled flowers that are a pale, rosy pink. The flowers are borne singly throughout summer. Stems and leaves exude a milky sap.

Habitat Madagascar periwinkle is native to the Indian Ocean island of Madagascar, but has been naturalized globally throughout tropical and subtropical regions and cultivated widely as an ornamental plant.

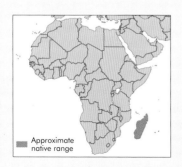

Approximate native range

Madagascar Periwinkle

Catharanthus roseus

DESPITE ITS NAME, MADAGASCAR PERIWINKLE IS NOT related to more familiar periwinkles such as *Vinca major* (greater periwinkle) and *Vinca minor* (lesser periwinkle). Madagascar periwinkle was once classified as *Vinca rosea* because the botanists who first observed it thought it resembled these other plants. But once its true characteristics were known, Madagascar periwinkle was reassigned to an entirely different genus: *Catharanthus*. Madagascar periwinkle hails from Madagascar, an island off Africa's southeastern coast that is known for its unique plant and animal inhabitants. Madagascar periwinkle is no exception. Despite its delicate appearance, this flowering herb is a virtual cornucopia of useful—and extremely toxic—chemical compounds. A number of these compounds formed the basis for several of the most powerful anticancer drugs ever discovered in the plant world.

Traditional and Current Medicinal Uses

GIVEN THE RIGHT CONDITIONS, MADAGASCAR PERIWINKLE IS A plant that naturalizes easily. Once it escaped from its homeland of Madagascar, it flourished in tropical environs around the world. Almost everywhere it grew, it found its way into the herbal medicine traditions of the local people. In Madagascar, extracts were used for hundreds of years to treat diabetes, stop bleeding, lower blood pressure, and as tranquilizers. In India, the herb's milky sap was applied to bee and wasp stings. Elsewhere in Africa, concoctions of the leaves supposedly relieved rheumatism and helped regulate unusually heavy or prolonged menstruation. In Vietnam, it was used for diabetes and malaria. Inhabitants of the Caribbean islands of Curacao and Bermuda used preparations of Madagascar periwinkle for reducing high blood pressure, while those in the Bahamas used the flowers for asthma and flatulence and other parts of the plant as a treatment for tuberculosis. In Central and South America, a gargle was made to sooth sore throats, cure laryngitis, and clear up chest conditions. In the Hawaiian Islands, an **extract** of the boiled plant was employed to stop bleeding.

More recently, *Catharanthus roseus* was considered a promising prospect in the treatment of diabetes and high blood pressure. But in the 1960s, researchers discovered the herb's real medicinal treasure. Madagascar periwinkle is the source of a number of bitter **alkaloids** that have pronounced anticancer properties.

Cultivation and Preparation

MADAGASCAR PERIWINKLE IS GROWN COMMERCIALLY FOR medicinal use in Australia, Africa, India, and southern Europe. Typically started from seed, the plant can also be propagated by cuttings taken in spring or summer. It prefers poor but well-drained soil in full sun or part shade. In warmer, frost-free climates, it develops a woody stem and can be pruned back to encourage fresh growth in late summer. It does best with lots of moisture but is able to withstand some drought.

Research

ALTHOUGH MADAGASCAR PERIWINKLE WAS A FOLK REMEDY for treating diabetes in some cultures, this historical use has not been supported by scientific research in human studies. However, the herb's alkaloids vincristine and vinblastine have been used successfully as anticancer medicines in chemotherapy since the 1970s. Vincristine is prescribed for lymphoma, leukemia, breast and lung cancer. Vinblastine is used to treat Hodgkin's disease. These injectable drugs, and drugs derived from them, interfere with cell division in cancer cells, although the drugs also affect healthy cells and have serious side effects. Recently, a lab study showed that other chemical compounds in Madagascar periwinkle may also inhibit growth of new blood vessels that form around many types of cancerous tumors and support their growth. This finding shows promise, but more research is needed.

CAUTION *Catharanthus roseus* preparations should never be used except under the strict supervision of a health care professional, as they can have serious, life-threatening side effects. Ingestion of the plants can cause poisoning and death.

ALL FROM A PERIWINKLE TEA

The story of the discovery of the anticancer drug vinblastine began in 1952. That was the year that Dr. Robert Laing Noble, a cancer researcher working at the University of Western Ontario in Canada, received a letter from his older brother, Dr. Clark Noble, who had recently retired from medical research. Inside the envelope were 25 plant leaves from the rosy periwinkle plant. Some time earlier, Clark Noble had developed an interest in this herb indigenous to Madagascar. When one of his patients in Jamaica told him that Jamaicans use a tea brewed from rosy periwinkle leaves to treat diabetes, and then sent him the leaves, the retired doctor passed them on to his brother for chemical analysis. Intrigued, Robert Noble set out to test the chemical properties of extracts from the leaves and see if the leaves contained some unknown compound that could cure diabetes. In studying the effects of leaf extracts in rats, Noble noticed that the rats' blood sugar levels were unchanged. But their white blood cell counts dropped significantly. Noble speculated that if he could find the chemical compound responsible for this effect, he might have a potentially powerful drug for the treatment of cancer on his hands. In 1954, Noble joined forces with Dr. Charles C. Beer. In 1958, after four years of intense research, they isolated the chemical they were looking for. Noble and Beer named it "vinblastine." Clinical trials of vinblastine administered to patients with lymphoid cancers at the Princess Margaret Hospital in Toronto were very successful. In 1979, Eli Lilly began marketing the drug under the brand name Eldisine.

See Also: *Nature's Medicine, Plants That Heal* by Joel Swerdlow, National Geographic, 2000; *A Field Guide to Medicinal Plants and Herbs: Eastern and Central North America, 2nd ed.* by S. Foster and J. Duke, Houghton Mifflin, 2000.

Common Names Marshmallow, white mallow, althaea, althea

Latin Name *Althaea officinalis*

Family Malvaceae

Parts Used Roots, leaves, flowers

Description Marshmallow is an erect perennial that grows to six feet in height. From a large, fleshy taproot arise woolly stems that bear grayish-green, velvety leaves. Attractive, five-petaled, lilac-pink flowers are succeeded by round, downy fruits that contain one seed.

Habitat Native to Europe and western Asia, marshmallow grows in moist to wet places, particularly salt marshes and coastal wetlands. It is naturalized in eastern North America and cultivated for medicinal purposes, primarily in Eastern Europe.

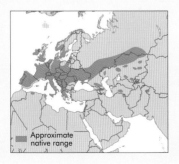

Approximate native range

Marshmallow
Althaea officinalis

I N HERBAL MEDICINE, MARSHMALLOW IS NOT THE SPONGY white confection roasted on sticks over campfires. But there is a link between plant and sweet. Gelatin gives today's puffy white marshmallows their soft, gooey consistency. But centuries ago, the French used the powdered roots of marshmallow to make soft lozenges, called *pâté de guimauve*, that were used to soothe coughs and sore throats. Marshmallow roots, as well as its leaves and stems, exude a sweet **mucilage** that is soothing, softening, and healing. This characteristic has made marshmallow a valued part of herbal medicine since the ancient Greeks, Romans, and Anglo-Saxons. Even the genus name, *Althaea*, comes from the Greek *altheo*, meaning "to cure" and referring to marshmallow's healing nature. The common name is derived from the fact that *Althaea officinalis* is a member of the mallow family that was typically found in marshy habitats. In the past, marshmallow preparations have been traditionally taken to soothe inflammation and irritation both inside and outside the body. This remains true today, as marshmallow continues to be used in modern herbal medicine whenever a soothing effect is needed in the digestive, respiratory, and urinary tracts.

Traditional and Current Medicinal Uses

THE MEDICINAL VALUE OF MARSHMALLOWS WAS FIRST NOTED by the ancient Greeks in the ninth century B.C. The Greek physician Hippocrates, writing in the fourth century B.C., described how marshmallow was used to treat wounds. Arab physicians made **poultices** from marshmallow leaves and applied them to the skin to reduce inflammation. Later Greek physicians recommended **infusions** of marshmallow as a cure for toothache and a soothing balm for insect stings; mixed into sweet wine it was taken for coughs. The Romans recognized the laxative properties of marshmallow roots and leaves. From ancient times, marshmallow was eaten to reduce sexual desire, counteracting the effects of aphrodisiacs and love potions. By the Middle Ages, marshmallow preparations were common remedies for coughs, chest and lung ailments, diarrhea, stomach upsets and ulcers, bladder infections, and insomnia. Lozenges such as *pâté de guimauve* were sucked for sore throat. Marshmallow gargles helped heal mouth infections and inflamed gums. Poultices of fresh marshmallow leaves were applied to wounds, bruises, insect bites, and sprains to reduce inflammation.

In modern herbal medicine, herbalists may recommend marshmallow for relieving asthma, bronchitis, colds and sore throat, cough, inflamed gums, stomach ulcers, inflammatory bowel diseases, and as an aid for weight loss. Marshmallow syrup is especially recommended for dry coughs.

Cultivation and Preparation

MARSHMALLOW IS EASY TO PROPAGATE FROM SEED OR BY root divisions. The herb will grow in average soil, but will thrive in moist, fertile, sandy soil with good drainage in full sun. Roots are the part primarily used in commercial herbal medicine. They are harvested in late autumn from three-year-old plants and dried for liquid **extracts**, syrups, and ointments. Leaves, harvested before the plant blooms, and flowers are popular for home remedies and used for **infusions** and ointments.

Research

ALL PARTS OF THE MARSHMALLOW PLANT CONTAIN VARYING amounts of mucilage (the highest concentration is in the roots) and pectin; these substances are primarily responsible for the herb's soothing properties in the digestive tract. The root is rich in sugars as well, which accounts for its sweet taste. Marshmallow also contains compounds that are antiseptic and **anti-inflammatory** and that mildly stimulate the immune system. However, the therapeutic applications for marshmallow in herbal medicine are based on history of use in traditional medicine, on **phytochemical** investigations, and in vitro studies and in vivo experiments in animals. No clinical studies have been conducted on the medicinal value of marshmallow. In Germany, marshmallow is licensed for use in medicinal teas and cough syrup medicines. In the United States, marshmallow is an ingredient in supplements sold for cough-suppressing and **expectorant** effects.

MARSHMALLOW THEN AND NOW

In the modern world, eating marshmallow may bring to mind toasted sugary blobs squeezed between graham crackers and chocolate bars to make s'mores, or bright yellow spongy treats in the shape of chicks sold at Easter. Centuries ago, eating marshmallow meant something quite different. The ancient Romans cooked the leaves of marshmallow as a vegetable. In medieval Europe, marshmallow was viewed as a food eaten during hard times when nutritious foods were scarce. Among the country folk, however, the tender growing tips of marshmallow stems were often eaten, famine or not. Collected in spring, they were made into a syrupy drink. The same young shoots, along with tender leaves, were a common ingredient in spring salads. They were also added to soups and stews. Marshmallow fruits, the unripe seed capsules, known as "cheeses," were eaten raw in salads, too. For a change of pace, the young roots of marshmallow were boiled and fried in butter, sometimes with onions. The original marshmallow confection was made by mixing powdered marshmallow root with water and allowing the mixture to swell and thicken. Sugar was added and it was then heated until it turned into a sweet paste. Today's marshmallows have only sugar in common with this original recipe.

See Also: *Herbal Medicine Expanded Commission E Monographs* by M. Blumenthal, A. Goldberg, and J. Brinckmann, American Botanical Council, 2000; *World Health Organization (WHO) Monographs on Selected Medicinal Plants, Vol. 2*, 2002.

ALTHAEA OFFICINALIS | Marshmallow

Common Names Maté, *yerba maté, erva maté,*
Paraguay herb, Paraguay tea, South American
holly, St. Bartholomew's tea, Jesuit's tea, Brazil tea

Latin Name *Ilex paraguariensis*

Family Aquifoliaceae

Parts Used Leaves

Description Maté is a medium-sized, white-flowered evergreen tree that grows near streams
throughout South America and thrives between
1,500 and 2,000 feet above sea level. It reaches
65 feet in the wild but is usually pruned to
between 12 to 25 feet for harvesting. It has large,
oval, broad-toothed, alternate leaves and small,
red, black, or yellow berries. A member of the
holly family, it has leathery, holly-like leaves.

Habitat Maté grows wild in Argentina, Chile, and
Peru, as well as in Brazil, Paraguay, and Uruguay,
where it is also most actively cultivated and abundant.

Approximate
native range

Maté
Ilex paraguariensis

YERBA, OR *HIERBA*, IS SPANISH FOR "HERB," AND *MATÉ*
means "cup" in the Quechua language. This
"cup-herb" is enjoyed at any time of the day
throughout South America. Many South American
countries consider it a national drink. Like the Japanese tea ceremony, the ritual of preparing and drinking maté is central to South American life. It is also
widely used throughout the United States, Europe, and
India as a stimulating beverage for healthful and
medicinal purposes.

Traditional and Current Uses

MATÉ HAS BEEN USED AS A MEDICINAL BEVERAGE BY NATIVE
Americans in Brazil and Paraguay for centuries. The
Guarani were first observed in the early 16th century
drinking the tea. Jesuit missionaries began cultivating
and drinking it, as well as spreading the practice. Though
maté is brewed like most teas from dried, ground leaves,
traditionally it is sipped from a *bombilla*, a distinctive,
hollow calabash with a metal strainer or straw. The
process of preparing and drinking maté often takes on
ceremonial significance. Many regions lay claim to the
finest method of preparation, but most methods involve
packing the gourd with maté and then adding hot, but
not boiling, water. The average Uruguayan consumes
some 20 pounds of maté a year. Throughout the
history of South America and Brazil, in particular, maté
has been used for energy, strength, concentration, alertness, and nourishment.

Today it is used as a stimulant, tonic, appetite suppressant, laxative, and **diuretic**, for headache, memory
enhancement, heart regulation, gout, neurasthenia,
rheumatism, and ulcers. This sustaining tea is often the
only refreshment a South American will carry on a journey of several days. Maté contains many vitamins, minerals, and 15 **amino acids**. Its medicinal use has spread
from its South American roots to North America,
Europe, and India. In Europe it is known as "the green
gold of the Indios." In India the *Ayurvedic Pharmacopoeia I* prescribes maté for headache, fatigue, nervous depression, and rheumatic pain.

Cultivation and Preparation

ONCE THE LEAVES HAVE BEEN STRIPPED FROM THE PLANT, THEY are baked green, or blanched and then toasted to deactivate **enzymes** and render the leaves brittle. One maté bush typically yields up to 85 pounds of dried leaves a year. Paraguay exports five to six million pounds annually. Though sustainable methods of farming maté are being researched, unrestricted harvesting of maté has devastated many parts of the rain forest's understory.

Research

RESEARCH CONFIRMS MATÉ'S EFFECTS AS AN **ANTI-INFLAMMA-tory, antioxidant,** antispasmodic, stimulant, and vasodilator. Because of the extensive research available on some of maté's active ingredients (such as theobromine, theophylline, and caffeine), few clinical studies have focused specifically on the plant's medicinal properties. Some studies indicate a slightly increased chance of cancer (oral, esophageal, bladder, and lung) among heavy maté drinkers. It has also been shown to interact with some medicines, increasing, for example, the absorption of aspirin and pain relief of acetaminophen. Researchers in Switzerland found that it increased the proportion of fat burned as energy in healthy drinkers. Other studies have found it relaxes smooth muscles, increases bile flow, and inhibits vaso-constriction (narrowing of blood vessels). There is controversy about whether its stimulant is caffeine or "mateine," purported to have all the stimulant effects of caffeine but without side effects such as anxiety, insomnia, heart palpitations, and jitteriness. Though most researchers reject the idea that mateine is something other than caffeine, doctors often prescribe maté as an alternative to coffee and caution against the same side effects as any other caffeinated drink. In comparing amounts of caffeine in an average six-ounce cup, maté (50–100 mg) contains a bit more than black tea (10–60 mg) and a bit less than coffee (100–250 mg).

> CAUTION Maté is on the FDA's GRAS (generally regarded as safe) list, but it should not be consumed by pregnant women, those allergic to caffeine or xanthenes, or those suffering from hypertension, cardiac disorders, ulcers, or anxiety, or those who are taking monoamine oxidase inhibitor drugs (MAOIs). Excessive and chronic consumption of maté tea is associated with an increased risk of certain cancers.

Commonly, the gourd is filled half to three-quarters full with maté. Many use this as the basis for adding additional herbs. Typically, the preparer will cover the top of the gourd with one hand, invert, give a quick, vigorous shake, then turn it back over, keeping the finer powder at the top. Bringing the maté to an angle, the preparer then gives a gentle shake to further settle the finest herbs at the top and layer the coarser leaves and stems of the maté on the side. Now, the gourd is set upright again, retaining the carefully arranged mound with its powdery peak. All of this careful arrangement is to ensure the smoothest, particle-free sips possible by keeping the finest particles filtered away from the end of the straw. It is also meant to extend the consistent flavoring of successive refills. In Uruguay, where maté is very popular, it is a common sight to see people toting a maté gourd along with a thermos of hot water. Once it was also common to see drivers pouring themselves a drink behind the wheel. Due to the high number of drivers burned while drinking maté, however, a national law now prohibits drinking maté and driving.

See Also: *Herbal Medicine Expanded Commission E Monographs* by M. Blumenthal, A. Goldberg, and J. Brinckmann, American Botanical Council, 2000; *Medicinal Herbs History, Use, Recommended Dosages & Cautions* by S. Foster, Interweave Press, 1998.

ILEX PARAGUARIENSIS | Maté

Common Names Mayapple, American mandrake, devil's apple, wild lemon, hog apple

Latin Name *Podophyllum peltatum*

Family Berberidaceae

Parts Used Rhizome (underground stem)

Description Mayapple is a small, hardy perennial with a long, creeping rhizome and usually unbranched stems. Each stem bears one or two large leaves that are deeply divided into four to nine triangular-shaped lobes. Drooping white flowers with yellow centers are succeeded by fleshy fruits full of dark browns seeds.

Habitat Native to eastern North America, mayapple grows in wet meadows and in damp, open woods.

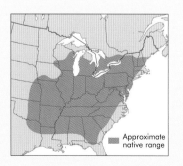

Approximate native range

Mayapple
Podophyllum peltatum

I N WOODLANDS IN THE EASTERN UNITED STATES, THE appearance of the umbrella-like leaves of mayapple is a sure sign of spring. Each round, smooth stem that rises from the damp ground is crowned by just one or two leaves and a single white, strong-smelling flower. A two-inch-long green fruit develops from the flower and ripens to yellow during the summer; it looks like a tiny lemon. This is the mayapple—also known as wild lemon, hog apple, and tellingly, devil's apple. The fruit of *Podophyllum peltatum* is the only edible part of an otherwise deadly poisonous plant. Another common name for mayapple is American mandrake, though it should not be confused with true mandrake, *Mandragora officinarum*, an unrelated Old World plant whose roots have been used throughout history for medicines and potions.

Traditional and Current Medicinal Uses

NATIVE AMERICANS VALUED THE MAYAPPLE AS A **PURGATIVE,** **emetic,** and liver tonic. The Cherokee nibbled the boiled roots as a strong laxative; they also made pills out of boiled root syrup for the same purpose. Drops of liquid from the fresh **rhizome** were used to improve hearing. Powdered root went into a remedy to cure skin ulcers and sores. The Delaware used the roots to make a "spring tonic." The Iroquois made a cold **infusion** of the root as a strong purgative and to increase strength, while the Meskwaki took a root preparation for rheumatism. A number of tribes used the fruit to remove warts and Maine's Penobscot Indians used mayapple to treat certain types of cancer. Young shoots of mayapple were reportedly eaten as a way to commit suicide. Mayapple was introduced into American folk medicine in the 1780s. By the 1800s, mayapple, particularly the resin extracted from the rhizome, was regarded by both herbal and conventional medical practitioners as one of the most powerful laxatives available. It was also used for a wide array of other disorders and diseases, including rheumatism, jaundice, typhoid, cholera, dysentery, hepatitis, gonorrhea and syphilis, as well as menstrual and prostate problems. Because of its toxicity, the use of mayapple declined in herbal medicine. The United States Food and Drug Administration declared it unsafe for use even as a laxative.

Then in the 1970s, pharmaceutical research into some of mayapple's most toxic chemical constituents led to development of several anticancer agents that stop cell division. These substances have been used in treating external carcinomas, venereal warts, and several types of cancers.

Cultivation and Preparation

MAYAPPLE NEEDS RICH, HUMUSY, MOIST SOIL AND PARTIAL shade to grow well. It is propagated by division of its rhizomous runners. Rhizomes are lifted in autumn for the extraction of the compounds used in commercial pharmaceuticals.

Research

MAYAPPLE RHIZOME CONTAINS A RESIN CALLED PODOPHYLLIN that has been used in preparations to kill certain types of benign skin tumors such as warts. These resin preparations, typically administered by health care professionals, are applied to very small areas in minute amounts and for limited times, because they are easily absorbed through the skin and can cause serious systemic side effects. Podophyllin is composed of several toxic **glycosides**, the most active of which is podophyllotoxin. Two derivatives of podophyllotoxin that have been formulated into anticancer drugs are etoposide and teniposide. These are powerful agents that kill cells, particularly those that are undergoing cell division. They are used in chemotherapy to inhibit the growth of tumors, which are characterized by uncontrolled cell division. Etoposide is used mainly to treat testicular cancer that has not responded to other treatment and as first-line treatment for small-cell lung cancers. It is also used to treat Kaposi's sarcoma, lymphomas, and malignant melanomas. Teniposide is used less often than etoposide; mainly, it is used to treat lymphomas.

CAUTION All parts of mayapple, except the ripe fruits, are extremely poisonous. Mayapple preparations should never be used by pregnant women due to their potential to cause birth defects or death of the fetus.

OLDTIMERS IN THE FOREST

Mayapple colonies are common sights in the woodlands of eastern North America where they often spread in the damp ground of hardwood forests. Mayapple spreads primarily through rhizomes, which run along or under the ground and produce shoots and roots for new plants. Over time, large colonies of mayapple are formed. There can be as many as a thousand stems in these colonies. Because all of them arise from a common root system, they are genetically identical, making the entire colony a single plant. These colonies expand very slowly, as the rhizomes only grow about four inches per year. As a result, a really large mayapple colony can easily be more than a hundred years old. New colonies are started by animals that eat ripe mayapple fruits and then deposit the undigested seeds (which are very toxic) in a new location. Box turtles, raccoons, and other animals seem to relish the fruits, and are the primary seed distributors.

Some people also eat the ripe fruits or make them into jelly or jam. They are said to have a pleasant aroma and a taste slightly reminiscent of strawberries. However, all other parts of the mayapple, including the unripe fruits, are toxic. They should never be eaten or taken orally.

See Also: A Field Guide to Medicinal Plants and Herbs: Eastern and Central North America, 2nd ed. by S. Foster and J. Duke, Houghton Mifflin, 2000; Medicinal Plants of the World by B. van Wyk and M. Wink, Timber Press, 2004.

Milk Thistle
Silybum marianum

M ILK THISTLE GETS ITS NAME FROM THE MILKY-WHITE mottling of its deeply lobed, spiny leaves. According to the **Doctrine of Signatures** espoused by medieval herbalists and alchemists—the idea that the appearance of a plant gave clues about how it should be used—milk thistle was thought to be good for stimulating milk flow in nursing mothers because of its milky-white coloration. Several of milk thistle's other common names, such as St. Mary's thistle and Marian thistle, refer to the belief that the Virgin Mary's milk once fell upon the herb, forever marking the leaves. Even the Latin species name, *marianum*, reflects this folkloric link. The milk connection notwithstanding, milk thistle has been used since ancient Greece and Rome as a remedy for a variety of ailments, but particularly for liver problems. Modern research supports this use.

Common Names Milk thistle, St. Mary's thistle, Marian thistle, silybin

Latin Name *Silybum marianum*

Family Asteraceae

Parts Used Fruits (achenes)

Description Milk thistle is an annual or biennial herb with a tall, erect, branched and furrowed stem. Its spiny leaves are mottled with white along the toothed margins and distinct veins. Stems are topped by solitary violet flowerheads composed of tiny tubular flowers. The fruits are brown-to-black achenes with hairy tufts.

Habitat Native to the Mediterranean region, milk thistle thrives in dry, stony soils in fields, ditches, and roadsides. It has been naturalized in North America, Australia, and other countries and is widely cultivated.

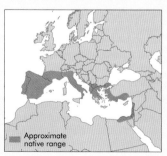

Approximate native range

Traditional and Current Medicinal Uses

MILK THISTLE HAS BEEN CULTIVATED AS A VEGETABLE AND AN herbal medicine for more than 2,000 years. Pliny the Elder, a Roman naturalist of the first century A.D., wrote that the juice of milk thistle mixed with honey was food for "carrying off bile." By the Middle Ages, herbalists were expounding on milk thistle's value to treat depression and other "melancholy diseases" that were generally thought to be caused by poor liver function. In the 17th century, the herbalist Nicholas Culpeper recommended milk thistle for clearing "obstructions" from the liver and spleen, and for treating jaundice. In the 19th and early 20th centuries, milk thistle fruits were widely used by physicians in the U.S. and Europe to treat liver, spleen, and kidney ailments.

In the late 1960s, however, German researchers undertook a chemical analysis of milk thistle fruits and isolated a complex of chemical compounds that collectively came to be called silymarin. The silymarin complex was shown to exhibit significant liver-protecting properties. Extensive research eventually led to creation of a standardized milk thistle **extract**. Similar extracts are now widely used in herbal medicine for the treatment of liver diseases including viral hepatitis as well as liver damage caused by drugs, industrial toxins, and alcohol. In Europe, milk thistle components are used as a primary treatment for poisoning by the deathcap mushroom (*Amanita phalloides*), which contains a toxin that can cause fatal, irreversible liver damage.

Cultivation and Preparation

MILK THISTLE GROWS WELL IN ANY WELL-DRAINED SOIL IN A sunny spot. Propagation is by seed; the plant self-sows freely. For medicinal use, the seeds are collected when ripe and used in preparing milk thistle extract. Most extracts are standardized to contain 70 to 80 percent silymarin, although different milk thistle preparations may vary in their silymarin content.

Research

SILYMARIN IS A COMPLEX OF THREE ACTIVE INGREDIENTS, OF which the compound silibinin seems to be the most active. Studies have shown that silymarin reduces inflammation, is a potent **antioxidant,** and helps to stabilize liver cell membranes; it alters the structure of the membranes in such a way as to prevent toxins from penetrating into the interior of the cell. Milk thistle extract also helps repair liver cells damaged by alcohol and other toxic substances and keeps healthy liver cells from being harmed. Clinical studies of alcohol-induced liver disease, including cirrhosis, have shown that taking milk thistle extract led to measurable improvements in liver function in a significant percentage of the participants. Trials of milk thistle's effects on hepatitis, particularly hepatitis C, have had mixed results. Because acute viral hepatitis can be life-threatening, treatment with milk thistle alone is not recommended by medical experts. Several preliminary studies suggest that milk thistle extract may exhibit some anticancer effects. In laboratory experiments, silymarin and silibinin have been shown to reduce the growth of human breast, cervical, and prostate cancer cells. More research is needed to determine whether milk thistle is safe or effective for human cancer patients. A limited number of animal and lab studies suggests that milk thistle may also lower cholesterol levels; human studies in this area of research have yielded unclear results.

WHAT YOU SEE IS WHAT YOU GET

The Doctrine of Signatures was based on the idea that God had endowed everything in nature with healing powers and marked his creations with a sign, or signature, as to its true purpose. This meant that plants had clues—in the shape of their roots or color of their leaves—as to how they should be used. The Doctrine of Signatures became an integral part of medical thinking in the 1600s—due largely to the efforts of Jakob Böhme (1575–1624), a shoemaker in the small town of Görlitz, Germany. He had a mystical vision in which he saw what he came to believe was the relation between God and humans. Böhme wrote a book about his vision, titled *Signatura Rerum: The Signature of All Things.* Although it began as a spiritual philosophy, Böhme's "doctrine" was adopted by medical men of the day and applied to medicinal herbs. For example, the yellow sap oozing from the herb celandine (*Chelidonium majus*) reminded medieval physicians of the yellowed skin of people suffering from jaundice; hence it was used to treat liver problems—probably successfully, as celandine is now known to stimulate bile secretion. The Doctrine of Signatures was a product of European alchemists and herbalists, but similar beliefs were held in several Asian cultures and by Native American tribes.

See Also: Herbal Medicine Expanded Commission E Monographs by M. Blumenthal, A. Goldberg, and J. Brinckmann, American Botanical Council, 2000; *World Health Organization (WHO) Monographs on Selected Medicinal Plants, Vol. 2,* 2002.

Common Names Monkshood, aconite, wolfsbane, soldier's cap, blue rocket, friar's cap

Latin Names *Aconitum napellus; A. carmichaelii,* synonym *A. fischeri,* is sometimes used in Chinese medicine

Family Ranunculaceae

Parts Used The entire plant, but especially the dried tuberous roots

Description A hardy perennial herb with a fleshy, tuberous root, *Aconitum* has tall stems and palmately divided leaves. The flowering stems, which may reach five to six feet, have terminal spikes of violet or dark blue, occasionally white, hood-shaped flowers.

Habitat Native to Europe and northern temperate regions in the Eastern Hemisphere, *Aconitum* has been introduced to England, the U.S., and many other countries.

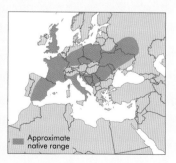

Approximate
native range

Monkshood
Aconitum napellus

A MEADOW FULL OF WILD *ACONITUM* IN BLOOM IS A STUN-ning sight. But the plant's beauty is deceptive: It is one of the most poisonous of all medicinal plants. Worldwide, there are about a hundred species of *Aconitum*, but *A. napellus* is most often used in herbal medicine. The genus name may have derived from the Greek word *akon*, which means "dart" and refers to the fact that in ancient times archers dipped their arrows in the plant's poisonous juice to make them more deadly. Ancient Chinese warriors were the first to use *Aconitum* to poison the tips of their arrows to make them twice as lethal. From there, the practice spread to India and Europe. Alternatively, the source may have been the Greek *akone*, which means "rocky or cliffy"; *Aconitum* is often found in mountain glens. The popular name "monkshood" (as well as "friar's cap") stems from the fact that the flowers are shaped like the hood of a medieval monk's garb. The downward-opening "hood" is one of five colorful and conspicuous sepals that surround the true flower parts.

Traditional and Current Medicinal Uses

ALTHOUGH *ACONITUM* HAS LONG BEEN CONSIDERED ONE OF the most dangerous plants in Europe, its use as a medicine dates back many hundreds of years there. It is administered in very small doses, as the active ingredient derived from the herb—the **alkaloid** aconitine—is deadly; it is one of the most potent nerve poisons in the plant kingdom. In the past, *Aconitum* has been used to treat arthritis, inflammation, heart disease, fever, and neuralgia. Externally, preparations of *Aconitum* in the form of a **liniment** or ointment were rubbed into the skin to help reduce pain and inflammation in muscles and joints.

In recent years, *Aconitum*'s primary use has been as a fast-acting **analgesic** for relieving pain, especially pain that is associated with rheumatism and neuralgia. It is very rarely used internally. In Tibetan medicine, where *Aconitum* is considered an important herb, aconitine is referred to as "the king of medicines." About a teaspoonful of some *Aconitum* preparations can kill an adult; much less can be fatal to a child. Because of its extreme toxicity, some experts recommend against using *Aconitum* in any herbal remedies and it is subject to legal restrictions in certain countries.

Cultivation and Preparation

ACONITUM GROWS BEST IN MOIST, FERTILE SOIL IN PART SHADE, flowering in May or June. It takes two to three years for plants sown from seed to flower. Propagation is by dividing the tuberous roots in autumn. *Aconitum* roots are unusual in that "daughter" tubers develop around the edges of the existing one, which dies at the end of the growing season. It is these new tubers that are then replanted. Although the plants are perennial, each individual root lasts only one year. *Aconitum*'s tuberous roots contain the highest concentrations of the important chemical compounds and are the primary source for use in herbal medicine. Tubers are collected in autumn after the stem has died down, then washed, trimmed, and dried. Active ingredients extracted from tubers are used to create **tinctures**, ointments, and liniments. Collection and preparation of *Aconitum* is best left to experts, as any contact with the plant is considered potentially dangerous.

Research

ACONITUM CONTAINS HIGHLY ACTIVE AND TOXIC ALKALOIDS, of which aconitine is the most important. Aconitine is extremely poisonous to humans and animals, causing cardiac arrest and respiratory failure in a short time after being taken internally. This can result not only from ingesting the alkaloid but also from external contact through cuts or cracks in the skin. Stories of the dangers of monkshood abound in herbals, and accidental poisonings are not uncommon. *Aconitum* is commonly sold as an ornamental plant, but gardeners should always wear gloves when handling it. Aconitine is a fast-acting poison—a very small dose causes numbness of lips, tongue, extremities, followed by vomiting and coma. Death is by asphyxiation.

CAUTION Under no circumstances should *Aconitum* ever be collected, prepared, or used for self-medication. The entire plant is extremely poisonous and can kill. Contact with the skin may cause allergic reactions and even poisoning.

THE PLANT FROM HELL

According to Greek mythology, *Aconitum napellus* arose from the drool that dripped from the mouths of the three-headed dog, Cerberus—hell's gatekeeper—when the Greek hero Hercules dragged him from the underworld. The herb also was thought to be the source of the poison used by Medea, one of the great mythical sorceresses of the ancient world. As the story goes, Medea prepared a poisonous drink for her stepson, Theseus, who stood in the way of her own son's chance to ascend to the throne of Athens. The deception failed, however, and Medea was forced to flee Greece with her own son in tow. The link between *Aconitum* and sorcery did not end there, however. In the Middle Ages, concoctions containing extracts of *Aconitum* and *Atropa belladonna* (also known as deadly nightshade) were said to be the "flying ointments" brewed by witches. The combi-nation of potent alkaloids that these two powerful herbs contain could very likely induce the sensation of flying—and also death, unless extreme caution was taken. For centuries, hunters tipped their arrows with *Aconitum* when they hunted wolves, a practice that gave rise to one of the herb's common names, "wolfsbane."

See Also: *A Field Guide to Venomous Animals and Poisonous Plants of North America Exclusive of Mexico* by S. Foster and R. Caras, Houghton Mifflin, 1994; *Pharmacognosy 9th ed.* by V. Tyler, L. Brady, J. Robbers, Lea & Febiger, 1988.

Mullein

Verbascum thapsus

WHEN IN BLOOM, MULLEIN IS HARD TO IGNORE. Its tall spires of bright yellow flowers resemble flaming torches held high above whorls of gray-green leaves. The flowers are also a magnet for bees, which seek the sweet but somewhat sparse nectar produced by these striking **biennials**. Closer inspection reveals that mullein's leaves and stems are cloaked in flannel-soft downy hairs. This characteristic is reflected in both mullein's scientific and common names: *Verbascum* is derived from the Latin *barbascum* (*barba* means "beard") while mullein is a corruption of the word *mollis*, meaning "soft," also from Latin. Both the downy leaves and glowing flowers of mullein—along with those of its very close relatives orange mullein (*V. phlomoides*), black mullein (*V. nigrum*), and common or large-flowered mullein (*V. densiflorum* syn. *V. thapsiforme*)—have been used medicinally since ancient times, primarily to treat coughs and congestion. Mullein flowers are favored over the leaves in herbal medicine today and are a common ingredient in herbal teas and other remedies given for respiratory complaints.

Traditional and Current Medicinal Uses

Mullein tea, brewed from either the leaves or the flowers of the herb, is a very old remedy for coughs and colds. The tea was prized for its ability to reduce mucus and as an effective **expectorant** for breaking up phlegm and relieving bronchial congestion. Tea made from mullein had to be carefully strained through fine cloth, however, to remove any fine and potentially irritating plant hairs from the liquid. During the Middle Ages, mullein preparations were commonly given to both people and cattle for respiratory ailments. **Poultices** of fresh bruised mullein leaves were applied to slow-healing wounds as well as skin rashes, ulcers, and tumors. **Infusions** of the flowers were said to cure burns, sores, and ringworm. Mullein was also given to promote sweating, as a mild **diuretic**, and to treat kidney infections, colic, and digestive upsets. At one point, mullein was included in herbal mixtures that were smoked to relieve the hacking cough of consumption and other types of respiratory distress.

Common Names Mullein, great mullein, Aaron's rod, candlewick, velvet dock

Latin Name *Verbascum thapsus*

Family Scrophulariaceae

Parts Used Leaves, flowers

Description Mullein is an upright biennial that forms a robust rosette of large gray-green leaves in the first year. In the second year, tall (up to six feet) stems emerge from the rosette; each terminates in a dense spike of yellow flowers. Leaves and stems are covered with downy hairs.

Habitat Native to central and southern Europe and western Asia, mullein has become naturalized in many temperate regions, including parts of North America. It thrives on sunny dry banks, roadsides, and waste ground.

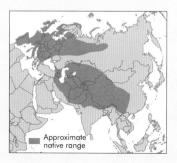

Approximate native range

During the 1800s, American **Eclectic** physicians recommended mullein for inflammatory diseases of both the respiratory and genitourinary tracts, as well as for earaches and ear infections; olive or mineral oil in which mullein flowers had been steeped made effective earache drops. By the end of the 19th century, mullein preparations were routinely prescribed in Europe, the British Isles, and the United States for coughs and congestion associated with tuberculosis.

In modern herbal medicine today, mullein is recommended by practitioners mainly for coughs, colds, influenza, whooping cough and other types of respiratory infections, laryngitis, and asthma. It is also suggested for digestive upsets, nervous tension, urinary tract infections, and insomnia, and externally for ear infections, rheumatic pain, chills, and skin conditions.

Cultivation and Preparation

MULLEIN THRIVES IN DRY, STONY, WELL-DRAINED SOIL IN FULL sun. The herb is easily propagated by seed and it also self-seeds freely under suitable conditions. For herbal preparations, flowers and leaves are collected in summer. Leaves are dried for infusions, **tinctures**, and liquid **extracts**. Flowers (preferred in European herbal medicine) are made into infusions, oils, and syrups, and are an ingredient in herbal teas. Much of the mullein used in herbal medicine comes from plants that are cultivated in Bulgaria, Czech Republic, and Egypt.

Research

DESPITE ITS LONG USE AS AN HERBAL MEDICINE, MULLEIN HAS not undergone extensive research. It is known to contain **triterpene saponins**, including verbascosaponin, as well as **mucilage** and **glycosides, flavonoids**, and acids. The herb's expectorant properties are most likely due to the saponins it contains. Mucilage acts to soothe and coat irritated or inflamed mucous membranes. Mullein's flavonoids are thought to exert a weak **diuretic** action, and its glycosides possess **anti-inflammatory** properties. In lab experiments, mullein flower infusions have exhibited antiviral activity against a number of viruses, including several strains of influenza A and B, and herpes simplex type I virus, but clinical studies are needed to confirm this in humans.

Mullein is a plant with no shortage of common names. Monikers such as "Aaron's rod," "shepherd's club," and "Jacob's staff" or "Jupiter's staff" most likely were inspired over the centuries by the staff-like appearance of the sturdy, upright flower spikes. The fact that the spikes of bright yellow flowers might—to the imaginative mind—resemble giant candles is thought to have been the source of names such as "hedge taper" and "Our Lady's candle." Another common name, "candlewick plant," stems from a practical use. During the Middle Ages, the downy hairs that cover the leaves and stems of mullein were collected and dried and used to make lamp wicks. The plant's dried leaves are also highly flammable and can be used to start a fire quickly. It was also thought that witches used lamps and candles with wicks made of mullein hairs while practicing their black arts. The nickname "torches" probably grew out of the practice of dipping the flower spikes into melted suet or some other fat to make torches that were burned at funerals and special occasions. A host of mullein's common names are undoubtedly the result of the remarkable softness of the hair-covered leaves and stems. Among these are "blanket leaf," "feltwort," "flannel-flower," "beggar's blanket," "velvet dock," and "woolly mullin." Names such as "cow's lungwort," and "cuddy's lungs" have their roots in mullein's use as a remedy for respiratory infections in cattle.

See Also: A Field Guide to Medicinal Plants and Herbs: Eastern and Central North America, 2nd ed. by S. Foster and J. Duke, Houghton Mifflin, 2000; Medicinal Plants of the World by B. van Wyk and M. Wink, Timber Press, 2004.

Myrrh

Commiphora myrrha

THE ANCIENT EGYPTIANS MAY HAVE BEEN THE FIRST TO use the fragrant resin that oozed from the bark of the myrrh tree's thorny branches. They collected the tear-shaped drops of dark resin and put them to use in embalming the dead, preserving their bodies to ensure a safe passage into the next world. Myrrh was prized in other ancient cultures of northeastern Africa and the Arabian Peninsula as a slow-burning incense and holy oil used in religious rituals. In Christ's day, the resins of both frankincense (*Boswellia* spp.) and myrrh were some of the most precious commodities bought and sold in that region. Even today, myrrh is a well-known fragrance in incense and perfumes. But myrrh has also been valued in Middle Eastern medicine for thousands of years for its **astringent** and antiseptic properties and its ability to soothe fevered brows, sore mouths, and troubled stomachs. The name myrrh comes from *mur*, an ancient Hebrew and Arabic word that means "bitter." Bitter, aromatic myrrh is still valued in modern herbal medicine for encouraging healing by relieving inflammation, spasms, and digestive discomfort.

Traditional and Current Medicinal Uses

SINCE BIBLICAL TIMES, MYRRH HAS BEEN A STANDARD REMEDY in Middle Eastern medicine for mouth sores, infected wounds, digestive ailments, and lung complaints. Myrrh has a long history of use as a healing and rejuvenating herb in Indian **Ayurvedic medicine**, being used as a remedy for mouth sores, gum disease, sore throat, congestion, and ulcers of the skin. It is thought that myrrh was introduced into traditional Chinese medicine from India, at least as early as A.D. 600. More recently, myrrh has been employed in eastern Africa and Saudi Arabia as an **anti-inflammatory** and antirheumatism drug. In Western herbal medicine, myrrh has long been recommended as an astringent, healing tonic and stimulant, primarily for treating digestive upsets, bronchial congestion, sore throat, inflamed gums, canker sores. Myrrh was also used for slow-healing skin sores, for ulcers, and also as an ingredient in mouthwashes and tooth powders.

Common Names Myrrh, common myrrh, *mo yao shu, mo yao*, Hirabol myrrh

Latin Name *Commiphora myrrha*

Family Burseraceae

Parts Used Oleo-gum-resin

Description Myrrh is an aromatic shrub or small tree with thorny branches and three-part leaves made up of leathery, oval leaflets. Yellow-red flowers are followed by tiny, pointed fruits.

Habitat Native to northeastern Africa and the Arabian Peninsula, myrrh is now found throughout the Middle East and western Asia. It grows in desert scrub.

Approximate native range

Today myrrh is still used for many of these same conditions: stomach problems, inflammations of the mouth and throat, asthma, and other bronchial conditions. In Europe, myrrh is approved by Germany's Commission E, a scientific panel that investiages and rules on herbal medicines, for the localized treatment of mild inflammations of mouth and throat. It is also used in Germany for treating bed sores and pressure sores caused by prosthetic limbs. Veterinarians use myrrh-based ointments to treat some types of wounds in animals, especially horses.

Cultivation and Preparation

MYRRH GROWS BEST IN WARM, ARID CONDITIONS, IN WELL-drained soil in full sun. Most of the myrrh used commercially is collected from wild trees in Ethiopia, Somalia, Sudan, and Yemen. Myrrh is also cultivated to some extent in Kenya, Tanzania, Ethiopia, and other North African countries. Myrrh is harvested by collecting hardened resin that has naturally oozed from the bark or by making incisions in the bark to encourage resin flow; naturally exuded resin is said to be of higher quality. The resin hardens into reddish-brown, tear-shaped crystals that are semi-transparent, oily, and highly aromatic. Different commercial varieties of myrrh resin are named according to their sources, such as Somali myrrh and Arabian myrrh. The resin is dried further and then distilled for oil or ground into a powder used in various medicinal preparations.

Research

MYRRH RESIN IS TECHNICALLY AN OLEO-GUM-RESIN, A mixture of **volatile oil**, gum, and resin. In animal studies, myrrh has been shown to reduce fever and exhibit anti-inflammatory effects. Also in studies with animals, myrrh **extracts** have been found to protect the lining of the stomach from damage by non-steroidal anti-inflammatory drugs and alcohol. In addition, some preliminary studies indicate that myrrh has **antioxidant**, thyroid-stimulating, and **prostaglandin**-inducing properties. Sesquiterpenes, chemical compounds that are ingredients of the resin component of myrrh, have been shown in animals to be potent inhibitors of certain solid-tumor cancers.

THE TEARS OF MYRRHA

Myrrh is named for Myrrha, a tragic character in Greek mythology. According to the legend related by Ovid, Myrrha was the daughter of a wealthy king of Cyprus, Cinyras. Myrrha was a beautiful young woman with many suitors, but she was attracted to none of them. Instead she developed a lust for her own father, an incestuous desire instilled in her by the goddess Aphrodite. Ashamed and horrified, Myrrha tried to hang herself, but was saved by her nursemaid. Believing sin to be a better solution than suicide, the nursemaid devised a scheme to rid Myrrha of her unnatural desire. While Myrrha's mother was away attending a religious festival, the princess disguised herself and slept with her father, who was intoxicated and in the dark, could not identify this mysterious young woman. After several nights, however, Cinyras gave in to his curiosity and lit a lamp. Disgusted and enraged to discover that he had been sleeping with his own daughter, the king tried to kill Myrrha, but she escaped and fled. Myrrha soon realized her situation was hopeless—she could neither live nor die because her terrible crime offended the living and the dead. So she asked the gods to release her from shame. They obliged by turning her into the myrrh tree. The drops of resin that ooze from the bark of the tree are said to be Myrrha's tears.

See Also: Herbal Medicine Expanded Commission E Monographs by M. Blumenthal, A. Goldberg, and J. Brinckmann, American Botanical Council, 2000; Medicinal Herbs History, Use, Recommended Dosages & Cautions by S. Foster, Interweave Press, 1998.

Common Names Native tobacco, Aztec tobacco

Latin Name *Nicotiana rustica*

Family Solanaceae

Parts Used Leaves

Description A large annual growing to three or more feet in height, wild tobacco is an erect plant with large, fleshy, lance-shaped leaves covered with sticky hairs and funnel-shaped, whitish yellow flowers.

Habitat Native to the Americas, tobacco is now cultivated in warm climates in many parts of the world. *Nicotiana tabacum* is grown primarily as smoking tobacco, while *N. rustica* is cultivated primarily for its use as an insecticide.

Approximate native range

Native Tobacco
Nicotiana rustica

E THNOBOTANISTS BELIEVE THAT PEOPLE BEGAN USING tobacco in prehistoric America, perhaps as much as 8,000 years ago. Archeological evidence is slim, but it is thought that the earliest use of tobacco may have been among forest-dwelling tribes in South America, where the wilted, dried leaves of wild tobacco plants were ritualistically smoked or otherwise ingested—usually by shamans—to induce an altered state of mind. The **alkaloid** responsible for tobacco's effects on the human mind and body is nicotine, a nervous system stimulant that is fatally toxic in large doses. It was wild tobacco, *Nicotiana rustica*, that was first rolled into cigars, stuffed into pipes, or ground into a fine dust that was inhaled through the nose. Later, *N. tabacum*, the now common species of the plant, went on to shape American history and spread worldwide. In addition to its familiar uses, tobacco has a long heritage as a medicinal plant. In recent decades, however, tobacco has been recognized as an addictive, cancer-producing substance. Ironically, nicotine, the compound in tobacco that is so addictive, is now the "medicine" in nicotine gum, skin patches, and other aids designed to help people break their tobacco habits.

Traditional and Current Medicinal Uses

T OBACCO WAS USED IN ANCIENT CIVILIZATIONS IN THE Americas to ease the pain of childbirth, treat the sick, and stave off hunger. Native Americans in North America smoked tobacco ceremonially, but also used it medicinally. Tobacco **poultices** were applied to boils, insect bites, and snakebites. The herb was used, often in the form of a tea, as a worm expellant, an **emetic, expectorant**, laxative, and **diuretic**, and for dizziness, fainting and headaches. The Iroquois used *N. rustica* as a wash to counteract poison, for insect bites, and for tuberculosis. By 1540, tobacco had arrived in Europe and was soon credited as being able to cure a host of illnesses, from joint pains and migraines to epilepsy and plague. The French called tobacco the *herbe a tous les maux*—the plant against evil, pains, and other bad things. Over the centuries, tobacco use continued medicinally while it grew recreationally. In 19th-century America, the herb was used to induce vomiting and as a sedative to calm "mental inquietude" as well as to treat fevers, rheumatism, cholera, tetanus, croup, hiccups, and laryngitis. Nevertheless, the narcotic and disease-causing effects of tobacco were already well-known by this time.

Today, tobacco is no longer used medicinally, although nicotine is an ingredient in many different types of antismoking aids.

Cultivation and Preparation

TOBACCO HAS TINY SEEDS THAT CANNOT BE SOWN DIRECTLY into fields. Instead, seedlings are raised and tended in sheltered seed beds and then planted by hand or mechanical transplanter. In the United States and in Canada, tobacco is often stalk-cut by machine. In many other parts of the world, however, it is still harvested by hand, leaf by leaf. Fully ripe leaves are harvested, dried, and cured.

Research

TOBACCO CONTAINS HUNDREDS OF CHEMICAL COMPOUNDS, but its most active and well-studied ingredient is the alkaloid nicotine. Wild tobacco contains up to 18 percent nicotine, which is more than the cultivated variety, *N. tabacum*. Research has shown that nicotine stimulates the nervous system by mimicking a natural **neurotransmitter** in the body called acetylcholine. In the body, nicotine activates specific types of acetylcholine receptors, which are involved in respiration, heart rate, memory, alertness, and muscle movement. By activating these receptors, nicotine disrupts normal brain function. It is addictive because the receptors develop a tolerance for nicotine and as nicotine levels fall, uncomfortable withdrawal symptoms begin to appear. Nicotine has also been shown to stimulate the release of dopamine in the brain; this is what underlies the pleasurable sensations experienced by smokers. Smoking tobacco causes respiratory problems, lung cancer, emphysema, heart problems, and peripheral vascular disease. Chewing tobacco causes cancers of the mouth, tongue, pharynx, larynx, and esophagus.

TOBACCO USE IN THE AMAZON

Tobacco use began in prehistoric times, but many indigenous tribes in the Amazon region of South America still use the herb in traditional ways. These customs provide a glimpse back in time as to how tobacco may have been used thousands of years ago. For these groups, tobacco is an extremely important plant, an essential component of rituals and ceremonies as well as of ordinary medical practices. In some tribes, preparations of tobacco leaves are used for treating sprains and bruises, or as poultices on boils and infected wounds and sores. Ground dried tobacco leaves are inhaled through the nose to treat lung and heart ailments. The men of at least one tribe use the juice of tobacco leaves to prevent balding. Typically, tobacco is only smoked on special occasions or as a part of certain rituals, including those designed to heal. Even then, it is usually medicine men, or shamans, who do the smoking. They may blow smoke or even spit tobacco juice over patients as part of a curative ceremony. Tobacco is used recreationally by many Amazonian tribes, but it is almost always taken as snuff. Chewing tobacco leaves is also common. A wad of leaves is held in the lower lip and gently sucked all day long, much like the indigenous people in Andean regions of South America use coca leaves.

See Also: A Field Guide to Medicinal Plants and Herbs: Eastern and Central North America, 2nd ed. by S. Foster and J. Duke, Houghton Mifflin, 2000; *Native American Ethnobotany* by D. Moerman, Timber Press, 1998.

NICOTIANA RUSTICA | Native Tobacco

Noni
Morinda citrifolia

THOUGH IT HAS BEEN USED AS A POLYNESIAN REMEDY for thousands of years and was at one time the most widely used medicinal plant in the region, only recently has the rest of the non-tropical world learned about noni. International noni production and sales began only a decade ago and are now growing into a billion-dollar industry. Islanders in Hawaii, Tahiti, and elsewhere are for the first time devoting hundreds of acres to noni cultivation for export to the rest of the world. What has been part of their tradition since their earliest history has now become famous worldwide for its healing powers. Along with its many medicinal uses, some cultures eat the fruit for food amd extract red dye from the bark and yellow dye from the root.

Common Names Noni, Indian mulberry, *nanu, nono,* och plant, cheese fruit, hog apple, *mora de la India,* wild pine

Latin Name *Morinda citrifolia*

Family Rubaiceae

Parts Used Fruit, bark, leaves, stems, roots

Description Noni is a small evergreen with large, shiny, dark green, oval leaves and small white flowers that bloom in summer and fall. Flowers grow into a bumpy, pitted, yellow-green fruit several inches long. When ripe, the fruit develops translucently thin skin and an odor offensive to people but attractive to bats, which help to disperse the seeds.

Habitat Noni is native to the Pacific islands, Polynesia, Asia, and Australia and is now cultivated on many tropical islands throughout the world.

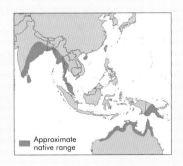

Approximate native range

Traditional and Current Medicinal Uses

NONI SEEMS TO HAVE WORKED WONDERS FOR POLYNESIAN healers for everything from headaches to broken bones, but the common traditional practice was an external application of the leaves, or leaf extracts, to treat infection, swelling, and pain. Another traditional practice was chewing the leaves, sometimes with other parts of the plant, as a treatment for diabetes.

In modern herbal medicine, noni is promoted for a variety of uses but primarily used for chronic fatigue, hypertension, menstrual cramps, arthritis, digestive and bowel disorders, wounds, pain, diabetes, and cancer. The fruit juice, because of its offensive smell and bitter taste, is said to ward off demons. In Pacific islands and Hawaii, the leaves, fruit, and bark are utilized for eye problems, wounds and abscesses, gum and throat problems, respiratory ailments, and constipation. In Malaysia, heated leaves are placed on the chest for cough, nausea, and colic and the juice of overripe fruit is taken to regulate menstrual and urinary problems.

Cultivation and Preparation

THE NONI TREE GROWS WELL ON THE SANDY, ROCKY SHORES of tropical islands like Hawaii where it flourishes in the rich ash and volcanic terrain. Because of the unpleasant odor emitted by mature fruit, noni are not widely cultivated as garden plants but propagated from seeds or cuttings for more utilitarian purposes. The noni plant can withstand drought in diverse soils. The tree also serves as a valuable stabilizer for coastal shores, preventing erosion and providing shade for less hardy plants like coffee. Noni trees appear to have a symbiotic relationship with weaver ants; the ants are attracted to the fruit and nest in the leaves, which offer them some protection from insect predators. Traditionally, noni is used as a **poultice**, with heated leaves applied directly to wounds. It is, however, flavored noni juice now shipped around the world, which is most commonly available. Unripe fruit are thick-skinned, hard, and difficult to process; typically a hydraulic press is employed to extract juice from the pulp and seeds. The traditional method of extracting juice by first letting the fruit steep is more time comsuming but produces juice higher in **polysaccharides**. Most Pacific island cultures allow the ripe fruit to steep in containers, fermenting it about two months, to allow the juice to separate from the pulp.

Research

PRELIMINARY RESEARCH ON ANIMALS SUGGESTS THAT NONI has immune-enhancing, anticancer, and pain-relieving properties. Noni-ppt, a polysaccharide-rich substance found in the fruit juice, appears to help regulate immune functions. The most referenced research confirms its potential for treating cancer. Mice injected with lung cancer and noni extract survived 20 days longer than the mice who did not received noni. Research confirmed noni's potential as a complementary alternative medicine to conventional cancer treatments but also noted added toxicity. Another animal study done on mice showed root extracts to have sedative and pain-relieving properties. Research also confirms the power of leaf **extract** to suppress the growth of infections in test tubes; however, there is no evidence that leaf extracts have the power to fight infections once symptoms start.

CAUTION Noni juice is high in sugar. Diabetics should consult medical professsionals before drinking the juice. Noni juice is also high in potassium. Patients with kidney problems should not consume noni. Noni is not recommended for pregnant or breastfeeding women.

NONI—THE MONEY TREE

Noni has been known to Polynesians and Hawaiians for centuries as one of the precious "canoe plants" brought as seeds in seafaring canoes to colonize the islands. But noni remained an island secret until a few years ago. Noni's resurgence began in the 1990s in Hawaii where it was promoted for everything from stress to cancer. Demand soon outstripped supply. Hawaii's Department of Health warned that many of noni's touted benefits were unsubstantiated, but this did not curb demand. In 1994, with the passage of the Dietary Supplement Health and Education Act, labeling and information became better, and packaging and palatability improved. The raw, foul-smelling fruit and juice were replaced in the marketplace by flavored juices and dried extracts. Leading the way in the marketing of noni juice was Tahitian Noni International (TNI). In the company's first seven years, it captured 2 billion dollars in sales, earning a place just behind Google, Fed Ex, and others as one of the fastest-growing companies in history. TNI's effective multilevel marketing distribution network capitalized on the gap between tradition and science. A University of Hawaii survey in 1999 on the use of herbal medicines found noni second only to aloe vera in Hawaii. Of the top five (aloe vera, noni, garlic, ginseng, and lemongrass), noni was the only herbal medicine without a clear biomedical basis for its health claims. But that gap "between tradition and science" has proved to be no problem for many users. Sales figures make that abundantly clear.

See Also: *Medicinal Herbs History, Use, Recommended Dosages & Cautions* by S. Foster, Interweave Press, 1998; *Native American Ethnobotany* by D. Moerman, Timber Press, 1998.

Opium Poppy
Papaver somniferum

THE OPIUM POPPY IS NATIVE TO THE REGION OF THE world now occupied by Turkey and its neighbors. The herb's pepper pot-shaped seed capsule is the source of both the familiar black poppy seeds that are used in baking and of opium, the powerful and highly addictive narcotic. Opium has been used medicinally for thousands of years, primarily as a painkiller and a sedative. It was probably introduced into southern Europe by Arabian physicians. Opium is also the starting point for two of the world's most powerful painkillers, morphine and codeine, as well as for the illegal drug heroin. Today opium and its derivatives can be legally administered only by professionally licensed medical practitioners.

Traditional and Current Medicinal Uses

IN ANCIENT GREECE, HIPPOCRATES WROTE ABOUT OPIUM'S USEfulness in killing pain and treating internal disorders. In the following centuries, opium use spread throughout Europe; poppy juice continued to be employed as a sedative and painkiller. In the 1600s, an alcoholic **tincture** of opium called laudanum was developed. By the 1800s laudanum was used in many patent medicines to relieve pain, induce sleep, calm nerves, and treat many common complaints. It was prescribed by physicians for everything from colds to cardiac diseases, in both adults and children. Countless women were given the drug for relief of menstrual cramps and "nerves." Opium in other forms was also regularly administered by physicians (although its addictive nature was well-known) for a wide variety of ailments, from pain, cough, and diarrhea to nephritis, angina, and insanity. In 1803 morphine was isolated and codeine a few years later. Thought to be more effective and safer than crude opium preparations, morphine was used to control pain and to relieve severe coughs and diarrhea. In the 1860s morphine was used extensively as a painkiller and to treat dysentery in the Civil War. Not surprisingly, addiction to morphine became a huge problem. In the 1870s a supposedly nonaddictive substitute for morphine was introduced: heroin. It was used as an effective cough suppressant for

Common Names Opium poppy, Oriental poppy, poppy, opium

Latin Name *Papaver somniferum*

Family Papaveraceae

Parts Used Fruits, seeds

Description Opium poppy is a tall annual herb with a slightly hairy, erect stem and oblong, deeply lobed, bluish-green leaves. Solitary, terminal flowers can be white, red, or lilac and have delicate, papery petals. They bloom in early summer and are followed by bulbous, bluish-green capsules that contain many gray-to-black seeds.

Habitat Native to southwestern Asia, opium poppy has been widely introduced elsewhere and is cultivated, both legally and illegally, in many regions of the world.

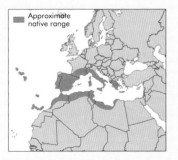

Approximate native range

tuberculosis patients and to combat morphine addiction, but its addictive properties far exceeded those of morphine. By the 1920s use of morphine, heroin, opium, and opium derivatives outside of medical practice was made illegal in the United States.

Today morphine is still used in treating severe pain. Codeine is an ingredient in some prescription cough and pain-relieving medications. Other **alkaloids** derived from opium are administered as painkillers and sedatives for surgical procedures.

Cultivation and Preparation

THE CULTIVATION OF OPIUM POPPY IS LEGALLY RESTRICTED IN the United States and many other countries. Most legal cultivation of the plant is in India and Turkey; it is cultivated illegally for the heroin trade. Poppies are also grown for their seeds for culinary use. Opium poppy grows in full sun in well-drained soil. Opium is collected by making shallow cuts in the unripe seed capsules and collecting the juice that oozes from the cuts. Poppy seeds are harvested when seed capsules are ripe.

Research

OPIUM CONTAINS 26 DIFFERENT ALKALOIDS. THE MOST potent is morphine. Possibly the most effective painkiller known to medicine, morphine exerts its effect on sensory nerve cells of the brain, blocking pain messages. It is also a stimulant that binds to endorphin receptors in the brain, inducing feelings of euphoria and eliminating anxieties. But morphine is highly addictive and fatal in large doses. Codeine, another opium alkaloid, is an ingredient in many prescription cough syrups and capsules. It has both cough suppressant and **analgesic** properties and is often recommended to relive minor pain. The opium alkaloid papaverine blocks nerve impulses responsible for muscular contractions and so acts as a very effective muscle relaxant. It is used in conventional medicine to treat spasms of stomach and intestinal muscles and to quell bronchial spasms triggered by asthma attacks.

CAUTION With the exception of the seeds, all parts of *Papaver somniferum* and other *Papaver* species are toxic if eaten.

OF FORGETTING AND REMEMBERING

The opium poppy and the narcotic properties of its juice were well known in ancient times. The first descriptions of the use of opium medicinally come from clay tablets, at least 6,000 years old, found in archeological excavations of ancient Sumerian cities. The Egyptians, Greeks, and Romans were also familiar with poppy's powers and the effect it can have on the mind. In Greece, the plants were called the "poppies of Lethe," a reference to the river Lethe in Greek mythology. Lethe was said to be one of the rivers that flowed through the underworld of Hades. Lethe was known as the "river of forgetfulness" or the "river of oblivion" because all the souls of the dead who passed into Hades had to drink from its waters to forget about their past lives on Earth.

It is remembrance, not forgetfulness, however, that is associated with *Papaver rhoeas*, the field or corn poppy. For thousands of years, these small, bright red poppies have grown wild in cornfields and meadows across Europe, western Asia, and North Africa. The flowers have been associated with both blood and rebirth since ancient Egypt and throughout history have been a symbol of remembrance for fallen warriors. Corn poppies (*P. rhoeas*) bloomed in vast numbers on World War I battlefields in western Europe and fittingly became the symbol associated with November 11 observations of Remembrance Day in the United Kingdom, Australia, and Canada, and of Armistice Day (now Veteran's Day) in the U.S.

See Also: Medical Botany: Plants Affecting Human Health by W. Lewis and M. Elvin-Lewis, John Wiley & Sons, 2003; *Pharmacognosy,* 9th ed. by V. Tyler, L. Brady, J. Robbers, Lea & Febiger, 1988.

Common Names Orange, neroli (flowers)

Latin Name *Citrus sinensis*

Family Rutaceae

Parts Used Fruits, fruit rind, flower

Description The orange tree is a small evergreen tree that grows 18 to 40 feet in height. The angular green twigs produce small spines when young; then the leaf stalks produce narrowly winged margins, tapered at both ends. The familiar orange fruits are well known to all.

Habitat As the species name *sinensis* implies, sweet orange is believed to have originated in China near the border between present-day China and Vietnam. Not known from the wild, orange trees are cultivated throughout the tropics and subtropics with 90 percent of the cultivation in Florida and Brazil grown for fruit juice.

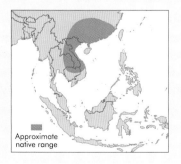

Approximate
native range

Orange
Citrus sinensis

THE GENUS *CITRUS*, WHICH INCLUDES ABOUT 16 SPECIES originating from southern and southeastern Asia, is one of the most economically important fruit-producing plant groups in the world. The genus has given us the sweet orange (*C. sinensis*), lemon (*C. x limon*), lime (*C. x aurantifolia*), grapefruit (*C. x paradisi*), and other lesser known citrus fruits such as bitter orange or Seville orange (*C. x aurantium*), pomelo (*C. maxima*), and mandarin orange or tangerine (*C. reticulata*), among others. The rinds and flowers of several *Citrus* species produce **essential oils,** and the dried rinds of *C. x aurantium* and *C. reticulata* are used in traditional Chinese medicine and in dietary supplements in the U.S. The medicinal use of citrus peels (*zhu pi*) was first mentioned in *Shen Nong Ben Cao Jing,* the first important Chinese herbal and medical text, about 2,000 years ago. The bitter orange was the first orange known to Europeans, introduced from Asia by Arab traders. Tenth-century Arab physician Avicenna wrote about use of the juice. The first bitter oranges to reach England arrived on a Spanish ship in 1290. Europeans quickly adopted the bitter, fragrant fruits, using the juice to quench thirst, particularly for fevers and inflammatory conditions. The rind was used to treat stomach disorders and malaria. The first sweet orange tree in Europe was introduced by Portuguese sailors and given to the prime minister of Portugal in the 15th century.

Traditional and Current Medicinal Uses

AS AN HERBAL MEDICINE IN TRADITIONAL CHINESE MEDICINE, dried citrus peels were used to regulate energy, strengthen the spleen, and treat coughs, vomiting, and diarrhea. They were also used for their **expectorant** and stomach-soothing qualities. The scurvy-preventing properties of citrus fruits was known for centuries though attributed to their vitamin C content only in the 20th century. Scurvy was once the scourge of British sailors who often died from the disease on long voyages with no fresh food available. In the 18th century British sailors became known as "limeys" after British naval surgeon James Lind began prescribing citrus fruits to curb scurvy.

In modern aromatherapy, minute amounts of neroli oil are used to treat diarrhea and circulatory problems, including high blood pressure. Aromatherapists also claim that smelling the oil can have antidepressive effects; it is used to combat nervous strain, anxiety, and fear. It also is said to be useful for fatigue and insomnia, but these claims are not scientifically confirmed.

Cultivation and Preparation

ORANGE IS A SUBTROPICAL RATHER THAN TROPICAL SPECIES and does best where there is a prominent change of seasons but without a hard freeze. Dozens of cultivated varieties are propagated by budding—from selections chosen for their flavor, fruit-bearing qualities, or resistance to disease. Irrigation is usually required. Citrus fruits are grown in warmer climates of the U.S., including Florida, Texas, and California. Elsewhere, they are grown as greenhouse specimens.

Research

FRESH ORANGES AND ORANGE JUICE ARE WELL KNOWN FOR their high vitamin C and vitamin E content. They also contain flavanones, a class of chemical compounds belonging to the **flavonoid** family. The **antioxidant** activity of oranges and orange juice, based on epidemiological evidence suggests that their consumption may reduce the risk of cardiovascular disease and perhaps certain forms of cancer, when included as a normal part of the diet. Health claims are allowed by the U.S. Food and Drug Administration (FDA) for the bone-building benefits of calcium-fortified orange juice products, though the calcium has been added to the juice. Following the ban by the FDA of ephedrine **alkaloids** (see Ephedra, page 146) in herbal weight loss products, herbal products with extracts of tangerine peel (*Citrus reticulata*) appeared on the market claiming the alkaloid synephrine, a component with a similar chemical structure to ephedrine would induce weight loss. Some of the products contained 25 percent more synephrine in the **extracts** compared with what is normally found in Chinese citrus peel products. Despite many advocates in the literature, there is little scientific evidence to support weight loss claims for synephrine-fortified citrus peel products.

EAU DE ORANGE

Citrus fruits and flowers produce various types of essential oils, used for their flavor and fragrance. Bitter orange oil is from bitter orange (*Citrus aurantium*). Sweet orange oil is from the fruit rinds of several varieties of *C. sinensis*. Both are quite similar in chemical composition, although sweet orange oil, by far the most widely used, does not have as bitter a flavor as the names imply. Both are used in the food industry as flavor components for a wide range of products. Neroli oil, also known as orange flower oil, which is steam-distilled from the freshly harvested flowers of varieties of *Citrus aurantium*, is used primarily as a fragrance component in perfumes, lotions, soaps, and cosmetics. The flowers have also been used in teas as a mild sedative and a sleep aid. The first mention of the distillation of neroli oil is in a 1563 publication by an Italian naturalist, J. B. della Porta. The name "neroli" honors the Duchess Flavio Orsini, princess of Neroli, a member of the Italian Orsini family. In 1680 she introduced the oil as a perfume in the courts of Europe. Since that time the oil has been regarded among perfumers as one of the finest of flower perfumes. It is still an important perfume ingredient in toilet waters, and in particular, eau de cologne. Historically, southern France is considered the most important production region. Sweet orange neroli is produced in Portugal from *Citrus sinensis*, but is not as prevalent in commercial trade.

CITRUS SINENSIS | Orange

See Also: Herbal Medicine Expanded Commission E Monographs by M. Blumenthal, A. Goldberg, and J. Brinckmann, American Botanical Council, 2000; Medicinal Plants of the World by B. van Wyk and M. Wink, Timber Press, 2004.

Pacific Yew

Taxus brevifolia

T HE PACIFIC YEW IS A SMALL, EXTREMELY SLOW-growing evergreen understory tree found in the cool, wet forests of the Pacific Northwest. Pacific yew produces dense, finely grained wood that was prized by Native Americans of the region for making canoe paddles, bows, and frames for snowshoes. Although native tribes did use yew medicinally to a limited extent, all parts of the tree—except for the fleshy fruit surrounding the seed—are extremely poisonous. In the 1960s, during a time when American medical researchers were investigating plants for new sources of medicines, an unusual chemical called paclitaxel was extracted from Pacific yew bark. Laboratory and clinical testing revealed that paclitaxel was a powerful anti-cancer drug, later marketed as Taxol, that was especially useful for combating ovarian and breast cancer. A number of other yew species have since been found to be additional sources of paclitaxel and similar compounds that are highly effective in cancer treatment.

Traditional and Current Medicinal Uses

NATIVE AMERICANS OF THE PACIFIC NORTHWEST USED YEW TO treat a variety of conditions. Both the Karok and the Yurok made a **decoction** of the bark that was taken to strengthen and purify the blood, while the Tsimshian used yew for treating cancer. The Quinault and Bella Coola made a lung medicine out of dried yew bark. The Kitasoo used yew wood and bark for stomach pain.

Despite these applications by native tribes, Pacific yew played no role in Western herbal or conventional medicine until 1966, when the tree was included in a massive screening of 35,000 species for new drugs by the National Cancer Institute. Paclitaxel, a substance extracted from the bark of the Pacific yew discovered in 1971, turned out to possess remarkable anti-cancer activity. In 1992 the United States Food and Drug Administration approved the use of paclitaxel for treatment of advanced ovarian cancer and, two years later, for breast cancer. However, the bark from huge numbers of trees were required to produce even small quantities of paclitaxel. Removing the bark killed the

Common Names Pacific yew, western yew

Latin Name *Taxus brevifolia*

Family Taxaceae

Parts Used Bark, leaves

Description Pacific yew is a small evergreen (20 to 30 feet high) with scaly, reddish-purple bark, slender, drooping branches and flattened, leathery, needle-like leaves. Male and female flowers are produced on separate trees. Female flowers develop into scarlet, berry-like fruits that contain a single seed.

Habitat Pacific yew occurs from southeastern Alaska to coastal British Columbia, Washington, Oregon, and northwestern California. A shade-tolerant species, it grows in damp forests in rich soil at low to mid elevations.

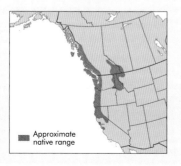

■ Approximate native range

trees. Fortunately, a related chemical compound easily converted to paclitaxel in the lab was discovered in the leaves of several related yew species, including English yew (*Taxus baccata*). In addition to yew's use in chemotherapy, yew **extract** has been recently marketed as an herbal medicine suggested both for antiviral and immune system-stimulating effects.

Cultivation and Preparation

PACIFIC YEW DOES BEST IN PART TO FULL SHADE IN MOIST, RICH soil. Propagation by seed can be difficult; the seeds may take two or more years to germinate. It is easier to start plants from cuttings. Even then, Pacific yew is one of the slowest-growing trees in the world. Bark is harvested from autumn through spring and leaves are harvestd in spring or autumn for the commercial extraction of paclitaxel and related compounds.

Research

PACLITAXEL STOPS CELLS FROM DIVIDING BY INTERFERING WITH structures known as microtubules. These microtubules form the cell's cytoskeleton—the framework that undergoes dramatic rebuilding when cells divide. Cancer cells are characterized by rapid cell division so their cytoskeletons undergo constant modification. Paclitaxel binds to proteins in microtubules and locks them into place, preventing microtubules from being disassembled and the cytoskeleton from rebuilding. In so doing, paclitaxel brings cell division to a halt. Research also has shown that paclitaxel triggers programmed cell death in cancer cells by binding to a "cell-death-stopping" protein. Paclitaxel is administered intravenously as a chemotherapy drug. It has significant side effects, including hair loss, nausea and vomiting, and joint and muscle pain. Research continues into its use to combat cancers, including colon, gastric, and lung cancers, as well as its potential to treat arthritis, Alzheimer's disease, and as an antiviral agent. Paclitaxel is one of the success stories of the National Cancer Institute's five-decade search for new cancer drugs from nature.

CAUTION Yew is very toxic and is not suitable for self-medication.

THE SACRED YEW

Yew trees are some of the oldest living things on Earth. In Scotland, at the eastern end of one of its longest glens, stands a yew that is that country's—and possibly Europe's—oldest tree. The famous Fortingall yew in Glen Lyon is estimated to be between 2,000 and 9,000 years old. Before the arrival of Christianity, the yew was held sacred by the Druids, an ancient Celtic priesthood. They worshipped the trees and built their temples near them. Yews were symbols of both death and everlasting life; the trees have remarkable regenerative powers if damaged, and their drooping branches can also root and form new trunks where they touch the ground. In ancient times, it was not uncommon for people to plant a yew where they expected to be buried. This continued with the arrival of Christianity. Churches were built next to established yew trees. Many churches in the British Isles once stood in a circle of yews, probably the remnants of sacred groves planted by the Druids. Yew trees were also planted next to churches and graveyards. One yew typically stood beside the path leading from the funeral gateway of the churchyard to the main door and another yew beside the path leading to a lesser doorway. During a funeral, the clergy gathered under the first yew to await the corpse-bearers.

See Also: *A Field Guide to Medicinal Plants and Herbs: Western North America* by S. Foster and C. Hobbs, Houghton Mifflin, 2002; *Medical Botany: Plants Affecting Human Health* by W. Lewis and M. Elvin-Lewis, John Wiley & Sons, 2003.

TAXUS BREVIFOLIA | Pacific Yew

Parsley
Petroselinum crispum

PARSLEY IS FAMILIAR TO MANY PEOPLE AS THE UBIQUITOUS sprig of green garnish that decorates steak and fish platters in restaurants. It is often ignored, yet parsley is not only edible but very nutritious, packed with protein (up to 22 percent), calcium, iron, potassium, magnesium, several B vitamins, vitamin A, and more vitamin C by volume than an orange. In cooking, parsley combines well with most foods and complements many flavors. It is an essential ingredient in classic dishes from diverse cuisines, such as Middle Eastern tabouleh and Mexican salsa verde. Parsley has the rare ability to mask strong odors, which is why chewing fresh parsley helps freshen the breath. Parsley is the most widely grown herb in Europe and the most heavily consumed fresh herb in the U.S. Though not a prominent plant in herbal medicine, it is valued, as it has been for centuries, for treating a number of complaints including bladder, kidney, and menstrual disorders.

Traditional and Current Medicinal Uses

THE ROMANS CULTIVATED PARSLEY PRIMARILY AS A CULINARY herb (Roman physician Pliny the Elder complained that every sauce and salad contained it). From southern Europe, parsley's use spread north and east. In India, parsley was and still is used in traditional Indian **Ayurvedic medicine** for stomach complaints, as a **diuretic**, and an **expectorant**. In Europe, however, it was not until the Middle Ages that parsley was widely used as a medicinal herb. Commonly grown in monastery gardens, parsley was credited with curing a range of ailments, but especially those having to do with the liver and kidneys, such as jaundice, gout, edema, and bladder infections. Parsley was also prescribed for menstrual problems, asthma, coughs, eye complaints, and plague. It was recommended for nursing mothers to encourage milk flow, and to stimulate appetite and settle upset stomachs. As a **poultice**, parsley leaves were applied to sprains, swellings, and insect bites. Parsley water or parsley tea was given to children and adults for flatulence and bloating. Fresh leaves were chewed as a breath freshener, especially after eating garlic.

Common Names Parsley, garden parsley, rock parsley

Latin Name *Petroselinum crispum*

Family Apiaceae

Parts Used Leaves, root, seeds

Description A clump-forming biennial, parsley has a short, stout taproot from which arise angular, grooved stems topped by dark green, deeply divided, three-pinnate leaves. In the second year, umbels (umbrella-like clusters) of small yellow-green flowers are followed by gray-brown seeds.

Habitat Parsley originated in the Mediterranean region of Europe, but has become naturalized in much of Europe and is now cultivated in many temperate regions of the world.

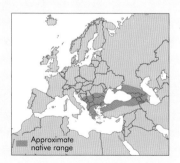

Approximate native range

In modern herbal medicine, parsley is popular in Europe, but less widely used in the United States. Preparations made from the seeds and leaves are frequently recommended for indigestion, gallstones, kidney stones, urinary infections, and asthma. Tea made from the leaves or roots is used to treat jaundice and coughs. The seeds in particular are prescribed as a diuretic in the treatment of gout, rheumatism, and arthritis. In the U.S. parsley tea is often suggested for bladder problems in young women. The root has laxative properties, and the leaves are sometimes applied to relieve itchy skin problems. Parsley juice has been successfully used to treat conjunctivitis and blepharitis (inflammation of the eyelids).

Cultivation and Preparation

PARSLEY REQUIRES RICH, MOIST, WELL-DRAINED SOIL IN FULL sun or part shade. Although parsley is a biennial, the herb is commonly grown as an annual propagated by seed. Leaves are harvested before flowering. Roots are lifted in late autumn of the first year or spring of the second year and dried; seeds are collected when ripe and dried for **infusions** and **extracts**. Oil is distilled from leaves and seeds.

Research

PARSLEY CONTAINS THE FLAVONOID APIIN ALONG WITH A **volatile oil** that has very high levels of the chemical apiole. Apiin is known to reduce allergic responses and act as an **antioxidant**. Apiole exhibits diuretic properties and is sometimes referred to as "parsley camphor" because it gives the herb much of its characteristic odor. In the urinary tract, apiole shows antiseptic activity; it also strongly stimulates uterine muscles. However, there is some evidence that apiole may be toxic in large quantities. Signs of toxicity include lowered blood pressure and pulse rate followed by muscle weakness and paralysis and possibly lung congestion and swelling of the liver. It can also act as an **abortifacient**.

> CAUTION Excessive amounts of parsley seed and oil can be toxic. Medicinal use of parsley is not recommended during pregnancy and in cases of kidney inflammation.

FOR GARLANDS AND GRAVES

The genus name for parsley, *Petroselinum*, comes from the Greek name given to the herb—*petros selinon*—by the Greek physician and botanist Dioscorides (A.D. 40–90). By the Middle Ages, this name had became corrupted to *petrocilium*, which was then anglicized and gradually transformed over the centuries from "persele" into "parsley." For such a common plant, parsley has an uncommon number of stories and superstitions associated with it. In Greek mythology, parsley sprang from the ground where the blood of the hero Archemorus (the forerunner of death) was spilled as he was devoured by serpents. In general, the Greeks associated parsley with death and oblivion. It was used in funeral rites and fashioned into wreaths for graves. Yet parsley was also associated with the heroic Hercules and garlands of parsley were given to the winners of athletic competitions. Both the Greeks and the Romans fed parsley to their chariot horses to give them stamina. Later, parsley's association went from death to the devil. The herb's slow germination was thought to be the devil's fault—he supposedly stole seed and the way to outwit him was to sow parsley seed on Good Friday. However, many country folk believed that only the wicked successfully grew parsley. It was also said that parsley grew well in the gardens of women who were masters of the house.

See Also: Herbal Medicine Expanded Commission E Monographs by M. Blumenthal, A. Goldberg, and J. Brinckmann, American Botanical Council, 2000; Medicinal Herbs History, Use, Recommended Dosages & Cautions by S. Foster, Interweave Press, 1998.

HEALING PLANTS OF
North America

A MODERN DICTIONARY DEFINITION FOR THE WORD "HERB" IS "ANY PLANT used for flavoring, fragrant, or medicinal purposes." If we take that definition literally, in any given area of the Northern Hemisphere, up to 25 percent of flowering plants can be documented as being used as herbs. So it is in the United States. The flora of North America (north of Mexico) has nearly 22,000 species of flowering plants (not including so-called lower plants such as mosses, liverworts, and algae). About 25 percent of those have been used medicinally. Daniel Moerman, an anthropologist at the University of Michigan, has documented Native American plant uses in Native American Ethnobotany, his monumental database; there he lists more than 44,000 uses for more than 4,000 kinds of plants among hundreds of indigenous Native American groups in the U.S. and Canada. All of the important American medicinal plants in use today—American ginseng, black cohosh, echinacea, goldenseal, saw palmetto, and more—begin with Native American use passed on to or observed by early European settlers to North America.

MEDICINAL PLANT REGIONS OF NORTH AMERICA

NORTH AMERICA IS A MICROCOSM OF DIVERSITY, NOT ONLY OF PEOPLES AND CULTURES but also of vegetation zones. Most of the world's major vegetation zones are represented in this diverse climatic expanse, which includes tundra and polar deserts, subarctic evergreen forests, mountain forests, temperate rain forests, prairie, shrub steppes, **deciduous** and evergreen forests, and warm deserts. These vegetation zones are home to herbs sold in today's market—up to 180 native medicinal plants are harvested from the wild for world markets.

The northeastern U.S. encompasses several vegetation zones. Much of northern New England and eastern Canada is boreal forest or taiga. These vast northern forests extend from central Alaska to eastern Canada, covering about 28 percent of the continent. The northeastern region has low species diver-sity, with a high percentage of evergreen trees. Among thick forest stands are bogs and meadows, home to cranberries and other important medicinal plants. The Northeast is also home to many alien intruders—nonnative plants that have intentionally been introduced or opportunist weeds that have made themselves at home. Columbus is often credited with "discovering" America. His greatest impact, however, may have been ushering

in an era of transoceanic migration of plants. Almost one-sixth of plant species growing wild in North America are of foreign origin. Many, such as Japanese honeysuckle (*Lonicera japonica*) and kudzu (*Pueraria lobata* var. *montana*), are considered weeds or invasive aliens—though both of these are used in traditional medicine in China. Up to 30 percent of New England's plant species are non-native and many of these are medicinal herbs, including valerian (*Valeriana officinalis*), yarrow (*Achillea millefolium*), dandelion (*Taraxacum officinale)* and tansy (*Tanacetum vulgare*), to name just a few.

Farther south lies the most important medicinal plant region of the country—the eastern deciduous forest. North America's most diverse collection of forest trees is found in the eastern deciduous forest, which covers 11 percent of the continent. The Appalachians and the Ozarks, famous for their medicinal plants, are largely within this forest. The greatest proportion of American medicinal plant species come from this vegetation zone.

Historically, as colonial America developed its own identity separate from Europe, settlers sought to develop medicines from American forests. Pre-Revolutionary naturalists and explorers observed medicinal plant use among Indians groups and wrote about it in travel accounts and journals.

Lush echinacea plants thrive under irrigation at Trout Lake Farm in Washington State. Echinacea (Echinacea purpurea) is the most popular American medicinal plant sold as a dietary supplement in the United States. Echinacea species were introduced into pharmacies in the 1890s and until the 1920s preparations of echinacea were the most widely used medicinal herb prescribed by physicians in the U.S.

PRECEDING PAGES: *Bogs of the northeastern U.S. are home to the cranberry (Vaccinium macrocarpon), a wet soil-loving shrub that produces edible berries. Once used to treat scurvy, cranberries are now valued as a treatment of urinary tract infections.*

In 1751 John Bartram (1699–1777), the foremost botanist in colonial times, wrote the earliest pamphlet on American medicinal plants. Published by young Philadelphia printer Benjamin Franklin, the pamphlet included a "newly discovered Indian Cure for the Venereal Disease"—blue lobelia (*Lobelia siphilitica*), the name by which the plant is still known today. Later, in the mid-19th century, on the cover of an herb catalog, a member of the communal Shaker religoius sect asked, "Why look to Europe's shores for plants that grow at our own doors?" The Shakers were the first in the United States to start a commercial herb business—in 1799 at the Sabbath-day Lake Maine Shaker Community. The only remaining Shaker group, they still sell herbs today.

Medicinal Plant Uses in North America

THE MAJORITY OF IMPORTANT AMERICAN MEDICINAL PLANTS IN WORLD COMMERCE today comes from the eastern deciduous forest. The most popular medicinal plants in North America include herbs such as American ginseng (*Panax quin-quefolius*), goldenseal (*Hydrastis canadensis*), black cohosh (*Cimicifuga race-mosa*), and wild yam (*Dioscorea villosa*). Others such as slippery elm bark (*Ulmus rubra*) and witch hazel (*Hamamelis virginiana*) are approved as non-prescription or over-the-counter drugs.

Goldenseal is one of the most popular herbs sold in health food markets in the United States. Surprisingly, it is little researched. Many herb consumers think of it as a natural antibiotic. Recently, goldenseal made the news as part of an attempt to mask detection of illicit drugs in urine. Though this attempt prompted further testing for detecting the presence of goldenseal in urine, there is no scientific evidence to support this use.

American colonists admired handsome, robust black cohosh with its spikes of brilliant white flowers and planted it in their perennial gardens. Today a new generation of baby boomers is exploring this traditional Indian remedy to treat symptoms associated with menopause. Extracts of black cohosh root have been used in Germany since the mid-1950s to treat menopausal symptoms. In the U.S., National Institutes of Health-sponsored clinical studies are under way at the University of Illinois, Chicago, and at Columbia University to explore the herb's value for treating menopausal symptoms.

If there is one medicinal plant that underscores the melding of history, commerce, and tradition, it is American ginseng. The Penobscots called it "man root" referring to the resemblance of the American ginseng root to the human form. The Menominee in Wisconsin consumed the roots as a tonic and to strengthen mental powers. Today, American ginseng is used by Asians and Americans alike as a general tonic and rejuvenator. American ginseng, both wild harvested and widely cultivated, is a major herbal export, primarily to Hong Kong and China. In 2004, wild American ginseng valued at more than $17 million was exported along with cultivated American ginseng worth some $15 million. Listed as a threatened species under the Convention of International Trade in Endangered Species (CITES), only wild American ginseng roots ten years old can be exported today.

South of the Appalachians, the southeastern coastal plain represents only 3 percent of the North American landmass. It is dominated by upland pine forests, wetlands, and at the southern tip of Florida, tropical hardwood vegetation. One of the most common species in the coastal plain is saw palmetto (*Serenoa repens*). Saw palmetto berries, once relished as a staple by Native Americans in Florida, are now valued as an important treatment for benign prostatic hyperplasia (BPH), a non-malignant enlargement of the prostate affecting many American men over the age of 60. Saw palmetto thickets blanket millions of acres in Florida, where up to 2 million pounds of berries are harvested each year, usually by migrant farm workers. In stifling humidity, the berries are gathered at dawn. An experienced crew of three pickers can harvest about 1,200 pounds of the fresh berries in a morning.

The late Hopi herbalist Soloho explains medical uses of Southwest native plants to participants of an herbal workshop on the Lummi Indian Reservation on the northern coast of Washington. He taught a generation of American herbalists about the spiritual and herbal healing traditions of his tribe.

As the most widely used alternative treatment for BPH—used in Europe for more than 60 years—saw palmetto has been closely scrutinized. Evaluating the scientific literature on saw palmetto, officials of the **United States Pharmacopoeia** concluded, "These studies provide evidence . . . that commercial extracts of saw palmetto at a dose of 160 mg twice a day are more effective than a placebo in relieving lower urinary tract symptoms of benign prostatic hyperplasia." It is likely that use of this Native American food-turned-herbal-medicine will continue to grow.

Across the Mississippi River in western Arkansas and Missouri, the eastern deciduous forest begins to fade, then merges with the vast grasslands of middle America, which once covered nearly 25 percent of the continent. This is the home of what has become the best-selling Native American herb in today's herb market—echinacea. *Echinacea* is a genus of nine species. Three of those species (*E. purpurea, E. angustifolia,* and *E. pallida*) enter commerce. Two species, the Tennessee coneflower (*E. tennesseensis*) and smooth-leaved coneflower (*E. laevigata*) are federally listed endangered species. The common purple coneflower (*E. purpurea*) is widely grown as a flower garden perennial. *Echinacea angustifolia* is most common in western prairies and was used by native groups of the Great Plains for more medicinal purposes than any other plant. Echinacea is best known as an immune system stimulant, primarily for the prevention of colds and flu. Today German physicians write more than 3 million prescriptions for echinacea each year—despite recent clinical studies that question the herb's effectiveness.

The first Spaniards who entered the vast southwestern deserts and saw plant forms such as the giant saguaro and other cactuses must have felt transported to another planet. The Chihuahuan, Sonoran, and Mojave Deserts and the semiarid intermountain regions of the Southwest are part of the vegetation zone known as desert scrub, about 5 percent of the North American landmass. This regional vegetation zone supports thousands of bioactive species, among them *Ephedra* (ephedra), *Larrea* (chaparral), *Yucca, Agave, Opuntia* (prickly pear), and *Simmondsia* (jojoba). Like the eastern deciduous forest, the southwestern desert is one of the most important regions for significant medicinal plants in commerce today.

In the western United States, from Oregon to Mexico are scrub and woodland vegetation zones. In California, there are more vegetative subzones than in any other state. Most of the plants associated with culinary and aromatic herbs in European tradition, such as sage, thyme, rosemary, and other familiar herbs, originate from similar climates in the Mediterranean region. The Pacific Coast coniferous forest contains some of the world's most diverse and long-lived tree species, covering about 3 percent of North America. This zone is famous for its redwoods and giant sequoias, Douglas firs, and Sitka spruces. Here the Pacific yew (*Taxus brevifolia*) became the focus of scientific research in the 1980s. Its bark was the original source of the anti-cancer drug paclitaxel (marketed under the more familiar name Taxol). The drug is used in chemotherapy for certain forms of ovarian cancer and breast cancer—a product of the National Cancer Institute's nearly five-decade-long search for anti-cancer drugs from plants.

Medicinal herb use in the United States took a dramatic turn in 1994 with the passage of the Dietary Supplement Health and Education Act—legislation that allowed herbs to be sold freely and to carry claims explaining how they affect the human body. This landmark legislation ushered in the rebirth of herbal medicine in the United States. What goes around, comes around: Now several North American medicinal plants, once relegated to an irrelevant past, are again commonly available not only in the United States but around the globe.

OPPOSITE PAGE: *Saw palmetto berries (*Serenoa repens*) are gathered in big pots as the sun rises across the pine-palmetto scrub of southern Florida. The berries are harvested by migrant farm workers in late August and September. An experienced crew of three can gather about 1,200 pounds of fresh berries between sunup and noon.*

Partridge Berry
Mitchella repens

Common Names Partridge berry, squaw vine, twinberry, checkerberry, one berry

Latin Name *Mitchella repens*

Family Rubiaceae

Parts Used Whole plant

Description A trailing, evergreen vine, partridge berry hugs the ground as it spreads via rooting stems. It has small, rounded, shiny, white-veined leaves with a distinct central rib. In late spring, pairs of white or pinkish flowers appear; they are fused at their bases. Each pair of flowers forms a single bright-red berry with two distinct dimples on its surface.

Habitat Native to eastern and central North America, partridge berry is a forest floor plant at home in moist, usually evergreen forests.

Approximate native range

PARTRIDGE BERRY IS A PRETTY LITTLE PLANT, WITH PAIRS OF shiny rounded leaves less than an inch long on a slim runner of a stem that forms a mat as it grows. When not in bloom partridge berry could be easily overlooked creeping about in the moss at the foot of trees and decayed stumps. But it commands attention when it flowers, because it typically produces pairs of tubular white flowers that are fused together at their bases. And if that's not eye-catching enough, the big, scarlet berries that follow the flowers—one berry for each pair—certainly are. Partridge berry is a distinctly American plant. It was used medicinally by many Native American tribes primarily as a woman's herb for everything from menstrual complaints to facilitating childbirth. Today it is still recommended by herbal practitioners in much the same way.

Traditional and Current Medicinal Uses

PARTRIDGE BERRY WAS WIDELY USED BY EASTERN NATIVE TRIBES. One of its most common applications was as a childbirth aid for women (hence the nickname "squaw vine"); it was typically taken in frequent doses for several weeks before delivery, to render labor easier and safer. Among the Cherokee, the herb was also taken to relieve menstrual cramps and soothe sore nipples for nursing mothers. It was administered just before newborns started to nurse. The Chippewa used partridge berry to ease muscular swellings and stiff joints as well. Strong **infusions** of the herb's roots and twigs were favored by the Delaware and Oklahoma for rheumatism and to stimulate menstruation. The Iroquois had a remarkable number of uses for partridge berry, ranging from **decoctions** designed to quiet vomiting, relieve labor pains, and treat uterine infections to preparations for controlling convulsions in children, easing back pain, reducing fever (especially fevers associated with infants and children, as well as those with typhoid-like fevers), and soothing stomachaches. The berries of the plant were also eaten raw by women of the tribe. European colonists adapted partridge berry for their own use to treat similar conditions. By the early 1800s, the herb had been adopted into American folk medicine and ultimately by American **Eclectic** physicians, who used medicinal herbs in their practices. In addition to its use in easing labor, partridge berry was found to be a valuable **diuretic** and **astringent**. In the 19th century, it was taken as a remedy for pain, urinary and kidney complaints, and for dysentery. As a wash for treating sore nipples it was said to be unsurpassed. A concoction that was made from partridge berry and from several other herbs, which was known as Sirup Mitchella or Mothers' Cordial, became very popular. This drink was adminstered for a wide variety of female complaints, not the least of which was to make childbirth easier and less painful.

In modern herbal medicine, partridge berry is reputed to promote an easy labor by aiding contractions of the uterus during childbirth. It is typically administered during the last two months of pregnancy as a uterine tonic (usually as a tea). In addition, the herb is said to exert a calming effect on the nervous system and to improve digestion. Partridge berry is also used as an eyewash and as an astringent skin wash—and it is still used today as a salve to alleviate nipple soreness in nursing mothers.

Cultivation and Preparation

PARTRIDGE BERRY IS A PERENNIAL THAT NEEDS MOIST, RICH, neutral-to-acid soil and shade. It transplants easily and grows quickly; it also can be started from seed, but this is not common and the plant is not widely cultivated. For herbal medicine preparations, partridge berry is cut in summer and dried for later use. Due to unsustainable harvesting of wild plants, the herb is considered threatened in some parts of its range.

Research

PARTRIDGE BERRY'S PRIMARY CHEMICAL CONSTITUENTS include **alkaloids, glycosides, saponins, mucilage,** and **tannins**. Little reliable laboratory or clinical research has been carried out on this herb. To date, there have been no toxic effects reported or precautions issued about the use of partridge berry, although herbal practitioners do not recommend it during the first six months of pregnancy.

Partridge berry belongs to the very small genus *Mitchella*. The famous Swedish botanist Carolus Linnaeus gave the genus its name. He named it after his friend, John Mitchell (1711–1768), a Virginia-born physician, botanist, naturalist, and cartographer educated in Scotland who returned to live and work in America around 1731. On his return to the colonies, Mitchell set up a medical practice but also began to pursue botanical studies in earnest. Mitchell provided Linnaeus with much valuable information on many American plants, partridge berry among them. Mitchell is well respected as an early American botanist. But as a cartographer, he made a remarkable contribution to American history. In 1750, Mitchell was asked to prepare a map of the British colonies in North America for the purpose of maximizing British territorial claims. The result of Mitchell's five-year effort was a map that extended the boundaries of Virginia, the Carolinas, and Georgia across the Mississippi River. It also depicted the Missouri River more accurately than any other map of the day. Mitchell correctly showed the northern branch of the Missouri as the river's main branch. Mitchell's map was used by Lewis and Clark on their expedition. It was also used during the Treaty of Paris peace negotiations and to settle many boundary disputes. The only map Mitchell ever produced, it is considered one of the most significant maps in American history.

See Also: *A Field Guide to Medicinal Plants and Herbs: Eastern and Central North America, 2nd ed.* by S. Foster and J. Duke, Houghton Mifflin, 2000; *Native American Ethnobotany* by D. Moerman, Timber Press, 1998.

MITCHELLA REPENS | Partridge Berry

Common Names Passionflower, maypop, passion vine, apricot vine

Latin Name *Passiflora incarnata*

Family Passifloraceae

Parts Used Flowers, leaves, stems

Description Passionflower is a climbing vine with stems 10 to 30 feet long; it climbs with coiled tendrils. It has large white-and-violet flowers and deeply lobed leaves. The fruit is a many-seeded berry about the size of a hen's egg.

Habitat Native to eastern and southern parts of North America, passionflower inhabits thickets, fence lines, and the edges of woodlands. It is widely cultivated in Europe.

Approximate native range

Passionflower
Passiflora incarnata

THE PASSIONFLOWER'S LINK TO CHRISTIANITY DATES BACK to the early 17th century, when Spanish missionaries in South America associated the intricate form of the climbing vine's flowers with the events surrounding the crucifixion, or the passion, of Christ. In the United States, *Passiflora incarnata*'s original range was from Virginia to Florida and west to Ohio and Texas, although today it is cultivated in many parts of the country as a garden ornamental. Its remarkably complex and showy flowers can be two to three inches across. They are succeeded by yellow-orange, egg-shaped fruits, known as maypops, that are filled with small seeds embedded in an edible, sweet yellow pulp. Native Americans valued passionflower medicinally for its ability to heal bruises and wounds. Later herbal practitioners prized the plant for its calming, sedative, and pain-relieving actions. Passionflower is still used in modern herbal medicine as a gentle herbal tranquilizer, but more so in Europe than in its native homeland of North America.

Traditional and Current Medicinal Uses

NATIVE AMERICANS OF THE EASTERN UNITED STATES APPLIED the crushed leaves of passionflower to heal and reduce swelling in bruises, wounds, and other injuries. **Infusions** of the pounded roots were used to wean babies and as drops for ear infections. Preparations of the plant were also used for boils and as a blood tonic. A tea made from the vine was drunk to soothe nerves. Throughout the last few centuries, passionflower continued to be used in folk remedies as a "calming" herb for anxiety, fatigue, insomnia, muscle spasms, seizures, hysteria, and even hyperactivity in children. In the early 20th century, passionflower was an ingredient in many over-the-counter (OTC) sedatives and sleep aids. However, in 1978, the U.S. Food and Drug Administration withdrew its support for passionflower in OTC sedatives, giving it a Category II listing (not generally recognized as safe and effective) due to a lack of the herb's proven effectiveness. In Europe, however, passionflower is still widely used. It is typically available as an OTC sedative in which passionflower **extract** is combined with other calming herbs such as valerian and lemon balm.

In modern herbal medicine, professional herbalists use passionflower as a gentle sedative. It is prescribed to treat insomnia, tension, restlessness, and other health problems related to conditions of nervous anxiety, as well as for nervous gastrointestinal disorders, especially in children.

Cultivation and Preparation

PASSIONFLOWER THRIVES IN RELATIVELY POOR, ACIDIC, SANDY soils in full sun where it has something to climb. The plant can be grown from seed, cuttings, or by dividing the rhizomous runners by which it naturally spreads. The above-ground parts of the plant are used in herbal medicine. Flowering shoots are typically harvested after the first fruits have matured. Cuttings can be used fresh or dried for use in pills, teas, **tinctures**, and infusions.

Research

FROM A RESEARCH STANDPOINT, PASSIONFLOWER HAS NOT been thoroughly investigated. Studies by various European research groups have confirmed that extracts exhibit sedative, antispasmodic, and antianxiety activity, but researchers have not been able to attribute these effects to any single chemical compound or group of compounds. A study involving patients with a generalized anxiety disorder found passionflower as effective in reducing anxiety as a leading antianxiety medication, but larger studies are needed to confirm these results. An extract containing passionflower and hawthorn has been studied in people with congestive heart failure for treating shortness of breath and difficulty exercising. People using this combination of herbs experienced improvement in symptoms, but positive effects may have been due to the hawthorn, commonly used for congestive heart failure. Some studies indicate passionflower may be useful in combination with certain drugs for opiate detoxification (for example, in heroin addicts). Some dietary supplements available for attention deficit hyperactivity disorder (ADHD) contain passionflower, but their safety and effectiveness have not been confirmed.

THE PASSION IN PASSIONFLOWER

Anyone unfamiliar with passionflower and its applications in herbal medicine might wonder if it was used as an aphrodisiac. But the devout missionaries who gave passionflower its name would have quickly set the record straight. In the 17th century, Jesuit missionaries working in South America professed to see symbols of the crucifixion in the plant's blossoms. They believed these showy flowers represented a sort of botanic "Calvary lesson." The three styles of the pistil so prominent in the center of the flower were said to represent the three nails used to nail Christ to the cross. The five anthers on the stamens stood for the five wounds in his body. The dramatic corona of white and purple threadlike filaments that surrounds these plant parts was thought to resemble the legendary crown of thorns. The five sepals and five similar petals beneath this corona were said to symbolize the ten apostles—leaving out Peter and Judas Iscariot, who both betrayed Christ. The lobed leaves and tendrils symbolized the hand and whips of his tormentors. Even the flower's colors, white and purple, symbolized purity and heaven. It may be that the Jesuits took the presence of the passionflower, coupled with their interpretation of its significance, as divine assurance of success in their quest to convert the natives of the region to Christianity.

See Also: *Herbal Medicine Expanded Commission E Monographs* by M. Blumenthal, A. Goldberg, J. Brinckmann, American Botanical Council, 2000; *A Field Guide to Medicinal Plants and Herbs: Eastern and Central North America, 2nd ed.* by S. Foster, J. Duke, Houghton Mifflin, 2000.

Patchouli
Pogostemon cablin

Common Names Patchouli, *guan huo xiang*, patchouly

Latin Name *Pogostemon cablin*

Family Lamiaceae

Parts Used Leaf, stem

Description Patchouli is a small, bushy, perennial herb with a unique scent that grows two to three feet high with white flowers blooming mid-autumn to early winter. A member of the mint family, it has mint-like, serrated leaves. Patchouli (*P. cablin*) has a hairy stem; Java patchouli (*P. heyneanus*) has a smooth stem. (Java patchouli is considered to have an inferior scent and is used as a cheaper adulterant oil to "true" patchouli oil.)

Habitat Patchouli likes tropical climates and is grown primarily in Indonesia, as well as Malaysia, China, Brazil, and India. It is cultivated around the world.

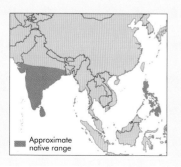

Approximate native range

THOUGH YOU MAY NOT KNOW IT, CHANCES ARE YOU HAVE smelled patchouli. It is hard to forget. Patchouli oil has been described as having a scent that is exotic, earthy, musty, spicy, sweet, balsamic, woody, and rich. Because it makes such an excellent base, and combines so well with so many other scents, it is used in at least a third of all perfumes and fragrances. Oil freshly distilled from the leaves has a green, slightly harsh aroma. But like a fine wine, patchouli improves with age, mellowing considerably, becoming sweeter, and finally becoming suave and fruity. It is used in soaps, detergents, deodorants, and cosmetic products. Its smooth scent is used for aromatherapy, massage, and romance. But patchouli is and has been used medicinally throughout India and Asia for centuries where it is valued not only for its fragrance but also for its healing. The name "patchouli" comes from the Hindustan words for "leaf" and "green." It is known worldwide as the scent of Indian silks and inks.

Traditional and Current Medicinal Uses

PATCHOULI HAS BEEN USED FOR AGES IN THE EAST AS AN ANTI-dote for snakebite, a repellant for leeches, moths, bedbugs and other insects, as a prophylactic, for menstrual cramps, colds, headaches, nausea, vomiting, diarrhea, abdominal pain, tumors, and bad breath. In Chinese medicine, the dried leaves and stems have long been used to inspire clarity and balance the *chi*, or life force. The discovery of patchouli by the West seems to have occurred somewhere in the early 1800s as silks from India arrived in Britain thick with the smell of patchouli leaves placed in the folds of the shawls to protect the cashmere from moths. The scent became an indicator of genuine Oriental goods which, with the help of a few patchouli leaves, was easily forged by local manufacturers to sell knockoffs. Patchouli's modern association is with the hippie culture of the 1960s.

As aromatherapy, patchouli is used today as an appetite suppressant, for constipation, stress and fatigue, and as an aphrodisiac, often as part of a massage oil, bath oil, or hair or skin care product. The oil is said to be good for sores, dandruff, eczema, dermatitis, acne, and athlete's foot. Patchouli is also used as a flavor in many foods and beverages.

Cultivation and Preparation

PATCHOULI IS A TENDER PERENNIAL, UNABLE TO WITHSTAND the cold and preferring partial shade. It can withstand full sun but then requires much more water. Seeds or cuttings can be used for propagation. Several years of frequent harvesting will weaken the plant to the point of needing to replant. Because it is easy on the soil, it is often grown between rotations of other crops. It is also often used as an understory plant, thriving in the dappled shade of the forest. After young patchouli plants have been harvested, the leaves are partially dried, stacked, and baled. Then the leaves can be fermented slightly in order to maximize the yield by weakening the cell walls that hold the oil. Patchouli is often grown on small farms and sold to regional steam distilleries, which combine harvests and successive distillations. Patchouli's high output of **essential oil**, up to 3.5 percent (as compared with an herb like rose oil which yields less than one percent), makes adulteration less of a problem than with other oil-yielding plants. Oil that has been tampered with may be identified by a heavy cedar or spicy clove smell.

Research

MUCH RESEARCH HAS BEEN DEVOTED TO STUDYING DIFFERENCES in composition between patchouli oils produced under varying conditions in different regions. But little research has focused on patchouli's medicinal uses. Patchouli's reputation as an antibacterial and antifungal oil was tested in one Indian study, which compared its effectivness against 22 strains of bacteria and 12 fungal strains. Patchouli oil inhibited the growth of 20 of the bacterial strains and all of the fungi. One recent study found that the the oils of patchouli, clove, and citronella provided two hours of complete mosquito repellence.

CAUTION Patchouli is generally regarded as nonirritating, nontoxic, and nonsensitizing but should not be taken internally without consulting a medical professional.

A SYMPHONY OF SMELLS

Why is patchouli so commonly used in fragrances? When creating a scent, fragrance makers blend essential oils into a perfume much the way a composer combines instruments to make an orchestra. In fact, fragrance makers use musical terms to describe the process. "Top notes" tend to be light, fresh, and uplifting. Peppermint, lemon, eucalyptus, and sage are all top notes. The so-called middle notes take a few minutes to establish their scent. As many top notes echo away, the slower evaporating middle notes step forward to take the lead as some lower notes begin to become apparent. Warm, soft, and balancing, middle notes generally make up the bulk of the oil. Black pepper, pine, rosemary, and bay are middle notes. As the middle stage peaks and dies, the deep, relaxing "bass notes" hold on to them, slowing the evaporation of all the oils. Rich and solid, the bass notes are usually the most expensive. Cedarwood, myrrh, rose, and vanilla are bass notes. Musk and patchouli are among the most tenacious and commonly used bass notes. It is patchouli's deep staying power that gives the scent a long life, and all the more ethereal scents time to develop and play off each other. Patchouli's strong earthiness grounds and complements the stronger smells, giving them a solid base from which to spring. Patchouli gives any scent a long, strong, rich, and relaxing life.

See Also: *Medicinal Plants of the Worlds* by B. van Wyk and M. Wink, Timber Press, 2004; *Aromatherapy: A Complete Guide to the Healing Art* by K. Keville and M. Green, The Crossing Press, 1995.

POGOSTEMON CABLIN | Patchouli

Pau d'Arco
Tabebuia impetiginosa

BRAZILIAN INDIANS HAVE USED PAU D'ARCO FOR MORE than a thousand years. From Brazil it has spread all over South America and the world. There are more than a hundred species in this genera of colorful trees, shrubs, and flowering vines known by their trumpet-shaped flowers. Several trees from the Bignoniaceae family native to tropical America are known as pau d'arco and used to treat skin conditions, cancer, and many other ailments. Apart from being valued medicinally for its bark, and somewhat for its leaves, the hardwood is particularly weather- and insect-resistant. *Tabebuia* wood was used to make the famous boardwalk in Atlantic City, New Jersey. It has been and still is used to make weapons, particularly bows, and gets its name from the Portuguese word for bow wood. European scientists learned of the tree in 1820 from an Austrian botanical expedition. Pau d'arco's recent recognition as a cancer treatment together with its popularity for building have put a high price on rain forest areas where it is cleared. Despite research judging it to have too many side effects for cancer treatments, **extracts** continue to be developed and grow in popularity.

Traditional and Current Medicinal Uses

PAU D'ARCO HAS LONG BEEN A TRADITIONAL MEDICINE OF the Guarani and Tupi tribes of Brazil for treating malaria, anemia, colitis, respiratory problems, colds, cough, flu, fungal infections, fever, arthritis and rheumatism, snakebite, poor circulation, boils, syphilis, and cancer. Tea from the bark is known as a blood purifier. It is said to have been popular among the Inca as well. Further, it may have been used against impetigo, a skin infection from which the species name *impetiginosa* comes.

Today it is used all over the Americas to treat a wide range of internal and external afflictions such as infection, fevers, colds, influenza, skin disease, ulcerations, dysentery, gastrointestinal inflammation, respiratory disease, arthritis, syphilis, cancer, prostatitis, circulatory problems, diabetes, leukemia, allergies, liver disease, and Parkinson's disease. But it is primarily used in Central and South America to treat insect or snakebite,

Common Names Pau d'arco, *lapacho, ipe roxo, taheebo*

Latin Names *Tabebuia impetiginosa*

Family Bignoniaceae

Parts Used Bark, wood, leaves

Description The pau d'arco is a deciduous tree that can grow to more than 100 feet in the wild but is often cultivated into a 25- to 75-foot tree for its attractive irregular canopy that blooms full of pink trumpet-shaped flowers.

Habitat Pau d'arco is native to Brazil and tropical America including some of the Lesser Antilles.

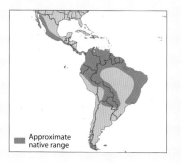

Approximate native range

minor skin injuries, and other skin conditions such as psoriasis. Pau d'arco has both antifungal and antimicrobial properties.

Cultivation and Preparation

THE PAU D'ARCO TREE NEEDS SUN AND WATER ALL SUMMER and grows on sunny ridge tops, on moist riverbanks, and in marshy forests, but not on the coast. In its native habitat of Brazil it loses all its leaves during the dry winter and blooms bright pink, before leaves grow back. It makes a stunning display, leafless and full of dense clusters of pink and purple or occasionally white trumpet flowers with yellow or orange throats, all to attract pollinators such as carpenter ants and hummingbirds. Skinny, brown seedpods hang from the tree in the winter; in the spring the pods release winged seeds that take several weeks to germinate. Pau d'arco can also be propagated by cuttings. As with many rare trees with medicinal bark, the bark can be harvested responsibly, in patches, so as not to kill the tree, but, out of ignorance or greed, the pau d'arco is frequently cut down or stripped, which kills the tree.

Research

MUCH RESEARCH HAS BEEN DONE ON COMPOUNDS KNOWN as quinones found in the pau d'arco tree. In small doses quinones stimulate the immune system; in high doses they repress it. The quinone compound found in pau d'arco is lapachol—believed to have **antioxidant,** anticoagulant, antiviral, **anti-inflammatory,** antimalarial, and anticancer properties. Lapachol is synthesized and taken in Brazil to reduce pain in cancer patients. Betalapachone, another quinone compound with antiviral and tumor-fighting properties, is used in combination with chemo- and radiation therapy. The National Cancer Institute and other organizations studied pau d'arco in the 1960s and 70s, but the research only confirms that it shows promise in animal studies. Dosage levels needed to be very high to see effects and research was discontinued.

CAUTION Pau d'arco can cause moderate to severe nausea, dizziness, vomiting, anemia, and bleeding. It should not be taken without the consultation of a doctor or by pregnant or breastfeeding women.

The first famous boardwalk in the U.S. was built in Atlantic City, New Jersey, in the 1880s, out of white cedar, a plant native to New Jersey and chosen for its resistance to dry rot. But overharvesting made it scarce and expensive, so the city switched to red cedar, native to the rain forests of the Northwest. Overlogging made it no longer viable after a few years. Next was pine, which, even when treated, lasts only ten years. Then in the 1960s, New York City became the first to use ipe (the name by which wood from pau d'arco trees is sold in the U.S.) for boardwalks at Coney Island, Brighton Beach, the Rockaways, Staten Island, as well as for benches and the deck on the Brooklyn Bridge. Atlantic City also chose the Brazilian hardwood. The city inspector explained, "With casino traffic, we were replacing pressure-treated pine every seven years. We project the ipe decking to hold up for 30 years." Ipe has continued to gain in popularity, especially in the last 10 years, not only for boardwalks but also for many waterside structures. Dense and resistant to warping, shrinking, splintering, chemicals, termites, fire, and marine borers, ipe is a dark reddish-brown that turns silver and needs no coating. All this puts pau d'arco trees in high demand, increasing the unsustainable and illegal harvesting of rain forest. Ipe is being cultivated, but not fast enough to quell serious concerns about the potential for driving the tree into extinction.

See Also: *Medicinal Herbs: History, Use, Recommended Dosages & Cautions* by S. Foster, Interweave Press, 1998; *Tyler's Honest Herbal*, 4th ed. by S. Foster and V. Tyler, The Haworth Herbal Press, 1999.

TABEBUIA IMPETIGINOSA | Pau d'Arco

Peppermint
Mentha x piperita

PEPPERMINT RANKS AMONG THE WORLD'S MOST POPULAR flavorings and the aromatic oil extracted from its leaves is the world's most extensively used **essential oil.** Peppermint oil is added to everything from antacids to ice cream to after-dinner mints. The secret to peppermint's intense, refreshing taste—simultaneously cooling and warming—is menthol. There are 25 different species of mints in the genus *Mentha*. Nearly all contain at least a little menthol, but peppermint and Japanese mint (*Mentha arvensis*) are the richest natural sources of menthol known. Peppermint has been valued for its minty fresh flavor since ancient Greece and Rome, but did not become an important therapeutic herb in Western medicine until the early 1700s. In modern herbal medicine, peppermint is respected as a soothing aid for stomach and intestinal complaints that is also employed to relieve pain and headaches and treat symptoms of the common cold.

Common Names Peppermint, brandy mint, lamb mint

Latin Name *Mentha x piperita*

Family Lamiaceae

Parts Used Whole plant, leaves, oil

Description Peppermint is a vigorous, aromatic perennial that grows about two feet tall and spreads by runners just under the soil surface. It has highly branched square stems and small, lance-shaped, toothed leaves that are dark green but often tinged with purple. Tiny purple flowers bloom in whorls on terminal spikes in summer.

Habitat Native to Europe and Asia, peppermint is a hybrid perennial that is mostly cultivated, but also grows wild in moist, rich soil environments in temperate parts of Europe and in the eastern United States.

Approximate native range

Traditional and Current Medicinal Uses

MINT (PROBABLY SPEARMINT) IS BELIEVED TO HAVE BEEN USED since Roman times. The Romans added mint sprigs to bathwater and perfumes. The Romans also appear to have introduced mint to other parts of Europe. References to "mint" appear in medieval texts and plant lists, but true peppermint did not appear on the scene until 1696, when a strongly aromatic plant that was a natural hybrid of spearmint (*M. spicata*) and water mint (*M. aquatica*) was discovered in an English field and subsequently cultivated. By 1721 peppermint was officially included in the *London Pharmacopoeia*. It was prescribed for treating indigestion, flatulence, colic, nervous headaches, fever, colds, and a variety of other ailments. Colonists carried peppermint to the New World. In the American folk medicine tradition, peppermint was used for indigestion, flatulence, colic, heartburn, to stop nausea and vomiting, to cure hiccups, for relief of headaches, and as a stimulant but also to induce sleep.

In modern herbal medicine, peppermint is suggested for relieving indigestion and bloating due to excess gas, for spastic complaints of the gastrointestinal tract, gallbladder and bile ducts, and for irritable bowel syndrome. It is also prescribed to relieve congestion, to ease tension headaches, to reduce muscles spasms in the colon, and to alleviate nerve and muscle pain.

Cultivation and Preparation

PEPPERMINT IS PROPAGATED BY DIVISION OR BY CUTTINGS; IT is a sterile hybrid and so does not produce viable seeds. Like most mints, peppermint needs rich, moist soil in sun or part shade. For medicinal use, the entire plant can be cut at the beginning of flowering or just the leaves can be harvested at any time during the growing season. Leaves and other above-ground parts are used fresh or they may be dried in various preparations and for oil extraction.

Research

THE MENTHOL IN PEPPERMINT'S ESSENTIAL OIL IS PRIMARILY responsible for its beneficial effects. Menthol is an antispasmodic that inhibits smooth muscle contractions, especially in the digestive tract. Menthol also stimulates production of bile. These two actions combine to calm stomach muscles and improve digestion. By relaxing the muscles of the esophageal sphincter at the top of the stomach, peppermint helps release trapped air, reducing bloating and belching. However, peppermint may worsen the symptoms of heartburn and indigestion in people with gastroesophageal reflux disease (GERD). Studies have shown that enteric-coated capsules of peppermint oil relieve many of the symptoms of irritable bowel syndrome (IBS). In one study comparing enteric-coated peppermint oil capsules to **placebo** in children with IBS, three-fourths of the subjects using peppermint oil had reduced symptoms. In a similar study with adults, almost 80 percent experienced relief. In laboratory studies, peppermint oil has been shown to be active against a wide variety of bacteria and several viruses, including herpes and West Nile. Research has shown that peppermint applied to the forehead and temples compares favorably with acetaminophen in relieving headaches. Menthol stimulates cold receptors in the nostrils and is an effective decongestant and **expectorant.**

THE HOSPITALITY HERB

The genus name for peppermint and other mints, *Mentha,* comes from Minthe, a nymph in Greek mythology. According to legend, the beautiful Minthe was changed into a nondescript little plant by Persephone when she discovered that her husband and lord of the underworld, Pluto, was in love with the nymph. Unable to undo Persephone's spell, Pluto tried to improve the situation as best he could. He endowed Minthe with a sweet scent, one that became sweeter the more she was walked upon. Over the centuries, mint has been put to many uses, but has also become a symbol for purity and hospitality. The Greek poet Ovid wrote about using mint to scrub the boards upon which food was set out for the gods. A related use of mint is described in another tale from Greek mythology. The gods Zeus and Hermes, disguised as poor wanderers, journeyed through the countryside of Phrygia. They knocked at every house, asking for food and a place to rest. Each time they were refused. Finally they came upon the poor hut of Philemon and Baucis, an old couple with few resources. Yet here the disguised deities were warmly welcomed and served food on a table freshly scrubbed with mint leaves. When the gods revealed themselves, Zeus rewarded the couple for their unselfish kindness by turning their humble hut into a beautiful temple and ensuring that they would always be together. Mint thus became a symbol of true hospitality.

See Also: *The ABC Clinical Guide to Herbs* by M. Blumenthal, T. Hall, and A. Goldberg, American Botanical Council, 2003; *World Health Organization (WHO) Monographs on Selected Medicinal Plants, Vol. 2,* 2002.

Common Names Pineapple, ananas, *piña*

Latin Name *Ananas comosus*

Family Bromeliaceae

Parts Used Fruit, stem

Description A tropical or near-tropical plant, *Ananas* is an herbaceous perennial with a stout stem surrounded by a rosette of pointed leaves that bear sharp spines along their margins. The plant grows two to five feet tall with a spread up to four feet. At blooming time, the central stem elongates and a cluster of small purple or red flowers emerge.

Habitat *Ananas* is native to southern Brazil and Paraguay, where its wild relatives still occur. It is cultivated in many tropical or subtropical locations, including Florida, California, Hawaii, many Caribbean islands, Australia, Southeast Asia, Africa, the Philippines, and Indonesia.

Approximate native range

Pineapple
Ananas comosus

WALKING IN A FIELD OF PINEAPPLES IS A FORMIDAble undertaking. The thigh-high plants bristle with spear-shaped leaves that bear sharp spines along their margins. At blooming time, the central stem of the plant elongates and a cluster of small purple or red flowers emerge at its tip. The familiar juicy, fleshy pineapple fruit is the result of a fusion of the many small fruits that develop from the individual flowers; the fibrous core of a pineapple is the plant's central stem. Depending on the variety, pineapple fruits may grow up to a foot long and weigh as much as ten pounds. Pineapples are widely enjoyed as a food for their sumptuous sweetness. But their inclusion in herbal medicine is largely attributed to the fact that pineapple juice aids digestion and contains an enzymatic substance called bromelain known for its ability to reduce swelling and fight inflammation.

Traditional and Current Medicinal Uses

PINEAPPLE HAS A LONG HISTORY AS A MEDICINAL PLANT IN tropical regions. As a folk remedy, it has been used to treat conditions ranging from constipation to varicose veins and venereal disease. The plant's most active chemical compound, bromelain, was isolated in 1876.

In Western medicine, bromelain was introduced as a therapeutic agent in 1957 by chemist Ralph M. Heinicke. Working for Dole Pineapple Company in Hawaii, Heinicke found bromelain in high concentrations in pineapple stems and was tasked with finding medicinal uses for it. In the ensuing years, bromelain was shown to reduce inflammation in arthritis as well as in injuries such as sprains and strains, and to help prevent tissue swelling after surgery. Bromelain has also been used in treating blood clots and bruises, reducing angina, accelerating wound healing, alleviating upper respiratory conditions, and calming indigestion. It may also help boost immunity, increase the efficacy of antibiotics, and possess anticancer properties. The fruits also contain alpha-hydroxy acid, a chemical effective in exfoliating the skin that is commonly added to wrinkle-reducing creams and cosmetic products.

Cultivation and Preparation

PINEAPPLE LOVES WARMTH AND SUN; IT REQUIRES A FROST-FREE environment. It does best in well-drained sandy soil that is somewhat acidic. It is drought tolerant, but plants that receive adequate water produce sweeter fruit. Cultivated varieties are propagated vegetatively in a number of ways: from slips arising from the stalk, from suckers, or from the spiky crowns. Bromelain and alpha-hydroxy acids are found only in small amounts in pineapple fruits; bromelain is concentrated in the plant's stem. Extracts of bromelain are available in supplement form.

Research

SINCE THE DISCOVERY OF BROMELAIN'S THERAPEUTIC PROPerties in 1957, hundreds of scientific papers have reported research on the chemical compound. Bromelain is not one substance, but a mixture of sulfur-containing **enzymes** that break down proteins. In 1972 researchers discovered that bromelain prevents the aggregation of blood **platelets**, which occurs during the blood clotting process following an injury. Subsequent studies have shown that bromelain appears to exert its **anti-inflammatory** effects by inhibiting the formation of fibrin and blocking the production of other substances that increase swelling and pain at the site of an injury. Bromelain also acts to break down clots in damaged tissue and hasten healing. Considerable laboratory and clinical evidence supports the long-held claim that bromelain speeds healing and disappearance of soft tissue bruises and similar injuries. Research also has revealed that bromelain assists in activation of T-cells, which play critical roles in the body's immune defenses. In a number of foreign countries, bromelain is administered along with certain antibiotics to intensify their effects in fighting infection or disease. The compound has been reported to speed healing of stomach ulcers in animals and to stimulate cytokine production, a substance known to inhibit development of tumors. Bromelain is considered to have low toxicity; few side effects in human clinical trials involving moderate doses of bromelain have been observed. However, enzymes in bromelain are potential allergens and may cause allergic reactions in some people.

THE PATH OF THE PINEAPPLE

The pineapple is a South American native that made its way into Central America and across the Caribbean to the islands of the West Indies as a result of trade among indigenous tribes. Highly prized for its intensely sweet, juicy fruit, it was a staple at feasts and the juice was fermented to make wine. In 1493, when the European explorer Christopher Columbus was making his second voyage to the Caribbean, he and his crew went ashore on the island of Guadeloupe where they encountered pineapples for the first time. Columbus dubbed the new culinary treat "the pine of the Indies," possibly because its rough, segmented exterior is somewhat reminiscent of a pine cone. He carried pineapples back to Spain, where the sweet fruit became a coveted treat on the tables of royalty and a novel species for avid horticulturists. After their "discovery" by the Spanish, pineapples were carried around the world on sailing ships as a means to stave off scurvy. Pineapples reached England in 1660. In colonial America, pineapples became the symbol of fine hospitality—serving the expensive fruit to guests was a reflection of the host and hostess's place in society. Pineapples did not reach Hawaii, a major source of pineapple production in the world today, until 1813.

See Also: *Medical Botany: Plants Affecting Human Health* by W. Lewis and M. Elvin-Lewis, John Wiley & Sons, 2003; *Pharmacognosy, 9th ed.* by V. Tyler, L. Brady, J. Robbers, Lea & Febiger, 1988.

Common Name Pomegranate

Latin Name *Punica granatum*

Family Punicaceae

Parts Used Fruits, seeds

Description A small tree growing to 20 feet or (rarely) more in height, pomegranate has glossy leaves about three inches long. The crinkled, orange-red to purplish flowers are solitary, growing in clusters at the ends of small branchlets. The rounded, yellowish to purple-red, thick-skinned fruits enclose an edible, juicy pulp and are filled with dark seeds that make up about half of the fruit's mass.

Habitat Pomegranate is thought to have originated in the Trans-Caucasus to Afghanistan, including the north of present-day Syria, Iraq, and Iran. Through cultivation it spread to India, China, Africa, and Mediterranean Europe centuries ago. Wild forms in Central Asia have great diversity in the size and sweetness of the fruits, time of ripening, juiciness, and the ratio of flesh to seeds.

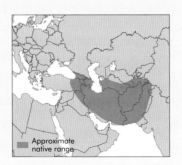

Approximate native range

Pomegranate
Punica granatum

POMEGRANATE SEEDS ARE FOUND IN MIDDLE BRONZE Age archaeological sites at Jericho and Nimrud in Israel, dating the cultivation of those seeds to at least 5,000 years ago. Sumerian records indicate pomegranates were planted under date palms from at least 3,000 B.C. In the Ebers Papyrus dating to 1530 B.C., an **infusion** of pomegranate root is recorded as a treatment for intestinal parasites, a use that continues today. The name "pomegranate" derives from the Lain *malum granatum* meaning "apple with many seeds." Early Jewish, Islamic, and Christian art all use pomegranates to symbolize concepts of unity and eternal life. The pomegranate is often cited in the Old Testament and is connected with myths of Middle Eastern and Mediterranean cultures relating to spiritual and agricultural abundance.

Traditional and Current Medicinal Uses

ANCIENT HISTORY EXPERTS HAVE THEORIZED THAT THE "APPLE with many seeds" could have been the famed "apple" of the Garden of Eden. That theory is based on many ancient texts. Second-century Greek physician Soranus, foremost writer on gynecology in the ancient world, included in his works five prescriptions using pomegranate for oral contraceptives and vaginal suppositories. Other writers who described the use of pomegranate seeds or rinds to prevent conception included Hippocrates, Dioscorides, and Ibn Sina (Avicenna, 980–1037). (Pomegranate is still used as a folk contraceptive in some parts of modern Africa.) Pomegranates arrived in China from Sumatra during the Han dynasty. The medicinal use of the fruit rinds first appears in the sixth-century Chinese work *Ming Yi Bei Lu* (*Miscellaneous Records of Famous Physicians*) by Tao Hong-jing.

In modern herbal medicine in China, pomegranate rinds (*shi liu pi*) are used to check diarrhea, treat dysentery, arrest bleeding, and to treat intestinal worms. Pomegranate is listed as an official drug in the *Pharmacopoeia of the People's Republic of China*. In the U.S. and Europe, pomegranate products are increasingly valued for their **antioxidant** activity and their potential in cancer prevention.

Cultivation and Preparation

POMEGRANATE THRIVES IN SEMI-ARID SOILS OF SUBTROPICAL climates that have hot summers and cool winters, making it suitable for the southwestern U.S. from southern Texas to central California. It likes a slightly alkaline soil and does well in a loamy, well-drained soil, but also grows well in barren soils where other fruit trees will not survive. It can be propagated by seeds, by hardwood cuttings, or by layering.

Research

ONLY IN THE 21ST CENTURY HAVE POMEGRANATES BEGUN to gain popularity in the U.S. A 2002 *New York Times* article cited a survey indicating that only 5 percent of Americans had ever tasted pomegranates. But in the past few years, pomegranate juice has become widely available as a beverage in the American market. Research on pomegranate fruit **extracts** has shown them to be rich in anthocyanidins known to have antioxidant and **anti-inflammatory** properties. Laboratory studies have also shown potential immuno-stimulating activity and antidiabetic activity (for flower extracts), and have confirmed the 1,500-year-old Chinese traditional medicine use of the rinds to treat dysentery and diarrhea. Fermented fruit extracts, a **polyphenol**-rich water extract of the rind, recently were found to promote differentiation of leukemia cells, causing them to revert to normal cells. Pomegranate extracts are suggested for further evaluation in breast, prostate, and colon cancer, among others. Future research will focus on a potential prevention role, as well as a role in supportive treatment in diagnosed cancers. Modern pharmacology also provides a scientific rationale to pomegranate's ancient use as a contraceptive. Lab studies in the 1970s and 1980s showed female rats fed pomegranate had 72 percent as many pregnancies as a control group. A similar study of female guinea pigs fed pomegranate and then paired with males resulted in no pregnancies. In both studies, four months after pomegranate feeding stopped, fertility returned to normal.

CAUTION Rare allergic reactions have been associated with pomegranate fruits and seeds.

OF LIFE AND DEATH

Since ancient times pomegranates have been associated with renewal of life, abundance, and also with blood and death. During the ancient Greek Thesmophoria festival, celibate female initiates were forbidden from eating pomegranates. The pomegranate was the emblem of the Greek goddess Demeter. According to Greek myth, Hades (Pluto), the god of death, abducted Persephone, the daughter of Demeter and Zeus, and took her to his underworld domain. Demeter was the goddess of the harvest. When Demeter discovered Hades had taken her daughter to the underworld, Demeter withdrew from her earthly duties, and the earth became infertile. Zeus intervened and ordered the release of Persephone. Hades reluctantly obliged, but before she was allowed to leave the underworld, Hades enticed her to eat a few pomegranate seeds. When she did, she was tied to the underworld forever, bound to return for one third to one half of each year. Each bite of pomegranate she consumed determined the number of months given to fall and winter, the time of year when crops and plants die and Earth is not fertile.

PUNICA GRANATUM | Pomegranate

See Also: American Botanical Council, www.Herbalgram.org/default.asp?c=pomehrt; *Eve's Herbs: A History of Conception and Abortion in the West* by J. Riddle, Harvard University Press, 1997.

Psyllium
Plantago psyllium

Common Names Psyllium, blond psyllium, Indian plantain, *ispaghul* (India)

Latin Names *Plantago psyllium, P. ovata*

Family Plantaginaceae

Parts Used Seeds, seed husks

Description *P. psyllium* is a small herbaceous annual with long leaves and straight stalks that shoot up about a foot, ending in clusters of many small white flowers. Flowers give way to seed capsules in about 60 days. The seeds are small, dark, and glossy, often with a reddish tint.

Habitat Psyllium likes sandy soil and dry, sunny weather. It is native to India and Iran and grows throughout the Mediterranean region, and in Europe, India, Pakistan, North Africa, Iran, and western Asia. It is cultivated in the southwestern United States.

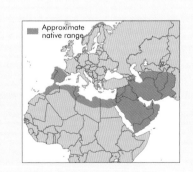

Approximate native range

P SYLLIUM IS THE SOURCE OF A SOLUBLE FIBER THAT IS extracted from the husks and seeds of several *Plantago* species. The genus *Plantago* contains more than 200 species; several members of the genus are commonly referred to as psyllium. Psyllium contains **mucilage**, a gelatinous substance that makes it useful as a thickening stabilizer, commonly used in foods and cosmetics. The same properties make it an intestinal regulator of constipation and diarrhea that acts to normalize the absorption of sugar and reduce cholesterol levels. Recently, psyllium has gained attention for its approval by the United States Food and Drug Administration (FDA) as an herb that reduces cholesterol and the risk of heart disease, which is still the number one cause of death in the United States. The United States is the world's largest importer of psyllium.

Traditional and Current Medicinal Uses

PSYLLIUM HAS LONG BEEN PART OF TRADITIONAL MEDICINE throughout Asia and Europe. *Plantago* species may have been used as a food source by the Aztecs. Blonde psyllium is part of the national **pharmacopoeias** of India, China, Japan, France, Germany, Great Britain, and the United States. Psyllium is used mainly for the mucilage (highest in *P. ovata*) milled from the seed coat or husk of the plant. The ground mucilage is a water-loving, white, fibrous material that swells to ten times its size in water. Psyllium is used primarily as a dietary fiber and a bulk laxative, which is not digested, but, by purely mechanical means, stimulates intestinal movement. In the intestines, psyllium creates a large, soft, thick, gooey mass that makes its way through the intestine, triggering contractions, coating the walls, slowing digestion, and evening out absorption levels. Such activity has some beneficial effects that may make psyllium worth taking even if constipation is not a problem.

In modern herbal medicine, psyllium is used as a treatment for irritable bowel syndrome, hemorrhoids, inflammatory bowel disease, colon cancer, high cholesterol, diabetes, obesity, high blood pressure, and heart disease.

Cultivation and Preparation

PSYLLIUM LIKES LIGHT, WELL-DRAINED, SANDY, LOAMY SOIL, and does not require many nutrients. Its odorless, tasteless seeds are small and vulnerable. Five hundred seeds weigh less than a gram. Seedlings are frost sensitive and are not planted until after the last frost. When the flower spikes ripen, they turn reddish brown as the lower leaves dry out and the upper leaves yellow. Two months after that, they are mature. Psyllium is vulnerable just before harvest time: It becomes brittle when ripe and is easily shattered by rain. A warm night and a cloudy, wet day can ruin a crop. A perfect harvest requires clear, sunny, dry weather and is gathered in the morning after the dew is gone. The plant is cut halfway up the stalk, bound, and dried for a few days. Thrashing and winnowing are involved processes of sifting and grinding with stone until finally the seeds are repeatedly sieved and screened through finer and finer mesh.

Research

IN A RANDOMIZED, DOUBLE-BLIND PLACEBO STUDY OF 20 patients with chronic constipation, all the subjects that took psyllium reported good results—all symptoms were reversed, and participants experienced no adverse effects. Another study compared psyllium to bran for regularity and alleviation of symptoms of irritable bowel syndrome. Though both bran and psyllium worked well, those taking psyllium experienced less gas and bloating. Research studies also show psyllium to be effective at lowering low-density lipoprotein levels (LDL) in the blood, both by preventing the absorption of LDL and by increasing consumption of the "bad" cholesterol. Psyllium also appears to be a cholesterol medicine that does not have a negative effect on weight, blood pressure, and HDL, glucose, iron, or zinc levels. Further, research also suggests that psyllium lowers blood sugar levels, requiring less insulin in insulin-dependent diabetics and helping to prevent the onset of diabetes in those who are vulnerable.

CAUTION Allergic symptoms may arise in a small percentage of psyllium users. Cases of asthma, rhinitis (with swelling), and nausea also have been reported.

PSYLLIUM PSNACKS IN PSPACE

On February 20, 1962, astronaut John Glenn, Jr., became the first American to go into orbit, 120 miles above Earth in the Friendship 7 space capsule. Thirty-six years later, on October 29, 1998, Glenn became the oldest person to go up in space, this time as a payload specialist on the space shuttle *Discovery*. Aboard the space shuttle and other spacecraft, astronauts eat rehydratable, thermostabilized, irradiated versions of anything from shrimp cocktail to fettuccine alfredo. On the *Discovery* flight Glenn requested apple crisp psyllium wafers during the nine-day flight. His fellow payload specialist, Japanese astronaut Chiaki Mukai, requested the cinnamon spice psyllium wafers. Since psyllium made it into space, it has become a major herbal supplement not just for the elderly but for everybody, particularly in breakfast cereals. The Kellogg Company, maker of many cereals, saw the research indicating psyllium's ability to lower cholesterol and prevent heart disease as a marketing message. They petitioned the FDA for the right to make such claims on psyllium products, citing 57 clinical studies since 1965. In 1997 the FDA amended the right to make therapeutic claims to include soluble fiber from psyllium husks. Psyllium has never been more popular or sold in so many forms and products, and John Glenn is still going strong.

See Also: Herbal Medicine Expanded Commission E Monographs by M. Blumenthal, A. Goldberg, and J. Brinckmann, American Botanical Council, 2000; *World Health Organization (WHO) Monographs on Selected Medicinal Plants, Vol. 1*, 1999.

PLANTAGO PSYLLIUM | Psyllium

Pulsatilla

Pulsatilla vulgarus

I N EUROPE PASQUEFLOWERS ARE BELOVED WILDFLOWERS and harbingers of spring as their bell-shaped, lavender-blue heads poke up through late-winter snows to bloom. This diminutive herb typically flowers around Easter. In fact, the 16th-century herbalist John Gerard named the plant "Pasqueflower" based on that coincidence. The word "Pasque" is derived from the French word for Easter, and so *Pasque floure* is literally "Easter flower." The genus name, *Pulsatilla*, comes from the Latin *pulso*, meaning "to strike or set in violent motion." The link to Pasqueflower is not entirely clear, although some sources suggest that the reference is to the fact that all parts of the herb are poisonous and, if eaten, can cause violent stomach upset.

Traditional and Current Medicinal Uses

PULSATILLA WAS VERY POPULAR IN HERBAL MEDICINE IN centuries past, and was employed in treating a wide variety of complaints. It was traditionally used as a remedy for cough, nervous distress and sleeplessness, and spasmodic pains of the reproductive system in both men and women. As such, it was often prescribed for premenstrual pain and menstrual cramps, especially in conjunction with nervous exhaustion. Pulsatilla was also recommended for gastrointestinal and urinary tract problems, indigestion, nerve pain, migraine headaches, and skin and mucous membrane inflammations. During the 19th century, pulsatilla was a popular treatment for menstrual problems, conjunctivitis (also known as pink-eye) and other types of eye inflammations, severe coughs (such as whooping cough), expelling tapeworms, eczema and syphilitic skin eruptions, and acute meningitis.

In modern herbal medicine, the herb is still used to relax spasms, relieve pain, and calm the nerves. The plant is taken for premenstrual syndrome, menstrual cramps, ovarian pain, inflammation of the male or female reproductive organs, tension headaches, stomach pains, neuralgia, insomnia, bacterial skin infections, spasmodic coughs such as those characteristic of asthma and whooping cough, and other lung ailments

Common Names Pulsatilla, European Pasque-flower, meadow anemone, windflower

Latin Names *Pulsatilla vulgarus*, synonym *Anemone pulsatilla*

Family Ranunculaceae

Parts Used Dried aerial parts

Description A petite perennial herb that grows 6 to 12 inches high, pulsatilla has stems covered with silky hairs, finely cut leaves, and large, bell-shaped, deep- to pale-purple flowers. The flowers are followed by fuzzy seed heads.

Habitat Native to Europe, pulsatilla thrives in chalky soils in dry grasslands and in alpine meadows.

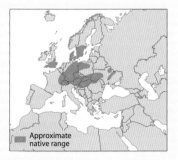

Approximate native range

such as bronchitis. Extracts of pulsatilla are used medicinally to treat certain inner eye diseases, including iritis (inflammation of the iris), scleritis (inflammation of the sclera, the coating of the eyeball), retinal disorders, cataracts, and glaucoma. Several other species of *Pulsatilla* are also used in herbal medicine. In China, for example, *P. chinensis* (*bai tou weng*) is considered to be a very effective treatment for gastrointestinal infections, especially amoebic dysentery.

Cultivation and Preparation

PULSATILLA PREFERS FULL SUN TO PARTIAL SHADE IN WELLdrained, slightly alkaline soil. It can be propagated by seed, division, or cuttings. For the herbal medicine market, aerial parts of pulsatilla is cut when the plants are in bloom. These are dried for medicinal use; fresh pulsatilla is not used because it is extremely irritating to skin and mucous membranes.

Research

PULSATILLA IS QUITE TOXIC WHEN FRESH. THIS IS BECAUSE THE fresh herb contains a compound known as ranunculin, a potent poison. Any crushing or cutting of the plant's tissues releases an **enzyme** that changes ranunculin into protoanemonin, which is a highly irritating, yellow **volatile oil**. Protoanemonin is very unstable, however, and gradually breaks down chemically into a nontoxic substance called anemonin. Protoanemonin can cause severe skin irritations, even blistering, and if ingested, leads to severe damage of the kidneys and urinary tract and paralysis of the central nervous system. As harvested pulsatilla dries, however, protoanemonin rapidly breaks down chemically until only a nontoxic byproduct (anemonin) remains. Nevertheless, the speed at which this chemical breakdown occurs in drying pulsatilla, and when and whether the chemical process is complete, is impossible to know without chemical analysis. For this reason, dried pulsatilla should always be used with great care by qualified practitioners.

> CAUTION Pulsatilla is poisonous and can be extremely irritating. Preparations made from this herb should be administered only by qualified practitioners.

Pulsatilla used to be classified as *Anemone pulsatilla* and is sometimes called windflower (as is another species, *P. pratensis*). The word "anemone" comes from the Greek, *anemos*, which means "wind." Two different legends account for the association of anemones and the wind. In Roman myth, a nymph named Anemone lived at the court of Flora, the goddess of flowers and springtime. Flora's husband, Zephyr, was god of the west wind. Zephyr fell in love with Anemone and when Flora discovered this, she banished the nymph from the court. Heartbroken, Anemone died of sadness. Zephyr then persuaded Venus to change Anemone's body into a flower that would come back to life each spring.

Another version appears in Greek myth. In this legend, the handsome mortal Adonis lived with the goddess Aphrodite, and the two often hunted in the woods. Adonis chased game, and Aphrodite followed in her chariot. Eventually Ares, Aphrodite's ex-lover, grew jealous. Disguised as a boar, he attacked Adonis, goring him to death. When Aphrodite appeared, she tried to save Adonis, but he died. As she carried his body out of the woods, crimson anemones sprang up where a drop of his blood fell. It was said that the wind caused anemones to open each spring, but soon blew the petals away. Anemone was a reminder that what brings forth life also ends it.

See Also: *A Field Guide to Medicinal Plants and Herbs: Eastern and Central North America, 2nd ed.* by S. Foster and J. Duke, Houghton Mifflin, 2000; *Herbal Medicine, 2nd ed.* by R. Weiss and V. Fintelmann, Thieme, 2000.

Pumpkin
Cucurbita pepo

TOGETHER WITH OTHER MEMBERS OF THE *CUCURBITA* genus, the familiar bright-orange pumpkin was cultivated in Central America and Mexico at least 14,000 years ago. Today we associate this vining herb's large fruits—which botanists classify as berries—with Halloween jack-o-lanterns and fragrant pumpkin pie. But Native Americans discovered the medicinal powers of pumpkin long ago. The large, plentiful seeds of the fruits have been used for centuries as an agent to expel intestinal worms. As a deworming treatment, pumpkin is quite effective and safe enough to be used by pregnant women and children. More recently, pumpkin has become a popular herbal remedy for relieving some of the annoying symptoms of enlarged prostate in men, at least in the early stages.

Traditional and Current Medicinal Uses

PUMPKIN WAS WIDELY USED IN TRADITIONAL NATIVE AMERICAN medicine to expel intestinal roundworms and kill and expel tapeworms. But the plant and its hefty, pulpy fruits had other medicinal uses as well. In Central America, the Maya applied the sap of pumpkin to burns. The Cherokee, Iroquois, and Menominee all used the seeds as a **diuretic**; the Cherokee also employed them as an aid to treat bedwetting in children. The Meskwaki made a **decoction** out of pumpkin stem that was helpful for a variety of female complaints, while the Navajo used the leaves to calm upset stomachs. The Cocopa rubbed the oily seeds on their hands for protection against cold. The Pima made a paste of the ground seeds to cleanse and soften skin. Pumpkin seeds were an ingredient in preparations that the Zuni used externally for swellings and rheumatism. In Central Europe, pumpkin has long been regarded as a remedy for the prevention and treatment of enlarged prostate, a condition known medically as benign prostatic hyperplasia, or BPH. Traditionally, men in Bulgaria, Turkey, and Ukraine ate handfuls of dried, ripe pumpkin seeds to alleviate this condition.

In modern herbal medicine, pumpkin seed and pumpkin seed oil continue to be used for the symptomatic relief of BPH, as well as for other bladder irritations. In

Common Names Pumpkin, vegetable marrow, field pumpkin

Latin Name *Cucurbita pepo*

Family Cucurbitaceae

Parts Used Seeds, flesh

Description Pumpkin is a robust, annual herbaceous vine with hollow trailing stems, large hairy leaves, coiling tendrils, and star-shaped yellow flowers. The large, tough-skinned fruits have numerous oval, flat seeds embedded in spongy flesh.

Habitat Pumpkin is native to Central America, but is grown worldwide in warm and temperate regions as a vegetable, for its oil, and as animal food.

Approximate native range

pediatric medicine in Germany, pumpkin seed preparations are used to treat irritable bladder and bed-wetting. Seed **extracts** are still employed in many parts of the world as an herbal remedy for intestinal worms. Pumpkin seed oil also is recommended for healing minor wounds, especially burns, and for chapped skin. The raw fruit is slightly diuretic and its juice is occasionally recommended for urinary complaints.

Cultivation and Preparation

THERE ARE NUMEROUS VARIETIES OF *CUCURBITA PEPO* THAT produce fruits of different shapes, sizes, and colors. Pumpkin and its relatives grow well in good soil in full sun. Vines may reach up to 30 feet in length. Flowering time is June to August, so fruits are produced for many months. The ripe pumpkins are harvested in late fall. Dried seeds are mainly used in herbal medicine preparations.

Research

PUMPKIN SEED OIL CONTAINS FATTY ACIDS, STEROLS, minerals, vitamin E, and a nonprotein **amino acid** called cucurbitin. This amino acid is thought to be responsible for the pumpkin's **anthelmintic** effects (ability to expel parastic worms). Cucurbitin is found only in the seeds, and its concentration varies widely among different species or cultivars and even among fruits of the same species. The sterols in the pumpkin seed oil exhibit **anti-inflammatory** properties, and it has been suggested that some of these sterols also may be involved in pumpkin's beneficial effects in treating enlarged prostate. One hypothesis is that the sterols inhibit a key chemical reaction associated with BPH, the conversion of the hormone testosterone into dihydrotestosterone, a chemical compound that causes prostate cells to divide (thus enlarging the prostate gland). Although more research is needed, some clinical studies have supported claims for pumpkin's use in effectively relieving many of the symptoms of early BPH.

> CAUTION Pumpkin seeds and preparations only relieve the symptoms of enlarged prostate. Treatment of this condition should be supervised by a health care professional.

Medicinal values aside, pumpkins are a delicious and versatile food that played an important culinary role in the life of many Native American tribes. Pumpkins and other types of squash were planted along with corn and beans; these three foods were the staples in the Native American diet. The Apache baked pumpkin blossoms into cakes; the Navajo used them as a seasoning for soup. Almost all tribes that grew pumpkins ate the flesh baked or roasted; sometimes it was mashed and sweetened or seasoned with salt and pepper. The Iroquois and several other tribes sliced up strips or rings of pumpkin flesh to dry and store for winter use. Dried pumpkin flesh was also ground or pulverized and then added to puddings, sauces, and other dishes or mixed with the flesh of stored whole pumpkins to improve their flavor.

Legend has it that Native Americans introduced European colonists to pumpkins. Although pumpkin pies as we know them today did not grace the first Thanksgiving table, colonists did prepare pumpkins as a dessert by slicing off their tops, removing the seeds, filling the interior with milk, spices, and honey, and then baking the fruit slowly in hot ashes. Pumpkins' bright orange flesh is rich in beta-carotene, a substance that is converted to vitamin A in the body and that is also a powerful antioxidant. Pumpkin seeds are rich in the minerals zinc and selenium.

See Also: Herbal Medicine Expanded Commission E Monographs by M. Blumenthal, A. Goldberg, and J. Brinckmann, American Botanical Council, 2000; Medicinal Herbs: History, Use, Recommended Dosages & Cautions by S. Foster, Interweave Press, 1998.

Common Names Pygeum, African plum, African cherry

Latin Name *Prunus africana*, synonym *Pygeum africanum*

Family Rosaceae

Parts Used Bark, leaves, fruit

Description This evergreen grows tall and straight with a domed crown. Its shiny leaves are serrated. White, fragrant flowers grow alone or in clusters. The red fruit, or drupes, are related to cherries, plums, and almonds. The blackish-brown bark smells like cherry or almond leaves, when broken.

Habitat Pygeum grows in central and southern Africa and Madagascar in tropical mountain forests where it likes high altitudes and lots of light at the forest's edge.

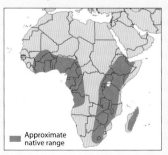

Approximate native range

Pygeum
Prunus africana

THE PYGEUM TREE HAS BEEN KNOWN BY AFRICANS FOR centuries to be good for its hard wood as well as for its healing properties. One of these healing properties applies to what is known in Africa as "old man's disease." Prostate enlargement occurs naturally in more than half of men over 50 and in 90 percent of men over 70. Benign prostatic hyperplasia, or BPH as it is known, interferes with the flow of urine as the prostate presses against the urethra and bladder. Prostate cancer can include the same symptoms, which may also be treated with pygeum. BPH can be treated with drugs, surgery, and herbal options. Drugs such as finasteride are usually a physician's first suggestion, but they can be accompanied by side effects such as nausea and fatigue. Surgery is routine, but risks include impotence and urinary incontinence. Pygeum bark has been shown to be an effective alternative for the treatment of BPH.

Traditional and Current Medicinal Uses

PYGEUM HAS BEEN USED IN AFRICA FOR CENTURIES TO TREAT prostate enlargement, inflammation, infection, malaria, fever, kidney disease, urinary tract problems, and sexual disorders.

In modern herbal medicine, uses vary by region in Africa. East Africans use pygeum as an inhalant for fevers and stomachaches and as a **purgative** for cattle and humans. In Cameroon the bark is commonly used to make a milk tea for fever and chest infections. But pygeum is known primarily to the rest of the world as a treatment for an enlarged prostate, as well as for hair loss and impotence. Use of pygeum bark for BPH was patented in 1966. Pygeum bark **extract** is the most common natural remedy for enlarged prostate in France and has been widely used in Italy and Germany for more than 30 years. In the United States, pygeum use is on the rise, especially among a rapidly increasing number of baby-boom seniors.

Cultivation and Preparation

PYGEUM CAN BE PROPAGATED BY SEED OR, SOMEWHAT LESS successfully, from cuttings. Pygeum trees grow at high altitudes—from 1,000 to 3,000 feet in Africa. Flowers bloom from fall through most of the winter and are pollinated by insects. About six months later, deep red fruits mature and fall to the forest floor. But it takes 15 years for pygeum trees to be harvestable

In Cameroon, the largest exporter of pygeum bark, overharvesting of this cash crop became a problem in the mid-1980s, when the amount of pygeum bark harvested doubled within 5 years, capturing more than 60 percent of the world market. Although harvesters had been trained to use sustainable methods—removing bark from opposite sides of the tree up to the first branch and allowing the tree to live and continue producing—things changed as prices contined to rise. When prices quadrupled, contractors abandoned responsible methods. They harvested large quantities of bark, which ultimately leads to the death of a tree, or they simply cut trees down for easier bark removal. Cultivation continues in Cameroon and Kenya, but on a small scale that does not meet international demand.

Research

PYGEUM'S ACTIVE INGREDIENTS INCLUDE **TRITERPENES** THAT produce **anti-inflammatory** effects and fatty acid compounds that prevent cholesterol buildup. Many clinical trials indicate pygeum's effectiveness for treating BPH, including reducing symptoms of urinary frequency, volume, and flow, as well as the reduction of secondary symptoms like headache and gastrointestinal discomfort. More than 600 subjects have been studied in 10 **double-blind, placebo**-controlled trials. Typically, notable improvement is reported within two months and lasts for at least a month after treatment. Other studies indicate pygeum's effectiveness for treating male sexual dysfunction and infections of the prostate and seminal vesicles. Preliminary animal research also suggests pygeum's potential for increasing semen viability, hair growth, and for treating urinary tract conditions and fever.

> CAUTION Pygeum should not be used before a proper medical evaluation is obtained to rule out prostate cancer. The most common side effect of pygeum is mild gastrointestinal distress. Pygeum appears to be nontoxic; however, safety in young children, pregnant or nursing women, or those with severe liver or kidney disease is unknown.

SEEDLINGS OF HOPE

Located on the Cameroon coast on the Gulf of Guinea, the Limbe Botanic Garden was founded in 1892 by a group of Germans and soon became one of the most important in the world for acclimatizing exotic crop species such as coffee, rubber, and sugarcane. After passing through British and Cameroonian hands, the garden ended up under governmental control and fell into a state of decline. But in 1988, just as overharvesting was devastating wild pygeum, a British-Cameroonian partnership led to renovation and redevelopment. The garden stresses the link between people and plants, featuring *P. africana* prominently in the medicinal plant section. Garden staff travel around Cameroon giving slide shows on the importance of plants, teaching sustainable harvesting of roots and barks, and educating people on the conservation of forest resources. The Botanic Garden helped the Cameroon Development Corporation establish the first plantation of pygeum trees in the town of Moliwe, providing 7,000 seedlings. Since then they have helped supply thousands more seedlings to projects around the country, consulted on the establishment of a gene bank for *P. africana*, and supplied materials to a forestry school to undertake further trials in *P. africana* propagation.

See Also: *Medicinal Herbs: History, Use, Recommended Dosages & Cautions* by S. Foster, Interweave Press, 1998; *Tyler's Honest Herbal,* 4th ed. by S. Foster and V. Tyler, The Haworth Herbal Press, 1999.

PRUNUS AFRICANA | Pygeum

Queen Anne's Lace

Daucus carota

THE GENTLY NODDING FLOWER HEADS OF QUEEN ANNE'S lace are a familiar summertime sight in meadows and roadsides throughout temperate regions around the world. *Daucus carota* is one of 22 species in the genus *Daucus*, but the only one widely used and cultivated. Centuries of selective breeding have transformed the wild variety (*Daucus carota carota*), with its nearly inedible bitter root, into the familiar vegetable (*Daucus carota sativa*) widely grown in North America, Europe, North Africa, and many parts of Asia. Cultivated carrots typically have orange roots, but other edible varieties range from yellow to dark red and purple. Carrots are easily digested and nutritious, being especially rich in beta-carotene, which is converted to Vitamin A in the liver. Both wild carrot and its cultivated cousins are used medicinally.

Common Names Queen Anne's lace, wild carrot, bird's nest, bee's nest

Latin Name *Daucus carota*

Family Apiaceae

Parts Used Root, seeds, leaves, stems

Description *Daucus carota* is a biennial herb with fernlike foliage and dense umbels (umbrella-like clusters) of small white flowers (the center flower is usually pink or purple). Small flattened seeds are covered with hook-tipped bristles. Queen Anne's lace (*D. carota* ssp. *carota*) has a thin, white, bitter taproot, while the widely cultivated subspecies (*D. carota* ssp. *sativus*) has an orange, succulent, edible taproot.

Habitat Wild carrot is native to Europe, temperate Asia, and North Africa but has become widely naturalized in many temperate regions worldwide, including North America where it is a common weed in fields and other grassy places.

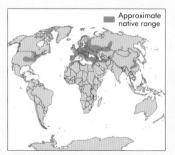

Approximate native range

Traditional and Current Medicinal Uses

WILD CARROT HAS BEEN VALUED FOR ITS MEDICINAL PROPERTIES since ancient times. More than 2,000 years ago, Hippocrates described how the crushed seeds of wild carrot were used as a contraceptive. In traditional **Ayurvedic medicine**, the seeds of the herb were considered to be an aphrodisiac and stimulant and were also used to treat kidney and nervous conditions. Throughout the Middle Ages, wild carrot was appreciated for its success in treating bladder and kidney conditions including urinary stones and cystitis, for relieving gas, as a mild laxative, and as a **diuretic** for **edema**. Preparations of wild carrot were used in **poultices** to soothe a wide variety of sores, and even cancerous skin tumors. Among Native Americans, wild carrot had significant medicinal value. It was used by the Cherokee to reduce external swellings, by the Micmac as a **purgative**, and by the Iroquois for blood disorders, paleness, and lack of appetite. The Delaware, Oklahoma, and Mohegan all used wild carrot to treat diabetes. Wild carrot also has been widely used to expel intestinal worms.

In modern herbal medicine, wild carrot is used primarily to treat kidney and bladder conditions, as an **anthelmintic**, for indigestion, flatulence, and gout. Raw carrots and carrot juice are highly recommended by many health practitioners because they contain high levels of beta-carotene, a Vitamin A **precursor** with anticancer effects. Vitamin A, in turn, is the source of substances that enhance eyesight, improving both keenness of sight and the ability to see well in dim light.

Cultivation and Preparation

WILD CARROT PREFERS WELL-DRAINED, FERTILE, ALKALINE SOIL in full sun or light shade. It is propagated by seed sown in spring or summer (it readily self-sows). Whole plants are cut in summer and dried for medicinal use. Seeds are collected in autumn when ripe, and then either dried for **infusions** or crushed and distilled for their oil. The fresh roots (primarily those of cultivated varieties) are used freshly grated as well as for their extracted juice.

Research

THE SEEDS OF WILD CARROT CONTAIN A **VOLATILE OIL** THAT is high in **flavonoids, monoterpenes, sesquiterpenes,** and a number of other active compounds. At least one of the monoterpenes exerts documented diuretic activity. Wild carrot's use as a contraceptive appears to have a scientific basis as well. Research conducted on laboratory animals found the wild carrot interferes with the implantation of fertilized eggs in the wall of the uterus. Chinese studies have also indicated that the oil from wild carrot seeds may block the synthesis of the hormone progesterone, which could also have a contraceptive effect. Cultivated carrots are especially rich in the **antioxidants** beta-carotene and alpha-carotene, calcium, potassium, Vitamins A, B1, B2, C, and E, and copper, iron, magnesium, manganese, phosphorous, and sulphur. Studies have shown that beta-carotene is a powerful antioxidant, an immune system booster, and may significantly help reduce the risk of heart attack and stroke. Along with alpha- carotene, beta-carotene also exhibits certain types of anticancer effects. Carrots are a healthful and natural source of Vitamin A.

TOO CLOSE FOR COMFORT

Wild carrot is one of many white-flowered members of the parsley family (Apiaceae), including several that are extremely poisonous. Unless you are a botanical expert, it can be very difficult to distinguish the safe herbs from the deadly ones because they so closely resemble one another. *Conium maculatum*, commonly known as poison hemlock, is an herb that could easily be mistaken for wild carrot. Like wild carrot, it has finely divided leaves and lovely umbels (umbrella-like clusters) of small white flowers. Poison hemlock has been misidentified not only as wild carrot but also as fennel and parsley; its fleshy, white, unbranched roots might also pass for parsnips. Such cases of mistaken identity can be fatal because poison hemlock is highly toxic, especially its roots and seeds. The plant contains a strong neurotoxin, composed of at least five poisonous alkaloids, which attacks the central nervous system in mammals, including humans. The poison is quite volatile. Simply touching the plant, or breathing the air around it, is enough to cause toxic reactions. Poisoning by poison hemlock is not uncommon in livestock, because the plant is widely distributed across the United States and is often found growing along roadsides, ditches, and field borders. Probably the most famous victim of poisoning from poison hemlock was the Greek philosopher Socrates (470–399 B.C.), who was sentenced to death for impiety and forced to drink a potent solution of the plant.

See Also: *A Field Guide to Medicinal Plants and Herbs: Eastern and Central North America, 2nd ed.* by S. Foster and J. Duke, Houghton Mifflin, 2000; *A Field Guide to Medicinal Plants and Herbs: Western North America* by S. Foster and C. Hobbs, Houghton Mifflin, 2002.

DAUCUS CAROTA | Queen Anne's Lace

Red Cinchona
Cinchona officinalis

RED CINCHONA BELONGS TO THE FAMILY RUBIACEAE, which also includes well-known shrubs and trees such as coffee and gardenia. *Cinchona* bark is the source of a bitter **alkaloid**, quinine, which has long been used to treat the parasitic disease malaria. There are a number of species in the genus *Cinchona*. Not all are used to produce quinine. In fact, some contain virtually no quinine at all. Species that reliably produce significant amounts of the substance and are thus important in herbal medicine are *Cinchona officinalis*, *C. succirubra*, and *C. ledgeriana*. In addition to its use as an herbal remedy, quinine has long been enjoyed as a flavoring—it is what gives tonic water its distinctive bitter taste. In fact, the drink gin-and-tonic was originally developed and consumed in the tropics, where malaria was typically rampant, as a palatable way to help prevent malaria attacks.

Common Names Red cinchona, quinine, Peruvian bark, Jesuit's bark

Latin Name *Cinchona officinalis*

Family Rubiaceae

Parts Used Bark, roots

Description A small tropical evergreen tree, *Cinchona officinalis* grows 15 to 50 feet, and in some cases taller, depending on the species. It has large, flat, broadly elliptical leaves that are glossy green with pronounced veins. Fragrant, pink flowers are produced in long panicles, followed by small seeds that are surrounded by a papery wing and dispersed by the wind.

Habitat *Cinchona* is native to the eastern slopes of the Amazonian region of the Andes in northwestern South America. It is widely cultivated in many tropical countries.

Approximate native range

Traditional and Current Medicinal Uses

FOR CENTURIES, INDIGENOUS TRIBES IN PERU BREWED A TEA made of *Cinchona* bark to treat fevers, including those caused by malaria. The bark was introduced to the European medical communy in the mid-1600s. Until the mid-1800s, *Cinchona* bark was the remedy of choice for malaria. It was also used for treating other fevers, mouth and throat ailments, indigestion, and cancer.

Today in the Amazon region of South America, *Cinchona* is still used in herbal medicine as a fever reducer, for stimulating poor appetite, and for treating gastrointestinal complaints. Among some tribes it is also viewed as a natural cancer treatment and is used to combat amoebic dysentery, flu and lung ailments, nerve pain, lower back pain, diarrhea, dysentery, and heart problems. In European herbal medicine, quinine derived from *Cinchona* is used for antispasmodic, antimalarial, and antibacterial properties and as a fever-reducer. It is recommended for liver, spleen, and gallbladder disorders, anemia, irregular heart beat, and alcoholism. In the U.S., the herb was formerly used as a tonic and digestive aid, to regulate heart rate, to treat colds, flu, and indigestion, for varicose veins, and to relieve leg cramps.

Cultivation and Preparation

NATIVE TO SOUTH AMERICA, CINCHONA IS INTENSIVELY cultivated in India, Indonesia, and parts of Africa. *Cinchona* trees are propagated from cuttings. Bark is harvested in much the same way it has been for hundreds of years. The trunks of the trees are beaten until the bark loosens enough so it can be peeled off. Bark partially regenerates, but a tree typically can only survive a few cycles of bark removal before it is uprooted and replaced. In the past, dried *Cinchona* bark was ground into a fine powder that could be mixed with water or wine. Now it is typically taken in tablet form, although it can also be administered intravenously. It is estimated that roughly half of the global production of quinine bark goes into the making of tonic water and bitter additives. The remainder is used in the manufacture of quinine-based drugs.

Research

THE PRIMARY ALKALOID EXTRACTED FROM CINCHONA BARK, quinine, is a powerful **antipyretic**—it helps lower body temperature. People suffering from malaria typically experience cyclical bouts of extreme chills and burning fever, when the body temperature can reach a dangerous 107 degrees Fahrenheit. By lowering fever, quinine helps malarial patients survive the most critical stages of the disease. It also seems to slow the reproductive rate of malarial parasites, and thus the speed of the infection. Over time, quinine was largely superceded by chemically synthesized antimalarial drugs such as chloroquine and mefloquine. But as more and more drug-resistant strains of the disease surface, quinine is experiencing something of a comeback as an antimalarial. Scientists are finding that some drug-resistant strains do respond to natural quinine bark **extracts**. A more recent use for quinine, in the form of the drug quinidine, is in relieving muscle spasms and nocturnal leg cramps, and in treating heart arrhythmia. In clinical studies, it has been found that quinidine is more effective than **placebos** in helping to restore normal heart beat in patients in atrial fibrillation and more effective at preventing relapses of atrial fibrillation after initial restoration of normal heart rhythm.

Malaria is a parasitic disease caused by several species of the one-celled protozoan, *Plasmodium*, which infects certain types of mosquitoes. The name "malaria" comes from the Latin *mal aria*, or "bad air," and refers to the early belief that the disease was caused by breathing the fetid air of swamps. Only later did people realize that it was not the air that was causing the problem, but the mosquitoes that were breeding in the swampy waters. Quechua Indians in the tropical forests of northwestern South America used *Cinchona* bark to treat malaria and other fevers long before Europeans arrived on the continent. But around 1630, Spanish Jesuits learned of the tree and its curative bark. According to legend, the name *Cinchona* came from a recovered malaria victim—the Countess of Chinchon, wife of a viceroy of Peru—cured of the disease by using the bark in 1638. By 1645, *Cinchona* bark had made its way to Rome. By 1677, *Cinchona* had been added to the London *Pharmacopoeia*. The powerful alkaloid quinine was isolated from *Cinchona* bark in 1820. Seeing an opportunity, British and Dutch entrepreneurs smuggled *Cinchona* seeds out of South America in the mid-1800s, eventually founding quinine plantations in Java, India, and Ceylon. By 1944, however, several synthetic quinine substitutes were developed and natural quinine was no longer in high demand.

See Also: Medical Botany: Plants Affecting Human Health by W. Lewis and M. Elvin-Lewis, John Wiley & Sons, 2003; *Pharmacognosy, 9th ed.,* by V. Tyler, L. Brady, J. Robbers, Lea & Febiger, 1988.

CINCHONA OFFICINALIS | Red Cinchona

Red Clover
Trifolium pratense

Common Names Red clover, cow clover, meadow clover, peavine clover, honeysuckle trefoil, king's crown, sweet kitty clover, sleeping maggie, and bee-bread

Latin Name *Trifolium pratense*

Family Fabaceae

Parts Used Leaves, flowers

Description One of the largest clovers, this short-lived perennial sometimes acts as a biennial. Red clover grows hairy stems one to three feet high from which leaves grow in threes, each with its distinctive, whitish "v." Red clover's round flowers blossom light pink to reddish-purple and occasionally white.

Habitat Red clover is native to the eastern Mediterranean and Asia and naturalized to Britain, the U.S., and many parts of the world.

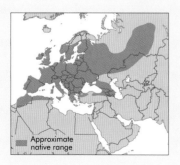

Approximate native range

R ED CLOVER, A MEMBER OF THE PEA FAMILY, HAS LONG been praised as an excellent forage crop for live-stock as well as a crop cultivated by good farmers as an excellent rejuvenator of the soil. For the ancient Celtic priesthood of Druids, clovers were symbols of Earth, sea, and heaven, and for Christians, a symbol of the Trinity. Its use as an herbal remedy, however, has always been in the realm of alternative medicines. In 19th-century pharmacological literature it was noticeably absent and in the 20th century it was at the center of a great deal of controversy (see sidebar).

Traditional and Current Medicinal Uses

MEDICINAL RED CLOVER TEAS WAS USED BY THE CHINESE FOR coughs and by the Russians for asthma. Europeans have used red clover for digestive ailments, and Native Americans used red clover as a remedy for sore eyes, burns, and as food. Red clover was never an official drug of the **United States Pharmacopeia**, though it was recognized in the National Formulary from 1916–1947, valued as a sedative for coughs and as a "blood purifier." It was introduced by, and widely used from the 1850s to the 1920s, by American **Eclectic** medical practitioners who relied upon herbal medicine in their practice. Medicinal uses of the herb were first championed in an 1876 edition of *The American Dispensatory* by John King, who called the red clover **extract** "an excellent remedy for cancerous ulcers . . . and burns" and also praised it for "prompt relief in whooping cough."

In modern herbal medicine, herbal practitioners attribute a wide range of healing effects to the **phyto-estrogen** compounds called isoflavones in red clover. It is increasingly taken for the effects of these isoflavones, for the regulation of sex hormones, maintenance of bone density and calcium storage, for cardiovascular health, and to inhibit the growth of numerous cancer cells and cancer cell adhesion. Red clover has grown as an alternative therapy for postmenopausal women, especially in recent years in light of the increased risks now recognized as side effects of hormone replacement therapy. Though it has received less attention for premenopausal use, red clover extract-based supplements have been patented and marketed for disorders associated with high estrogen levels in pre-menopausal women.

Cultivation and Preparation

APART FROM A FEW BUTTERFLIES, BUMBLEBEES ARE THE only insects with a long enough nose to reach the nectar at the bottom of the red clover flower. Red clover depends on bees for fertilization, but it can be grown from seed sown from late winter through spring, or in late summer with a companion crop such as alfalfa or corn. Red clover likes open meadows, dry forests, and paths or borders with well-drained, loamy soil, rich in calcium and potassium. It can take more shade as a seedling than most **legumes** and tolerates poor soil and poor drainage better than alfalfa. For herbal remedies it is often taken as a tea, made from dried flowers, but is also available in pills, capsules, and **tinctures**.

Research

ISOFLAVONES ARE THE PRIMARY ACTIVE INGREDIENT FOUND in red clover. The isoflavones in red clover are known as phytoestrogen isoflavones because they activate estrogen receptors. Researchers speculate that isoflavones may attach to estrogen receptors, in the bladder, arteries, bones, and heart, relieving symptoms of premenstrual syndrome, or PMS, in some women. Interest in the health benefits of phytoestrogens has produced a new body of research on red clover. Though studies have not found red clover to reduce hot flashes, the isoflavones may act as hormone replacements to relieve symptoms in postmenopausal women. Further study is needed to understand red clover's mechanism of action in both PMS and postmenopausal symptoms. Red clover has been shown to limit development in men of benign prostate hyperplasia (BPH), a noncancerous enlargement of the prostate. Further, a pilot study in Australia reported red clover extract produced a 23 percent increase in elasticity of arteries compared with **placebo**. This study suggests potential benefits for red clover extracts in reducing risk of cardiovascular disease associated with menopause.

HOXSEY'S HOAX?

Harry M. Hoxsey (1901–1974) learned medicine from his father, a veterinarian who claimed to have cured both horses and people of cancer. On his deathbed, Harry's father left his son his secret cancer-cure formula based on red clover. Harry Hoxsey went on to become one of the longest practicing alternative healers of the 20th century. But the secret formula was as much curse as blessing. It brought him an unending stream of patients; however, he was hounded by the medical community throughout his life. After years of ridicule, Hoxsey eventually closed his treatment center in Dallas, Texas, and left the country, setting up just across the border in Tijuana, Mexico, where he continued to draw patients for his therapy. Using the Hoxsey formula, he administered a preparation known as Red Clover Tonic, taken internally or as a paste applied externally to tumors. The tonic provoked unending vehemence, particularly from Morris Fishbein, longtime editor of the *Journal of the American Medical Association*. Hoxsey was sued more than a hundred times! When the U.S. Food and Drug Administration broadened its labeling requirement to interstate shipments, Hoxsey finally revealed his herbal formula, only to be dismissed outright without even a scientific investigation. Subsequently, isolated studies have begun to demonstrate some cancer-fighting properties for ingredients in his tonic. Research continues.

See Also: A Field Guide to Medicinal Plants and Herbs: Eastern and Central North America, 2nd ed. by S. Foster and J. Duke, Houghton Mifflin, 2000; A Field Guide to Medicinal Plants and Herbs: Western North America by S. Foster and C. Hobbs, Houghton Mifflin, 2002.

Rhodiola
Rhodiola rosea

RHODIOLA, OR GOLDEN ROOT AS IT WAS KNOWN IN ancient legends, has long been considered a cure-all. The use of rhodiola goes back at least 2,000 years. The first-century Greek physician Dioscorides wrote about *rodia riza* in 77 A.D. in his *De Materia Medica*, perhaps the first drug reference book of the Western world. In the 18th century, Swedish botanist Carolus Linnaeus renamed it *Rhodiola rosea* for the rose-like fragrance of the freshly cut root. It has long been a Russian folk medicine—a bouquet of rhodiola roots is still presented to Russian couples before marriage for fertility and healthy offspring. Chinese emperors ordered expeditions to Siberia to retrieve golden root. Native Americans ate fermented rhodiola root. In clinical trials in Russia and Scandinavia, research has confirmed that rhodiola is both a stimulant and an antistress agent.

Traditional and Current Medicinal Uses

TRADITIONALLY RHODIOLA WAS USED THROUGHOUT EASTERN Europe and Asia as a tonic to increase physical and mental performance, endurance, and strength. It has been used for depression, fatigue, anemia, cardiovascular disease, impotence, infection, altitude sickness, and many gastrointestinal ailments and nervous system disorders. Linnaeus wrote, in the mid-1700s, of rhodiola's **astringent** properties. In 1755 *R. rosea* appeared in the first Swedish **pharmacopoeia.** Rhodiola tea has been used for winter colds and flus throughout Asia and prescribed in Mongolia for tuberculosis and cancer.

Botanist and taxonomist G.V. Krylov of the Russian Academy of Sciences made an expedition to Siberia in 1961 to retrieve golden root. That investigation marked the beginning of modern scientific inquiry into rhodiola and its uses, and led to the isolation of bioactive ingredients believed to be responsible for its effectiveness. In 1975 the Ministry of Health registered and approved rhodoiola **extract** as a medicine and tonic, and large-scale commercial production began in the Soviet Union. It was recommended for memory enhancement, increased attention span, to combat fatigue, and for a host of neurological conditions. Sweden followed

Common Names Rhodiola, golden root, roseroot, Arctic root

Latin Names *Rhodiola rosea, Sedum roseum*

Family Crassulaceae

Parts Used Root, stem, leaves, flowers, seeds

Description Growing to three feet, rhodiola is a small perennial with unbranched stems surrounded by fleshy, alternate leaves. At the end of the stems, small flowers, usually yellow or pale-green, appear from spring through summer. Small, deep-brown fruits contain seeds.

Habitat Rhodiola is native to the Himalaya and grows in the Northern Hemisphere at high elevations in Asia, Europe, and North America.

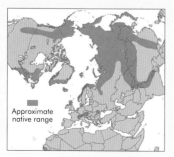

Approximate native range

suit in 1985, recognizing rhodiola as a stimulant and antifatigue agent. Animal and human research has continued to confirm rhodiola's worth as a physical and mental enhancer and tonic for a wide range of ailments, including cancer and cardiovascular disease.

Cultivation and Preparation

RHODIOLA LIKES SANDY SOIL AND SUNNY SPOTS AT HIGH altitudes. It is tolerant of damp conditions but prefers well-drained soil and, once established, fares well in droughts. Extremely resistant to cold, rhodiola is often called Arctic root because it grows at high northern latitudes. Flowers bloom from May to August and seeds ripen from July to August. Cultivators usually use a sunny greenhouse to protect new plants for their first winter. Seeds are sown in spring. Rhodiola can also be grown easily from roots divided between August and October. Most of the plant is edible, but it is generally taken as a root extract in pill form, or as a tea.

Research

RHODIOLA IS STILL BEING DISCOVERED IN THE WEST. Though research has been done since the mid-1960s, it has occurred mostly in Russia, has been published in Russian, and is rarely translated into English. Russian science dubbed rhodiola an **adaptogen,** an herb that increases an organism's ability to adapt to stress with few side effects. It has been observed to have antifatigue, antistress, anticancer, **antioxidant**, and immune-enhancing effects in vitro, as well as in animals and humans. A number of randomized, **double-blind, placebo**-controlled human studies have shown rhodiola to improve mental and physical performance under stress. Rhodiola extract has been shown to significantly improve performance of students during exam periods as well as the endurance of young, healthy exercisers. A study of 112 athletes in track and field, swimming, speed skating, and skiing competitions showed 89 percent made rapid improvements in speed and strength. In higher doses, rhodiola can be a sedative and sleep enhancer. Rhodiola also shows promise in treating some types of cancer, but more human studies are needed. In animal studies, rhodiola inhibited tumor growth and decreased metastasis.

In 2002 the American Botanical Council published several case studies on the successful use of rhodiola. The studies are anecdotal, not controlled clinical trials. Among the case studies are the stories of two 45-year-old women suffering from depression.

The first, Ms. W., a writer, for many years faced writer's block, which prevented her from finishing her doctoral thesis. She did not think of herself as depressed or qualify as dysthymic (chronically depressed, but with less severity than major depression). For seven years she tried psychotherapy and prescription antidepressants. Then she tried 100 mg of *Rhodiola rosea* extract twice a day. Within six weeks she was productive; she completed her thesis and felt happy with herself and in her marriage. She then stopped taking rhodiola and within six months felt as she had before taking it. Back on her twice-daily dose, she fully recovered again.

Ms. B., a mental health professional, for five years suffered from fibromyalgia and depression, which was unresponsive to many psychotropic drugs. Then she found sertraline, known as Zoloft, which helped her function. She added 600 mg of *R. rosea* extract to her daily dose and within two months she became productive and enjoyed herself again. After six months, she stopped taking rhodiola. Within three weeks she relapsed. Returning to her rhodiola-sertraline treatment, she experienced a full remission.

See Also: Medicinal Plants of the World by B. Wyk and M. Wink, Timber Press, 2004; *Rhodiola rosea: A Phytomedicinal Overview* by R. Brown, Herbalgram 56: pp. 40–53.

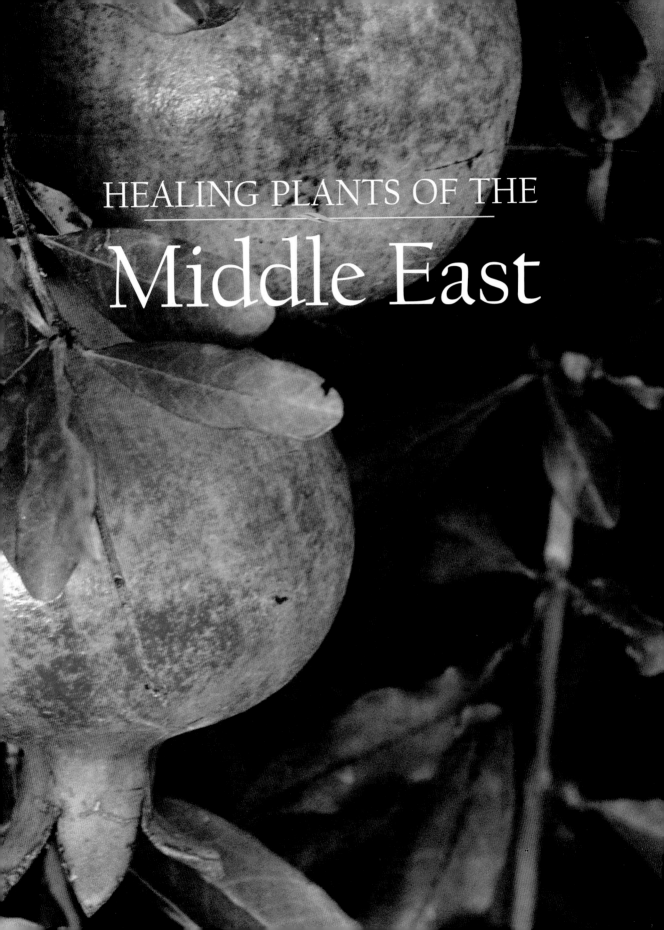

HEALING PLANTS OF THE
Middle East

NEAR THE PRESENT-DAY CITY OF SHABHAT, ALONG THE northeastern coast of Libya, lies a UNESCO World Heritage site—the ancient city of Cyrene. The site dates to 631 B.C. In classical times it was one of the five most important Greek cities in the region. Later it fell to Alexander the Great who ruled it until his death in 323 B.C. In the first century B.C. Cyrene became a Roman province. It remained an important center on the western edge of the Middle East until its economy collapsed when its main export—a medicinal plant—was overharvested.

MEDICINAL PLANTS, MYTH, AND HISTORY

SILPHION, AS IT WAS KNOWN TO THE ANCIENT GREEKS, WAS A SPECIES OF GIANT fennel that grew in the hills near Cyrene. The principal export of Cyrene, silphion's economic importance was underscored by its image on Cyrenian coins. Bundles of the plant, which commanded a price said to exceed its weight in silver, were exported throughout the Mediterranean region. However, silphion grew in a limited range. Attempts to cultivate silphion in Greece and Syria failed. Eventually, demand resulted in it being harvested to extinction. The roots of silphion were the premier oral contraceptive and early-term **abortifacient** of the ancient world. What does its loss represent to humanity?

In a history classroom at North Carolina State University in Raleigh, Professor John M. Riddle attempts to answer such questions. Here, for more than four decades, Riddle, a distinguished scholar in the field of historical pharmacology, has focused on the early reaches of human history. To him, anything after 1500 is a current affair. Selected by students as the best teacher at North Carolina State on several occasions, Riddle is not only a fine teacher but also a keen observer, looking for clues in the contemporary world to answer questions about the ancient world. In conversations with Iranian students, Professor Riddle became curious about the origins of a wedding tradition. The bride was always given pomegranates as a wedding gift. Why pomegranates? What might history reveal?

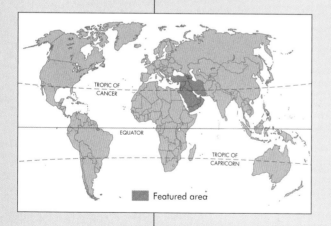

In the myth of Persephone, Riddle sees a link between mythology and historical pharmacology. Long before Greek physician Hippocrates (460–377 B.C.) and his contemporaries, the use of pomegranates occurs in mythology. According to Greek myth, Hades (Pluto), god of the underworld, abducted

These statues of Demeter, goddess of the harvest, and her daughter, Persephone, stand outside a Greek temple in Cyrene. They recall the ancient Greek myth that explains why we have the seasons: Because Persephone must spend part of every year in the underworld, Demeter grows sad and neglects the Earth and lets the plants die in fall and winter. When Persephone returns to Earth, Demeter is happy and tends the plants so that they bloom and flourish, and we have spring and summer.

PRECEDING PAGES: Pomegranate trees (Punica granatum) occur throughout the Mediterranean region and the Middle East. Some have speculated that the pomegranate may have been the forbidden "apple" of the Garden of Eden. Pomegranate seeds have been used as a contraceptive folk medicine since ancient times. Today pomegranate fruits are valued for their strong antioxidant activity.

Persephone while she collected flowers on the plain of Enna. Persephone was the daughter of Demeter, goddess of the Earth and harvest. When she discovered Persephone was missing, she stopped taking care of crops to search for her. Persephone's father, Zeus, secured her release from Hades. But before Persephone left the underworld, Hades tempted her to eat a few pomegranate seeds. When she took a bite, she was bound to the underworld forever. Each pomegranate seed that she had eaten meant that she would have to return for part of each year.

Professor Riddle explains the connection: The virgin goddess Persephone was infertile because she ate pomegranates—hence the association with fall and winter when nothing grows. Confirmations of this link are revealed throughout history. Second-century Greek physician Soranus, the foremost writer on gynecology in the ancient world, included prescriptions in his works for oral contraceptives. Five recipes, recorded by John Riddle in

The Caucasus Mountains of Armenia and Georgia are known for many endemic medicinal plants that do not occur anywhere else in the world. Important plant groups include Angelica *species (dong quai and others),* Symphytum *species (comfrey),* Verbascum *species (mullein), and* Thymus *species (thyme).*

Contraception and Abortion from the Ancient World to the Renaissance (published in 1992), include pomegranates. Others who described the use of pomegranate seeds or rinds to prevent conception included the Greek physicians Hippocrates and Dioscorides and Arab physician Ibn Sina (Avicenna, 980–1037). In classical and medieval references and in ancient Indian medical literature, pomegranates are also recognized as abortifacients.

Today in parts of Africa, pomegranates are folk contraceptives. Modern pharmacological studies of the 1970s and 1980s offer scientific confirmation. Laboratory studies in which female rats were fed pomegranate led to fewer pregnancies than in a control group not fed pomegranate. A similar study with female guinea pigs resulted in no pregnancies. In both studies, four months after pomegranate feeding stopped, fertility returned.

Herbal Medicine Rediscovered

The Middle East, where pomegranates grow wild, is the birthplace of civilization tself. It is also the birthplace of both Eastern and Western medical traditions. Middle East cultures blended with myths and cultures of ancient Greece, India, and China to create traditional medical systems. Nowhere is this more evident than in modern Armenia.

Located among Muslim countries, Armenia adopted Christianity in the year 300, the first nation to do so. At the crossroads of ancient traditions and cut off from neighbors with whom it does not have diplomatic relations, Armenia's southern border with Iran is its trade route to the world. Armenia—from the Aras River Valley to the Caucasus—has a wide diversity of flowering plants. More than 3,200 species represent 50 percent greater biodiversity than temperate regions of North America of similar size. (Armenia is slightly smaller than the state of Maryland.) Some 1,500 of the species growing in Armenia have been used historically as folk medicines, with 150 species still in common use today and 60 species harvested in the wild.

At the end of the main thoroughfare of Yerevan, Armenia's capital city, sits a library filled with ancient manuscripts. During Soviet times, it was a storage building. Now its treasures are being discovered by the outside world. In a dusty office, Stella Vadanyan studies ancient Armenian manuscripts. One of these is the work of 15th-century Armenian scholar Amirdovlat Amasiatsia, who wrote extensively on medical subjects, including folk medicine and traditional medicine systems of the Middle East. His medieval encyclopedia includes a dictionary of simple medicinal compounds in 36 chapters—one for each letter of the Armenian alphabet. Amasiatsia, a relative latecomer to the medicinal plant kingdom, was not alone. King Vagharshak created medicinal plant gardens across Armenia to improve sanitation about 200 B.C.; a century later, King Artashes II gathered medicinal plants from the wild and cultivated them in his garden in the first century B.C.

Armenia lies along the Silk Road, the main trade route connecting East and West. Against this ancient backdrop herbalist Armen Mehrabyan learned herbal traditions from his grandmother in the snow-capped mountains in northern Armenia. Today he is creating a line of herbal teas called Ancient Herbals. The herbs are wild harvested in the mountains. Mehrabyan trains collectors and harvesters to identify each herb species and each plant part. Using traditional herbal recipes, Mehrabyan packages the herbs in cotton bags with Armenian embroidery on each bag and markets them to specialty groceries and hotels in New York and Boston.

The transition from an industrial economy after the collapse of the Soviet Union to a small agrarian economy in today's Armenia has forced career shifts for many. Dr. Hakob Barseghian, a mechanical engineer who lost his job after the fall of the Soviet Union, has since focused his attention on herbs. Once a designer of industrial meat-processing equipment, he now designs and makes equipment for use in herb processing. This includes efficient drying systems and equipment for grinding, powdering, and sifting herbs. He gathers, dries, processes, and packages dried, culinary herbs and herbal teas in handmade packaging, each with his own hand-drawn picture of the plant. Like many herb producers in the Middle East, his is a one-man operation.

Traditional Medicine in the Middle East

FROM THE NINTH THROUGH THE THIRTEENTH CENTURIES, ANCIENT GRECO-ROMAN medicine was assimilated by the Arabs, and with the spread of Islam, Arabian traditional medicine emerged. Arabian physicians such as Ibn Sina (Avicenna) were to have wide-ranging influence. Traditional Arab medicine is known today as **Unani-Tibb**, practiced in Pakistan, Iran, Afghanistan, the Arabian Peninsula, and other parts of the Middle East. Like classical Greek medicine, it is based on the four elements (earth, water, air, and fire), and relates to bodily humors (blood, phlegm, yellow bile, and black bile). Concepts of quality (hot, cold, dry, and wet) are integrated into an understanding of equilibrium and imbalance. Disease is a result of imbalance.

Frankincense (*Boswellia sacra*), the gum resin of a plant growing on the Arabian Peninsula, is an important herbal medicine in the Middle East. It is collected by making cuts on the plant's stems so that they exude the resin. It is used as a perfumed smoke to cleanse homes and ingested to strengthen teeth and stimulate digestion. In Saudi Arabia it is considered a **diuretic** and **purgative**. Thought to be an aid to memory, frankincense also is added to coffee. Myrrh (*Commiphora myrrha*), a close botanical relative of frankincense, also produces a gum resin. Myrrh has **anti-inflammatory** and antibacterial properties. Studies have shown that it also may lower cholesterol.

Few plants have had such an intimate relation with humans as the olive tree (*Olea europea*). Probably originating from Asia Minor and Syria, the olive tree was introduced throughout the Mediterranean centuries ago. The food value of olives and olive oil is well known. Traditionally, the olive leaf also has been valued as an **astringent** and antiseptic. Olive leaf teas were used to treat fevers, as was the bark. The bitter leaf tea also was used as a mild diuretic and to treat malaria. For external conditions, the leaves were made into a **poultice** to treat boils, skin rashes, and sprains. In the late 1800s, scientists isolated a chemical compound called oleuropein from olive leaves. The compound has strong antibacterial and antifungal activity. It occurs throughout the tree, usually at levels of up to 0.3 percent in the leaf. It is also found in the fruits and the oil and is one of the compounds of olive oil that protects it from spoiling. Recent European studies have confirmed that olive leaf extracts exhibit **antioxidant** activity and may be beneficial in combating aging and cardiovascular disease and in protecting the nervous system.

The herbal traditions of the Middle East are among the least known medical traditions in the West. New discoveries, such as the antioxidant activity of the olive leaf or the contraceptive potential of pomegranate, developed from observations of traditional uses of these plants. New discoveries no doubt will arise out of the Middle East's rich herbal heritage.

OPPOSITE PAGE: The leaves of the olive tree are an ancient symbol of good will and peace. Olive trees have been cultivated for millennia, with a history of use by the Assyrians, Egyptians, Greeks, Romans, and other ancient civilizations of the Middle East. The green fruits must be processed to make them edible, as they are too bitter to eat straight from the tree. Ripe black olives do not require processing. The fruits contain up to 40 percent oil, which is cold-pressed to make olive oil. Olives are rich in vitamins and minerals and have the highest energy value of any fruit.

Rosemary
Rosmarinus officinalis

ROSEMARY HAS A LONG HISTORY IN MYTHOLOGY AND literature. In ancient Greek mythology, Minerva, the goddess of knowledge, is associated with rosemary, and the nine daughters of Mnemosyne, or memory, are sometimes depicted holding sprigs of rosemary. Dioscorides, the ancient Greek physician, wrote about rosemary's "warming faculty" in his *De Materia Medica*. It is said to have been found in Jesus's manger and associated with the Virgin Mary. Shakespeare referred to rosemary in his plays, too; in *Hamlet*, Ophelia hands Hamlet a sprig of rosemary and bids him to remember her: "There's Rosemary, that's for remembrance: pray, love, remember." It is traditionally added to wedding bouquets to remind couples of their wedding vows and also used at funerals as a token of remembrance. Egyptian mummies have been found wrapped with rosemary. Australians wear it on Anzac Day to remember the dead. Rosemary's medicinal attributes include its **antioxidant** and **analgesic** properties; rosemary tea has been used as a therapy for all sorts of ailments, including headaches, indigestion, and depression.

Traditional and Current Medicinal Uses

ROSEMARY WAS USED THROUGHOUT THE ANCIENT WORLD. IN Greece, scholars hung rosemary around their necks during examinations to improve memory and concentration. In Europe rosemary was a tonic for tension, headache, and indigestion. In Azerbaijan, rosemary baths were prescribed for low blood pressure. In Chinese medicine, it has long been used to treat headaches as it has in **Unani** and **Ayurvedic medicine**. Rosemary was listed in the *Pharmacopoeia of the United States* from 1820 to 1950.

In modern herbal medicine, rosemary tea is commonly prescribed in Germany for digestive problems. Rosemary is also applied externally, in oils and ointments for rheumatism and to increase circulation. Rosemary is used in baths, aromatherapy, potpourris, soaps, and cosmetics. In the U.S. rosemary is widely used in dietary supplements. Rosemary tea is used to treat colds and flus, rheumatic pain, arthritis, aching muscles,

Common Name Rosemary

Latin Name *Rosmarinus officinalis*

Family Lamiaceae

Parts Used Leaves, twigs

Description An evergreen shrub, rosemary grows about three to five feet high, with thin, dark green leaves and pale blue flowers in summer. It is a perennial, woody bush with a fresh piney scent.

Habitat Rosemary is native to Spain, Portugal, southern France, and the western Mediterranean region and is now grown around the world with most production coming from Spain, France, Morocco, and Tunisia. It is commonly found in American, British, European, Indian, and Chinese gardens.

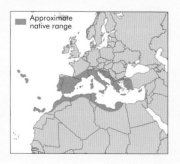
Approximate native range

muscle spasms, indigestion, headache, fatigue, and depression. Rosemary also is used as a mouthwash, dye, preservative, and in shampoos to combat dandruff and thinning hair and balding.

Cultivation and Preparation

ONLY ABOUT 30 PERCENT OF ROSEMARY SEEDS GERMINATE, so taking cuttings or layering branches is an easier way to propagate the plant. Rosemary likes lots of sun and well-drained soil. It is grown as a perennial in warmer areas but is susceptible to frost. It is typically planted as an annual or potted and brought in for the winter. A bit can be snipped fresh at any time for use in the kitchen or the bath. However, no more than 20 percent of the plant should be removed. Rosemary is fast growing, particularly if pruned. **Infusions** are prepared by adding the dried leaves to hot water for a tea.

Research

ROSEMARY HAS BEEN SHOWN TO BE AN ANTISPASMODIC, antidepressive, and antimicrobial. It relaxes smooth muscles of the gastrointestinal tract and is a strong antioxidant. Researchers have associated both oxidative stress and inflammatory processes in the development of factors leading to Alzheimer's. Deficiency of choline and acetylcholine in the brain have also been linked to contributing factors. In addition, researchers speculate that oxidation in cells produces many disabling changes in the elderly—and rosemary is known to have more than a dozen antioxidant compounds. Rosmarinic acid, found in rosemary and many species of the mint family, has antiviral, antibacterial, **anti-inflammatory**, and antioxidant properties. In a recent study, rosemary was tested against lavender and a control for mood and memory enhancement. Rosemary improved the quality of memory in objective tests. Rosemary also exhibits evidence of inhibiting cancer in lab animals. One study showed that a one percent **extract** of rosemary fed to laboratory animals produced a 47 percent decease in the incidence of experimentally-induced mammary gland tumors when compared with controls In another study, colon and lung cancer incidence was cut in half for animals ingesting rosemary.

The herb world lost one of its great patrons when herbalist extraordinaire Bertha Reppert passed away in 1999. An herbal student and teacher, Bertha Reppert wrote dozens of books and hundreds of columns on herbs and lectured across the United States. She also established Rosemary House in Mechanicsville, Pennsylvania, in 1968, when herb shops hardly existed. Today her shop—one of the oldest herb shops in the country—continues, run by Reppert's daughter Susan. Bertha Reppert's herbal heritage came from generations of oral instruction from other herbalists. In addition to spreading the word about rosemary (her favorite herb) and other herbs, Bertha Reppert documented (in one of her books) what it takes for herb shops to survive. Chief among necessities, Ms. Reppert said, is knowledge of how to grow herbs. When Rosemary House started, most herbs were not available, so she grew them and made them available. Her business practices also included employing handicapped helpers or stay-at-home mothers to do packaging. She was famous for declaring "Let the herb become the teacher." Today that phrase is engraved on her headstone in the herb garden at Cornell University.

See Also: Herbal Medicine Expanded Commission E Monographs by M. Blumenthal, A. Goldberg, J. Brinckmann, American Botanical Council, 2000; *Herbal Renaissance: Growning, Using, and Understanding Herbs in the Modern World* by S. Foster, Gibbs Smith, 1993.

Common Names Sage, broadleaf sage, common sage, dalmatian sage, garden sage, kitchen sage, salvia

Latin Name *Salvia officinalis*

Family Lamiaceae

Parts Used Leaves and flowers

Description A small perennial evergreen shrub, sage grows only a few feet high. Its wooly, gray-green, oval leaves grow several inches long in opposing pairs, and give off a strong, slightly bitter, lemony scent. The square stems start to become woody in the second year. The blue, lilac, or white flowers have two lips like an open mouth and grow up along shooting stems.

Habitat *Salvia officinalis* comes from the Mediterranean region, particularly the Adriatic coast. Sage is commercially grown in the U.S., Canada, Argentina, Germany, and France. Most of the world's supply is wild harvested along the Adriatic coast.

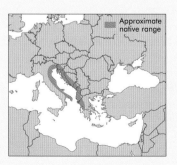

Approximate native range

Sage
Salvia officinalis

WHEN USED IN COMMON REFERENCE, SAGE USUally refers to *Salvia officinalis*, or common sage, though it is often used to describe any of the 900 species that come from the genus *Salvia* and a few that do not. *S. officinalis*, with its characteristic aroma, is the sage to which all other sages are compared. There are many ornamental and nonaromatic varieties of *Salvia* that may have a smell but are not considered medicinal. There are chia sages, whose seeds are used as laxatives, and many aromatic sages—of which *S. officinalis* is one—which are used medicinally. *S. officinalis* was used medicinally by the ancient Greeks, Romans, and Egyptians. The Greek physician Dioscorides recommended sage for treating wounds and coughs in the first century. An ancient proverb goes, "Why should a man die who has sage in his garden?" It has been a European garden plant since medieval times and is currently most avidly used in Italy. In the 17th century, as it was arriving in America, Dutch merchants would get three chests full of green tea from the Chinese for every one of sage. It is most famous today as a culinary herb, raw, cooked, or dried and used to flavor salads, soups, stews, meats, and vegetables as well as oils, vinegars, and teas. It also is a common ingredient in soaps, cosmetics, and perfumes.

Traditional and Current Medicinal Uses
FOR EGYPTIANS SAGE WAS A FERTILITY DRUG. GREEKS USED IT to stop bleeding and clean wounds, ulcers, sores, and snakebite, and drank **infusions** for consumption and throat problems. To Romans, sage was a sacred herb, harvested with solemn ceremony. "Sage" and "salvia" come from the Latin *salvere*, meaning "to be saved"; it has been associated with longevity since ancient times and used as a cure for a wide variety of ailments, serving as a digestive and nerve tonic, a gargle for sore throats and bleeding gums, an antiseptic in vaginal infections, a **poultice** for insect bites, and a cure for diarrhea. Sage also made its way into traditional medicines of India—**Ayurvedic**, **Siddha**, and **Unani**—for indigestion and any soreness or swelling of the mouth and throat.

In modern herbal medicine, sage is widely used in Asia to treat hemorrhoids, blood or phlegm in urine, excessive breast milk or fluid in the abdomen, insomnia, hepatitis, and more. In Germany, sage is administered in pills or drunk as sage tea or juice for colds, congestion, and fevers. In the U.S., sage is commonly taken as a dietary supplement to treat hot flashes, night sweats, and estrogen loss, as well as a tonic for fighting fatigue and nervous exhaustion, and providing immune enhancement and memory improvement.

Cultivation and Preparation

SAGE LIKES DRY, WELL-DRAINED, SANDY SOIL AND FULL SUN and is fairly frost resistant, once established. Heavy, wet, or acidic soil can kill the plant. It flowers from June to August. Sage can be propagated by root division, by stem or leaf cuttings, or by seed, preferably sown in spring and kept inside its first winter. Commercially, each plant is harvested just prior to bloom. Leaves can be dried in a warm, shady place. Fresh leaves can be boiled into a tea or soaked in oil, such as olive oil, or in wine.

Research

ACCORDING TO GERMANY'S COMMISSION E, A SCIENTIFIC panel of experts that regulates herbal medicines, sage possesses antibacterial, antifungal, antiviral, and **astringent** properties. Though most modern treatments with sage have a long history of use, and many animal studies have been done to confirm these traditions, further clinical studies are needed. Human studies on patients using sage to treat herpes have shown reduction in size, number, severity, and time between outbreaks of genital and oral cold sores. Sage also shows promise in treating Alzheimer's disease. Sage has been shown to be an acetylcholinesterase inhibitor, the only type of drug approved by the U.S. Food and Drug Administration to treat Alzheimer's. Sage appears effective at managing cognitive loss and agitation in patients with mild to moderate Alzheimer's disease.

> CAUTION Sage reportedly reduces milk supply and is not recommended for medicinal use during pregnancy or lactation, though it is considered to be safe in the low doses used as a culinary flavor.

SAGE IN OLD AGE

Alzheimer's disease affects one in ten people over 65 and almost half the people over 80, causing just over half of the cases of dementia worldwide. The number of people with Alzheimer's has doubled since 1980. Wherever life expectancy is long, Alzheimer's is a growing problem—and sage may offer hope. Alzheimer's is characterized by loss of memory and sage is known for improving it. English herbalist John Gerard wrote of sage in the 16th century, "It is …good for the head and brain, and quickeneth the nerves and memory." Following this historical hint, numerous studies have been done testing sage's ability to prevent and treat Alzheimer's disease. Alzheimer's prevention seems to be linked to a diet high in antioxidants and use of nonsteroidal anti-inflammatory drugs. These apparently help guard against low levels of the neurotransmitter acetylcholine (Ach) that leads to loss of brain function in Alzheimer's patients. Drug treatment usually focuses on inhibiting the Ach enzyme (AchE). In vitro tests show that both S. officinalis and S. lavandulafolia have Ach-inhibiting compounds. But S. officinalis has higher levels of the neurotoxin thujone, making S. lavandulafolia better for treatment. Its inhibition of AchE was confirmed in rats. One rigorous study of sage's effects on human cognition shows promise for sage's AchE-inhibiting and antioxidant effects. Research continues.

See Also: Herbal Medicine Expanded Commission E Monographs by M. Blumenthal, A. Goldberg, J. Brinckmann, American Botanical Council, 2000; A Field Guide to Medicinal Plants and Herbs: Eastern and Central North America, 2nd ed. by S. Foster, J. Duke, Houghton Mifflin, 2000.

Common Names Sassafras

Latin Name *Sassafras albidum*

Family Lauraceae

Parts Used Leaves, roots

Description Sassafras can be a large shrub or a scraggly tree that reaches 50 feet, with deeply furrowed bark and leaves that often have two or three distinct lobes. Clusters of yellow-green flowers are followed by small, oval, dark blue fruits.

Habitat Native to eastern North America, sassafras' original range in the United States extended from Maine to Florida and west to Texas and Kansas. It typically grows in dry, infertile soils.

Approximate native range

Sassafras

Sassafras albidum

SASSAFRAS IS KNOWN FOR ITS DISTINCTLY SHAPED leaves—mitten-shaped, with one or two "thumbs"—and their distinctive citrusy scent. Supposedly the scent of sassafras played a role in Columbus's discovery of the New World. It is said that he detected it above the briny notes of the sea air and simply followed his nose toward land. Sassafras is a North American herb and it was used for many centuries by Native American tribes who lived within its range. Sassafras tea was said to cure many ills, both among the Indians and later the settlers who adopted its use. Some authorities believe that sassafras was the first medicinal herb sent back to Europe from North America. The plant was christened "sassafras" in the 16th century by a Spanish botanist who encountered it in Florida. The odd name is thought to be a corruption of the Spanish word for saxifrage, an entirely unrelated plant. Sassafras was more than just a medicinal herb. It became widely used as a flavoring agent, added to enrich the taste of chewing gum, toothpaste, root beer, and many foods. In the 1960s, however, researchers discovered that one of sassafras oil's main ingredients, safrole, was a carcinogen. At that point, the use of sassafras **extracts** and oil in food was banned in the U.S. (and in Europe in 1974), unless the safrole was removed. Sassafras continues to be used in herbal medicine, but cautiously.

Traditional and Current Medicinal Uses

NATIVE AMERICAN TRIBES OF THE EASTERN WOODLANDS OF North America used sassafras both as a food and a medicine, often brewed as a pleasant-tasting tea from the bark of the roots. The Cherokee used preparations of sassafras bark to help heal wounds, banish fever, cure diarrhea, expel worms, ease rheumatism, and cure colds. Sassafras was a blood thinner for the Chippewa and a cure for eye diseases for the Mohawk. The Iroquois used sassafras as a blood strengthener and for wounds, bruises, fever, nosebleeds, and swellings. Settlers from Europe found sassafras to be something of a cure-all. It was used as a spring tonic and blood purifier, to induce sweating and as a **diuretic,** and to treat bronchitis, gastritis, gout, rheumatism, indigestion, kidney ailments, and skin sores. It was also considered to be a cure for syphilis (later shown to be completely ineffective). Large amounts of sassafras bark were exported to England and Europe; many early English colonies were founded on the promise of profits from the sassafras trade. In the 1800s, sassafras was taken as a remedy for syphilis, rheumatism, skin eruptions, eye diseases, and disorders of the chest, bowels, kidneys, and bladder. The gummy core (pith) of the branches was used to soothe tired eyes. It was also used topically for sprains and bruises and to stop the progress of gangrene.

In modern herbal medicine, sassafras is no longer considered safe for internal use (although sassafras tea is still available). Sassafras is primarily used for treating insect bites and getting rid of lice, and is also suggested as a remedy for poison ivy and poison oak.

Cultivation and Preparation

SASSAFRAS PREFERS GOOD SOIL THAT IS MOIST, WELL-drained, acidic, and deep. It thrives in full sun or part shade. The tree can be grown from seed (often a slow process), from root cuttings, or from runners sent out by mature trees. Roots are lifted in spring, before leaves appear, or in autumn, after the leaves have fallen. The roots are dried for powders, **tinctures**, and other preparations. Root bark is distilled for its oil. Safrole-free extracts (see sidebar) are now used as flavorings.

Research

SASSAFRAS CONTAINS AN **ESSENTIAL OIL** THAT HAS SAFROLE as a major (at least 80 percent) ingredient. Safrole is common in many plants and commercially is used in insecticides and the perfume industry. Safrole is, however, a known liver toxin shown to cause liver cancer in lab animals. Even with safrole removed, sassafras oil has caused tumors in lab animals. Although sassafras teas and other preparations are available in health food stores, some herbalists recommend against taking sassafras internally, in any form.

CAUTION Pure sassafras oil is extremely toxic. Just a few drops can kill a child, and not much more can be fatal to adults. The pure oil is also a skin irritant.

SEASONING WITH SASSAFRAS

Some people link the taste of sassafras with old-fashioned root beer. For others, it is the essence of gumbo filé, a unique dish synonymous with Cajun cuisine. Filé (pronounced either FEE-lay or fee-LAY) is fine powder made from pulverized sassafras leaves. Louisiana's Choctaw Indians were the first to discover that the powdered leaves, when mixed with water, made a mucilaginous but flavorful thickening agent that could be added to soups and stews to give them color, body, and a special, spicy taste. The Cajun and Creole cultures adopted the ingredient, added garlic and some other spices, and created the classic seasoning called filé. Added to gumbo—a tasty soup made from seafood, crawfish, or chicken—the result was the ultimate Cajun dish: "gumbo filé." Although sassafras is now eyed with suspicion because of high safrole content, the leaves contain much less of this chemical than the roots. Because of the low safrole content in sassafras leaves, and in filé powder, the seasoning is generally thought harmless on the scale used in cooking. Experienced cooks add filé late in the process of making gumbo. If the powder is heated too long, it becomes stringy and disgustingly thick. Adding a pinch to the pot just before serving will yield a gumbo with classic filé taste.

See Also: *A Field Guide to Medicinal Plants and Herbs: Eastern and Central North America, 2nd ed.* by S. Foster and J. Duke, Houghton Mifflin, 2000; *Tyler's Honest Herbal, 4th ed.* by S. Foster and V. Tyler, The Hawthorn Herbal Press, 1999.

Saw Palmetto
Serenoa repens

SAW PALMETTO, OR SABAL AS IT IS OFTEN CALLED IN Europe, is indigenous to the southeastern United States, particularly Florida. It is the single species in the genus *Serenoa*, which was named for Harvard botanist Sereno Watson (1826–1892). Before the arrival of Europeans in North America, indigenous tribes ate saw palmetto berries as a dietary staple. The fruits were also used medicinally, particularly as a remedy for urinary complaints. Impressed with the effects saw palmetto berries had on their health, settlers adopted the fruits as a food for themselves and their animals, which grew "sleek and fat" from eating them. Saw palmetto found its way into conventional medicine in the United States in the late 1800s, and was very popular during the early 1900s. After a lull in interest, saw palmetto resurfaced in American herbal medicine. In fact, since the mid-1990s, saw palmetto has been one of the top-selling herbs in the United States.

Traditional and Current Medicinal Uses

SINCE AT LEAST THE 1700S, NATIVE AMERICANS IN WHAT IS NOW the southeastern United States used saw palmetto berries to treat digestive problems, dysentery, genitourinary inflammation, as a tonic to increase strength and weight, and as an aphrodisiac. Early American settlers ate the fruits and used their juice to promote reproductive function, as a sedative, and as a tonic to improve general health. By the late 1800s, physicians were recommending saw palmetto as a sedative, **diuretic**, sleep inducer, **expectorant** and cough suppressant, digestive aid, and to build body tissues and promote weight gain. By the early 1900s, both conventional and American **Eclectic** physicians commonly recommended saw palmetto to alleviate symptoms of prostate enlargement in men and to treat urinary tract infections in both men and women.

Today, saw palmetto is very widely used by natural health practitioners, both in the U.S. and Europe, for a variety of problems. But its reputation is based largely on its well-documented ability to help alleviate bladder and urinary tract problems in men with benign prostate hyperplasia (BPH), a common nonmalignant,

Common Names Saw palmetto, sabal palm, palmetto berry, American dwarf palm tree, cabbage palm

Latin Name *Serenoa repens*

Family Arecaceae

Parts Used Fruit

Description Saw palmetto is a low-growing, clump-forming palm with fan-shaped leaves that have thorny teeth along the stems. Tiny, sweet-smelling flowers grow in dense clusters and are followed by single-seeded, blue-black fruits.

Habitat Saw palmetto is native to the southeastern United States, from South Carolina to Florida and west to Texas. The plant grows in dense thickets in areas of well-drained, somewhat sandy soil, primarily along coastal plains.

Approximate native range

age-related enlargement of the prostate gland. Saw palmetto is also recommended for inflammation of the urethra, cystitis, prostatitis, gallbladder problems, bronchial complaints, and general debility.

Cultivation and Preparation

SAW PALMETTO THRIVES IN MOIST, WELL-DRAINING SOIL AND dappled shade. It is propagated by seed or by separation of suckers. Most saw palmetto fruit is still wild-harvested; Florida is the largest producer. Fruits are harvested when ripe and dried for use in preparations.

Research

CHEMICALLY, SAW PALMETTO IS COMPOSED OF VARIOUS compounds, including a **volatile oil** rich in fatty acids. It is this fatty component that appears to give saw palmetto its therapeutic action. Since the 1960s, extensive clinical research has been carried out on saw palmetto, largely in Europe. Clinical trials have shown saw palmetto is not only effective in reducing the symptoms of BPH (such as painful, frequent urination) but also works better than the commonly used prescription drug (finasteride) for the condition. And while the prescription drug can cause serious side effects including impotence and breast enlargement, saw palmetto has few side effects. Saw palmetto does not reduce prostate enlargement, which is thought to be caused by an increase in the conversion of the male hormone testosterone into a related compound, dihydrotestosterone (DHT). Rather, the herb works to alleviate the symptoms of the condition, first by inhibiting chemical conversion of testosterone, and second, by interfering with production of estrogen and progesterone, two other hormones involved in DHT production. Several years ago there was a concern that taking saw palmetto supplements could mask readings of prostate-specific antigen (PSA), a marker used in lab tests to detect prostate cancer. Since then, several studies have found no effect by saw palmetto on PSA secretion, even in men who have been using the herb for many months.

CAUTION BPH cannot be self diagnosed. To rule out the possibility of prostate cancer, a physician should be consulted before using saw palmetto.

SAW PALMETTO REDUX

Native American tribes inhabited the Florida peninsula at least 12,000 years ago, and ethnobotanists believe saw palmetto fruits were part of their diet. In 1879, Dr. J. B. Read of Savannah, Georgia, introduced saw palmetto in an article in the *American Journal of Pharmacy*. In 1906, saw palmetto was listed in the *U.S. Pharmacopoeia* and soon after the pharmaceutical firm Eli Lilly & Company set up a saw palmetto drying facility in Vero Beach, Florida. People harvested the fruits from wild populations, much as they do today, and sold them to the facility. They were dried and used to produce medicinal products. The herb was included in the National Formulary in 1926, but was dropped in 1950. By that time, medicinal use of herbs, including saw palmetto, had declined dramatically in the U.S. Saw palmetto use increased in Europe, however, and research there confirmed its therapeutic effects. European companies were among the first to produce standardized extracts of saw palmetto. In the 1990s, its popularity skyrocketed in the U.S.; the herb was reintroduced into the National Formulary in 1998. In 2000, saw palmetto ranked sixth in total herb sales in the United States. In Europe, it is the most commonly used plant-based therapeutic agent for BPH.

See Also: The ABC Clinical Guide to Herbs by M. Blumenthal, T. Hall, and A. Goldberg, American Botanical Council, 2003; *World Health Organization (WHO) Monographs on Selected Medicinal Plants, Vol. 2,* 2002.

Schisandra
Schisandra chinensis

Common Names Schisandra, magnolia vine, star vine, bay star vine, *wu wei zi*.

Latin Name *Schisandra chinensis*

Family Schisandraceae

Parts Used Fruit/berries, leaves

Description Schisandra is a deciduous, woody vine that winds its way up into trees and along trellises. Little white flowers in May and June give way to clusters of red berries that ripen in August and September.

Habitat Schisandra originates in China, Japan, and Korea and is grown in gardens throughout the world.

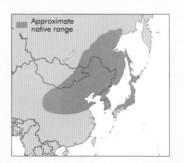

Approximate native range

S CHISANDRA IS BOTH A GENUS AND AN ANCIENT ASIAN vine (*Schisandra chinensis*) of that genus, often grown in fine gardens around the world. Its use in Chinese medicine goes back 5,000 years; in China, it is still considered one of the 50 fundamental herbs. Sometimes a substitute for ginseng, schisandra is also considered in China and Russia to be an **adaptogen**—used to fight stress and as an overall tonic to enhance physical and mental performance. It has been in the *Russian Pharmacopoeia* since 1961. The vine grows bunches of berries, like little red grapes, which can be eaten, dried like raisins, or ground into a medicinal powder and flavor. The berries are known to the Chinese as *wu wei zi*, or "five taste fruit," for their combination of the four basic tastes: sweet, sour, salty, and bitter, plus a spicy-warmth. To Japanese the berries are known as *gomishi*, and to Koreans, *omisha*. In the U.S., *S. chinensis* is known as "magnolia vine," "star vine," or "bay star vine." It and a related species, *S. glabra*, grow in undisturbed woods from North Carolina to Louisiana. Schisandra arrived in the western U.S. from Russia in the 1850s. It is a common ornamental vine in English or western European gardens, but relatively unknown and rarely cultivated in the U.S.

Traditional and Current Medicinal Uses

SCHISANDRA HAS A LONG HISTORY IN THE TRADITIONAL MEDicines of China and Russia, where it was used to treat respiratory ailments such as coughs, wheezing, or asthma, for insomnia, impotence, diarrhea, and kidney problems. Athletes and sportsmen, hunters, and soldiers have used schisandra for endurance and to fight stress and fatigue. Travelers often pack dried berries for the sugars, flavors, and sustenance. The fruit can be eaten raw, dried, cooked, or ground up. Russians make a schisandra paste mixed with hardy kiwi. The young leaves are sometimes cooked as a vegetable.

Today schisandra is used as an adaptogen—to prevent cancer, enhance mental, physical, and sexual performance, for kidney and liver health, and as a sleep aid. It is also associated with lung problems, and taken for conditions such as chronic cough, bronchitis, and asthma. In Chinese medicine, schisandra is used for lung, kidney, liver, and heart health, and to calm the heart and ease the mind.

Cultivation and Preparation

SCHISANDRA LIKES WELL-DRAINED, RICH, SANDY SOIL, AND partial or full shade. In the wild it is often found in the deep, dappled shade of the woods, near running water, or in a garden along a north- or east-facing wall. It can can be propagated by cuttings or layering. Seeds are best soaked for 12 hours, sown in autumn, and kept in a cold frame in a greenhouse for at least the first two winters. Schisandra is frost sensitive and will continue to prefer the greenhouse to winters outside. Cuttings are best with half-ripe wood, and layering of long shoots should take place in fall. In August or September, when the fruits are ripe and bright red, they can be harvested for eating or dried like raisins.

Research

OF THE 25 SPECIES IN THE GENUS *SCHISANDRA, S. CHINENSIS* contains the highest concentration of **lignans**, the main active ingredient. Most research has appeared in Chinese, Japanese, or Russian journals and has focused on adaptogenic, liver-protecting, cardiovascular, and **anti-inflammatory** effects. Research has focused on the lignans—or lignan **extracts**—regarded as the main active ingredients. For more than 50 years, experiments have tested schisandra's adaptogenic powers on athletes, airline attendants, hunters, and soldiers, demonstrating increases in stamina and concentration and decreases in fatigue and recovery time. **Double-blind** studies point to schisandra's potential for treating hepatitis. Research on rats recognizes schisandra's potential for protecting the liver from toxins, increasing cardiac health, and increased sleep time when used with sedatives or anesthesia. Schisandra studies on rats have shown improved tolerance to extreme temperatures. Other studies have pointed toward schisandra's application as an antidepressant and anticonvulsive.

CAUTION Side effects may include a depression of the central nervous system or heartburn.

SCHISANDRA AND SHEN NONG

Shen Nong, whose name means "the divine farmer," is the legendary plowman and emperor of China who is said to have lived some 5,000 years ago. His life's work marks the starting point of Chinese medicine, which because of Shen Nong, is often referred to as being 5,000 years old. He personally tested and identified hundreds of herbs—and poisons—for their medicinal properties. He is often depicted as a horned recluse, covered in a suit of leaves, holding a plant to be tasted in one hand. He is credited with discovering grain agriculture and transitioning his people from a meat diet to one of grains and vegetables. The discovery of tea is also credited to Shen Nong. He laid the groundwork for Chinese herbal medicine in *Shen Nong Ben Cao Jing* (*Shen Nong's Herbal Classic*), which arranges herbs by type and material and categorizes them by rank and rarity. Shen Nong left a legacy of experimentation and first-hand knowledge of herbal properties. He also created the classification of herbs into three categories (upper/superior, middle, and lower/inferior) still used today. Shen Nong defined schisandra as a superior herb, having the gentle, persistent ability to protect health and prolong life. Today, schisandra functions in Chinese medicine as a warm and sour tonic for the lungs, kidneys, liver, and heart. Schisandra is usually taken in combination with other herbs, according to many ancient recipes.

See Also: *Herbal Emissaries: Bringing Chinese Herbs to the West* by S. Foster and Y. Chongxi, Healing Arts Press, 1992; *Tyler's Honest Herbal*, 4th ed. by S. Foster and V. Tyler, The Haworth Herbal Press, 1999.

Seneca Snakeroot

Polygala senega

SNAKEROOT IS A COMMON NAME FOR PLANTS WITH ROOTS or **rhizomes** that have twisted, tortuous shapes. It has been given to many different species, and seneca is no exception. Seneca snakeroot is *Polygala senega*, a perennial member of the milkwort family that is native to woodlands of eastern North America. The herb was named for the North American Seneca Indians, who used it as a remedy for rattlesnake bites. In the 1730s, Virginia physician John Tennant noticed that the symptoms of snakebite can be remarkably similar to those of pneumonia and pleurisy, an epidemic disease in colonial Virginia. Tennant promoted seneca root's use, but not until after his death did the herb gain widespread acceptance in the colonies. As Tennant had predicted, seneca snakeroot is good for treating respiratory ailments. By the late 1700s, it was enjoying great popularity in medicine and was being cultivated and used in Europe as a respiratory cure.

Traditional and Current Medicinal Uses

THE SENECA INDIANS USED SENECA ROOT TO MAKE A TEA, WHICH was drunk as a treatment for coughs, sore throat, and colds. To treat snakebite, pieces of seneca root were chewed to make a mash that was then applied to the bite (after the skin had been cut and the poison sucked out). Other Native American tribes in the region also used preparations of the roots to treat various conditions, including respiratory diseases, rheumatism, as an **expectorant**, for reducing swelling, for pleurisy and croup, convulsions, heart trouble, bleeding wounds, and more. European colonists eventually adopted the herb for many of the same reasons the Indians used it, but it was particularly popular for treating respiratory conditions. In the 1800s seneca continued to be well regarded for its expectorant action and was a common ingredient in syrups, lozenges, and other remedies for coughs and colds. Great quantities of the dried root were exported to Europe. In the 1900s, it was used in

Common Names Seneca snakeroot, senega snakeroot, rattlesnake root

Latin Name *Polygala senega*

Family Polygalaceae

Parts Used Roots

Description Seneca is a short perennial with erect stems that arise from a branched root. The leaves are narrow, lance-shaped, and almost stalkless. Spikes of small, pea-like, usually white flowers bloom at the tips of stems.

Habitat Typically found in rocky woodlands, seneca is native to eastern North America, from New Brunswick to Georgia and west to South Dakota and Arkansas. It is cultivated in several countries.

Approximate native range

patent medicines and cough medicines to treat bronchitis. Demand declined about 1960 after the introduction of chemically synthesized expectorants.

In modern herbal medicine seneca root is still used to treat bronchitis, asthma, and other respiratory conditions. It is often incorporated into cough medicines to treat chronic bronchitis, asthma, dry coughs, whooping cough, and emphysema. A gargle is sometimes recommended for throat infections. Though it is a native American herb, seneca root is more commonly used in Japan and Germany than in the United States.

Cultivation and Preparation

SENECA GROWS WELL IN MOIST SOIL THAT IS WELL-DRAINED, in sun or part shade. It can be propagated with difficulty by seed; starting new plants from shoot cuttings is far easier. The roots of the herb are typically lifted in summer, sliced and dried, and then powdered for use in herbal preparations. A resurgence of interest in natural-product medicine led to a considerable increase in the use of seneca in the past two decades. Most root material is obtained either by harvesting wild plants in North America, or from plants cultivated in Japan, China, India, and Russia. As demand increased, over-harvesting of natural populations became a concern, but today most of the commercial supply is from cultivated material.

Research

SENECA IS RICH IN COMPOUNDS CALLED TRITERPENOID **saponins**. These compounds are the most likely candidates for the herb's **anti-inflammatory**, cough controlling, expectorant, and mucus-thinning effects in the body. Their mechanism of action has not been studied in detail, but it is likely that they directly reduce the viscosity of thickened bronchial secretions and irritate the stomach lining enough to cause a reflex action that induces coughing as well as sweating. Seneca is still widely used in Europe in syrups, lozenges, and teas for controlling coughs. Because of the herb's potential to cause nausea, its use is less common in the U.S.

CAUTION Large doses of seneca can cause vomiting and diarrhea. An overdose can be poisonous.

THE MILKWORTS

The botanical family Polygalaceae includes about 500 different species of plants. There are more than a handful of milkworts making up the genus *Polygala*. The genus name comes from the Greek, meaning "much milk." It was believed that cattle feeding on milkwort would produce more milk. (Contrary to this traditional superstition, milkworts do not increase lactation.) Several species of *Polygala* are used in traditional medicine worldwide. *Polygala amara*, also known as bitter milkwort, has long been used in central European folk medicine as an expectorant. *Polygala vulgaris*, known as common milkwort, has similar properties but is less potent. *Polygala tenuifolia* is native to Asia and its medicinal use was first recorded in writings of traditional Chinese medicine practitioners during the Han dynasty, from 206 B.C. to A.D. 23. It contains chemical compounds similar to those in *P. senega* but is used to strengthen gastric function and relieve urinary tract problems. *Polygala fruticosa* and *P. virgata* are both used in Zulu traditional medicine in Africa.

See Also: World Health Organization (WHO) Monographs on Selected Medicinal Plants, Vol. 2, 2002; A Field Guide to Medicinal Plants and Herbs: Eastern and Central North America, 2nd ed. by S. Foster and J. Duke, Houghton Mifflin, 2000.

POLYGALA SENEGA | Seneca Snakeroot

Common Name Senna

Latin Names *Cassia angustifolia*, synonym *Senna alexandrina*

Family Fabaceae

Parts Used Leaflets, fruit (pods)

Description A perennial herb that grows three to six feet high, senna has erect, woody stems and leaves that are divided into small, oval, leathery green leaflets arranged on either side of a narrow, grooved stalk. Stems terminate in spikes of yellow flowers from which two-inch-long, pea-like pods develop. The pods contain six or more seeds.

Habitat Native to northern Africa, parts of the Middle East, and southern India, senna is found all across Africa but is cultivated primarily in India, Egypt, and Sudan.

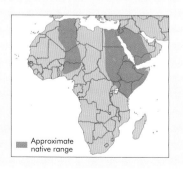

■ Approximate native range

Senna
Cassia angustifolia

WIDELY USED IN BOTH CONVENTIONAL AND HERBAL medicine, senna is a powerful **cathartic**—a very strong laxative. There are more than 400 different species of *Cassia*, but only a few are commonly used commercially as remedies for constipation: *Cassia angustifolia*, *C. lanceolata*, and *C. acutifolia*; they are all now known by the botanical synonym *Senna alexandrina*. Senna is so powerful in its action that it can cause sharp, severe stomach pains as well as intestinal cramping. To counteract this, senna is often mixed or taken with various aromatic herbs such as ginger, cloves, fennel, mint, or cinnamon—which tend to soothe the gastrointestinal tract and relax the muscles of the stomach and intestines. Mixing senna with other more palatable herbs also helps in getting the medicine down, since it has a bitter, unpleasant taste.

Traditional and Current Medicinal Uses

SENNA HAS BEEN USED FOR MANY CENTURIES AS A STIMULANT laxative in both the Eastern and the Western medical traditions, typically drunk as a tea or swallowed in powdered form. The first record of senna and its medicinal use comes from the writings of two Arab physicians who lived during the ninth century. In fact, the herb's common name is Arabian in origin, derived from the Arabic word *sena*. The herb senna also appears in traditional Chinese medicine as a treatment for atherosclerosis (characterized by fatty deposits in the arteries), as well as constipation, and also to clear "heat" in the liver, and brighten the eyes. It had additional uses in Indian **Ayurvedic medicine**, too, where it was employed as a remedy for anemia, jaundice, bronchitis, and certain types of skin problems. Through the centuries, the herb has also been used as a treatment for dysentery, ringworm, fever, hemorrhoids, wounds, and dermatitis.

Today many over-the-counter laxatives contain senna as at least one of their active ingredients. Senna preparations were until recently approved in the United States for use as laxatives. They are currently approved in the national **pharmacopoeias** and

formularies of China, France, Austria, Germany, Great Britain, India, Japan, Russia, Switzerland, and several other countries. In Germany, senna is used in more than a hundred different preparations.

Cultivation and Preparation

SENNA IS GROWN FOR COMMERCIAL USE PRIMARILY IN SOUTHern and northwestern India and in Pakistan. Senna is grown from seed in spring, or it can be started from cuttings in early summer. Plants need warmth and plenty of sun. Leaves are picked during the summer; pods are harvested in autumn. Pods have a milder laxative effect than the leaves and are more commonly used in making laxative pills and other preparations.

Research

MODERN THERAPEUTIC APPLICATIONS OF SENNA ARE SUPported by the history of its use as well as by many laboratory studies, pharmacological research with animals, and human clinical trials. Like any laxative, senna should only be taken occasionally and not for long periods of time; overuse leads to weakening of the muscles and contractions in the large intestine, which can aggravate constipation.

Research has demonstrated how senna's active constituents—**anthranoid glycosides**—work within the body. These chemical compounds are initially inactive, passing unabsorbed and unchanged through the stomach and small intestine. However, once they pass into the large intestine, the compounds become activated. They irritate the intestinal lining, causing the muscles in the intestinal wall to contract vigorously and rhythmically in waves. The compounds also inhibit fluid uptake by the cells lining the large intestine. This keeps material in the bowel abnormally soft, making its evacuation from the body all the easier.

Senna is often used in situations where easy bowel evacuation is necessary—in cases of hemorrhoids and anal fissures. Senna is also used before x-ray exams and prior to and following various types of surgery.

> CAUTION Senna can cause cramping in single doses; chronic use can disturb electrolyte balance, or cause dependency or severe side effects. Consult with a physician or other health care provider before using.

Senna, collected from the wild in southern Egypt and Nubia, was for centuries carried from the mountains by camel caravans to the Nile or to Red Sea ports. Senna was introduced into Arab medicine sometime in the ninth century and soon thereafter made its way to Western Europe. Ninth-century Egyptian writer Isaac Judaeus wrote about the use of senna leaves as a laxative as early as 850 A.D., noting that the best quality senna came through Mecca. At the close of the 12th century, senna was listed among the commodities at Acre in Palestine that were charged a duty. In 1542, a pound of senna leaves brought the same price as a pound of black pepper or ginger. Leaves were harvested in September at the end of the rainy season and again in April. The leaves and pods were dried in the sun, then packed into bags made of palm leaves and transported by camel to the Nile, and on to Alexandria or elsewhere in Egypt for export. The highest quality leaves fetched a price four times higher than other types of senna. Sold in the trade as Alexandrian senna, this product was *Cassia acutifolia*. Its cousin, *Cassia angustifolia*, was known in the trade as Arabian *moka senna* when it was shipped from Red Sea ports to Europe. In the 19th century, extensive production of senna was initiated in India, where the cultivated plant was sold as Tinnevelly senna. Today, much of the world's senna still comes from India.

See Also: Herbal Medicine Expanded Commission E Monographs by M. Blumenthal, A. Goldberg, and J. Brinckmann, American Botanical Council, 2000; *World Health Organization (WHO) Monographs on Selected Medicinal Plants, Vol. 1,* 1999.

Skullcap
Scutellaria lateriflora

Common Names Skullcap, scullcap, blue skullcap, Virginia skullcap, mad-dog weed, helmet flower

Latin Name *Scutellaria lateriflora*

Family Lamiaceae

Parts Used Dried aerial parts

Description A slender, heavily branched perennial growing one to three feet high, skullcap has pointed leaves and numerous two-lobed, violet-blue (sometimes pink or white) flowers produced in one-sided racemes (flowers borne on short stalks along an elongated axis).

Habitat Indigenous to eastern North America, *Scutellaria lateriflora* grows wild in damp woodlands, thickets, swamplands, and along riverbanks. It is wildly cultivated in Europe and other parts of the world.

Approximate native range

S KULLCAP WAS SO NAMED BY NATIVE AMERICANS because its hooded, two-lobed flowers bore a slight resemblance to the military helmets worn by early American soldiers. The genus name, *Scutellaria*, comes from the Latin *scutella*, meaning "a small dish," and refers to the shape of the small fruits that follow the flowers. Native tribes in the eastern United States were the first to use skullcap medicinally, primarily for treating menstrual problems and other female conditions. Skullcap rose to fame in the 1700s, when it was promoted as a cure for rabies, then called hydrophobia. This connection spawned other skullcap nicknames: mad-dog skullcap and mad-dog weed. Over time, the herb came to be widely used as a sedative and nerve tonic in Western herbal medicine. Today it is still prescribed by herbal practitioners for various nervous conditions including tension, anxiety, and insomnia. However, questions have been raised about the safety of some herbal skullcap products because there have been cases of contamination with another herb known to cause liver problems.

Traditional and Current Medicinal Uses

CENTURIES AGO, THE CHEROKEE USED SKULLCAP TO PROMOTE menstruation, for nerves, to help expel the placenta after childbirth, and for kidney problems. The Iroquois used preparations made from the powdered roots to prevent smallpox and to cleanse the throat. Use of the herb was introduced into American conventional medicine in 1773 by Lawrence Van Derveer, a physician who used and promoted skullcap as a cure for rabies because of its calming effects on the nervous system. Skullcap tea remained a folk remedy for rabies for some time; the herb may have helped moderate the symptoms but did not cure the disease. Subsequently, skullcap came to be utilized primarily for its tonic, calming, and antispasmodic effects. It was prescribed for hysteria, convulsions, epilepsy, St. Vitus's dance (a neurological disease later called Sydenham's chorea), rickets, neuralgia, headaches, and severe hiccups. In the early 1900s, **Eclectic** physicians in America prescribed skullcap for nervous excitability, insomnia, restlessness, and irritability.

It was also used in treating some serious mental illnesses, such as schizophrenia.

In modern herbal medicine, skullcap is suggested for treating tension, anxiety, insomnia, and muscular tension caused by stress and tension. It is also prescribed for tension headaches, **anorexia nervosa**, fibromyalgia, mild cases of Tourette's syndrome (a condition characterized by motor and vocal tics), and some types of seizure disorders. Some herbal practitioners also use skullcap in cases of delirium tremens (a delirium with tremors induced by excessive use of alcohol) and for treating withdrawal from both tranquilizers and barbiturates.

Cultivation and Preparation

SKULLCAP WILL GROW IN ORDINARY GARDEN SOIL IN SUN OR part shade, but it is a moisture-loving perennial that does best in damp conditions. It can be propagated by seed, by division, or by cuttings. For the herbal medicine market, above-ground parts of skullcap are typically collected in June from three- to four-year-old plants. These are dried and powdered and used in making **infusions, tinctures,** and capsules.

Research

DESPITE THE EXTENSIVE USE OF SKULLCAP IN AMERICAN AND British herbal medicine, few scientific studies have been conducted on its medicinal properties. (A related species used in traditional Chinese medicine, *S. baicalensis*, has been relatively well researched, although the chemical makeup of these two species is not identical.) Chemically, *Scutellaria lateriflora* contains diverse and abundant **flavonoids**; most of its effects are thought to be due to the action of these compounds. One flavonoid in particular, scutellarin, exhibits confirmed sedative and antispasmodic activity. In one rare clinical study, an extract of scutellarin was shown to improve blood flow in patients with blood clots, cerebral thrombosis, or stroke-induced paralysis. However, much more research is needed on skullcap before conclusions can be drawn about its efficacy and safety. There have been a number of reports of liver damage following the consumption of herbal products mislabeled as skullcap.

An herb closely related to *Scutellaria lateriflora* is Chinese or Baikal skullcap (*S. baicalensis*), which is native to China, Japan, Korea, Mongolia, and Russia. Chinese skullcap roots have been used in traditional Chinese medicine since at least the second century. The herb was first mentioned as a medicinal plant in the ancient Chinese medical text known as the *Shen Nong Ben Cao Jing*, written between A.D 25 and 220. Chinese skullcap has been quite extensively researched, especially in China. In studies carried out on both animals and human subjects, the herb has been shown to have antioxidant, anti-inflammatory, and antihistamine (antiallergenic) effects. In Chinese herbal medicine, skullcap root preparations are used to treat allergic conditions such as hay fever, asthma, eczema, and contact dermatitis. The herb is also used to treat tumors. There is some evidence from laboratory studies that compounds in skullcap roots may be effective in combating bladder, liver, and several other types of cancer, but this research is still preliminary. Furthermore, Chinese researchers have isolated a compound from Chinese skullcap roots that may be effective against the virus that causes hepatitis B and may also be useful in preventing heart disease or at least limiting the damage following a heart attack.

See Also: *A Field Guide to Medicinal Plants and Herbs: Eastern and Central North America, 2nd ed.* by S. Foster and J. Duke, Houghton Mifflin, 2000; *Tyler's Honest Herbal, 4th ed.* by S. Foster and V. Tyler, The Haworth Herbal Press, 1999.

Slippery Elm
Ulmus rubra

THE ELM IS A VERY AMERICAN TREE NATIVE TO NORTH America. Many Native American tribes used its bark for food and medicine and its wood for building. George Washington's army survived on porridge made from slippery elm bark during the brutal winter at Valley Forge. In the mid-1960s, Chicago Cubs Hall-of-Fame pitcher Gaylord Perry, famous for the spit ball pitch, is said to have tried slivers of the slippery elm bark that he harvested on his father's farm to perfect his pitch (he also tried mud, sweat, petroleum jelly, and spearmint gum) before major league baseball outlawed the spitball. The fragrant inner bark of slippery elm, mixed with a little water, is exactly that—slippery—making it a medicine that soothes and coats the digestive tract, relieving all sorts of gastrointestinal tract stress. Though it is backed by few scientific claims and clinical studies, slippery elm is widely available in dietary supplement products. It is approved by the United States Food and Drug Administration (FDA) and sold as an over-the-counter (OTC) or nonprescription drug.

Traditional and Current Medicinal Uses

SLIPPERY ELM'S INNER BARK HAS LONG BEEN USED FOR HERBAL medicines. Tawny in color and highly **mucilaginous** or "slippery," it has a faint fenugreek-like scent and a bland taste. The first work on American medicinal plants, *Materia Medica Americana* written by J. Schoepf in 1787, listed slippery elm as "salve bark." Skin ulcers, abscesses, inflammations, burns, chilblains, boils, broken bones, syphilitic eruptions, and even leprosy were treated with the bark **poultice**. The Cherokee used the bark for coughs, skin conditions, and as an eye wash. During the American Revolution, poultices of slippery elm were the chief means of treating gunshot wounds. In the 19th century, slippery elm emerged as an important domestic remedy for gastrointestinal tract ailments, such as sore throat, cough, gastritis, peptic and other ulcers, diarrhea, dysentery, and many other irritations of the stomach or intestines. Nineteenth-century physicians and herbalists also recommended slippery elm tea for pneumonia, consumption, pleurisy, and other lung

Common Names Slippery elm, Indian elm, moose elm, red elm, sweet elm, winged elm, gray elm, soft elm

Latin Names *Ulmus rubra*, synonym *Ulmus fulva*

Family Ulmaceae

Parts Used Bark, wood

Description Slippery elms are tall trees, growing up to 150 feet tall, out in the open. Branches start high upon the trunk and grow into a wide canopy. Leaves are serrated, rough, and lopsided. Small, light green flowers bloom in tight clusters of three to five in spring before the leaves unfurl. Seeds are surrounded by a thin, round, green wing.

Habitat Slippery elm is native to the eastern and central United States and into Canada, from Florida to Quebec, and from Texas to North Dakota.

Approximate
native range

afflictions. Elm broth was often recommended for infants and invalids.

In modern herbal medicine, slippery elm preparations are still taken as they were traditionally and available the way they have always been, as a coarse powder for making poultices and a finer powder for making drinks. Slippery elm preparations are now also available as teas, lozenges, syrups, and pills. High in calcium, slippery elm products are also taken to promote bone healing. The U.S. Food and Drug Administration recognizes slippery elm as a safe and effective option for sore throat and cough. Slippery elm is one of four main ingredients in two of the most widely used herbal cancer treatments, flor-essence and essiac.

Cultivation and Preparation

THE FLAT BROWN SEEDS, WRAPPED IN A GREEN WING, FLY away on the spring wind and ripen in early summer. In the forest, only a small percentage of seeds are fertile. Seedlings first establish a taproot and later grow a fibrous root system. Slippery elm does well in loamy soil, alkaline or acidic, but also grows in average, dry ground in full or partial sun. Slippery elm often grows as a small understory tree as well as a giant elm. It occurs in wetter soils than the American elm (*Ulmus americana*) and is less vulnerable to Dutch elm disease.

Research

THOUGH FEW STUDIES HAVE BEEN DONE TO CONFIRM THE traditional uses of slippery elm, recent trials suggest it contains **antioxidants**, which bolster the immune system and reduce intestinal inflammation. Because it cannot be digested, the mucilage swells and becomes slippery as it passes through the gastrointestinal tract. It coats and soothes the throat and stomach, speeding digestion, absorbing toxins, softening waste, and enhancing growth of beneficial bacteria. Though there is a conspicuous lack of research, this seems to be in part because there is little doubt about slippery elm's benefits.

CAUTION Though it is thought to be safe for pregnant or nursing women, it has not been tested. Mucilage may interfere with the absorption of other medicines.

THE BANE OF MAIN STREET, USA

It seems every small town has an Elm Street and American elms (cousin to the slippery elm) were once commonly seen along walks and roads, grown for their wide canopies. Since the onslaught of Dutch elm disease, however, those stately elms are not so common a part of the landscape. Dutch elm disease is caused by a fungus (*Ophiostoma ulmi*), which probably came from Asia. This deadly scourge of elm trees around the world got the name "Dutch elm disease" because it was first described by a Dutch biologist. It made its way to Europe after World War I and to the United States around 1930 where it spread quickly through the abundant population of native and urban American elms (*Ulmus americana*). The fungus blocks the flow of water through the tissue of the tree, wilting branches, turning leaves yellow, and usually killing the tree in a year. Once 25 percent of the crown is wilted, the tree cannot be saved. Carried by elm bark beetles, the disease also spreads along entwined roots, common among elm trees less than 50 feet apart. Prevention requires blocking the fungus from traveling from sick to healthy trees. Trenches dug between adjacent trees can sever underground transfer of the fungus between root structures and save trees. In 1950 the disease was discovered in Illinois, where some communities did nothing and lost all their elms; others established rigorous prevention programs and maintained most of their trees. All American elms are susceptible to the disease, but immune hybrids have been developed.

ULMUS RUBRA | Slippery Elm

See Also: A Field Guide to Medicinal Plants and Herbs: Eastern and Central North America, 2nd ed. by S. Foster and J. Duke, Houghton Mifflin, 2000; Tyler's Honest Herbal, 4th ed. by S. Foster and V. Tyler, The Haworth Herbal Press, 1999.

Soy Bean
Glycine max

A MEMBER OF THE PEA FAMILY, SOY BEAN HAS BEEN CULtivated for thousands of years in Asia. Some 5,000 years ago, Emperor Shen Nong of China named five sacred plants—soy beans, rice, wheat, barley, and millet. The modern species, *Glycine max*, has never been found growing in the wild. It is thought to be the result of a cultivar developed long ago in China from a related wild species, *G. soya*. Soy bean is a high-protein **legume** and a major world food crop. Sometimes called the "king of legumes," soy bean contains 30 to 40 percent protein. A field of soy beans may yield 15 to 20 times as much protein as cattle raised on the same amount of land. Although soy bean is not a plant that most people think of as a medicinal herb, it has several therapeutic applications.

Traditional and Current Medicinal Uses

ANCIENT CHINESE TEXTS SPEAK OF THE MEDICINAL VALUES OF soy bean. In traditional Chinese medicine, soy bean was a remedy for fever, headaches, insomnia, irritability and restlessness, lung congestion, and measles. Preparations of soy bean were considered to be a tonic for the heart, liver, kidneys, stomach, and intestines. The crushed leaves were applied to cure snakebite. Soy bean flowers were used to treat blindness and other eye diseases, while chewed seedpods were helpful when applied like a **poultice** to ulcers of the skin and cornea. Soy bean sprouts were used as a laxative and to relieve **edema**, stimulate perspiration, and ease painful urination.

In modern herbal medicine, soy bean **extracts** are often suggested for reducing blood cholesterol levels. They may enhance liver function and are therapeutic in cases of chronic liver disease and hepatitis. Because soy bean contains compounds that are essentially the botanical versions of female hormones, it has also been widely promoted as a natural treatment for some of the unpleasant symptoms of menopause and also as an inhibitor of estrogen-dependent cancers, such as breast, ovarian, and prostate malignancies. The use of soy bean and soy extracts in hormone replacement therapy remains controversial.

Common Names Soy bean, soy

Latin Name *Glycine max*

Family Fabaceae

Parts Used Seeds

Description Soy bean is an erect, bushy annual with hairy leaves and stems that grows up to six feet tall. The leaves each consist of three large leaflets. Small white or mauve pea-shaped flowers grow in clusters from the bases of the leaves, followed by hairy pods containing up to four seeds that can vary in color.

Habitat Native to central and eastern Asia, soy bean is widely cultivated in China, Japan, Korea, Indonesia, the U.S., Brazil, and Argentina.

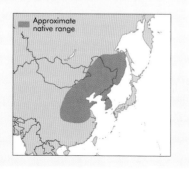

Approximate native range

Cultivation and Preparation

A PLANT THAT GROWS WELL IN TROPICAL AND TEMPERATE regions, soy bean thrives in fertile, well-drained soil in full sun. It is grown from seed sown in spring. Green seeds can be harvested late in the summer for fresh use. Ripe seeds are harvested in autumn and soaked or cooked before being ground, fermented, or otherwise used in herbal preparations.

Research

SOY BEAN EXTRACTS CONTAIN A LARGE AMOUNT OF FATTY OIL, a wide variety of **amino acids**, the phospholipid lecithin, phosphatidylcholine, and several **phytoestrogens**. Lecithin is a fat emulsifier; it breaks down fat and enhances its absorption and use in the body. Numerous studies have shown that diets high in soy lecithin tend to lower **triglycerides** and harmful **low-density lipoproteins** (LDLs) in the bloodstream, while boosting levels of helpful **high-density lipoproteins** (HDLs). It appears that a soy-based diet provides a certain amount of protection from the risk of cardiovascular disease. Phosphatidylcholine is known to exhibit liver-protecting activity and to help prevent clots from forming in blood vessels. Soy bean's phytoestrogens act like much weaker forms of the natural hormones. In menopausal and postmenopausal women, these compounds may help compensate for declining levels of estrogen and progesterone, lessening the symptoms of menopause and possibly preventing osteoporosis. More study is needed in this area, however, as results are conflicting. Epidemiological studies show soy bean-rich diets are associated with a lowered risk of leukemia as well as cancers of the breast, lung, and prostate. Supportive evidence has been found in studies utilizing cultured human breast cancer cells, leukemia cells, and prostate cancer cells. Research has demonstrated that the phytoestrogen genistein inhibits the process by which cancer cells stimulate growth of blood vessels that support tumor development. Genistein may also play a role in the prevention or treatment of autoimmune diseases. There is also evidence that soy bean exhibits **anti-inflammatory** properties, confirming observations made several thousand years ago in the Chinese medical literature.

A CORNUCOPIA OF USES

Soy bean is an immensely useful plant, both as a food and for many industrial materials and products. For centuries, soy bean seeds have been made into bean curd (tofu) and flour (miso), particularly in eastern Asia. Over the past few decades, soy protein has become popular in the U.S. as well. Soy bean goes into making dairy product substitutes such as soy milk, soy yogurt, and soy cream cheese. Soy products are popular with diabetics because the sugars in soy bean are on the whole not absorbed in the body. Soy protein can be spun into fibers that become textured vegetable protein (TVP), the foundation for many meat substitutes popular among vegetarians. Soy bean oil is widely used for cooking and in the manufacture of many other food products.

In industry, soy bean oil is used in the manufacture of paints, linoleum, oilcloth, printing inks, plastics, soap, insecticides, and disinfectants. Lecithin, a by-product of the soy bean oil industry, is used as a stabilizing agent in food, pharmaceuticals, and detergents. Both soy bean meal and protein are used to make synthetic fibers, adhesives, and fire-fighting foam. Soy bean meal makes nutritious animal feed. The entire plant is used for making biodiesel fuels.

See Also: Herbal Medicine Expanded Commission E Monographs by M. Blumenthal, A. Goldberg, and J. Brinckmann, American Botanical Council, 2000; *Medicinal Plants of the World* by B. van Wyk and M. Wink, Timber Press, 2004.

Spikenard
Aralia racemosa

ARALIA RACEMOSA IS INDIGENOUS TO NORTH AMERICA and was widely used by native peoples as both a food and a medicine. *A. racemosa*'s root is pleasantly aromatic and imparts a licorice-like flavor to foods. The Menomini, for example, made a dish of spikenard root, wild onion, and wild gooseberries. The tender young shoots of the plants were relished by the Potawatomi and other tribes as an ingredient in soups. The tiny purplish fruits were eaten raw or cooked. Spikenard and its close cousin wild sarsaparilla (*Aralia nudicaulis*) are both members of the ginseng family and have been used since colonial times to make pleasantly flavored beverages, including root beer.

Traditional and Current Medicinal Uses

THE GENUS NAME *ARALIA* IS LIKELY A LATINIZATION OF AN OLD French-Canadian name *aralie*, which may have come from the Iroquois language. This is fitting, as *Aralia* was an important medicinal herb for many Native American tribes. A root tea was widely used for treating coughs and lung ailments such as asthma, for menstrual irregularities, and to improve the flavor of other medicines. The Cherokee and other tribes made **poultices** from the root and applied them to burns, cuts, swellings, and boils. Among the Iroquois, an **infusion** of the roots was taken to purify the blood, to relieve the pain of rheumatism, and to treat miscarriage and cases of prolapsed uterus; parts of the plant were chewed to induce tapeworms to pass out of the body. The herb was also widely used in various forms to encourage sweating and thus detoxify the blood and the body. The juice of the berries and oil from the seeds was thought to cure earache and deafness if poured into the ears.

More modern herbal medicine uses of spikenard, which focus largely on the treatment of respiratory complaints and skin conditions, were derived directly from their Native American counterparts. In the last century, **extract** of the herb was commonly made into a syrup used in treating chronic coughs, asthma, and rheumatism. A poultice was applied as a remedy for a variety of skin conditions.

Common Names Spikenard, American spikenard, Indian spikenard

Latin Name *Aralia racemosa*

Family Araliaceae

Parts Used Roots

Description *Aralia* is an indigenous perennial that grows as a widely branched bush three to five feet high. The leaf stalks arising from the plant's smooth stems are each divided into three partitions; each partition bears large, leathery, oval leaves with saw-toothed edges. In early summer, clusters of small greenish-white flowers appear, succeeded by purplish berries in late summer. The roots are large and fleshy and exude a spicy and balsamic aroma. The entire plant, when bruised, gives off the same aroma.

Habitat Found from Canada to Georgia, and westward to Kansas, spikenard thrives in moist woodlands, thickets, along rocky riverbanks, and bluffs. It is often found in rock crevices in full or semi-shade.

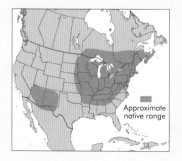

Approximate native range

Cultivation and Preparation

SPIKENARD IS AN EASILY GROWN PLANT SOWN FROM FRESH, ripe seed or propagated from root cuttings or the division of suckers late in the year. It prefers fertile, moist soil, and a semi-shady, somewhat sheltered location. For medicinal preparations, the root is collected in late summer and autumn and dried for later use.

Research

SPIKENARDS CONTAIN A VOLATILE OIL, TANNINS, AND **saponins**. In general, saponins act as **expectorants** and may aid in the body's absorption of nutrients. Spikenard and the five other North American species of *Aralia* are surprisingly little researched, given the economic importance of their cousin in the ginseng family, American ginseng (*Panax quinquefolius*). The genus *Aralia* contains about 36 species, most of which are native to East Asia. An Asian species closely related to American spikenard is *A. cordata*, known as *udo* in Japan. It is a spineless, perennial herb growing to nine feet, which occurs along streams in thickets and woods from Japan, Sakhalin, northeast China, and Korea. It is cultivated for its edible shoots. Components extracted from the roots have shown strong pain-relief properties and anti-ulcer activity. The shoots of another spikenard, *A. elata*, are also eaten in China. *A. elata* is by far the best-studied species. Like ginseng, spikenard and its relatives contain triterpene saponins. In Japan, *A. elata* shoots are known as *taranome*. In Japan and in many other parts of Asia, the herb is used as a folk remedy for the treatment of diabetes. Recently, researchers have isolated a new group of chemical compounds called elatosides from taranome shoots. Three of the five elatosides isolated in taranome shoots were found to have potent antidiabetic activity in laboratory animals. Similar antidiabetic activity has been attributed to components in the root bark, along with a strong ability to inhibit alcohol absorption. **Antioxidant** activity, cholesterol-lowering effects, and anticancer activity also have been attributed to components of *A. elata*. However, much more research is needed on all species of *Aralia*, especially the North American ones, to explore potential uses suggested in preliminary studies.

American spikenard (*Aralia racemosa*) is one of six species of spikenards indigenous to North America. The others are California spikenard (*A. californica*), American or wild sarsaparilla (*A. nudicaulis*), Sonora spikenard (*A. humilis*), hairy sarsaparilla (*A. hispida*), and angelica tree or toothache tree (*A. spinosa*). All belong to the ginseng family and have been used as tonics in herbal medicine. Wild sarsaparilla was used in folk medicine to treat many of the ailments for which *A. racemosa* was used. It was also a substitute for true sarsaparilla (a tropical plant in the genus *Smilax*) in brewing refreshing, foamy drinks similar to root beer, and was a common ingredient in patent medicines in the late 19th century. A large industry for collection of wild sarsaparilla existed in the mid- to late 19th century. *A. nudicaulis* is the most abundant native member of the ginseng family found in woods in the Northeast. Indians of California also used *A. californica* as a tonic. The root was made into a tea, or the berries eaten for a tonic effect. The largest North American member of the genus, *A. spinosa*, grows into a small tree. Its berries were made into a tincture for toothaches (hence the name toothache tree). In recent years, Koreans in the Washington, D.C., area have used *A. spinosa* shoots as a folk remedy to lower insulin requirements of diabetics, presumably a substitute for the closely related *A. elata*, which occurs in Korea, Japan, and China.

ARALIA RACEMOSA | Spikenard

See Also: A Field Guide to Medicinal Plants and Herbs: Eastern and Central North America, 2nd ed. by S. Foster and J. Duke, Houghton Mifflin, 2000; *Native American Ethnobotany* by D. Moerman, Timber Press, 1998.

St. John's Wort
Hypericum perforatum

PINCH THE BRIGHT YELLOW PETALS OF ST. JOHN'S WORT and they will turn red, appearing to bleed. Long associated with St. John the Baptist, this herb was said to bloom on the saint's birthday, June 24, and to bleed red oil from its flowers on August 29, the day that John the Baptist was beheaded. It is not blood, of course, but an oil that oozes from glands in the petals. The leaves of St. John's wort are also covered with oil glands. They are visible as translucent dots that look like tiny punctures when the leaves are held up to the light. To the Knights of St. John of Jerusalem, the tiny perforations looked like wounds and so the plant was used to heal the wounds of Crusaders. For centuries, St. John's wort was also credited with the power to drive away devils. In the modern herbal pharmacy, St. John's wort is used to banish demons of a different sort: It is respected as one of the best antidepressants that nature has to offer.

Traditional and Current Medicinal Uses

SINCE ANCIENT GREECE AND ROME, ST. JOHN'S WORT HAS been regarded as a healing remedy for wounds—particularly deep sword cuts—as well as sores, burns, bruises, sprains, inflammations, and nerve pains. It was also used to treat lung ailments and coughs, stomach complaints, nervous exhaustion, epilepsy, insomnia, depression, and even madness. In the Middle Ages, St. John's wort was recommended as a healing remedy for pulmonary complaints, jaundice, chronic urinary problems, dysentery, bleeding, worms, diarrhea, hysteria, and nervous depression. It was said to help children troubled by bedwetting and ease the troubled mind so the body could rest. In the 19th and 20th centuries, American **Eclectic** physicians prescribed St. John's wort to treat hysteria and "nervous affections with depression." When the herb's fresh flowers were steeped in oil, the result was "hypericum oil." Rubbed into the skin, it hastened healing of bruises, swellings, wounds, and sores. The oil was still available in pharmacies in the early 1900s. But by then, St. John's wort had fallen out of favor as a medicinal herb. During the late 20th century, however, it underwent a revival

Common Names St. John's wort, Johnswort, hardhay, amber, goat weed, Klamath weed

Latin Name *Hypericum perforatum*

Family Clusiaceae

Parts Used Dried flowering tops

Description A hardy perennial about two feet in height, St. John's wort has erect, woody-based stems and small, linear-to-oval, gland-dotted leaves. The bright yellow, five-petaled flowers are also edged with small dark-colored glands. The entire plant smells faintly of turpentine or balsam.

Habitat Native to Europe and temperate regions of Asia, St. John's wort has been naturalized in North America and Australia. It is found in open woods, meadows, and along roadsides.

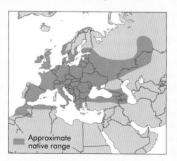
Approximate native range

when clinical studies showed that it was very effective in relieving mild to moderate depression.

Today, St. John's wort is primarily used to relieve anxiety, nervous tension, insomnia, seasonal affective disorder (SAD), and depression. It is also prescribed for menopausal disturbances, premenstrual syndrome, shingles, bladder control problems, and for pain and inflammation caused by nerve damage. Recently, St. John's wort has also been found to be a potent antiviral agent.

Cultivation and Preparation

ST. JOHN'S WORT IS EASILY GROWN IN WELL-DRAINED TO DRY soil in sun or light shade. It self-sows readily. In fact, it has become a noxious weed in many regions where it has been introduced. For herbal medicine use, the plants are cut just as they begin to flower. They can be used fresh or dried or in the making of **extracts**. Herbal preparations include teas, **tinctures**, and tablets using either the plant in crude form or as a standardized extract.

Research

CHEMICALLY, ST. JOHN'S WORT CONTAINS TANNINS, **flavonoids**, and—most importantly—the compounds hypericin and hyperforin. Hypericin exhibits pronounced antiviral activity against herpes, hepatitis, and HIV. Research points to hyperforin (and possibly to a lesser degree, hypericin) as the substance responsible for the herb's antidepressant effects. In many controlled, clinical studies involving thousands of people, preparations produced significant improvement in depression and symptoms, such as inability to sleep and concentrate, without the side effects of conventional antidepressants. Exactly how the herb improves depressive states is still being investigated; a recent hypothesis is that hyperforin blocks neurotransmitter re-uptake in the brain. In lab studies, hypericin has also shown potent antitumor activity, while extracts of the herb exhibit significant antibacterial action.

> CAUTION Use of St. John's wort can induce severe photosensitivity that can lead to dermatitis, inflammation of mucous membranes, and more toxic reactions.

Over the centuries, St. John's wort has been credited with many mystical and magical properties. It was thought to be powerful enough to protect people from thunderbolts and lightning, and to drive away demons and witches. The herb's genus name, *Hypericum*, comes from Greek words that mean "over a picture or icon," possibly referring to flowers that were placed above religious images to ward off evil, especially on Midsummer's Day. According to one superstition, anyone treading on St. John's wort after sunset might be carried away by a magic fairy-horse and not return until the break of day. The tiny glands around the edges of the leaves (once thought to be "perforations") were said to have been caused by the devil in a vain attempt to stab the plant to death with a needle. *Fuga daemonium* was once another name for St. John's wort. Literally translated, the phrase means "devil's flight," a reference to the belief that the herb's scent was so abhorrent to the devil that he would always flee its presence. In medieval times, people believed that if a woman gathered St. John's wort on St. John's Eve with the dew still on its leaves, she would find a husband. Gathered by a childless wife, it could guarantee conception. Other superstitions associated with St. John's wort had a darker side. In Wales, a long-held custom involved taking sprigs of the herb, naming one for each member of the family, and then hanging them from the rafters to dry overnight. The degree to which a sprig had shriveled overnight was thought to indicate how soon the person it was named for would die.

See Also: Herbal Medicine Expanded Commission E Monographs by M. Blumenthal, A. Goldberg, and J. Brinckmann, American Botanical Council, 2000; *World Health Organization (WHO) Monographs on Selected Medicinal Plants, Vol. 2,* 2002.

HYPERICUM PERFORATUM | St. John's Wort

Stinging Nettle
Urtica dioica

THE COMMON OR STINGING NETTLE IS AN UNPOPULAR weed, but over the centuries it has provided food, fiber, and medicine to many cultures. The genus name, *Urtica*, comes from the Latin *urere*, meaning "to burn." And burn is the best word to describe a close encounter with a nettle plant. Its leaves and stems—seemingly every inch of the plant—are densely covered with tiny sharp hairs that break at the slightest touch to release irritating substances that cause burning, itching, and even blistering of the skin. Strangely enough, when nettles come into contact with a part of the body that is already in pain, the chemicals the plant injects into the skin ease that original pain, partly by encouraging blood flow to the skin. The effect is called counterirritation. Fighting pain with pain is what has made nettle popular for hundreds, if not thousands, of years in treating rheumatism, arthritis, and similar painful conditions. Today, nettle is also used as a natural remedy for many other ailments, including hay fever, anemia, eczema, and benign prostatic hypertrophy (BPH).

Traditional and Current Medicinal Uses

USE OF NETTLES AS A COUNTERIRRITANT WAS KNOWN TO ROMAN legionnaires, who lashed themselves with nettles to feel warm during northern European winters. Flogging with nettles, or urtication as it came to be called, later was an accepted remedy for chronic rheumatic pain, muscle paralysis, rashes, and even sciatica. In medieval times, nettles were widely used medicinally to treat gout, arthritis, anemia, eczema, and other skin diseases as well as to heal wounds and ulcers and staunch bleeding. Nettle tea was given to stimulate circulation and to increase the flow of milk in nursing mothers. Later, nettle became a traditional remedy for purifying the blood, clearing up chronic skin conditions, as a therapeutic **diuretic**, and for treating rheumatism and gout. Smoke from burning nettle leaves was inhaled to ease asthma and bronchitis.

In modern herbal medicine, nettle preparations are employed in treating rheumatism, preventing and treating kidney and bladder stones, and easing inflammation

Common Names Stinging nettle, garden nettle, common nettle

Latin Name *Urtica dioica*

Family Urticaceae

Parts Used Leaves, roots

Description Nettle is a tall (to five feet) erect perennial herb with creeping roots, square stems, lance-shaped leaves with serrated edges, and clusters of small green flowers. All parts of the plant bristle with stinging hairs.

Habitat Native to Eurasia, nettle is a common invasive weed that inhabits the edges of woodlands, ditches, fields, waste places, and neglected gardens. It grows in temperate regions worldwide.

Approximate native range

of the urinary tract. Dried roots or root **extracts** are suggested for treating the symptoms of enlarged prostate (BPH). Nettle is also prescribed for anemia, for hay fever, asthma and other allergic conditions, to rid the body of uric acid in treating gout, to stimulate circulation, to clear inflammatory skin conditions such as eczema, and to control uterine hemorrhage and heavy menstrual bleeding.

Cultivation and Preparation

NETTLE GROWS WELL IN DAMP, NITROGEN-RICH SOIL IN FULL sun or light shade. It can be grown from seed, cuttings, or divisions of the roots. Nettle is cut in early summer before flowering. It quickly regrows and three or four harvests of the above-ground parts are possible with commercially grown nettle plants. Once dried, nettle loses its sting. Nettle roots are harvested in autumn.

Research

THE STINGING HAIRS OF NETTLE ACT LIKE MINIATURE SYRINGES that inject a mixture of histamine, formic acid, and acetylcholine into the skin; these chemicals cause extreme irritation. The plant itself contains **polysaccharides** and large protein-sugar molecules known as lectins; these substances have been shown to stimulate the immune system. Other active compounds in nettle include various **flavonoids**, which have been shown in animal studies and clinical trials to exhibit strong **diuretic** action. Nettle leaf extracts also have proven **anti-inflammatory** effects. The polysaccharides in nettle are thought to be largely responsible for this anti-inflammatory activity. In Germany, clinical trials in which nettle extracts were given to people with rheumatic complaints showed the herb does significantly reduce pain. In another study, nettle preparations enhanced the activity of a prescription anti-inflammatory drug used to treat rheumatoid arthritis. Other research has demonstrated that nettle root preparations provide symptomatic relief of urinary difficulties associated with benign prostatic hyperplasia (BPH); nettle was shown to be as effective as treatment with the most common BPH drug, finasteride, but with fewer side effects.

The idea of making clothes from nettles initially sounds about as inviting as wearing a hair shirt. After all, nettle is a plant most famous for causing extreme irritation. But beneath the stinging hairs that cover the surface of a nettle plant are strong fibers imbedded in the stem tissue. In Europe, nettle fibers were used for thousands of years to make cordage, cloth, and other materials in much the same way as the fibers from two better-known plants, hemp and flax. Processing nettle fibers is tedious work. After tall, healthy plants are cut, the stems are dried, steeped, and then the fibers inside them teased out, separated, cleaned, and dried. The fibers are then spun into yarn. Nettle fibers are especially sturdy and fabrics made from them are extremely durable and less prone to tearing than any other type of fabric made from natural fibers. Nettle has been used to make heavy, rugged fabrics such as sailcloth and sacking. But the finest nettle fibers can be spun and woven into fabrics supple and strong as silk. During World War I, Germany ran short of cotton for making military uniforms. The plant chosen as a substitute source of fabric fibers was nettle. Nettle fibers are still used on a small scale to make specialty fabrics. These are known for their ability to absorb and release moisture as well as petroleum-based microfiber fabrics.

See Also: *Herbal Medicine Expanded Commission E Monographs* by M. Blumenthal, A. Goldberg, and J. Brinckmann, American Botanical Council, 2000; *World Health Organization (WHO) Monographs on Selected Medicinal Plants, Vol. 2,* 2002.

URTICA DIOICA | Stinging Nettle

Common Names Sweet wormwood, *qing hao*, sweet Annie, annual wormwood

Latin Name *Artemisia annua*

Family Asteraceae

Parts Used Leaves

Description Common in grasslands and open areas, *Artemisia annua* is a fast-growing, bushy annual that has a neat growth habit and can reach three feet in height. It has green, finely divided leaves that are covered with a soft down of fine hairs. Very tiny, green-yellow flowers are produced in clusters.

Habitat Native to Asia and Eastern Europe, *Artemisia annua* has dispersed throughout temperate and subtropical regions around the world. It has become naturalized in the United States.

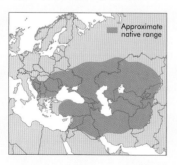

Approximate native range

Sweet Wormwood
Artemisia annua

A T FIRST GLANCE, A CLUMP OF *ARTEMISIA ANNUA* COULD be mistaken for the feathery foliage of asparagus. But its distinctive scent would give it away as sweet wormwood or sweet Annie—or as it is known in much of the Asian world, as *qing hao*. The plant is highly aromatic; when crushed the leaves have a sharp, slightly balsamic aroma, one that appeals to some people but is irritating to others. Qing hao was traditionally used by Chinese herbalists for millennia in the treatment of many illnesses, including malaria. To the rest of the world, it was just another *Artemisia* until research revealed that the herb is the source of a powerful antimalarial agent that has relatively few side effects. Easy to grow and highly adaptable, qing hao offers hope against a disease that annually affects 500 million people around the globe, and may kill more than two million every year.

Traditional and Current Medicinal Uses

FOR MORE THAN 2,000 YEARS, THE CHINESE HAVE BREWED THE leaves of qing hao into a bitter tea that was used to reduce fevers, including those brought on by malaria, and in treating inflammation, headaches, dizziness, chills, nosebleeds, and some digestive complaints. Externally, it was used on abscesses and boils. Much more recently, the herb was an ingredient in the flavoring of beverages in Europe, but the plant was not much used as a medicinal.

That situation changed in the 1980s, when the Western world became keenly aware of qing hao's potential through an article published in a Chinese medical journal. That article discussed a substance extracted from qing hao and its effective use in treating malaria. The substance is called *qinghaosu* in Chinese, but it is now known as artemisinin to scientists and doctors worldwide. Artemisinin was discovered in 1972 by Tu Youyou, a Chinese researcher involved in a program to test the efficacy of nearly 200 traditional Chinese medicines in treating malaria. In the decades following artemisinin's discovery, it has been shown to have marked antiparasitic and antibacterial activity. In clinical trials, it has proven extremely effective in fighting malaria, a disease caused by the protozoan malarial parasite *Plasmodium*; the parasite is introduced into the body through the bite of a mosquito. Artemisinin is especially effective in treating chloroquine-resistant strains of the disease. (Chloroquine has been one of the most commonly used antimalarial drugs for years and the malaria parasite has developed resistance to it and other chloroquine-derived drugs.) Many countries have now approved the use of artemisinin for the treatment of malaria. *Artemisia annua* also contains substances that act as immunosuppressants. These may be helpful in treating diseases such as lupus.

Cultivation and Preparation

ARTEMISIA ANNUA PREFERS A SUNNY SITE AND SANDY TO loamy, well-drained soil; it does well even in poor soil. In fact, plants grown in poor soil are typically hardier and more aromatic. Propagation is by seed sown in spring or by root division in autumn. *Artemisia annua* plants are vigorous and essentially disease- and pest-free. Leaves are typically harvested in summer before flowering.

Research

ARTEMISIA ANNUA'S KEY CONSTITUENTS INCLUDE AN **essential oil, flavonoids,** and artemisinin. As part of its chemical structure, artemisinin contains a peroxide that is key to the substance's disease-fighting actions. When the peroxide encounters high iron concentrations it makes the artemisinin molecule unstable, so that it breaks apart, releasing **free radicals** in the process. Malaria parasites congregate inside red blood cells, which are full of hemoglobin, an iron-containing compound. Thus, when artemisinin molecules enter iron-rich red blood cells, they release free radicals, which kill the malarial parasites. Two other potent malaria-fighting chemicals have been synthetically derived from artemisinin: artemether and artesunate. Artesunate also has been shown to inhibit the growth of some types of cancer cells.

NEW HOPE FOR A MALARIA CURE

An estimated 700,000 to 2.7 million persons die of malaria each year—75 percent of them African children. Artemisinin, derived from *Artemisia annua*, is now widely used as an effective and affordable anti-malaria drug. Administered as a mixture of artemisinin (or its derivatives artemether and artesunate) and other "partner" antimalarial drugs, this treatment is called ACT, short for artemisinin-based combination therapy. Clinical trials have shown that ACT is more than 90 percent effective in curing malaria; recovery typically occurs after only three days. The artemisinin compounds kill malaria parasites more quickly and effectively than any other known antimalarial drug. The World Health Organization recommends ACT as the best strategy for malaria treatment in countries where chloroquine-resistant strains occur. Artemisinin and its derivatives are now a standard component of malaria treatment in China, Vietnam, and several other countries in Asia and Africa. Up until recently, China and Vietnam were the primary producers of *A. annua* for production of artemisinin. However, worldwide demand for ACTs quadrupled from 2003 to 2004 and shortages of artemisinin resulted from this increased demand. This, in turn, has led to the herb's cultivation in other parts of the world, including countries in East Africa.

See Also: A Field Guide to Medicinal Plants and Herbs: Eastern and Central North America, 2nd ed. by S. Foster and J. Duke, Houghton Mifflin, 2000; A Field Guide to Medicinal Plants and Herbs: Western North America by S. Foster and C. Hobbs, Houghton Mifflin, 2002.

Common Names Tea, green tea, black tea, oolong tea

Latin Name *Camellia sinensis*

Family Theaceae

Parts Used Leaves, buds

Description Tea grows as a large evergreen shrub or small tree. In the wild it may reach 30 feet in height, but under cultivation tea plants are typically less than seven feet tall. *Camellia's* lance-shaped leaves are glossy dark green with finely serrated edges. White, fragrant flowers are succeeded by small, brown fruits with three partitions; each of these contains a single seed.

Habitat Native to Southeast Asia, *Camellia* has been cultivated in China and India for thousands of years. It is now widely cultivated throughout Asia and parts of Africa and the Middle East. Camellia grows best in tropical or subtropical climates where it receives plenty of sun and moisture.

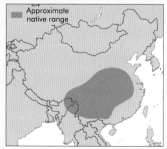

Approximate native range

Tea
Camellia sinensis

AN ANCIENT CHINESE SAYING STATES, "IT IS BETTER TO BE deprived of food for three days, than of tea for one." The Chinese should know—as a culture, they are thought to have been drinking tea, brewed from the dried leaves of *Camellia sinensis*, for thousands of years. The first surviving records actually documenting tea's use there date to the tenth century B.C. Tea was introduced to Europe by Dutch traders in the 1700s, and from there it spread to England, and later to North America. Today, hundreds of millions of people drink tea every day. It is second only to water as the world's most common beverage. Tea is such a familiar drink, in fact, that most people do not think of it as an herbal medicine. Yet tea is an integral part of the traditional medicine cultures of China, Japan, Korea, and Hong Kong. *Camellia sinensis* has been extensively studied. The results of many experiments suggest that tea can contribute to a healthy lifestyle as it exhibits a wide variety of medicinal effects.

Traditional and Current Medicinal Uses

THERE ARE THREE MAIN VARIETIES: GREEN TEA, OOLONG TEA, and black tea. All are derived from the leaves of *Camellia sinensis*. But because of differences in processing, these three teas have different characteristics and varying concentrations of active chemical constituents. Green tea is made from leaves that have simply been steamed and dried. To make oolong tea, the leaves are partly fermented and then dried. Black tea is made from fully fermented leaves that are then roasted. Green tea has been drunk for thousands of years in China, India, Japan, Thailand, and other countries in Southeast Asia. It is an important component of both traditional Chinese and Indian medicine, used as a stimulant, **diuretic**, to help regulate blood sugar and body temperature, and to improve the condition of the heart. Green tea also is regarded as a treatment for controlling bleeding and healing wounds, preventing tooth decay, and promoting digestion and mental clarity. Oolong teas are thought to be effective in lowering blood cholesterol levels and possibly reducing high blood pressure. Black tea has

astringent properties and is an age-old remedy for upset stomachs and treating diarrhea. Recently, tea—and green tea in particular—has been shown to possibly reduce the risk of atherosclerosis, lower total cholesterol while raising "good" **high-density lipoprotein** (HDL) levels in blood, reduce risk of heart attack, protect against a wide variety of cancers, positively stimulate the central nervous system, and guard against diabetes and liver disease.

Cultivation and Preparation

TEA GROWS BEST ON WELL-DRAINED, FERTILE ACID SOIL AT fairly high altitude in tropical to subtropical climates. Cultivated tea plants seem to thrive in locations where daytime temperatures are reasonably cool (as they are at higher altitudes) and where morning mists shield the plants from the sun. Tea is harvested by hand. For high quality teas, only the youngest leaves—the leaf bud and the second and third leaves below it—are plucked. After tea leaves are harvested, they are processed in various ways to produce the different varieties of tea.

Research

THE YOUNG LEAVES OF *CAMELLIA* PLANTS CONTAIN A WIDE range of chemical compounds. The most important in terms of tea's medicinal value are **phytochemicals** known as polyphenol catechins. These are powerful **antioxidants,** substances that scavenge destructive **free radicals** produced in the body. Free radicals can induce mutations in DNA (the genetic material), damage cell membranes, and destroy cells. The presence of free radicals has been linked to a number of diseases and health conditions. Neutralizing free radicals is thought to reduce, and even prevent, the damage and diseases they may foster. Clinical studies indicate that regular tea drinking is safe and may contribute to the prevention of heart disease, heart attack, and atherosclerosis; several kinds of cancer including cancer of the mouth, breast, bladder, skin, stomach, pancreas, lungs, prostate, and esophagus; diabetes; liver disease; and irritable bowel syndrome. Some studies suggest that green tea or green tea extract may help burn fat by raising the body's metabolic rate, but more research in this area is needed.

THE BIRTH OF TEA

According to legend, the drinking of tea got its start with the early Chinese emperor, Shen Nong, about 5,000 years ago. In addition to being a clever and fair ruler, Shen Nong had a scientific mind and a health-conscious attitude. One of his edicts required that all drinking water be boiled in order to prevent disease. One summer day while visiting part of his kingdom, or so the story goes, Shen Nong and his attendants stopped to rest. In accordance with his ruling, the servants began to boil water to drink, setting up their cooking fire near a tall bush with glossy green leaves. A puff of wind dislodged several dried leaves clinging to the bush's branches. The leaves fell into the boiling water, transforming it into a clear brown liquid. Intrigued, Shen Nong swallowed some of the hot drink and found it very refreshing. And so tea was born, becoming an integral part of Chinese culture, diet, and medicine. From there its use and enjoyment spread to Japan and other Asian countries, and ultimately, to the rest of the world.

See Also: The ABC Clinical Guide to Herbs by M. Blumenthal, T. Hall, and A. Goldberg, American Botanical Council, 2003; *Medicinal Plants of the World* by B. van Wyk and M. Wink, Timber Press, 2004.

HEALING PLANTS OF
Oceania

PELA LILO DID NOT LOOK NOTICEABLY DIFFERENT FROM THE OTHER women of Falealupo village on the Samoan island of Savaii. Each morning at sunrise she was out picking up breadfruit leaves on the white sands fronting her thatched house. Like other women in the village, she was devoted to children and grandchildren, weaving Pandanus leaf mats for them to sleep on, and washing their clothes in the swamp nearby. But the massage oil Pela prepared each month by laying grated coconut in large pans underneath the hot tropical sun *was* completely different from that prepared by other village women. In addition to the fragrant gardenia and ylang-ylang flowers she added to scent the oil, she also included ifiifi fruits that grew on a tree tended by her sister-in-law. When subjected to careful pharmacological analysis, the oil produced by Pela and other women in the Lilo family was shown to have an extraordinary property: It completely blocks cellular inflammation due to the presence of a substance called a COX-2 inhibitor. This activity was traced to the ifiifi fruits. With them, Pela Lilo was producing the Samoan version of Vioxx.

Word of Pela's healing touch spread not only through her village but throughout the island. Samoans with various forms of inflammatory disease would journey to Pela's hut, where, without any request for remuneration, Pela would rub them with the leaves of healing plants after first laying down a soothing coat of her special massage oil. Not only did her massage oil lead to the discovery of one of the first known COX-2 inhibitory compounds, but a bark she used led to a major advance in AIDS therapy.

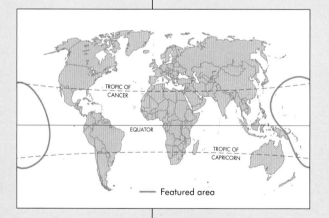

MEDICINAL PLANTS OF OCEANIA
USED THROUGHOUT THE PACIFIC ISLANDS, KAVA IS a healing plant presented to visitors as a sign of hospitality. Known as 'ava in most Polynesian languages, the medicinal extract is manufactured from the underground stems and roots of kava (*Piper methysticum*) and mixed with water. Originating in Vanuatu and other Melanesian islands to the east, kava is always accompanied by elaborate rituals and rhetoric. In Polynesia, kava is a sacred plant, and is used with care and respect. In Melanesia, visitors to Fijiian villages bring slender roots of kava, carefully tied and wrapped in newspaper to show respect. Elsewhere, villagers present large ceremonial kava roots to visitors as a gift. In Samoa, kava is traditionally prepared by village maidens—

guarded 24 hours a day to ensure their virginity—while orators extol the sanctity of the occasion with references to both nature and mythology: "Our meeting is as sacred as the touching of the tips of two clouds in the heavens, as sacred as the motionless mating of sea turtles in the ocean. This morning, we have the joy of a pigeon hunter in his jungle blind. Our morning is clear, and its sanctity derives from the sacredness of our gathering."

Protocol at a kava ceremony is strict: Chiefs and visitors face each other across woven mats, sitting cross-legged in a strict hierarchy. Kava, unlike peyote, mescaline, or other psychoactive plants used in indigenous rituals elsewhere, has a subtle effect. Rather than ushering the participants into another world, kava serves to bind them to their duties and each other in this one, reinforcing the existing social order, particularly the status of village chiefs.

The kava cup is distributed in strict order of hierarchy, with the young man serving the kava holding the cup high above his head as he moves across the *alofi sa,* or sacred space, within the hut. Before drinking from the kava cup, the recipient pours a few drops on the ground, to symbolize returning goodness to Earth, and then ceremoniously intones "*ia manuia*" ("Let there be blessings").

The village virgin in Saipipi, Savaii Island, Samoa, ceremonially prepares kava for village visitors. Village chiefs sit behind her on mats. Kava is a drink used to welcome visitors throughout Oceania. It is also sold in village markets as a relaxing drink and as a stress reliever.

PRECEDING PAGES: *Samoan healer Pela Lilo (left) applies an herbal remedy to a sick villager. She is assisted by her daughter-in-law, Fa'asaina Lamositele (right).*

Within seconds, kava's chemical compounds take effect in the body. Molecules—known as kavalactones—pass through mucous membranes of the mouth and cheeks, producing a tingling sensation in the lips and tongue. Acting on the central nervous system, kavalactones and other compounds produce a tranquilizing effect. One feels subdued, but the mind remains clear.

Believing kava to be an indigenous analogue of valium, health food stores throughout North America and Europe began selling kava extracts as mild sedatives and stress relievers: Kava bars appeared in places as disparate as Maui and Amsterdam. But recently, the pills were withdrawn from the market because of a possible association with liver failure noted in Germany. Interviews with villagers who drink kava regularly and analysis of hospital admission records in Samoa demonstrate no such linkage. Are German cases associated with excessive use of kava pills? Are Europeans who use kava more likely to consume alcohol or anti-depression medications? Could organic solvents used in commercial extractions—different from the water infusions made in Polynesia—produce dangerous residues? Until such questions are answered, what seems to be a gentle stress reliever will be kept off the market in the U.S., Germany, and elsewhere.

Primarily a ceremonial plant, kava is sometimes used to treat back pain or muscle aches. More serious ailments are treated by a village healer. Women predominate in Polynesia as healers. In Tonga, healers typically gain knowledge of medicinal plants from their mothers and grandmothers. This pattern of passing down knowledge matrilineally also occurs in Samoa. In Tahiti, some healers even hold the island equivalent of patents—even if their mixture of roots and leaves can be reproduced by another villager, the remedy will not be efficacious.

MEDICINAL PRACTICES IN OCEANIA

THROUGHOUT OCEANIA, INDIGENOUS HEALERS BELIEVE THEIR HEALING VOCATION IS A call—a divine assignment—that comes to only a few. Since causes of disease in their world view are disparate—infection, trauma, interpersonal hostility,

A remedy for hepatitis is prepared by Samoan healer Ake Lilo in Falealupo village, Savaii Island, Samoa. Bark from the mamala tree is scraped onto a clean coth, collected in a bag, and boiled to produce a tea.

poor diet, and even neglect of deceased ancestors are all believed to cause disease—the cures themselves are diverse in nature. Medicinal plants are only part of a healer's repertoire: Specialized massage, bone setting, counseling, midwifery, even the use of ritual incantations all play a role. But Oceania healers typically differ from other members of their society in their remarkable knowledge of healing plants.

In Samoa, for example, Pela Lilo could easily identify more than a hundred species of medicinal plants by name and had memorized more than twice that many herbal formulations. Years of study with her mother and grandmother had made Pela a highly valued member of Falealupo village. As she became infirm with age, Pela would diagnose villagers' diseases, and then send her daughter-in-law to the rain forest to collect appropriate plants. Then she would pound the medicinal plants in a rock bowl and mix them with water to produce an **infusion** that could be drunk or rubbed on the skin to produce a slow, controlled dose.

When analyzed by modern laboratory methods, the centuries-old herbal wisdom possessed by Pela and other healers led to startling scientific breakthroughs. Consider, for example, a remedy Pela prepared from the mamala tree (*Homalanthus nutans*) to treat hepatitis. The bark of the mamala tree is scraped into a clean cloth, and the resultant tea bag is immersed into boiling water. After the mamala tea cools, the patient is allowed to drink the **astringent**, bitter liquid. Analysis of this tea by scientists at the National Institutes of Health showed it to be effective in protecting cells against the AIDS virus. Trials with laboratory animals of the resultant drug, prostratin, are promising. As prostratin advances to human clinical trials, an important question arises: Who should profit from the drug if it is approved?

The AIDS drug candidate prostratin, a chemical compound found in a remedy made from the bark of the Samoan mamala tree (Homalanthus nutans), is used by Samoan healers to treat hepatitis.

The not-for-profit AIDS Research Alliance of California, which licensed prostratin rights, was required by the National Institutes of Health to negotiate an equitable return to the people of Samoa. The landmark agreement between ARA and Samoa grants the people of Samoa 20 percent of ARA's profits from prostratin, to be divided between the Samoan government, the village where the plant was first collected, and the families of the healers who originally taught researchers about it. Recently, researchers at the University of California, Berkeley have begun attempts to clone prostratin-producing genes within the mamala tree so that an inexpensive supply of the drug can be generated. Agreement was reached between the University of California and the people of Samoa to share equally in the proceeds from the research.

Polynesians can also profit in other ways from their medicinal plants. A decade ago, juice from the fruits of *Morinda citrifolia*—called *noni* in Hawaii, *nonu* in Tonga and Samoa, and *nono* in Tahiti—was introduced to the American market. Touted as a tonic, "noni juice" has gained significant market share in North America, Europe, and Japan, even though healers typically use the leaves of the plant rather than the odorous fruits used to produce the commercial juice. In Hawaii, Tahiti, Tonga, and Samoa hundreds of acres are devoted to production of noni, now a major export crop.

Polynesian medicinal plants are also used to heal external as well as internal ailments. The round, coin-size leaves of gotu kola (*Centella asiatica*) are applied as a plaster to wounds, abrasions, and coral cuts. Containing antibacterial and wound-healing components, gotu kola leaves are the Tongan equivalent of antibacterial ointments such as Neosporin.

Another example of a Polynesian healing plant used for cosmetic purposes as well as health is forest ginger (*Zingiber zerumbet*). Each juicy bulb of this plant, when compressed, produces nearly half a liter of fragrant fluid. Used as a shampoo and hair conditioner, this fluid leaves the hair feeling silky and smooth. The prevalence of such island beauty aids, coupled with alluring advertisements, perhaps masks the real power of the healing plants of Polynesia. Researchers have found, for example, that the bark of the indigenous gatae tree (*Erythrina variegata*), used by healers to treat insect stings and inflammation, contains compounds that function much like ibuprofen.

The future of healing in Oceania faces serious challenges. Apprenticeships for healers—up to seven years—leading to unpaid service to the village is not attractive to young people enticed by the lures of capital cities. Foreign radio and television programs compete for the attention of impressionable youth. The chain of oral transmission of healing lore, from generation to generation, is in danger of being broken, and many healers die without communicating their knowledge. Further, modern marketing of Polynesian plants, such as kava or noni, often sidestep or ignore the experience of healers. And the plants themselves are at risk—throughout the Pacific islands native forests are felled by logging companies with precious plant species disappearing forever. Despite these challenges, throughout New Zealand, Hawaii, and the islands of Fiji, Samoa, Tonga, and Tahiti, there is a resurgence of interest in traditional customs and healing. Should a major pharmaceutical, such as prostratin, be developed from a Polynesian medicinal plant, the validation and benefits to island people will do much to stabilize interest in healing plants of Oceania. ✍

OPPOSITE PAGE:
*Researchers have recently discovered new anti-inflammatory molecules in the bark of the Samoan gatae tree (*Erythrina variegata*), used by villagers to treat bee stings.*

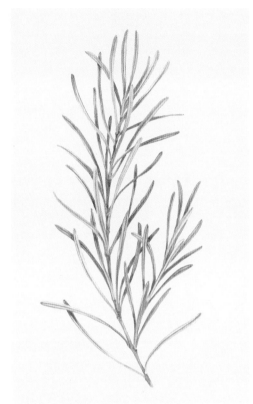

Common Names Tea tree, ti tree

Latin Name *Melaleuca alternifolia*

Family Myrtaceae

Parts Used Leaves

Description The tea tree is a small, narrow tree, growing to a height of only about 20 feet, with soft, alternate leaves and yellowish flowers shaped like bottle brushes. *Melaleuca*, from the Greek *melas* ("black") and *leukos* ("white"), most likely refers to the contrast between its dark green leaves and its loose, flaky, paper-thin, white bark.

Habitat The tea tree grows naturally only in a small, swampy area of northeastern New South Wales, Australia, where rivers often flood the lowlands. Tea tree production has spread to north Queensland and western Australia.

Approximate native range

Tea Tree
Melaleuca alternifolia

IN AUSTRALIA, "TEA TREE" REFERS NOT JUST TO A single tree but to aromatic trees of the myrtle family well known for their use as beverage teas. In international commerce, however, tea tree has come to refer to just one species of *Melaleuca*—*M. alternifolia*, a shrub or small tree of Australia's ubiquitous myrtle family, with papery bark, alternate leaves, and cream-colored flowers. Tea tree oil is one of the strongest natural antiseptics known, useful for treating many bacterial and fungal infections. The clear **essential oil** has a spicy smell, similar to eucalyptus oil, and can be found in a wide array of pharmaceutical, cosmetic, and household products. *M. alternifolia* is only one of more than 300 species of tea trees native to Australia, but because of the economic success of its oil over the past few decades, it is by far the most well known—often referred to as "the wonder from down under." Australia exports 80 percent of its tea tree oil to the United States and other countries.

Traditional and Current Medicinal Uses

AUSTRALIAN ABORIGINES HAVE MADE USE OF *MELALEUCA* FOR centuries, applying the pulp of crushed leaves to a host of ailments. They used it to treat headaches and repel insects, and washed themselves in the healing waters of the swamp where the trees grow. In 1770, when Captain James Cook and his crew made their first voyage to Australia, they observed Aborigines brewing the leaves and first called it a "tea tree," returning to England with samples for study. Not until early in the 20th century did research confirm the antibacterial, antifungal and **anti-inflammatory** effects of tea tree oil. In 1925, Australian scientist Arthur Penfold, credited with discovering the benefits of the tea tree, showed that as an antiseptic, tea tree oil is 13 times stronger than carbolic acid, which was the standard at the time. When Australian soldiers in World War II used tea tree oil from their first aid kits as a disinfectant, the rest of the world took notice of its medicinal properties—and high demand followed. With the commerical production of penicillin in the mid-1940s, tea tree oil use declined.

In the 1980s, an intense marketing campaign touted tea tree oil as "a medicine chest in a bottle"—and demand has grown exponentially ever since. Today, tea tree oil is used for a wide array of ailments including cuts, wounds, warts, acne, sore throat, cold, flu, congestion, athlete's foot and other fungal infections, vaginal infections, hemorrhoids, body odor, bad breath, cold sores, burns, dandruff, eczema, insect bites, sore muscles, joint injuries, and HIV support.

Cultivation and Preparation

TEA TREE REQUIRES A RICH, WELL-DRAINED, MOISTURE RETENtive soil, free of lime and nitrogen. The species likes full sun and is not cold hardy, but will tolerate shade and favors wetlands—making it difficult to harvest. The resilient tea trees are harvested every 12 to 18 months; oil is steam distilled from leaves and terminal branches.

Research

RESEARCH HAS SHOWN TEA TREE OIL TO BE AN EFFECTIVE treatment for acne and for fungal infections. A 1990 clinical trial involving 124 patients provided evidence of the effectiveness of *M. alternifolia* oil in the treatment of acne. A **double-blind** study showed a concentration of 5 percent tea tree oil was less effective because of slower onset of action than a 5 percent benzoyl peroxide lotion. However, clinical assessment and self reporting of side effects indicated that the tea tree oil preparation was better tolerated with subjects experiencing less scaling, dryness, and irritation of the skin than those using the benzoyl peroxide preparation. Another double-blind study found 100 percent tea tree oil as effective as clortimazole (used in over-the-counter creams) for treating fungi affecting toenails. Further studies are needed to confirm claims of effectiveness of the oil in the treatment of athlete's foot, varioius types of dermatitis, hemorrhoids, vaginal infections, chicken pox, and herpes zoster (shingles) infections.

> CAUTION Though it is sometimes used for mouth rinses or toothpastes in small amounts, tea tree oil should never be swallowed or taken internally and can cause nerve damage and coma in addition to burning and rashes on sensitive skin.

MELALEUCA ALTERNIFOLIA | Tea Tree

Among the many species in the *Melaleuca* genus is a cousin of *M. alternifolia* known as the cajuput tree or the broadleaf paperbark tree (*M. quinquenervia*). Like *M. alternifolia*, its famous cousin, *M. quinquenervia* is also harvested and sold under the name cajuput oil, though with much less success. Unfortunately, its claim to fame is as the nemesis of south Florida. Miami forester John Gifford was the first to bring seeds to Florida in 1906; as recently as the 1980s, however, the U.S. Department of Agriculture imported and grew *M. quinquenervia* for research. By 1990, a Florida task force reported that the tree constitutes "one of the most serious ecological threats to the biological integrity of south Florida's natural systems." Thriving in wet or dry soils, it chokes out natural vegetation and provides little benefit to wildlife. The *M. quinquenervia* infestation has increased 50-fold in the last 25 years, spreading across 450,000 acres of south Florida. Attempts to burn trees revealed the cajuput tree's resistance to fire. Thick, spongy bark protects the tree, which not only resprouts quickly, but, once burned, sends forth millions of seeds from hard seed capsules. Currently, Florida's plan focuses on containment. Dense groves are left alone, but outlying trees are prevented from invading new territory and worsening the problem.

See Also: *World Health Organization (WHO) Monographs on Selected Medicinal Plants, Vol. 2, 2002; Medicinal Herbs: History, Use, Recommended Dosages & Cautions* by S. Foster, Interweave Press, 1998.

Thuja
Thuja occidentalis

THUJA IS A COMMON LANDSCAPING SHRUB. THERE ARE only a half dozen species in the genus *Thuja*, but these have numerous cultivars that come in many different sizes, colors, and growth habits. Most are relatively slow-growing and all have a pungent, cedar-like aroma that some people find refreshing and others irritating. *Thuja occidentalis* is indigenous to southeastern Canada and the northeastern United States. It was used by Native Americans of that region as a source of wood and fibers for canoes, bows, rope, and baskets. They also burned the fragrant wood of thuja in smoky fires, both for its scent and to banish evil spirits. The name *thuja* is a Latinized form of a Greek word that means "to fumigate or sacrifice." Native Americans also used thuja medicinally to banish fevers and colds and for a variety of other ailments. Thuja remains a useful herbal medicine, but it contains thujone, a known neurotoxin. One of thuja's most common uses is in removing warts.

Common Names Thuja, eastern arborvitae, eastern white cedar, northern white cedar, swamp cedar, tree of life

Latin Name *Thuja occidentalis*

Family Cupressaceae

Parts Used Young leafy twigs

Description Eventually reaching 40 to 50 feet, arborvitae is slow-growing, narrow, aromatic conifer with flattened branches covered with tiny, scale-like leaves. Branches bear tiny, black male cones and erect, yellow-green female cones with overlapping cone scales.

Habitat Native to eastern North America, thuja thrives on wet, marshy ground and along river banks. It is widely planted as an ornamental.

Approximate native range

Traditional and Current Medicinal Uses

NATIVE AMERICAN TRIBES OF THE NORTHEASTERN UNITED States prized thuja for its power to heal fever, headache, coughs, and aching joints. They also used it for menstrual problems, swelling, and heart disease. A tea made from thuja branches was a folk remedy for rheumatism among loggers who harvested the trees in centuries past. During the 19th century, American **Eclectic** physicians and herbalists used thuja to treat colds, bronchitis, severe cough, rheumatism, uterine and menstrual complaints, and some types of cancer. It was also a known **abortifacient**, and was used to combat the side effects of smallpox vaccinations. Thuja was listed in the **United States Pharmacopoeia** briefly at the end of the 19th century as both a **diuretic** and uterine stimulant.

In modern herbal medicine, the herb is used—under the supervision of a professional qualified practitioner—as an **expectorant** and decongestant associated with colds, for bronchial complaints, especially those linked to congestive heart failure, and for rheumatism, urinary tract infections, skin rashes, and eczema. **Extracts** can be painted on the skin to relieve rheumatic aches and pains, neuralgia, and strained or stiff muscles; **tinctures** can be applied to warts and polyps. Thuja also has been suggested as an anti-cancer agent.

Cultivation and Preparation

THUJA DOES BEST IN RICH, WELL-DRAINED SOIL THAT IS consistently moist—hence its common name "swamp cedar." The trees are usually propagated from seed or by cuttings. The tender tips of the branches are used in herbal medicine; these include both the leaves and the underlying bark. Cuttings are dried and then used in **decoctions**, tinctures, and in liquid extracts. Thuja is commonly combined with witch hazel (*Hamamelis virginiana*) to make a preparation used to treat the skin condition eczema.

Research

THUJA CONTAINS FLAVONOIDS, TANNINS, POLYSACCHARIDES and a **volatile oil**. The herb has well-established antiviral activity and some of the polysaccharides in thuja have been shown in the laboratory to have immune system-stimulating properties, especially in activating certain types of white blood cells. A combination of *Thuja occidentalis*, *Baptisia tinctoria*, and *Echinacea* spp. has been used as an immune stimulant to treat chronic bronchitis and genital herpes; results of very limited clinical trials have been mixed. Thuja has also been tested, in combination with several other herbs, to stimulate white cell activity in cancer patients, but with little or no effect. The most active component of thuja's volatile oil is thujone, a known central nervous system toxin. Prolonged use of thujone is not recommended because its effects can be cumulative. In small amounts, used for a an appropriately limited period, thujone is considered safe. Applying the volatile oil of thuja has been shown to be quite successful for eliminating small warts and polyps, although large, solid warts do not typically respond as well to this treatment.

CAUTION Arborvitae and its preparations should only be used under the supervision of qualified practitioners.

TREE OF LIFE

Another common name for thuja is "tree of life," which is a literal translation of the Latin words *arbor* (tree) and *vita* (life). The name dates from 1535, when French explorer Jacques Cartier was exploring eastern Canada and the Saint Lawrence River. Around mid-November, Cartier's three ships and crews of more than a hundred men became trapped in the ice as the river's surface froze over. There was nothing to do but wait for winter to pass, and Cartier's men were forced to pass the season living off their stores. Only a few weeks had passed by the time the first cases of scurvy appeared; it would be centuries before the cause of the disease was known to be a lack of vitamin C. As Cartier's men began to die from scurvy, he sought help from the Iroquois who were in their winter camps along the shore. The Iroquois eventually showed Cartier how to make a scurvy remedy by boiling the branch tips of the thuja tree to make a tea. Cartier did as they instructed and administered the tea to his ailing crew. The men recovered rapidly. Out of gratitude for this new scurvy cure, Cartier carried a specimen of thuja (also known as arborvitae) back to France at the end of his expedition and presented it to the king, who dubbed it "l'arbor de vie" and had it planted in the royal medicinal gardens. Thuja is thought to be the first North American tree introduced into Europe.

See Also: *A Field Guide to Medicinal Plants and Herbs: Eastern and Central North America, 2nd ed.* by S. Foster and J. Duke, Houghton Mifflin, 2000; *Native American Ethnobotany* by D. Moerman, Timber Press, 1998.

Thyme
Thymus vulgaris

Common Names Thyme, common thyme, garden thyme

Latin Name *Thymus vulgaris*

Family Lamiaceae

Parts Used Leaves, flowers, oil

Description Thyme is a low-growing perennial herb with thin, branching stems and small grayish green leaves. Tiny white or purplish flowers are arranged in dense whorls on terminal spikes.

Habitat Native to the Mediterranean region, thyme is grown in herb gardens and cultivated commercially in most temperate regions of the world.

Approximate native range

G ARDENERS LOVE THYME FOR ITS NEAT GROWING HABIT, colorful flowers, and fragrant foliage. Cooks have favored thyme for centuries. It is a classic culinary herb, one of the *fines herbes* of French cuisine, as well as an ingredient in *bouquet garnis*. Thyme is added to soups and stuffings, salads and sauces, sausages and stocks, and it complements nearly every kind of meat, fish, fowl, and vegetable dish imaginable. "When in doubt, use thyme," is a time-honored cook's adage. Thyme's preservative properties have been known since the time of the ancient Egyptians, who used oil of thyme to embalm the dead. The Greeks were very fond of thyme's fragrance—to tell someone they smelled of thyme was considered a compliment. The scent of thyme is also apparently irresistible to bees, which hover in clouds above the plant's diminutive flowers and produce an exceptionally fragrant honey from its nectar. Thyme has been valued as a medicinal herb for as long as it has been cultivated and cooked with. It has proven antiseptic, antibacterial, and antifungal properties, and has long been a remedy for coughs and colds, as well as digestive upsets.

Traditional and Current Medicinal Uses

IN THE FIRST CENTURY A.D. THE ROMAN PHYSICIAN PLINY THE Elder wrote that thyme cured melancholy and aberrations of the mind and could bring people out of epileptic convulsions. The Greeks used thyme for nervous conditions and valued it for its antiseptic properties. In the Middle Ages, thyme was a remedy for gastric upsets, flatulence, bronchial complaints, coughs, colds, laryngitis, colic, rheumatism, and menstrual disorders. Tea brewed from thyme was a folk cure for hangovers. Thyme tea was also used to treat flu as well as gum, mouth, and throat infections. Pillows of thyme were thought to cure depression and banish nightmares. Medieval herbalists boiled it in wine for a digestive tonic. Throughout the past few centuries, thyme was considered effective in relieving acute bronchitis, laryngitis, and coughs and a good remedy for asthma and whooping cough. Thyme was also taken for stomach upsets, lack of appetite, diarrhea, flatulence, colic, and headache. A **poultice** of mashed thyme leaves was used to soothe sores and ease inflammation. Thyme baths and massages with thyme oil were recommended for neuralgia, rheumatism, bruises, and sprains.

Today, thyme is recognized as a powerful antiseptic that also exhibits antibacterial, antispasmodic, antifungal, and **anthelmintic** properties. In modern herbal medicine, the herb is taken for spasmodic coughs, throat and chest infections, and digestive upsets. Thyme oil is used externally to relieve pain.

Cultivation and Preparation

THYME GROWS BEST UNDER HOT, DRY CONDITIONS IN FULL sun and well-drained, slightly stony soil. The herb can be started from seed in spring or by cuttings or division. Harvesting thyme for the herbal medicine market begins just as the plants are starting to flower. Leaves and flowering tops are distilled for their oil or dried and used in a variety of preparations. Fresh thyme is also used.

Research

THERE ARE DOZENS OF SPECIES OF THYMES AND ALL OF THEM are rich in a **volatile oil** that in many consists largely of thymol. Thymol is a powerful and proven antiseptic, a strong antibiotic, and an effective antifungal agent. In pure form, it is also toxic in large quantities; only small amounts are used in herbal preparations and commercial products, such as cough drops, gargles, and antiseptic ointments. Thymol is the primary chemical components of thyme responsible for its antispasmodic, **anti-inflammatory**, and **antitussive** effects. In the 1990s, Scottish researchers found that laboratory animals fed with thyme oil aged more slowly than animals that did not receive the oil in their diets. Researchers hypothesized that thyme oil somehow counters effects of aging, possibly through its **antioxidant** effects. Extracts of thyme have also been shown to destroy the bacterium *Heliobacter pylori*, which has been linked with the formation of stomach ulcers.

> CAUTION Because thyme oil is a uterine stimulant, medicinal doses of thyme and thyme oil should be avoided during pregnancy.

THYME FOR COURAGE

In addition to its culinary and medicinal virtues, thyme has been known since ancient times for its magical and spiritual powers. The Greeks believed that thyme imparted courage to those who used it, especially soldiers. Greek men were said to rub the herb on their chests to anoint themselves with its fragrance. The Romans added thyme to bath water to impart vigor, courage, and strength. One suggestion for the origin of the genus name *Thymus* is that it is derived from the Greek *thumus*, which means "courage." Other sources propose that the origin is the Greek word for "fumigate," a reference to the fact that the herb was burned as incense in ceremonies designed to instill courage for whatever task lay ahead. Thyme was one of the chief ingredients in ritual altar fires that purified sacrifices to make them acceptable to the gods. It was also burned as a part of funeral rites and placed with the dead inside coffins and tombs; thyme was thought to ensure the passage of the dead into the afterlife. There was a long-held belief that the souls of the dead took up residence in the tiny flowers of thyme plants, and that the scent of thyme could often be detected in places where murders had been committed. In medieval times, thyme's link to courage and strength continued. It was customary for ladies to present their bravest knights with scarves on which they had embroidered a sprig of blooming thyme, often with a bee hovering over it.

See Also: *Herbal Medicine Expanded Commission E Monographs* by M. Blumenthal, A. Goldberg, J. Brinckmann, American Botanical Council, 2000; *A Field Guide to Medicinal Plants & Herbs: Eastern & Central North America, 2nd ed.* by S. Foster, J. Duke, Houghton Mifflin, 2000.

Turmeric
Curcuma longa

LOVERS OF INDIAN AND ASIAN CUISINE ARE INTIMATELY familiar with turmeric's bright yellow color and musky, somewhat sharp flavor. This ancient herb from southern Asia is the source of a yellow powder that is widely used as a food coloring and vegetable dye and is one of the principal ingredients in curries and curry powder. It also lends its distinctive flavor to Worcestershire sauce and color to prepared mustard. Turmeric has long been used in the **Ayurvedic, Unani, and Siddha** systems of herbal medicine, as well as in traditional Chinese medicine, for treating liver and digestive problems. It was largely ignored in the West until the 1970s, when research confirmed many of turmeric's traditional uses and revealed its **anti-inflammatory, antioxidant**, antimicrobial, and possible anticancer properties.

Traditional and Current Medicinal Uses

TURMERIC HAS ITS ROOTS DEEP IN TRADITIONAL INDIAN medicine. For centuries it has been used in that country to treat digestive disorders and as a blood purifying tonic for fever, skin conditions, morning sickness, and liver disorders. It was also a remedy for skin infections and sores, sprains, conjunctivitis, arthritis, hemorrhoids, eczema, and to reduce hair growth. In Thailand, turmeric was prescribed for dizziness, peptic ulcers, and gonorrhea. It was administered to stimulate the appetite and control diarrhea, and to treat insect bites, fungal infections of the skin such as athlete's foot, and minor wounds. In China, turmeric was considered a cure for abdominal pain, bloating, chest pain, jaundice, menstrual conditions, and pain after childbirth.

In modern herbal medicine, turmeric is recognized for its beneficial effects in treating stomach upset, flatulence, abdominal cramps, and other digestive disorders. Because of its ability to reduce inflammation, the herb is often recommended by herbal practitioners for rheumatoid arthritis and osteoarthritis. Turmeric is also suggested for treating certain types of cancerous skin lesions, and it is considered a useful antibacterial agent when applied to wounds. Other uses for turmeric include

Common Names Turmeric, Indian saffron, *jiang huang*, yellow ginger

Latin Name *Curcuma longa*

Family Zingiberaceae

Parts Used Root, rhizome (underground stem)

Description A member of the ginger family, turmeric is a stemless, leafy perennial that grows to three feet tall. Its large, shiny, lanceolate leaves and dense spikes of pale-yellow, tubular flowers emerge from a fleshy, tuberous rhizome that is a dull orange color inside.

Habitat Turmeric is thought to be indigenous to India. It is extensively cultivated in all parts of that country and in many other tropical parts of the world, including southern mainland China, Taiwan, Burma, Indonesia, and Japan, as well as continental Africa and Madagascar.

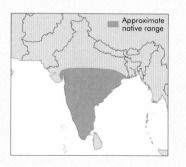

Approximate native range

asthma, skin conditions such as eczema and psoriasis, prevention of cardiovascular disease, reducing cholesterol, and to improve stomach and liver function.

Cultivation and Preparation

A TENDER, TROPICAL PLANT, TURMERIC NEEDS WELL-DRAINED moist soil, sun or light shade, warm temperatures, and high humidity. The herb is propagated by root division, although it can also be started from seed. The roots are harvested during the plant's dormant period. Then they are steamed or boiled before being dried for several days and ultimately ground into the familiar deep yellow powder that, for the herbal medicine market, is used in **decoctions**, **tinctures**, pills, **poultices**, and powders.

Research

TURMERIC'S YELLOW PIGMENTS ARE KNOWN AS CURCUMINOIDS, one of which is curcumin, the herb's most active ingredient. Curcumin has been shown in studies to have antioxidant properties, possibly as strong as those of vitamins C and E. Scientific studies of the herb's anti-inflammatory effects began in 1971 and research has revealed turmeric may rival hydrocortisone for reducing the pain and stiffness associated with various forms of arthritis. Curcumin seems to increase bile production and flow from the liver, enhancing the breakdown of fats during digestion. Some studies indicate it may protect the liver from damage caused by alcohol and various toxins. In some animal studies, curcumin reduced the secretion of stomach acid and seemed to protect the lining of the stomach and intestines. Research on turmeric's effect on the circulatory system indicate it could help prevent atherosclerosis because it tends to reduce levels of **low-density lipoproteins** (LDLs) in the bloodstream and prevent clots in injured blood vessels that could lead to vessel blockage. Laboratory and animal studies also suggest that the herb may be valuable in preventing and treating several forms of cancer, but more research is needed to confirm those results. Turmeric preparations applied to wounds have been shown to prevent bacterial infections such as those caused by *Staphylococcus aureus* and to speed healing.

IT'S GOLDEN

The Chinese name for turmeric is *jiang huang*, which translates as "yellow ginger." In many other languages turmeric is called "yellow root." The name "turmeric" even derives from the Latin *terra merita*, a phrase that refers to a yellow mineral pigment. Turmeric is notorious for its intense yellow color. As most cooks who have ever used the spice know, the yellow stains left by ground turmeric on wooden and plastic utensils, countertops, and fabric are difficult, if not impossible, to remove. Turmeric's gift for imparting such a vivid hue has been exploited for thousands of years. The powdered root has been used as a natural yellow dye for silk, cotton, and wool. Turmeric is still used in Hindu rituals and as a dye for the holy robes of priests. Turmeric water is an Asian cosmetic applied by women to their faces to give their complexions a golden glow. In cooking, a pinch of turmeric added to rice dishes can sometimes fool the eye as a substitute for saffron, but rarely the tongue. Neither its color nor its flavor has the same subtlety as the much costlier saffron. Turmeric has found its way into dozens of products lining the shelves of grocery stores. It is used as a coloring agent in canned beverages, dairy products, ice cream, yogurt, cakes and icings, biscuits, microwave popcorn, cereals, sauces, and gelatin desserts. Combined with another coloring agent called annatto, turmeric is also used to tint cheeses, salad dressings, butter, and margarine.

See Also: Herbal Medicine Expanded Commission E Monographs by M. Blumenthal, A. Goldberg, and J. Brinckmann, American Botanical Council, 2000; World Health Organization (WHO) Monographs on Selected Medicinal Plants, Vol. 1, 1999.

Common Names Valerian, garden valerian, garden heliotrope

Latin Name *Valeriana officinalis*

Family Valerianaceae

Parts Used Rhizome (underground stem), root

Description Growing to four feet, valerian is a clump-forming perennial herb with a yellow-brown rhizome, hollow stems, deeply divided leaves, and small white or pinkish flowers that form flat-topped clusters.

Habitat Valerian is native to Europe and Asia, but is naturalized in North America. In the wild, it grows in grasslands, damp meadows, and along streams. It is also cultivated in several European countries, Japan, and the United States.

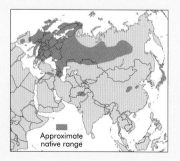
Approximate native range

Valerian
Valeriana officinalis

THE STATELY VALERIAN PLANTS THAT GRACE THE BACK border of many perennial gardens are the same species that first-century Greek physician Dioscorides and others called *phu* because of the offensive odor of its roots. Not all people find the musky odor of valerian roots unpleasant, however, and most cats find it quite irresistible—at least on par with catnip. Despite their disdain for valerian's aroma, the ancient Greeks used the herb medicinally as a **diuretic**. Valerian's popularity blossomed in Europe in the ninth, tenth, and eleventh centuries and the belief that this herb could cure almost everything was reflected in the common name given to it during medieval times: "all-heal." The genus name, *Valeriana*, was given to the herb during this time as well. It comes from the Latin *valere*, meaning "to be in good health." Today the most well-known medicinal use for valerian is as a natural tranquilizer, a safe and effective sedative that is often suggested for insomnia, nervous tension, and stress.

Traditional and Current Medicinal Uses

VALERIAN WAS USED AS EARLY AS THE FOURTH CENTURY B.C., recommended by the Greek physician Hippocrates. Both the Greeks and Romans used valerian medicinally, primarily for digestive problems, nausea, liver complaints, and urinary tract disorders. The Greek physician Galen (A.D. 131–201) was the first to write of valerian's use as a treatment for insomnia. In medieval Europe, valerian was esteemed as a tranquilizing agent that could cure, or at least treat, epilepsy. It was also used during this period as a remedy for stomach and intestinal upsets and as an antidote to the plague. Mixed with cinchona, it was given as a cure for fevers. Use of valerian for insomnia and nervous conditions gained momentum in the 1500s. From the 1700s to the 1900s, it was widely taken as a sedative, a treatment for sleeplessness, as a remedy for nervous disorders characterized by digestive tract distress, trembling, headaches, and heart palpitations.

Valerian root, prepared in teas and **tinctures** and taken as capsules, continues to be used in modern herbal medicine to treat insomnia and other sleep disorders, stress and nervous anxiety, hyperactivity, muscle spasms, depression and despondency, and fatigue. Valerian preparations also are said to slightly lower blood pressure. For several decades, valerian-based herbal medicines were not available in the United States. But today valerian is sold widely in health food stores as a dietary supplement. Further, valerian is often combined with other herbs recognized for sleep-promoting effects, such as hops, passionflower, lemon balm, lavender, and chamomile.

Cultivation and Preparation

VALERIAN IS RELATIVELY EASY TO GROW IN RICH, MOIST, humusy soil in full sun to partial shade. It can be propagated from seed, or by division of the roots. Valerian self-sows and spreads by root runners. For the herbal medicine market, the **rhizomes** and roots of second-year plants are used. These are harvested in autumn after the leaves have died back. Dried roots are prepared as teas or tinctures and **extracts** made into capsules and tablets.

Research

VALERIAN CONTAINS MORE THAN 150 DIFFERENT CHEMICAL constituents, but it is still not clear which are responsible for the herb's sleep-promoting effects. Two groups of constituents, however, appear to be the most likely candidates. The first includes the substances that make up valerian's **volatile oil**, including valerenic acid and its derivatives, which have been demonstrated to induce sleep in animals. Other evidence points to a second group of compounds called iridoids (sometimes known as valepotriates) that in some studies have been shown to affect nervous system functioning. Over the past few decades, several hundred scientific studies on valerian's active ingredients and their effects have been carried out, primarily in Europe. Several of the best-designed and most highly regarded clinical studies have shown that valerian is better than a **placebo** for improving the sleep quality of people suffering from mild insomnia, especially if it is taken for several weeks. One advantage of valerian over many prescription sedatives and sleep aids is that it does not interact with alcohol.

Valerian affects the nervous system of several animals, especially cats, which seem to enter into a kind of intoxicated frenzy when they get a good whiff of it. Crushing the leaves of valerian growing in a garden is an open invitation for cats in the neighborhood to come and roll on the unfortunate plant. It has been said that some cats are so attracted to dried valerian root that they will aggressively destroy containers in which the herb is kept. One famous 18th-century English physician is said to have remarked that the quality of valerian for sale in apothecary shops could be assessed by watching how a cat responded to it. The higher the quality, the more potent the herb, and the more agitated the cat's behavior. Unlike catnip, however, valerian is also attractive to rats. It was once used by rat-catchers to bait their traps, and some people still plant valerian around the borders of their property to lure rats away from the buildings. The folktale of the Pied Piper of Hamlin relates the story of a young musician who led rats out of a village by enchanting them with music he played on his flute. In early German versions of the story, however, the Piper is described as both a musician and an herbalist. It has been suggested that he carried pieces of valerian root in his pockets to entice the rats to follow him. If so, then it raises an interesting question: Did the villagers of Hamlin lose their cats as well as their rats?

See Also: The ABC Clinical Guide to Herbs by M. Blumenthal, T. Hall, and A. Goldberg, American Botanical Council, 2003; World Health Organization (WHO) Monographs on Selected Medicinal Plants, Vol. 1, 1999.

VALERIANA OFFICINALIS | Valerian

Common Names White bryony, bryony, black-berried bryony

Latin Name *Bryonia alba*

Family Cucurbitaceae

Parts Used Root

Description *Bryonia* is a perennial vine that climbs with spiraling tendrils and can reach a length of 15 to 18 feet. The leaves are five-lobed (hand-shaped) and roughly hairy. In early summer, small yellow-green flowers are produced that are succeeded by thin-skinned black berries. Roots are light-colored, branching, and turnip-like.

Habitat *Bryonia alba* is native to Europe and central to western Asia, but has become naturalized elsewhere, including England and the northwestern United States. In Washington State it is classified as a noxious weed.

Approximate native range

White Bryony
Bryonia alba

BOTH THE NAMES *BRYONIA* AND *BRYONY* MAY POSSIBLY be derived from the Greek words *bruein*, which means "to grow vigorously," or *bryo*, which means "to sprout." *Bryonia* is a fast-growing vine that is at home scrambling through hedges, bushes, and the undergrowth at the edges of woods. It grips as it grows, hanging on to whatever support is available with spirally coiled tendrils that arise from the sides of the leaf stalks. The species name, *alba*, means "white" and refers to the color of the roots. Both *Bryonia alba*, and a closely related, red-berried species, *B. dioica*, have light-colored roots, a characteristic that distinguishes them from black bryony (*Tamus communis*), which has black roots. Black or white, however, the roots—and other plant parts—of all the "bryonies" are poisonous. Once used in human and veterinary medicine, it is today used mostly in **homeopathic** preparations for treatment of gastrointestinal, rheumatic, and respiratory conditions.

Traditional and Current Medicinal Uses

ALTHOUGH IT IS POISONOUS, *BRYONIA* HAS BEEN VALUED MEDicinally since ancient times. Due to the extremely irritating nature of its sap, *Bryonia* was long used as an herbal remedy for its severe **cathartic** laxative effect. However, even in small doses *Bryonia* **extracts** can be very irritating to the stomach and intestines and its use as a **purgative** was discontinued over time. Applied to the skin, *Bryonia* extract can be a harsh irritant, causing itching, inflammation, and blisters. Nevertheless, used in very small doses, *Bryonia* has been praised as a remedy for acute lung or bronchial disorders, especially those characterized by a dry, sharp, painful cough (including whooping cough) and chest congestion; in such cases *Bryonia* was often administered in conjunction with minute amounts of *Atropa belladonna*. *Bryonia* also has been used as a treatment for severe inflammation in the intestines (enteritis), lungs (pleuritis), nerves (neuritis), and the joints (synovitis and bursitis).

In herbal medicine it is employed to treat rheumatism and arthritis, to reduce fevers, to alleviate backache and various types of myalgia, for severe, pounding headaches, as a laxative, **emetic**, and **diuretic**, and to ease inflammation of breast tissue in nursing mothers. *Bryonia* is also used to treat intestinal ulcers, hypertension, and endometriosis.

Cultivation and Preparation

THIS HERB GROWS VERY RAPIDLY, AND IS SOMETIMES USED AS an ornamental to provide a quick leafy cover for unsightly fences or walls. Bryonia is easily grown from seed. The plants prefer moist, well-drained, nonacidic soils in sun or part shade. Only the root is used in herbal medicine. Roots are harvested late in the summer and are used fresh or dried. Homeopathic remedies prepared from the root are mixed with alcohol to formulate extremely dilute solutions.

Research

BRYONIA IS VERY TOXIC AND DEATH CAN RESULT FROM ingesting too much of any part of the plant. Symptoms of poisoning include cold perspiration, slowing of the heart beat, severe headache, nausea leading to vomiting, severe diarrhea, and ultimately convulsions. Death can occur within a few hours. Large but nonfatal doses of *Bryonia* can also cause kidney and liver damage and abortion. The roots of *Bryonia alba* contain several **glycosides**, a number of cucurbitacins, **tannins**, the **alkaloid** bryonicine, and resin. Cucurbitacins are bitter-tasting chemical compounds present in most plants of the family Cucurbitaceae. Some cucurbitacins have strong cell-destroying properties and a number of those in *Bryonia* may have anticancer and antitumor activities; however, considerably more research is needed to determine the herb's cancer-fighting properties. At least one study has shown that extracts of *Bryonia alba* are helpful in correcting some of the major metabolic abnormalities that are associated with severe diabetes. Nevertheless, Germany's Commission E, a panel of scientific experts that regulate and approve the use of herbal medicines, currently does not classify *Bryonia* as an approved herb because the effectiveness of its preparations for medicinal applications is not sufficiently documented.

Both white bryony (*Bryonia alba*) and its close relative *Bryonia dioca* (often called white bryony as well) have been linked to witchcraft and the black arts for centuries. Witches supposedly kept bryony hidden on their bodies. They also had a knack for growing the herb; it was said that a witch could grow bryony anywhere—in a garden, in a pot, even without dirt! Bryony was also thought to possess wicked powers of its own. Digging up a bryony plant was to tempt fate; a person who did so was destined to destroy his or her own happiness. For this reason, people in ages past fenced in bryony plants found growing near their houses. Bryony inside a house was also considered unlucky. Another belief was that bryony roots screamed when they were pulled from the ground, in the same way that mandrake roots (*Mandragora officinarum*) supposedly did. Mandrake roots were believed to possess magical powers and were used in witches' brews and spells. The large, white fleshy roots of bryony were sometimes cleverly cut into human shapes by unscrupulous "herbalists" trying to pass them off as mandrake roots. A more subtle way to create mandrake fakes was to unearth the root of a young bryony plant and then insert a mold—fashioned in the rough shape of the human form—around it. Over time the root grew to fill the mold, taking on its exact shape. These little bryony root "sculptures" were known as puppettes or mammettes and were believed to possess great power.

See Also: *Medical Botany: Plants Affecting Human Health* by W. Lewis and M. Elvin-Lewis, John Wiley & Sons, 2003; *Medicinal Plants of the World* by B. van Wyk and M. Wink, Timber Press, 2004.

BRYONIA ALBA | White Bryony

Common Names White willow, European willow, *bai liu*

Latin Name *Salix alba*

Family Salicaceae

Parts Used Bark

Description White willow is a large tree, growing to 80 feet in height, with upright branches, rough gray bark, and narrow, lance-shaped leaves. Male and female flowers occur on separate trees, appearing in catkins at the same time as the new leaves emerge.

Habitat Common in wetlands and near rivers and streams, white willow is native to Europe, central Asia, and North Africa. It was introduced into eastern North America and is now naturalized from Nova Scotia to Georgia.

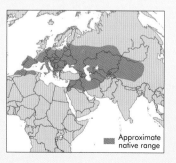

Approximate native range

White Willow
Salix alba

WHITE WILLOW IS WIDELY KNOWN AS A SOURCE OF salicylic acid, the **precursor** of one of the world's most commonly used painkilling drugs: aspirin. The "white" in the common name comes from the leaves, which have a whitish cast due to a covering of very fine silky hairs. White willow thrives in damp soil, flooded areas, and along streams and ponds. This characteristic is reflected in its genus name, *Salix*, which is derived from a Celtic word meaning "near water." The medicinal power of white willow lies in its inner bark, which has been used therapeutically for several thousand years. Willow bark has been used throughout the centuries in both the West and the East, and continues to be used by herbal practitioners for the treatment of fever, pain, headache, and inflammatory conditions such as arthritis. Although the bark of the white willow is most commonly used, related species such as black or basket willow (*S. purpurea)* and crack or brittle willow (*S. fragilis*) are also sources of willow bark in herbal medicine.

Traditional and Current Medicinal Uses

CHINESE MEDICAL PRACTITIONERS USED WHITE WILLOW BARK TO combat pain and relieve fever at least as early as 500 B.C. White willow was also used in ancient Egyptian, Assyrian, and Greek medicine. The Greek physicians Galen, Dioscorides, and Hippocrates all praised the tree for its therapeutic powers; they advised their patients to chew on the bark to reduce fever and inflammation. In medieval Europe, willow bark was similarly employed to alleviate pain, relieve headaches, and reduce fever. It was also a common remedy for rheumatism, arthritis, inflammation, colds, gout, heartburn, and digestive problems. Preparations of willow bark were applied to skin to heal burns, sores, cuts, and rashes. Across the Atlantic Ocean, the Cherokee, Blackfoot, Iroquois, and other Native American tribes used closely related species of willow for headache relief, to reduce fever and chills, and for alleviating muscle and joint pains. In the 18th century, willow bark was used as a substitute for cinchona bark in treating malaria. (Although it may have lowered malarial fevers, it would not have had the effect that quinine did on malarial parasites in the body.) The active ingredient in white willow bark—salicin—was isolated in 1828. By the end of the 19th century, synthetic salicylic acid was produced in the laboratory and aspirin was born. As use of aspirin grew, white willow lost its popularity as a pain and fever remedy.

Modern herbal medicine, however, has seen a resurgence in the use of white willow bark, as studies have shown its **analgesic** effects—while initially slower to act—last longer than aspirin. Preparations of the bark are given for tendinitis, bursitis, rheumatoid arthritis, back pain, and muscle cramps and aches as well as headaches and fever. Willow bark also contains additional chemical compounds that are known to have **antioxidant**, antiseptic, and immune system-boosting effects.

Cultivation and Preparation

WHITE WILLOW GROWS BEST IN DAMP SOIL. PRIMARILY THE bark is used in herbal medicine. It is harvested in spring from branches of trees two to three years old. The grayish bark is separated from the tree and used fresh or dried for use in tablets, capsules, powders, or teas.

Research

WHITE WILLOW BARK CONTAINS A NUMBER OF TANNINS, **flavonoids**, and numerous **glycosides**, of which salicin is the most important. In the body, salicin is gradually converted into salicylic acid, which is the precursor to acetylsalicylic acid, better known as aspirin. Because of the time required for this conversion, the therapeutic properties of willow bark take effect more slowly but continue for a longer period of time than those of aspirin. Salicin, unlike aspirin, does not irritate the stomach as much. White willow's analgesic activity is the result of salicin's inhibition of the production of **prostaglandins**, hormone-like chemicals produced by the body in response to injury that cause aches, pains, and inflammation. Recent clinical studies support the painkilling and fever-reducing properties of willow bark. The clinical effects of salicylic acid are very well documented.

TREE OF SADNESS

Many people believe that the "weeping" willow (*Salix babylonica*) gets its nickname from its drooping branches that almost touch the ground. But in folklore the willow is often associated with death, heartbreak, sorrow, and lost love. In the Bible, the children of Israel sat down and mourned their captivity in Babylon beneath a willow tree. In medieval times, sprigs of willow were worn as signs of grief and mourning. Garlands made from leaves and twigs were worn by those who had been forsaken or rejected by a lover. Willow also had a darker side. According to one superstition, a person could bind or even kill an enemy by tying knots in a supple willow branch. Sorcerers were said to favor magic wands made of willow. Sarifices by Druids—members of a Celtic priesthood—were offered in willow-wicker baskets. The word "witchcraft" is derived from the word "willow," and willow branches were used to bind birch twigs to an ash stake for a witch's broom. Despite these evil associations, willow was also linked with protection. Willow branches were brought into homes to guard against evil. Some believed that a secret confessed to a willow would be forever trapped in the tree. Another belief held that evil could be averted by knocking on a willow tree—perhaps the source of the expression, "knock on wood."

SALIX ALBA | White Willow

See Also: *Nature's Medicine, Plants That Heal* by Joel Swerdlow, National Geographic, 2000; *A Field Guide to Medicinal Plants and Herbs: Eastern and Central North America, 2nd ed.* by S. Foster and J. Duke, Houghton Mifflin Co., 2000.

Wild Yam

Dioscorea villosa

THE GENUS *DIOSCOREA* IS A LARGE ONE, WITH AT LEAST 800 species widely distributed in tropical and subtropical regions around the world. Most are twining, climbing vines that produce underground tubers. The tubers of some species are edible. The word "yam," in fact, comes from Portuguese *inhame* or Spanish *ñame*, both of which are derived from the West African word *nyami*, meaning "to eat." White yam (*Dioscorea alata*) is an edible species that produces hefty tubers weighing more than a hundred pounds. The tubers of wild yam (*Dioscorea villosa*), however, have an acrid, bitter taste and would never grace a table. But this herb is the source of **steroid**-like substances that have been used by the pharmaceutical industry as a starting point in the laboratory synthesis of human sex hormones and the steroid cortisone. Although wild yam was largely responsible for the advent of inexpensive oral contraceptives, the herb itself was not used as a contraceptive in traditional herbal medicine, but rather as a treatment for colic, muscle spasms, and rheumatism.

Traditional and Current Medicinal Uses

NATIVE TO NORTH AMERICA, WILD YAM WAS USED BY SOME Native American tribes in a root tea given to relieve labor pains and menstrual cramps. Both the Aztec and the Maya used wild yam medicinally, possibly as a pain reliever. European settlers found in wild yam a remedy for colic—hence its common name, "colic root." It was also used traditionally to treat inflammation, muscle spasms, gastrointestinal irritations, morning sickness, asthma, persistent hiccups, and rheumatism.

In modern herbal medicine, wild yam continues to be used for treating menstrual cramps, nausea associated with pregnancy, rheumatoid arthritis, and intestinal upsets. As an **anti-inflammatory** it relaxes muscle spasms, stimulates bile flow, and dilates blood vessels. In conventional medicine, however, wild yam was the original source of diosgenin, a steroid-like substance that was processed in the laboratory to produce various steroid hormones. Most of the steroid hormones used

Common Names Wild yam, colic root, rheumatism root, China root

Latin Name *Dioscorea villosa*

Family Dioscoreaceae

Parts Used Roots, tuber

Description Wild yam is a deciduous, perennial vine with heart-shaped leaves that have prominent veins. It has tiny drooping, greenish-white flowers and long, woody, knotted tuberous rhizomes (underground stems) that produce long, creeping runners. The herb can reach 30 feet in length.

Habitat *Dioscorea villosa* is native to North America, growing in tropical and subtropical climates.

Approximate native range

in modern medicine today, including those used in birth control pills and widely prescribed cortisone and hydrocortisone preparations, were developed originally from wild yam's diosgenin.

Cultivation and Preparation

WILD YAM FLOURISHES IN DAMP WOODLANDS AND THICKETS. In cultivation, it needs rich, well-drained soil in sun or partial shade. The herb is propagated by seed sown in spring, by division of tubers in autumn or spring, or by small **bulbils** planted in spring. **Rhizomes** are harvested in autumn and dried for use in liquid **extracts** or to make capsules or tablets of the powdered root. The fluid extract can be made into an herbal tea. Fresh rhizomes are also used in **homeopathic** preparations.

Research

WILD YAM CONTAINS DIOSGENIN, A TYPE OF PLANT CHEMICAL known as a **saponin**. Saponins are plant steroids. Diosgenin was first identified in wild yam by Japanese researchers in 1936. A few years later, it was discovered that diosgenin could form the starting point in the laboratory synthesis of the human steroid hormones progesterone and testosterone. This discovery made wild yam a remarkably rich source of material for the mass production of human steroid compounds, which in turn were used in the manufacture of oral contraceptives and corticosteroids such as cortisone and hydrocortisone. Few herbs have had such a profound impact on modern medicine and modern life. Until diosgenin itself was synthesized in the laboratory in 1970, wild yam was the sole source of this **precursor**.

It is important to note that wild yam rhizome is not itself a source of progesterone, estrogen, or any other human steroid compound. Diosgenin can be converted into human steroids in the laboratory, but not in the body. Nevertheless, wild yam has been marketed in recent years as a cure for menopausal disorders, despite the fact that the plant itself has no proven hormonal action and no studies have shown it to be effective in treating hormone-related disorders. This marketing effort has been dubbed by some as the "wild yam scam."

In 1940, an eccentric American biochemist named Russell E. Marker published the results of his work on diosgenin, the saponin isolated from wild yam. Starting with diosgenin, Marker had been able to chemically synthesize the human sex hormone progesterone in five steps, and testosterone in eight. Unable to interest American pharmaceutical companies in the process, however, Marker went to live in Mexico where in a makeshift laboratory he began to manufacture progesterone from a Mexican species of wild yam. Tons of yams later, Marker had managed to produce about six and a half pounds of the hormone. That got the attention of a tiny Mexican pharmaceutical company, Laboratorios Hormona. In 1944, owners of the company entered into a partnership with Marker. They formed a new company, Syntex, to synthesize progesterone for the pharmaceutical market. In a year Marker had a fight with his partners and left—taking critical steps of the synthesis process with him. The Syntex owners looked for someone to fill Marker's role and found George Rosenkranz, a Hungarian chemist, who figured out the missing steps. Syntex went on to patent the diosgenin-to-progesterone process. In a few years, Rosenkranz and a Syntex team figured out how to synthesize testosterone, the female hormones estrone and estradiol, and inflammation-reducing cortisone. In 1952, they synthesized the active ingredient for what would become the birth control pill.

See Also: A Field Guide to Medicinal Plants and Herbs: Eastern and Central North America, 2nd ed. by S. Foster and J. Duke, Houghton Mifflin, 2000; *Nature's Medicine, Plants That Heal* by Joel Swerdlow, National Geographic, 2000.

DIOSCOREA VILLOSA | Wild Yam

Common Names Wintergreen, teaberry, checkerberry, mountain tea, Canada tea

Latin Name *Gaultheria procumbens*

Family Ericaceae

Parts Used Leaves

Description A prostrate evergreen shrub growing only six inches high, wintergreen has creeping stems that send up erect branches that bear dark green, glossy leaves and small, white, bell-shaped flowers. The edible fruits are scarlet berries.

Habitat Wintergreen is a native North American shrub that grows in moist woods and clearings from Newfoundland to Manitoba and south to Georgia, Michigan, and Indiana.

Approximate native range

Wintergreen
Gaultheria procumbens

G*AULTHERIA PROCUMBENS* IS A SOURCE OF THE ORIGInal, natural oil of wintergreen used as a flavoring agent in candy, chewing gum, and toothpaste and an ingredient (often combined with eucalyptus and menthol) in rheumatic rubs and other products. Wintergreen was used medicinally by Native American tribes long before European contact. The genus name, *Gaultheria*, refers to Canadian physician and botanist Jean-Francois Gaulthier (1708–1758), who made botanical studies of the flora of Quebec. In 1753, the Swedish scientist and taxonomist Carolus Linnaeus named the genus *Gaultheria* in honor of this Canadian botanist. The species name, *procumbens*, comes from the Latin word for "prostrate" and refers to wintergreen's low-growing habit. The common name "wintergreen" is a reference to the fact that the herb's tough, dark-green leaves persist throughout the cold winter months. Today, most wintergreen oil is produced synthetically in the laboratory. But the naturally derived oil is still used in herbal medicine, as are the leaves of this small evergreen shrub. Wintergreen is valued for its antiseptic and pain-relieving properties.

Traditional and Current Medicinal Uses

WINTERGREEN WAS USED MEDICINALLY BY MANY NATIVE American tribes, typically to relieve aches and pains but also to improve breathing while hunting or carrying heavy loads. The Algonquin brewed a tea from the leaves of wintergreen for relieving headaches. **Infusions** of the leaves were also remedies for colds and stomachaches. Crushed into a **poultice**, the leaves were applied to aching, arthritic, or overexerted muscles and joints, or to the chest for treating colds. The Cherokee chewed wintergreen leaves to alleviate diarrhea and soothe tender gums; the Quebec rolled the leaves around aching teeth. **Decoctions** of the leaves were used by the Chippewa as general tonics and to fight colds. The Delaware, Oklahoma, Menominee, Potawatomi, and Ojibwa all took preparations of wintergreen for rheumatism and other aches and pains. During the Revolutionary War (1776–1783), colonists sometimes steeped wintergreen leaves as a substitute for heavily taxed imported tea (*Camellia sinensis*). Colonists adopted the use of wintergreen for medicinal purposes as well, mainly for treating headaches, inflammation, and rheumatism.

Modern herbalists recommend using wintergreen (particularly wintergreen oil) for rheumatism, minor stomach upsets, and colic, and in **liniments** and ointments to relieve sciatica (inflammation of the sciatic nerve) as well as swollen or inflamed muscles and joints. Wintergreen oil is sometimes used to treat cellulitis, a bacterial infection of the skin.

Cultivation and Preparation

WINTERGREEN SPREADS BY UNDERGROUND STEMS INTO A dense mat that can be several feet across. It does best in moist, acidic soil in partial shade. Most wintergreen used in the herbal medicine market is wild harvested but a limited amount of the plant is cultivated in the United States and Canada. Leaves can be gathered from spring to fall. These are used fresh or dried for teas and **tinctures**. The oil is extracted from fresh leaves and used in a variety of massage oils, liniments, and ointments.

Research

WINTERGREEN'S ACTIVE INGREDIENT IS METHYL SALICYLATE, which is found in the herb's **essential oil**. In fact, methyl salicylate can make up as much as 99 percent of the oil. (Growing conditions affect the concentration in wintergreen plants.) Methyl salicylate is an aspirin-like compound, and like aspirin, is a proven **anti-inflammatory**. In the body, methyl salicylate appears to block the formation of **prostaglandins**, natural chemical substances involved in inflammation and pain. Methyl salicylate thus gives wintergreen its anti-inflammatory, antirheumatic, and **analgesic** properties. Aspirin is an effective pain reliever but tends to cause ulcers and intestinal bleeding if taken regularly. In a recent study, researchers assessed wintergreen as a natural alternative to aspirin; results suggested fewer side effects. Clinical studies are needed to confirm these preliminary findings.

CAUTION Wintergreen oil is highly toxic and can be absorbed through the skin.. Avoid ingestion or topical use, except under medical supervision. It should not be used by those who are allergic to aspirin

People who grew up in the 1940s, 1950s, and 1960s might remember a popular chewing gum called teaberry with an image of wintergreen berries on the wrapper. Teaberry chewing gum was first manufactured in the early 1900s by the Clark Gum Company. Flavored with wintergreen oil, teaberry gum was a big seller in the southeastern U.S., where people knew wintergreen by its southern nickname: "teaberry." Wintergreen oil also was used in many other kinds of gum and candy manufactured in the U.S. Kids who grew up on teaberry gum might also have loved wintergreen-flavored Wint-O-Green Lifesavers—but for more than their minty taste. These donut-shaped candies are renowned for giving off mysterious sparks when snapped in two. The light is produced by friction. When sugar crystals are stressed, positive and negative charges in the crystals separate, generating an electric potential. When enough charges accumulate, electrons jump across a fracture in the crystal, colliding with and exciting electrons in the surrounding air. The result is a tiny, bluish-white flash. The flashes given off by wintergreen candies when they break are brighter than in hard candy made from sugar alone, however, because the main ingredient in wintergreen oil—methyl salicylate—is fluorescent. When wintergreen candy breaks, the light given off excites methyl salicylate electrons, causing them to glow and make wintergreen "sparks."

See Also: A Field Guide to Medicinal Plants and Herbs: Eastern and Central North America 2nd ed. by S. Foster and J. Duke, Houghton Mifflin, 2000; Tyler's Honest Herbal 4th ed. by S. Foster and V. Tyler, The Hawthorn Herbal Press, 1999.

Witch Hazel

Hamamelis virginiana

LTHOUGH WITCH HAZEL IS A SMALL WOODLAND TREE that could easily go unnoticed in midsummer, it is an eyecatcher in late fall. Surrounded by trees that have long since lost their autumn leaves, witch hazel stands cloaked in clusters of spidery yellow flowers that may bloom well into winter. The "witch" in witch hazel has nothing to do with witches. It is a corruption of the old English word *wych*, meaning a tree with bendable branches. The reference is to the pliable branches used by dowsers to locate underground water or precious metals. In colonial America, the forked branches of *Hamamelis virginiana* were a favorite source of "witching sticks." An interesting botanical phenomenon is the source of another of witch hazel's common names— "snapping hazel." Capsules that develop after the tree blooms in fall ripen the following summer and then eject twin black seeds with a loud POP! and enough force to propel them some 20 feet from the tree. In herbal medicine, witch hazel has been used for centuries as a mild **astringent** that reduces inflammation.

Traditional and Current Medicinal Uses

WITCH HAZEL WAS WELL KNOWN AS A MEDICINAL PLANT BY Native Americans. The Cherokee, Chippewa, Iroquois, Mohegan, and Potawatomi tribes used the leaves and bark in many ways. They brewed a tea to relieve mouth and throat irritations, reduce fever, and relieve menstrual cramps. Witch hazel steam baths were effective in providing relief from feverish colds and coughs with heavy phlegm. A wash or compress made from leaves or bark was used to treat skin irritations, to check bleeding, and for bites, burns, poison ivy rash, inflamed eyes, headaches, strained muscles, back pain, and arthritic joints. Witch hazel was subsequently adopted as a medicinal herb by European settlers, who used it in similar ways, as well as for diarrhea and dysentery. It was also widely prescribed to stop internal bleeding and to tighten distended varicose veins. By 1860, witch hazel was listed in the *Pharmacopoeia of the United States*; by then it had also been introduced into England and Europe.

Common Names Witch hazel, hamamelis, snapping hazel, winterbloom

Latin Name *Hamamelis virginiana*

Family Hamamelidaceae

Parts Used Leaves, bark, twigs

Description Witch hazel is a shrub or small tree with smooth, grayish-brown bark, twisting stems, and long forking branches. Its broad, green leaves have scalloped margins. Yellow flowers with long, threadlike petals bloom in autumn. They mature into paired, urn-shaped, woody seed capsules.

Habitat Native to eastern North America, witch hazel typically grows in moist, light woods and along rocky streams.

Approximate native range

Today, distilled witch hazel water is widely available as an easy-to-use, household first aid for minor injuries and as an **astringent** for skin irritations. The **tinctures** and other preparations typically used by herbal medicine practitioners are stronger. These are suggested for mouth irritations, sprains, bruises, varicose veins, sore nipples, muscular aches, eye and skin inflammation, and sore throat. Less commonly, witch hazel is administered for internal bleeding, diarrhea, and dysentery. Witch hazel is also an ingredient in some commercial hemorrhoid preparations, and distilled witch hazel is used in commercial eye drops, skin creams, and skin tonics.

Cultivation and Preparation

WITCH HAZEL CAN BE PROPAGATED BY SEED OR SUCKERS THAT arise from the roots. It prefers moist, rich, neutral to acidic soil in sun or part shade. The plant is wild-harvested in the United States. Leaves are picked in summer for dry and liquid **extracts** and ointments. Branches are cut in spring and stripped of bark, which is used to make **decoctions** and tinctures. Twigs, which are also harvested in spring, are used to make distilled extracts.

Research

WITCH HAZEL CONTAINS LARGE QUANTITIES (UP TO TEN PERcent) of several **tannins** as well as **flavonoids** and **essential oil**. The tannins strongly interact with proteins and exhibit well-documented astringent, antiseptic, and **hemostatic** (serving to check bleeding) properties. Laboratory and animal studies have shown that witch hazel also has significant **antioxidant** effects. Animal studies in Europe also have demonstrated that extracts of witch hazel do cause constriction of veins—thus supporting the herb's folk use for tightening distended varicose veins. One study, which used a specially filtered fraction of witch hazel extract, found pronounced evidence that the plant exhibited antiviral activity against the herpes simplex virus.

CAUTION Internal consumption of witch hazel tinctures, teas, or extracts is not recommended because witch hazel has a very high tannin content.

It's as close as the corner drugstore. Millions of gallons of bottled witch hazel are sold every year in drugstores and pharmacies across the U.S. It is one of the few widely available commercial medicines made from a wild native plant. This is not the extract used by herbal medicine practitioners or what is sold in Europe under a similar name. It is witch hazel water, a distilled preparation made from the dried leaves, twigs, and branches of *Hamamelis virginiana*. To make witch hazel water, plant parts are soaked in water and the resulting infusion is distilled. Alcohol is added to keep the distillate from spoiling. Tannins are removed in the process. Though some question its medicinal value, witch hazel water has been sold for more than 150 years in the U.S.

The man behind the original product was Theron Pond, a pharmacist from Utica, New York. In the 1840s, he befriended the Oneida tribe of central New York State and learned that they used the plant for treating wounds and burns. Pond studied extracts from the herb and in 1846 marketed a patent medicine called "Golden Treasure." It was promoted for treating burns, bruises, sprains, rheumatism, toothaches, sore throats, and insect stings. Today witch hazel water is marketed as a mild astringent and antiseptic for minor skin irritations and as a skin toner.

See Also: World Health Organization (WHO) Monographs on Selected Medicinal Plants, Vol. 2, 2002; A Field Guide to Medicinal Plants and Herbs: Eastern and Central North America, 2nd ed. by S. Foster and J. Duke, Houghton Mifflin, 2000.

Common Names Wormwood, artemisia, green ginger

Latin Name *Artemisia absinthium*

Family Asteraceae

Parts Used Leaves, stems, flowers

Description A two-to-three-foot perennial herb with tall, erect, furrowed stems, *Artemisia* has silvery green, deeply serrated, almost lacey leaves. Small rounded, pale yellow, gently drooping flower heads are arranged in elongated clusters and appear in midsummer. Both the leaves and the stems are covered with a silvery-white down of fine hairs.

Habitat Native to Europe and the British Isles, *Artemisia* also grows wild in central Asia and in the eastern United States and is cultivated in many temperate parts of the world. It is common along dry roadsides and similar sites.

Approximate native range

Wormwood
Artemisia absinthium

A VERY OLD HERBAL REMEDY, *ARTEMISIA* IS A COMMON sight in herb and perennial gardens, with its gray-green feathery leaves forming a pleasing contrast to the brighter greens of other plants. *Artemisia* is an extremely bitter-tasting herb that emits a dry, pungent scent. In fact, the species name, *absinthium*, means "lacking in sweetness." One of the herb's common names, "wormwood," possibly derives from the Anglo-Saxon words *wer mod*, which meant "man's courage" and may have been a reference to the herb's reputation for helping overcome bodily weakness. The name of the liquor "vermouth," which originally was flavored with extracts of *Artemisia absinthium*, seems to have the same linguistic origin. Because of its pungent scent, *Artemisia* was once common as a strewing herb and also used as an effective insect repellent when placed in pantries and drawers. It was sometimes used by German brewers as a substitute for hops in the making of beer, and it was used by the French and others in preparing the liquor absinthe. *Artemisia* was also used as an ingredient in some love potions and thought to be a cure for hemlock poisoning. Modern herbal preparations of *Artemisia* are used primarily for treating a variety of stomach upsets and other digestive complaints.

Traditional and Current Medicinal Uses

WORMWOOD HAS BEEN EMPLOYED IN HERBAL MEDICINE FOR centuries on both sides of the Atlantic Ocean in semi-arid and temperate regions where the plants are found. Native Americans used wormwood to help relieve digestive upsets and expel intestinal worms. **Infusions** were also taken for head colds, flu, and tuberculosis. In England, Europe, and elsewhere, the herb was valued for its tonic effect on the liver, gallbladder, and the digestive system, and for helping rid the body of worms. The extremely bitter leaves were chewed to help stimulate the appetite.

In modern herbal medicine, extracts of wormwood have been shown to stimulate the production of both stomach acid and bile, which helps improve digestion and the absorption of nutrients. In addition to its effects on the digestive tract, wormwood is used as an ingredient in **poultices** applied to bruises, insect bites, and sprains to reduce swelling and inflammation. The herb is occasionally given as a mild antidepressant and because of its appetite-stimulating properties has been employed with some success in the treatment of **anorexia nervosa** (an eating disorder characterized by prolonged loss of appetite.)

Cultivation and Preparation

WORMWOOD NEEDS VERY WELL-DRAINED SOIL BUT IS OTHER-wise undemanding. It grows best in full sun to partial shade and is quite drought tolerant. Plants grown in poor, dry soil are actually hardier and more aromatic than those cultivated under richer soil conditions. The plant is typically propagated from semi-hardwood cuttings taken in late summer or autumn. It also can be propagated by seed in spring or by dividing the roots in autumn. In herbal medicine, the above-ground parts of wormwood are used. Leaves and flower heads are collected in July and August, when the plant is in bloom; these are dried for later use.

Research

A BITTER **VOLATILE OIL** IS EXTRACTED FROM WORMWOOD THAT contains the chemical comounds known as **sesquiterpene** lactones (including absinthin, anabsinthin, and artabsin), azulenes (which give the oil a blue-green color), and thujone. Thujone is a nerve stimulant that is considered safe by many herbal medicine practitioners if administered in very small doses. However, when taken in excess, it is also a convulsive poison. Prolonged consumption or large doses of thujone can lead to epileptic convulsions, brain and nervous system degeneration, and death. Recent research studies have revealed that thujone works by blocking brain receptors for gamma-aminobutyric acid, or GABA. Without access to GABA, which is a natural inhibitor of nerve impulses, neurons fire too easily and their signaling goes out of control.

> CAUTION *Artemisia absinthium* can be toxic. It should only be taken in small doses and under the strict supervision of a qualified medical or herbal practitioner.

ABSINTHE AND ART

A*rtemisia absinthium* is the plant from which the hallucinogenic drink absinthe is made. In the bars and clubs of late 19th-century and early 20th-century Paris, absinthe was the favored drink of many artists and writers. It may have been an addiction to this emerald-green liqueur that drove Vincent Van Gogh to suicide. Edgar Degas, Henri de Toulouse-Lautrec, and Pablo Picasso all portrayed absinthe drinkers in their art, depicting the drink's popularity and its destructive impact. Absinthe gets its mind-bending properties from the chemical compound thujone. Over time, thujone becomes habit-forming and eventually will cause serious brain damage.

Despite warnings about its dangers, absinthe became very popular a century ago, especially in France. Between 1905 and 1913, Switzerland, Belgium, Italy, and the U.S. banned absinthe. In 1915, France followed suit. In parts of Eastern Europe, absinthe is still available, but in a less potent form than was available in the Parisian world of Degas and Toulouse-Lautrec. Then, absinthe contained 260 parts per million of thujone. Today, absinthe has less than 10 parts per million. That is below the maximum concentration permitted in Europe.

See Also: A Field Guide to Medicinal Plants and Herbs: Eastern and Central North America, 2nd ed. by S. Foster and J. Duke, Houghton Mifflin, 2000; Tyler's Honest Herbal 4th ed. by S. Foster and V. Tyler, The Haworth Herbal Press, 1999.

Yarrow
Achillea millefolium

YARROW IS A VERY OLD MEDICINAL PLANT THAT HAS potent properties. Dried specimens of yarrow were found in a 60,000-year-old Neanderthal grave, along with other herbs. Whether yarrow was actually used medicinally by our ancient ancestors, however, remains unknown. It is known that yarrow has been used traditionally to treat a variety of ailments for many centuries, especially to heal wounds and to stop blood flow. In addition to its medicinal properties, yarrow has long been associated with fortune telling and magic. In the British Isles, the Druids (a Celtic priesthood) used the stems of the plant to foretell the weather. In the Hebrides, a leaf held against the eyes supposedly gave "second sight." In China, yarrow stems were the "stalks of divination" used by masters of the ancient guide known as the *I Ching* to predict future events. In Eastern Europe, where the herb's common name was yarroway, the interior of the nose was tickled gently with fresh leaves. If this treatment induced a nosebleed, it was taken as a sign that one's love was true.

Common Names Yarrow, milfoil, woundwort, carpenter's weed, staunchweed, nosebleed, *herbe militaris,* yarroway

Latin Name *Achillea millefolium*

Family Asteraceae

Parts Used Leaves, stems, flowers

Description This hardy, herbaceous perennial grows one to three feet tall and is entirely covered with tiny, silky white hairs. The rough, erect stems and deeply cut, feathery leaves are gray-green and aromatic. Small, strongly scented white to pale pink or lilac flowers appear from summer to autumn; the densely arranged flowers are borne on stems that branch at the top to form flattened terminal clusters, or cymes.

Habitat Native to Europe and Asia, *Achillea* is found in temperate regions worldwide. A sun-loving plant, it grows wild along roadsides and in meadows but is widely cultivated in gardens.

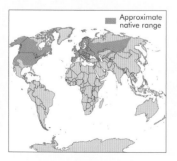

Approximate native range

Traditional and Current Medicinal Uses

YARROW HAS LONG BEEN VALUED FOR ITS USE IN STAUNCHING the flow of blood from wounds by encouraging clotting, a fact reflected in many of its common names such as "woundwort," "staunchweed," and "carpenter's weed." Traditionally, the herb was dried, powdered, and mixed with plantain or comfrey water (both are also wound herbs), or used fresh as a **poultice**, and applied to wounds that would not stop bleeding. One of its most common applications is to treat respiratory infections. Tea made from an **infusion** of the plant's leaves has long been considered a remedy for colds; chest rubs made from a distillation of the flowers may aid in reducing congestion in the respiratory tract. The herb has also been found to help lower blood pressure, alleviate hay fever, and reduce inflammation of gums and skin. Among Native Americans, it was well known as a medicinal plant.

Many modern herbals credit yarrow with **anti-inflammatory**, antispasmodic, antiallergenic, **diuretic,** diaphoretic, and **astringent** properties. Herbalists use it to treat colds and fevers, digestive problems, and hay fever, as well as to lower high blood pressure and improve circulation.

Cultivation and Preparation

YARROW GROWS WELL IN FULL SUN AND MODERATELY RICH, moist soil. In the United States, it blooms from June to September. All of the plant's above-ground parts—stems, leaves, and flowers—are used medicinally. They have a pungent odor and a bitter, astringent taste. Yarrow is typically collected for medicinal purposes while it is in bloom and is prepared in various ways: as fresh or dried herb, as capsules or tablets, and as **tinctures** or similar **extracts**. Boiling water is poured over the dried herb to make an infusion drunk as a tea. Tinctures and extracts are also added to water or juice to make an herbal drink. A dark blue **essential oil**, extracted from the flowers, is used in chest rubs and in other preparations. Externally, a **decoction** is used to treat slow-healing wounds, skin rashes, and eczema, and as a gargle and skin soak.

Research

DESPITE ITS MANY USES, ONLY LIMITED RESEARCH HAS BEEN carried out on *Achillea*'s medicinal properties. However, clinical experience and some laboratory studies support the use of *Achillea* for many of the conditions for which it has been used traditionally. The plant is chemically complex and contains many compounds, including the **alkaloid** achilleine, salicylic acid (the **precursor** of aspirin), and **flavonoids**. Its most notable compounds are azulenes, responsible for the dark blue of the herb's essential oil (azulenes turn blue after distillation). Azulenes have both anti-inflammatory and antiallergenic properties. Achilleine helps stop bleeding. Flavonoids are most likely the chemical compounds that are responsible for the herb's antispasmodic effects.

> CAUTION Prolonged contact with *Achillea* may trigger allergic rashes and cause skin photosensitivity in some people. Pregnant women should avoid using this herb because it may induce uterine bleeding and, possibly, miscarriage.

MANY LEAVES AND MANY NAMES

Yarrow is a plant with many names. The genus name, *Achillea*, derives from the hero Achilles, the famous figure in Greek mythology who is thought to have used the herb to stop the bleeding of soldiers' wounds during the Trojan War. However, other sources attribute the name to the plant's discoverer, who was also named Achilles. The species name, *millefolium*, refers to the many segments of the finely divided leaves. The French called the plant *millesfeuilles*, a possible source of the English nicknames "milfoil" and "thousand weed." "Woundwort," "bloodwort," and "staunchweed" all refer to *Achillea*'s ability to arrest blood flow. The common name "yarrow" is a corruption of the plant's Anglo-Saxon and Dutch names, *gearwe* and *yerw*, respectively. On account of the pungency of its foliage, *Achillea* was once dried and used as inexpensive snuff, which led to its being dubbed "old man's pepper." In some cultures, *Achillea* was also connected with witchcraft and was supposedly dedicated to Satan. In this context it was sometimes known as "devil's nettle" and "bad man's plaything" and was widely used in charms and spells.

See Also: Herbal Medicine Expanded Commission E Monographs by M. Blumenthal, A. Goldberg, J. Brinckmann, American Botanical Council, 2000; A Field Guide to Medicinal Plants and Herbs: Eastern and Central North America, 2nd ed. by S. Foster, J. Duke, Houghton Mifflin, 2000.

Common Names Yellow dock, curled dock, garden patience, sour dock

Latin Name *Rumex crispus*

Family Polygonaceae

Part Used Root

Description A robust erect perennial, yellow dock has a spindle-shaped yellow taproot from which a smooth, slender stem arises that can reach one to three feet. Wavy-edged, lance-shaped, light green leaves are larger at the bottom of the stem and shorter near the top. Loose whorls of pale green flowers appear on drooping panicles in midsummer, followed by small heart-shaped winged fruits.

Habitat Native to Europe and Africa, yellow dock has become naturalized along roadsides and in ditches and abandoned places in many temperate regions; it is considered a noxious weed in places.

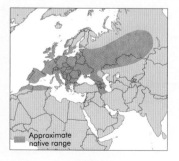

Approximate native range

Yellow Dock
Rumex crispus

THE GENUS *RUMEX* IS MADE UP OF TWO RELATED GROUPS of plants. The first are the sorrels, which are often cultivated for use in cooking. Some add a lemony spark to salads while others are classic accompaniments to meat dishes. The docks form the second group in the genus. They are generally wild, difficult to eradicate once established, and far less tasty than their sorrel cousins. Although the tender leaves of both sorrel and dock were once eaten as pot herbs, the fresh leaves of dock should never be eaten. Like rhubarb (*Rheum* spp.), another relative in the family Polygonaceae, dock leaves contain oxalic acid, which can aggravate certain conditions such as rheumatism and gout. Despite these drawbacks, docks, and yellow dock in particular, have real medicinal value. Docks were formerly classified in the genus *Lapathum*, a name derived from the Greek, *lapazein*, meaning "to cleanse." And cleanse they do. Yellow dock has long been respected in herbal medicine as a bitter **astringent** herb that acts as a mild laxative, cleanses toxins from the body, and helps clear up chronic skin problems.

Traditional and Current Medicinal Uses

SINCE THE MIDDLE AGES, YELLOW DOCK HAS BEEN USED TO treat skin complaints, liver disorders, and respiratory problems. Roots were used in laxative preparations and in tonics designed to strengthen the blood. Rubbing the fresh leaves on nettle stings was supposed to lessen the pain. Yellow dock was introduced into North America from Europe and quickly naturalized. American Indians applied crushed leaves from the plant to boils and pulverized roots to cuts. During the 19th century, yellow dock was widely prescribed by American herbal practitioners and by physicians of the American **Eclectic** school, who regularly prescribed herbal medicines, as a blood purifier, a gentle laxative, a tonic for rheumatism, liver ailments including jaundice, upset stomach, and as a remedy for boils and other eruptive skin diseases. Ointments made from the boiled roots were commonly given for itching sores, swellings, and scabby conditions of the skin. The seeds were given to treat dysentery, and the cooked leaves were eaten to prevent scurvy, as they are high in vitamin C. In rural Appalachia, fresh dock preparations are still used to treat hives and ringworm. Traditionally, preparations of the roots were also a remedy against intestinal worms, and the whole plant was used to treat internal bleeding and vascular disorders.

In modern herbal medicine, yellow dock is used primarily in the treatment of digestive problems, skin disorders such as psoriasis, eczema, acne, poison ivy, and rashes, and liver and gallbladder conditions, as it is thought to help support and restore liver function. Applied externally as an antiseptic and an astringent, yellow dock has been used to treat cuts, wounds, swellings, tumors, boils, burns, bleeding hemorrhoids, and insect and animal bites. Other conditions for which traditional herbalists recommend yellow dock include fibroids, anemia, swollen glands, and irritable bowel syndrome.

Cultivation and Preparation

YELLOW DOCK GROWS LIKE A WEED AND IS NOT FUSSY ABOUT soil, but it needs full sun. It can be propagated by seed or by division. Leaves are picked when young and used fresh. Roots are dug in late summer or early autumn and cleaned and split lengthwise for drying. Ground or crushed dried root is used in preparing ointments, **tinctures**, **decoctions**, and teas.

Research

VERY LITTLE RESEARCH HAS BEEN CONDUCTED ON YELLOW dock and its specific effects. Chemical analysis of the plant reveals that it contains small amounts of chemical compounds called **anthraquinone glycosides**, along with **tannins** and various **oxalates**, including potassium oxalate. In large doses, anthraquinone glycosides are strong laxatives. However, since yellow dock contains fairly small amounts of these chemicals, its effects on the intestinal tract are relatively mild. Anthraquinones also stimulate bile flow and trigger excretion of toxins. Oxalates are poisonous in large quantities. However, oxalates act medicinally as mild **diuretics**, can be somewhat effective against skin disorders, and help to control bleeding.

There are some 200 species in the genus *Rumex*. Like yellow dock, broad-leaved dock (*Rumex obtusifolius*) has been used as a remedy for various skin conditions and has mild laxative effects. *Rumex aquatica*, as its name suggests, is better known as water dock. Internally it was used much like yellow dock, but had the added advantage, when powdered, of being a serviceable tooth cleaner. *Rumex acetosella* is not a dock but a sorrel. Called sheep's sorrel, this herb is the most famous *Rumex*, known for being one of four ingredients in essiac, an herbal mixture promoted as a cancer remedy.

Essiac was popularized in Canada in the 1920s as a cancer treatment. The Canadian Cancer Commission investigated essiac and concluded there was only limited anecdotal evidence to explain its effectiveness. It continued to be promoted as a cancer cure, but no appropriate clinical trials were carried out. Then in 2004, a mixture of essiac herbs was shown to inhibit growth of prostate cancer cells in a test tube. Lab and animal experiments have shown essiac to have antioxidant, anti-inflammatory, and anticancer activity, but more research is needed to reach scientifically based conclusions about this herbal mixture.

See Also: *A Field Guide to Medicinal Plants and Herbs: Eastern and Central North America, 2nd ed.* by S. Foster and J. Duke, Houghton Mifflin, 2000; 101 *Medicinal Herbs: History, Use, Recommended Dosages & Cautions* by S. Foster, Interweave Press, 1998.

Yellow Jasmine
Gelsemium sempervirens

ELSEMIUM IS THE STATE FLOWER OF SOUTH CAROLINA and widely cultivated as an ornamental climber. The vine can reach more than 20 feet in length and, covered with dozens of fragrant yellow blossoms, is a truly stunning sight. Yellow jasmine also can be deadly unless handled with extreme care. This is a plant that should never be used for self-medication—it is very poisonous. Eating a single flower has been known to be lethal. *Gelsemium sempervirens* is closely related to *G. elegans*, another poisonous vine native to Southeast Asia, traditionally used for murder and suicide in Indonesia, and in Hong Kong to execute condemned criminals. As is the case with other plant toxins such as strychnine and curare, however, minute amounts of *Gelsemium*—when administered by medical experts— can heal rather than harm. In **homeopathic** medicine, *Gelsemium* is used as a sedative, antispasmodic, and to relieve nerve pain.

Traditional and Current Medicinal Uses

NATIVE TO THE SOUTHEASTERN UNITED STATES, *GELSEMIUM* WAS not widely used by Native Americans, although both the Delaware and Oklahoma made preparations from it to purify the blood. The plant was brought into conventional and herbal medicine circles in the U.S. in the mid-1800s after its effects were discovered by chance in a remarkably nonfatal case in Mississippi (see sidebar). Not long afterward, the herb was included in many of the major **pharmacopoeias** of the day, including the *Pharmacopoeia of the United States*, where it was listed from 1863 until 1926. During the 19th and early 20th centuries, *Gelsemium* was administered to relieve acute fevers, muscle spasms and twitches, spinal meningitis, nervous headaches and migraines, appendicitis, dysentery, nerve pain, epilepsy, rheumatism, tetanus, and other ailments. In folk medicine, *Gelsemium* was even considered to have cancer-fighting properties and to be a remedy for some kinds of cancerous tumors.

In homeopathy, *Gelsemium* is carefully administered in very dilute doses to treat neuralgia (especially facial and dental nerve pain), pain from pinched nerves (such

Common Names Yellow jasmine, yellow jessamine, false jasmine, evening trumpet flower, Carolina jasmine, wild woodbine

Latin Name *Gelsemium sempervirens*

Family Loganiaceae

Parts Used Rhizomes (underground stems), root

Description *Gelsemium* is a perennial, climbing vine with glossy green leaves and large, bright yellow, tubular flowers. It has a long, knotted rhizome (underground stem).

Habitat Native to North America, *Gelsemium* is found in thickets and moist woodlands from Virginia to Texas and south into Mexico and Central America.

Approximate native range

as sciatica), convulsive coughing that is associated with whooping cough, asthma, and muscle spasms. Homeopathic practitioners also recommend *Gelsemium* for migraines, irregular heartbeat, fever, and for treating anxiety.

Cultivation and Preparation

GELSEMIUM NEEDS MOIST, WELL-DRAINED SOIL AND FULL SUN. It can be propagated by seed sown in spring or by cuttings planted in summer. The **rhizomes** and some of the attached roots are unearthed in autumn and dried for use in **decoctions** and **tinctures**. *Gelsemium* was once exported from the United States in large quantities for the herbal medicine market. But it has fallen from favor and is not as widely used as it once was because of the extreme toxicity of the plant. The plant and its active ingredients are subject to legal restrictions in some countries.

Research

GELSEMIUM CONTAINS A NUMBER OF TOXIC **ALKALOIDS**, particularly gelsemine and gelsemicine, along with **glycosides**, and **steroids**. All parts of the plant contain the alkaloids and so are very poisonous, including the nectar in the sweetly fragrant flowers. Children have been poisoned by mistaking *Gelsemium* for honeysuckle and sucking the nectar from the flowers. The nectar is even toxic to honeybees, and if gathered by worker bees, can decimate an entire hive. Gelsemine is a powerful depressant of the central nervous system; it quickly paralyzes motor neurons and interferes with nerve impulse transmission. Carefully controlled, the effect can ease pain and calm muscle spasms. But the margin between therapeutic and toxic doses is slim. Even slight overdoses can cause vertigo, headache, blurred vision, drooping eyelids, clammy skin, difficulty swallowing, and muscular weakness. Poisoning brings on nausea, weak pulse, and shallow, irregular breathing. Death results from respiratory failure.

CAUTION *Gelsemium* is extremely toxic. It should never be used except under the supervision of an experienced medical expert. Skin contact causes allergic reactions in some individuals and may even cause systemic poisoning.

A LUCKY ACCIDENT

According to one historical account, *Gelsemium*'s potential as a healing drug was discovered by accident. A Mississippi planter who was suffering from a severe fever sent a farmhand out to collect a certain medicinal root. The man collected the rhizomes of *Gelsemium* by mistake, made a decoction from them, and gave the remedy to the ill planter. Within minutes, the planter began to show the signs of *Gelsemium* poisoning—drooping eyelids (and the inability to open them), loss of strength in all the limbs, and very shallow breathing. Death seemed imminent. But the planter did not die. Instead, the effects of the *Gelsemium* poison gradually wore off. The planter also was cured of his fever and it did not recur. The physician who had observed the case went on to concoct his own remedy from the herb and began marketing it as a cure for fever under the enigmatic name, Electrical Febrifuge. *Gelsemium* remedies were popular with doctors of the Eclectic school of medicine in the United States. Eclectic practitioners were known for combining both homeopathic and conventional treatments in their work, and for being open to the use of herbal remedies in treating disease.

See Also: *A Field Guide to Medicinal Plants & Herbs: Eastern & Central North America*, 2nd ed. by S. Foster, J. Duke, Houghton Mifflin, 2000; *A Field Guide to Venomous Animals & Poisonous Plants of North America Exclusive of Mexico* by S. Foster, R. Caras, Houghton Mifflin, 1994.

GELSEMIUM SEMPERVIRENS | Yellow Jasmine

Yohimbe
Pausinystalia johimbe

SEXUAL POTENCY DRUGS HAVE BEEN IN GREAT DEMAND in the last decade. In this market, yohimbe has experienced a double resurgence—as both herbal remedies and sexual enhancers such as Viagra have grown in popularity. Yohimbe is the only herbal remedy generally approved for erectile dysfunction by both the medical community and the United States Food and Drug Administration. Despite these endorsements and despite considerable research confirming its effectiveness, yohimbe is known to interact with other drugs and to produce a number of potential side effects. It is not yet approved in Germany for lack of data and because of safety concerns.

Traditional and Current Medicinal Uses

YOHIMBE BARK HAS HISTORICALLY BEEN USED IN WESTERN Africa for coughs, fevers, leprosy, heart disease, to dilate the pupils, as an anesthetic, hallucinogen, and aphrodisiac. Yohimbe's stimulant properties have made the herbal **extract** a part of rituals and ceremonies for centuries. It has played a part in many rituals—from orgies to spiritual visions. In the 19th century, word of yohimbe bark's powers spread from West Africa to Europe where the bark remains popular as a sexual stimulant.

Drug companies have extracted and patented yohimbe's most active ingredient, yohimbine, making it available in pill form. A prescription drug containing yohimbine hydrochloride, completely synthesized in the laboratory and not derived from the bark of the yohimbe tree, has been available for decades. Reports that the raw bark is stronger suggest that there are other active ingredients not present in pill form, helping to explain why the pill is milder and results in fewer side effects. Today yohimbe is most often used as a treatment for sexual dysfunction or to enhance sexual performance. It is also used as a weight-loss drug, for narcolepsy, and is marketed to athletes as a steroid substitute.

Cultivation and Preparation

THE HERBAL MEDICINE IS DERIVED FROM THE BARK OF A WEST African tree, *Pausinystalia johimbe,* which grows in

Common Names Yohimbe, johimbe, johimbi

Latin Names *Pausinystalia johimbe*

Family Rubiaceae

Parts Used Bark

Description The yohimbe tree is a skinny, fast-growing, tropical evergreen that can grow almost a hundred feet high. Its glossy, dark-green leaves are oblong; clusters of white, yellow, or pink flowers bloom in winter followed by winged seeds.

Habitat Yohimbe trees are native to the coastal forest of Africa along the Gulf of Guinea from Cameroon to southern Congo.

Approximate native range

Cameroon, Gabon, and Congo. The trees propagate by means of winged seeds that travel on the wind. Demand for yohimbe bark has risen so sharply that yohimbe plantations cannot satisfy the market fast enough to reverse the unsustainable overharvesting of tens of thousands of wild yohimbe trees each year. Poor governmental control is driving the yohimbe tree, once common along 500 miles of African coastal forest, to the verge of extinction. During the rainy season, from May to September, when yohimbine levels are highest, locals harvest the trees (see sidebar). Though yohimbine occurs in the branches, stems, and leaves, usually only the bark of the yohimbe tree is removed after the tree is felled. Preparation usually consists of making a powder out of the bark that is commonly ingested in a tea but also can be smoked.

Research

RESEARCH HAS FOCUSED PRIMARILY ON THE ACTIVE INGREdient, the isolated **alkaloid** yohimbine. Many human trials have focused on yohimbine's benefits for treating erectile dysfunction and impotence. A systematic review of this research concludes that yohimbine is better than a **placebo** for treating erectile dysfunction and that benefits generally outweigh risks. Yohimbine is effective in 30 percent of men who use it and less so in women. It has been found to be more effective for sexual disorders like erectile dysfunction and female sexual arousal disorder taken in combination with arginine. Risks may outweigh benefits when taking extracts of the crude bark. Risks for both raw yohimbe and yohimbine extract can be high. Use is unpredictable based on the dosage and the individual. Yohimbe contains alkaloids with stimulant effects and other alkaloids with tranquilizing effects. Taken in lower doses, yohimbe often causes sweating, fever, anxiety, nausea, vomiting, and increased blood pressure. In higher doses, yohimbe may cause a sudden drop in blood pressure, abdominal pain, fatigue, hallucination, and even paralysis.

CAUTION Yohimbe or yohimbine should not be taken by pregnant or nursing women or by those with high blood pressure, kidney or liver disease, or by those with stomach ulcers.

TOO MUCH OF A GOOD THING

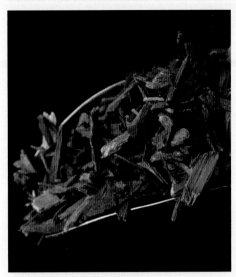

Most yohimbe comes from Cameroon, where it is among the most popular medicinal plants sold in urban markets. It is also popular worldwide—making it a cash crop for villagers who harvest it from the wild to sell to drug companies, often without knowledge of, or concern for, yohimbe's scarcity. Though it is a hardy grower, wild harvesting of the plant is outstripping its natural reproduction. Like many nationally grown herbal resources, yohimbe is being overharvested. Supply cannot keep up with the demands of an exploding market that continues to grow—in Cameroon and worldwide. Consider the process by which Plantecam, the supplier of yohimbe to Europe, gathers the bark. Formally, Plantecam gets a license from the Forestry Department and agrees not to accept plant material from anyone without a license. In fact, the majority of the bark is provided by locals without any authorization to harvest the wild forest. Because the natural habitat of so many of Cameroon's 14,000 species is being lost so rapidly, the need for research into use, conservation, and cultivation is urgent. In the 1980s the government of Cameroon formed the National Institute of Medicinal Plants (NIMP) to perform research, but funding dried up shortly after it opened. However, the National Institute of Medicinal Plants was reopened in 2002. The public perception that yohimbe is abundant in the wild in Cameroon must be changed. Until that happens, yohimbe's future looks bleak.

See Also: Herbal Medicine Expanded Commission E Monographs by M. Blumenthal, A. Goldberg, and J. Brinckmann, American Botanical Council, 2000; Medical Botany: Plants Affecting Human Health by W. Lewis and M. Elvin-Lewis, John Wiley & Sons, 2003.

Abortifacient A substance that causes or promotes abortion.

Adaptogen Herbs that act in a nonspecific way to strengthen the body and increase resistance to disease and stress with few side effects.

Alkaloid Any of numerous, usually colorless, complex, and bitter organic bases (such as as morphine or codeine) containing nitrogen and usually oxygen that occur especially in seed plants. An alkaloid is a basic organic compound with alkaline properties and generally a marked physiological effect on the nervous and circulatory systems. Alkaloids show varying pharmacological effects; for example, they can act as analgesics, local anesthetics, tranquilizers, vasoconstrictors, antispasmodics, and hallucinatory agents.

Amino acid Any of a class of 20 molecules that are combined to form proteins in living things. The sequence of amino acids in a protein and hence protein function are determined by the genetic code.

Amphetamine A central nervous system stimulant that increases energy and decreases appetite; used to treat narcolepsy and some forms of depression.

Analgesic A medication for the relief of pain.

Anorexia nervosa A psychophysiological disorder usually occurring in young women that is characterized by an abnormal fear of becoming obese, a distorted self-image, a persistent unwillingness to eat, and severe weight loss.

Anthelmintic An agent that destroys and expels worms from the intestines.

Anthranoid glycoside (Also known as anthraquinone glycosides or anthraquinones) Any one of a number of plant-produced glycosides that tend to exert laxative effects in the body; they are present in many plants, including aloes, senna, and rhubarb.

Anthraquinone glycoside A glycoside that contains a glycone group that is a derivative of anthraquinone. Glycosides are present in senna, rhubarb, and aloe, and have a laxative effect.

Antihistamine A drug that blocks histamine, typically used to treat allergic reactions.

Anti-inflammatory An agent that reduces heat, redness, and swelling associated with inflammation.

Antioxidant Chemical compound that protects against cell damage by molecules called oxygen-free radicals that are major causes of disease and aging.

Antipyretic An agent that relieves or reduces fever.

Antitussive A substance that relieves coughs.

Arteriosclerosis Any of several diseases characterized by thickening and inelasticity of arterial walls.

Astringent An agent that contracts or shrinks tissues; it is used to decrease secretions or control bleeding.

Ayurvedic medicine The ancient Indian medical system of maintaining health and fighting disease based upon equilibrium with nature. Ayurvedic medicine utilizes thousands of plants.

Biennial A plant whose life cycle extends over two growing seasons.

Bronchioles Tiny branches of air tubes in the lungs.

Bulbil A small bulb that is produced on the above-ground parts of plants.

Calcium-channel blocker A medication that slows the flow of calcium to the lining of the coronary arteries. This medication enhances blood flow and decreases blood pressure.

Cardiac glycoside A plant-derived glycoside used in the treatment of congestive heart failure and cardiac arrhythmia.

Carminative An agent that relieves and removes gas from the digestive system.

Carotenoid Natural, fat-soluble pigments found in certain plants that provide the bright red, orange, or yellow coloration of many fruits and vegetables.

Cathartic (Also called a purgative) An agent used to relieve severe constipation.

Coumarin A vanilla-scented plant constituent, used in perfumes and flavorings, and in remedies to reduce blood clotting.

Deciduous A plant that sheds its leaves annually.

Decoction A preparation made by simmering a plant part in water.

Diaphoretic A substance having the power to increase perspiration.

Dioecious A species in which the male and female reproductive organs occur on separate individuals.

Diuretic A substance that increases the flow of urine from the body.

Doctrine of Signatures The concept that plants are marked with signs that indicate their purpose. It has been used for centuries in herbal medicine to draw a correspondence between a particular plant and its medicinal use.

Double blind A clinical trial in which neither the doctor nor the patient knows whether the patient is being administered a placebo or the test drug.

Eclectic Referring to a medical movement that flourished in the United States from 1850 to 1940. Physicians who used the Eclectic approach relied heavily on American medicinal plants. Eclectic physicians introduced echinacea and black cohosh, as well as other botanical remedies.

Edema Swelling caused by fluid retention in the tissues of the body.

Emetic Medicine that induces nausea and vomiting.

Enzyme Protein that accelerates chemical reactions.

Essential oil (Also called volatile oil) Aromatic volatile oil found in specialized glands (as in the mint family). Many plants containing essential oils are known for their fragrance and cultivated for the food and perfume industries. Medicinally, essential oils have varied effects when used appropriately.

Estrogenic A substance that induces female hormonal activity.

Expectorant A substance that stimulates removal of mucus from the lungs.

Extract A concentrated active constituent that is obtained from a plant using a solvent.

Flavonoid A group of chemical compounds, low molecular weight phenylbenzopyrones, found in all vascular plants. In the diet, flavonoids are found in many fruits, vegetables, teas, wines, nuts, seeds, and roots. Many of the medicinal actions of foods, juices, herbs, and bee pollen are directly related to their flavonoid content. They exhibit antioxidant properties and other effects.

Formulary A book containing a list of pharmaceutical substances as well as their formulas, uses, and methods of preparation.

Free radical A chemical that is highly reactive and can oxidize other molecules.

Glycoside A product of secondary metabolism in plants. Glycosides break down into two parts—the glycone component, or sugar, and the nonsugar, or aglycone component. The therapeutically active constituent is the aglycone, which can selectively affect a particular organ in the body. Glycosides include some of the most effective plant drugs and some plants containing them are highly toxic.

Hemostatic An agent that controls or stops bleeding.

High-density lipoprotein (HDL) Lipoprotein that contains a small amount of cholesterol and carries cholesterol away from body cells and tissues to the liver for excretion from the body. Lower levels of HDL increase the risk of heart disease, so the higher the level of HDL in the bloodstream, the better. The HDL component normally contains 20 to 30 percent of total cholesterol.

Homeopathy A medical approach developed by German physician Samuel Hahnemann (1755–1843). This approach is based on a system of medical practice that treats a disease by administering minute does of a remedy that would in a healthy person produce symptoms similar to those of the disease.

Homeopathic Containing infinitesimal doses of a substance that would, in normal doses, produce symptoms of the disease it is intended to treat

Hyperglycemia The presence of abnormally high levels of glucose in the blood, often associated with diabetes.

Inflammatory response The immune system's natural response to tissue injury or harmful stimulation caused by physical or chemical substances. Blood flow to the affected area increases and results in swelling, redness, and pain.

Infused oil The result of an herb or plant part being soaked or macerated in oil and heated. The infused oil is then strained out.

Infusion Tea made by steeping herb(s) in hot water.

Iridoid glycosides A type of terpene-related glycoside; iridoid glycosides are one of several types of iridoids, a widely distributed class of plant compounds that have been shown to exhibit anticancer, immunostimulant, and liver-protective functions.

Ischemic Insufficient blood flow and oxygen to the body tissues.

Legume Plant belonging to the pea family that typically hosts nitrogen-fixing bacteria.

Lignan A diverse group of plant-derived compounds that form the building blocks for plant cell walls. Lignans can influence hormonal metabolism and may also be anticarcinogenic.

Liniment A thin medicinal fluid rubbed on the skin to reduce pain.

Low-denisity lipoprotein (LDL) The major cholesterol carrier in the blood. LDL transports cholesterol from the liver and intestines to various tissues. LDL is known as "bad" cholesterol because high levels are linked to coronary artery disease.

Metabolite Any organic substance produced by metabolism or enzymatic reactions.

Monoterpenes A broad category of 10-carbon, terpene-based compounds that may prevent, slow, or reverse the progression of various cancers and affect blood clotting and cholesterol levels.

Mucilage A gelatinous substance produced by some plants that is often used in herbal medicine as a soothing agent.

Neurotransmitter Chemical compound that transmits nerve impulses across synapses between nerve cells and between nerve and muscle or gland cells.

Oxalate Hard lump of crystals formed when oxalic acid combines with calcium, iron, sodium, magnesium, or potassium.

Peristalsis Wavelike muscle contractions that push food and liquid through the digestive tract.

Pharmacopoeia A book containing an official list of medicinal drugs together with articles on their preparation, usually produced by legislative authority.

Phytochemical A chemical found naturally in plants that has metabolically active qualities.

Phytoestrogen A plant compound with estrogen-like actions.

Phytomedicine A medicine based on active ingredients within an herbal base, sometimes used to describe all plant-based medicines.

Placebo An inactive pill, liquid, or powder that has no treatment value.

Platelet One of the main components of the blood that forms clots, sealing up injured areas and preventing hemorrhage.

Platelet aggregation The process of platelets clumping together in the blood; also known as clotting.

Polyphenol A large group of phytochemicals responsible for the coloring in some plants.

Poultice A preparation of fresh, moistened, or crushed dried herbs, applied externally.

Polysaccharide Any of a class of carbohydrates consisting of chains of simple sugars.

Precursor A substance from which a different substance is formed, especially in a metabolic sequence of reactions.

Prostaglandins Compounds made in the body from fatty acids, with a range of effects, including inhibition or stimulation of smooth muscle contractions.

Purgative (Also called cathartic) Agent used to relieve severe constipation, often with intense effects.

Rhizome A somewhat elongated, usually horizontal, subterranean plant stem, often thickened by deposits of reserve food material, that produces shoots above and roots below; distinguished from a true root in having buds, nodes, and usually scale-like leaves.

Saponin Any of several glycosides, found widely in plants, that produces a soapy lather when mixed with water.

Serotonin A neurotransmitter involved in many functions, including emotion, behavior, and thought.

Sesquiterpene A terpene-based compound that when taken from a plant can stimulate glands in the liver. Sesquiterpenes may have antiallergenic, antispasmodic, and anti-inflammatory properties.

Siddha An ancient system of medicine prevalent in southern India that comes from the Tamil word for perfection. Siddha medicine aims at the immortality of body and soul, and uses drugs that supposedly arrest the degeneration of cells in the body. Meditation and diet are also part of the system.

Steroid Any member of a complex group of compounds (all of which contain a characteristic chemical ring structure) found in both plants and animals and that exhibit powerful metabolic effects.

Steroidal hormone A type of steroid; examples of steroidal hormones include sex hormones such as estrogen and progesterone, which affect secondary sex characteristics, and hormones produced by the adrenal glands, which help regulate a variety of functions including fluid balance in the body.

Steroidal saponin A type of plant-produced steroid compound similar in chemical composition to the sex hormones of animals, including humans; some saponin-containing plants are the source of substances used in the manufacture of contraceptives.

Steroid glycoside A glycoside that contains a steroid ring structure; cardiac glycosides, which affect heart function and are used in the treatment of various heart diseases, are a type of steroidal glycoside.

Synapse The gap between two neurons, over which impulses lead to learning; specialized junctions through which cells of the nervous system signal to one another and to non-neuronal cells such as muscles or glands.

Tannin A group of simple and complex phenol, polyphenol, and flavonoid compounds, bound with starches, and often so amorphous that they are classified as tannins simply because at some point in degradation they are astringent and contain variations on gallic acid. Produced by plants, tannins are generally protective substances found in the outer and inner tissues, such as the bark and inner bark.

Terpene A class of hydrocarbon compounds produced by a wide variety of plants; terpenes, along with closely related compounds called terpenoids, are major constituents of many plant essential oils.

Tincture A plant medicine prepared by soaking an herb in alcohol (ethanol, never isopropyl alcohol); traditional herbal preparations dispensed as alcohol-based liquid medicines.

Triglyceride A type of fat made up of glycerol and three fatty acids.

Triterpene glycoside A glycoside that has a 30-carbon structure as part of its chemical composition.

Triterpene saponin A type of triterpene glycoside; triterpene saponins are known for their anti-inflammatory effects and ability to cause hemolysis (breaking apart) of red blood cells; some have also been shown to be selectively toxic to tumor cells.

Triterpinoid A type of terpene-based compound.

Unani (Also known as Unani-Tibb) Greco-Arab system of traditional medicine. Unani is primarily practiced by Muslims in the Indian subcontinent. Tibb (also Tibbi or Tibabat) is a related Muslim traditional medicine, incorporating more folk medicines of the East, and mainly practiced in the Middle East.

U.S. Pharmacopoeia Not-for-profit organization of scientists, physicians, pharmacists, and others that produces the *Pharmacopoeia of the United States*.

Volatile oil See Essential oil.

Zoopharmacognosy The use of drugs or plants for medicinal purposes by animals.

CAMPTOTHECA ACUMINATA
Happy tree
page 202

CENTELLA ASIATICA
Gotu kola
page 188

CANNABIS SATIVA
Hemp
page 208

CHONDRODENDRON TOMENTOSUM
Curare
page 128

CAPSICUM ANNUUM
Cayenne
page 92

CICHORIUM INTYBUS
Chicory
page 102

CASSIA ANGUSTIFOLIA
Senna
page 328

CIMICIFUGA RACEMOSA
Black cohosh
page 54

CATHARANTHUS ROSEUS
Madagascar periwinkle
page 242

CINCHONA OFFICINALIS
Red cinchona
page 302

CAULOPHYLLUM THALICTROIDES
Blue cohosh
page 60

CINNAMONUM VERUM
Cinnamon
page 108

CITRUS SINENSIS
Orange
page 264

CYMBOPOGON CITRATUS
Lemongrass
page 228

COLCHICUM AUTUMNALE
Autumn crocus
page 30

DAUCUS CAROTA
Queen Anne's lace
page 300

COMMIPHORA MYRRHA
Myrrh
page 256

DIGITALIS PURPUREA
Foxglove
page 174

CRATAEGUS LAEVIGATA
Hawthorn
page 204

DIOSCOREA VILLOSA
Wild yam
page 368

CUCURBITA PEPO
Pumpkin
page 296

ECHINACEA PURPUREA
Echinacea
page 138

CURCURMA LONGA
Turmeric
page 360

ELEUTHEROCOCCUS SENTICOSUS
Eleuthero
page 142

EPHEDRA SINICA
Ephedra
page 146

GALEGA OFFICINALIS
Goat's rue
page 184

ERYTHROXYLUM COCA
Coca
page 112

GAULTHERIA PROCUMBENS
Wintergreen
page 370

EUCALYPTUS GLOBULUS
Eucalyptus
page 148

GELSEMIUM SEMPERVIRENS
Yellow jasmine
page 380

EUPHRASIA OFFICINALIS
Eyebright
page 164

GENTIANA LUTEA
Gentian
page 178

FOENICULUM VULGARE
Fennel
page 166

GERANIUM ROBERTIANUM
Herb-Robert
page 210

FRANGULA PURSHIANA
Cascara sagrada
page 76

GINKGO BILOBA
Ginkgo
page 182

GLYCINE MAX
Soy bean
page 334

HYDNOCARPUS KURZII
Chaulmoogra
page 100

GLYCYRRHIZA GLABRA
Licorice
page 230

HYDRASTIS CANADENSIS
Goldenseal
page 186

GUAIACUM OFFICINALE
Guaiacum
page 190

HYPERICUM PERFORATUM
St. John's wort
page 338

HAMAMELIS VIRGINIANA
Witch hazel
page 372

ILEX PARAGUARIENSIS
Maté
page 246

HARPAGOPHYTUM PROCUMBENS
Devil's claw
page 132

INULA HELENIUM
Elecampane
page 140

HUMULUS LUPULUS
Hops
page 212

JUNIPERUS COMMUNIS
Juniper
page 220

LAMINARIA DIGITATA
Kelp
page 224

LYCOPODIUM CLAVATUM
Clubmoss
page 110

LARREA TRIDENTATA
Chaparral
page 96

MATRICARIA RECUTITA
Chamomile
page 94

LAVANDULA ANGUSTIFOLIA
English lavender
page 144

MEDICAGO SATIVA
Alfalfa
page 12

LIGUSTRUM VULGARE
Common privet
page 116

MELALEUCA ALTERNIFOLIA
Tea tree
page 354

LINUM USITATISSIMUM
Flax
page 170

MELISSA OFFICINALIS
Lemon balm
page 226

LOBELIA INFLATA
Lobelia
page 240

MENTHA X PIPERITA
Peppermint
page 286

MITCHELLA REPENS
Partridge berry
page 278

PANAX GINSENG
Asian ginseng
page 24

MONARDA DIDYMA
Beebalm
page 34

PANAX QUINQUEFOLIUS
American ginseng
page 16

MORINDA CITRIFOLIA
Noni
page 260

PAPAVER SOMNIFERUM
Opium poppy
page 262

NEPETA CATARIA
Catnip
page 88

PASSIFLORA INCARNATA
Passionflower
page 280

NICOTIANA RUSTICA
Native tobacco
page 258

PAULLINIA CUPANA
Guarana
page 192

OENOTHERA BIENNIS
Evening primrose
page 154

PAUSINYSTALIA JOHIMBE
Yohimbe
page 382

PETASITES HYBRIDUS
Butterbur
page 68

PLECTRANTHUS BARBATUS
Forskohlli
page 172

PETROSELINUM CRISPUM
Parsley
page 268

PODOPHYLLUM PELTATUM
Mayapple
page 248

PHYSOSTIGMA VENENOSUM
Calabar bean
page 70

POGOSTEMON CABLIN
Patchouli
page 282

PILOCARPUS PENNATIFOLIUS
Jaborandi
page 218

POLYGALA SENEGA
Seneca snakeroot
page 326

PIPER METHYSTICUM
Kava
page 222

PRUNELLA VULGARIS
Heal all
page 206

PLANTAGO PSYLLIUM
Psyllium
page 292

PRUNUS AFRICANA
Pygeum
page 298

PRUNUS SEROTINA
Black cherry
page 52

ROSA CANINA
Dog rose
page 134

PULSATILLA VULGARIS
Pulsatilla
page 294

ROSMARINUS OFFICINALIS
Rosemary
page 316

PUNICA GRANATUM
Pomegranate
page 290

RUMEX CRISPUS
Yellow dock
page 378

RHEUM OFFICINALE
Chinese rhubarb
page 104

SALIX ALBA
White willow
page 366

RHODIOLA ROSEA
Rhodiola
page 306

SALVIA OFFICINALIS
Sage
page 318

RICINUS COMMUNIS
Castor bean
page 78

SAMBUCUS NIGRA
European elder
page 150

SANGUINARIA CANADENSIS
Bloodroot
page 58

STRYCHNOS IGNATII
Ignatius bean
page 216

SASSAFRAS ALBIDUM
Sassafras
page 320

SYMPHYTUM OFFICINALE
Comfrey
page 114

SCHISANDRA CHINENSIS
Schisandra
page 324

TABEBUIA IMPETIGINOSA
Pau d'arco
page 284

SCUTELLARIA LATERIFLORA
Skullcap
page 330

TANACETUM PARTHENIUM
Feverfew
page 168

SERENOA REPENS
Saw palmetto
page 322

TARAXACUM OFFICINALE
Dandelion
page 130

SILYBUM MARIANUM
Milk thistle
page 250

TAXUS BREVIFOLIA
Pacific yew
page 266

THEOBROMA CACAO
Chocolate
page 106

UNCARIA TOMENTOSA
Cat's claw
page 90

THUJA OCCIDENTALIS
Thuja
page 356

URTICA DIOICA
Stinging nettle
page 340

THYMUS VULGARIS
Thyme
page 358

VACCINIUM MACROCARPON
Cranberry
page 126

TRIFOLIUM PRATENSE
Red clover
page 304

VACCINIUM MYRTILLUS
Bilberry
page 40

TRILLIUM ERECTUM
Bethroot
page 38

VALERIANA OFFICINALIS
Valerian
page 362

ULMUS RUBRA
Slippery elm
page 332

VERBASCUM THAPSUS
Mullein
page 254

VERNONIA AMYGDALINA
Bitterleaf
page 50

VITEX AGNUS-CASTUS
Chaste tree
page 98

VIBURNUM PRUNIFOLIUM
Black haw
page 56

WITHANIA SOMNIFERA
Ashwagandha
page 22

VISCUM ALBUM
European mistletoe
page 152

ZINGIBER OFFICINALE
Ginger
page 180

CONTRIBUTORS

Consultants and Writers

JIM ADAMS worked at the U.S. National Arboretum for twelve years and was curator of the National Herb Garden there for nine years. During that time he contributed to many projects and publications about herbs and their uses. The National Arboretum is a U.S. Department of Agriculture facility whose main 446-acre campus is located in Washington, D.C. The National Herb Garden is one of many features at the Arboretum. The 2.5-acre garden features herbs from cultures and traditions around the world. Currently Adams is head horticulturist at the British Embassy in Washington, D.C.

MICHAEL J. BALICK has studied the relationship between plants and people for three decades and has become a leading figure in the field known as ethnobotany, with a specialty in ethnomedicine, the study of how traditional cultures use plants in healing. Most of his research is in remote regions of the tropics, where he works with indigenous cultures to document their plant knowledge, understand the environmental effects of their traditional management systems, and help develop sustainable utilization systems for the region—while ensuring that benefits from such work are always shared with local communities. Dr. Balick also conducts research in the urban environment in New York City. He directs The New York Botanical Garden's Institute of Economic Botany, the largest and most active such program of its kind in the nation.

PAUL ALAN COX is Director of the Institute for Ethnomedicine in Jackson Hole, Wyoming. A Harvard Ph.D., Dr. Cox was chosen by *Time* magazine as a Hero of Medicine for his discovery of the anti-AIDS drug prostratin. For his efforts to protect the Samoan rain forest, Cox was awarded the Goldman Environmental Prize. Seacology, the not-for-profit foundation he created, has protected tens of thousands of hectares of island rain forests and coral reefs. Cox's recent studies of disease among the Chamorro people of Guam have led to new approaches in understanding amyotrophic lateral sclerosis (ALS), Alzheimer's disease, and other neurodegenerative illnesses.

NINA L. ETKIN is Professor of Anthropology and Graduate Chair at the University of Hawaii. She is appointed as well to the Cancer Research Center and the Department of Ecology and Health (UH Medical School). She is a past President of the International Society for Ethnopharmacology. She is best known for her pioneering work on the pharmacologic implications of plant use, especially the interrelations among medicines and foods. She has field and laboratory experience in northern Nigeria (among the Hausa), eastern Indonesia, and contemporary Hawaii. Her work reflects an interdisciplinary perspective that links physiology, culture, and society to understand the dialectics of nature and culture in diverse ecologic and ethnographic settings.

STEVEN FOSTER is a best-selling author, photographer, international consultant, and lecturer with more than three decades of experience in the herbal field. His career began in Maine at the Sabbathday Lake Shaker Herb Department, America's oldest herb business, which dates to 1799. He is the senior author of three Peterson Field Guides for identifying North American herbs and bioactive plants, and a dozen more books, including *Tyler's Honest Herbal* and the award-winning *101 Medicinal Herbs*. Foster's photographs of herbs and medicinal plants appear in numerous books and magazines, and are regularly featured in *HerbalGram*, the journal of the American Botanical Council. Foster makes his home in Eureka Springs, Arkansas, in the heart of the medicinal plant–rich Ozark Mountains.

REBECCA L. JOHNSON is a 20-year veteran of publishing who has authored more than 60 books for adults and children on diverse scientific subjects ranging from polar exploration and climate change to the ecology of coral reefs. To gather firsthand information for her books, she has worked side by side with scientists in far-flung parts of the world, including those studying ice-bound algae in Antarctica, mangroves in northern Queensland, and marine invertebrates living in the eternal darkness of the deep sea. Johnson has been an author for National Geographic since 2000. Several of her books have received national awards from *Scientific American*, the National Science Teachers Association, and the Children's Book Coucil. An avid gardener and herb enthusiast, Johnson maintains an extensive herb garden at her home in Sioux Falls, South Dakota.

JASON MOLIN is a writer, teacher, web designer, and singer/songwriter living in Austin, Texas. He holds a bachelor's degree from New York University and a master's degree in instructional design from the University of Texas. His latest CD is entitled *J*. His website is www.jasonmolin.net.

Photographers

JUDY KARPINSKI is a commercial and fine arts photographer living in Wilmington, North Carolina. She specializes in nature and landscape photography. Her images appear in various books and publications and she has exhibited and won numerous awards for her photography. Her website is www.judykarpinski.com.

DENNIS AND BETTY LIGHT are Chicago-based photographers. Early interest and training in health and nutrition led them to develop a large collection of images of medicinal plants. They travel the country photographing these and other select subjects. Their work is published throughout North America and Europe. Their website is www.photosourcebook.com/1124

MARTIN WALL collected and used his first medicinal plant from the wild at the age of eleven. He continues his studies of medicinal plants while also photographing, writing, and teaching about them. His photographs of plants have appeared in dozens of books and magazines around the world. He resides in North Carolina with his wife and daughter.

Illustrators

MARY E. EATON painted 672 botanical watercolors for the National Geographic Society between 1915 and 1928. Although then National Geographic editor Gilbert H. Grosvenor considered Eaton's work "exquisitely beautiful," he was willing to pay only $12.50 per painting. In 1926, the Society agreed to increase the payment to $15 but attempted to make up the difference by offering only $10 for the paintings of less colorful specimens. When Eaton complained that "the less colorful subjects take as long to paint—sometimes longer," the Society wisely reconsidered and agreed to meet her price.

JANE WATKINS is a botanical painter and Royal Horticultural Society medallist. She has illustrated for many publications and her work is displayed commercially. She exhibits locally in the West Country. Her work is sold through Leicester Galleries in London.

Bown, Deni. *The Herb Society of America New Encyclopedia of Herbs and Their Uses, revised edition.* Dorling Kindersley, 2001.

Brown, Donald J. *Herbal Prescriptions for Health and Healing.* Lotus Press, 2003.

Bunney, Sarah, ed. *The Illustrated Encyclopedia of Herbs.* Barnes and Noble Books, 1996. (Published originally in the Czech Republic as *The Illustrated Book of Herbs* by Jiri Stodola and Jan Volak. Artia, 1984)

Chevallier, Andrew. *Encyclopedia of Herbal Medicine, 2nd ed.* Dorling Kindersley, 2000.

Duke, James A. *Handbook of Medicinal Herbs.* CRC Press, 1985.

Duke, James A. *The Green Pharmacy Herbal Handbook.* Rodale Press, 2000.

Duke, James A. *The Green Pharmacy.* St. Martin's Press, 1997.

Foster, Steven, and James A. Duke. *A Field Guide to Medicinal Plants and Herbs: Eastern and Central North America, 2nd ed*; Peterson Field Guides. Houghton Mifflin, 2000.

Foster, Steven, and Varro E. Tyler. *Tyler's Honest Herbal, 4th ed.* The Haworth Herbal Press, 1999.

Foster, Steven, and Yue Chongxi. *Herbal Emissaries: Bringing Chinese Herbs to the West.* Healing Arts Press, 1992.

Foster, Steven. *Herbal Renaissance: Growing, Using, and Understanding Herbs in the Modern World.* Gibbs-Smith, 1993.

Grieve, Maud. *A Modern Herbal.* Dover Publications, 1971. (An unabridged republication of Harcourt, Brace & Company edition published in 1931.)

Houdret, Jessica. *Herbs.* Hermes House, 2002. (originally published by Anness Publishing Limited, London, 1999)

Kowalchik, Claire, and Willian H. Hylton, editors. *Rodale's Illustrated Encyclopedia of Herbs.* Rodale Press, 1998.

Lust, John. *The Herb Book: The Complete and Authoritative Guide to More Than 500 Herbs.* Beneficial Books, 1974 (reprinted 2001).

Tyler, Varro E. and James E. Robbers. *Tyler's Herbs of Choice.* Haworth Herbal Press, 1999.

Uno, Gordon, Richard Storey, and Randy Moore. *Principles of Botany, 1st ed.* McGraw-Hill, 2001.

Van Wyk, Ben-Erik, and Michael Wink. *Medicinal Plants of the World.* Timber Press, 2004.

Weiss, Rudolf Fritz. *Weiss's Herbal Medicine, 6th ed.* Thieme, 1985 (reprinted 2001).

Foster Group, Inc; 121, © Steven Foster, Steven Foster Group, Inc; 122, © Steven Foster, Steven Foster Group, Inc; 123, © Steven Foster, Steven Foster Group, Inc; 125, © Steven Foster, Steven Foster Group, Inc; 126, Jane Watkins; 127, Dennis Light/Light Photographic; 128, Jane Watkins; 129, Michael J. Balick; 130, Mary E. Eaton; 131, © Steven Foster, Steven Foster Group, Inc; 132, Jane Watkins; 133, © Steven Foster, Steven Foster Group, Inc; 134, Jane Watkins; 135, Tony Wharton, Frank Lane Picture Agency/CORBIS; 136, Jane Watkins; 137, © Steven Foster, Steven Foster Group, Inc; 138, Mary E. Eaton; 139, Annie Griffiths Belt; 140, Mary E. Eaton; 141, © Steven Foster, Steven Foster Group, Inc; 142, Jane Watkins; 143, © Steven Foster, Steven Foster Group, Inc; 144, Jane Watkins; 145, © Steven Foster, Steven Foster Group, Inc; 146, Jane Watkins; 147, © Steven Foster, Steven Foster Group, Inc; 148, Jane Watkins; 149, Bil Ellzey; 150, Mary E. Eaton; 151, Dennis Light/Light Photographic; 152, Mary E. Eaton; 153, Mattias Klum; 154, Mary E. Eaton; 155, Dennis Light/Light Photographic; 156-157, Lynn Johnson; 159, © Steven Foster, Steven Foster Group, Inc; 160, Lynn Johnson; 163, © Steven Foster, Steven Foster Group, Inc; 164, Jane Watkins; 165, © Steven Foster, Steven Foster Group, Inc; 166, Jane Watkins; 167, © Steven Foster, Steven Foster Group, Inc; 168, Jane Watkins; 169, © Steven Foster, Steven Foster Group, Inc; 170, Jane Watkins; 171, © Steven Foster, Steven Foster Group, Inc; 172, Jane Watkins; 173, Martin Wall/herbslides.com; 174, Mary E. Eaton; 175, Judy Karpinski Photography; 176, Jane Watkins; 177, Dennis Light/Light Photographic; 178, Courtesy of Hunt Institute for Botanical Documentation, Carnegie Mellon University, Pittsburgh, PA; 179, © Steven Foster, Steven Foster Group, Inc; 180, Jane Watkins; 181, © Steven Foster, Steven Foster Group, Inc; 182, Jane Watkins; 183, Dennis Light/Light Photographic; 184, Jane Watkins; 185, © Steven Foster, Steven Foster Group, Inc; 186, Jane Watkins; 187, © Steven Foster, Steven Foster Group, Inc; 188, Jane Watkins; 189, © Steven Foster, Steven Foster Group, Inc; 190, Jane Watkins; 191, Judy Karpinski Photography; 192, Jane Watkins; 193, © Steven Foster, Steven Foster Group, Inc; 194-195, © Steven Foster, Steven Foster Group, Inc; 197, © Steven Foster, Steven Foster Group, Inc; 198, © Steven Foster, Steven Foster Group, Inc; 201, © Steven Foster, Steven Foster Group, Inc; 202, Jane Watkins; 203, Judy Karpinski Photography; 204, Jane Watkins; 205, © Steven Foster, Steven Foster Group, Inc; 206, Jane Watkins; 207, © Steven Foster, Steven Foster Group, Inc; 208, Jane Watkins; 209, © Steven Foster, Steven Foster Group, Inc; 210, Mary E. Eaton; 211, © Steven Foster, Steven Foster Group, Inc; 212, Mary E. Eaton; 213, G. Rossenbach/zefa/CORBIS; 214, Courtesy of Hunt Institute for Botanical Documentation, Carnegie Mellon University, Pittsburgh, PA; 215, © Steven Foster, Steven Foster Group, Inc; 216, Jane Watkins; 217, Gregory G. Dimijian/Photo Researchers, Inc.; 218, Jane Watkins; 219, Michael J. Balick; 220, Jane Watkins; 221, Dennis Light/Light Photographic; 222, Jane Watkins; 223, © Steven Foster, Steven Foster Group, Inc; 224, Jane Watkins; 225, David Doubilet; 226, Courtesy of Hunt Institute for Botanical Documentation, Carnegie Mellon University, Pittsburgh, PA; 227, © Steven Foster, Steven Foster Group, Inc; 228, Jane Watkins; 229, © Steven Foster, Steven Foster Group, Inc; 230, Jane Watkins; 231, © Steven Foster, Steven Foster Group, Inc; 232-233, Lynn Johnson; 235, Lynn Johnson; 237, © Steven Foster, Steven Foster Group, Inc; 239, Lynn Johnson; 240, Jane Watkins; 241, © Steven Foster, Steven Foster Group, Inc; 242, Jane Watkins; 243, Judy Karpinski Photography; 244, Mary E. Eaton; 245, © Steven Foster, Steven Foster Group, Inc; 246, Missouri Botanical Garden; 247, © Steven Foster, Steven Foster Group, Inc; 248, Mary E. Eaton; 249, Dennis Light/Light Photographic; 250, Jane Watkins; 251, Dennis Light/Light Photographic; 252, Mary E. Eaton; 253, Martin Wall/herbslides.com; 254, Mary E. Eaton; 255, Dennis Light/Light Photographic; 256, Jane Watkins; 257, Dennis Light/Light Photographic; 258, Mary E. Eaton; 259, © Steven Fos-

ter, Steven Foster Group, Inc; 260, Jane Watkins; 261, © Steven Foster, Steven Foster Group, Inc; 262, Jane Watkins; 263, © Steven Foster, Steven Foster Group, Inc; 264, Mary E. Eaton; 265, Kirk Weddle/Getty Images; 266, Jane Watkins; 267, © Steven Foster, Steven Foster Group, Inc; 268, Jane Watkins; 269, Dennis Light/Light Photographic; 270-271, Betty Light/Light Photographic; 273, © Steven Foster, Steven Foster Group, Inc; 275, © Steven Foster, Steven Foster Group, Inc; 277, © Steven Foster, Steven Foster Group, Inc; 278, Jane Watkins; 279, © Steven Foster, Steven Foster Group, Inc; 280, Mary E. Eaton; 281, Dennis Light/Light Photographic; 282, Jane Watkins; 283, © Steven Foster, Steven Foster Group, Inc; 284, Jane Watkins; 285, © Steven Foster, Steven Foster Group, Inc; 286, Mary E. Eaton; 287, © Steven Foster, Steven Foster Group, Inc; 288, Jane Watkins; 289, © Steven Foster, Steven Foster Group, Inc; 290, Missouri Botanical Garden; 291, CORBIS; 292, Courtesy of Hunt Institute for Botanical Documentation, Carnegie Mellon University, Pittsburgh, PA; 293, © Steven Foster, Steven Foster Group, Inc; 294, Jane Watkins; 295, © Steven Foster, Steven Foster Group, Inc; 296, Jane Watkins; 297, Martin Wall/herbslides.com; 298, Jane Watkins; 299, Martin Wall/herbslides.com; 300, Mary E. Eaton; 301, Judy Karpinski Photography; 302, Jane Watkins; 303, Martin Wall/herbslides.com; 304, Mary E. Eaton; 305, © Steven Foster, Steven Foster Group, Inc; 306, Courtesy of Hunt Institute for Botanical Documentation, Carnegie Mellon University, Pittsburgh, PA; 307, Niall Benvie/CORBIS; 308-309, © Steven Foster, Steven Foster Group, Inc.; 311, Patrick Syder/Lonely Planet Images/Getty Images; 312, © Steven Foster, Steven Foster Group, Inc.; 315, William Albert Allard/NGS Image Collection; 316, Courtesy of Hunt Institute for Botanical Documentation, Carnegie Mellon University, Pittsburgh, PA; 317, © Steven Foster, Steven Foster Group, Inc; 318, Courtesy of Hunt Institute for Botanical Documentation, Carnegie Mellon University, Pittsburgh, PA; 319, Dennis Light/Light Photographic; 320, Mary E. Eaton; 321, © Steven Foster, Steven Foster Group, Inc; 322, Jane Watkins; 323, © Steven Foster, Steven Foster Group, Inc; 324, Jane Watkins; 325, Dennis Light/Light Photographic; 326, Jane Watkins; 327, © Steven Foster, Steven Foster Group, Inc; 328, Courtesy of Hunt Institute for Botanical Documentation, Carnegie Mellon University, Pittsburgh, PA; 329, © Steven Foster, Steven Foster Group, Inc; 330, Mary E. Eaton; 331, © Steven Foster, Steven Foster Group, Inc; 332, Courtesy of Hunt Institute for Botanical Documentation, Carnegie Mellon University, Pittsburgh, PA; 333, © Steven Foster, Steven Foster Group, Inc; 334, Jane Watkins; 335, Dennis Light/Light Photographic; 336, Mary E. Eaton; 337, Martin Wall/herbslides.com; 338, Jane Watkins; 339, Dennis Light/Light Photographic; 340, Mary E. Eaton; 341, © Steven Foster, Steven Foster Group, Inc; 342, Jane Watkins; 343, © Steven Foster, Steven Foster Group, Inc; 344, Jane Watkins; 345, © Steven Foster, Steven Foster Group, Inc; 346-347, Paul Alan Cox ; 349, Paul Alan Cox ; 350, Paul Alan Cox ; 351, Paul Alan Cox ; 353, Paul Alan Cox ; 354, Jane Watkins; 355, Martin Wall/herbslides.com; 356, Jane Watkins; 357, Dennis Light/Light Photographic; 358, Jane Watkins; 359, © Steven Foster, Steven Foster Group, Inc; 360, Jane Watkins; 361, Judy Karpinski Photography; 362, Mary E. Eaton; 363, © Steven Foster, Steven Foster Group, Inc; 364, Jane Watkins; 365, Survival Anglia/Photo Library; 366, Jane Watkins; 367, © Steven Foster, Steven Foster Group, Inc; 368, Jane Watkins; 369, © Steven Foster, Steven Foster Group, Inc; 370, Mary E. Eaton; 371, © Steven Foster, Steven Foster Group, Inc; 372, Mary E. Eaton; 373, © Steven Foster, Steven Foster Group, Inc; 374, Jane Watkins; 375, © Steven Foster, Steven Foster Group, Inc; 376, Mary E. Eaton; 377, Dennis Light/Light Photographic; 378, Mary E. Eaton; 379, © Steven Foster, Steven Foster Group, Inc; 380, Mary E. Eaton; 381, © Steven Foster, Steven Foster Group, Inc; 382, Jane Watkins; 383, Photolibrary.

DESK REFERENCE TO NATURE'S MEDICINE
by Steven Foster and Rebecca L. Johnson

PUBLISHED BY THE NATIONAL GEOGRAPHIC SOCIETY

John M. Fahey, Jr. *President and Chief Executive Officer*
Gilbert M. Grosvenor *Chairman of the Board*
Tim T. Kelly *President, Global Media Group*
Nina D. Hoffman *Executive Vice President;
    President, Book Publishing Group*

PREPARED BY THE BOOK DIVISION

Kevin Mulroy *Senior Vice President and Publisher*
Leah Bendavid-Val *Director of Photography Publishing
    and Illustrations*
Marianne R. Koszorus *Design Director*
Barbara Brownell Grogan *Executive Editor*
Elizabeth Newhouse *Director of Travel Publishing*
Carl Mehler *Director of Maps*

STAFF FOR THIS BOOK

Barbara H. Seeber *Editor and Project Manager*
Kate Griffin *Illustrations Editor*
Carol Farrar Norton *Art Director*
Teresa Neva Tate *Illustrations Specialist*
Steven Foster *Map Researcher and Editor*
Matt Chwastyk and Sven M. Dolling *Map Production*
Ric Wain *Production Project Manager*
Margo Browning, Barbara Johnson *Contributing Editors*
Michael Greninger *Editorial Assistant*

Jennifer A. Thornton *Managing Editor*
R. Gary Colbert *Production Director*

MANUFACTURING AND QUALITY MANAGEMENT

Christopher A. Liedel *Chief Financial Officer*
Phillip L. Schlosser *Vice President*
John T. Dunn *Technical Director*
Chris Brown *Director*
Maryclare Tracy *Manager*
Nicole Elliott *Manager*

Founded in 1888, the National Geographic Society is one of the largest nonprofit scientific and educational organizations in the world. It reaches more than 285 million people worldwide each month through its official journal, NATIONAL GEOGRAPHIC, and its four other magazines; the National Geographic Channel; television documentaries; radio programs; films; books; videos and DVDs; maps; and interactive media. National Geographic has funded more than 8,000 scientific research projects and supports an education program combating geographic illiteracy.

For more information, please call
1-800-NGS LINE (647-5463)
or write to the following address:

National Geographic Society
1145 17th Street N.W.
Washington, D.C. 20036-4688 U.S.A.

Visit us online at
www.nationalgeographic.com/books

For information about special discounts
for bulk purchases, please contact
National Geographic Books Special Sales:
ngspecsales@ngs.org

For rights or permissions inquiries,
please contact National Geographic Books
Subsidiary Rights: ngbookrights@ngs.org

First paperback printing 2008

ISBN: 978-1-4262-0293-3

Printed in China